MW00637656

Praise for

TO OVERTHROW THE WORLD

"Following the collapse of the Soviet Union, many in the West were lulled into a sense of complacency. Fast-forward to today, and the United States is locked in yet another struggle with a communist superpower, even as our liberal system is under attack at home. In his thoroughly researched but readable and entertaining new book, historian Sean McMeekin charts the evolution of communism from Karl Marx to the Tiananmen Square massacre while explaining how this political system endured through the trials and tribulations of the twentieth century. Students, scholars, and policymakers will all benefit from the lessons contained in this bold and lively book."

—Walter Russell Mead, author of *The Arc of a Covenant*

"An essential read. McMeekin is one of the few historians who understands the history of communism from the ground up. He has written a powerful and urgent book, revealing communism in all its ugly detail, and showing how its pernicious influence still lingers on into the twenty-first century."

—Nick Lloyd, author of *The Western Front*

"This vivid history of communism, from the day Marx penned *The Communist Manifesto* in 1848 to the present, contains valuable insights, including that of Bakunin, the Russian anarchist who immediately pointed out the crippling contradiction of Marxism—it merely substitutes one power-hungry form of government for another. McMeekin follows this skeptical thread through the Soviet and Chinese experiences, from Lenin and Stalin to Mao and Xi, detailing the economic weakness and political madness of communist regimes in Europe and Asia that have been kept afloat over the decades as much by Western gullibility and indulgence as by their own ruthless, incompetent managers."

—Geoffrey Wawro, author of *The Vietnam War*

"With amazing scholarship, McMeekin tells the story of the rise and fall of communism in *To Overthrow the World*. The utopian promises of communism have always led to dictatorship, bloody repression, and war. McMeekin punctures one myth after another, including the legend that the Soviets won World War II without much help from the West. Many people today are too young to remember the Cold War, and it is vital that they learn the facts about communism found in *To Overthrow the World*."

—David Gordon, senior fellow, Ludwig von Mises Institute

"In *To Overthrow the World*, McMeekin describes in telling detail how no communist regime in history has gained power through the vote or public approval, and how its social and economic policies invariably bring about mass repression and poverty. No other book to my knowledge has demonstrated so damningly the endemic falsity of the ideology's doctrines, together with the appalling consequences of the social experiment in a worldwide setting."

—Nikolai Tolstoy, historian

TO OVERTHROW THE WORLD

Also by Sean Mcmeekin

Stalin's War: A New History of World War II

The Russian Revolution: A New History

The Ottoman Endgame: War, Revolution, and the Making of the Modern Middle East, 1908–1923

July 1914: Countdown to War

The Russian Origins of the First World War

The Berlin-Baghdad Express: The Ottoman Empire and Germany's Bid for World Power

History's Greatest Heist: The Looting of Russia by the Bolsheviks

The Red Millionaire: A Political Biography of Willy Münzenberg

TO OVERTHROW THE WORLD

THE RISE AND FALL AND RISE OF COMMUNISM

SEAN
MCMEEKIN

BASIC BOOKS
New York

Basic Books
Hachette Book Group
1290 Avenue of the Americas, New York, NY 10104
www.basicbooks.com

Printed in the United States of America

First Edition: September 2024

Published by Basic Books, an imprint of Hachette Book Group, Inc. The Basic Books name and logo is a trademark of the Hachette Book Group.

The Hachette Speakers Bureau provides a wide range of authors for speaking events. To find out more, go to hachettespeakersbureau.com or email HachetteSpeakers@hbgusa.com.

Basic books may be purchased in bulk for business, educational, or promotional use. For more information, please contact your local bookseller or the Hachette Book Group Special Markets Department at special.markets@hbgusa.com.

The publisher is not responsible for websites (or their content) that are not owned by the publisher.

Print book interior design by Amy Quinn

Maps created by Philip Schwartzberg of Meridian Mapping

Library of Congress Cataloging-in-Publication Data

Names: McMeekin, Sean, 1974- author.
Title: To overthrow the world : the rise and fall and rise of communism / Sean McMeekin.
Description: New York : Basic Books, [2024] | Includes bibliographical references and index.
Identifiers: LCCN 2024007123 | ISBN 9781541601963 (hardcover) | ISBN 9781541601987 (ebook)
Subjects: LCSH: Communism.
Classification: LCC HX21 .M397 20245 | DDC 335.009—dc23/eng/20240329
LC record available at https://lccn.loc.gov/2024007123

ISBNs: 9781541601963 (hardcover), 9781541601987 (ebook)

LSC-C

Printing 1, 2024

For my children

CONTENTS

CONTENTS

PREFACE

I t is now more than three decades since the fall of the Berlin Wall and subsequent collapse of the USSR prompted Francis Fukuyama to proclaim the "End of History." Like most Americans who lived through those heady and exciting times, I felt a surge of pride as one Eastern Bloc country after another discarded single-party Communist rule for pluralism and political freedom—even Russia itself, which for a time seemed just as eager to embrace the West. For the first time, Soviet archives were thrown open to Western researchers such as myself, who happily descended on them to probe the secrets of Soviet and global Communism. Confident postmortems of Communism then filled the airwaves, with a sense of relief and "goodbye to all that." At the height of American triumphalism in 2001, the historian Richard Pipes described his short *Communism: A History* as not only "an introduction to Communism" but also "at the same time, its obituary."[1]

Twenty years later, things look rather different. Russia may no longer be Communist, but it is ruled by Vladimir Putin, a proud and unrepentant former KGB officer. Joseph Stalin is more admired in Russia today than at any other time since his death in 1953, his manifold crimes against the peoples of the Soviet Union now

1

either forgiven or forgotten. Since the Ukraine crisis of 2014 and the Russia-Ukraine war that broke out in February 2022, relations between Russia and the West have been thrown into the deep freeze, frostier by some measures than at the height of the Cold War, with nearly all trade and travel cut off. Meanwhile, thrown off its perch by the 9/11 attacks, ineffectual "forever war" military interventions, deindustrialization, and debts eroding the value of the dollar, the United States has bled prestige in uncanny parallel with the return of Russian military power to the world stage and the rise of Communist China in economic power and global influence. With the COVID-19 lockdowns of 2020–2022, the China model spread globally, as once inviolable rights, from freedom of speech and dissent to freedom of movement and travel, were temporarily abandoned in the West. For many young westerners, Communism is no longer a cause banished from mainstream discourse for its association with totalitarian regimes, for they have no living memory of them. Liberal democratic capitalism seems bereft of energy, if not moribund, while Chinese Communism rapidly assimilates much of the world. How did this happen, and why did no one see it coming?

What follows is an attempt to grapple with this question, and to approach it with a greater sense of humility than I might have done in those heady early years of the post-Communist era. Owing to several decades of historical research in partly open Chinese, mostly open Eastern Bloc, and until recently relatively open Soviet archives, we also know far more today than in the past about how Communism worked in practice, and about why, and exactly how, so many Communist regimes fell—while others endured—between 1989 and 1991. There was nothing fated about the collapse of Soviet power that allowed the Eastern Bloc Communist satellites and the three Baltic Republics to spin free from Moscow's orbit in 1989, and that prompted the collapse of the USSR itself two years later—the cause of Fukuyama's premature gloating—nor in the violent reassertion of Chinese Communist Party (CCP) control in Tiananmen Square earlier in 1989, which should have rendered his thesis null on arrival. Much as we like to imagine that Communism failed because of a cascading groundswell of heroic popular opposition from below, it was actually the disappearance of coercion from above that counted. More than any other system of government known to man, Communist rule required the strong hand of the military and heavily armed security services, all under strict party control. Once the regime's sword was lifted, Communist parties crumbled quickly; if the sword remained, the party did too.

Nor, for that matter, was the emergence of Communist governments in the twentieth century in the first place preordained by some Hegelian-Marxist law of history, however much Karl Marx and his acolytes would have wished it so. As we will see in the pages ahead, the emergence of Communism in Russia, China, and their satellites required a series of world wars that rent the social fabric and put lethal arms in the hands of millions of angry and impressionable young men. Despite the party's claim to speak for the proletarian masses of humanity, and several much ballyhooed near misses, Communists nowhere came to power through the ballot box. As some of Marx's earliest critics, particularly those on the anarchist left, such as Mikhail Bakunin, perceived, the maximalist Marxist program, requiring state control of the banks, industry, agriculture, and economic exchange, could only be achieved with massive violence and a preponderance of force. Absent the catalyst of war, Communist revolution was inconceivable. Marx, like Vladimir Lenin after him, saw the revolutionary potential of modern wars, such as the Franco-Prussian War of 1870–1871 and the Russo-Japanese War of 1904–1905, for the losing side—in the former case, France, and in the latter, Russia. Following Marx's own reading of the first conflict and his interpretation of the second,

Lenin forged the doctrine of "revolutionary defeatism," by which he meant that, if a country lost a modern war decisively enough, the resulting collapse of military discipline and prestige could weaken its government to the point that it might then be toppled by armed revolutionaries. But these relatively contained bilateral wars, however lethal and destructive to social order, leading to the short-lived but sanguinary Paris Commune of 1871 and the equally violent but ultimately contained Russian Revolution of 1905, were not destructive enough for Marx's or Lenin's purposes. Only the utter devastation of the First World War did enough damage, and mobilized and armed enough angry and embittered young men, to make Communist revolution possible. Even then, in order to succeed, Lenin's ruthless program of promoting mass mutinies in Russia's army and navy in order to transform the country's "imperialist war" into "civil war" required a fortunate sequence of events breaking his way—Lenin was extremely lucky in his enemies—and his new Communist government was on the defensive from day one.

Contrary to Lenin's hopes, the advent of Communism in Russia did not inspire a global wave of revolution. Aside from a few short-lived upheavals in Germany and Hungary—countries that, like Russia, had been devastated by the First World War and found themselves on the losing side in 1918—Communism failed to gain traction anywhere outside Russia. Marx might have prophesied in *Das Kapital* that, once capitalist "centralization of the means of production and the socialization of labor" reached some critical threshold, the "knell of capitalist private property" would ring globally, all at once—but nothing of the kind happened either in Russia in 1917 or elsewhere by imitation. Lenin tried gamely to speed the revolution along, creating a Communist International, or Comintern, in 1919 to coordinate global propaganda and paramilitary efforts to overthrow "capitalist" governments worldwide, but these efforts failed on all fronts.

It was only with the collapse of international order in the 1930s that Communism once again began to make inroads, first in Spain, in the wake of a devastating civil war, and then in Eastern Europe and North Asia, after the Second World War, which unleashed social and economic devastation on those regions even more terrible than the First World War had. Try though Soviet Comintern leaders and their foreign agents did to update the Communist theory of revolution on the fly, it was not doctrine that mattered, but force of arms. Only in the exceptional circumstances of war did Communists stand a real chance of sniffing power, and it usually required years of attrition to weaken traditional regimes enough for them to fall—along with the extra muscle and funding Moscow provided. Sometimes, as in the imposition of Communism by Soviet conquering armies in Poland or Hungary, this was obvious enough. But even the most famous "native" Communist conquerors, such as Tito in Yugoslavia and Mao Zedong in China, as we shall see below, needed heavy doses of foreign assistance to overwhelm their enemies. The real secret of Marxism-Leninism, as the reigning doctrine of Communism was called after 1917, was not that Marx and Lenin had discovered an immutable law of history driven by ever-intensifying "class struggle," but that Lenin had shown how Communist revolutionaries could exploit the devastation of war to seize power by force—if the devastation was severe enough, and if they armed enough fanatics and foot soldiers to prevail over their opponents. The rise and fall and surprising non-death of Communism was always the work of real, live men (and some women), with results sometimes reflecting, but more often defying, human intention. Marx, a much better historian than a prophet, once wrote that "men make their own history, but they do not make it just as they please."[2]

I have written the history of Communism with Marx's aphorism in mind, knowing that the story, despite its seeming resolution in

1989 or 1991, is far from over. As long as people dream of brotherhood between men, of equal rights for women or for racial or ethnic minorities, or, in the current jargon, of "social justice," some version of Communism will retain broad popular appeal, enticing young idealists—along with ambitious older politicians who may or may not share in the idealism but are tempted by the promise of an all-encompassing state granting them vast power over their subjects—to champion its cause. The history of Communism may not always be edifying or reassuring, but it is worth reexamining dispassionately, without either prejudice or wishful thinking. Let us begin.

INTRODUCTION

SOCIAL EQUALITY: GENEALOGY OF AN IDEA

Communism as a ruling doctrine is a relatively recent phenomenon in historical terms, dating back just over a century—or, if we count parties bearing the name, such as the Communist League of Marx and Engels (c. 1847–1848), about 175 years. But the idea of material or social equality lying at the heart of Communist theory traces back deep into antiquity, and it is worth examining the different strands of thought that have informed and inspired modern Communists. In *The Republic* (c. 375 BC), Plato has Socrates observe that the proliferation of "such words as 'mine' and 'not mine' and 'someone else's'" must lead to the dissolution of the social fabric. By contrast, the best-governed city would be one in which "all the citizens rejoice and are pained by the same successes and failures," as the "sharing of pleasures and pains bind[s] the city together." A thoughtful ruler, or philosopher-king, should thus establish a kind of political equality among active citizens, who by sacrificing selfish interests would come to equate their own fortunes with those of the polity to which they belonged. In his wicked satire *Ecclesiazusae* (*Assemblywomen*, c. 391 BC), Aristophanes went further, with his false-bearded female philosopher-queen Praxagora

7

vowing to make "land, money, everything that is private property, common to all." This dictum, she said, would include sexual relations: men must court the "ugliest and most flat-nosed [women] . . . side to side with the most charming [women]," and women were enjoined not to "sleep with the big, handsome men before having satisfied the ugly shrimps."[1]

Speaking to the individual soul rather than to the Greeks' pagan philosopher-kings, Jesus warned followers soon known as Christians that it would "be easier for a camel to go through the eye of a needle than for a rich man to enter the kingdom of heaven," and he advised one wealthy petitioner, who asked him what he must do to attain eternal life, "If you would be perfect, go, sell what you possess and give to the poor." Generations of Christian saints, inspired by the example of Martin of Tours (AD 316–397), who died on a bare floor clothed in rags, have taken Christ's words to heart, renounced their material possessions, and devoted their lives to helping the needy—to charity, as we now call it. As Saint Martin himself preached, a true Christian must act as "the helper of the lowliest, the protector of the weak, the shelter of the hopeless, the savior of the rejected." In this way early Christians introduced to the world the novel, counterintuitive idea that the weak, the poor, and the humble had as much human value as great statesmen, mighty warriors, and their wealthy patrons. If Christ was right, the meek might even find true salvation in the afterlife, while the selfish rich were judged and suffered the torments of the damned. While not every believer has obeyed this radical precept to devote their lives to helping the poor or become poor themselves, the Christian idea of material renunciation added a powerful allure to the Platonic ideal of a collective-minded political community. People might not be equal in wealth or social status, but in the eyes of God all souls might be equal, or at least judged by a universal moral standard to which all were equally bound.[2]

Still, even at its most radical, Western Christianity has stopped short of advocating for outright equality of wealth and material differences as proposed by Plato and Aristophanes (the latter satirically). The rich might be judged by God and found wanting; but not even the most devout Christian theologians have proposed, like Robin Hood, to rob them and redistribute their wealth in order to level out the social order. Theft is, indeed, expressly forbidden in the Ten Commandments of the Old Testament ("Thou shalt not steal"), fundamental to the faith of both Jews and Christians. The embrace of poverty, or the practice of charity, for a Christian believer, is the conscious act of a free human soul, not a coercive act or something to be mandated in law.

Nonetheless, there is no denying the explosive implications of the Christian faith for social evolution in the direction of greater social equality. The story of Genesis, of an unclothed Adam and Eve in the "Garden of Eden," central to both Judaism and the Christianity that emerged from it, posits a lost innocence or paradise. The first couple's sin leads to the need for clothing to conceal the human body, has implications for the temptations and complications of sex, and foreshadows the greed of humanity that leads in turn to inequalities of wealth, and ultimately to the sundry evil acts plaguing the fallen world. These evils then must be proscribed by the moral lessons of the Ten Commandments and by the other laws and holy texts of the three monotheistic faiths. Implicit in the idea of an earlier fall from grace is the possibility of redemption, whether through the restoration of a lost world or the repentance of an individual for one's actions. History thus proceeds inexorably in the Judeo-Christian worldview toward judgment and redemption (or everlasting damnation). Christianity and Judaism differ in the pacing of the linear progression, with Christians generally believing more strongly in the idea of a *final* judgment for all mankind, a branch of the faith known as eschatology. The central point, for understanding the evolution of Western intellectual life and ideas, is that the arc of time for Jews—and more especially Christians—moves forward in a linear fashion from one dramatic point toward another, with each decision, each action and event, pregnant with meaning in a world ruled by a unitary deity (God), rather than in random or cyclical fashion, or via the continual (though inconsistently paced) revelation of the sages and sagas of a polytheistic faith such as Hinduism. From the stories in the Bible to modern-day literature, this set of ideas has given Western thought its great narrative pull, as saints, poets, philosophers, novelists, and historians have wrung drama and meaning out of individual and collective struggle.

Islam, born of the same Abrahamic monotheistic tradition as Judaism and Christianity, shares the ideal of the equality of believers, and has its own ideas about how they will be judged worthy of heaven—or suffer eternal damnation. The Islamic tradition places less emphasis on voluntarism and free will in determining how believers (and unbelievers) are judged, ascribing all the proceedings of human life, even those that take place while we are unconscious, to an all-powerful God, or Allah. As revealed to Mohammad in the Koran, "Allah takes the souls unto Himself at the time of their death, and that which has not died in its sleep. He keeps those on whom he has decreed death, but looses the others until a stated term." The upshot is that, while Islam rejects fatalism, events are not random. Although, time, for Muslims, is not cyclical, nor does it proceed with such inexorable forward momentum as it does in Christian thinking.[3]

The eschatological and egalitarian impulses in Christian thought received a further shot in the arm with the (accidental) discovery of the New World after Columbus's famous voyage of 1492. When European Christians encountered more "primitive" peoples, it was perhaps natural that these "native" Americans were viewed as pre-Revelation innocents who lived in an unspoiled garden like that of Eden (although, after the arrival of Europeans, it would not remain unspoiled for long). Columbus himself claimed to observe, of the native inhabitants of what are now the Bahamas, Haiti, and Cuba, in his letter reporting to King Ferdinand of Spain, who had sponsored his voyage, that "all go naked, men and women, as their mothers bore them, although some of the women"—like Eve— "cover a single place with the leaf of a plant." Economic and social innocents, too, these inhabitants of the New World were, according to Columbus, "so guileless and so generous with all that they possess, that no one would believe it who has not seen it. They refuse nothing that they possess, if it be asked of them; on the contrary, they invite any one to share it."[4]

Columbus was, of course, defective in his understanding of the peoples he encountered, whose languages he did not speak, and whose societies were far more sophisticated and socially differentiated than he assumed. But the excitement born of his discovery of such radically different cultures, however much may have been lost in translation, inspired a whole new tradition of Christian writing about New Worlds that might be less corrupted, less fallen, than the Europe they lived in. The archetypal example, which gave its name to the genre, was Thomas More's *Utopia* (1516).[*] More presents a strange but oddly compelling vision of a society without money, law, or lawyers, where economic activity is rationally planned by "magistrates who never engage the people in unnecessary labour." "The chief end of the constitution," he wrote, "is to regulate labour by the necessities of the public, and to allow all the people as much time as is necessary for the improvement of their minds, in which they think the happiness of life consists." And yet social equality

---

[*] The book was published in Latin as *Libellus vere aureus nec minus salutaris quam festivus de optimo reip[ublicae] statu, deq[ue] noua Insula Vtopia* (*The Best State of a Commonwealth and the Island of Utopia*). It is simplified to *Utopia* in most English editions.

remains distant in More's utopian society: slavery is allowed, and we are told that "wives serve their husbands."[5]

The Christian Reformation, launched by Martin Luther when he posted his famous "Ninety-Five Theses" on the door of the church at Wittenberg in 1517—the year after More's *Utopia* was published—also spawned radical visions of the remaking of society. Luther's critique of the Church's material corruption was radical enough, proposing a more democratic "priesthood of all believers" in place of the increasingly ornate hierarchy of the Catholic Church, which was financed by taxes (the tithe) and the sale of "indulgences." Nonetheless, Luther balked at the idea of overturning the social order, disowning, and then denouncing, the German Peasant Rebellion of 1524–1525 in a bluntly titled polemic, *Against the Robbing Murderous Hordes of Peasants*. Other Reformation thinkers were willing to go further. Jean Calvin (1509–1564) and his followers, in service of their belief in the predestination of human souls for heaven or hell, created a number of small, tight-knit communities defined by austere morality and principled renunciation of materialism, most famously the Republic of Geneva, which would inspire Jean-Jacques Rousseau (discussed below).

Still more extreme were the Anabaptists, who seized control of Münster in February 1534. Inspired by the idea that not only faith, but even baptism, should be a matter of individual conscience and free will—that is, left to the discretion of rational adults, rather than imposed on infants too young to understand the ritual—Anabaptists were already radical by Reformation standards, with many of them participating in the German Peasant Rebellion. Given the chance to reorganize society in Münster, one Anabaptist sect, led by a former baker of Dutch origin named Jan Matthys, began by cleansing Catholics and Lutherans, then seized all the gold and silver in the town, looted Catholic monasteries of their wealth, abolished money, and declared food stocks common property. The radical new social order was enforced by terror, with public executions of critics, and by the edict that all houses keep their front doors open, so as to ensure that no private space be allowed for dissent. In this frenzied atmosphere of enforced social conformity, all books other than the Old and New Testaments were banned, and then collected and burned in great public bonfires. Matthys's ever more radical Anabaptist commune lasted about six weeks, until the tyrant of this theocratic utopia was cut down in battle and dismembered in early April—on Easter Sunday—with his head erected on a pole above the town to discourage future radical experiments.[6]

Not all "utopian" thinkers, of course, wanted to set history's clock backward to simpler times in the manner of Calvinists and Anabaptists. In *New Atlantis* (1626), Francis Bacon dreamed up a world enriched by the systematic study of plants, animals, and the heavens, enabled by the construction of observatories, nature parks, fish pools, and experimental facilities for agriculture, along with "brewhouses, bake-houses and kitchens." Inspired by Bacon and the tinkerers who ushered in Europe's scientific revolution, Denis Diderot and Jean d'Alembert set out to "assemble all the knowledge scattered on the surface of the earth" in a great *Encyclopédie* (1751–1772), so that, in Diderot's words, "our descendants, by becoming more learned, may become more virtuous and happier." In this way the Enlightenment rationalism of the philosophes secularized Christian eschatology, establishing a kind of European religion of social progress.[7]

By separating divine revelation from reason, however, the philosophes also forfeited much of the beauty and power of the Christian faith while also shunting Christian ideals about virtuous poverty and charity to the side. The hyper-rational "republic of letters" envisioned by Diderot, d'Alembert, and the famously irreligious Voltaire in the *Encyclopédie* was elitist rather than democratic, appealing more to enlightened despots, such as Frederick II of Prussia and

Catherine the Great of Russia, than to ordinary Christians, or even the growing numbers of literate Europeans.

In the end, it was the skeptical *enfant terrible* of the French Enlightenment, the Genevan autodidact and itinerant tutor Jean-Jacques Rousseau (1712–1778), who left behind the era's most enduring vision of social equality. Only in a "happy and tranquil republic," Rousseau argued in his *Discourse on the Origin and Foundations of Inequality Among Men* (1755), could humanity avoid the corruptions that led to the "different privileges enjoyed by some at the expense of others, such as being richer, more honored, more powerful than they, or even causing themselves to be obeyed by them." Like Christian saints and Columbus misinterpreting American natives (whom Rousseau revealingly described as "savages"), he looked back to a mythical lost Eden. Unlike Bacon and the philosophes, he did not believe that reason and scientific "progress" would improve lives. "The more we accumulate knowledge," Rousseau warned, "the more we deprive ourselves of the means of acquiring the most important knowledge of all." Civilization and material improvement were morally corrupting, depriving people of their natural freedom, entrenching inequality and slavery, and rendering men selfish and ambitious. "The first person who, having enclosed a plot of land, took it into his head to say, 'This is mine,'" Rousseau surmised, "and found people simple enough to believe him, was the true founder of civil society. What crimes, wars, murders, what miseries and horrors would the human race have been spared, had someone pulled up the stakes or filled in the ditch and cried out to his fellowmen, 'Do not listen to this impostor. You are lost if you forget that the fruits of the earth belong to all and the earth to no one!'"[8]

In this celebrated passage, Rousseau came as close to the vision of a propertyless world of social equals as any thinker had done since Plato and Aristophanes. But he did not repudiate private wealth entirely, recognizing that "the idea of property . . . was necessary to make great progress, acquire many skills and much enlightenment, and transmit and augment them from one age to another." In the famous opening of his 1762 work *On the Social Contract*, Rousseau proclaimed that "man is born free, but is everywhere in chains"— but his program for liberating them did not include the abolition of private property. Rather, "in accepting the goods of private individuals," a justly organized community "assures them of legitimate possession." Rousseau did insist that "each private individual's right to own his own land is always subordinate to the community's right to all," and thus conditional on one's civic status. As Rousseau explained in his most notorious passage, in order for any "social compact to avoid being an empty formula, it tacitly entails the commitment—which alone can give force to the others—that whoever refuses to obey the general will [*volonté générale*], will be forced to do so by the entire body." By "violating the laws" of the community, such a "malefactor" must be "put to death," Rousseau argued, "less as a citizen than as an enemy." Nonetheless, as long as a citizen obeyed the laws embodied in the "general will" of his political community, his right to own property was upheld. Radical republican Rousseau might have been, but he was not, quite, a Communist.[9]

A large part of the reason Rousseau's works became a standard part of the Western educational curriculum is that they so clearly influenced the course of the French Revolution. Rousseau's idea of the "general will," a nebulous notion of consensus public opinion or mandate he never quite defines in the *Social Contract*—there is no implication that it need reflect an actual democratic vote—made it into clause 6 of the Declaration of the Rights of Man and Citizen passed by the French National Assembly in August 1789 ("Law is the expression of the general will"), to which all other clauses are subordinated. In the language he used to justify the "Terror" of

1793–1794, Maximilien Robespierre channeled Rousseau's views on the purging of disloyal citizens when he wrote that "if the mainspring of popular government in peacetime is virtue, amid revolution it is at the same time [both] *virtue* and *terror.*" With the guillotining of more than 20,000 traitorous "enemies of the people," Robespierre brought Rousseau's draconian vision to life, establishing a precedent for apocalyptic revolutionary terror that has alternately inspired or terrified westerners ever since.[10]

The story of Robespierre's rise to power and his spectacular downfall on the ninth day of the revolutionary month of Thermidor, Year II (July 27, 1794), when he was guillotined along with eighty-three key collaborators, retains its dramatic appeal today. But in the history of Communism, Thermidor represents a dead end. The furthest Robespierre had been willing to go in socioeconomic reform was the "Law of the General Maximum," passed by the National Convention in September 1793, which established price ceilings on grain, meat, oil, soap, salt, shoes, and other essentials; punishments for violators; and a cap on wages. In the end, it may have been the national military draft, or *levée en masse*, of August 1793, not the short-lived Maximum of September, that established the more significant precedent for Communism. France's government began forcibly conscripting soldiers and workers—from foundrymen and tanners and tailors to bakers—into war industry, thus establishing a model for state direction and control of the economy, at least in wartime.[11]

However radical their ideas seemed at the time, from the perspective of the modern socialist or Communist Rousseau and his Robespierre were not radical enough. Widely read in the West, Rousseau's writings were never part of the Marxist-Leninist canon. For this reason it is worth examining the work of one of Rousseau's lesser-known contemporaries, who took his critique of social inequality further than Rousseau was willing to go. This was Étienne-Gabriel Morelly (1717–1778), who, like Rousseau, started out as a tutor of modest means. Morelly, from Vitry-le-François, published an anonymous pamphlet, *Code de la nature, ou le véritable esprit de ses lois* (*The Code of Nature, or the True Spirit of Her Laws*), in 1755, the same year that Rousseau published his *Discourse on Inequality*.

Morelly began his pamphlet in much the same vein that Rousseau began his own treatise, lamenting the fall of mankind into its present state of corruption, using the "noble savages" of the Americas as a rebuke to materialistic European civilization, and attributing the bulk of human misery to social inequality. But Morelly, a truer (or at least more literal-minded) Christian than the Genevan autodidact, ascribed man's descent to a single sin, a vice originating in the Garden of Eden itself: greed (*avarice*). "The sole vice that I can recognize in the universe," Morelly thundered, "is *greed*; all the others, whatever name we give them, are only tones, only degrees of [greed] itself, which is the Proteus, the Mercury, the base, the vehicle of all vices." The "desire to possess," he continued, was the "universal plague . . . of selfish interest" that tore at the social fabric. "Where no property exists," Morelly prophesied, "none of its pernicious consequences will exist either."[12]

In Morelly's view, it was not only the increasing prosperity and complexity of European society, compared to the material simplicity of life among "savages," that had brought the evils of property and inequality to society, but also the corruption of Christianity. Once upon a time, Christians had been persecuted, and by this persecution had been "made to feel the equality of all men," even slaves, whose suffering they had so nobly "softened." Saints such as Martin of Tours had "recommended that the rich surrender their possessions and spread them in the bosom of the poor." But this "spirit of charity" was destroyed by the greed of the Church, which erected "mediators between God and man" and siphoned off wealth from the poor to rich ministers of the faith.[13]

To restore the true spirit of Christianity, and usher man into a modern utopia mimicking the humbler virtues of mankind's lost Eden, Morelly proposed a series of laws "aligned with the intentions of Nature." The first was that "nothing in society must belong to anyone, either as personal possession nor as capital goods, except those things of which an individual makes immediate use for his need, his pleasure, or his work." Second was that "every citizen must be a man of public sustenance, maintained and occupied at public expense." Third, all citizens must "contribute on their part to the public utility according to their strengths, their talents, and their age." The key to his system, the "Economic and Distributive Law," would stipulate that "all durable goods must be amassed in public storage facilities, whence they will be distributed, some daily and some for fixed terms to all citizens, in order to serve the ordinary needs of life, and the material requirements of the works of different professions; other goods will be furnished to people who use them." In order to prevent anyone from profiting from the variable distribution of goods, Morelly said further that "nothing can be sold, according the *sacred laws*, or be exchanged between citizens." The exchange of all goods must instead be regulated at "the public storage facility . . . where they will be supplied by those who cultivate them, and distributed only for fixed terms to those who collect them"—Morelly noted, in a nod to tradition, "to each family patriarch, for his use and that of his children." To discourage hoarding, those "fixed terms" must be short. "Someone who needs . . . greens, vegetables or fruits," Morelly explained, "will go to the public square, which is where these items will have been brought by the man who cultivated them, and take what he needs for one day only." In a foreign trade corollary, Morelly's final law specified that "if the state is aided by a neighboring nation, or gives aid to the same, this exchange can only take place . . . in public, and one must take scrupulous care that it not introduce any private wealth into the republic."[14]

Here was a powerful vision of a propertyless commonwealth of radical social equality. It uncannily blended together the most promising post-pagan elements in the Western tradition, from Christian eschatology and early Christian notions of material renunciation and charity to Columbian romanticization of the "noble savage" and post-1492 theorizing about "utopia." As French scholars have noted, Morelly cites (or channels) with equal enthusiasm Thomas More, Rousseau, and the philosophes. His vision is somewhat crude and reductionist, jettisoning More's curious tolerance in *Utopia* for slavery and enduring class and sex differences (with the exception of Morelly's embrace of the *paterfamilias*), and subsuming the skeptical and tragic elements in Rousseau's work inside the rationalist optimism of the philosophes. But Morelly is more honest, too, taking Rousseau's premise about the "unnatural" evil of social inequality as the original sin of human civilization to its logical policy conclusion: the forcible abolition of private property, sale, and trade and the monopoly of all economic activity by the state. Small wonder Morelly's work, though mostly ignored in his own lifetime, was embraced by early French socialists such as Charles Fourier, and later became a staple of the Marxist-Leninist canon under Soviet Communism.[15]

Long before Morelly's *Code of Nature* was made into dogma by Soviet academics, however, it inspired a real-life French political movement. What Rousseau's *Social Contract* was to Robespierre's radical republican experiment with Terror in 1794, Morelly's work was to Gracchus Babeuf's ambitious Conspiracy of the Equals, launched in the aftermath of Thermidor.

PROLOGUE

CONSPIRACY OF THE EQUALS

R obespierre's political rivals, along with the thousands of Frenchmen destined shortly to face the guillotine's blade, could breathe a sigh of relief after Thermidor. The excesses of the Terror, along with the persecutions of draft resisters and hoarders falling afoul of the Maximum, wound down even as France's military situation stabilized. There remained political intrigue, but uprisings of the hard Robespierrist Left on April 1 and May 20, 1795 (12 Germinal and 1 Prairial Year III, by the republican calendar), and then a putsch by the royalist Right on October 5, 1795 (13 Vendémiaire Year IV), were crushed. The coup de grace came with Napoleon Bonaparte's "whiff of grapeshot" at the Vendémiaire insurrection—the firing of "grape," or small-caliber round shot, into crowds at short range, to mass-wound and terrorize rather than kill (although many royalists were killed in the operation). In this way the French army imposed its will on the street mobs of Paris, paving the way for a new regime headed by a Five-Man Executive Directory, which vowed that "the strictest observance of laws [would] be its rule."[1]

Not everyone was pleased with the stilling of Parisian revolutionary fervor and the authoritarian turn of the Directors. Beaten and battered though they were by the Thermidorian purges, there remained a residue of hard-left revolutionaries who still believed in the revolutionary trinity of *liberté*, *égalité*, and *fraternité* (liberty, equality, and brotherhood)—especially the central plank, social equality. Among these was a thirty-something political activist named François-Noël Babeuf, who had tasted power and fame in the early years of the Revolution and was loath to sink back into the obscurity of his pre-1789 existence as a clerk managing manorial property rolls, where his job had involved assessing the dues and obligations owed by French peasants to their lords. Although he had been well paid, in the euphoria of the Revolution Babeuf had come to despise his role as caretaker of "the repulsive secrets of the nobility and the story of the usurpation of the land of France."[2]

The convening of the Estates-General by King Louis XVI in 1789 presented Babeuf with a tempting opportunity. Knowing intimately as he did the ins and outs of feudal land tenure, Babeuf was ideally placed to advocate for fairer tax laws—though possibly at the price of his job. In October 1789 he made the break, publishing a short work calling for the abolition of all of France's ancient feudal taxes, despite their having provided him his métier. No longer the paid client of landowners, Babeuf launched a political career, writing screeds attacking unpopular taxes (including the salt tax, or *gabelle*), and urging shopkeepers not to pay their taxes—a campaign that landed Babeuf in prison in July 1790. He was imprisoned again in August 1793 for fraud, in a case involving the disposition of Church lands (which had been nationalized in 1790), though the radical Paris Commune offered him protection. Babeuf took up work on a food supply committee, championing Robespierre's Maximum. Clearly in his element, Babeuf took the name "Gracchus" in honor of the famous populist Roman tribune, grew his hair long, and began accusing other officials of withholding grain for profit. Predictably, this made him new enemies, who had him arrested again in November 1793. In a fortunate accident, a revolutionary tribunal exonerated Babeuf, releasing him on July 18, 1794—just nine days before the executions of 9 Thermidor.[3]

Trying to reactivate his radical base, in November 1794 Babeuf restyled his newspaper *Le Tribun du Peuple* (The tribune of the people) and defended the fallen Robespierre as a "sincere patriot," father of the Maximum and the *levée en masse*. Babeuf attacked war profiteers and demanded an end to France's war, the redistribution of land to the poor, and a return to the Constitution of 1793, which had granted universal male suffrage—a constitution suspended indefinitely owing to the war. "What," he asked in the first issue, "is the French Revolution? An open war between patricians and plebeians, between rich and poor."[4]

Boldly, Babeuf attacked republican leaders of the National Convention by name, all but ensuring that he would be arrested again, as he was in February 1795. Transferred to a prison in Arras, where a number of former Robespierrists were being held, Babeuf recruited followers into a souped-up Jacobin faction, which soon referred to itself as the Conspiracy of Equals. Babeuf's radical prison clique was transferred to Paris on September 10, 1795, and then amnestied by the Convention, which, having suppressed the left-wing uprisings of Germinal and Prairial, was gearing up for its showdown with the Right and thought a few Jacobin firebrands might be useful. Babeuf was thus ironically allowed to relaunch his *Tribun du Peuple* as part of the anti-royalist crackdown remembered for Napoleon's whiff of grapeshot. He even went public with his burgeoning group of conspirators, although camouflaging its name as the "Society of the Pantheon," because they met in the Panthéon atop the Montagne Sainte-Geneviève in the winter of 1795–1796—until Napoleon, turning his sights again on the Left, invaded the monument in February and closed its doors. A warrant for Babeuf's arrest was issued, but he escaped and went into hiding.[5]

Fearing that time might be short, Babeuf put together a shadow revolutionary cabinet styled, in homage to the body Robespierre had sat on in 1793–1794, the "Secret Committee of Public Safety." Babeuf's committee included hardened revolutionaries such as Félix Lepeletier, a wealthy ex-aristocrat and former Jacobin Club secretary; the Marquis Pierre Antoine d'Antonelle, a Jacobin president who had served on the revolutionary Tribunal of Paris in 1793; and Augustin-Alexandre-Joseph Darthé, a public prosecutor in Arras and Calais during the Terror. Alongside these experienced political hands were two talented writers: Philippe Buonarroti, an expatriate Italian descended from the family of Michelangelo, and Sylvain Maréchal, an author who had dabbled in philosophy, poetry, and playwrighting, and who would make a more immediate splash by composing a Manifesto of the Equals for Babeuf's revolutionary committee.[6]

Like Babeuf, Maréchal was an admirer of Étienne-Gabriel Morelly's *Code of Nature*. Maréchal, too, had fallen afoul of pre-Revolution censors with a work advocating for social equality (*Livre de tous les âges* [Book for all ages], 1779). Also like Babeuf, Maréchal spent the revolutionary years consumed by public feuds, though he still found time to write a blood-curdling play that envisioned the mass extinction of European royalty. As if to erase all doubt about his message, Maréchal's *Le jugement dernier des rois* (The last judgment of kings) premiered on October 17, 1793—the day after Queen Marie Antoinette was guillotined. ("A volcano explodes," Maréchal's stage notes say, cheerfully describing the play's final scene, represented by "stones, hot coals, etc. flying down on the stage": "An explosion ensues: fire envelops the kings from all sides, and they fall, consumed in the bowels of the half-opened earth.")[7]

Already notorious for his militant atheism and his regicidal drama, Maréchal outdid himself with the Manifesto of the Equals. "People of France!" he begins, "During fifteen centuries you have lived as slaves. . . . [F]rom time immemorial does the most degrading and monstrous inequality insolently oppress the human race." Despite its promising beginning, all Maréchal, Babeuf, and the conspirators now heard from the corrupt leaders of the French Revolution was "Be silent, miserables! Absolute equality is nought but a chimera; be contented with conditional equality; you are all *equal before the law*." Rather than *civic* equality, "the Equals" demanded "equality of fact, the final aim of social art." "We demand," Maréchal proclaimed, "henceforth to live and to die equal, as we have been born so. We demand real equality or death." The new "Republic of the Equals" would make "disappear, once and for all, the revolting distinction of rich and poor, of great and little, of masters and servants, of governors and governed," leaving "no other differences in mankind than those of age and sex." In a flourish meant to echo down through the generations, Maréchal prophesied that "the French Revolution is but the precursor of another, and a greater and solemn revolution, which will be the last!"[8]

Whether out of caution or jealousy, Babeuf did not allow Maréchal's Manifesto to be published in the *Tribun du Peuple*— it is known to us through Buonarroti's reproduction of it in his history glorifying the Equals, published in 1836. Instead, Babeuf condensed its themes into his own Manifesto. Because "nature has given to every man an equal right to the enjoyment of all goods," Babeuf declared, "in a true society there ought to be neither rich nor poor." Transferring the vector of Robespierre's Terror from citizenship to class, Babeuf said that "the rich who are unwilling to renounce their superfluity in favor of the indigent are *the enemies of the people*." Babeuf called Frenchmen to resume the Revolution thwarted by Thermidor, restore the radical 1793 Constitution, and judge the Directors "guilty of treason against the people."[9]

In retaliation for the ever more seditious rhetoric emanating from the Babeuvists, on April 16, 1796, the Directors made advocacy of the 1793 Constitution a capital crime. Babeuf now moved from seditious rhetoric to actual sedition, recruiting followers among the Paris police and local army units, dividing the capital up into neighborhoods under the control of trusted committee members, and printing up copies of an "Insurrectionary Act" to distribute around the city when the moment came for the hoped-for uprising. This document called for the restoration of the Constitution of 1793, the dissolution of both the Directory and the two captive legislative houses as "usurpers of the popular authority," and the arrest of all their members, who "shall be immediately judged by the people." The judgment envisioned for these and other class enemies would be harsh: "All opposition shall be instantly put down by force. The parties resisting shall be exterminated. Also shall be put to death all those who beat, or cause to be beat, the generals of the people [e.g., the Babeuvists], all foreigners, no matter of what nation, who shall be found in the streets, along with all the presidents, secretaries, and commandants of the royalist conspiracy of Vendémiaire, who may dare show their faces in public."

The object of this salutary political violence was to seize "all the property of . . . the *enemies of the people*" and redistribute it "without delay amongst the defenders of the country [e.g., Babeuf and his co-conspirators] and the unhappy poor." All property would be nationalized, and the poor would be domiciled "with lodging and furniture" confiscated from usurpers. In a nod to Morelly, Babeuf emphasized that "provisions of all sorts shall be brought to the people on the public places," where they would be distributed equally, according to need. An accompanying declaration, seized by authorities, scaled this up to the country at large: "A great national community of goods shall be established in the republic," such that "the property belonging to the national community shall be exploited in common by all its healthy members," who must, in turn, "perform all labour of which [they] are capable in agriculture and in industry," with the only exceptions being the sick and those over sixty years old. All active citizens not exterminated or expropriated as class enemies would be assured, by regional committees tasked with sharing out property, "a healthy, convenient, and well-furnished dwelling; clothes for work and clothes for leisure, of linen or wool . . . washing, lighting, heating; a sufficient quantity of the means of nourishment," and "medical aid."[10]

Babeuf's call to arms was not subtle, but it contained enough appreciation of the balance of forces to distinguish it from utopian literature of the kind Morelly, Rousseau, and Maréchal had indulged in. Anticipating resistance, Babeuf emphasized tactics, from the recruitment of mutineers from police and military units to the adoption of "tri-coloured ribands . . . around their hats" as a Babeuvist uniform to distinguish friend from foe. "Rendezvous points" would be designated for the distribution of arms to insurrectionists and volunteers, and insurgents were instructed to raid "every magazine, public or private, containing provisions, ammunition of war, or military stores." Moreover, "the barriers and the course of the [Seine] river" would be "sedulously guarded," and "no person" would be permitted to leave Paris "without a formal and special order of the Insurrectional Committee." There was no airy-fairy assumption here that a government could be overthrown, that property could be seized and redistributed, without ruthless organization and cleansing revolutionary violence.[11]

Unfortunately for Babeuf, he was not as effective a putschist as a pamphleteer. Although the uprising was planned for May 19, 1796, trigger-happy recruits from the Paris police mutinied three weeks earlier, April 28, tipping off the authorities. The police mutiny was suppressed, with seventeen Babeuvist policemen executed. On May 10, Babeuf and Buonarroti were rounded up, soon followed by eight other committee members arrested in the capital and another forty-eight conspirators in the provinces. One last mutinous spasm, which saw a group of underground Babeuvists march out to an army camp at Grenelle, outside Paris, in September, was likewise crushed with malice. The Conspiracy of the Equals was snuffed out before it really got going.[12]

Still, Babeuf had one card left to play. As the Directors wanted to hold a grand public trial to snuff out the insurrectionary movement for good, he was given the chance to defend himself. In April 1797, Babeuf delivered a courtroom address lasting nearly three days, and it was not so much aimed at securing his acquittal as outlining his principles for posterity. What was truly on trial, Babeuf insisted, was not a mere "conspiracy against established authority," but "ideas the ruling class deems inconceivably dangerous; dangerous, because such ideas are subversive of the power and privilege that our rulers have themselves usurped; dangerous, because they are based upon self-evident truths and elementary notions of justice, and may, therefore, all too easily spark a revolutionary fire among the masses." "Of this," he added, "our leaders stand in mortal dread."

Blazoned in his indictment as "Confiscation of Private Property," these ideas, Babeuf freely admitted, included published statements that "in a truly just social order there are neither rich nor poor"; that "the rich, who refuse to give up their superfluous wealth for the benefit of the poor, are enemies of the people"; and that "the purpose of the Revolution is to abolish inequality and to restore the common welfare." Unashamed, Babeuf read out long passages from the *Tribun du Peuple*, including quite explicit ones, such as the Morelly-esque exhortation "to organize a communal regime which will suppress private property, set each to work," and "require each to deposit the fruits of his labor in kind at the common store, and establish an agency for the distribution of basic necessities." Were these ideas really, Babeuf asked the jury members of the High Court of Vendôme, "as the prosecution alleges, damnable, vicious, and subversive"?[13]

As Babeuf must have himself expected, these ideas advocating the overthrow of a government and the confiscation of private property were indeed judged subversive, and he was condemned on May 26 and guillotined for sedition on May 27, 1797. Writing a farewell to his wife and children on the night before his execution, Babeuf declared that he had "no regrets that I have given my life to the best of causes. Even if all my efforts have been in vain, I have done my duty." As he must have hoped, Babeuf's "Defense Before the High Court of Vendôme" was later transcribed and published in multiple languages. His co-conspirator Philippe Buonarroti, wiggling out of a death sentence, survived long enough to witness France's 1830 Revolution, which furnished a platform for him to publish a memoir-history memorializing Babeuf's "Conspiracy for Equality." It sold more than 50,000 copies and inspired the French socialist tradition that emerged later in that decade; Marx's theory of Communism, a decade later; and the Paris Commune of 1871. Babeuf had thus died a martyr's death for Communism, dramatizing his principles in a doomed courtroom stand and ensuring that they would live on.[14]

PART I
COMMUNISM IN THEORY

1
KARL MARX AND THE UTOPIANS

Dramatic though Babeuf's trial might have been, in truth his Conspiracy of the Equals never had a realistic chance at power. By the time Babeuf appeared on the scene, the French revolutionary government had acquired considerable practice in suppressing sedition, displaying a ruthlessness King Louis XVI had lacked in 1789. Napoleon Bonaparte had successfully suppressed the royalists with his "Whiff of Grapeshot" in October 1795, and he had cut off the oxygen to the Babeuvists and other Jacobin clubs in the spring of 1796 by closing down the Panthéon. So it is not surprising that he also snuffed out the last revolutionary embers by mounting an armed coup d'état during the month of Brumaire (i.e., December) in 1799. Completing the Roman cycle from monarchy to republic to one-man dictatorship, Napoleon had himself proclaimed first consul, then first consul for life (1802), and finally emperor of the French (1804).

For an aspiring European radical, there was little left of the dream of greater social equality that had been brought to the fore by the Revolution of 1789. Despite his claims to be a "Liberator," because he brought French-style constitutions to many of the lands he conquered, Napoleon had little interest in social reform beyond toppling decrepit ruling houses and humbling his well-born military enemies. The Code Napoléon, first promulgated in 1804 and still the basis for much of Europe's civil law to this day, firmly upheld private property rights, restored legal prerogatives of male heads of households, and even made slavery legal again. Napoleon's military comeuppance in Russia in 1812, which culminated in his defeat at Waterloo in 1815, led Klemens von Metternich and the other statesmen rearranging Europe at the Congress of Vienna (1814–1815) to restore the monarchical principle in France and across Europe. They further enlisted three Great Powers (Prussia, Austria, and Russia) in a pledge, signed at Troppau in 1820, to suppress popular revolutions breaking out anywhere in Europe "by peaceful means, or if need be by arms." Revolution was out, reaction was in.[1]

With no realistic hope of obtaining political power, social reformers turned to smaller-scale benevolent projects instead. Henri de Saint-Simon, a French count with a lineage dating all the way back to Charlemagne, sought to revive the old Christian ideal of charity, which he thought had gotten lost amid material progress and Enlightenment rationalism. "Remember," he counseled readers of his *New Christianity* (1825), "that Christianity commands you to use all your powers to increase as rapidly as possible the social welfare of the poor!" Although Saint-Simon never really put his ideas into practice, his eloquence and magnetic personality inspired legions of disciples.[2]

Going Saint-Simon one better, Robert Owen, an idealistic mill owner, sought to rationalize and improve conditions for workers after taking over the cotton mills at New Lanark, near Glasgow, Scotland, providing them with schooling and various incentives to improve productivity. Owen then purchased land and attempted to create a planned agro-industrial community from scratch in New Harmony, Indiana, in 1825. It was to be devoted to "liberty, equality and fraternity in downright earnest," which would "unite all interests into one, and remove all causes for contest between individuals"—including the institution of marriage, which Owen denounced as "unnatural," though with less success. Many settler families, offended by Owen's attacks on marital chastity, left the community or were expelled for failing to get with the program. By 1827, Owen had given up, laying blame on the community members who had failed him. "Families trained in the individual system," he concluded, "have not acquired those moral characteristics of forbearance and charity necessary for confidence and harmony." Another dozen-odd efforts by Owen's followers to found similar planned economic utopias all failed in similar ways, none of them lasting more than two years.[3]

Charles Fourier, a wealthy French merchant from the textile hub of Lyon, who had become shocked at the conditions of its workers, proposed a radical restructuring of industrial plants into voluntary *phalanges*, or "phalanxes." In this system, laborers would receive a larger share of the profits, and they would change tasks frequently so as to stay stimulated and avoid monotony. A dose of freer sexual morals—like Owen, Fourier regarded marital chastity as unrealistic—would be thrown in as a sweetener. In 1833, Fourier tried to build his first phalanx on 500 hectares of virgin land at Condé-sur-Vesgre, near Rambouillet, forming a joint stock company and setting laborers to work clearing the land and building provisional living and farm quarters. Unfortunately, the architect he hired wasted much of the seed capital building a "pigsty with stone walls eighteen inches thick and no entrance," which convinced Fourier his project was being sabotaged, and he abandoned it within a year. Blaming its failure on souls corrupted by materialism and the other compromises of civilized life, he vowed to try again someday, but next time, he intended to build his utopia using only children, who would be uncorrupted by civilization.[4]

Despite the failure of these utopian projects to bear fruit, the intellectual soil in the Restoration era for social reformers was not entirely barren. France's short-lived July Revolution of 1830, though a disappointment to radicals, ushered forth a golden age of social critique. The franchise in the new "July" constitutional monarchy of Louis Philippe I (r. 1830–1848) was restricted to a thin crust of fewer than 200,000 wealthy taxpayers, a mere 1 percent of the population. The glaring material inequality of citizens under the July Monarchy furnished the backdrop to the "equality of conditions" in the early United States described by Alexis de Tocqueville in his 1835 masterwork *Democracy in America*. "Do you think," Tocqueville asked in his introduction, "that after having destroyed feudalism and vanquished the kings, democracy will retreat before the bourgeois and the rich?" The dominant social and political position of the *haute bourgeoisie* under the July Monarchy also inspired new French terms, such as *socialism(e)*, coined by Henri Leroux, one of Saint-Simon's disciples, in 1831 (Owen had used the word "socialist" in 1828, but never "socialism"). While its meaning was somewhat vague at first, during the years of the July Monarchy "socialism" caught on among radicals hoping the next revolution would bring about more equal social conditions.[5]

Another French social theorist of the time, beginning from a similar premise, went in a different direction. "What is property?" asked Pierre Proudhon in an 1840 treatise of that name, and not rhetorically. Answering his own question, Proudhon declared that "property is robbery" (or *theft*). Because it upheld property rights, "government" was, in Proudhon's view, a mere enforcer of "vengeance and repression." He meant it, too, noting that social reformers from Plato to Rousseau to Babeuf had all advocated for a stronger government, one that deployed tyrannical violence and injustice to eradicate private wealth while also producing a "pious and stupid uniformity." The "communism" that promoters of forced social equality strove for, Proudhon declared baldly, was "oppression and slavery." Rather than socialism or communism, he envisioned a world without the inequities of property or the established authorities to uphold it, declaring himself an "anarchist," and defining anarchy as the "absence of a ruler or a sovereign."[6]

In this way, French thinkers, inspired by their country's potent revolutionary tradition, created the vocabulary of modern socialism and anarchism. It was left to a more systematic German thinker to iron out the multiplying contradictions. Karl Marx (1818–1883), born in Trier, a once independent electorate absorbed into the Prussian Rhineland in 1815, was heir to both the atheistic (or at least irreligious) French revolutionary, socialist tradition, which he studied intently, and the German philosophical tradition, more heavily infused with Christian themes. The philosopher who most shaped Marx's thinking, Georg Wilhelm Friedrich Hegel (1770–1831), was a self-avowedly Orthodox Lutheran Christian, but one who took Enlightenment rationalism seriously. Unlike Rousseau, Morelly, the philosophes, and the socialists, Hegel used reason not to critique the existing order but to find an inner logic and harmony in the evolution of human society. True, Hegel admitted, "the history of the world is not a scene of happiness." But he insisted that it was in the course of struggle against injustice, through a dialectical process between opposing forces—the collision of *thesis* and *antithesis*, producing *synthesis*—that mankind had become self-aware and free. "World history," Hegel proclaimed, "is the progress of the consciousness of freedom." Christianity had bequeathed "moral dignity" to all souls, overriding the "distinction between classes of society" in places such as caste-ridden Hindu India, instead ushering in the modern concept of "equality before the law" and the "rights of person and property." Channeling Rousseau's "general will" in a more conservative direction, Hegel saw its fulfillment in bourgeois family life, civil society, and the modern state, asserting, in *Elements of the Philosophy of Right* (1820), that "it is only through being a member of the state that the individual himself has objectivity, truth, and ethical life." Whatever disgruntled French atheists might say, Hegel pointed out, life under secularized European Christianity was pretty good, and it was getting better all the time.[7]

Of course, the eschatological "dialectic" animating Hegel's secularized Christian philosophy, however conservative in his own interpretation, could easily be inverted into a profound critique of the existing order. In his *Critique of Hegel's Philosophy of Right* (c. 1843), Marx inverted Hegel's Christian rationalism into a frontal critique of religion, while retaining the eschatology. "Religion is indeed man's self-consciousness and self-awareness," Marx agreed, but only "so long as he has not found himself." In reality, "*man makes religion*; religion does not make man." Christianity, Marx conceded, gave men solace in suffering: religion was the "sigh of the oppressed creature, the sentiment of a heartless world," or, in his famous aphorism, "the opium of the people." But the "task of history" was not, contra Hegel, to enrapture men and women in religious superstition and obedience to families and secular authority, but to "establish the truth of this world," however dark. The "task of philosophy" was not to soothe, but to "unmask human self-alienation." As Marx put it in his "Theses on Feuerbach" in 1845, "The philosophers have only *interpreted* the world, in various ways; the point, however, is to *change* it."[8]

But how were philosophers to change the world, and why was Marx the man to do it? A critique of religion and the social order it helped uphold did not necessarily imply a critique of private property or social inequality as such. Rousseau and Morelly had lambasted inequality in part owing to their own precarious circumstances, as marginally employed itinerant tutors and scribblers. Babeuf had drawn on his expertise in feudal law in his blistering critiques of feudalism, which he attempted to realize through political action. Owen and the French utopians, all wealthy men, had been motivated out of a sense of Christian charity or *noblesse oblige* to improve the lot of workers. By contrast, Marx, still in his early twenties when he began writing his Hegelian commentaries, had no experience of business or politics; he was a kind of perennial student, who had done stints at the Universities of Bonn and Berlin before submitting a philosophy thesis for a doctorate at the University of Jena in April 1841.* All the while, he was living off subsidies provided by his father, Heinrich Marx, a successful attorney in Trier, who was increasingly frustrated by his son's refusal to train for a real profession. "As though he were made of gold," Heinrich complained, "my gentleman son disposes of almost 700 Thalers in a single year, in contravention of every usage and every agreement, whereas the richest spend no more than 500."⁹

Karl Marx represented a new, though soon familiar, social type, the *déclassé* bourgeois intellectual, not rich or well-born enough to live a life of social consequence, but content to spend down his inheritance as long as his parents allowed him to. He spent his time in Berlin in informal social clubs of Left Hegelian students, who, Marx's biographer Isaiah Berlin tells us, "met in beer cellars, wrote mildly seditious verse, professed violent hatred of the [Prussian] King, the church, the bourgeoisie, and above all argued endlessly on points of Hegelian theology." Rather than appreciating the good fortune that allowed him to live this agreeable life of leisure, Marx wrote poetry that, like his philosophy, was angry and misanthropic. In *Savage Songs*, published in January 1841, a twenty-two-year-old Marx lamented that humans were "shattered, empty, frightened,"

---

* Marx did not attend the University of Jena, but submitted his doctoral thesis (on the "theories of nature" in the philosophies of Democritus and Epicurus) by mail. He had been dropped from the rolls of the more prestigious University of Berlin after his mentor, Bruno Bauer, had left that institution. While his thesis was a serious piece of work, in view of his failure to complete a proper diploma with Bauer in Berlin it is not surprising that Marx never won an academic position.

the "apes of a cold God," a God who warned his apes, "I shall howl gigantic curses at mankind."[10]

Marx's social radicalism did not arise from his own economic situation or any unpleasant experience of business or factory life. He was certainly embittered after learning, in June 1841, upon returning to Trier after earning his Jena doctorate, that he would not receive anything substantial from his deceased father's estate (his share of 362 thalers was dwarfed by the debts he had incurred to his mother, Henrietta). "My family, in spite of its affluence," he complained in a letter to his friend Arnold Ruge, had "exposed" him "to the most wretched conditions." Still, not everyone disappointed in a meager inheritance concludes, as Marx later did when writing to Ruge, that philosophy must be driven by a "ruthless criticism of everything existing."[11]

It was the power of rhetorical flights of fancy like this, along with the air of sublime self-confidence they reflected, that began to win Marx attention and admirers. Moses Hess, a wealthy Jewish Hegelian student from Cologne who, in October 1842, offered Marx his first real job—editing and writing for the *Rheinische Zeitung* (Rhineland news)—gushed that Marx was his "idol," someone who "combine[d] the deepest philosophical seriousness with the most cutting wit." Readers seemed to agree, as the newspaper's circulation climbed steadily after he was hired. Curiously, Marx did not take a radical economic line in the *Rheinische Zeitung*, declaring that, as editor, he would not allow the "smuggling of communist and socialist dogmas" into reporting or cultural reviews, as had happened prior to his coming aboard. (If "communism . . . has to be discussed," Marx insisted, this "demanded a . . . more thorough discussion.") Marx's first article on economics, a discussion of the pilfering of fallen wood from privately owned land, took a pro-property line. He argued, in Hegelian style, that the recent codification of property laws had rendered old customary traditions, such as communal access to forests, obsolete. He took a more critical line on the *Zollverein*, or tariff union, which Prussia pushed through in 1834, but his criticism was rooted less in economics than in the heavy-handed actions of the Prussian government. Unfortunately for Marx, even this relatively mild criticism of the authorities led to the paper being shut down in February 1843.[12]

Still, his brief tenure had made an impression. Marx's friend Ruge, a fellow Left Hegelian—whose own publication had been prohibited in the Kingdom of Saxony—proposed that the two of them edit a radical journal in Paris, out of the range of German censors. It would be supported by a wealthy German émigré who offered Marx an annual salary of 550 thalers. Although not princely, this sum was enough to support a family, allowing Marx to marry his childhood sweetheart, Jenny von Westphalen, in June 1843. They enjoyed a brief honeymoon in Switzerland before moving to the chic Faubourg Saint-Germain neighborhood in Paris (though living at first in Ruge's flat, to save money).[13]

Leaving the travails of Prussian politics and journalism behind, Marx used his salaried leisure time to plunge back into political theory and the abstractions of Hegelian philosophy, which had been his passion all along. It was in his Paris days that he first embraced socialist themes, already ubiquitous in French radical circles. The key term in Marx's Hegelian pivot toward class was "proletariat," first used by a Swiss economist, Jean Charles Léonard de Sismondi, in 1819. For Sismondi, it denoted "unemployed and poorly employed laborers living in misery," threatened by competition driving wages down and machines that might make their jobs obsolete. Proudhon, too, had used the term. In the second part of *What Is Property?* (1841), he had meant it in the general sense of the poor, whether peasants ("the *proletaire* of the country") or urban workers ("the *proletaire* of the city"). In both cases, attaining greater social equality required the "intellectual and political emancipation of the proletariat."[14]

In his *Critique of Hegel's Philosophy of Right* (1843), Marx took Sismondi's concept of the proletariat to a level of abstraction beyond Proudhon's, describing a social class that did not even exist. "A class must be formed," Marx wrote, "which has *radical chains*, a class in civil society which is not a class of civil society, a class which is the dissolution of all classes, a sphere of society which has a universal character because its sufferings are universal, and which does not claim a *particular redress* because the wrong which is done to it is not a *particular wrong* but *wrong in general*." This imaginary class, "the proletariat," Marx said, must demand "the negation of private property," which will produce "the dissolution of the existing social order." He conceded that, in his native "Germany," the proletariat "was only beginning to form itself." But in the Hegelian dialectic—requiring conflict between opposing social forces to bring progress—backwardness could be an advantage. "Germany," Marx explained, "which likes to get to the bottom of things, can only make a revolution which upsets the *whole order of things*. The *emancipation of Germany* will be an *emancipation of man*. *Philosophy* is the *head* of this emancipation and the *proletariat* is its *heart*. Philosophy can only be realized by the abolition [*Aufhebung*, or self-cancellation] of the proletariat, and the proletariat can only be abolished by the realization of philosophy."[15]

It is worth pausing here to note the incongruity of Marx's increasingly apocalyptic rhetoric, composed at a time when he had just married his childhood sweetheart and been given a dream job writing occasional essays for a generous salary in one of the most fashionable districts of Paris. As his critics have observed, at the time he began banging on about proletarian revolution in 1843, Marx had not yet set foot in a factory, or met or talked to any factory workers. Nor had he done any research on industrial processes or wages, as he would in later years in London. In a series of unpublished manuscripts written in 1844, Marx's analysis of labor consists not of real-world observations, or any kind of data, but of clever Hegelian opposites, which he delighted in expressing: "The worker becomes all the poorer the more wealth he produces." "The more the worker produces, the less he has to consume." "The worker no longer feels himself to be freely active in any but his animal functions," thus "what is animal becomes human and what is human becomes animal." "In the wage of labour, labour does not appear as an end in itself but as the servant of the wage." By working for these wages, man was "estranged from the product of his labor," and this "alienated labor" was the "source" and "consequence" of "private property."

These antithetical formulations led Marx, in his essay on "Private Property and Communism," to the advocacy of the latter as the antithesis that dissolved the former, in the dialectical process, again, of *Aufhebung*, or self-cancellation. In a passage that brought the Hegelian dialectic to the point of parody, Marx declared that "socialism is man's *positive self-consciousness* no longer mediated through the annulment of religion, just as real life is man's positive reality, no longer mediated through the annulment of private property, through *communism*. Communism is the position of the *negation of the negation*, and is hence the *actual* phase necessary for the next stage of historical development in the process of human emancipation and recovery." Showing that this was no accidental turn of phrase, Marx repeated himself when he described communism as the "negation of the negation, as the appropriation of the human essence which mediates itself with itself through the negation of private property." Patting himself on the back, Marx declared that "communism"—his long-delayed exam answer to the questions Hegel asked his students—"is the riddle of history solved, and it knows itself to be the solution."[16]

Marx thus came to believe in Communism during his Paris years not out of real-world experience, but by applying the Hegelian dialectic to his historical studies (mostly of the French Revolution). It was really just a word game, the solving of an intellectual "riddle"— but Marx was good at it. Good, but not quite good enough for prime time. However revealing as a glimpse into his thought process, "negation of the negation" and the "riddle of history solved" was not much of a recommendation for Communism to anyone not already steeped in Hegelian philosophy.

Marx was maturing as a rhetorician, however, and it was not long before his writing was too sharp and original to ignore. What made the difference was the period of soul-searching and networking that followed his expulsion from Paris (on the request of the Prussian government, still smarting from the attacks from his Cologne days) in January 1845. It was in this period, as Marx found an uncomfortable refuge in Brussels (after giving a written pledge to the Belgian authorities not to engage in political activity), that he began spending time with Friedrich Engels, the German socialist who would become his muse, writing partner, and sponsor for the rest of his life. Like Marx, Engels was a well-born Left Hegelian, but one with experience in his family's German textile firm, which had a branch in Manchester. Engels had also served in the Prussian army. Engels's fiery Irish mistress and partner, Mary Burns (on socialist principle they refused to marry), was also, unlike Marx's Jenny, genuinely working-class—she had worked in his family's Manchester textile factory and had done stints in domestic service. Although Engels was two years younger than Marx and tended to regard him as an intellectual mentor, in truth Engels was the one with real-world experience—which kept his Hegelian musings honest and gave them heft.

In the summer of 1845, Engels showed Marx around Manchester and London. This was Marx's first trip to the great industrial powerhouse of England, and he did not visit factories or talk with English workers—he did not yet speak English. But in London Engels did introduce him to members of a "German Workers Educational Association," a proto-union, which pooled resources as a kind of insurance fund for members who fell ill or lost their jobs. Marx was not impressed with the workers' intellectual acumen, however. After one of them, a journeyman tailor named Wilhelm Weitling, tried to justify organizing workers into collectives to negotiate better conditions with their employers, an angry Marx was seen "pound[ing] on the table with his fist" before shouting that "ignorance has never yet helped anyone!" Marx told Weitling that "at the moment there can be no talk of the realization of communism; the bourgeoisie must first take control."[17]

Marx's first experience with labor and labor organizers, then, did not enflame him with a desire to change the world to improve their lot. Rather, the lack of intellectual sophistication of real workers reinforced his belief that doctrine must come first, and that the historical dialectic must be respected. Even so, Marx was game enough to take Engels's advice and begin organizing committees of the like-minded to promote Communist doctrine, although these were still largely made up of bourgeois intellectuals like them. (Despite his straitened circumstances, reduced to selling what was left of the family silver and gold and relying on handouts from Engels and others, Marx still employed servants to help Jenny with the children and housework.) In 1846, Marx and Engels formed a "Communist Committee of Correspondence" in Brussels. Mostly they recruited exiled German intellectuals, but Marx was game enough to invite the French thinker Proudhon to join his correspondence society to promote "an exchange of ideas." Proudhon, alas, told Marx he would be unable to "write to you either at length or often," owing both to his "natural laziness" and to certain philosophical objections. In this letter, datelined

Lyon, May 17, 1846, Proudhon registered the first anarchist critique of Communism, painfully comparing the fierce young German atheist to Martin Luther, the dogmatic prophet of German Protestantism:

> By all means let us work together to discover the laws of society, the ways in which these laws are realized and the process by which we will discover them. But, for God's sake, when we have demolished all the *a priori* dogmas, do not let us think of indoctrinating the people in our turn. Do not let us fall into your compatriot Martin Luther's inconsistency. As soon as he had overthrown Catholic theology he immediately, with constant recourse to excommunications and anathemas, set about founding a Protestant theology. . . . [S]imply because we are leaders of a movement let us not instigate a new intolerance.[18]

Unfazed by this rebuff, Marx attacked Proudhon in *The Poverty of Philosophy* (1847). "Does this mean," he asked rhetorically of Proudhon, "that after the fall of the old society there will be a new class domination culminating in a new political power? No. The condition for the emancipation of the working class is the abolition of every class." After the revolution, Marx promised, the "working class . . . will substitute for the old civil society an association which will exclude classes and antagonism, and there will be no more political power properly so called." In Marx's version of the Hegelian dialectical *Aufhebung*, class would abolish itself, thus making class conflict impossible. The "total revolution" to bring this about would, Marx admitted for the first time, require political violence. The last word in human affairs, he wrote almost with gleeful anticipation, was "combat or death: bloody struggle or extinction."[19]

Marx's own manner of dealing with political opponents was true to this battle cry. It was in the course of his public feuds with the Prussian authorities, with Proudhon, and with rival German

KARL MARX AND THE UTOPIANS

socialists that Marx refined his pugnacious rhetorical style. Owing to his penchant for insulting those he corresponded with, his correspondence committee never quite got going. But he was still an obvious choice when Engels, to launch a new Communist League in November 1847, wanted someone to write up its political program. Although it took Marx two months to complete the task, the resulting *Manifesto of the Communist Party* was a masterpiece of political rhetoric, full of catchy and memorable aphorisms that would soon be world-famous.

Marx opens the *Manifesto* by asserting, plausibly, if with a bit of exaggeration, that "a spectre is haunting Europe—the spectre of Communism." Leaving aside, for now, his quarrels with fellow German socialists, Marx denounced instead a "holy alliance" of authorities who were trying to "exorcise this spectre." These included "Pope and Czar, Metternich and Guizot [the conservative French prime minister], French Radicals [e.g., center-left but non-socialist politicians] and German police-spies." Rather than let the political establishment defame Communism with a "nursery tale" caricature, Marx said it was now "high time that Communists should openly, in the face of the whole world, publish their views, their aims, their tendencies." This he would do in the "following Manifesto, to be published in the English, French, German, Italian, Flemish and Dutch languages."[20]

Although Marx was working from an original draft by Engels, the final *Manifesto* bears his unmistakable stamp, hypnotic in its Hegelian thrust. "The history of all hitherto existing society," Marx begins, "is the history of class struggles" between "freeman and slave, patrician and plebeian, lord and serf, guild-master and journeyman, in a word, oppressor and oppressed." In the grand and wholly unsourced style of Hegelian history-writing, Marx asserted that ancient Rome was defined by class conflict between "patricians, knights, plebeians, slaves," the Middle Ages by struggle between "feudal lords, vassals, guild-masters, journey-men, apprentices, serfs." The French Revolution had then "sim-plified the class antagonisms," dividing "society as a whole . . . into two great classes directly facing each other: Bourgeoisie and Proletariat."[21]

Building on the theme of "alienation" he had explored in his Paris years, Marx deplored the cold hand of industrialization and "free trade," which, though unleashing "more massive and more colossal productive forces than have all preceding generations together," and "rescu[ing]" peasants from "the idiocy of rural life" by driving them into factories, had torn apart the "motley feudal ties that bound man to his 'natural superiors,'" leaving "no other nexus between man and man than naked self-interest, than cal-lous 'cash payment,'" dissolving all human relations into "the icy water of egotistical calculation." The human family, Marx claimed, had been stripped of "its sentimental veil" and "reduced . . . to a mere money relation." Even the "differences of age and sex," Marx claimed, with some justification in view of the employment of women and children in English textile sweatshops, "no longer have any distinctive social validity for the working class." Less plausi-bly, Marx asserted that modern industry had also "stripped" the wage-earning "proletarian" of "every trace of national character. Law, morality, religion, are to him so many bourgeois prejudices." Admitting that he and other "Communists" were not "proletari-ans" themselves, Marx insisted that they had "over the great mass of the proletariat the advantage of clearly understanding the line of march, the conditions, and the ultimate general results of the prole-tarian mass movement." Above all, they knew and could teach "the theory of the Communists," which "may be summed up in a single sentence: Abolition of private property."[22]

Spelling out what this radical doctrine might mean in practice, Marx condensed Engels's original twenty-five points into a pithier and more memorable ten, headlined by (1) "the abolition of property in land and application of all rents to public purposes," (2) "a heavy progressive or graduated income tax," (3) "abolition of all right of inheritance," and (4) "confiscation of the property of all emigrants and rebels" who might flee the scene. The "state," by which Marx meant whatever proletarian government would assume the reins after the revolution, would be tasked with (5) "centralization of credit . . . by means of a national bank with state capital and an exclusive monopoly," (6) "centralization of the means of communication and transport," (7) the ownership, planning, and management of all "factories and instruments of production," the "bringing of cultivation of waste-lands, and the improvement of the soil . . . in accordance with a common plan," (9) the "combination of agriculture with manufacturing industries," the "more equable distribution of the population over the country," and (10) the dispensation of "free education for all children in public schools," and the "combination of education with industrial production." In view of its ominous implications, the most significant clause of all may be no. 8, in which Marx proclaimed a kind of universal work obligation ("equal liability of all to labour") and demanded the "establishment of industrial armies, especially for agriculture."[23]

Knowing that objections to his astonishingly radical and authoritarian program, whether from property and business owners threatened by it or from skeptical workers themselves, were inevitable, Marx welcomed the criticism. Liberals, conservatives, and even anarchists like Proudhon had warned that forcibly eradicating social inequality must entail "the abolition of individuality and freedom." "Rightly so," Marx declared, if "by freedom is meant, under the present bourgeois conditions of production, free trade, free selling and buying." Critics reproached Communists with "intending to do away with your property," to which Marx replied, "Precisely so; that is just what we intend." Conservative concerns about family life, if education, like property, were taken over by a centralized state, Marx conceded, were well-founded; he boasted proudly that after the Communist revolution "the bourgeois family will vanish as a matter of course." In a notorious passage, Marx denounced such objections as "bourgeois clap-trap about the family and education, about the hallowed co-relation of parent and child," which were "all the more disgusting" in view of what "Modern Industry" had already done to families. As for the "reproach" that Communists aimed "to abolish countries and nationality," Marx again pled guilty, proclaiming that "working men have no country," and that the proletarian revolution would abolish not only the "antagonism between classes" but also "the hostility of one nation to another."[24]

As for the friendly fire Marx expected from rivals on the left, he attacked them preemptively, too, with characteristic vituperation. The work of radical economists such as Sismondi, who had coined the term "proletariat" Marx had adopted, he dismissed as "petty-bourgeois socialism." His fellow German Left Hegelian socialists, Marx wrote, had taken their "schoolboy task so seriously and solemnly" that their work was now relegated to the "domain of . . . foul and enervating literature." The "Socialist and Communist systems" of "Saint-Simon, Fourier, Owen and others," Marx chided, were enervated by naïveté and pacifism. Because they "reject[ed] all political, and especially all revolutionary action," and sought "to attain their ends by peaceful means," their "small experiments . . . of a purely utopian character" were "doomed to failure."[25] Unlike socialists and utopian dreamers, Marx's movement would not shy away from violence. "The Communists," he wrote, concluding the Manifesto in a rousing finale, "disdain to conceal their views and aims. They openly declare that their ends can be attained only by the forcible overthrow of all existing social conditions. Let the ruling classes tremble at

Communistic revolution. The proletarians have nothing to lose but their chains. They have a world to win. Working men of all countries, unite!"[26]

In addition to the mesmerizing rhetorical power of Marx's *Manifesto of the Communist Party*, the timing of its release was exquisite. It went to the printers in February 1848, just days before Paris erupted once again in revolution, with protesters (including, though hardly limited to, industrial workers) throwing up barricades, forcing Guizot to resign, toppling the July Monarchy of Louis Philippe, and proclaiming another French Republic (the second) on February 24. While the *Manifesto* cannot have inspired the events in Paris, the prospect of a French revolutionary wave engulfing Europe was more than enough to provoke the Belgian authorities into arresting Marx on March 3 and deporting him from the country. To his surprise, Marx was invited, by the new provisional republican government in Paris, to return to France, along with Engels and the other German members of his Communist League. They were not long in Paris before the revolution spread across the Rhine, prompting Marx and Engels to return to Cologne and plunge into German politics, reviving the old *Rheinische Zeitung*, now with *Neue* (New) in the title.

Curiously, with a genuine revolution underway in his native Prussia, and its outcome still far from certain, Marx did not endorse Communism in the paper, perhaps hoping to avoid arrest. Only once the revolution had fizzled out in April and May 1849, after the Prussian king, Friedrich Wilhelm IV, refused the crown of a unified German empire, offered him by the constituent German National Assembly gathered in Frankfurt, did Marx finally let fly in the *Neue Rheinische Zeitung*, publishing a kind of farewell issue on May 19, "printed in revolutionary red," calling for "the emancipation of the working class." As the issue was going to press, Marx and Engels fled the Prussian Rhineland, making their way back to Paris, before both men settled down in England more or less permanently as exiles, Engels in Manchester and Marx in London.[27]

The revolutions of 1848 were bitterly disappointing for European radicals. The failure of the Frankfurt Assembly demonstrated the impotence of Germany's liberal constitutionalists, reinforcing Prussian authoritarianism and paving the way for the more cynical (and violent) approach to German unification later taken by Chancellor Otto von Bismarck. Conservative Austria, too, weathered the revolutionary storm, brutally suppressing liberal-nationalist rebellions launched by Italian and Hungarian rebels, in the latter case with the help of Russian troops. France's Second Republic was snuffed out by Louis-Napoleon Bonaparte, nephew of the great conqueror, who won the presidency largely on name recognition in December 1848. He proceeded to make himself Emperor Napoleon III in a coup d'état in December 1851, inspiring Marx's most famous historical work, *The Eighteenth Brumaire of Louis Bonaparte*, the title a reference to the month when the original Napoleon had dissolved the French legislature in 1799, ending the Directory.

For Marx and his *Manifesto of the Communist Party*, the revolutions of 1848, however disappointing their ending, had provided a welcome jolt of publicity. First printed (in German) in London in February 1848, the *Manifesto* came out in French shortly before the "June Days" violence in Paris that spring, with an English translation following in 1850. Soon there were editions in all the main European languages. Catapulted to fame by the revolutions of 1848, Marx had become a household name in Europe. The *Communist Manifesto* has never been out of print since.

This did not mean, however, that Marx had won everyone over. By sheer force of conviction, the Left Hegelian exile from Trier had clambered his way to the top of the heap in European radical politics, planting the flag for "Communism" as the revolutionary doctrine *par excellence*. But he had made plenty of enemies along the way. For the rest of his life, Marx, assisted by his loyal partner Engels, would ruthlessly police the boundaries of his movement. Proudhon was the first to call him out for his authoritarianism, but he would not be the last.

2
THE FIRST INTERNATIONAL AND THE BAKUNIN PROPHECY

Just as Marx's influence and fame had waxed with the European revolutionary wave of 1848–1849, it waned with the era of reaction that followed. The failure of the German revolution ensured that he would not be able to settle down anywhere in Prussia or the German Confederation, consigning him to a life of exile for the foreseeable future. After Napoleon III's "Eighteenth Brumaire," Paris was no longer a viable refuge for notorious radicals like Marx and Engels. London was friendlier to political refugees, but, as Britain's financial and political capital, the beating heart of a global capitalist empire, it was also frightfully expensive. Even Engels, from whom Marx had sponged money for years, was cut off by his wealthy parents after his revolutionary escapades in 1848–1849. By the summer of 1850, so desperate were these German Communist exiles that Engels proposed to his parents that he would abjure radical politics and cross the Atlantic to represent the family cotton business in America, his real idea being that he and Marx might rejuvenate their political fortunes among the huge

German-speaking community in New York City. Alas, Engels's mother, sniffing out her son's intentions, proposed instead that he represent the family firm in Calcutta, a city empty of German radical exiles. Unable to scrape together money for the passage, Marx and Engels abandoned their idea of moving to New York and thus planting the seeds of Communism in America.[1]

In the end, Engels agreed to sacrifice his pride and work for the family business in Manchester. Even so, in the early days of his business career he could offer his friend only modest subventions, "moving the Marx family's financial situation," as one biographer observed, "from impossible to merely desperate." It was enough to allow Marx to avoid regular employment and continue his career as a pamphleteering political activist. But it was a lonely existence. While Marx scraped together a new Communist League, there were so few members in London that he had to relinquish leadership to the larger faction in Cologne—until it was smashed by the Prussian authorities, who put eleven defendants on trial in October 1852 and convicted seven. Conceding defeat, Marx dissolved the Communist League.[2]

Discouraging though this latest setback was, it allowed Marx time to return to his true métier, which was not politics as such but political writing. Whatever Marx might have lacked in organizational acumen and interpersonal skills, he was a talented wordsmith. In the hands of Hegel and most Hegelians, the dialectic was a slog, a recondite code language designed to repel understanding by those uninitiated into the jargon. In Marx's more capable hands, "dialectical materialism," as his application of the dialectic to the "class struggle" was soon called, becomes not only comprehensible but rhythmic and memorable. Reading Hegel, as students the world over have noticed for more than two centuries, is difficult in any language. The prose of Marx, by contrast, works in English, French, Italian, and Russian just as well as in German. "Working Men of All Countries, Unite!" loses none of its power in translation.

Marx wrote better history, too. Some of his historical works, such as the *Eighteenth Brumaire*, can be read with profit today. "Hegel remarks somewhere," Marx begins, "that all great, world-historical facts and personages occur, as it were, twice. He has forgotten to add: the first time as tragedy, the second as farce." Marx turns his aphorism into a philosophy of history pithier and more profound than anything Hegel had come up with. "Men make their own history, but they do not make it just as they please; they do not make it under circumstances chosen by themselves, but under circumstances directly found, given and transmitted from the past," he wrote: "the tradition of all the dead generations weighs like a nightmare on the brain of the living."[3] Marx does not jettison his Hegelian class-struggle theory entirely in the *Eighteenth Brumaire*, but it never overwhelms what is basically a traditional narrative of fast-moving events. Nor are the classes in play reduced to a mere binary opposition of "proletariat" and "bourgeoisie." Marx can barely contain his amusement at the *déclassé* "bohemian" antics of his well-born antihero Louis-Napoleon Bonaparte, whose "lumpen-proletarian" followers he describes as "vagabonds, discharged soldiers, discharged jailbirds, escaped galley slaves, swindlers, mountebanks."[4]

Class does play a role in Marx's narrative, but it is fluid and not necessarily dispositive. Despite the sarcasm with which he judges Bonaparte and his motley bohemian partisans, Marx notes that the election of Napoleon III to the presidency in December 1848 was genuinely democratic. Whereas the Bourbons had been a "dynasty of big landed property," and the July Monarchy a "dynasty of money, so the Bonapartes," Marx observes of both uncle and nephew, "are the dynasty of the peasants, that is, the mass of the French people." Sounding a theme that conservative statesmen such as Bismarck would later exploit to shore up popular support for monarchy, Marx notes that France's "small-holding peasants," who had taken over the land from the old feudal lords, formed families that were "almost self-sufficient," and therefore had little need to band together: they were "incapable of enforcing their class interest in their own name." Unlike Bismarck, Marx did not approve of the "superstition" of the innately "conservative peasant," with his "stupefied bondage to the old order," but he recognized its political significance.[5]

Marx's eminently quotable *Eighteenth Brumaire* (1852) forms an interesting contrast to *Das Kapital* (*Capital,* first volume published in German in 1867), the grand theoretical synthesis he produced during his long London years camped out in the Reading Room of the British Library. *Capital* was something of a mess during Marx's lifetime, with his original plans for three (or as many as six) volumes never coming together before his death in 1883. It was only thanks to Engels's efforts to impose order on Marx's notes that the second and third volumes, *The Process and Circulation of Capital* and *The Process of Capitalist Accumulation as a Whole,* were published at all—and they remain largely unread. Volume One of *Capital,* meant as a capstone of Marx's theories and the only one published in his lifetime, lays out his overarching views on currency, commodities, manufacturing, industry, and especially labor, which he sees as the ultimate source of the "surplus value" that allows capital accumulation. Despite the carapace of data on the British industrial economy with which Marx decorates his account, *Capital* is just as firmly rooted in the Hegelian dialectic as the *Manifesto.* Primitive economic transactions—the trading of basic commodities—become more complex over time as money and wage labor are introduced, leading to the "alienation" of workers from their product. The modern industrial era witnesses a culmination in the "appropriation of supplementary labour-power" by the "capitalists" owning the means of production, who drive down the price of labor by introducing machines, employing women and children at lower wages, and so on. In a typical Hegelian formulation, Marx concludes that the modern wage-laborer, who no longer makes goods for his own use or to sell himself, only "produces surplus value for the capitalist, and thus works for the self-expansion of capital."[6]

A critic might object that wage laborers, by definition, were compensated for their work, even if not earning nearly as much as their employers did. And it was conceivable, as Marx himself admitted, that productive workers contributing to an increase in a firm's profitability might even share in its profits, whether in the form of increased wages or by paying lower prices for its (or other firms') goods. In such ways, laborers might be able to "extend the circle of their enjoyments," as they could "make some additions to their consumption-fund of clothes, furniture, &c. and . . . lay by small reserve-funds of money." Common sense would suggest that this would be desirable, something to be encouraged and celebrated when it happened. But this is not how Left Hegelians think. Rather, as Marx improbably claims in his chapter on "The General Law of Capitalist Accumulation," "a rise in the price of labour, as a consequence of the accumulation of capital," does nothing but increase "the length and weight of the golden chain the wage-worker has already forged for himself," though perhaps allowing a "relaxation of the tension of [the chain]." The point is that the chain is still there. As soon as rising wages begin to "interfere with the process of [capital] accumulation," that is, with a firm's profits, "the price of labor falls again to a level corresponding with the needs of the self-expansion of capital." Labor, in Marx's formulation, is always secondary to capital, always the "dependent" variable in any equation, and the "very nature of accumulation excludes every diminution in the degree of exploitation of labor."[7]

Nor, Marx claims, does economic growth in the modern industrial era lead to greater prosperity overall. Taking on Adam Smith's attribution of wealth, in *The Wealth of Nations* (1776), to the specialized division of labor, competition, and expanding trade, Marx cries foul, claiming that, by reducing the proportionate cost of labor, any increase of labor productivity (owing, say, to the investment in new tools or machinery) simply tilts the share of wealth ever more heavily toward the owners of capital, impoverishing workers. Marx gives no data to support this assertion, arguing instead that the "growing productiveness of labor" must lead to "the diminution of the mass of labor in proportion to the mass of labor in the means of production moved by it," by which he means the "diminution of the subjective factor of the labour process compared with the objective factor" (the example Marx offers is of a hypothetical 50/50 split between capital investment in a plant versus wages changing to 80/20). One might suppose, following Smith, that increased labor productivity will lead to cheaper products, higher wages, or both, as well as a higher standard of living as a country's economic "pie" grows ever larger. But Marxist economics are a zero-sum game. Growth brings only ever more alienated and impoverished workers, whose bargaining power, paradoxically, decreases the more productive they are. Banking and stock issue ("credit"), by allowing large firms to invest in modern production techniques, accelerates the process whereby large firms dominate and crush competitors, leading to "the ruin of many small capitalists."[8]

It is not that Marx saw capitalist competition as inherently a bad thing. Like any good Hegelian, he relished conflict; it was the "antagonistic character of capitalistic accumulation" that propelled history forward. True, what economists saw as the "'sacred' law of supply and demand" was cruel to workers, who were impoverished in proportion to how productive they were becoming, but this, too, reflected the wages of progress. Were it not for competitive innovation; labor cost-cutting; bank credit to large firms, enabling consolidation; and the resulting "accumulation" and "concentration" of capital, Marx mused, "the world would still be without railroads."[9]

Still, Marx was not a complacent economist like Adam Smith, admiring technologies that helped increase a nation's wealth. Rather, he saw industrial progress as a prelude to sharpening class conflict. "In proportion as capital accumulates," he proclaims, as if stating a natural law (channeling, without attribution, the "iron law of wages" proposed by the "laissez-faire" economist David Ricardo), "the lot of the labourer, be his payment high or low, must grow worse. . . . [T]he accumulation of wealth at one pole is . . . at the same time accumulation of misery, agony of toil, slavery, ignorance, brutality, mental degradation, at the opposite pole." As the laborers of the "working class" learn the dirty truth—presumably from Marx instead of Ricardo—about "the ruinous effects of this natural law of capitalistic production," which saw their bargaining power dwindle the harder they worked, they must unite and oppose the existing order.

As the "centralization of capital" proceeds, it brings about "the entanglement of all peoples in the net of the world market, and with this, the international character of the capitalistic regime." But with this, too, everyone from artisans and farmers to managers and investors will join the growing ranks of "proletarian" wage laborers, says Marx. The process will not be unique to Britain, but will engulf the whole earth. "Along with the constantly diminishing number of the magnates of capital, who usurp and monopolise all advantages of this process of transformation," he explains with curious zeal, "grows the mass of misery, oppression, slavery, degradation, exploitation; but with this too grows the revolt of the working-class, a class always increasing in numbers, and disciplined, united, organised by the very mechanism of the process of capitalist production itself." Carried away with enthusiasm, Marx concludes with a famous eschatological prophecy: "The monopoly of capital becomes a fetter upon the mode of production, which has sprung up and flourished along with, and under it. Centralization of the means of production and socialization of labour at last reach a point where they become incompatible with their capitalist integument. Thus integument is burst asunder. The knell of capitalist private property sounds. The expropriators are expropriated."[10]

Whether or not Marx's thesis in *Capital* (later called the *Verelendung*, or "immiseration thesis") about the ever-diminishing bargaining power of labor and the accumulation of capital in fewer and fewer hands was borne out by economic data (already implausible in the Britain of 1867, his thesis was completely demolished by developments there over the next few decades), his moral critique of the unequal returns to capital was and remains plausible enough to sympathetic readers. Marx's "expropriators are expropriated" line, however vague in specifics, was hypnotic in its promise of apocalyptic revolutionary violence. Were it not for this rousing finale—or for the punchier *Communist Manifesto*, and the long shadow cast by the turbulent political career that followed—*Capital* might not be read today at all.[11]

Marx had always been a keen observer of current affairs. Like many of his acolytes, he was what we today might call a "news junkie," an obsessive reader of newspapers who had opinions on everyone and everything. Unlike Owen and the French utopians, Marx had never shown much interest in the design of factories or worker housing, or the living conditions of laborers. His passions were high theory and high politics, not the nitty-gritty of economics and factory life, which bored him, no matter how much he pretended to be interested in them in *Capital*.

It was therefore natural that Marx's return to the political arena in the 1860s was prompted not by anything happening in London, where he lived, or in Prussia or the Rhineland, where he had the most on-the-ground experience of political life, but by the American Civil War (c. 1861–1865) and an 1863 uprising in a region of Poland ruled at that time by Russia. By the end of the Polish uprising, thousands had died in battle or had been executed or sent into exile. Marx had no direct knowledge of the events either in America or Poland. The 1863 uprising, however, furnished the pretext for a meeting of English and French trade union and labor leaders at St. Martin's Hall in London on September 28, 1864, and the American Civil War became the inspiration for a charter document Marx wrote in October to launch the international organization these men were trying to found. The details of the negotiations remain obscure. Marx's support was solicited, to some extent, by the French and English unionists at St. Martin's Hall, although he seems also to have bulldozed his way in, writing a founding mission statement on his own after they had given up. Or, as Marx informed Engels upon reading their initial draft, "if possible not one single line of that stuff should be allowed to stand." Marx's "Address to the Working Class," later grandly relabeled the "Inaugural Address of the Working Men's International Association," was approved on November 1, 1864.[12]

Second in the Marxist canon only to the *Manifesto*, the "Inaugural Address" is a strange document. Marx dryly outlines some of the practical concerns the trade union leaders had discussed in St. Martin's Hall—worker health and nutrition, wages and the cost of living, and the "Ten Hours' Bill" limiting the length of the English working day—before returning to high politics, where he makes his own unmistakable contribution. Saluting the "heroic resistance" of the "working classes of England" to the Anglo-French policy of diplomatic support for the Confederacy in the American Civil War, despite the detrimental impact of the Union blockade on the cotton mills of Manchester, Marx said these politically savvy labor leaders had "saved the West of Europe from plunging headlong into an infamous crusade for the perpetuation and propagation of slavery on the other side of the Atlantic." Contrasting the selflessness of such workers with the reaction of Europe's elite toward the uprising in Poland, Marx lambasted the latter's "shameless approval" and "idiotic indifference" as they "witnessed . . . heroic Poland being assassinated by Russia." Russia's brutal crushing of Poland's aspirations for independence had, Marx asserted, "taught the working classes the duty to master themselves the mysteries of international politics," and to "counteract them . . . by all means in their power." What these two cases showed, to Marx at least, was that union leaders and organizers must realize the centrality of "foreign policy" in the "general struggle for the emancipation of the working classes." He signed off with his signature line from the *Manifesto*: "Proletarians of the World, Unite!"[13]

Under Marx's direction, the touchstones of the International Working Men's Association would be high politics and high theory. "To conquer political power," Marx declared in his founding address, was "the great duty of the working classes." The "one element of success" workers possessed was their numbers, "but numbers weigh only in the balance, if united by combination and led by knowledge." Workers must also cast aside the national prejudices that had undermined the "bond of brotherhood which ought to exist between the workmen of different countries, and incite them to stand firmly by each other in all their struggles for emancipation." They must become international news junkies like Marx, making connections between far-flung events in the headlines and coming to the correct conclusions about them.[14]

The wind was under Marx's sails again. His mother, Henrietta, had died in December 1863, leaving Marx with £700, a substantial sum. A German admirer called Wilhelm Wolff died in the spring of 1864 and left Marx even more than his mother had—nearly

£1,000. The combined windfall allowed Karl, Jenny, and their children to move into a spacious and comfortable dwelling in the Modena villas in Maitland Park, where they would remain until Marx's death in 1883.* In an ironic confluence of timing, Jenny threw a formal ball in the new family villa in October 1864, complete with "gold-rimmed invitations," "liveried servants," and a dance band, just as Marx was seizing the reins of the International Working Men's Association.[15]

Whether or not Marx's belated achievement of a high bourgeois lifestyle was appropriate for the sage of Communism, it did not hurt the impression he made on recruits. His Maitland Park villa in London became the nerve center of a growing international movement. Although English trade unions furnished the bulk of the members—and the financial contributions—branches were established in Spain, Italy, Prussia, Austria-Hungary, and Switzerland. The governments in Paris and Brussels, with past experience of Marx's conspiracies, made things difficult for local organizers, but even so, sections emerged there too. The French branch became the largest in Europe, with 433,785 members by June 1870, more than half of the European total of 811,513, according to the public prosecutor in Paris. The Vienna police reported membership numbers to be more than 1 million, and the *London Times* estimated (likely with exaggeration) 2.5 million.[16]

With help from the well-endowed English unions, Marx's International raised funds to support labor strikes in Berlin in 1865 (printers and typesetters), London itself in 1866 (tailors), Paris in 1867 (bronze workers), and Geneva in 1868 (construction workers). Owing to the relative leniency of the Swiss government, three of the first four congresses were held there, including in Geneva in

---

* They moved to a smaller villa a few doors down in 1875. The area was mostly destroyed by bombs in the Second World War and rebuilt, but there remains a plaque to commemorate the location of Marx's last known residence on Maitland Park Road.

1866, Lausanne in 1867, and Basel in 1869. Marx himself did not attend the congresses, preferring to remain in London drafting resolutions on Polish independence from Russia, and Irish Home Rule (both of which he favored), and keeping up with his correspondence. He even declined an offer to take over as president of the General Council of the International in 1866. Nonetheless, Marx was clearly, as he confessed on one occasion, "in fact the head of the whole business."[17]

For this reason, it is not surprising that the critical event in the history of the International Working Men's Association was not a labor strike, or a new law affecting labor organization, but the Franco-Prussian War of 1870–1871. In an apposite bookend to his farcical seizure of power in the "Eighteenth Brumaire" coup of December 1851, Napoleon III was lured into war by a ruse concocted by Bismarck, who, by releasing a carefully edited diplomatic insult to the press (the "Ems Dispatch"), convinced the French emperor, and large swaths of patriotic Frenchmen, that the Hohenzollern dynasty of Prussia was far more interested in assuming the throne of Spain than was really the case. France mobilized and declared war on July 19, 1870. This "aggression" by an outside power allowed Prussia to mobilize forces of the North German Confederation, paving the way for the political unification of Germany under Prussian leadership at the conclusion of the war. When Napoleon III was captured on the battlefield at Sedan in early September, his "Second Empire" was history. Although a rump (Third) French Republic was declared in Paris, which fought on until January 1871, Sedan heralded the end of France's role as the leading military power on the European continent, soon to be usurped by Bismarck's new German Reich.[18]

These were just the sort of world-historical newspaper headlines Marx lived for. Curiously enough, he did not condemn the war as such, but rather the "hideous farce" of French chauvinism, which he blamed for it. Still, Marx could not hide his relish in the Hegelian drama of it all, writing to his son-in-law Paul Lafargue, on the outbreak of hostilities, that "for my own part, I should like that both, Prussians and French, thrashed each other alternately." But in view of the reaction for which Napoleon III stood, Marx hoped that in the end, "the Germans got *ultimately* the better of it." Or, as he told Engels, "the French need a thrashing." "I wish this," Marx explained, "because the definite defeat of Bonaparte is likely to produce revolution in France."[19]

A cynic might object that Marx, for all his talk of worker solidarity and internationalism, was taking the position of Prussian patriots on the war. Certainly Marx had never pretended to be a pacifist or a humanitarian. But to accuse him of chauvinism is not fair. Marx did not endorse Prussian designs on French territory, authorizing a General Council resolution denouncing any "imperialistic" annexations Bismarck might demand. Once he got wind of Prussian designs on Alsace-Lorraine, Marx thundered that "history will measure its retribution, not by the extent of square miles conquered from France, but by the intensity of the crime of reviving . . . the policy of *conquest*." On the Franco-Prussian War, as on all political issues, he was a revolutionary Hegelian, seeing a Prussian victory as the "right" outcome, propelling history forward instead of backward, as a reactionary French regime was defeated and Paris saw another revolution.[20]

Nor was Marx wrong in his prediction. The French military humiliation at Sedan not only killed off the Napoleonic regime but left its rump republican successor prostrate, utterly at the mercy of the Prusso-Germans, who laid siege to Paris and continued the war through the winter. Marx's prediction of "revolution in France" was borne out on March 18, 1871, when an uprising in the capital prompted the formation of a Paris Commune just as radical as its predecessor in the first French Revolution. The Commune of 1871 abolished the death penalty and the military draft, took over charity and education functions from the Church, banned child labor, and enacted populist economic policies on worker pensions, debt, and rent relief. Nothing in the program was Communist, exactly. Its key figures were inspired more by French revolutionary figures such as Robespierre, Babeuf, and the French anarchist Proudhon than by doctrinaire German social theorists like Marx. The French section of the International, which had been raided by the French police after Napoleon III's declaration of war, was not involved in the Commune. There was no general strike against employers. Private property was not nationalized, as would have been suggested by Marxist doctrine. Nonetheless, the Commune was "socialist" enough to reject the French tricolor, adopt the red flag of revolution, and issue appeals to Marx's International for support.[21]

Would Marx's International support the Commune, despite having played no role in its organization, and despite its unorthodox policies? In view of the likely fate of this radical governing experiment, likely to be crushed by either the Prusso-German occupying army or the French Republic's troops as soon as the warring countries worked out a settlement, a public endorsement of the Paris Commune was risky. There was little political benefit in backing a doomed cause. Marx and his International were already suspected by the rump French republican government, now based outside Paris at Versailles, of being behind the Commune, even if this was not really the case. There was even a story going around that Marx was a double agent, working for Bismarck to undermine and humiliate France. Nor were the English unionists who provided much of the International's funding terribly keen on the Paris Commune, seeing it as an illegal usurpation of power from a legal republican government. To avoid legal headaches and distance himself from any violence and mayhem to come in Paris, Marx could easily have disowned the Commune as a new Eighteenth Brumaire—a reckless and pointless adventure from which good socialists and Communists should distance themselves.[22]

Instead, Marx embraced the Commune, at first privately, and then—once it was going down in a blaze of violence—as loudly and publicly as possible. In a letter to a German friend in Hanover on April 12, 1871, Marx all but takes credit for the Paris uprising, noting that he had predicted, in *Eighteenth Brumaire*, that in the next French revolution the goal would be "no longer, as before, to transfer the bureaucratic-military machine from one hand to another, but to *smash* it." Five days later, Marx struck a Hegelian tone when he wrote that "the struggle of the working class with the capitalist class and its State has entered upon a new phase through the struggle in Paris. Whatever the immediate outcome, a new point of departure of world historic importance has been gained."[23]

The immediate outcome for the Commune was unhappy. In a bloody weeklong campaign from May 21 to 28, 1871, the loyal armed forces of the French Republic, with tacit backing from Bismarck and the Prusso-German occupying army, crashed into Paris from the western suburbs and reconquered the city block by block. Whatever foreign support the Paris Commune had vanished quickly as tales of their scorched earth defense reached the outside world. Communards set fire to the Tuileries, burned down the Hôtel de Ville and other government buildings, took hostage and then executed the archbishop of Paris and 63 other "bourgeois" notables, and finally armed female civilians and sent them into battle against hardened professional troops, with predictably horrendous casualty rates. The army was scarcely less cruel, as soldiers gleefully hunted down and killed Communards in the streets, including women and children. Émile Zola, the future novelist, observed that "the slaughter was atrocious": "Corpses lay scattered everywhere, thrown into corners. . . . [F]or six days Paris has been nothing but a huge cemetery." Somewhere between 10,000 and 15,000 Communards were killed in the brutal fighting, and another 95 were sentenced to death after being captured. So terrible was the violence that a great basilica was built to commemorate—almost to exorcise—the tragedy, the famous Sacré Coeur, or Basilica of the Sacred Heart, which still dominates the skyline of Montmartre in north Paris today.[24]

Although it was unfair to blame the Communards alone for the horrific violence of May 1871, from which they themselves suffered more than anyone else, this was the general consensus in London and most other Western capitals as people read the mainstream news coverage. More than this, much of the coverage in the British press, in particular, held Marx himself, and his Working Men's International, responsible. The *Pall Mall Gazette* denounced Marx by name as the "head of a vast conspiracy" behind the Commune and its crimes.[25]

On May 30, 1871, just as the last Communards were being rounded up and "civilized Europe" was uniting in denunciation of the Paris Commune and of Marx himself, Marx addressed the General Council of the International in London. Rather than distancing himself, Marx doubled down. Addressing the key charges against the Communards, incendiarism and the use of women in battle, Marx did not deny but amplified. It was true, he declared defiantly, that "the working men's Paris, in the act of heroic self-holocaust, involved in its flames buildings and monuments." But "in war," Marx observed, "fire is an arm as legitimate as any," and it was rich for "the bourgeoisie of the world" to lament the "desecration of brick and mortar" instead of the "wholesale massacre after the battle." That the "people of Paris joyfully gave up their lives at the barricades," Marx said, illustrated only the "heroism of the defense." As for the execution of the archbishop and "sixty-four hostages," Marx observed that Communards taken prisoner had been executed in turn, exposing bourgeois "civilization and justice" as nothing but "undistinguished savagery and lawless revenge." All but daring his enemies to come after him, Marx laced his address with vitriol against Adolphe Thiers, the French Republic's chief executive ("that monstrous gnome"); the French foreign minister, Jules Favre (a "forger" who "lived in concubinage with the wife of a drunkard"); and Bismarck, who "gloats over the cadavers of the Paris proletariat."[26]

The very attacks on the Paris Commune, to Marx's dialectical mind, proved its worth. The measures it enacted may not have followed the program of his *Communist Manifesto*, but by exposing the united bourgeois front against them, the Communards had come to embody the cause. "The Commune, they exclaim, intends to abolish property, the basis of all civilization!" To this charge, Marx responded, "Yes, gentlemen, the Commune intended to abolish that class-property which makes the labour of the many the wealth of the few. It aimed," he continued with relish, if a bit of exaggeration, "at the *expropriation of the expropriators*." And yes, he went on, this was "Communism, 'impossible' Communism!" The Commune was "international," he added, noting that just as it had been denounced by bourgeois capitalists across Europe, so, too, had "the Commune annexed to France the working people all over the world." As for the charge that he and the International were "acting in the manner of a secret conspiracy" to unleash Communism on Europe, Marx responded that there was nothing "secret" about it. "Our Association is, in fact, nothing but the international bond between the most advanced working men in the various countries of the civilized world." The revolution may have failed, but it had ensured that "working men's Paris, with its Commune," would be "forever celebrated as the glorious harbinger of a new society," with "its martyrs enshrined in the great heart of the working class."[27]

Marx's vigorous public endorsement of the Paris Commune at the moment of maximum publicity over its bloody conclusion was a coming-out party for his Communist ideas while at the same time marking his final alienation from respectability. Now referred to regularly in the press as the "Red Terror Doctor," Marx reveled in his pariah status. "I am overrun by . . . newspapermen and others of every description," he wrote to a friend in Hanover in July 1871, "who want to see the 'monster' with their own eyes." Marx was given full-color treatment in a cover story in the Paris *Illustrated News* in November 1871, reprinted in five other countries.[28]

Not everyone was amused by Marx's grandstanding. The English trade unionists who had provided most of the funding for the International began to distance themselves from the organization, taking their money with them. Mikhail Bakunin, a charismatic Russian aristocratic anarchist whose international profile was beginning to rival Marx's, pulled back still further. Although he admired Marx's forthright radicalism enough to join the International Working Men's Association in 1864—he even gallantly offered to translate Marx's *Das Kapital* into Russian, before realizing how difficult a text it was—Bakunin had kept his distance, not joining a national section until 1868, and even then he joined the Swiss one in Geneva, so loosely controlled by the General Council in London that Bakunin scarcely had to pretend to obedience. A prolific correspondent and a man of great charm, Bakunin developed his own network of loyalists inside the International. His faction was especially strong in France, Switzerland, Italy, and Spain, where Marx's doctrinaire German theorizing had less appeal than direct action of the kind Bakunin favored.[29]

Whereas Marx had endorsed the Paris Commune *in theory*, from a comfortable distance in his London villa, Bakunin had set off for Lyon after Sedan while the Franco-Prussian War was still underway, rousing opposition to the republican government and posting placards calling for the abolition of "the administrative and governmental machinery of the state." It was enough for Bakunin to be arrested, although he somehow escaped and fled to Switzerland in disguise. True, the uprising in Lyon he supported failed, but then so did the Paris Commune. The point, for the rapidly growing ranks of Bakuninists, was that Bakunin, as usual, was actually *there*, risking his skin, while Marx was issuing pronouncements from on high and taking credit for the deeds of others. Indeed, Marx's very residence in London was beginning to seem suspect to more hardened revolutionaries facing arrest and prosecution on the Continent. The British government, despite numerous complaints from European authorities, especially in Bismarck's Germany, refused to extradite Marx and other radicals. As the *Norddeutsche Allgemeine Zeitung* complained, what was the point of "taking precautions" against Marx's International if "English soil provides free territory from which the other European states may be harassed under the protection of English law?"[30]

Sensing that an anarchist rebellion, coupled with dissension from the English labor unions, might sunder the International he had come to view as his own project and legacy, Marx convened a rump conference in the safety of London in August 1871, to be held in closed session with a strict lid on press leaks, allowing him to reassert control. The procedural resolutions were arcane, amounting to a more rigid and centralized administrative structure, and demanding that only properly "working-class" political parties be permitted to represent the movement. In the aggregate, they represented a shot across the bow at both the English labor unions, most of whose members still voted for the Liberal Party, and Bakunin, along with his anarchist factions in the Latin countries, who hated political parties in general. This was certainly how Bakunin interpreted the news after these decisions were passed on to him by a sympathizer present at the secret London conference. Rebellion spread through the ranks in the International sections of Switzerland, Italy, and Spain (the one in France, which had been more closely affiliated with Marx, had been suppressed completely after the Commune was crushed). The Belgian section, although not Bakunin-affiliated, demanded that an open congress of the International convene to clear the air.

The question of where to hold the Congress now became a political football, with Bakunin plumping for Switzerland, and Marx's faction favoring The Hague in the Netherlands, closer to London. The latter, as a relatively conservative and law-abiding Dutch city, would be less friendly to Bakunin and less approving of his methods. The Hague was chosen, and the Congress was scheduled for September 1872. Marx attacked his anarchist rival by name in a March 1872 pamphlet, titled *Purported Schisms in the International*, and Bakunin responded in turn. While both were talented polemicists, Marx was clearly the superior organizer, and he succeeded in stacking the Hague Congress with loyal supporters. The result was a rout: Bakunin, who was unable to travel to the Congress for legal reasons, was expelled from the International Working Men's Association, and his sub-organization, variously referred to as the Franco-Swiss Federation, the Democratic Alliance, or the International Alliance of Social Democracy, was formally condemned as "sectarian." "The history of the International," Marx wrote triumphantly, with a revealing hint about his approach to dissent, has been "a ceaseless battle . . . against dilettantist experiments and sects." Marx had won the day.[31]

Bakunin did not take political defeat quietly, however. The anarchist vowed, in a candid letter to his friend, the Russian socialist Alexander Herzen, to wage "war to the knife" on Marx and Engels, "against their false theories, their dictatorial presumptions . . . foul insults and infamous slanders, so characteristic of the political struggles of almost all Germans and which they have now, unfortunately, dragged into the International." Marx himself was, Bakunin thundered, "as a German and a Jew, an authoritarian from top to toe."[32]

In a blistering polemic later published as *Statism and Anarchy*, Bakunin produced a powerful critique of Marx and what would soon be known as Marxism. Although he drew on some of the same philosophical themes Proudhon had first sounded against Marx's Communism, Bakunin had also experienced Marx's rigid, top-down leadership style, which left a bad taste in his mouth. Most of all, it was the stale and lifeless Germanic quality of Marxism that repelled this Russian romantic. Somehow, the "adherents" of Hegel and other vaunted German philosophers, Bakunin observed in a curiously timeless passage, despite their "lofty ideals," could still "serve as obedient and even willing agents of the inhumane and illiberal measures prescribed by their governments." Marx and the Left Hegelian "doctors of philosophy" fancied themselves heroic radicals who "would leave the boldest figures of the 1790s far behind them and would amaze the world with their rigorously logical and relentless revolutionism." Instead, the German revolutions of 1848 had fallen flat because of "the special historical character of the Germans, which disposes them much more to loyal obedience than to rebellion." Even the most avowedly radical of them, like Marx with his *Communist Manifesto*, had "proceeded not from life to thought but from thought to life."

In the end Marx was nothing but a "metaphysician," a "worshipper of the goddess science," prophet of a desiccated approach to human affairs that, if ever realized, would mean that "life would dry up, and human society would be turned into a dumb and servile herd." By contrast, "we revolutionary anarchists," Bakunin declared, "are proponents of universal popular education, liberation, and the broad development of social life, and hence are enemies of the state and of any form of statehood." As against this, Marxian Communists were "the most impassioned friends of state power." "If the proletariat is to be the ruling class," Bakunin pointed out, "then whom will it rule? There must be yet another proletariat which will be subject to this new rule, this new state." True, the new ruling minority, the Communists claimed, would "consist of workers." If so, then they would soon be "*former* workers." "As soon as they become rulers," he wrote, they "will cease to be workers and will begin to look upon the whole workers' world from the heights of the state. They will no longer represent the people but themselves and their own pretensions to govern the people. Anyone who doubts this is not at all familiar with human nature."

Alternatively, and more likely, the new rulers would not be workers at all, but "learned" or "scientific socialists" of Marx's ilk—forming a government of intellectuals that, following Marx's example in running the International, would likely become "the most oppressive, offensive, and contemptuous kind in the world." What must happen after any such revolution was that "the leaders of the Communist party, in other words Marx and his friends," would strive to "concentrate the reins of government in a strong hand, because the ignorant people require strong supervision. They will create a single state bank, concentrating in their own hands all commercial, industrial, agricultural and even scientific production, and will divide the people into two armies, one industrial and one agricultural, under the direct command of state engineers, who will form a new privileged scientific and political class." Marx's "theory of so-called revolutionary dictatorship,"* Bakunin explained, could work only "by means of the dictatorial power of this learned minority, which *supposedly* expresses the will of the people." The real aim of "*doctrinaire revolutionaries*" like Marx, he concluded, was "to overthrow existing governments and regimes so as to create their own dictatorship on their ruins."[33]

---

* At this stage, Marx had not yet used the phrase "dictatorship of the proletariat," at least in print, although it does appear in his correspondence. The first "official" endorsement of the concept was in his *Critique of the Gotha Programme* published in 1875, when he spoke of the "revolutionary dictatorship of the proletariat."

Marx might have won the political battle in London and The Hague, but Bakunin had issued a clarion call of rebellion that could not be ignored. By expelling Bakunin from the International and letting the British unions drift free, Marx had effectively conceded that he could not control anarchists or reformist labor leaders—that he had not won them over with his ideas. It is a curious but revealing detail that the 1872 Hague Congress was the first and also the last one that Marx ever attended in person, in part because he put through a resolution there, much to the surprise of his own closest allies, to move its headquarters across the Atlantic to New York—a city he had never visited. The move was a poison pill, a kind of suicide pact that would allow the International to pass quietly from the scene, unsullied by any more dissident rebellions. As Marx explained in 1873 in a letter to his designated successor as head of the General Council of the International, one Friedrich Adolph Sorge, residing in Hoboken, New Jersey, it was "useful for the formal organization of the International to move to the background for the moment," to ensure that "no idiots . . . or adventurers seize the leadership and compromise the cause." Ideologically purified, the International would become a kind of still life, captured (or ossified) at the moment of Marx's maximum influence. To ensure that he would control its history, Marx kept the organization's records in London.[34]

The International died a quiet death in New York a few years later, officially disbanding in 1876 just as Marx had intended, and while he was still alive: Marx outlived his creation by seven years. But as Marx had perceived with his Hegelian sense of history, heroic failures—whether of the Paris Commune he endorsed or the International Working Men's Association he created and then killed off—could be turned into legends to inspire future generations. Bakunin might have been right that the realization of Marx's Communist program must demand both extreme political violence and a government more authoritarian than any seen before, but to radical activists in Marx's time and those yet unborn, these features were a central part of the attraction. Despite the revolutionary setbacks of 1848 and 1871, the idea of Communism was just getting started.

3
THE SECOND INTERNATIONAL AND THE PATH NOT TAKEN

With the *Communist Manifesto* and his stewardship of the First International, Karl Marx had put an indelible stamp on European socialism. But he had not won over everyone. By shunting the less doctrinaire English labor unions to the side and expelling Bakunin's anarchists, he had purified the International Working Men's Association, but he had also deprived it of the manpower and energy it needed to thrive. To Marx, it was more important that the doctrine was sound than that the organization outlive him. So long as he got this right, others could pick up where he left off, carrying the flame of Marxism beyond his death in London in 1883, drawing inspiration from his doctrinaire example. In doing so, however, they could also repeat many of his mistakes.

Despite Marx having spent his last decades in London, his posthumous legacy was strongest in the new Prussia-dominated German Empire, or *Kaiserreich*, land of his birth, where the socialist movement had begun to coalesce into a coherent national political party despite (or perhaps because of) Marx's long absence from the German political scene. Followers of the late Ferdinand Lassalle, a labor agitator in the vein of Bakunin, a man less interested in theory than action—Lassalle was killed in a duel in 1864, the same year the International was founded—had long wanted to honor their hero by forming a national party to advocate for the interests of German workers. Lassalle himself had been a kind of patriot, who saw nothing wrong with blending national pride with pro-labor activism in his General German Workers' Association (founded 1863). Lassalle did not live long enough to witness the Franco-Prussian War, but if he had he would have likely embraced the new unified Germany, as did many of his followers. Marx, after all, had taken an equivocally supportive position—a position more pro-war than his disciples in Germany. Indeed, several of Marx's followers, including Wilhelm Liebknecht and August Bebel, incurred the wrath of the Prussian government by voting against war credits, or the issuance of public bonds to help finance the war, in the North German Diet. Despite their reservations about the Prussian-dominated Kaiserreich, Liebknecht and Bebel teamed up with Lassalle's followers to form a new German Social Democratic Party (Sozialdemokratische Partei Deutschlands, SPD) in 1875 at a founding congress at Gotha.

The "Gotha program," as it came to be known, offers an intriguing vision of what a German labor movement might have looked like absent Marx's domineering influence: he was still alive when it was formulated, allowing him to pen a withering response. Despite talk of the "international character of the labor movement" and the duty of workers to "realize the international brotherhood of peoples," the Gotha program made clear that the German working class was better off "striving for its emancipation first of all *within the framework of the present-day national state.*" Moreover, it endorsed non-socialist liberal reforms such as universal suffrage, free elections, and a free press, along with a shorter workday, a ban on all female and child labor "injurious to health and morality," stricter health and safety regulations, and progressive taxation. The Gotha program for the SPD, that is, was fairly close to the moderate left line of the modern German SPD and other European socialist parties, or American liberals, today.[1]

Reading over the Gotha program, Marx was aghast. Its concessions to liberalism, he thundered, were "pernicious and demoralizing." In marginal notes later canonized as the "Critique of the Gotha Program," he denounced the party's nod to "the international brotherhood of peoples" as "a phrase borrowed from the bourgeois League of Peace and Freedom": it whitewashed the distinction between international *working-class* unity and the "bourgeois . . . ruling classes and their governments" that were united in false "brotherhood" against the workers. As for the bourgeois "freedom" in the Gotha program, Marx reminded socialists that their goal was a future in which "bourgeois society will have died off." The final goal must always be clear, with no backsliding. "Between capitalist and communist society," Marx explained, "lies the period of the revolutionary transformation of the one into the other. There corresponds to this also a political transition period in which the state can be nothing but *the revolutionary dictatorship of the proletariat.*" So focused on present-day concerns was the Gotha program that it ignored "the future state of communist society." For this reason Marx declared that he and Engels would "distance" themselves from it "and have nothing to do with it."[2]

In the short run, Marx's tantrum fell flat. The SPD adopted the Gotha program over his objections, and both Marx and Engels tacitly accepted the new party's right to speak for German socialism, or at least not to air Marx's sour grapes in public. The party did surprisingly well in the German Reichstag elections in 1877, and it continued to thrive in the coming years despite a ban on the party and its doctrines applied by Bismarck in 1878. (Confusingly, despite targeted arrests and the shuttering of party newspapers, SPD leaders could still stand for election, and thus legally tout their ideas, at least when running for office.) Bismarck then applied a carrot meant to undermine the party's appeal, pushing a series of social insurance laws through the Reichstag providing for health, accident, and disability programs as well as old-age pensions; together they constituted the most generous labor laws in all of Europe. With these reforms Bismarck tried to steal the SPD's thunder, but he seems to have actually increased its appeal instead. Freed of the need to kowtow to Marx, and given free publicity by Bismarck's ban, the party's popularity only grew throughout the 1880s, paving the way for a triumph in 1890, the year the ban was lifted. In that year, the SPD won the most votes of any party in the federal elections, nearly 1.5 million—almost 20 percent of the total—though the peculiarities of German federal election law meant the party controlled less than a tenth of the seats.[3]

Electoral politics had never been of great interest to Marx. To the extent he paid attention to the SPD from his London villa in his final years, it was only to police doctrine in the party's newspaper, which was published (owing to Bismarck's ban) in Zurich, Switzerland. Marx had all but given up on Germany by this time, paying much closer attention to Russian affairs, which had begun to engage his interest in the wake of the Russo-Ottoman War of 1877–1878. Owing to his deep antipathy to Russia as a hotbed of authoritarian reaction, Marx found himself lining up alongside Benjamin Disraeli and the Tories, who took a much stronger anti-Russian line than William Gladstone and the British Liberals. The rise of radicalism in Russia in the wake of this war, which culminated in the assassination of Tsar Alexander II in 1881, seemed so promising to Marx that he began to learn Russian. Owing to an oversight by the otherwise zealous tsarist censors, *Das Kapital* had been published in Russian and sold surprisingly well. As Marx observed in 1880, it was in Russia, home of the strongest autocracy in Europe and also the most baroque and violent political radicalism, that his book was "more read and appreciated than anywhere else."[4]

It might seem, to anyone not familiar with the Hegelian dialectical way of thinking, that Marx's news-junkie perspectives on international affairs, which sometimes lined him up alongside conservative politicians,* betrayed a lack of commitment to working-class politics. But this is to misunderstand the essence of Marxist internationalism, which is nothing if not news-obsessed. Whether in Marx's endorsement of the Paris Commune, his expulsion of Bakunin and direct-action anarcho-syndicalists, his vitriol against the reform-minded Gotha program, or his hopes for a cataclysmic Russian revolution following a military defeat that might destroy tsarist despotism, the point is to focus on world-historical *international* instead of local affairs.[5]

Marx had only mixed success during his own lifetime in winning over European socialists to his doctrinaire and eccentric worldview, but he was fortunate in his disciples. Liebknecht, Bebel, and other German socialists, forgiving him his insults, resolved to turn the rapidly growing German Social Democratic Party into a vehicle for the propagation of Marxism. Curiously, it was in the year after the SPD's relegalization and electoral triumph in 1890 that the party jettisoned the promising Gotha program and embraced Marxist orthodoxy. While the SPD's new program, ratified at Erfurt in 1891, did allow for participation in "bourgeois" elections and endorse practical measures such as an eight-hour workday, it was otherwise rigid in its adoption of Marxist dogma.

---

* One of Marx's last known political statements, in a letter to his daughter in April 1881, heaped praise on British conservatives, including Lord Randolph Churchill, father of the famously anti-Communist Winston, for their principled opposition to Russian tsarism.

The Erfurt program was based on the *Verelendung* (immiseration) thesis of ever-deepening inequality and class conflict. "Ever greater," the Erfurt program asserts as fact, "becomes the number of proletarians, ever more massive the army of excess workers, ever more stark the opposition between exploiters and the exploited, ever more bitter the class struggle between the bourgeoisie and the proletariat, which divides modern society into two hostile camps and constitutes the common characteristic of all industrialized countries." The role of the SPD, then, was not so much to advocate for the interests of German workers as to use its size and prestige to set the ideological agenda for the international socialist movement. "The German Social Democratic Party," the program insisted, "does not fight for new class privileges and class rights, but for the abolition of class rule and of classes themselves."[6]

Marx had never enjoyed quite the same level of devotion among French socialists as in his native Germany. Nonetheless, his son-in-law Paul Lafargue did his best to ensure that the master's message was not forgotten in France. Along with a Marx disciple called Jules Guesde, Lafargue formed France's first Marxist political party in Marseilles in 1879, the French Workers' Party (Parti ouvrier français, POF). It did not help the party's fortunes that Guesde lacked charisma. Émile Zola, the great French novelist, described Guesde as "rather hairy, stooping and with a perpetual cough." In a country with a proud revolutionary tradition, Guesde and Lafargue struggled to win a following, making little headway against "native" French socialist parties such as the radical Socialist Revolutionary Party (Parti Socialiste Révolutionnaire, PSR), led by Edouard Vaillant, and the moderate "Possibilist" movement, led by a former doctor, Paul Brousse, who memorably objected to the "unacceptable pretension" of Marx and Engels to "keep the whole Socialist movement within the limits of their brains."[7]

For all Marx's fame and prestige, France was still the trendset-
ter in radical politics. As the centenary of the great Revolution
of 1789 approached, it was thus natural that its socialist parties
would maneuver for position in claiming the mantle of revolution.
Brousse's Possibilists were first off the mark, announcing an international congress, to be held in the rue de Lancry in July 1889, on
the centenary of the storming of the Bastille. Urged on by Engels,
Jules Guesde announced that French Marxists would hold their
own congress on Bastille Day in the rue Petrelle. So tense was the
atmosphere that July that, according to a protocol of the Marxist
Congress, a team of "wicked Possibilists lay in wait at the [Paris]
railway stations to lead unsuspecting delegates from the provinces
off to the wrong Congress." In fact many socialists did attend both
congresses, as did uninvited anarchists, who were said to have been
better treated in the rue de Lancry than at the Marxist Congress
in the rue Petrelle (likely true). A motion proposed by the German
SPD leader, Wilhelm Liebknecht, to merge the two congresses—
i.e., to absorb the Possibilists into the Marxist organization—led
nowhere. Socialists were far from united, and the Possibilists actually had greater numbers than the Marxists in Paris (about 600 to
400).[8]

When it came to international organization, though, the Marxists had a distinct advantage. Although Brousse's Possibilists did
draw in a few foreign delegates, their congress at the rue de Lancry
was mostly a French affair. Owing to Marx's fame and the prestige
of the German SPD, its main organizational backer, the Marxist
Congress attracted delegates from twenty different countries—even
if three-quarters of them came from France (221) and Germany
(81). The Marxist Congress had a more dramatic *mise-en-scène*, too,
with the Salle Petrelle "festooned with red cloth, reinforced by red
flags," and crowned by a giant gold inscription above the rostrum

of Marx's closing lines from the Manifesto: "Working Men of All Countries, Unite!"[9]

The greatest advantage the Marxists had was doctrine. Possibilists, labor unions, and non-doctrinaire political organizations such as the British Labour Party might have more practical goals, and better ideas as to how to achieve them at the national level, but they did not have ideological cohesion. Indeed, the very idea of international coordination of doctrine ran against the needs of nationally or regionally focused reform movements, which must, after all, be particular to their local circumstances. Perhaps inevitably, despite plenty of talk in the rue de Lancry of future Possibilist congresses in Brussels or other cities, the 1889 one proved to be a one-off. There would be no reform-minded "Possibilist" International. In any international congress involving delegates speaking different languages, simplicity of messaging was essential, and there was nothing simpler than Marx's idea, endorsed in the Marxist Congress in Salle Petrelle, that workers had no homeland and must forge cross-border connections and objectives. This notion was embodied in a resolution creating an international holiday on May 1 (May Day) to demonstrate international labor solidarity on questions such as the eight-hour workday (which was officially endorsed as a standard). The international principle was also expressed in a Salle Petrelle resolution condemning standing national armies and declaring that "war, the sad product of economic conditions, will only disappear when the capitalist mode of production has given way to the emancipation of labor and the international triumph of socialism."[10]

It was one thing to agree on Marxist principles, however, and another to put them into practice. The central and most lasting achievement of the Paris Marxist Congress of 1889, and of the "Second International" to which it gave birth, after its delegates decided to revive Marx's old International in new form, was the advent of May Day, which is still practiced in some form in most European countries today. And yet there was disagreement from the start about it. The Russian delegation in Paris, led by the founder of the Marxist Russian Social Democratic Labor Party, G. V. Plekhanov, abstained from voting on the May Day resolution, knowing that a national labor protest of any kind in Russia would be quickly crushed by the tsarist police. Liebknecht and Bebel, representing the huge and influential German SPD, added a rider to the resolution stipulating that the "workers of the various nations will have to implement the rally in a manner prescribed for them by the conditions in their country." As both men knew, German workers tended, well, to *work*, including on May Day. At an SPD congress in 1890, several practical-minded delegates proposed marking German May Day on the Sunday nearest it, only for Liebknecht to object that this defeated the whole point. Try mightily though they did, neither Liebknecht nor Bebel were ever able to get Germans to stop working on May Day; the best most workers would do was to gather around in biergartens after work, singing songs.[11]

The one thing on which nearly all of Europe's Marxists agreed was that anarchists would not be allowed to disturb their discussions. While a few anarchists were allowed to speak at the inaugural Marxist Congress in Paris in 1889, and again at the follow-up Second International Congress in Brussels in 1891, they caused such a ruckus that, at the next assembly in Zurich (1893), the socialists prepared an ambush. On behalf of the leading SPD delegation, Bebel got a resolution passed limiting membership in the Second International to "groups and members who accepted political action" rather than "direct action." This was more than a semantic distinction. Inspired by the assassination of Tsar Alexander II carried out by Russian Narodnaya Volya (People's Will) terrorists in 1881, Europe's anarchists were unleashing a wave of carnage.

France alone had seen a bomb dropped from the galleries of the Paris stock exchange in 1886 and another in the Chamber of Deputies in 1893; the assassination of President Sadi Carnot in 1894 in Lyons; and yet another attacker on the Paris stock exchange in 1896 firing bullets into the crowd. Nor was the violence slowing down: Spain's premier, Antonio Cánovas del Castillo, would be assassinated in 1897, Austria's Habsburg empress Elizabeth in 1898, King Humbert of Italy in 1900, and US president William McKinley in 1901. Like Bakunin's rebellion against Marx in the First International, anarchist assassinations undermined the claim of the Marxists to be the true revolutionaries, while provoking police crackdowns that might also target socialists. Bebel's resolution at the Zurich Congress therefore stipulated that, however revolutionary the Erfurt program was in theory, in practice "workers' parties should make full use of political and legal rights in an attempt to capture the legislative machine and use it in the interests of the working class and for the capture of political power." The idea of legality was so offensive to anarchists that many of them tried to rush the stage when Bebel read this out. But this reaction only furnished a pretext to eject the lot of them from the hall—and the Second International.[12]

The expulsion of the anarchists at the Zurich Congress was a rare moment of socialist unity. Building on the victory in Zurich, large majorities of delegates to the London Congress of 1896 agreed to prioritize "political" over direct action, whether of the anarchist variety (e.g., targeted assassinations) or the "syndicalist" kind (e.g., industrial strikes, or collective refusal to pay rents, in order to achieve local objectives). Anarchists were formally excluded from membership in any of the national sections of the International, and trade unionists, though tolerated, were instructed to leave "political and parliamentary activity" to the socialist parties. The objective of all member parties in the Second

International, it was agreed in accordance with the Erfurt program, was "to transform the capitalist system of ownership and production into Socialism."[13]

For all the pretense of unity, however, the national parties were far from in agreement on what political action meant in practice. France, after all, had a proud revolutionary tradition in which the line between legal and illegal demonstrations was often blurred. French socialists of one stripe or another had engaged in "direct" (as opposed to merely "political") action from Babeuf's Conspiracy of Equals to the Paris Commune. In the wake of the "Dreyfus affair," in which a Jewish artillery officer in the French army, assigned to the War Ministry, was falsely accused and convicted in 1894 of treasonous contact with the Germans, French (non-Marxist) socialists took up his cause. These supporters included Alexandre Millerand, a lawyer who defended working-class clients, and Jean Jaurès, a charismatic philosophy professor who had come to fame supporting a strike in Carmaux, and had then been elected to the French Chamber of Deputies in 1893. Dreyfus, the son of a wealthy textile manufacturer, was no proletarian (for this reason Guesde and the Marxist POF kept their distance from the case). But the Dreyfus affair radicalized French politics, galvanizing both the Left and the monarchist Right, and mainstream center-left politicians began courting the socialists as a bulwark to defend the Republic. In June 1899, the new premier, René Waldeck-Rousseau, offered a cabinet position—minister of commerce—to Millerand, who proudly accepted. To the shock of French Marxists and monarchists alike, a socialist was now sitting at the seat of power in Paris.

At a French socialist congress in Paris held in December 1899, Guesde and the Marxists assailed Millerand for succumbing to the temptations of capitalism. Defiantly, Millerand argued that the working class must not resign itself to agitating "from a futile distance" when the opportunity was presented to fight "from the heart of the citadel." At one point Guesde cited Wilhelm Lieb-knecht, senior figure in the German SPD after the death of both Marx and (in 1895) Engels, as the ultimate authority on political tactics. Offended to be bossed around by a German who wasn't even in the room, Millerand's supporters shouted out "Down with Liebknecht!"—to the shock of Guesde's Marxists, one of them comparing the effect to shouting "Down with God" in Notre Dame. The final resolution asked French delegates, "Yes or no, does the class struggle permit a Socialist to enter a bourgeois govern-ment?" A majority voted no—only for a compromise resolution to save face for Millerand's supporters, allowing it under "exceptional circumstances."[14]

German socialism had its own civil war in 1899, not in the polit-ical arena but in the realm of ideas. This did not make the crisis any less serious, though, as the German who launched what became known as "Revision," Eduard Bernstein, was the closest intellectual heir of Marx and Engels. In 1878, at the age of nineteen, Bern-stein had gone into exile after Bismarck laid down his socialist ban, turning up in London, where he studied with the Master, and was named editor of *Der Sozialdemokrat* (The Social Democrat), the main SPD newspaper for socialists in exile. Bernstein had helped Engels craft the Erfurt program of 1891. Like his mentor Marx, Bernstein holed up in the Reading Room of the British Museum for years on end, poring over factory reports and industrial statis-tics, studying the movement of prices and wages. Unlike Marx, he remained open to data that undermined his convictions. At first gradually, and then with the galloping force of revelation, Bernstein realized that the *Verelendung*, or immiseration, thesis, on which all Marxist thought was premised—that capital was accumulating in fewer and fewer hands, and classes were being melted down into an ever poorer proletarianized "mass"—was not happening, at least not in England. In fact, wages were rising, along with consumption of foodstuffs, durables, and living standards: productivity gains were leading to lower prices and a higher quality of life for nearly everyone.

In a series of articles written for *Neue Zeit* (New times) between 1896 and 1898, later expanded into a book-length 1899 study, Bernstein attacked the core ideas of Marxism. Against the immiseration thesis, he noted that the "better organization of industry" and "the greater perfection of machinery" had been accompanied by "a rise in the price of human labor," and that all these things were "advantageous to the general well-being." Far from prophesying—and promoting—the proletarianization of society, socialists should set as their goal the "raising of the worker from the social position of a proletarian to that of a citizen," capable of exercising civic rights to improve the lives of other laborers. As for Marx's insistence on the nationalization of agriculture, Bernstein observed, most farm laborers did not want state control of agriculture, but "to get their own land." Against the collectivist compulsion for all workers to think and act en masse, Bernstein defended "individual responsibility" and even economic "liberalism," noting that there was a healthy balance to be struck between *laissez-faire* capitalism and trade and excessive "protectionism and subventionism." Democracy itself, Bernstein noted, required a balance of interests, and "nothing is more injurious to its healthy development than enforced uniformity." Bernstein disputed the "socialist theory of a catastrophic development of society" in capitalism, noting that Marxists were always crying "wolf," predicting doom, only to be proved wrong. "The movement," Bernstein declared in a reverse catechism of Marxist eschatology, "is everything: the final goal of socialism is nothing." Bernstein then returned to Germany, reasoning that he should work on behalf of the workers of his country instead of a mythical international class of them.[15]

Coming from a disciple of Marx and Engels, Bernstein's heresy was shocking. At the SPD congress in Hanover in October 1899, Bebel was gracious enough to salute Bernstein as "a man who, up to now, has justly been regarded as one of our leading Marxist theoreticians." But it was clear to Bebel that Bernstein was "no longer in the camp of Social Democracy." Bernstein's Revision, Liebknecht thundered, was "a solemn denial of socialist principles." To Bebel and Liebknecht, guardians of the Marxist flame in Germany, it was ultimately a matter of faith. As Liebknecht explained in a revealing analogy, "Islam was invincible as long as it believed in itself. . . . [B]ut the moment it began to compromise . . . it ceased to be a conquering force." Islam may not have been "the true, world-saving faith" it had claimed to be, but Marxist socialism now *was* that faith, and "Socialism can neither conquer nor save the world if it ceases to believe in itself."[16]

To restore the faith, ambitious German socialists competed to issue the most stinging denunciations of Revision. Karl Kautsky, a Czech-Austrian theorist who had edited *Neue Zeit*, was the first to publish a rebuttal. Called *Bernstein and the Social-Democratic Program* (1899), it established his reputation as a shrill guardian of Marxist Orthodoxy. Rosa Luxemburg, a Polish-Jewish exile from tsarist Warsaw who had joined the SPD, published a more stylish, though equally shrill, critique later that year. Channeling Shakespeare, she argued that the question of whether to pursue social reform or revolution amounted to the existential dilemma "To be or not to be?" Either Social Democracy aimed at cataclysmic social revolution, as Marx had dictated, or, as Bernstein now proposed, it did not. "In the controversy with Bernstein and his followers," Luxemburg insisted, "everybody in the Party ought to understand clearly that it is not a question of this or that method of struggle, or of the use of this or that *tactic*, but of the very *existence* of the Social Democratic movement." Accept Revision, that is, and socialism would cease to exist.[17]

Erupting in the socialist world almost simultaneously, the "Millerand case" and Bernstein's Revision presented serious challenges to the cohesion of the Second International before its fourth Congress, which met in Paris in September 1900. The circumstances of the day, however, augured well for a compromise. As Paris was then hosting an Exposition Universelle, or World's Fair, to mark the new century, the city was deluged with journalists, and the socialist delegates did not want to embarrass the International with a scandalous breach. For this reason debate on the question of "the conquest of State power and the alliance with *bourgeois* parties" remained civil. A compromise was worked out whereby socialist participation in "bourgeois" governments was "permissible only as a temporary expedient, adopted in exceptional cases under the force of circumstances"—and with the approval of the socialist party in question (an implied rebuke to Millerand, but only implied). Everyone agreed to reject Bernstein's Revision—including Jaurès and his faction of French non-Marxist socialists, who appreciated the revolutionary goals of the Erfurt program, disagreeing only over political tactics. As Jaurès said in support of Kautsky's majority resolution, "We are all good revolutionaries; let us make that clear and let us unite!"[18]

Although the Millerand question took up most of the time at the Paris Congress, it was a question raised by Rosa Luxemburg that proved to have the most legs. With the Boer War raging in South Africa, the United States having just fought the Spanish-American War and occupied the Philippines, and the Boxer Rebellion against European and Japanese colonialist trading colonies in China underway, she proposed an interesting update to Marxist theory whereby the final collapse of capitalism must come about as a consequence of imperialist rivalries. While no formal revision of the Erfurt program was proposed, Luxemburg won over a majority of delegates behind a resolution condemning the British suppression of the Boers, the "savage oppression of Finns and the Poles by Russian Tsarism," and the "colonial policy of the bourgeoisie" more generally, and urging that socialists unite to "educate and organize [Europe's] youth, in order to combat militarism . . . and colonial military expeditions." More provocatively, Luxemburg also tabled a proposal that the International establish a "permanent standing commission" to coordinate, "in the case of any important international [crisis]," "uniform anti-militarist agitation and protests to be conducted commonly in all countries."[19]

Although Luxemburg did not get her anti-militarist, anti-imperialist commission just yet, she had put her finger on an issue destined to dominate international socialism—the kind of hot-button, international-headline-leading topic Marx would likely have plunged into himself had he still been alive. Marx may or may not have been wrong that capitalism was destined to collapse as a result of capital concentration and proletarianization (the immiseration thesis). Even so, great power rivalry in the age of European imperialism might produce a violent cataclysm all the same. Could not socialists plan to act in the case of a European war, choosing whether to stop it with some kind of coordinated international strike action, or perhaps use the violence as a springboard to power?

This idea had occurred to Jean Jaurès, too. Having come to fame against the backdrop of the Dreyfus affair, Jaurès was a national figure in France. He could easily have become a candidate for higher office if the International's strictures were loosened. At the Amsterdam Congress in 1904, Jaurès raised a direct challenge to Bebel, who, after Liebknecht's death in 1900, was the unquestioned leader of the SPD. The challenge arose over the rules on joining "bourgeois" governments that now seemed hell-bent on imperialist expansion. Pointing out that the SPD, despite winning an impressive 3 million votes in the 1903 Reich elections, had still not *done* anything with its supposed political power—not only Germany's social insurance laws but even universal male suffrage had simply been handed down by Bismarck—Jaurès argued that "what at present most weighs on Europe and the world, on the guarantee of peace, the safeguarding of political liberties, the progress of socialism and the working class, what presses hard on the political and social progress of Europe, is not the alleged compromises . . . of the French Socialists who had allied themselves with democracy . . . but . . . the political powerlessness of German Social Democracy." Swallowing the insult, Bebel retorted that "however much we may envy you French your republic, and wish we had one, we don't intend to get our heads smashed in for its sake."[20]

Jaurès might have had popularity and eloquence on his side, but the Germans had the votes. Even Luxemburg, despite agreeing with Jaurès about the need to fight militarism, rejected his plea for permission to join bourgeois governments, denouncing the Frenchman as "the Great Corrupter." Bebel's resolution, which reiterated the Erfurt program's rules, updated at an SPD congress in Dresden in 1903 against "participating in governmental power within capitalist society," passed decisively. On the bright side, once Jaurès accepted defeat, the two French socialist factions did agree to unite in a new unified party, called the French Section of the Workers' International (Section française de l'Internationale ouvrière, SFIO). But Jaurès was quietly seething. As he left the hall, he told the Belgian socialist Jean Vandervelde, "I think, my friend, that I am going to apply myself to the study of military questions."[21]

The Bebel-Jaurès duel at Amsterdam almost perfectly encapsulated the contradiction at the heart of Marxist internationalism. Despite the pretense that workers everywhere were the same, both social and political conditions varied dramatically from country to country, as Bebel himself had plainly confessed. The real subtext of the argument in Amsterdam over participating in government was the war question, and how socialists might do something about it. With the Congress taking place against the backdrop of the Russo-Japanese War, there was a dramatic moment when the leaders of the Russian and Japanese Marxist parties, G. V. Plekhanov and Sen Katayama, rose and shook hands, to thunderous applause. Luxemburg, as an anti-tsarist exile, and Jaurès, a pacifist Frenchman devoted to reconciliation with Germany in a republic with laws safeguarding free speech, could both aspire to destroy Russian and French "militarism" in good conscience—and relative safety. Bebel and the German socialists he spoke for were less sanguine. As Bebel had mused painfully to a *London Times* correspondent in 1892, as they watched a battalion of Prussian Guards on parade in Berlin, "Look at those fellows—80 percent of them are Berliners and Social Democrats but if there was trouble they would shoot me down at a word of command from above." Moreover, Bebel retained some German patriotic pride, as Marx and Engels had also done during the Franco-Prussian War. As Bebel had once written, "If Russia, the champion of terror and barbarism, were to attack Germany to break and destroy it . . . we are as much concerned as those who stand at the head of Germany." For all the talk of internationalism, if his country went to war, Bebel, like the German socialists he spoke for, was a German first, and a socialist second.[22]

The Russian Revolution of 1905 injected new urgency to the question of how socialists might respond to a war between European powers. The dramatic events in Russia in the wake of Russia's humiliating defeats in the Russo-Japanese War, to be sure, were not planned or organized by socialist parties. The leading lights of Russian Marxism, including Plekhanov and the leaders of the two groups into which the Russian party split at the Brussels Congress in 1903—Vladimir Ulyanov Lenin of the "Bolshevik," or majority, faction, and Julius Martov of the "Menshevik," or minority, faction—were in exile when Cossacks and Imperial Guard troops fired into a massive crowd in St. Petersburg on "Bloody Sunday,"

January 22, 1905, killing 200 people and wounding another 800. The event ignited months of escalating protests. In the absence of senior party leadership—Lenin and Martov returned to Russia only in November 1905, after most of the revolutionary drama had played out—it fell to younger activists to make hay on the ground. These included one Joseph Stalin, a rough-and-ready Georgian activist who organized a Bolshevik Battle Squad in Baku, and Leon Trotsky, a twenty-six-year-old Menshevik firebrand from Kherson, Ukraine, who returned to Russia in February 1905. On October 26 of that year, Trotsky helped found a Soviet [Council] of People's Deputies in St. Petersburg. But not even Stalin and Trotsky could claim credit for the most successful Russian revolutionary action of 1905, the cascading labor walkout, which began with a print workers' strike in Moscow on September 30, spreading to railwaymen and telegraph and telephone workers, shutting down the country's communications. The impact was so dramatic that Tsar Nicholas II issued an "October Manifesto" to restore order, allowing the first-ever Russian parliament, or Duma, to convene, and even legalized labor unions. The October events in Russia entered socialist lore as a "general strike" of the kind Luxemburg and Jaurès had been speaking of since 1900.[23]

In truth, the dynamic of cause and effect in the Russian Revolution of 1905 had been far more muddled than Luxemburg and other socialists would have liked. By the time the "general strike" played out in October, Russia had already sued for peace with Japan. The strike had not stopped the war, nor had revolutionaries ridden to power on its back. The most radical faction in Russian Marxism, the Bolsheviks, had played little role in the Revolution, whether in Bloody Sunday, in the Petrograd Soviet (dominated by Trotsky and the Mensheviks), or in the October strike; Lenin himself returned to St. Petersburg only in November. Rosa Luxemburg tried to join in the revolution after she learned about the strike, returning to her native Poland—but only in December 1905, once it had largely run its course. The Russian Revolution may have shown the potential of mass protests to achieve political change, but if so, the general strike that wrested concessions from the tsar was effective largely *because* it was spontaneous, not the carefully planned-out work of some Marxist central committee.

Nonetheless, it was natural enough that Marxist revolutionaries would claim credit for the general strike and try to replicate its success. After being arrested by the tsarist authorities in March 1906 and fleeing police custody, Rosa Luxemburg penned an orthodox Marxist endorsement. In Russia, where the conditions facing workers were more "backward" than elsewhere in Europe, "the mass strike" (Luxemburg's preferred term) had served as a "means of creating for the first time in the proletariat the conditions of daily political struggle, and especially of parliamentarism." For the French SFIO, which Jaurès now led, the idea could serve as an antiwar lever, because France was entangled in military alliances with both Russia and Britain. The alliance with Russia dated back to 1894, but the one with Britain was more recent, originating in the Entente Cordiale of 1904. This was set against the "Triple Alliance" of Germany, Austria-Hungary, and (a more loosely affiliated) Italy, dating to 1882. As Jaurès proposed at the SFIO Congress in 1905, socialists should struggle against war and militarism "by all means[,] from parliamentary intervention, public agitation, [and] popular manifestations, to a general strike of the workers and insurrection." His resolution was carried.[24]

At the first Congress of the Second International after the Russian Revolution, held in Stuttgart in August 1907, there was a frisson of excitement surrounding the general strike question. In a curious mirroring of the military bloc antagonisms that now divided Europe, it was French and (exiled) Russian Marxists who lined up together behind the mass strike idea, and the Germans who were staunchly opposed. Debate over the "Militarism" resolution took up five whole days. Jaurès put up a staunch fight, trying to put together a plan for coordinated mass strikes in the case of a European conflict: stop war production, and presumably the war would never happen. The problem was that absent precise international coordination, any country that saw a successful strike in munitions factories or rail transport would consign itself to a crushing defeat from an enemy that suffered no such disruption. And SPD delegates had no confidence that a *Massenstreik* in Germany would survive an inevitable regime crackdown—nor did they necessarily want it to. "Do not fool yourselves," Bebel told an English delegate in Stuttgart. If war came, "every [German] Social-Democrat [would] shoulder his rifle and march to the French frontier." Another SPD delegate, Georg von Vollmar, also objected to Jaurès's plan, saying, "It is not true that workers have no Fatherland. The love of humanity does not prevent us from being good Germans." Nor were ordinary German laborers any less patriotic than the SPD politicians who spoke for them. As one foreign delegate observed, "Now I've seen German proletarians in the streets of Stuttgart. My naïve illusions are destroyed, they are all good contented and satisfied petite bourgeois [*Spiessbürger*]." It took all Jaurès's eloquence to get Bebel to back a vague compromise resolution, stipulating it as "the duty of the working classes and their parliamentary representatives in the countries taking part . . . to do everything to prevent the outbreak of war by whatever means seem to them most effective, which naturally differ with the intensification of the class war and the general political situation."[25]

Of greater lasting significance was the tactical alliance formed at Stuttgart between Luxemburg and Lenin on the war question. The two onetime tsarist subjects had clashed violently over doctrine in the past. Lenin had argued, in *What Is to Be Done?* (1902), for top-down direction of the party by a professional cadre of elites (sometimes called "vanguardism"). Luxemburg, in a rebuttal published in 1904 as "Organizational Questions of Russian Social Democracy," had advocated instead for a policy of building the organization from the ground up, educating the workers about Marxism and emphasizing the importance of "spontaneity" in revolutionary action. However much they disagreed on party tactics, Luxemburg and Lenin were both devoted Marxists and revolutionaries. They shared the aim of toppling the tsarist government—and ultimately all others. To them, the question of stopping war, as Jaurès so ardently wished to do for genuine humanitarian reasons, was secondary to the goal of revolution. It was these two who contributed a final flourish to the resolution on militarism at Stuttgart that struck a note of pessimism on the war question alien to Jaurès's positive spirit—though it was more optimistic, from the Marxist perspective, on where a European war might ultimately lead. "Should war break out in spite of all this," the Luxemburg/Lenin passage concluded, "it is the duty [of socialists] to intercede for its speedy end, and to strive with all their power to make use of the violent economic and political crisis brought about by the war to rouse the people, and thereby hasten the abolition of capitalist class rule."[26]

In the end, the delegates papered over their differences at Stuttgart long enough to pass this and other resolutions pretending to socialist unity. But the gap between the French and German socialist views on "Militarism," as earlier on the question of Millerand and "Ministerialism," was fundamental. True, there was probably no way socialists from opposite sides of the two main power blocs—France/Russia and Germany/Austria-Hungary—could really have coordinated a mass transport-and-production strike in the case of mobilization for war in such a way as to handicap all belligerents equally and render war inoperable.

When it came to Ministerialism, however, the German insistence that French socialists refuse to take on a responsible role in government had fateful consequences. After a long and illustrious career in French politics, Jean Jaurès was ready to take his turn at last after a sweeping victory for the parties of the Left in France's May 1914 parliamentary elections. While the center-left Radical Republican Party led by Joseph Caillaux tallied the most votes, the SFIO finished a strong second, consigning the conservative Democratic Republican Alliance party of France's recently elected president, Raymond Poincaré, to a distant third. Jaurès was a natural candidate for foreign minister in the new cabinet—in which post he was likely to repudiate the Franco-Russian alliance dating to 1894, possibly by exposing the role of Russian subsidies in the belligerently anti-German Poincaré's presidential election campaign in 1913. Russia, after all, even after the changes of 1905, was still the most reactionary autocracy in Europe, and was far from a desirable alliance partner for a democratic republic like France. However much Frenchmen might resent Imperial Germany for seizing Alsace-Lorraine after the Franco-Prussian War, the Russian alliance that French statesmen had embraced as a counterweight to Germany's growing military power was deeply controversial, and, after twenty years, long overdue for reconsideration. It was the Franco-Russian alliance that had alarmed German military planners enough for them to devise the fateful "Schlieffen Plan," with its daunting timetable for knocking France out of a two-front war requiring the invasion of neutral Belgium, whose neutrality was guaranteed by Britain. Absent the threat of a joint Franco-Russian invasion, the German government could have radically revised its strategic posture, slowing down the European arms race. The assassination of Archduke Franz Ferdinand, heir to the Habsburg throne of Austria-Hungary, by Serbia-backed assassins on June 28, 1914, might then have remained a tragic footnote rather than the spark that produced a terrible war. Cooler heads might have prevailed in Berlin, Paris, and St. Petersburg, and some kind of a

Balkan settlement satisfying both Habsburg honor and Serbian pride might have been possible.[27]

Alas, it was not to be. Back in March 1914, Caillaux's wife, Henriette, had murdered a powerful French news editor from *Le Figaro*, Gaston Calmette. Calmette had been threatening to publish scandalous stories about her affair with Caillaux when he had still been married to another woman. As Henriette was now on trial for murder, Caillaux could not take office, which deprived him and Jaurès of the chance to revamp France's foreign policy in June 1914, shortly before the Sarajevo incident plunged Europe into the "July crisis." It was Jaurès's tragic fate to embody the failure of the Second International to stem the march to war when, on July 31, he was assassinated by a French hyperpatriot in Paris after returning from Brussels, where the socialists had held one last, futile antiwar congress.[28]

For all the dramatic contingency in the Jaurès story, which saw France's great antiwar conscience silenced by the baroque Caillaux affair and cut off too soon by an assassin's bullet, we should not forget that Jaurès could easily have put his learned eloquence to use in reshaping French foreign policy in a less dangerous direction long before 1914, had his wings not been cut off by German bullying over his deviations from Marxist orthodoxy. The demographic weight and electoral popularity of the SPD, combined with the enduring prestige of Marx and Engels, had allowed Bebel to dominate the Second International, ensuring that its dictates imposed on member parties followed the German political line: theoretically revolutionary-internationalist, yet in practice timid, lawful, and deferential to the ambient pro-military patriotism of German political culture. In the development of German Social Democracy, this made good sense—the party was evolving this way organically, destined to become a stolid left-of-center bulwark of the German political scene, and building on a broad consensus behind a generous social welfare system originally bequeathed to the country by Bismarck from above—as indeed it remains to this day. But it made little sense in France, a country with a proud revolutionary tradition, where suffrage itself and labor rights far less sweeping than in Germany had been won on the barricades, where the entire political spectrum was tilted further left than in Germany, and where non-doctrinaire socialists like Jaurès could easily have joined majority coalitions and exercised real power.

Nor did the German model make sense in Russia, where the lack of intermediary institutions, such as labor unions and a parliament—at least before 1905—left Marxist socialists, like Bakunin-inspired anarchists and Narodniki populists before them, with few political means other than terrorism and violent protest. It was in recognition of these limitations that Lenin had formulated his views on top-down party organization, and Luxemburg had embraced the "spontaneous" general strike as a way of forcing political change. Unlike Jaurès and the French, neither Luxemburg nor Lenin were willing to take orders from German authority figures on party doctrine, however august their lineage. The failure of the Second International to coordinate protests and strike action to stop the outbreak of war in August 1914 was, for Jaurès and the French socialists he spoke for, a tragedy. For Lenin and Luxemburg, the war presented opportunity.

4
TURNING THE ARMIES RED
LENIN UPDATES MARX

Just as Mikhail Bakunin's self-purging protest walkout had eliminated the anarchist alternative to Communism, so did the failure of the pacifist wing of the Second International to prevent the outbreak of European war in August 1914—after Serbia's rejection of Austria-Hungary's ultimatum on July 25, the latter's declaration of war on the former on July 28, and the terrible doomsday machine of Great Power ultimatums, mobilizations, and war declarations that followed Russia's general mobilization on behalf of Serbia on July 30—discredit the antiwar version of Social Democratic Marxism. Jean Jaurès's principal German antagonist, August Bebel, had died (of natural causes) in August 1913, leaving the Social Democratic Party, too, without its anchor. While Bebel would not likely have taken a strong antiwar line in the feverish atmosphere of these events, the absence of his authority and gravitas made it that much easier for the German chancellor, Theobald von Bethmann Hollweg, to convince hesitant SPD parliamentary leaders—such as Hugo Haase, who claimed to be personally opposed to the war—to vote in favor of war credits in the Reichstag. In the end, the ostensibly revolutionary SPD, enforcer of the orthodox Erfurt program of Marxist internationalism, voted unanimously for what Marxists had called a "bourgeois" war in the Reichstag on August 4, 1914. Haase, thoroughly cowed, stood up before the Reichstag and declared that "in the hour of danger, we will not leave our own Fatherland in the lurch."[1]*

Coupled with similar votes the same day in Paris and Vienna, this "Fourth of August betrayal" buried the internationalist pretensions of the Second International, which was now dead in all but name. Far from uniting against their class oppressors in a general strike to halt the imperialist war, Europe's workers would take up arms on their behalf with the full endorsement of the Marxist parties that supposedly spoke for them. So distraught was Rosa Luxemburg—who, though an SPD party member, did not have a Reichstag seat enabling her to vote—that she contemplated suicide the night of August 4, only to be "talked out of it by her friends."[2]

Curiously enough, it was only in autocratic Russia that Marxist parliamentary deputies failed to support the war, with both Mensheviks and Bolsheviks (fourteen in all) abstaining from the vote in the Duma. (Lenin and Trotsky, exiled abroad, and Stalin, exiled in Siberia, were unable to vote.) In Russia-aligned Serbia, two socialist deputies also registered protests. In Britain, there was scattered opposition from a few Labour deputies in the House of Commons and five resignations in the Liberal cabinet of Herbert Asquith, but none of these politicians were Marxists. While historians continue to debate just how widespread "war enthusiasm" was in the belligerent countries whose men marched off to fight in 1914, there is no denying that, when war came, the leaders and broader membership

---

* One relatively obscure SPD deputy, Fritz Kunert, slipped out of the Reichstag before the vote, marking his opposition by his absence, but not registering a formal abstention. That was it.

of the Second International folded their arms and let it happen. Strikingly, Youth Socialist organizations in most of the belligerent countries, composed primarily of teenage men of arms-bearing age (or soon to be of that age), dissolved themselves in a frenzy of patriotism. Robert Danneberg, the Austrian chairman of the Second International's Youth Bureau, headquartered in Vienna, closed down his office and hung a note on the door explaining that "during the war the [International Youth Bureau] will be temporarily closed."[3]

Not everyone in the movement had given up on revolution. Rosa Luxemburg, after recovering from her shock at the August 4 betrayal, was the first SPD leader to organize an antiwar meeting in Berlin, sending out no less than 300 invitations—although she received a "pitiful response," in the words of her biographer J. P. Nettl. In the first several months, Luxemburg was able to recruit only seven German comrades to her antiwar "Internationale Group," founded on August 5, 1914; it was dismissed by the SPD leadership, with some justification, as simply the "Rosa group." Even so, her recruits included some big names, including the former editor of the party newspaper in Leipzig, Franz Mehring; the economics editor of the party's flagship newspaper *Vorwärts*, Ernst Meyer; and a young Wilhelm Pieck, a future president of East Germany. Karl Liebknecht, son of the party's founder and a radical antiwar firebrand—he had been tried for treason in 1907 and sentenced to an eighteen-month term in prison—had voted for war credits in the Reichstag (after voting against them in the party caucus) to ensure party discipline. He did not immediately respond to Luxemburg's entreaties. As a Reichstag deputy, and a reasonably fit adult male just forty-two when the war erupted (he turned forty-three in August 1914), Liebknecht was treading carefully, trying not to fall afoul of the government again; he even agreed to serve in an army construction battalion. This time it was Luxemburg's turn to be arrested for antiwar agitation, when, at a rally near Frankfurt in February 1915, she provocatively urged army draftees not to fire on "French workers" if they were sent to the front.[4]

With socialist men in the belligerent countries flummoxed, like Liebknecht, by their draft obligations, and Rosa Luxemburg in prison, it fell to Luxemburg's friend and comrade Clara Zetkin to organize the first socialist antiwar congress. Zetkin, who headed the Second International's Women's Bureau, and is credited as the creator of International Women's Day in 1911, published an appeal "To the Socialist Women of All Nations" in December 1914, proposing that they gather in neutral Switzerland to protest the war. Thirty or so of them did just that in the Volkshaus of the Swiss capital, Bern, from March 26 to 29, 1915. A week later, a new Youth Socialist Secretariat, led by Willi Münzenberg, a German exile based in Zurich who took advantage of Danneberg's self-cancellation of the Youth Bureau in Vienna, convened an antiwar congress in the same venue. Without Luxemburg present, both congresses were relatively genteel affairs, passing vague antiwar resolutions that did not commit delegates to any seditious program.[5]

The only fireworks in Bern were provided by the radical Bolshevik editor of *Rabotnitsa* (Working woman), Inessa Armand, the mistress of Vladimir Lenin, who was working secretly on his behalf. It was Armand who had convinced Zetkin to publish her appeal in December 1914, and she made clear why when, at the female socialist congress in Bern, she shocked the delegates by denouncing their "pacifist phrases about peace," and proposed a resolution, drafted by Lenin, that socialists use the European conflict as a springboard to "insurrectionary activity." "Of course," Armand allowed, "we do not claim that civil war will come about immediately, but we must guide our activity in this direction." Armand's radical resolutions were defeated at both the women's congress and the youth congress, but she and Lenin had laid down a marker for the movement.[6]

The outbreak of the war found Lenin in Poronino, near Cracow in the contested borderland of Galicia in what was then Austria-Hungary, agitating among local Ukrainians for autonomy from Tsarist Russia. Lenin was arrested as an enemy alien and suspected spy, a move that may have saved his life. Whatever his political views, he was still a Russian subject, and local tempers were running hot after casualties from the front began arriving in the local train station. Lenin's wife, Nadya Krupskaya, later recalled overhearing "some peasant women coming out of a Catholic church," enraged by the "horrible scene" of the dead and wounded arriving, and insisting that "even if the authorities released the spy [i.e., Lenin], the peasants would put his eyes out." Far from a Russian spy, of course, Lenin was a "bitter enemy of Russia," as an Austrian socialist admirer informed the Cracow prison director. It helped Lenin's case that a search of his flat turned up just the kind of dry research material one would expect to find in the study of a Marxist monomaniac. Under police questioning, this is exactly what Lenin showed himself to be. Along with his agitation for Ukrainian separation from Russia, this suggested to Vienna that Lenin might be a useful tool of the Central Powers. He was released by special order of the Habsburg War Ministry and dispatched on a military mail train to Switzerland, where he and Nadya took an apartment in Bern on the Distelweg, a short walk away from Inessa's flat on the Drosselweg.[7][*]

In the safety of the Swiss capital, Lenin swiftly formulated an original position on the war, which saw the European conflagration not as tragic carnage but opportunity. Many socialists protesting the war, such as Robert Grimm, a senior figure in the Swiss socialist party, and the majorities at the women's and youth congresses

---

* Curiously, Lenin's wife, Nadya, did not especially seem to mind that he was having an affair with Inessa Armand. All three were devoted Bolsheviks who believed that "bourgeois" marriage was an oppressive institution, and they (usually) got along well together.

in Bern, were temperamental pacifists, and thus willing to "be thrown together with the petty bourgeoisie, sentimental liberals, etc.," Lenin wrote to his Bolshevik friend Alexander Shliapnikov on November 14, 1914. But "the slogan of peace is in my mind incorrect," he continued, insisting that "a proletarian solution must demand civil war." Any support for one's own country was "chauvinism": a true socialist must strive to "awaken hatred for *one's own regime*" and help usher in "civil war."[8]

It was Lenin who had stage-managed Armand's interventions at the women's and youth antiwar congresses, sending instructions via couriers from a nearby café. Grimm, keen to preserve his party's legal standing, monitored the gatherings and influenced the direction they took. Lenin and Armand did not win majority support for their insurrectionist program, but they were quietly building a network among socialist exiles in Switzerland.[9]

An important test of Lenin's recruitment efforts occurred at the first adult and "co-ed" antiwar socialist congress, which convened on September 5, 1915, in the quaint Alpine village of Zimmerwald, south of Bern. Once again Grimm oversaw logistics on behalf of the Swiss hosts, ensuring that moderate delegates would predominate. The only real surprise came in the form of a "prison letter" from Karl Liebknecht, which was read aloud to great fanfare. After a sobering visit to the front as a Reichstag deputy in October, Liebknecht had recovered his antiwar morale and voted against a renewal of war credits in December 1914. In June 1915, Liebknecht was arrested in Berlin for antiwar sedition just as Rosa Luxemburg had been, despite his immunity as a Reichstag deputy—and for an even longer term of two and half years (later extended to four). Striking a militant tone in his prison letter, Liebknecht all but endorsed Lenin's position when he called for "civil war, not civil peace," and urged the delegates to form a new International "on the ruins of the old." Lenin himself (acting at first via a surrogate, the chain-smoking Polish-Jewish journalist Karl Radek) attacked the "passive revolutionism" of the SPD and other parties that supported the renewal of war credits, who had proven themselves "more dangerous enem[ies] than the bourgeois apostles of imperialism." But there was little appetite for the purges and denunciations of socialist comrades Lenin wanted. The final antiwar resolution passed at Zimmerwald, penned largely by Leon Trotsky, who belonged to the tamer Menshevik faction of Russian Marxism, urged socialists to "summon the working class to reorganize and begin the struggle for peace," but advocated no specific actions to do so, not even a binding pledge on socialists to refuse war credits.[10]

Lenin's own proposals, that the Second International be dissolved—and that a "ruthless struggle" be conducted inside each socialist party to purge socialist "traitors" who had voted for war credits—were defeated, and even provoked counter-resolutions. The final conference report stated, in a personal rebuke to Lenin, that "in no way must the impression be created that this conference aims to provoke a split in or to establish a new International." In his most explosive resolution, Lenin proposed that the delegates formulate a detailed plan "for transforming the imperialist war into civil war." Other delegates denounced this idea as "unacceptable." One delegate called it "childish [and] dangerous nonsense," and another objected stoutly that "the task of the conference was to end the world war, not to unleash a civil war."[11]

Nonetheless, Lenin won over a core group of supporters for his radical vision at Zimmerwald, including Radek, his fellow Russian Bolsheviks Grigory Zinoviev and Jan Berzin, and the Swiss socialist Fritz Platten. Behind the scenes, Lenin was circulating a blood-curdling pamphlet titled *Socialism and War* that would soon be required reading in the European radical underground. Inspired, in his own way, by the furies of conflict on the Western and Eastern Fronts in 1914–1915, Lenin had been reading Carl von Clausewitz's

On War and was heavily influenced by it. However, he reversed Clausewitz's premise: whereas Clausewitz had famously called war "the continuation of politics by other, namely violent, means," Lenin aimed to transform politics into warfare. Socialists may have failed to stop the war, but now that the Powers had foolishly armed the masses to fight their "imperialist war," Lenin thought the time was ripe to exploit their mistake. Channeling Marx's studies of the Franco-Prussian and Russo-Turkish Wars, Lenin pointed out that "despite all the horrors, atrocities, distress and suffering that inevitably accompany all wars," modern Great Power wars had also been "progressive, i.e. benefited the development of mankind by helping to destroy the most harmful and reactionary institutions (e.g. an autocracy or serfdom) and the most barbarous despotisms in Europe (the Turkish and the Russian)."[12]

Not all wars were the same, of course, but Lenin took as given that the war of 1914 was an "imperialist war" par excellence, fought not to liberate peoples but to further enslave them. None of the belligerents' "national defense" cases for war were, in Lenin's view, truly just, not even that of Belgium, whose territory might have been violated by Germany—but whose cause was really nothing more than a pretext for Belgium's "Allies" to grab territory elsewhere. With impressive foresight, in view of Allied secrecy over war aims, Lenin pointed out that "Britain is grabbing at Germany's colonies and Turkey; Russia is grabbing at Galicia and Turkey; France wants Alsace-Lorraine and even the left bank of the Rhine; a treaty has been concluded with Italy for the division of the spoils (Albania and Asia Minor); bargaining is going on with Bulgaria and Romania, also for the division of spoils." The "defense of the fatherland" was, at least on the Allied side, nothing more than a fig leaf for "chauvinism," for "perpetuating the imperialist oppression of nations."[13]

A cynic might object that Lenin was attacking the imperialist designs of only one of the warring coalitions, sparing those of Germany and Austria-Hungary, the latter having arranged his comfortable exile in Switzerland so that he could work against Russian interests. And this is true. But to Lenin, the mark of a real revolutionary was precisely his opposition to the "chauvinism" of his own country. In the most striking, and shocking, passage in *Socialism and War*, Lenin argued that a true socialist must aim for the "defeat of one's 'own' government in the imperialist war," using scare quotes for emphasis. "A revolutionary class cannot but wish," he explained, "for the defeat of its government in a reactionary war, and not fail to see that the latter's military reverses must facilitate its overthrow." It was therefore the task of socialists to "explain to the masses that they have no other hope of salvation except the revolutionary overthrow of their 'own' governments, whose difficulties in the present war must be taken advantage of for that purpose."[14]

The implications of Lenin's new doctrine, later called "revolutionary defeatism," were far-reaching. Lenin was not the first to notice that states reeling from a devastating military defeat, such as France in the Franco-Prussian War of 1870–1871 and Russia in the Russo-Japanese War of 1904–1905, tended to suffer political turmoil, in the first case with the Paris Commune Marx had endorsed, in the second by Bloody Sunday and the Revolution of 1905. But Lenin was the first to turn this historical pattern into a political *program*, whereby Marxist revolutionaries would crow after a government endured military setbacks and openly undermine its military effort. Lenin was arguing for mutiny: organized mutiny, on a scale large enough to poison and ultimately destroy a country's armed forces. For political-messaging reasons, and to avoid legal scrutiny, he preferred the term "fraternization," but the idea was the same. The "example set by fraternization in the trenches," he wrote carefully, "shows us how possible it would be to shorten the present criminal, reactionary and slave-holders' war and to organize a revolutionary international movement, if systematic work were conducted in this direction . . . by the Left-wing socialists in all the belligerent countries." The goal, which Lenin shortened into a "Zimmerwald Left" slogan, was the "transformation of the imperialist war into a civil war."[15]

At a time when the European powers had mobilized mass armies to conduct a war of unprecedented scale under conditions of strict military discipline, encouraging soldiers to mutiny was dangerous, if not treasonous, even if Lenin himself was protected as a resident alien exiled in neutral Switzerland. Genuinely pacifist socialists, such as Grimm and Zetkin, recoiled from such language. Trotsky, the principal author of the majority resolution at Zimmerwald, denounced Lenin's Zimmerwald Left faction as "extremists and sectarians." But was it really so discordant with the Marxist tradition of internationalism, with the formula laid down in the *Communist Manifesto* that the "workers of the world," who had no real homeland, must "unite" against their ruling-class oppressors? The anthem of the Second International, Eugène Pottier's "The Internationale," openly celebrated mutiny:

> *The kings intoxicate us with gunsmoke,*
> *Peace between ourselves, war on the tyrants.*
> *Let us bring the strike to the armies,*
> *Fire into the air and break ranks!*
> *If they insist, these cannibals,*
> *On making us into heroes,*
> *They'll know soon enough that our bullets*
> *Are for our own generals!*[16]

Among Lenin's earliest converts was Willi Münzenberg, secretary of the Socialist Youth Secretariat in Zurich. Although Münzenberg's funds mostly came from the more moderate socialist youth organizations in Scandinavia, his sympathies lay with

Lenin, particularly after the Bolshevik firebrand began spending time in Zurich in the fall of 1915 and moved there in February 1916. Famously, Lenin lived in a flat on Spiegelgasse across from a sausage factory, the stench from which was so overpowering that he kept the windows permanently closed.* Münzenberg was a frequent guest in the Spiegelgasse, and Lenin began attending his Youth Socialist rallies in the Zurich Volkshaus, drawing energy and inspiration from the youthful crowds.[17]

Because most of the members of Münzenberg's Youth International were men of arms-bearing age (or soon to be so), they were a perfect test market for Lenin's new doctrine of revolutionary defeatism. Prior to his conversion to Leninism in the winter of 1915–1916, Münzenberg's propaganda had focused on attacking the iniquities of the war, the military draft, and a nebulously defined "militarism," while being careful not to counsel draft resistance. One of the common catchwords was *Entwaffnung*, or disarmament. Beginning in the spring of 1916, Münzenberg's organs began talking about *Bewaffnung* instead, or the "arming" of the proletariat—that is, young working-class radicals receiving their rifles upon mobilization. While Münzenberg was careful to avoid explicit and potentially actionable calls for mutiny, Youth Socialist circulars advocated for "the placement of revolutionary soldiers" and "practical measures taken as a consequence." After an antiwar march in August 1916 by his supporters on Bahnhofstrasse, Zurich's ritzy shopping thoroughfare, turned violent—the police opened fire, wounding several protesters and bystanders in the resulting stampede—Münzenberg was called into police headquarters to explain himself. His testimony provides a perfect snapshot

---

* Lenin's Spiegelgasse apartment, long a shrine for Communists and Communist sympathizers, is now a recognized historic site with its own "attraction page" on Tripadvisor.com. Reviews by mere tourists are middling, averaging, at the time of writing, 3.5 stars out of 5.

of evolving Marxist theory at the moment of Lenin's wartime intervention. "I am a Marxist," Münzenberg said defiantly, "and the goal of disarmament is incompatible with this [ideology] at the present moment. I am thus against the refusal of military service."[18]

Lenin was less careful with his language. At the follow-up socialist antiwar conference to Zimmerwald, held in the Bernese Oberland at Kiental in April 1916, Lenin proposed a resolution instructing proletarian-soldiers, "Lay down your weapons. Turn them against the common foe!—the capitalist governments." While this and Lenin's other exhortations to purge social "chauvinists" did not pass at the conference, Lenin's Zimmerwald Left faction was growing. The conference Manifesto, addressed "To the People Driven to Ruin and Death," moved in Lenin's direction by declaring that the only "effective means of preventing future wars" was through "the seizure of political power and the abolition of capitalist property by the working class." The Liebknecht-Luxemburg faction of the German socialist opposition, now styling itself "Spartacus," was also closer to Lenin's than the majority line at Zimmerwald and Kiental, stating, in a "political letter" penned in response to Kiental in May, that "international socialism does not consist of conferences, resolutions, or manifestos, but of deeds, of struggle, of mass action." Lenin himself viewed Kiental as a "step forward . . . toward a break with the social patriots."[19]

In the wake of Kiental, Lenin refined his ideas about war and revolution, writing one of his most ambitious theoretical works in his Spiegelgasse flat in Zurich. Clearly influenced by a 1902 critique by the British liberal economist John Hobson, *Imperialism: A Study*, to which he gives a hat tip, Lenin's own study of *Imperialism, the Highest Stage of Capitalism* is more strictly Marxist in interpretation—and also written with hindsight about the outbreak of world war in 1914. Whereas Hobson saw in British imperialism a "depraved choice" reminiscent of the decadence of ancient Rome, a lazy way out of the hard work of domestic economic development for a polity past its prime, Lenin saw the war marking the "stagnation and decay" of capitalism, as European empires reached the limits of expansion and began squabbling over a shrinking pool of new markets. Just as Marx's immiseration thesis envisioned an ever smaller pool of capitalists lording it over the proletarianized masses, so did Lenin see the elite imperial powers, France and Britain with their "vast colonial possessions," lording it over lesser European rivals in a zero-sum game to achieve "a monopolist position in the world market." By unleashing the fury of unrestrained imperialist rivalries, the world war had destroyed the "vain, hypocritical, and cowardly" dreams of liberal and socialist reformism, bringing forward a darker "epoch of wars and revolutions."[20]

Blending together the ideas of *Socialism and War* and *Imperialism, the Highest Stage of Capitalism*, Lenin formulated a "Military Program of the Proletarian Revolution" in October 1916. Rejecting pacifism, he asserted that "socialists have never been, nor can they ever be, opposed to all wars." True, the ongoing war, marked in 1916 by the twin horrors of the futile and bloody German offensive at Verdun, and the no less futile and bloody Allied offensive at the Somme, was in Lenin's view being waged by the "bourgeoisie" as a classic "reactionary, slave-owners' and criminal war." But "what about," he asked his fellow socialists, "a war *against* this bourgeoisie?" What about a war "waged by peoples oppressed by and dependent upon this bourgeoisie, or by colonial peoples, for liberation?" So, too, was "civil war just as much a war as any other," and anyone who "accepts the class struggle cannot fail to accept civil wars, which in every class society are the natural . . . continuation, development and intensification of the class struggle."[21]

Nor, in Lenin's view, would a successful socialist revolution "in one country," contrary to the wishful sentiment expressed in the majority Kiental manifesto, "eliminate all war in general." Because other countries, at different stages of development, would "remain bourgeois or pre-bourgeois" even after socialism emerged in one, "this is bound to create not only friction, but a direct attempt on the part of the bourgeoisie of other countries to crush the socialist state's victorious proletariat." In case of such a counter-revolutionary attack, "such a war on our part would be a legitimate and just war. It would be a war for socialism, for the liberation of other nations from the bourgeoisie." The world war, as Lenin explained, would engender the "possibility and inevitability, first, of revolutionary national rebellions and wars; second, of proletarian wars and rebellions *against* the bourgeoisie; and, third, of a combination of both kinds of revolutionary war." The "social parsons and opportunists" in the ranks of socialism, Lenin scoffed, preferred to "build dreams of future peaceful socialism," betraying a refusal to "think about and reflect on the fierce class struggle and class *wars* needed to achieve that beautiful future."[22]

The foolish decision of Europe's ruling classes to arm "proletarians" to fight their imperialist war would pave the way for their own destruction now that the "oppressed class" could finally fight back. Rather than draft resistance, conscientious objection, or other forms of pacifist protest, socialists must turn the armies red, infiltrating the ranks with indoctrinated revolutionaries. Channeling Clausewitz and Marx, Lenin observed that "every war is but the continuation of policy by other means." He demanded that proud "proletarian women" drill this message into their sons: "You will soon be grown up. You will be given a gun. Take it and learn the military art properly. Proletarians need this knowledge not to shoot your brothers, the workers of other countries, as is being done in the present war, and as the traitors to socialism are telling you to do. They need it to fight bourgeoisie of their own country, to put an end to the exploitation, poverty and war . . . by defeating and disarming the bourgeoisie."[23]

Having armed their sons to launch a cataclysmic class war, these mothers should not shy from joining the fight themselves. Marx himself had observed that "women and teen-age children fought in the Paris Commune side by side with the men." It would be "no different," Lenin said confidently, "in the coming battles for the overthrow of the bourgeoisie," as "proletarian women . . . will take to arms, as they did in 1871." Imperialism had led to world war and the "militarization of all countries, even in neutral and small ones." Bourgeois women, and chauvinist traitors to socialism, might urge disarmament, but "the women of an oppressed and really revolutionary class will never accept that shameful role." From the "cowed nations of today," Lenin predicted, "there will undoubtedly arise, sooner or later, but with absolute certainty, an international league of the 'terrible nations' of the revolutionary proletariat."[24]

At a time when most European socialists, alongside conscience-stricken citizens of all political stripes, were genuinely horrified by the ongoing carnage on numerous fronts of a world war, Lenin was prophesying—endorsing and promoting, basically—a whole age of unending armed conflict, of imperialist wars and civil wars and revolutionary and counter-revolutionary struggle, one war begetting another in a global bonfire of violence as Marx's prophesy from *Das Kapital* came true and the "expropriators were expropriated."

However bold his theory of inevitable proletarian revolution, Lenin was not certain he would live to see the bonfire. On January 22, 1917, he lamented, in a speech to Münzenberg's Youth Socialists in Zurich, on the somber anniversary of Bloody Sunday, that "we of the older generation may not live to see the decisive battles of the coming revolution." Although Russia's 1905 Revolution, born of the last Great Power war, had ushered in hopes of revolutionary change, these had been quickly dashed: the tsar and his ministers had neutered the new parliament (Duma) by giving the tsar full veto power over its legislation, the right to dissolve it at any time, and the right to rule by emergency decree when it was not in session. The "Fundamental Laws" promulgated in April 1906, loosely the equivalent of a Russian constitution, even reaffirmed the "Supreme Autocratic Power" of the tsar as sovereign. By wartime, all that was left of the old revolutionary spirit of 1905 was an annual march in solidarity with the victims of Bloody Sunday—and even then, turnout in January 1917 was pitiful, lower by an order of magnitude than the one the year before. Significantly, the January 1916 Bloody Sunday demonstration in Petrograd, unlike the January 1917 one, had been subsidized by the German Foreign Office, to the tune of a million rubles. As a brutally cold winter savaged Russia, Lenin's pessimism seemed warranted.[25]

By 1917, even the military situation had turned against Lenin's hopes for a crushing Russian defeat midwifing revolution. The year 1915 had been a catalog of misfortunes for Russia, with the Germans breaking through Russian lines at Gorlice-Tarnów in May and sweeping through Russian Poland and up the Baltic coast that summer. So catastrophic was Russia's "Great Retreat," blamed in the popular press on "shell shortage" and government corruption and malfeasance, that it nearly led to the collapse of the tsarist regime in August 1915. A "Progressive Bloc" in the Duma began demanding that Tsar Nicholas II appoint a government composed of "persons enjoying the confidence of the public," that is, answering to parliament instead of the tsar. Only the tsar's own brave—if foolhardy—decision to assume the military command himself, and thus take personal responsibility for Russian victory and defeat, staved off a political meltdown.[26]

In 1916, by contrast, Russia's armies had been mostly victorious, helped along by a surge in war-industrial production that turned the "shell shortage" into a distant memory. The Brusilov Offensive in Galicia was the big story of the summer, as Russia's armies reconquered some 40,000 square kilometers (15,000 square miles) of territory—an area larger than Belgium. This gain produced "an electrifying effect on Russian morale," as one Allied military attaché reported. In the Ottoman Empire, the Russian Caucasian army rode from one triumph to another that year, conquering the reputedly impregnable fortress at Erzurum in February, landing amphibious forces at Rize and Trabzon, and pitching the Ottoman Third Army into headlong retreat. The food situation on the Russian fronts had improved so dramatically in 1916 that, during a pause in fighting on Christmas Day, desperate Germans came across Russian lines begging for food. As one Russian soldier in the Fifth Army gloated in a letter home, "Now our roles have reversed. Last year we were retreating, but now the Germans are preparing to run away." At a planning conference of the Allies held in Petrograd in January 1917, a British commander reported home with confidence that "Russia's generals were full of fight."[27]

Little did Lenin know that, after years in the political wilderness, events in Russia outside his control would soon change his fortunes dramatically, along with those of Communism.

5
THE BOLSHEVIKS TAKE POWER

A t first the atmosphere in Petrograd on International Women's Day was festive, peaceful, and relatively apolitical. It was Thursday, February 23, 1917 (or March 8, according to the Gregorian calendar used in the West), and many women, both labor activists and those simply frustrated by surging bread and fuel prices, had come out for the march. Their event had been scheduled to show solidarity with an ongoing strike at the Putilov arms works, and the protests rapidly merged into a great human wave. People had been cooped up indoors for weeks during a brutally cold winter, and they were happy to come out to enjoy the unseasonably warm weather. Although detachments of police and mounted Cossacks were patrolling the city, few of them wanted to harass peaceful crowds full of women.

Events took a darker turn over the weekend as the strike spread to other factories. Rougher elements from the working-class neighborhoods of Vyborg and Vasilyevsky Island joined the growing crowds on Nevsky Prospekt and the squares around it. Despite the warm spring weather, the Neva River was still frozen, which allowed protesters to bypass police checkpoints on the bridges and simply walk across the ice. Saturday, February 25 (March 10), saw the first serious violence: three protesters were killed at the covered shopping bazaar known as Gostinnyi Dvor, ten more wounded, and one police officer hacked to death by Cossacks (who objected to his threats after they refused to engage protesters). The police chief of Vyborg was dragged from his horse and beaten (though he survived), and the nearby police station in his district was set on fire by rioters.[1]

On Sunday, Tsar Nicholas II called in the army, which nearly succeeded in restoring order—but by methods that rapidly backfired. After two inexperienced training companies of the Volynsky Guard Regiment fired into a crowd of protesters in Znamenskaya Square, killing forty and wounding a similar number, several guard regiments resolved not to obey further orders to fire at the unruly crowds, including the regiment that had shed blood at the square. Late that night, one or more of the Volynsky guardsmen shot their commanding officer, Major I. S. Lashkevich, and he died. This act unleashed a mutiny that spread like wildfire through the Petrograd garrison. Hundreds, then thousands of soldiers deserted, sold their weapons, commandeered vehicles and ran up the red flag, or joined the milling crowds. Police stations were overwhelmed, and some of them were torched to the ground, though usually only after inmates were freed (freed inmates were often the ones doing the torching). Uniformed policemen were lynched, shops and markets raided, and the main city arsenal looted of weapons. In a symbolic coup, the headquarters of the tsarist secret police (Okhrana) on the Moika Canal was stormed late on Monday afternoon, February 27 (March 12). Smoke poured out the chimneys as files were burned. By nightfall, the tsarist authorities had clearly lost control of Petrograd, although it was still unclear who was in charge of the city.[2]

In the back rooms of Taurida Palace, where the Duma had met, a furious power struggle was underway between a group of Duma

"elders" led by the Speaker, Mikhail Rodzianko, and a more radical body styling itself the Executive Committee of the Petrograd
Soviet, convened in homage to the one formed by Trotsky in the
1905 Revolution. Had Tsar Nicholas II stuck to his original orders,
issued on February 28 (March 13), that a punitive "St. George battalion" of loyal frontline troops proceed to the city, he might have
consigned these self-appointed revolutionary bodies to irrelevance.
Instead, Russia's sovereign, after he was cornered by generals worried
about the impact of a counter-revolutionary crackdown in Petrograd
on frontline morale, agreed, on March 2 (15), 1917, to call off the
St. George battalion. He then abdicated his throne to his brother
Michael in a letter addressed to the army command "in agreement
with the State Duma." "Nicholas Romanov" was now a mere private
subject—and was promptly placed under house arrest at his former
Summer Palace at Tsarskoe Selo. There, in his newfound idleness,
he helped shovel snow.[3]

Far from resolving the succession problem, the tsar's hurried and
chaotic abdication threw Russia's political future into turmoil. To
begin with, his brother Michael had not asked to, and did not desire
to, assume the throne. Nor were the Duma elders in Petrograd in
agreement about what to do. Rodzianko was quickly pushed to the
curb by a Council of Ministers of the Provisional Government that
was meant to be a caretaker cabinet until a Constituent Assembly was elected later in 1917. Michael Romanov abdicated to the
council, and the council's defense minister, Alexander Guchkov,
founder of the center-right "Octobrist" party, drew up new loyalty
oaths pledging the Russian army to fight on its behalf. The Executive Committee of the Petrograd Soviet, or Ispolkom, issued an
"Order No. 1" on March 1 (14) instructing soldier "committees" to
seize control of weapons and ammunitions in order to forestall any
counter-revolutionary push against mutineers. It forbade officers
from addressing their men with the informal "you" (in Russian, *tyi*

instead of the more respectful *vyi*) and stipulated that the Petrograd garrison answer to Ispolkom. Although addressed only to the Petrograd garrison, not to frontline troops, Order No. 1 was published in Ispolkom's new newspaper, *Izvestiya* (News) with thousands of copies printed, and the text was sent out over the telegraph wires. As one radical sailor who witnessed its drafting in Taurida Palace observed, "Educated folk will read it differently. But we understand it straight: disarm the officers."[4]

From his comfortable exile in Zurich, Lenin could observe the dramatic events of what we now call the "February Revolution" only at second hand. Aside from Alexander Shliapnikov, who had joined the Menshevik-led Ispolkom, and Lenin's friend Vladimir Bonch-Bruevich, a well-connected party loyalist who, by seizing control of the printing works used to publish *Izvestiya*, was instrumental in publicizing Order No. 1, the Bolsheviks had played only a minor role in the February Revolution. Lenin's doctrine of revolutionary defeatism had not really factored in—at least, not yet. Russia's armies had performed well in 1916 and were poised for major spring offensives. It was not a military setback at the front, but a Petrograd garrison mutiny that had toppled the Russian tsar. Lenin had neither foreseen this course of events nor done anything to catalyze it.[5]

Nonetheless, Lenin was ideally placed to capitalize on the unfolding political chaos in wartime Russia—if he could return home to take a hand. Getting there, however, was politically delicate. To avoid breaching the Western and Eastern Fronts, the only practical way to get from Switzerland to Russia was by way of Germany, which might look suspicious to Russians still locked in war with that country. Having already established contact with Lenin via a range of intermediaries, the German consul in Bern was eager to help the Bolshevik firebrand return home to wreak havoc with Russia's war effort, but he needed to proceed carefully, lest his collaboration with Lenin be too obvious and damage Lenin's political credibility. Lenin's Swiss socialist convert to the Zimmerwald Left, Fritz Platten, agreed to handle all negotiations and purchase rail tickets and passes for Lenin and his nineteen Bolshevik associates (including his wife and his mistress, along with Karl Radek and Grigory Zinoviev). He would also act as Lenin's "host" while the train passed through Germany, ensuring that Lenin need not contact or speak to any German officials. Platten and the Germans released a cover story, parroted by credulous journalists (and repeated to this day by incurious historians), that Lenin's train car was "sealed" and would not open its doors while crossing Germany, satisfying "extraterritoriality" requirements, enabling Lenin to deny that the Germans had organized his trip (as they did, appropriating 5 million gold marks for Lenin's return voyage and his initial operations in Russia).[6]

The story of Lenin's "sealed train" ride through Germany was a convenient lie. Lenin and the other Russian passengers broke the seal right after they crossed the Swiss border, stepping foot on German soil to switch over to a German train. On the new train, they were accompanied by three German state officials. Lenin's party missed their connection in Frankfurt, necessitating a stopover there. When Lenin's train reached Berlin, it remained at a standstill for twenty hours. Because of the delay, Lenin's party missed the ferry connection at Sassnitz for Denmark. They spent an entire night on German soil, staying in a port hotel as they waited for the morning ferry.[7]

Lenin was playing with political fire by collaborating with the Germans. However sincere his belief in Marxism and the revolution, his position on the war was incendiary: he wanted "his" side to lose it and would work to bring this about. Nor did Lenin moderate his extreme views on returning to Russia, despite being warned by party comrades—including Stalin and Lev Kamenev, who had toiled away at home in the underground during the war—to tone it down so as not to associate the Bolsheviks with treason. Whisked away to party headquarters upon his arrival at Finland station on the historic night of April 3–4 (16–17), 1917, Lenin unloaded for two hours at his party colleagues, denouncing the "piratical imperialist war" and the party "backsliders" who had gone along with the Fourth of August betrayal and supported Russia's war. Lenin's April Theses, memorialized in Communist lore for the phrase "All Power to the Soviets," were largely devoted to foreign policy, rejecting even conditional support for the war and demanding the outright abolition of the Russian Imperialist Army. His April Theses were voted down by the Bolshevik Central Committee 13 to 2. Kamenev, editor of the party organ *Pravda* (Truth), refused to publish them, disavowing the "demoralizing influence of 'revolutionary defeatism' and . . . comrade Lenin's criticism." Stalin denounced Lenin's "Down with the War" slogan as "useless."[8]

There was nothing subtle about any of this. Even without being published in *Pravda*, Lenin's "extreme radical and pacifist" program was the talk of the town, as an American historian, Frank Golder, wrote in his diary the day after Lenin's dramatic entrance. "Germany," Golder observed, "is doing its best to bring about discord. Lenin . . . has been given special permission and special facilities to come through Germany from Switzerland in order that he and his party might preach pacifism and demoralize the army and the country." As a German army intelligence officer in Stockholm reported to the German high command on April 4 (17), "Lenin's entry into Russia successful. He is working exactly as we would wish."[9]

Of course, Lenin had his own objective in Russia, namely, toppling the tsarist government to bring about a revolutionary proletarian dictatorship—the first, he hoped, of many to come. The "imperialist war," he hoped, would give way to a series of civil wars, and then wars between "Communist" and "capitalist-imperialist" states, as the world was plunged into an age of unceasing violence. However helpful his advocacy of army demoralization and the promotion of mutinies and revolutionary strife might be to Russia's wartime enemies in the short run, his objective was not the same as that of his German sponsors. To be sure, the German government was using Lenin for its own ends—but then Lenin was using the Germans, too. German funds allowed Lenin to purchase a private printing press on Suvorovsky Prospekt in Petrograd for 250,000 rubles (equal to some $12.5 million today). The Bolsheviks were soon using it to print party propaganda in virtually unlimited quantities. Within days, Lenin's party was publishing separate versions of *Pravda* for the Petrograd army garrison (*Soldatskaia Pravda*), sailors in the Baltic Fleet (*Golos Pravdy*), and Russian frontline troops (*Okopnaia Pravda*), this last broadsheet achieving a circulation well into six figures. Because it was Lenin's German connections that enabled him to fund this publishing bonanza, Kamenev and Stalin relented and let him flood Russia's armies and naval forces with his defeatist antiwar propaganda, openly encouraging mutinies in wartime.[10]

Flush with cash, the Bolsheviks took over the Kshesinskaya Mansion, a grand Art Nouveau residence built for a famous ballerina, Mathilde Kshesinskaya, a former mistress of Tsar Nicholas II. Strategically located opposite the Peter and Paul Fortress in the city center, the mansion was transformed into a fortified political compound. It housed the editorial offices of the soldier and sailor editions of *Pravda* and became the headquarters of the Bolshevik Military Organization, which dispatched "commissars" to army and navy units to convert enlisted men to the cause. A printing office downstairs turned out automobile passes and identity cards for party operatives and soldiers, along with protest signs, which the party paid Russians to carry around Petrograd. In the "April Days" rioting, Bolshevik activists were witnessed handing out ten-ruble notes—real money, akin to $500 today—to Russians holding up protest placards carrying borderline-treasonous slogans such as "Down with the war" and "The Germans are our brothers."[11]

Lenin's "revolutionary defeatism" messaging was most potent—and effective—in eroding Russian morale in the frontline armies. With remarkable timing, the first Bolshevik agitators from Petrograd reached Russia's southwestern front in Galicia just days before Russia's Provisional Government, and, on the urging of its new war and naval minister, Alexander Kerensky, launched an offensive targeting Lemberg (Lvov) on June 16 (29), 1917. At first the Russians advanced easily into the pulverized Austro-Hungarian trenches, pushing the front forward two miles, seizing twenty-nine guns, and taking 18,000 prisoners while suffering only minimal losses. But the congratulations Kerensky offered proved premature, as even victorious units soon halted the offensive to convene fractious "soviets" similar to those that had undermined the Petrograd garrison. The very act of occupying Austrian territory was, from the Leninist viewpoint, a crime of rapacious capitalist-imperialism. "Comrades! Whose land are we on anyhow?" a soldier in the Thirty-Fifth Division asked his fellow Russians. He proposed, "Let's give the Austrians back their land and return to our own borders" (adding that if the Austro-Hungarian armies tried crossing the old frontier, it would be "over our dead bodies"). Tellingly, the unit physician then pulled out a copy of *Okopnaia Pravda* and read out a kind of Bolshevik "sermon" to the men. Getting the message, they agreed on a resolution that nicely encapsulated the new quasi-Leninist disposition of Russia's frontline armies: "Ours we will not yield, but others' [lands] we do not seek."[12]

Russia's armies were not the only ones beginning to crack under the strain in 1917 as the Great War approached the three-year mark. France's offensive at Chemin des Dames on the Western Front, launched in mid-April, had fallen apart by April 20 (May 3) after many French soldiers had refused to continue making fruitless assaults against German lines—while insisting, like the Russians in Galicia, that they would still defend their own trenches. While morale in the German armies held strong in 1917, on the home front the Social Democratic Party (SPD) shattered in two over the question of war aims. Like the Russians in the soviets in Galicia, or the mutinous French soldiers at Chemin des Dames, many German socialists wanted to renegotiate the compromise (or "betrayal") of August 1914, disowning the increasingly aggressive war aims of the belligerent powers.

The difference in Russia was that Lenin wanted to go further still, not simply pausing the war to reconsider "imperialist" war aims, but using it as a springboard to a civil war. The Bolshevik contagion spread rapidly through the armies on the Galician front, bringing one unit after another to the point of mutiny. Banners began appearing in frontline areas not just questioning imperialist war aims, but proclaiming "Down with the War" and "Down with the Provisional Government." As General P. N. Baluev reported to General Aleksei Brusilov, who was directing the Galician offensive, it was "impossible to expel the main agitators in view of the fact that they were armed." The Russian Eleventh Army, flooded with Bolshevik agitators, suffered 346 desertions in a single rifle regiment, who all left with their arms. Another army company, it was reported, "not only willfully deserted the trenches on the night of June 19 [July 2], but ridiculed those soldiers who remained in the trenches." Just as Lenin had planned, Russia's armies were turning "red."[13]

After Kerensky ordered reinforcements from Petrograd to the Galician front, the cascading Bolshevik mutinies reached the capital, nearly toppling the beleaguered Provisional Government. The First Machine Gun Regiment that Kerensky had tried to send to

Galicia, as Kerensky knew, had been infested with Bolshevik agitators for weeks, led by a young ensign named A. Y. Semashko. Semashko had deserted the regiment back in March only to show up at its soviets to organize Bolshevik "collectives" in each of its units—recruiting 500 activists in the First Machine Gun Regiment alone. Other "Red Guards" reporting to the Bolshevik Military Organization at Kshesinskaya's were recruited from the naval regiment at Kronstadt, on Kotlin Island in the Gulf of Finland. So heady was the atmosphere at Kshesinskaya's that Leon Trotsky, the Menshevik who had written the tepid majority resolution at Zimmerwald, joined forces with Lenin and delivered a "passionate, harsh and heated" speech on July 2 (15), 1917, at the Petrograd People's House, proclaiming, "Down with the Minister-Capitalists," "Down with Kerensky." According to some eyewitnesses, he urged Semashko's First Machine Gun Regiment Bolsheviks to "kill Kerensky."[14]

Trotsky may have overplayed his hand. Owing, in part, to Lenin's disappearance from Petrograd between June 29 and July 4 (July 12 and 17), when he was hiding in Finland, the Bolsheviks were unable to storm Taurida Palace and depose the Provisional Government. Although reinforcements from factories and placard-holders recruited at Kshesinskaya's allowed the Bolshevik mob marching on Taurida Palace to swell to nearly 10,000, the core armed muscle provided by F. F. Raskolnikov's Red Guard sailors and Semashko's machine-gunner mutineers was much smaller—likely no more than a few thousand. The mob also became dispersed more widely throughout the city as they tried to secure strongpoints—including railroad stations, key intersections on Nevsky Prospekt, the Mariinsky Palace (where the Provisional Government periodically sat), and the printing offices of the liberal newspaper *Novoe Vremya* (New times). Another unit of armed Bolsheviks tried to hunt Kerensky down at the central rail station, only to get there ninety minutes after the war minister had passed through. For a few heady hours, as Raskolnikov's sailors and Semashko's soldiers took over the square in front of Taurida Palace, it seemed that Lenin's Bolsheviks would take over from Kerensky's beleaguered government, which was insisting on continuing an increasingly unpopular war. Strangely, however, Lenin shied away from addressing the crowd and proclaiming a revolutionary government. By midnight on July 4 (17), the armed but increasingly fractious Bolshevik mob in front of Taurida Palace began to disperse.[15]

Lenin's passivity nearly proved fatal to the Communist cause. Even while the rudderless Bolshevik revolution was losing momentum in Taurida Palace square, Kerensky's ministers gathered to plot a counter-move. Although the Justice Department was still assembling evidence of Lenin's treasonous German contacts, Kerensky agreed to leak a summary of their findings to date to the press to impugn Lenin's reputation. On the morning of July 5 (18), the liberal paper *Zhivoe Slovo* (Living word) led with the banner headline "LENIN, GANETSKII & CO. SPIES," printing enough copies to blanket Petrograd. After hearing the news, Lenin was overheard telling Trotsky, "Now they are going to shoot us," before shaving his beard and going to ground in the Finnish countryside. Abandoned by their leader, the Bolsheviks could only watch as the *Pravda* printing press was smashed and Kshesinskaya headquarters raided by loyal Russian army troops, who arrested 2,000 Bolsheviks and swept up a motherlode of intelligence. The next day 11 leading Bolsheviks, including Lenin in absentia, were charged with "high treason and organizing an armed uprising." In a curious irony, Trotsky, who had been far more involved in the insurrection than Lenin, was spared, as he was still a Menshevik—until July 23 (August 5), when he joined the Bolsheviks and was promptly arrested. By moving against the government before enough support in the army was secured—by showing his hand too soon and then abandoning the field at the critical moment—Lenin had consigned the Bolsheviks to mass imprisonment and apparent political oblivion.[16]

Lenin, however, proved fortunate in his enemies. Kerensky's Justice Department assembled evidence all summer for a treason trial against the Bolshevik Party. But Kerensky lost heart after a bitter showdown with the man he had appointed to restore discipline to Russia's armies, General Lavr Kornilov, whom Kerensky, owing to a baroque saga of miscommunication, accused of treason, too. The accusation itself led Kornilov to order troops to Petrograd, committing the treasonous act of which he had been accused. Bizarrely, Kerensky issued orders that Kornilov, though guilty of treason, was to be obeyed until a suitable replacement was found, and a bewildered Kornilov surrendered without a fight. On August 31 (September 13), 1917, Kerensky amnestied all Bolsheviks not already "proved guilty of acts of a criminal nature" and allowed the party to rearm in order to help defend the government against the alleged threat of "Kornilovism": the Bolsheviks promptly seized 40,000 rifles from a government arsenal. A cautious Lenin remained in hiding in Finland, but his rejuvenated movement was now stronger than ever in Petrograd and Moscow. The Bolshevik Party won majorities in the soviets of both cities for the first time in mid-September, and it was gaining influence in the army on the fronts nearest Petrograd, where Lenin's "end the war now" message was resonating more powerfully every day. Key Baltic units, such as the Latvian Brigades of the Twelfth Army, were now thoroughly bolshevized, providing nearby muscle to the Bolsheviks in case they chose to overthrow Kerensky, who, by moving against Kornilov, had forfeited the support of what remained of the Russian officer corps. With evidence mounting of Bolshevik plans for a coup, Kerensky wired northern front headquarters at Pskov, requesting loyal troops to defend the capital. The front commander replied coldly, "This is political and has nothing to do with me."[17]

As we saw in his hesitation during the "July Days," Lenin was not an infallible political tactician, but in his ideological conviction, confidence, and stubbornness he was a worthy heir to Marx. Lenin had updated Marxist doctrine in significant ways. In his top-down "vanguardism," for example, the broad participation of the working masses, though desirable in theory, was not strictly necessary in practice, but converting soldiers to the cause might provide enough muscle to topple a government absent this mass support. Lenin had also learned from the history of the Paris Commune and Russia's Revolution of 1905 that military failure undermined a government's legitimacy—drawing the lesson that revolutionaries might speed along that government's collapse if they actively promoted such failure. So it was that Bolshevik activists had arrived in Galicia just as Kerensky launched his ill-fated offensive there in June 1917, and then blanketed the northern front defending Petrograd in August–September, just as the German armies took Riga and the Russian armies fell back on Petrograd.

In his view of politics as sublimated warfare, Lenin reduced revolution to its Marxist essence: Who had more men under arms, the government or its enemies? In an October 1917 memorandum, Lenin insisted that the Bolsheviks must achieve a "gigantic preponderance" of armed force over Kerensky's government, only to be told that he could rely on only about 10,000 armed Red Guards, roughly half from army units and half from Russia's Baltic Fleet, which he reckoned was "not enough" to conquer Petrograd. Briefed by his military advisers, however, Lenin was convinced that his armed supporters now outnumbered Kerensky's in the capital.[18]

In the Bolshevik Central Committee on October 10 (23), 1917, Lenin argued, over the objections of most of his colleagues, that the party must not wait for the national parliamentary elections scheduled for November—which the Bolsheviks did not expect to win—but must seize power now. Trotsky chimed in with a proposal that the party wait until the Second Congress of Soviets, an urban body in which the party might win a majority, convened on October 25 (November 7). Trotsky's compromise proposal carried 10 to 2. With Lenin—with warrants for his arrest plastered around Petrograd—still hiding, traveling about the city only at night and in disguise, Trotsky emerged as party spokesman. Asked by a Menshevik, named Fyodor Dan, in the Petrograd Soviet on October 16 (29), whether Lenin's party was "getting ready for [armed] action," Trotsky replied, mischievously, "We have still not decided on an insurrection."[19]

A curious waiting game now ensued. The Bolsheviks had resolved to seize power by force, and both the Petrograd Soviet and Kerensky's Provisional Government expected a putsch to be sprung any day. In view of all the ink spilled over doctrine during the seventy years since the publication of Marx's *Communist Manifesto*, all the furious debates at socialist congresses about revolutionary eschatology, tactics, and the timing of the moment when (in Marx's words) the "knell of capitalist private property" would finally sound, the fate of the revolution seemed entirely up to chance—not least whether or not Lenin would be arrested before it happened (as he nearly was on October 24 [November 6] by a picket near Taurida Palace; Lenin feigned drunkenness and was let go). True, the party, and its increasingly well armed Red Guards, was better prepared than it had been in July, and Kerensky's government much less popular. But when the cards were dealt, would Lenin, who had fled the scene so quickly when things turned sour in July, really succeed in toppling Russia's government in wartime—a government still defended by an army 7 million strong?[20]

There was nothing secret or unexpected about the Bolshevik putsch. Kerensky moved into the military headquarters of the Petrograd garrison at Mikhailovsky Palace on October 23 (November 5) to meet fire with fire and publicly paraded evidence of Lenin's insurrectionary plans the next day, accusing the Bolsheviks of "treason and betrayal of the Russian state." Kerensky cut off the phone lines to the Smolny Institute where the Bolsheviks had moved their headquarters, and even instructed government employees to return home early (at 2:30 p.m.), to avoid getting hit in the cross fire. Kerensky sent a wire to the northern front headquarters at Pskov, requesting army reinforcements.[21]

Unlike in July, however, Kerensky did not have popular opinion on his side, nor did he have strong military support. Toward dawn on October 25 (November 7), armed Bolshevik Red Guards fanned out across the city, walked up to young cadets guarding key choke points, and told them they were being relieved. In this way, the Bolsheviks gained control of bridges, railway stations, and critical buildings such as the Peter and Paul Fortress; Mariinsky Palace, where the body preparing for November's parliamentary elections was sitting; and the Central Telegraph Office, where Red Guards disconnected the phone lines to the Winter Palace, and where the Provisional Government was sitting. Tentatively, Lenin issued a public appeal to the "citizens of Russia" at 10 a.m., declaring the Provisional Government "deposed." Authority, he said, had passed to the Petrograd Soviet and its Military-Revolutionary Committee (Milrevkom), which the Bolsheviks dominated. Even so, the Bolsheviks hesitated before storming the Winter Palace, guarded by cadets, Cossacks, and a "Women's Death Battalion" that Kerensky had created to shame Russia's men into fighting harder. It was the latter force that held out the longest. Just past midnight on October 25–26 (November 7–8), 1917, the Women's Death Battalion was overwhelmed; its members were reportedly raped as the Bolsheviks stormed the building. At 2:10 a.m., Red Guards burst into the room where the Provisional Government was meeting, arrested the ministers, and stopped the palace clock, marking the moment the world's first Communist regime was born.[22]

To give the Bolshevik coup—or, as the Bolsheviks and much of the world would soon call it, the "October Revolution"—a patina of democratic legitimacy, Lenin convened the "Second All-Russian Congress of Soviets" in the Smolny Institute at 10:40 p.m. on October 25, while the Winter Palace was still under siege. When news trickled in toward 3:00 a.m. of the successful putsch, most of the Menshevik and Socialist Revolutionary (SR) deputies walked out to protest Lenin's "criminal venture." Taking advantage of the walkout, the Bolsheviks rubber-stamped their own revolution with a series of resolutions creating a provisional "Workers' and Peasants' Government to be known as the Soviet of People's Commissars [Sovnarkom]." They abolished "private ownership of land," granted amnesty to Bolshevik prisoners, and ended Russia's war against the Central Powers. "To those who have left," Trotsky taunted his opponents, "we say: you are miserable bankrupts, your role is played out, go where you ought to go—into the dustbin of history."[23]

It was Lenin's moment. For all his faults, the Bolshevik leader had seen the opportunity presented by the war of 1914 more clearly than others, understanding that it accentuated class divisions between ruler and ruled, with the latter foolishly armed by the former. He had drawn the Marxist dialectical conclusion that imperialism had begotten world war, and that the military conflagration could bleed into a series of civil wars—helped along by the Bolsheviks giving history a shove. The next step was to end the "imperialist war," as Lenin did on November 8 (21), when Trotsky handed over a "proposal for an immediate armistice on all fronts" to the ambassadors of the Entente Powers in Petrograd, and wired an order to cease hostilities to Kornilov's hapless successor as Russian commander-in-chief at military headquarters in Mogilev, General N. N. Dukhonin. When Dukhonin, viewing the order as illegitimate—Defense Ministry employees had gone on strike to protest Lenin's coup, such that it came through undated and without proper stamps—refused to comply, Lenin dismissed him for insubordination and replaced him with a bolshevized ensign, N. V. Krylenko. In a national radio broadcast, Lenin denounced Dukhonin, insisting, with a hint of menace, that Russian soldiers "not permit counter-revolutionary generals to frustrate the great cause of peace." Getting the message, on November 20 (December 3), 1917, soldiers from Krylenko's punitive battalion, sent to arrest the commander-in-chief, "dragged the unfortunate Dukhonin out to the platform, mercilessly beat him, and ran him through with bayonets." Having thus seized control of the Russian army command, the Bolsheviks sued for peace with Germany and the Central Powers, ending the war on the Eastern Front.[24]

As Lenin's theory of revolutionary defeatism suggested, the campaign to turn imperialist war into civil war bore fruit first in the defeated country that now lay prostrate before its enemies: his own. Revolution might come later to Germany and the Entente Powers, but for now the action was in Russia. Taking over Stavka, Ensign Krylenko reported to Lenin that a "catastrophic situation" had emerged in army logistics, with shortages of food, fodder, and rolling stock so horrendous that the Russian army needed to shed "three or four million soldiers" immediately. In a directive on December 8 (21), 1917, Krylenko noted that Lenin had asked him to come up with a "plan to transform a standing army into an armed population." He set up a demobilization commission, instructing departing soldiers to keep their weapons. Combined with the controversial ceasefire and the flight of hundreds of patriotic Russian officers (such as Kornilov, sprung from military prison by Dukhonin shortly before the latter was lynched) to Rostov-on-Don, where they began organizing armed resistance to the Bolsheviks under the protection of the Don Cossacks, the demobilization of "three to four million" heavily armed soldiers primed the pump for civil war.[25]

Already battles were raging across Russia after the October Revolution between Red Guards and loyalists, the latter fighting, if not for Kerensky, then for Russia's honor and the integrity of the upcoming parliamentary elections. The fiercest fighting took place in Moscow, where a force of some 15,000 armed Bolsheviks—including not just Red Guards recruited locally but an entire bolshevized infantry regiment (the 193th), which deployed ten machine guns and two "mobile heavy artillery columns"—fought their way down Tverskaya and Strastnaia Boulevards, shot up the Bolshoi and Malyi Theaters and the great central market at Okhotnyi Ryad, and shelled the red brick walls of the Kremlin across the Alexander Garden from the Hotel National before storming into the Kremlin through the famous Manezh Gate. On November 2 (15), 1917, they announced "an end to combat operations in Moscow."[26]

While much of European Russia, and nearly all of Asiatic Russia beyond the Urals, remained outside of Bolshevik control, with the capture of Russia's two capital cities and Russian military headquarters in the October Revolution Lenin's Bolsheviks had raised high the red flag. After decades of theorizing and talk, the world would now learn what Communism looked like in practice.

PART II
COMMUNISM IN PRACTICE

6
COMMUNISM IN POWER

The putsch in Petrograd and the conquest of the Moscow Kremlin were the first battles in an emerging Russian Civil War. In Minsk and areas in west European Russia close to the front, the struggle was mostly decided by soldier committees, who simply shunted aside those officers who had not already fled and declared loyalty to the new government. In regions of European Russia farther removed from the front, the "advent of Soviet power," as the overthrow of Russia's governing institutions was styled by the Bolsheviks, followed a different pattern, although soldiers were usually still involved. In Saratov, southeast of Moscow on the Volga, the Bolsheviks staged a rump election in the Soviet at 3:00 a.m. on October 26 (November 7), 1917, purging Mensheviks and Socialist revolutionaries after they walked out in protest, just as Trotsky and Lenin had done in Petrograd. The deposed Soviet deputies then rallied a loyalist "army" in the City Duma comprising cadet officers, machine-gunners, and some women and children. On October 28 (November 9), the Bolsheviks shelled their opponents into submission, though suffering a dozen casualties themselves (mostly from machine-gun fire). By afternoon it was all over.[1]

East of the Ural Mountains, the "advent of Soviet power" took place considerably later. In Viatka province, the Bolshevik military revolutionary committee sent a commissar from Petrograd named F. G. Luparev to effect the coup, but he did not arrive until December. Luparev did succeed in shutting down non-Bolshevik newspapers, but he was unsure what to do next. As Viatka provincial commissar Luparev reported to Moscow, "All agencies [of the local government] have announced a strike and I cannot obtain a credit from the Provisional Treasury to support the Commissariat's employees." To help him assemble a Communist government in Viatka, Commissar Luparev requested that the Bolsheviks send him 1,000 rubles—by courier. Farther east, in Siberia, the first Bolshevik emissaries did not arrive until spring 1918.[2]

Despite wresting control of the Petrograd Soviet and its local equivalents in the cities and towns of European Russia, the Bolsheviks were unable to secure the loyalty of the civil servants who ran Russia's government. On October 29 (November 10), Lenin abolished the tsarist Table of Ranks—a list of government, military, and court positions and their ranks that had been instituted in 1722. Lenin's decision angered Russian state employees who had worked their entire lives to achieve their ranks. As early as October 28 (November 9), a group representing them, the All-Russian Union of State Employees, issued a protest against "the usurpation of power by the Bolshevik group in the Petrograd Soviet," resolving that "work in all the administrative departments of the state shall cease immediately." On October 29, the Central Committee of the All-Russian Union of Railwaymen announced a "complete stoppage of all train movements." When Trotsky introduced himself as "the new Minister of Foreign Affairs" on October 28, he was "greeted," according to a news report, "with ironic laughter." Trotsky ordered everyone "to go back to work," but 600 employees left. Employees at the Ministry of Agriculture struck next, then those at the Ministries of Education and Food. On November 7 (20), telegraph and telephone workers walked out, followed by transport workers and schoolteachers. "The Bolsheviks," the state employee union declared on November 8 (21) in announcing a general strike, "making use of brute force, have declared themselves at the head of government," and were now "aiming to get control . . . of the entire machinery of government. . . . [W]e defy [their] threats, and refuse to offer our experience and knowledge." The world's first avowedly proletarian government was thus forced to devote its primary energies in its first days in power to strikebreaking.[3]

The most stubborn resistance to the imposition of Communist rule came, as we saw in Luparev's report from Viatka, from the banking community. For Lenin, banks were target number one for property nationalization. "The proletariat will use its political supremacy," Marx had written in the *Communist Manifesto*, "to wrest, by degrees, all capital from the bourgeoisie," though ominously, he noted that such a program could not "be effected except by means of despotic inroads on the rights of property," including the "centralization of all credit in the hands of the State, by means of a national bank with State capital and an exclusive monopoly." As Lenin had written earlier in 1917, "The big banks are that 'state apparatus' which we *need* for the realization of Socialism and which we *take ready-made* from capitalism."[4]

The bank employees of Petrograd, however, did not see things as Lenin did. Private banks shut their doors in protest of the Bolshevik power seizure. The State Bank and Treasury remained open to honor obligations to soldiers and state employees, but refused to release funds to the Bolsheviks. The Soviet of People's Commissars, Sovnarkom, issued a decree threatening the director of the State Bank, I. P. Shipov, with arrest if he did not authorize its withdrawals, but Shipov still refused. On November 4 (17),

Shipov announced that since the coup, the bank had authorized 600 million rubles in withdrawals to employees and beneficiaries of Russia's "real" government, including charities and soup kitchens for the poor. To the new Bolshevik authorities, he would give nothing.[5]

Lenin was not deterred. On November 7 (20), he dispatched a battalion of Red Guards to the State Bank. They were unable to force their way in, and so Lenin dispatched an even larger force four days later with an ultimatum. Unless Shipov relented, the Bolsheviks would fire all State Bank employees, who would lose their pensions, and those of military age would be drafted and sent to the front. At this threat Shipov gave himself up, but it did the Bolsheviks little good, as the employees all walked out in protest, leaving no one to help them access the vaults. To break the bank strike, Lenin ordered commissars to seize "capitalist" hostages, including Shipov and four more bank directors. Lenin demanded a billion tsarist rubles for each hostage before settling for a million instead. Even then the bank directors required Lenin to produce the proper paperwork to withdraw 5 million rubles, and the employees slow-walked Lenin's request.[6]

Although Lenin's withdrawal bought the Bolsheviks time and allowed them to pay the Red Guards, the bank strike persisted, soon encompassing 6,000 employees in Petrograd. In the absence of help from the staff, the Bolsheviks stationed "commissars" at banks in Petrograd and Moscow, charged with overseeing salary disbursements to workers, but they soon ran out of ready cash, as they had no access to the vaults. It was largely to break the bank strike that the soon-to-be-dreaded Soviet secret police, CHEKA—forerunner of the NKVD and KGB—was formed. As Lenin instructed the man named to head this "All-Russian Extraordinary Commission to Combat Counterrevolution, Speculation, and Sabotage," Felix Dzerzhinsky, on December 7 (20), 1917, "The bourgeoisie are still persistently committing the most abominable crimes. . . . The accomplices of the bourgeoisie, notably *high-ranking function-aries and bank cadres*, are also involved in *sabotage and organizing strikes* to undermine the measures the government is taking with a view to the socialist transformation of society. . . . [E]xceptional measures will have to be taken to combat these saboteurs and counter-revolutionaries."[7]

The Bolshevik bank war was just getting started. On December 14 (27), the Soviet Finance Ministry abolished private banks in Russia. A young Communist activist named Grigory Sokol-nikov (with no prior experience in the finance sector) was given the revealing title of "Managing Director of the Commissariat of Formerly Private Banks." Sokolnikov's new Banks Commissariat laid claim to private bank *deposits*, with the exception of accounts held by "proletarians" and other Russians not belonging to the "rich classes," with the cutoff set at 5,000 rubles in savings, or a monthly income of 500 rubles. In this way, Sokolnikov vowed to "annihilate" private property in Russia.[8]

Sokolnikov performed his duties with Communist aplomb, almost maniacal in literal-mindedness. First, he began assembling data on Russia's thousands of banks, beginning with their addresses and phone numbers. The first reports he received from Bolshevik bank commissars bristled with talk of sums of "incredible size" soon to be at Lenin's disposal. A quick inventory of the "formerly private banks" of Moscow taken in late December 1917 turned up nearly 200 million rubles' worth of equities and bonds on the books. Of course, as Sokolnikov would discover, every bank asset was someone else's liability—namely, whoever had issued the equity or bond shares. This was not to count savings accounts, personal or corporate checks recently drawn, employee salaries, or dividend and interest payments coming due. Nationalizing banks meant far more than simply confiscating cash, coin, and gold bullion—and even that the Bolsheviks were still unable to do, owing to the lack of cooperation from bank employees.[9]

Nonetheless, Lenin and Sokolnikov plowed on. Sokolnikov's December nationalization decree ordered that "all holders of safe deposit boxes are under obligation to appear at the bank upon notice, bringing the keys to their safe deposit boxes." On December 21, 1917 (January 3, 1918), Sokolnikov decreed that Bolshevik commissars must be appointed to every single bank in Russia. In a telegram sent simultaneously to 102 different cities, not all of them yet under Bolshevik control, Sokolnikov ordered that Bolshevik bank commissars in each city transfer to the State Bank for inspection, as quickly as possible, all "gold coin and ingots discovered" in their banks.[10]

And so it came about that on December 21, 1917 (Old Calendar)—just four days before Christmas in an Orthodox Christian country—notices appeared all over Petrograd announcing that "the late private banks have been occupied by armed forces" and everyone's money would be seized by the government. Bolshevik commissars were instructed to record "the quantities of: foreign valiuta [currency], gold and silver coin and ingots and bars of gold, silver, and platinum, all of which are confiscated and handed over to the State Treasury." This process was euphemistically called "safe revision," accompanied by menacing instructions like this (on January 4 [17], 1918): "Owners of safes from Nos. 1 to 100 at the said banks are to appear with their keys at 10 a.m. Safes belonging to those not presenting themselves within 3 days will be opened . . . at each bank with a view to the confiscation of the contents."[11]

Intimidating as these decrees were, it was not enough to get more than a small fraction of people to turn their life savings over to the Bolsheviks. Owing to the bank employee strike, the Bolsheviks did not know which account number at which bank belonged to the right person. Holders of account numbers 1–100 at the banks listed in the January 4 (17) decree could just stay home (if they had not already fled the country). And so Sokolnikov switched to a reference system general enough not to require assistance from bank staff, but specific enough to frighten depositors into compliance. Each day a new letter of the alphabet would be called, marking out safeholders whose family names began with that letter as "public enemies" if they did not show up to empty out their safe-deposit boxes. By late February 1918, the Bolsheviks had moved on to the letter *L* in Petrograd, which prompted Max Laserson, commercial director of the Shuvalov Mining Company, to visit his bank, bringing, as ordered, the key to his safe-deposit box. Laserson recalled the remarkable scene:

> All around stood the safe deposit boxholders whose boxes were to be opened. The plan followed was to remove all valuables (precious metals in bars, objects of platinum, gold, silver, precious stones, pearls, foreign currency, etc.), which were subject to confiscation for the welfare of the state, and to make it impossible for the owner of any particular object later to identify his property. . . . In a case such as mine, where the valuables were wrapped up in packages, the wrappers were torn open and the . . . object was tossed on the pile.[12]

In the first six months of 1918, 35,493 safes were "revised" by Sokolnikov's bank commissars in Moscow alone, yielding the Bolsheviks half a ton of gold, silver, and platinum bullion, 700,000 rubles' worth of gold and silver coin, 65 million tsarist rubles, 600 million rubles' worth of public and private bonds, and foreign "hard" currencies. This was only a fraction of the bank safes, though. Laserson's was the exception, not the rule: most Russian safe-owners (about 75 percent) had either fled by the summer of 1918 or refused to cooperate. Owing to the lack of cooperation from "capitalists," Sokolnikov would establish a sub-branch of the

Commissariat of Formerly Private Banks devoted to safe-cracking, the "Safes Commission" (Seifovaia Komissiia).[13]

Beyond breaking the bank strike, another important task Lenin gave the new CHEKA in the first winter of Communism was damage control from the recent parliamentary elections. Considering the circumstances, the elections of November 1917 were conducted with integrity, with a turnout of 41 million, half of eligible voters. As expected, Kerensky's old party—the Socialist Revolutionary (SR) Party—won a clear plurality, scoring just above 40 percent, with the Bolsheviks coming in a distant second at 24 percent (though Lenin's party won nearly 50 percent of the army vote, including the votes of 70 percent of men serving in the heavily propagandized garrisons of Moscow and Petrograd, which helps explain why the revolution triumphed there). Impressive though this was in comparison to where the Bolsheviks had stood earlier in 1917, it was not reassuring to Lenin that more than three-quarters of the Russian people had voted against his party, leaving them with only 175 seats out of 707. And so Sovnarkom, refusing to ratify the results as legitimate, postponed the convocation of Russia's long-awaited Constituent Assembly, originally scheduled for November 28 (December 11), until "electoral abuses" could be investigated. It shut off Taurida Palace with CHEKA agents, Red Guards, and pro-Bolshevik troops to prevent opposition forces from gathering there.[14]

At a Central Committee party meeting on December 12 (25), 1917, Lenin and other leading Bolsheviks laid down the gauntlet for Russia's elected Constituent Assembly, which they viewed as hostile to the Communist cause. Nikolai Bukharin, a bookish intellectual who spoke for the "Left Bolsheviks," proposed to let the body assemble, expel recalcitrant non-leftists, and then call the rump body a revolutionary convention—as the French revolutionary radicals had done in 1789 (and again in 1792). Lenin argued that the entire Constituent Assembly was illegitimate, as it "was conceived against the people and we carried out the insurrection [i.e., the October Revolution] to make certain that it will not be used against the people." Because the Bolsheviks represented the "revolutionary class" of proletarians, who were "struggling against the propertied classes," there was no choice but that "resistance has to be suppressed." Lenin vowed, "We shall suppress it by the same methods by which the propertied classes suppressed the proletariat." Trotsky then spelled out what Lenin had only implied, namely, that within "a month's time"—i.e., when the assembly was scheduled to meet in January 1918—"the mild terror which we are directing against our class enemies . . . will assume very violent forms after the example of the great French revolutionaries. The guillotine will be ready for our enemies and not merely the jail." Trotsky did not mean that the Bolsheviks would *literally* guillotine their enemies, the guillotine being a rather inefficient killing instrument by twentieth-century standards, now that machine guns were available. Rather, he meant that, since the "bourgeoisie as a class" was "passing away from the scene of history" anyway, the merciless "measures of violence" the Bolsheviks proposed to deploy were "for the good of the bourgeoisie, since they help the latter to disappear more rapidly."[15]

Lenin and Trotsky meant what they said. When the Constituent Assembly convened in Taurida Palace, home of the old Russian Duma, on January 18, 1918 (in this month Russia switched over to the Gregorian calendar), Red Guards surrounded the building and dispersed the elected parliament, killing at least eight. Denouncing deputies elected in the broadest democratic election ever held in Russia as "hirelings of bankers, capitalists, and landlords," the Bolsheviks convened a rump "Third Congress of Soviets," composed exclusively of party members and Left SRs, which rubber-stamped "Sovnarkom" as the only legitimate authority in a country now called the Russian Soviet Federative Socialist Republic (RSFSR). Once the Petrograd bank strike was broken at the end of March 1918—a compromise allowed 4,000 out of 6,000 bank employees to keep their jobs in exchange for their cooperation in withdrawing state funds and gold bullion for the Bolsheviks—Lenin kicked the Left SRs out of Sovnarkom too. To camouflage the dictatorship of his minority party, Lenin renamed it the "All-Russian Communist Party (Bolsheviks)."[16]

Despite its claim to be the world's first "proletarian dictatorship," in its first months in power Lenin's government still relied heavily on German occupation troops to defend itself. Nor could Lenin entirely trust the Germans, despite their having financed his return to Petrograd and the initial Bolshevik operations in Russia. With his government viewed by the Entente Powers, and by critics inside Russia, as a German puppet regime, Lenin had hesitated before signing the punitive terms that German diplomats had offered during armistice negotiations at Brest-Litovsk, which would strip from Russia nearly 3.4 million square kilometers (1.3 million square miles) of prime land—one-fourth of its prewar territory—on which 62 million people, or 44 percent of its population, lived, and which accounted for a third of the country's agricultural production, three-quarters of its iron and coal output, and over half (56 percent) of its industrial and manufacturing capacity. True, this land was not annexed by Germany—Ukraine, Finland, Georgia, and the Baltic provinces were invited to declare independence—but the presence of a million German occupying troops gave the game away. So reliant on Germany was Lenin's government that, when Lenin announced the terms of Brest-Litovsk to Sovnarkom in Taurida Palace on February 23, Left SR delegates greeted him as a "German spy" and proclaimed, "Down with the Traitor!" The first plot to topple Russia's Communist government, launched on July 4, 1918, in Moscow—after Lenin had transferred the capital there—saw Left SR assassins murder the German ambassador, Count Wilhelm Mirbach, whom they viewed as Russia's real ruler.[17]

Despite his embarrassing dependence on the German "imperialists," Lenin was doing his best to assemble a new "proletarian" army. On January 28, 1918, Sovnarkom formally created the Red Army of Workers and Peasants (RKKA, or "Red Army") to replace the now demobilized Russian Imperial Army. It would be under the leadership of Trotsky as commissar of war (he resigned his post as foreign affairs commissar, where he was replaced by Georgy Chicherin). Significantly, Lenin and Trotsky decided—overruling fervent opposition from the outgoing commander-in-chief, ex-ensign Krylenko, and the Bolshevik Central Committee—to hire ex-tsarist officers as "military specialists" (*voenspetsy*) to train new Red Army recruits, a policy ratified by Sovnarkom on March 31 in one of its last joint resolutions before the Left SRs were kicked out. Because these mostly aristocratic "class enemies" could not be trusted ideologically, each officer had a political "commissar" assigned to keep watch on him. On May 8, Lenin and Trotsky reassembled the old Russian General Staff, or Stavka, now styled the "All-Russian Main Staff."[18]

Still, given the geopolitical circumstances of Russia in 1918, assembling the armies of Communism was difficult work. Russia's agony in the world war had produced the crisis Lenin had used as a springboard to power, allowing the Bolsheviks to carry out a hostile takeover of the Russian Imperial Army. But the war was still raging, and so long as the European Powers were mobilized, it was hard to see how Trotsky's ramshackle new Red Army could compete. In a fit of pique, Bolshevik sailors had scuttled what remained of Russia's Black Sea Fleet, denying it to the Germans, but also enraging the German high command, which kept Lenin's government on a very short leash. The only units of the Imperial Army to survive intact and declare loyalty to Lenin were a few bolshevized Latvian rifle brigades from the Baltic front—and even these

Latvian Rifles were subsidized by the German imperial government (via its new embassy in Moscow). For much of 1918, Lenin relied on these 35,000-odd Latvians to put out counter-revolutionary fires, now holding down Petrograd during a cholera outbreak in June, now suppressing an SR uprising in Yaroslavl heralded by the murder of the German ambassador in early July, then being dispatched to Perm to see off a threat to prevent hostile freed Czechoslovak Legion prisoners of war from taking Yekaterinburg, where the ex-tsar, Nicholas II, and his family were being held prisoner.[19]

The Bolsheviks were able to hold Yekaterinburg just long enough for a special execution squad, led by Yakov Yurovsky, to execute the Romanov family on the night of July 16, 1918, including the tsar and tsarina, her ladies-in-waiting, their five children, and their doctor. The finale was gruesome. Because the four Romanov daughters wore special corsets into which diamonds and other jewels had been sown, the girls survived the initial machine-gun volleys and had to be finished off with bayonet thrusts. Then, in Yurovsky's clinical recollection, "the detachment began to undress and burn the corpses." To prevent the nearby Czechoslovak Legion from discovering the bodies, Yurovsky had the Romanov remains dumped into the nearby "Four Brothers Mine" only to realize it was not deep enough. The bodies were lifted up and tossed into a ditch along the Yekaterinburg–Moscow road, doused with sulfuric acid, and covered with sticks and branches. Yurovsky's men drove over the makeshift grave with trucks to mangle everything beyond recognition. It worked, too: when the Czechoslovak Legion conquered Yekaterinburg ten days later, and a team of investigators from the Committee of the Constituent Assembly (KOMUCH) assembled in Samara to carry on the legacy of the deposed Russian parliament, they found just a few scattered, unidentifiable body parts in the Four Brothers Mine. The Romanov remains were only discovered (with identities confirmed by DNA testing) in 1989.[20]

The Bolsheviks' just-in-time murder of the Romanov family won Lenin's beleaguered government some macabre prestige at a dire moment for Communism.* But it was not long before the Czechoslovak Legion, fighting on behalf of KOMUCH, had captured not only Yekaterinburg and Perm but also Kazan, just 800 kilometers (500 miles) from Moscow, on August 7. Responding to the fall of Kazan, Trotsky proclaimed the restoration of the death penalty for desertion in the Red Army on August 14. Not even commissars were immune. Trotsky decreed bluntly that "if any part of the army retreats of its own . . . the first to be shot will be the commissar and the second, the commander. Cowards and traitors will not escape the bullets." In this way the Bolsheviks neatly completed the circle, from Order No. 1 and inciting mutinies in the Russian Imperial Army, in 1917, to restoring the most draconian military discipline to the Red Army in 1918.[21]

A further blow to Lenin's strategic position came when, on August 3, 1918, KOMUCH invited the Western Allies to intervene in the Russian Civil War on its behalf. British, French, American, and Japanese troops were already on the ground in Russia, but they had initially been invited in by Trotsky back in March and April as a counterweight to the German occupiers. Now open war was declared between the Allies, some of whose representatives (such as a British diplomat named Bruce Lockhart) were caught funneling money to the former Imperial Russian Army generals Mikhail Alekseev and Lavr Kornilov and their "Volunteer Army" assembling in the Don region under Cossack protection, and the Bolsheviks, who responded by arresting British and French nationals in Moscow. The assassination of Lenin's CHEKA chief in Petrograd, Moisei Uritsky, on August 30, followed that same day by an

---

* The tsar's blood relatives who were held at nearby Alapaevsk, including two Romanov grand dukes, a grand duchess, and their children, were also shot and dumped in a mine shaft on July 18.

attempt on Lenin himself in Moscow (three bullets were fired, one of them hitting his shoulder and another his lung), gave the Bolsheviks the pretext to launch what was soon called the Red Terror. On August 31, the chairman of the Bolshevik Central Executive Committee, Yakov Sverdlov, summoned "all Soviets of Workers', Peasants', and Red Army Deputies" to launch "merciless mass terror against the enemies of the revolution." By September 3, the Soviet press organ *Izvestiya* announced that "over five hundred hostages" had been shot by the CHEKA. Red Terror now spread outward from Moscow and Petrograd to the areas of Russia the Bolsheviks controlled. Significantly, a Sovnarkom decree on September 5 legalized summary executions without trial as well as the erection of concentration camps (*kontsentratsionnye lageri*) near all military fronts. Trotsky proclaimed, on August 31, that "twenty deserters were shot yesterday. The first to go were the commissars and commanders who left their posts; next came the cowardly liars who played sick; and finally the Red Army soldiers who deserted. Death to the coward! Death to the traitor-deserter!" The Red Terror claimed nearly 15,000 lives in the first two months, or more than twice the total number of prisoners of all kinds executed in the *century* of tsarist rule before 1917 (6,321).[22]

The German collapse on the Western Front in September–October 1918 came just in the nick of time for Lenin. Aghast at Germany's role in midwifing the Red Terror, the German general staff had just issued orders, now moot, to occupy Petrograd and depose the Communist regime. With *Schadenfreude* the Bolsheviks turned the tables, confiscating diplomatic bags used by German embassy staff in Moscow and looting the German consulate in Petrograd, helping themselves to 250 million tsarist rubles. Lenin and Trotsky could now build the Red Army, which they had been forbidden to do by Article 5 of Brest-Litovsk, in earnest. On October 1, 1918,

Lenin ordered general conscription to begin, aiming to enlist 3 million men by the spring of 1919.[23]

The German collapse clarified the stakes in the hitherto confusing Russian Civil War. Allied landings at Murmansk, Vladivostok, and Archangel in the spring of 1918 had been small in scale and anti-German rather than anti-Bolshevik as such. Only in August had relations between the Entente Powers and Moscow tipped over toward outright hostility, and even then it stopped short of armed combat (beyond Bolshevik arrests of British and French nationals). After the November armistice ending the European war, any continued Allied military presence in Russia would be *ipso facto* hostile—something the Bolsheviks could plausibly describe to peasant recruits, or ex-tsarist officers, as a foreign invasion, thus salting their war against "class enemies" with a patina of patriotism. In Marxist terms, it was the perfect storm, allowing Lenin to complete the transformation of the imperialist war into an anti-imperialist civil war. The message worked, judging by raw numbers: 3.6 million had enlisted in the Red Army by the summer of 1919, surpassing Lenin's goal. This included 75,000 former tsarist officers, 775 of them generals—more than the 60,000 who had joined the "Volunteer Army" coalescing under Cossack protection in the South, although another 40,000 former tsarist officers later joined other anti-Communist forces in the Civil War. True, neither Trotsky nor Lenin trusted these ex-bourgeois officers, which is why political "commissars" were appointed to keep watch over them—a practice that endured throughout Soviet history. But most of them fought bravely to defend Lenin's government, whether or not they endorsed its Communist ideals and policies. It helped Trotsky's recruitment drive that the "White" armies, as the Bolsheviks called their armed opponents, were sponsored, armed, and (in a few areas) directly aided by outside "capitalist" powers—principally Britain,

France, the United States, and Japan, alongside nascent states that had won a fragile independence from the Russian Empire in the wake of Lenin's revolution and wished to retain it, such as Poland, Finland, and Estonia.[24]

In reality, the Russian Civil War was murkier than this. None of the three counter-revolutionary armies—neither the Volunteer Army fighting north from the Don Cossack region; nor the Siberian People's Army under Admiral Alexander Kolchak, trying to reconquer European Russia across the Urals; nor the Northwestern (NW) Army of Nikolai Yudenich, threatening Petrograd from the Baltic region—called itself "White," a Bolshevik term of abuse meaning "counter-revolutionary" (e.g., the White color of the pre-1789 Bourbon monarchy of France). All of the "White" generals vowed publicly to restore the deposed Russian Constituent Assembly, not to bring back tsarism.

Nonetheless, Trotsky and Lenin could and did plausibly claim that the Reds were fighting to expel the Whites and foreign imperialists to save the Communist revolution. Although there were dark moments, none darker than the advance of Yudenich's NW Army to Pulkovo, just twenty-five kilometers (fifteen miles) from Petrograd, in October 1919, the Reds held on and ultimately defeated the White forces. Trotsky himself vowed to defend Petrograd "to the last drop of blood" and rallied Red troops at Pulkovo on horseback. His application of stringent, though not inflexible, discipline—some 600 Red deserters were publicly executed in 1919, a small percentage of the 1.7 million believed to have deserted at some point—held the Red Army together long enough to see off the threat to Petrograd, expel the Siberian People's Army eastward into Siberia, and break the back of Anton Denikin's Volunteer Army, most of which evacuated across the Black Sea in the winter of 1919–1920, but for a rump army under General Pyotr Wrangel, which held out in Crimea into the summer of 1920.[25]

Complicated though its military course might have been, the political outcome of the Russian Civil War was unambiguous. Facing a world of "capitalist" enemies in the civil war Lenin had prophesied and helped to bring about, and having lost his only Great Power ally after Imperial Germany collapsed in 1918, the forces of Communism had won. In doing so, moreover, Lenin had not so much paused his experiment in socialist governance as brought it to its most radical crescendo—more radical, in certain respects, than what Stalin would later achieve in peacetime.

In the early flush of revolutionary enthusiasm, Sovnarkom had passed decrees outlawing "all payments of interest on investments and dividends on shares" (January 11, 1918), nationalizing iron and steel production and the insurance industry (February 5 and 10) and annulling (or "annihilating") Russia's external debts to foreign banks and the Western powers (February 10). Those powers seized Russia's foreign assets in turn in an enduring Mexican standoff between the new Communist regime and the capitalist world. In April another Sovnarkom decree nationalized commercial and industrial enterprises. Because most of these enterprises had been owned by "capitalist" banks whose assets were confiscated in December 1917, the upshot of these decrees was the choking off of cash from industry. Compounded by fuel shortages and the fact that contact with foreign investors and managers was cut off, the result was a mass shuttering of factories. By May 1918, unemployment in Petrograd's factories had reached 90 percent. Urban employment figures across Russia soared to similar levels, as so many idled workers fled to the countryside—like Dr. Zhivago—to get closer to the food supply.[26]

Cut off from the world by both their own default in 1918 and the knock-on effects of war and blockade, the Bolsheviks were forced to improvise a new kind of command war economy—later known retroactively as "War Communism"—entirely on their own. In a sense, the autarky imposed by the German (and then, after the Germans surrendered, British) blockade of the Baltic was ideologically appropriate, giving the regime a tabula rasa to build Communism without capitalist "infection" from abroad. What remained of Russian industry would be exclusively state-owned and state-controlled, under the auspices of the Supreme Council of the National Economy (Vysshyi Sovet Narodnogo Khoziaistva, or VSNKh). Created on paper in December 1917, VSNKh became truly operational in August 1918 when Sovnarkom delineated its powers and gave it a budget. Comprising delegates from the Communist Commissariats of Food, Transport, Labor, Agriculture, and Finance, VSNKh was authorized "to regulate and organize all production and distribution and to manage every enterprise of the Republic."[27]

The unveiling of VSNKh in 1918 was a seminal moment for Communism. Later renamed (in 1921) the State Planning Commission, or Gosplan, VSNKh was the "brains" of Communism— of the planned economy of the utopian future. With private property abolished, the state—that is, the ruling Russian Communist Party (Bolsheviks)—now controlled, in theory at least, all economic activity in Russia. Entire sectors of the Russian economy were assigned to planning agencies named after the commodities produced (Glavsol for salt, Glavlak for paint, Glavbum for paper, etc.). As one Russian industry after another was subordinated to VSNKh, the planning leviathan grew and grew, reaching 25,000 full-time employees by early 1920, nearly all of them stuffed into a huge building in central Moscow on Myasnitskaya ulitsa, a street near the Kremlin.[28]

In material terms, the early returns of all this VSNKh paper-shuffling were disappointing. Economic indices, already trending down, declined still more precipitously despite rampant inflation caused by runaway money printing, with monthly ruble emissions hitting 13 trillion by 1921. The inflation was by then so bad that

Sovnarkom issued a resolution, in January 1921, on the "abolition of money payments for all products that are issued by the People's Commissar for Provisions" (that is, rationing), along with the "abolition of money payments for rent on dwellings of workers, clerks, and their families," and "for fuel of all kinds." It also mandated the "abolition of fees for railway transportation of all freight, and of almost all passengers." In this way the Bolsheviks, in a kind of Communist *reductio ad absurdum*, tried to abolish money itself—only to realize that economic activity of any kind was impossible without it. They were forced to introduce a gold-backed ruble, worth ten old tsarist rubles, or five dollars, at the time, called the *chervonetz*. (Lenin, throwing up his hands, vowed that in the Communist future, gold would be used only to build toilets.) As for economic output, in the revolutionary chaos of 1917, industrial production had already declined to 77 percent of Russia's last prewar year, 1913. In 1919, it fell to 26 percent of the 1913 total, and in 1920 to a mere 18 percent. This was true even of sectors that had long been Russian strengths, such as energy and raw materials. Oil production fell to 42 percent of prewar levels, coal to 27 percent, cotton yarn to 5 percent, and iron ore to a woeful 2.4 percent. Agricultural production declined less in relative terms from 1913 to 1920 (40 percent) but massively in volume, from 78 million tons to 48 million, basically to famine levels.[29]

Owing to transportation problems, the impact on Russia's northern cities was devastating: there was simply nothing to eat. Nor was there fuel to heat residences, leading to a cannibalization of the housing stock as Russians tore down empty buildings for firewood. Water pipes cracked in the cold, and streetlamps ceased to function, leaving cities dark and menacing at night. By 1920 Moscow and Petrograd were ghost towns, the population of the latter, once the imperial capital and Russia's glittering urban crown jewel, reduced from a population of 2.5 million to scarcely 700,000. An

American Red Cross commissioner, Colonel Edward Ryan, came over from Estonia to investigate the situation in Russia's cities in April 1920 and was shocked at what he saw. "Both Moscow and Petrograd," Ryan observed, were "indescribably filthy in outward appearance." Informed that "the streets had not been cleaned for more than three years," he noted that "the dirt and rubbish is in all places at least ankle deep and in most places it is up to one's knees, and there are many places where it is as high as one's head. . . . There has obviously been no attempt to haul anything away."[30]

In such conditions, epidemic disease was rampant, although Russians suffering from flu, cholera, typhus, or dysentery found little solace in the hospitals, because so many nurses and doctors were dying, too. In even one of the best-equipped hospitals in central Moscow favored by Bolshevik commissars, Ryan was told that "during the previous three months seventy-five percent of the personnel of the hospital had died." There were sheets and mattresses, but surgeries could not be performed, as there were "very few surgical instruments and few anesthetics." In still more frigid and desolate Petrograd, Ryan learned that so many residents were dying that "morgues and cemeteries could not cope, and corpses lay around for months waiting to be buried."[31]

If conditions under War Communism were this harsh in Russia's richest cities, it is not hard to imagine what they must have been like elsewhere. Following a series of poor harvests and an ever more bitter war between Bolshevik food requisitioners and peasants determined to guard their dwindling reserves of grain and livestock, famine spread across huge swaths of European Russia in 1920–1921, even as the "proper" civil war between the Red Army and the Whites and foreign forces wound down. Vladimir Antonov-Ovseenko, the Red Army commander in charge of suppressing one of the largest peasant rebellions, in Tambov province, admitted in a report to Moscow in January 1921 that "half the peasantry was starving." In Samara province, the Red commander of the Volga military district reported that "crowds of thousands of starving peasants are besieging the barns where the [armed Bolshevik] food detachments have stored the grain," and that "the [Red] army has been forced to open fire repeatedly on the enraged crowd." Even while fighting an increasingly desperate rearguard war against Russia's recalcitrant peasants—this "peasant war" cost the Red Army 237,908 casualties against farmers who fought mostly with pitchforks and farm tools—Lenin's Communist government was forced to admit in *Pravda*, on June 21, 1921, that some 25 million people in Russia's Volga basin were on the brink of starvation, including 7 million children. CHEKA reports, discovered after the Soviet archives were opened in 1991, noted that another 7.5 million Ukrainians were in imminent threat of starving to death, too.[32]

The crisis was desperate enough by June 1921 that Lenin temporarily allowed the American Relief Administration (ARA) run by Herbert Hoover, along with "bourgeois" charity organizations such as the American Red Cross, to ship over 2 million tons of grain, seed, and foodstuffs into Soviet Russia and even help distribute them, albeit under strict CHEKA surveillance. It was enough to feed 11 million people, along with seed sufficient for the next two years' harvests. Although more than 5 million Russians and Ukrainians starved to death that summer and fall, by early 1922 reports of starvation had virtually ceased. So efficient was the ARA's work that the Soviet government requested that Hoover's men curtail aid shipments into Baltic ports in February, "owing to their inability to handle such large quantities."[33]

Ukraine, one of the most fiercely contested regions in the Russian Civil War, saw mortality rates skyrocket after the final Communist takeover in 1920, and not only from the famine. As a result of shortages of fuel and medical supplies, 2.5 percent of the population of Soviet Ukraine died of typhus alone in the first two years of Communist rule, about 660,000 people. In Odessa, the prewar "death rate" of about 23 per 1,000 had risen to 90 by the end of 1921, some five to six times higher than the birth rate. Not only was food scarce, but also water for drinking and washing: water was "sold by weight" to residents lining up in long queues. Conditions were so atrocious in 1922, even after the famine had eased, that, as one foreign witness observed, "hundreds of corpses daily were taken off the streets—many partially eaten by dogs." When independent Ukrainian National Republic (Ukrainska Narodnia Respublika, UNR) forces retook the town of Zviahel, in Volyn province, they reckoned that the pre-revolution population of 28,000 had shrunk to 2,000. Ukrainian Jews were particularly hard hit by War Communism, as so many of them were urban traders whose livelihoods were now outlawed. Kiev (Kyiv), reported a Jewish UNR official named Mikhail Gorenshtein after the Ukrainian capital was reconquered by the Bolsheviks in 1920, "has become a graveyard, all the shops are closed, there is no electric light or water, no trams, no telephones, and the population has been turned into slaves."[34]

In part owing to the wretched caloric intake of their "proletarian" subjects, the Bolsheviks found it difficult to get anyone to work at all. As early as October 31, 1918, a Sovnarkom decree introduced "universal labor duty," soon expanded to include compulsory weekend work battalions, referred to as *subbotniks* (*subbota* being the Russian word for Saturday). Trotsky channeled Marx's advocacy of "equal liability of all to labor" in the *Manifesto* when he explained Communist labor policy: "As a general rule, man strives to avoid work. . . . [T]he only way to attract the labor power necessary for economic tasks is to introduce *compulsory labor service.*" "Compulsory labor" was expressly written into the Soviet labor code of 1919 for all healthy Russians between the ages of sixteen and fifty, with the exception of pregnant women "for a period of 8 weeks before and 8 weeks after confinement." There was one day of rest per week. In place of the old Orthodox Christian "saints' days," which had given Russian workers many weekdays off during the year, a decree on "Proletarian Holidays," passed in March 1920, coughed up a few non-workdays: on New Year's Day; January 22 (the anniversary of Bloody Sunday); March 12 (the anniversary of the "overthrow of the autocracy" in 1917); March 18 (to commemorate the Paris Commune); May 1 (May Day, International Workers' Day); and November 7 (the "day of the Proletarian Revolution" in 1917). Workers' rights were, theoretically, protected by "officers of labor inspection authorized to adopt special measures . . . for the removal of conditions endangering the lives and health of workmen." And yet these rights depended on the good faith of government inspectors, because all private labor unions and worker advocacy organizations were abolished. Compounded by the "compulsory labor" requirement, this effectively eliminated the right of Russian workers to strike for better pay or work conditions.[35]

The *subbotniks*, or "Communist Saturdays," were celebrated in *Pravda* and other state media organs, which claimed, dubiously, that Soviet workers had all "volunteered to work twelve hours" every Saturday. "Workers and peasants," one editorial boasted in March 1920, had "repeatedly achieved wonders of valor and endurance." The Saturday workdays had "barely begun, and yet the institution is already of immense importance. It is the beginning of a new revolution." But this revolution would be a victory "over indolence, over disorder, over petty bourgeois egoism, a victory achieved by the working class themselves, a victory over all the bad habits bequeathed to the workers and peasants as a legacy of capitalistic anarchy." In this way forced labor was not simply enshrined in Soviet law, but turned into a proud achievement of Communism, publicly touted by the government.[36]

Soviet Communism introduced many other Marxist causes to the world. Marx's critique of "bourgeois" marriage made its way into Soviet "domestic relations law," which withdrew all legal force from any "marriage contracted by a religious ceremony performed by a clergyman," replacing church weddings with secular civil ceremonies. Divorce law was radically simplified, with either party to a marriage able to dissolve it at any time for any reason ("mutual consent of the husband and wife, or the desire of either of them to obtain a divorce, shall be considered a ground for divorce," and this "desire" could be presented "orally or in writing"). As if to render marital obligations superfluous, a further stipulation was that "the change of residence by one of the parties to a marriage shall not impose an obligation upon the other party to follow the former." Soviet marriage was less "til death do us part" than "insofar as it remains convenient." A similar principle animated the Communist legalization of abortion in November 1920—Lenin's Soviet government being the first in the world to do so, and also the first to subsidize the practice. Abortions, it was stipulated, could be obtained "freely and without any charge in Soviet hospitals," although (in a nod to Marxist preference for the modern) only licensed doctors in state hospitals could perform them. "Any nurse or midwife found guilty of making such an operation," or a doctor doing so in private practice, would be "called to account by a People's Court."[37]

Communist governance also brought a can-do positivist spirit to culture and education, epitomized most famously in Soviet mass literacy campaigns. True, the early returns, against the chaotic backdrop of the Civil War, were relatively meager. Even Cherepovets, a regime showcase city of 700,000 some 320 kilometers (200 miles) north of Moscow, improved from a pre-revolution literacy rate of 42.8 percent in 1917 to a mere 51.1 percent by 1926. But the priority was established, and mass literacy campaigns were a defining feature of early Soviet Communism.[38]

So, too, was the brief of the new Commissariat of Enlightenment (Narodnyi Kommissariat po Prosvescheniiu, or Narkompros) to "direct all scholarly, scientific, educational, and artistic activity . . . of a general as well as professional character," mostly aspirational at first. To run Narkompros, Lenin appointed a college dropout from Zurich called Anatoly Lunacharsky, best known for his role in promoting the Proletarian Culture (Proletkult) movement in 1917. Vowing to "democratize" classical music, ballet, theater, literature, and the fine arts, Lunacharsky found it difficult to recruit Russia's top artists and writers. When he summoned 150 cultural figures to come work for him in December 1917, only five showed up—although these did include real talents, such as the poet Vladimir Mayakovsky, the stage director Vsevolod Meyerhold, and the novelist Maxim Gorky. Lunacharsky's network of Proletkult studios, with "poetry circles, folk theaters, extension courses, libraries, exhibitions," and factory "culture" cells, were staffed mostly by second-rate artists, who embraced the opportunity to have the state subsidize their work—and censor their rivals. Perhaps the best illustration of the Communist approach to culture came in Lenin's rejoinder to a deputy at the Fourth Congress of Soviets in March 1918. The man had shouted out a complaint that all of Russia's independent periodicals and "thick journals," such as the venerable old *Vestnik Evropy* (Herald of Europe), *Russkii vestnik* (Russian herald), and *Russkaia mysl'* (Russian thought), printed since the eighteenth century, had been closed down. "Unfortunately not all, but we *will* close them all," Lenin replied. He was good to his word, and by 1919 these thick journals had all been shut down, giving the Communist government a monopoly over the press, education, culture, and Russian intellectual life more broadly.[39]

As suggested by its approach to censorship and state media, the Communist government was uncertain of the loyalties of the "workers and peasants" from whom Lenin claimed a mandate to rule. True, Russia remained "backward" by European standards, economically and culturally, which gave Lunacharsky's Commissariat of Enlightenment both a mission and an excuse for its failures. So, too, was Lenin's "proletarian dictatorship," just as he had predicted in his "Military Program of the Proletarian Revolution" in October 1916, surrounded by hostile neighboring "capitalist" governments, such as Poland and Japan, along with more distant capitalist Great Powers—Britain, France, and the United States—that had intervened in the Russian Civil War. If Communism was going to survive, the revolution would have to spread beyond Russia.

7
THE COMMUNIST INTERNATIONAL

Soviet Communism was never meant to remain confined to a single country—certainly not to Russia, the least advanced of the European Great Powers. Marx had headquartered the First International in the great imperial capital of London before allowing it to die a quiet martyr's death in New York, after Mikhail Bakunin's rebellion had sapped it of its energy. The Second International, founded in 1889, had never had a central headquarters, but it was born in Paris, where a revolutionary tradition provided inspiration, even though the movement drew its demographic and political energy from the German Kaiserreich. The central axis of the International between 1889 and 1914 was Franco-German, not Russian. The leading Russian exile figures of the prewar International, such as Lenin, Rosa Luxemburg, and Trotsky, had spent nearly all their time in Europe.

It may seem natural to us today that Red Square, the parade marching ground of the Red Army and home to Lenin's tomb, abuts the red brick walls of the Moscow Kremlin, but this would not have struck many revolutionary socialists as inevitable or appropriate before 1917. Tsarist Russia was the worst autocracy in Europe, despised by Marx along with European socialists and liberals as a symbol of reaction. Moreover, Moscow itself was the beating heart of old Orthodox Russia, conservative antipode to St. Petersburg, which was Russia's one reasonably modern city, built by Peter the Great as a Window to the West. St. Petersburg, Russified to Petrograd in 1914 when Russia went to war with Germany, was not only the capital of the Russian Empire but also the scene of the October Revolution, which is why the Bolsheviks renamed it Leningrad. Moscow was an accidental capital at best, a convenient refuge for Lenin's government after the Germans began battering Petrograd in March 1918 to force his diplomats to sign the humiliating Brest-Litovsk Treaty. The crenellated fortress walls of the Kremlin sent a message as far from the kind of forward-looking modernist positivism of Communism as one could possibly imagine.

Nonetheless there was an undeniable austere grandeur to the place. Symbol of reaction and medieval autocracy though it might have been, the Kremlin was also a fortress and command center, which suited Lenin's Soviet government well in an era when Communism was under siege. It was not an accident that Petrograd, but not Moscow, had nearly fallen to the "Whites" in the Civil War. The former city was pinched in between newly independent Estonia and Finland, reached overland in a matter of hours by a force invading from those territories, or in mere minutes by warplanes. Moscow, by contrast, was more than 800 kilometers (500 miles) from the nearest frontier or power center, whether Brest-Litovsk, Kiev, or Helsinki, and farther still from Warsaw and Berlin.

It was also difficult to travel to in the early days of Communism. For most of 1918, the German Imperial Navy was blockading the Baltic, and German armies were occupying the Baltic region, Belorussia, and Ukraine. Nor was it any easier in 1919 after the Royal Navy moved into the Baltic, with the Russian Civil War raging across the Baltic area, Ukraine, and parts of Belorussia. For this reason the inaugural Congress of the Third, or Communist, International—meant to replace the discredited Second International after the Fourth of August betrayal—which convened in the Moscow Kremlin on March 2, 1919, did not amount to much. Only five out of forty-four delegates were able to make it there from outside Russia, and of these, only one (Hugo Eberlein, from Germany) had a mandate from an existing political party. The remaining thirty-nine delegates were either Russian Communists or already in Moscow, such as the freed prisoners of war now "representing" Germany, Austria, and Hungary. To give the body a patina of international flavor, Lenin appointed the polyglot Italian socialist Angelica Balabanoff as "general secretary." Still, it was clearly Lenin's show, and he closed the founding congress by assuring delegates that "victory is assured for the workers' revolution throughout the world." Lenin appointed Grigory Zinoviev president of the Communist International, or "Comintern," although its impresario was Karl Radek, the chain-smoking polyglot journalist from tsarist Poland. Radek had accompanied Lenin on the "sealed train car" in April 1917, and his good relations with him, his fluency in German, and his contacts in Berlin would prove critical as the Bolsheviks sought to spread Communism westward.[1]

The Communist International got off to a slow start. The inaugural congress took place in the wake of the conspicuous failure of the German Communist Party (Kommunistische Partei Deutschlands, KPD), formed under Karl Radek's supervision out of Luxemburg's "Spartacus" faction in Berlin over New Year's Eve 1918–1919, to seize power in the "Spartacist" uprising launched on January 4 in protest of the firing of a socialist Berlin police president. Confusingly, the KPD had not organized the protests itself so much as piggybacked on them, and the leading figure in the party, Luxemburg, had not even wanted to do that. In the "Spartacus program," published on December 14, 1918, Luxemburg had disavowed Lenin's coup-followed-by-the-dissolution-of-parliament in Russia, vowing that "the Spartacus Union will never take over the power of government otherwise than by a clear manifestation of the unquestionable will of the great majority of the proletarian mass of Germany." When the National German Congress of Soldiers' and Workers' Councils voted on December 19 *not* to seize power, but to bow to the will of a new "bourgeois" parliament to be elected in January, Luxemburg resolved that German Communists would stand down in obeisance to this democratic verdict. In a painful irony, her devotion to the democratic process meant that she had to go along with the outcome when she was outvoted in the KPD Central Committee on January 5, and it resolved to overthrow the German Provisional Government, headed since the Kaiser's abdication in November 1918 by the Majority Socialist leader of the old SPD, Friedrich Ebert. Forced to join a Lenin-style uprising she had not endorsed, Luxemburg was then captured, along with Karl Liebknecht, and both were killed while in German army custody. While sympathy "Spartacist" uprisings broke out in many other German cities, by mid-January it was over, and the KPD was reeling.[2]

Only in Munich did something like a Communist revolution take place in Germany. Bavaria had been somewhat ahead of the curve in German politics, as King Ludwig III of the old Wittelsbach dynasty had abdicated his throne on November 7, 1918, two days before Kaiser Wilhelm II did so for the Reich. Parliamentary elections were held there earlier, too, on January 12, 1919, although before a new coalition government could be formed, the assassination of the interim head of the Bavarian Provisional Government, a socialist politician named Kurt Eisner, threw Munich into turmoil. On April 6, a shadowy group of intellectuals seized power in the name of the "soldiers' and workers' councils" or *Räte*, but this Lenin-style *Räterepublik* was rejected by the Munich KPD as a "coffee-clatsch of writers" (its leading lights were indeed writers, including the anarchist poet Erich Mühsam and the expressionist playwright Ernst Toller). Only after delegates from the Majority Socialist Party, relying on disgruntled Bavarian army officers for muscle, tried to overthrow the writers' *Räterepublik* in the "Palm Sunday Putsch" on April 13 did the KPD take over the Bavarian Soviet Republic—just in time to take the blame for "Red Terror" when this short-lived regime was crushed by a coalition of reactionary militias in early May. The bitter struggle cost at least 557 Bavarian lives, including some 93 "Reds" and 38 counter-revolutionary troops killed in battle, another 186 Reds executed, along with 200 civilians caught in the cross fire—far more lives than the 46 Bavarians who died violently in the "revolutionary" period between November 1918 and the end of the Bavarian Soviet Republic on April 30, 1919.[3]

Because the bloody end of the Bavarian Soviet Republic helped fuel the emergence of Nazism in Munich, it has received more press than it may have merited on its own terms. The government lasted just over three weeks, of which only the final two involved the KPD itself. Even so, the fact that its emergence occurred just weeks after the founding of the Communist International, and that the Soviet-affiliated KPD was involved, gave it "internationalist" frisson. It further helped—or hurt, depending on one's perspective— that some 53 Russians were executed as spies, lending political credibility to the Comintern, albeit on largely false pretenses (in fact the Russians were mostly freed prisoners of war, whose only role in the Bavarian Soviet Republic was that its officials offered them money to return home). Communists and Nazis had equal motivation to exaggerate the significance of this sordid episode as a world-historic event.[4]

Lending notoriety to the Bavarian revolution was the almost simultaneous advent of a longer-lasting Soviet Republic in nearby

Hungary. In reality, the Hungarian Revolution was no more planned by the Comintern Executive in Moscow than the Bavarian one had been, but unlike the rudderless writers' collective in Munich, the revolution in Budapest was led by an experienced Communist veteran. This was Béla Kun, born in 1886 in a small Transylvanian village in a region of Austria-Hungary now located in the northwestern corner of Romania near Ukraine. A talented middle-class striver, Kun won a scholarship, attended university and law school, and dabbled in journalism and labor activism, only to be drafted into the army when war broke out in 1914. Taken prisoner by the Russians on the Galician front in 1916, Kun was interned in Siberia near Tomsk, an experience that further radicalized him. Freed after the February Revolution, he joined a local Bolshevik faction and traveled to Petrograd after the October Revolution, where he met Lenin and won his trust by fighting at the head of a Hungarian ex-prisoner-of-war detachment in the armed suppression of the Left SR uprising in July 1918. As a reward, he received the chairmanship of the Confederation of Foreign Communist Groups in Moscow.[5]

Following the European armistice in November 1918, Kun was sent to Budapest, ostensibly to help negotiate for the return of Russian prisoners of war from Hungary, but likely with the aim of stirring the political pot, judging by his rapid arrest by police authorities in Budapest for agitation. Being imprisoned in the terrible winter of 1918–1919 turned out to be a political advantage, as Hungary's beleaguered post-Habsburg government, a Provisional National Council headed by a moderate liberal named Count Mihály Károlyi but reliant on the majority Hungarian Social Democrats, faced the same desperate political calculus as Ebert did in Germany, assuming power of a defeated country being dictated to by its conquerors. On March 20, 1919, just days after the founding of the Communist International, the Allied armistice commissioner in

Budapest, Lieutenant-Colonel Ferdinand Vix, handed over a note ordering the Hungarian army to complete its evacuation of Debreczen and declaring that the imposing demarcation lines would be permanent. This "Vix note," prefiguring the "Trianon Treaty" that would truncate prewar Hungary by nearly two-thirds, was a death blow to Károlyi's hopes for negotiating a better peace in Paris, prompting his resignation. The imprisoned Communist leader, Béla Kun, was now the man of the hour. As a veteran of the Russian Civil War with ties to Lenin, Kun had military experience and diplomatic prospects that looked enticing to the Social Democrats who had been backing Károlyi. Unbeknownst to Károlyi, a delegation of socialists met with Kun in prison and negotiated—according to legend, it took only thirty minutes—a united socialist-Communist front in a new "Hungarian Soviet Republic," with Kun as dictator, charged with organizing a Moscow-backed Hungarian Red Army to resist the "imperialist peace" imposed by the Western Allies.[6]

Such, at any rate, was the idea. It would not be easy, however, in view of Hungary's precarious strategic position, so similar to that facing Lenin's Russia in 1918. A Romanian army, already occupying Transylvania, was poised before Debreczen, even while a French-sponsored and French-trained Czechoslovak army was pushing down from Slovakia toward Budapest. Nor had Kun, despite his experience in Russia, imbibed the key lesson of Brest-Litovsk: faced with an impossible situation, Lenin had chosen *not* to resist the Germans, but to cut a deal allowing the Bolsheviks to remain in power and fight another day. When a British envoy in Budapest proposed a compromise in early April 1919 that would have pushed back the demarcation lines in exchange for a promise to demobilize and refrain from spreading Communist propaganda, Kun went the other way. Arguing that cutting a deal with the Entente Powers, then at war with Soviet Russia, was a betrayal of the world revolution, Kun convinced the Council of People's Commissars to

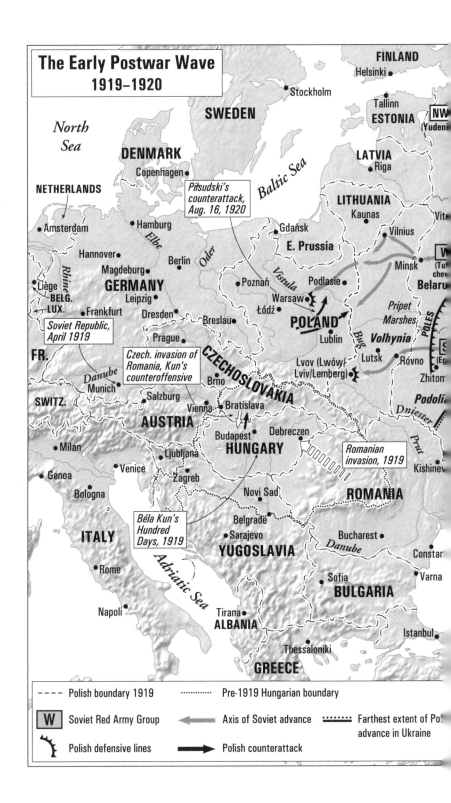

The Early Postwar Wave
1919–1920

FINLAND
Helsinki •

• Stockholm

*North
Sea*

SWEDEN

Tallinn •
ESTONIA   NW
(Yudeni

DENMARK
Copenhagen •

LATVIA
• Riga

Baltic Sea

NETHERLANDS

Piłsudski's
counterattack,
Aug. 16, 1920

LITHUANIA
Kaunas •

Vil

• Amsterdam

• Hamburg

Elbe

Gdańsk •

• Vilnius

Hannover •

• Berlin

Oder

E. Prussia

• Minsk
(Tu
che

W

Liège •
BELG.
LUX.

Magdeburg •

GERMANY
Leipzig •

• Frankfurt

• Poznań

Podlasie •

Belaru

Rhine

• Vistula

Warsaw •
Łódź •

*Pripet
Marshes*

Vistula

Soviet Republic,
April 1919

• Dresden

Prague •

• Breslau

POLAND

Lublin •

Bug

Volhynia

POLES

FR.

Czech. invasion of
Romania, Kun's
counteroffensive

CZECHOSLOVAKIA

Lvov (Lwów)
Lviv/Lemberg)

• Lutsk

• Rovno

(E

Danube
• Munich

Brno •

Zhiton

SWITZ.

• Salzburg

Vienna •

• Bratislava

Podoli

Dniester

AUSTRIA

• Debreczen

Romanian
invasion, 1919

Prut

• Milan

• Ljubljana

Budapest •

HUNGARY

• Kishinev

• Venice

Zagreb •

• Novi Sad

ROMANIA

• Genoa

• Bologna

Béla Kun's
Hundred
Days, 1919

Belgrade •

• Sarajevo

Bucharest •

Danube

• Constar

ITALY

YUGOSLAVIA

Sofia •

• Varna

BULGARIA

• Rome

Adriatic Sea

Napoli •

Tirana •
ALBANIA

Istanbul •

• Thessaloniki

GREECE

- - - - Polish boundary 1919   ·········· Pre-1919 Hungarian boundary

W   Soviet Red Army Group   Axis of Soviet advance   ······· Farthest extent of Po!
advance in Ukraine

Polish defensive lines   Polish counterattack

Farthest advance
of Siberian Army,
April 1919

•Perm

Volga   Kazan

Frunze's breakthrough,
April 28, 1919

•Vladimir
•Moscow

Farthest advance of
Volunteers, Oct. 1919

etrograd

•Smolensk

•Tula

ogilev

RUSSIA   •Samara

Orenburg

Bryansk   •Tambov

Saratov•

Uralsk

•Kursk   •Voronezh

Chernigov

Don Cossacks

Volga   Ural

Kiev

Ukraine

Donbass
Coalfields

Tsaritsyn
•

Farthest advance
of Siberian Army,
April 1919

Dnieper

Yekaterinoslav•   •Aleksandrovka

Don

Astrakhan•

Makhno's
Partisans

•Rostov-Na-Donu

dessa

Sea of
Avoz

Denikin's Volunteers,
March 1919

Caspian Sea

ench
ndings

Wrangel
1920

•Novorossiysk

Sevastopol

Black Sea

Georgia   Tbilisi
•

Batumi•

Baku•

Armenia   Azerbaijan

Yerevan•

•Ankara

TURKEY

IRAN

0   300 miles

refuse the deal.* Kun's new Hungarian Red Army promptly coun-
terattacked the Romanians at Debreczen and launched an offensive north into the former Hungarian lands of Czechoslovakia, as
if daring the Allies to do their worst—while hoping that the (Russian) Red Army would intervene from Ukraine to tie down Romanian and Czech forces.[7]

Béla Kun's Communist Holy War never quite got off the ground.
On March 25, Trotsky did order a Soviet offensive from Kiev across
independent Ukrainian territory to establish "direct contact with
the Soviet armies of Hungary," but it took the Red Army nearly
two months to get a bridgehead on the western side of the Dnieper
River, by which time Trotsky's forces were threatened in the rear
by a Volunteer Army advance into the Donbass. Lenin and Trotsky
assured Kun they were doing all they could, but by June 18, it was
clear that no Red Army breakthrough to Romania was possible.
Lenin cabled Kun that he was best advised to request a ceasefire.[8]

Meanwhile, the Hungarian Soviet Republic was floundering at
home. Despite an initial surge of patriotism around the militant
new Soviet Republic willing to resist the Allies, and some initial
military gains on the Czech front, Kun rapidly alienated urbanites by nationalizing all businesses with more than twenty workers
(then those larger than ten, and finally all of them). At the same
time, he enraged farmers with aggressive grain requisitions. Going
further than Lenin had yet done, Kun's government decreed the
nationalization of land while refusing to redistribute nationalized
estates to local farmers. Instead, the existing owners of the great
aristocratic latifundia in eastern Hungary were appointed "production commissars" over their own estates. Resistance was still fiercer
west of the Danube, where "nationalization" mostly entailed expropriation of modest Hungarian peasant smallholders. Kun deputized

---

* Formally, Kun's only title in the new government, in a nod to his Russian connections,
was commissar for foreign affairs. Nonetheless there was little doubt he was in charge.

a radical ex-journalist named Tibor Szamuely to lead a punitive detachment against recalcitrant peasants of western Hungary. Szamuely applied a Communist version of the old Roman practice of decimation, ordering patrols to shoot the first three peasants they encountered on entering a village, without regard for guilt. By summer Red Terror had engulfed Budapest as well, carried out by a gang of demobilized soldiers given the grandiose title of "Terror Group of the Revolutionary Council of the Government," but who called themselves "Lenin boys." This was hardly a misnomer: Lenin himself sent a "message to the Hungarian workers" on May 27, 1919 (by way of Kun), instructing them that "the dictatorship of the proletariat requires the use of swift, implacable, and resolute violence to crush the resistance of exploiters, capitalists, great land-owners, and their minions. Anyone who does not understand this is not a revolutionary." Translated into local idiom, Lenin's message was scrawled across one Budapest street placard announcing menacingly that "in the proletarian state, only the workers are allowed to live!"[9]

Meanwhile, a counter-revolutionary "White" army had been organized in southern Hungary by a Habsburg naval war hero, Admiral Miklós Horthy. Areas conquered by the Hungarian Whites saw terrible pogroms, with Christian peasants blaming Jews for the excesses of the urban-dominated and heavily Jewish Kun government. (It was widely reported that eighteen out of twenty-six of Kun's "people's commissars," including Kun, were of Jewish origin.)[*] With southern Hungary falling to Horthy's Whites, and Romanian troops approaching Budapest from the east, Kun's position was desperate. After wiring Lenin one last time to ask for a Russian supporting offensive and being rebuffed, Kun dissolved

---

[*] A more recent scholarly estimate, which broadens the definition of "commissar" to include lesser officials, yields a higher number of Jews but a lower percentage (thirty out of forty-eight).

the Hungarian Soviet Republic on August 1, 1919, and fled with his family to Vienna. There, he negotiated asylum for himself and trusted aides, including Mátyás Rákosi, a production commissar, and György Lukács, people's commissar for education and culture. Most of Kun's other commissars were left behind to Horthy's mercy, although their fate was delayed for months. The Romanians occupied Budapest first, and the Western Allies bogged Horthy down in negotiations until November, which spared the city the horrors of a White sacking. Even so, the ensuing "White Terror" was likely no less bloody than Kun's Red Terror (Kun's government admitted to carrying out 234 executions; the Whites claimed the true number was 590). Casualty estimates were harder to come by for the counter-revolution, however, as the Horthy government remained in power until 1944 and had little incentive to investigate its own crimes.[10]

Béla Kun's Hungarian Soviet Republic had lasted a bit more than four months—longer than its Bavarian counterpart, but just a fraction of the duration of Lenin's government. Kun himself declared it a failure, admitting, in his concession speech on August 1, 1919, that "the proletariat was dissatisfied with our domination, already it shouted in the factories, in spite of all our agitation: 'Down with the dictatorship!' Now I realize that we have tried in vain to educate the masses of the proletariat in the country to be self-conscious revolutionaries."[11]

Nonetheless, Kun's Hundred Days, as they came to be known in popular lore (the real number was 133), cast a long shadow. Kun himself lived to fight another day for the world revolution, chastened but undaunted. His comrade Rákosi, who had overseen property nationalizations before taking a Hungarian Red Army Command, had acquired so much experience in four months that he was promoted to the Executive Committee of the Comintern. Rákosi would end his career as general secretary of the post-1945

Hungarian Communist government. But it was Lukács who may have cast the longest shadow of all. As commissar of culture in 1919, he took a more radical line than Lunacharsky had in Russia, introducing sex education as early as primary school. His aim was overturning "bourgeois" morals on monogamy, premarital sex, and female chastity. Drawing on the lessons of the Hundred Days, Lukács argued, in *History and Class Consciousness* (1922), that Communism could "come into existence only as a *conscious transformation of the whole of society*." Or, as Lukács recalled in a memoir essay, he had come to see "revolutionary destruction as the one and only solution to the cultural contradictions of the epoch." Embraced and embellished by the avant-garde Marxists of the Institute for Social Research at Frankfurt University (the "Frankfurt School"), Lukács's ideas later helped inform the "sexual revolution" that swept across the Western world in the 1960s, by way of Frankfurt School disciples such as Herbert Marcuse and Charles Reich.[12]*

Disappointing as the results were, the revolutions in Bavaria and Budapest seemed to augur well for Communist fortunes. As Comintern president Grigory Zinoviev wrote, in May 1919, "The Third International has as its main basis three Soviet Republics, Russia, Hungary, and Bavaria. No one will be surprised, however, if by the time these lines appear in print, we shall have not merely three, but six more, Soviet Republics. Europe is hurrying towards the proletarian revolution at breakneck speed." Even after Kun's fall, Karl Radek saluted the Hungarian Revolution as a "revolutionary

---

* Lukács reprised his role as commissar of education in the short-lived Hungarian Reform Communist government in 1956. Statues of him were taken down in Budapest in 2017, whether out of antipathy to his controversial views on education and sex—or, as critics of the current Hungarian government believe, because of his Jewish origins. Of course, Lukács cannot be blamed for how his ideas have been interpreted by others. Nonetheless, it is rich for his defenders to claim that Lukács did not really mean what he said when he advocated for "revolutionary destruction" and the "conscious transformation of the whole of society."

outpost on an advanced redoubt." It had reminded Europe's proletarian masses, he said, that there was "only *one* party willing to fight till the last drop of blood: the Communists."[13]

The prospects for world revolution were given further impetus by the Polish invasion of Ukraine on April 25–26, 1920, which reignited the war between Soviet Russia and the "capitalist world" just when it had been petering out. It was not hard for the Bolsheviks to spin this new conflict as a war against imperialism, as the invading Polish force, commanded by Marshal Józef Piłsudski, a Polish nobleman, had been armed by Entente suppliers, and aimed squarely at territorial expansion. Making things still spicier ideologically, Piłsudski had cut a deal with the reactionary Ukrainian Cossack hetman Semen Petliura, who conceded eastern Galicia in exchange for recognition of his authority in Kiev, from which city Piłsudski's Poles expelled the Red Army on May 7. The agitprop concerning this imperialist aggression against the "workers' state" nearly wrote itself, and it came at an opportune time, as the Bolsheviks were preparing to relaunch the Comintern that summer. After the fall of Kiev hit the news wires, English stevedores at the London East India docks went on strike, refusing to load field guns and ammunition destined for Piłsudski's forces in Poland. An up-and-coming Labour leader, Ernest Bevin, called on all British workers to boycott the manufacture or transport of "munitions for purposes which outrage our sense of justice." By May 17, the battle was won when cabinet spokesman Andrew Bonar Law assured the House of Commons that no "assistance" was "being given to the Polish government."[14]

Buoyed by the resistance of English workers to "British imperialism," Lenin's confidence in the world revolution was restored. In *"Left-Wing" Communism: An Infantile Disorder*, written as a handbook for revolution to be handed out to delegates at the upcoming Second Comintern Congress, Lenin singled out British workers as promising revolutionaries, despite the Labour Party being traditionally reformist. Huge strikes had broken out in 1919 in Clydeside, Glasgow, and Belfast, and now London dockworkers, too, had shown their teeth. In the handbook, Lenin cited a Lloyd George speech in which the prime minister had darkly warned that "four-fifths of [Britain] was industrial and commercial," marking it out as "more top-heavy than any country in the world. If it begins to rock, the crash here, for that reason, will be greater than in any land." From these terrified remarks of the "the leader of the British bourgeoisie," Lenin concluded that "the conditions for a successful proletarian revolution are obviously maturing in Britain."[15]

Lenin's optimism was buoyed by a strategic turnaround in Ukraine. Foolishly, Piłsudski's troops, despite having failed to destroy any large Red formations in their rapid march on Kiev, had thrown bridgeheads across the Dnieper in a hope of pursuing the Reds into Left Bank Ukraine. In early June, the Red Southwestern Army Group crossed the river both north and south of Kiev, threatening the city's encirclement and forcing Piłsudski to order a swift retreat on June 12. This marked the sixteenth change of regime in Kiev since the October Revolution, and, as it turned out, the last. While Piłsudski's forces escaped the Red pincers, the Red Western Army Group in Belorussia, commanded by the brilliant ex-tsarist officer Mikhail N. Tukhachevsky, launched an offensive that pitched Polish forces into headlong retreat. Channeling his orders from Trotsky and Lenin, Tukhachevsky himself, a former nobleman, caught the revolutionary fever, exhorting his men on July 2, "Over the corpse of White Poland lies the path to world conflagration. . . . On to Vilno, Minsk, Warsaw! Forward!" Backing up his vow, Tukhachevsky's forces conquered Minsk on July 11, Vilnius on the 14th, Grodno on the 19th, and the old Polish fortress city of Brest-Litovsk on August 1. Warsaw, it seemed, would be next to fall.[16]

It was in this heady atmosphere that the Second Congress of the Comintern convened on July 19, 1920, just as the Red Army was entering Poland. A Polish revolutionary committee in attendance, handpicked in Moscow, included Felix Dzerzhinsky, the Polish-born founder of the CHEKA. As Trotsky recalled of the mood in the Kremlin, Lenin "calculated, in view of the revolutionary situation in Germany, Italy and the other countries, that the military blow [into Poland] would let loose the avalanche of revolution which had been momentarily halted." Through back channels, Lenin had been informed that the German government, to weaken Poland, was quietly supporting the Red offensive by holding up French arms deliveries. This cynical German assistance, along with the British dockyard strike, likely inspired the language of condition 14 of the "21 Conditions" placed before aspirant member parties at the Second Comintern Congress, namely, that Communists must "give every possible support to the Soviet Republics in their struggle against counter-revolutionary forces," such as by "induc[ing] the workers to refuse to transport munitions of war intended for enemies of the Soviet Republic."[17]

With Bolshevik prestige soaring and the expectation that revolutions would soon engulf Central Europe in the baggage train of the Red Army, Lenin brooked no compromise as he laid down the law for global Communism. The "21 Conditions" were rigorous and thorough. In line with Lenin's premise that "the class struggle in almost all the countries of Europe is entering the phase of civil war" (condition 3), the Comintern mandated the purging of "reformists" from "all responsible posts in the labor movement" (condition 2). This directive was pursuant to a "complete rupture with reformism and the policy of the center" in all European socialist parties, with a specific list of English, French, German, and Italian reformists who must be expelled "with the least delay" (condition 7). Also to be expelled were those who had succumbed to "social patriotism" (e.g., by supporting their country in the war), or the kind of "social pacifism" embodied in supporting the new League of Nations (condition 6). Based on the model of Lenin's successful revolution in 1917, Communists were enjoined to carry out "systematic propaganda in the army" (condition 4), while doing the same "in the rural districts" (condition 5) and "in the trade unions" (condition 9), targeting all sectors of capitalist society. In the present "acute time of civil war," Communist parties must adopt the Leninist structure of "democratic *centralism*," organizing themselves "in the most centralized manner, [with] iron discipline, bordering on military discipline" (condition 12). To that end, all parties were required to obey the new Executive Committee of the Comintern (ECCI), whose every dictate was "binding," and to rename themselves *Communist party* of such-and-such country (Section of the Third Communist International)" (conditions 16–17). Last, Communists were directed to convene a "special party congress" within four months, to expel reformists, and to bind the loyal new Communist party "sections" to Moscow (conditions 19–21).[18]

Although the First Congress, held in isolated Moscow in March 1919, had been a dud, the Second Congress was a serious affair. Upon arrival in Petrograd and receiving, in their hotel welcome packet, complimentary copies of Lenin's *"Left-Wing" Communism: An Infantile Disorder*, delegates were shown the revolutionary sights. Highlights included the Summer Palace of Tsarskoe Selo (Tsar's Village), which, after being occupied by grubby soldiers during the Civil War (when locals had referred to the town as *Soldatskoe Selo*, Soldiers' Village), was now a showcase home for orphans of the revolution, or "proletarian children" (*Detskoe Selo*, Children's Village). Back in Petrograd, the delegates were shown around the Smolny Institute, Bolshevik headquarters during the October Revolution. On Nevsky Prospekt, they were treated to a dramatic reenactment of *The Storming of the Winter Palace*, staged under Maxim

Gorky's direction on the steps of the now silenced Petrograd Stock Exchange. Red flags blustered atop the Winter Palace, while warships on the Neva lit up a giant replica of the Soviet hammer-and-sickle flag with searchlights. As Lenin's now starry-eyed comrade from Zurich, the Youth Socialist and now Youth Communist chairman Willi Münzenberg, later recalled, "It was like a dream."[19]

After a few ceremonial days in Petrograd, everyone took the train to Moscow on July 23, where the real business began. The Comintern president, Zinoviev, boasted in his opening speech that "the Second International has been knocked on its head by the Communist International." Lenin then mounted the rostrum in the Kremlin throne room, three gold-embroidered tsarist thrones at his back, to deliver the keynote address. When the moment comes "for direct action to achieve the Communist revolution," Lenin warned, delegates must ensure that their parties were ready by purging them all from the "yoke of the labour aristocracy and the opportunists." Lenin's speech was received, according to multiple witnesses, with a "deafening standing ovation."[20]

Feeling their oats, Lenin and Zinoviev nearly ruined Communism's coming-out party by arranging a victory tour for forty European Congress attendees through recently reconquered areas of Soviet Ukraine. The delegation's specially outfitted military train was ambushed three separate times by the partisan army of Nestor Makhno. The Comintern VIP train made an inviting target for Makhno's men in a land ravaged by years of civil war; it was so lavishly outfitted that the curtains were drawn when it passed through populated areas, lest hungry Ukrainians storm the train. Somehow, Makhno kept missing his target, blowing up one bridge a moment too late, then tearing up the tracks too early, then occupying a station just after the VIP train had pulled through. If Makhno's partisans had blown up Lenin's foreign guests under a Soviet military escort, Bolshevik prestige in Europe would have likely plummeted, with potentially fateful consequences for the adoption of the "21 Conditions" and the future autonomy of the German, French, and Italian Communist parties. Makhno's misfires instead turned a near debacle for Moscow into a beatification. As a Ukrainian peasant told a German Communist passing through his village, "If even the Popes from abroad are in favor, then the Bolsheviks, these scoundrels, must be in the right and will win."[21]

In a coda to the Second Congress meant to activate Lenin's anti-imperialist program outlined in condition 8 of the 21 ("on the question of colonies and oppressed nationalities"), the Bolsheviks convened a "Congress of the Peoples of the East" in Baku on September 1, 1920. Whereas the First and Second Congresses in Moscow aimed at capturing European socialists, the Baku Congress targeted those of Asia, the Middle East, and Africa, broadcasting the message that Soviet Russia stood with the world's colonized and oppressed against European imperialism. Owing to logistical problems, the Congress was predictably dominated by Russians, along with a few Tatars from Central Asia, Azeri Turks from Baku or neighboring Iran, and a few Turks from Ankara, with still tinier contingents from China and India. Because Christian Armenia and Georgia boycotted the conference, it took on the air of a Communist-Muslim alliance against the West. In his opening address, Zinoviev suggested that delegates should launch a "holy war" against "British imperialism." His abandonment of the Whites and Piłsudski's Poles notwithstanding, Lloyd George was burned in effigy (as was US president Woodrow Wilson).[22]

As promising as the idea of a Muslim-Communist holy war was in propaganda terms, the Baku Congress, muted by the darkening strategic picture for Moscow, had little immediate effect. While Lenin and Zinoviev addressed Comintern delegates in the Kremlin throne room, the Red Army had been moving from triumph to triumph as it entered Polish territory. Piłsudski, falling back for a last-ditch defense of Warsaw on the eastern bank of the Vistula River, was outnumbered nearly two to one, with 220,000 Red troops facing 120,000 Poles. On August 14, just after the Second Congress, Trotsky issued orders for the final push against Warsaw. Despite facing imposing odds, Piłsudski launched a blistering counterattack against Tukhachevsky's flank on August 16, capturing 95,000 Russian prisoners and forcing three Red armies to pull back in what Poles famously christened the "Miracle on the Vistula." By September, the Reds were retreating all along the line, falling back all the way through Belorussia into Ukraine, where Pyotr Wrangel's rump White Army was still encamped in Crimea.[23]

Realizing this, Lenin and Trotsky swallowed their pride, gave up temporarily on Lenin's dreams for a Communist conquest of Central Europe, and sued Warsaw for peace. On October 12, Soviet diplomats signed a treaty at Riga, marking the final Polish boundary 200 kilometers (125 miles) east of the Curzon Line drawn at Versailles. Eight days later, after transferring troops east to achieve a crushing superiority over the Whites holed up in Crimea, the Red Army attacked. It was all the overmatched Wrangel could do to screen an evacuation from Sevastopol across the Black Sea to Constantinople. On November 14, the last White troops, along with Russian or Ukrainian civilians lucky enough to talk their way aboard Allied vessels—83,000 people in all—left the Crimea; most would never see their homeland again. Some 300,000 unfortunate "collaborators" who had retreated to Sevastopol with Wrangel's army were left behind to face Bolshevik firing squads or be interned in concentration camps.[24]

In view of the altered strategic situation, Europe's socialists had reason for caution as they convened "special congresses" within the mandated four months to evaluate the "21 Conditions." After the Soviet retreat from Poland, did it really make sense to hitch a party's fortunes entirely to Moscow? Nor was it clear that Europe was really entering an "acute time of civil war." Perhaps Lenin's best hope outside Poland in 1920 was Italy, where a series of strikes swept through Milan and Turin that summer, and where the Italian socialist party, led by Giacinto Serrati, possessed the largest delegation in parliament. "The *absolutely vital thing* for the victory of the revolution now," Lenin wrote in *Pravda* on November 7, was to make sure there was "a real Communist party to act as vanguard for the revolutionary workers of Italy." But as Serrati pointed out in reply, the strike movement "was really just a deep-rooted and broadly based trade-union campaign which went off quite peacefully, apart from one or two sporadic incidents." Delicately, Serrati wrote in this public letter to Lenin that "we are very much afraid that you do not fully understand the position in Italy." To believe that, after purging reformists, "pure Communists . . . would bring about revolution in Italy," Serrati objected, "would be to diminish the whole meaning of revolution." Unsurprisingly, Lenin responded to this public criticism by insisting that Serrati, too, be purged, as he duly was.[25]

Serrati's fate was a harbinger of things to come: Comintern operatives descended upon Europe's venerable socialist parties one by one and pried them apart over the question of obedience to Moscow. The "great splitting," as it came to be known in socialist lore, was carried out on the Independent Social Democratic Party of Germany (Unabhängige Sozialdemokratische Partei Deutschlands, USPD) at Halle in October 1920, on the French socialists at Tours in December, and on the Italian party at Leghorn (Livorno) in January 1921. In Germany, the Communists did win over a majority, even if this was only of the USPD—the larger SPD being the party that had crushed the Spartacist uprising, and was thus hostile to the KPD and Moscow almost by definition. Still, the USPD was a force in its own right, boasting 800,000 members and having won nearly 5 million votes in Reichstag elections in June 1920, finishing second to the SPD. By comparison, the pre-Halle KPD had received less than a tenth as many votes, and had all of 2 Reichstag deputies to the USPD's 81. Winning over the rump of the larger USPD to the KPD, by a vote of 393 to 237, was thus a real coup for the Comintern, even if the end result was a kind of addition by subtraction: so many USPD members (200,000) left the party in disgust that the new unified KPD boasted not 800,000, or even half this, but about 350,000 members.[26]

The story in France was similar. At Tours, owing in part to the mistaken view of French socialists that a country with such a proud revolutionary tradition would enjoy leeway with the "21 Conditions," delegates voted to affiliate with the Comintern by nearly 3 to 1 (3,028 to 1,022). This result allowed the ECCI to take control of a mass party with 140,000 members as well as a newspaper, *L'Humanité*, founded by Jean Jaurès. *L'Humanité* had a daily circulation of 200,000 (and is still in print today). Still, it was an open question whether or not everyone in the new French Communist Party (Parti Communiste français, PCF) would reliably obey Moscow. As the party's theoretical journal, *Cahiers du bolchévisme*, estimated after an internal canvass, its ideological composition was "20 per cent Jaurèsism, 10 per cent Marxism, 20 per cent Leninism, 20 per cent Trotskyism, and 30 per cent confusionism."[27]

The Italian "splitting congress" of January 1921 may have been the most counterproductive. To ensure that Serrati and his associates were purged along with the "reformers," Lenin and Zinoviev sent two credentialed non-Italian Comintern agents to Livorno, including Rákosi, one of Kun's former Hungarian commissars, and Christo Kabakchiev of the embryonic Bulgarian Communist Party, as if to remind Italians of their subordinate place. "Those who refused to accept the separation of the reformists," Kabakchiev said, reading out an ECCI directive at Livorno with his eyes on Serrati, "violate an essential order of the Communist International and, by that alone, place themselves outside it." So egregious was the interference, and so popular was Serrati, that a clear majority voted against affiliation with Moscow, and those joining the new Italian Communist Party (Partito Comunista Italiano, PCI) were forced to leave the hall. Curiously, despite decisively losing the vote and getting only a rump party—the PCI would get only about a tenth of the votes won by the socialists in elections held four months later—Lenin declared the Livorno splitting congress "a great success."[28]

The rationale of these purges, as Lenin saw it, was that the new Communist parties would be leaner and purer in doctrine, ready to seize the moment and take power when opportunities presented themselves. Of course, although this part was not widely publicized, joining the Comintern also meant that the stripped-down parties had access to Moscow funds, which could be used to subsidize mass strikes and insurrections. After the Second Congress, favored delegates were given diamonds to bring home. Others carried cash, including German marks, Swiss francs, and especially US dollars, which soon became the official currency of the Comintern, in which all accounts were kept (the official language, owing to the importance of the KPD and the enduring prestige of Marx, was German). A special body called the Department of International Communication (Otdel mezhdunarodnoi svyazi, OMS), headed by a loyal Bolshevik, Osip Piatnitsky, was created to facilitate money transfers between Moscow and Comintern member parties.[29]

In practice, the streamlined and Moscow-financed new Communist parties had no more success in fomenting revolution than the Spartacists had earlier. Contrary to Lenin's hopes for Britain, Italy, and Poland in 1920, Kun's ill-fated Hundred Days in the spring of 1919 turned out to be the high-water mark of the postwar revolutionary surge. The first stab at a Comintern-planned and Comintern-financed insurrection after the Second Congress, the

German "March Action" of 1921, was a bloody fiasco, exemplified by an embarrassing episode in Breslau that saw a local Communist party committee blow up a toilet at its own party headquarters. Elsewhere, Communists tried to call a general strike and sent unemployed activists to factories such as the Krupp works in Rheinhausen only for workers to bludgeon them with clubs. At Rheinhausen, the workers wounded about eight Communists and then went to work. As Paul Levi, the departing KPD chairman whose pleas to stand down had been overruled by the Comintern liaison in Berlin, the former Hungarian dictator Béla Kun, complained in his postmortem, "It was a terrible thing to watch how the unemployed, crying loudly at the pain of the thrashings they had received, were thrown out of the factories." So disgusted were the party's rank and file, many of whom had belonged to the USPD before the Halle splitting congress, that 200,000 of them tore up their membership cards. Levi, although right about the failure of the putsch, was purged from the KPD for insubordination and, in effect, for airing the party's dirty laundry in public.[30]

The streamlined PCI fared just as poorly in action. Although there was no attempt to seize power akin to the German March Action, the PCI might still have done something to rouse Italian workers against Benito Mussolini's "Blackshirt" fascist militias, which had begun fighting with organized labor and socialists in Milan and Turin in the aftermath of the general strike of the summer of 1920. But the post-purge PCI, led by the uninspiring but loyal Amadeo Bordiga, refused to cooperate with Italian socialists. Following ECCI orders from Moscow, Bordiga banned PCI members from joining Arditi del Popolo (The People's Braves), a combat organization combining the forces of Italian liberals and socialists against Mussolini's Blackshirts, and resolved, at a party congress in March 1922, that any invitation to join a coalition government of the Left could "only be a trap." Italian Communists, Bordiga declared in July, would not even back the beleaguered coalition government in Rome if it chose to "use the official force of the state in the legal repression of fascism." When Mussolini staged his "March on Rome" that October, Italian Communists did not lift a finger to protest—only for Bordiga and most of the party leadership to be arrested by Mussolini anyway.[31]

Although Lenin was not the kind of man to admit to political error, at least not publicly, the lessons of the March Action were obvious enough, even before the fascist debacle in Italy, to prompt a reconsideration of the hyper-revolutionary line he had taken at the Second Comintern Congress. At the Third Congress, held in Moscow in July 1921, Lenin warned that anyone who "fails to understand that in Europe—where nearly all the proletarians are organized—we must win over the majority of the working class, is lost to the Communist movement." Translated into policy terms, this meant that Communists must go a bit easier on reformists and go "to the masses" to create a "united front" before resuming the offensive, while also purging overeager leftists whose failures in the "first round of proletarian revolutions" from 1919–1921 were clear to all.[32]

Still, putschism was a hard habit for Communists to shake. In 1923, Germany again plunged into chaos after French armies occupied the industrial Ruhr region to seize reparations "in kind" that Berlin was failing to pay in cash, prompting the German government to declare "passive resistance" and print money to pay Germans not to work. By the fall of 1923, hyperinflation had arrived, leading to a push to political extremes, with Adolf Hitler's Nationalist Socialist German Workers' Party (Nationalsozialistische Deutsche Arbeiterpartei, NSDAP) and the KPD both gaining strength. To capitalize on the chaos, Zinoviev sent arms, Comintern funds ($1 million, equivalent to roughly $100 million today), and Soviet officers to Germany to train Communist paramilitaries ("red" or "proletarian hundreds"), with an eye to seizing power in Saxony and marching to Berlin. With Lenin out of commission after a series of strokes, it fell to Zinoviev and Stalin, now general secretary of the Russian Communist Party, to approve the putsch. Perhaps hastily, Stalin saluted German Communists, in a letter published in the KPD newspaper *Die Rote Fahne* (The red flag) on October 10, on "the approaching revolution in Germany," which would soon "shift the center of world revolution from Moscow to Berlin." Thus alerted to the insurrection, the Saxon authorities declared martial law, disarmed the Red Hundreds, arrested hundreds of activists, and rendered the Communist "German October" dead on arrival.[33]

In Comintern policy terms, the German Communists' latest failure did little more than reaffirm the moderate "united front" line adopted at its congresses of 1921 and 1922 (even if it had obviously not been followed in Germany in 1923). Still, the spectacular failure of the German October, transpiring in the midst of a furious succession struggle as an ailing Lenin stood at death's door (he would succumb on January 21, 1924), reshuffled the political deck in the Kremlin. Although Zinoviev ran the Comintern and Stalin had written the damning public letter to *Rote Fahne*, both men claimed to have been less enthusiastic about the revolutionary line than Trotsky and Radek, who had been on the ground in Berlin as the revolution went up in smoke. Trotsky and Radek shouldered the blame for the German October, accused of "right opportunist deviations" that had led them to pursue a "united front from above" rather than a "united front from below." The German October became an albatross to hang around Trotsky's neck.[34]

A similar template was followed after the next conspicuous Comintern failure, which took place in China. As part of the "rightward" tilt of the "united front from below," Stalin and the ECCI threw support behind Chiang Kai-shek in the Kuomintang

(KMT), a nationalist-revolutionary party-cum-army founded by
Sun Yat-sen, which had come to dominate much of urban coastal
China in the chaos following the dissolution of the Qing dynasty
in 1912. While China also had a Moscow-funded Communist
Party adhering to the "21 Conditions" (the CCP), the real energy
in the 1920s lay with the nationalist and "anti-imperialist" KMT,
especially after Stalin backed Chiang, an energetic young military
chieftain who visited Moscow in 1923, to supplant the aging Sun
in 1924, before the latter's death in 1925. Red Army experts organized a "Whampoa Military Academy" near Canton (Guangzhou)
to help train and modernize KMT forces. As late as July 1926, Stalin ordered loyal CCP members to "occupy various leading posts"
in the Kuomintang, and sent military advisers to support Chiang,
referred to in Moscow as the "Red General." The ECCI printed
up autographed portraits of Chiang for distribution, and ordered
the Communist Party in Shanghai to disarm workers in the Communist General Labor Union, who had launched a general strike
in February 1927, and to tell them to stand down. But Chiang,
wary of Soviet interference after decades of European meddling
in China, had other ideas. In April, the Red General led his army
into Shanghai and crushed the General Labor Union and the Communist network in the city. Aghast, CCP leaders, urged on by a
hotheaded German Comintern agent named Heinz Neumann,
launched an insurrection in December 1927 in Canton, the party's last urban stronghold—an uprising crushed no less brutally by
Chiang than the Shanghai general strike had been.[35]

The Chinese debacle of 1927 was just as damaging to Communist prospects as the German failures of 1921 and 1923, and
the political fallout just as severe. In February 1927, Lenin's old
comrade from wartime Zurich, Willi Münzenberg, the former
Youth Communist secretary who now ran the Comintern's public outreach media campaigns, had organized an "anti-imperialist"

congress in Brussels, hoping to reignite the cause after the fizzling out of the Baku "Congress of the Peoples of the East" in 1920. Münzenberg had invited Chiang Kai-shek, hoping that the Kuomintang chieftain could headline his Brussels conference. But Chiang, more interested in the mechanics of governance in China than in burnishing the image of Communism, never showed up, and his nationalist turn against the now moribund CCP later that year undermined the credibility of Münzenberg's "League Against Imperialism," which never really got off the ground.[36]

Once again, Stalin contrived to hold the "leftist" opposition (Trotsky and Zinoviev) responsible for the Chinese debacle, notwithstanding the fact that it was Stalin and Bukharin who had thrown support behind the man who had just crushed the Communists in Shanghai and Canton, whose Kuomintang was now denounced as a front for "the imperialists, landlords, and national-bourgeoisie" in China. The new, hard-left line at the ECCI stated that a "third period" was beginning, marked by a "severe intensification of the general capitalist crisis" in which the "imperialist" powers would soon launch an "armed attack . . . on the Soviet Union," leading to a "tremendous revolutionary explosion" that would "bury capitalism under its ruins."[37]

The significance of these Moscow sectarian purges for international Communism lay not in their recondite ideological subtleties, but in the fact that the party line in this or that country in Europe or Asia was now being determined by the sordid internal politics of the Kremlin. Marx had once purged those guilty of Bakununist (read: leftist) and "reformist" (read: rightist) deviations from the First International not so much to ensure doctrinal purity— although that was surely part of it—as to ensure his own personal dominance. Stalin, like Lenin before him, could now do the same for international Communism. Unlike Marx, however, Bolshevik leaders ruled over a once mighty empire and could deploy Soviet

Russian prestige and treasure, however truncated state resources might have been owing to Communist disruption of the Russian economy, to ensure international compliance with his directives. So long as Communist rule in Russia was secure against real or phantom threats from the "imperialist powers," Stalin could impose his will and define Communism for the world.

8
STALIN RESUMES THE COMMUNIST OFFENSIVE

For all the grand ambitions of the Comintern, the number one priority of all Communists around the world, as stated unambiguously in membership condition 15, was to ensure the survival of Communism in its Russian birthplace. And growing pains were hard to miss. By the time the Volga famine began to bite in the spring of 1921, the combination of civil war and "maximalist" War Communism policies had brought the Russian economy to its knees. Russia's twin capitals of Moscow and Petrograd, despite being given priority in distribution of scarce foodstuffs, were starving. On February 22, a "Plenipotentiary Workers' Assembly" was formed that demanded an end to Bolshevik dictatorship, freedom of speech and assembly, and a release of political prisoners; it also called for a general strike. The CHEKA responded with force, firing into a group of workers on February 24 and killing twelve. On February 26, Grigory Zinoviev, then party boss in Petrograd, warned Lenin that if he did not receive reinforcements, "we are going to be overrun."[1]

Just when it seemed things could not possibly get worse for Communism, the rebellion reached Kronstadt, which had supplied most of Lenin's Red Guards in 1917. On March 8, the local *Izvestiya* hit the Bolsheviks where it hurt. "In carrying out the October Revolution," the paper announced, "the working class hoped to achieve its liberation. The outcome has been even greater enslavement of human beings." Instead of freedom, Russia's urban workers now faced "the daily dread of ending up in the torture chambers of the CHEKA," while its peasant masses were being "drenched with blood." A "third revolution" was at hand in which "the long suffering of the toilers has drawn to an end." To ensure this did not happen, Trotsky went to Petrograd to take charge of the counterattack. On the night of March 16, 50,000 Red troops set out over the ice. Kronstadt's anarcho-socialist freedom fighters fought fiercely, inflicting 10,000 casualties, but succumbed two days later. Trotsky had vowed the rebels would be "shot like partridges," and he was good to his word. Of Kronstadt's rebel survivors, 2,103 were executed and 6,459 sent to concentration camps in the Soviet arctic region, where nearly three-quarters died within a year.[2]

Notwithstanding Trotsky's victory in Kronstadt, Lenin was forced to abandon the Communist offensive at home, at least in terms of economic policy. In painful recognition of policy failure, on March 23 Lenin announced the end of the hated grain requisition, or *pradrazvërstka*, replacing requisition quotas with a lower "tax in kind" on agricultural produce, the *prodnalog*. The old rural communes, and not Gosplan in Moscow, would determine the obligations of each peasant household. While there was never any formal announcement of the end of War Communism, the climbdown on grain requisitions heralded the relegalization of many private markets in Soviet Russia, from the retail sale of grain, and then agricultural and manufactured goods (July 19, 1921), to real estate transactions (August 1921), publishing (December 1921), and small-scale manufacturing (June 1922). The critical month was April 1922, when the Bolsheviks, by abandoning rationing and restoring the right to own hard currency, brought back money: Russians would again pay cash for food, public transport, and postal service. By the summer of 1922, the consequences of this "New Economic Policy" (NEP) were clear. With the exception of heavy industry, banking, and foreign trade, which Lenin called the "commanding heights" of the economy and maintained under state control, Russia's Communist rulers appeared to have brought back capitalism, not least in the reappearance of prosperous fur-clad manufacturers, traders, and speculators, who were soon referred to as *nepmen*. Lenin himself was game enough to admit, in a speech to a party congress in October 1921, that the implementation of NEP could not "be called anything but a very severe defeat and retreat" for Communism.[3]

Trying to account for the failure of Communism to achieve the bounty Marxist theory had predicted, Lenin blamed Russia's comparative economic backwardness, lamenting, in March 1922, that "nobody could foresee that the proletariat would gain power in one of the most underdeveloped countries." Still, Lenin admitted that the inexperience of Communist intellectuals factored in too. "The idea of building Communism with communist hands," Lenin chided delegates to a party congress, "is childish, completely childish. Communists are only a drop in the sea of people," and even the best Communist "does not know how to carry on trade, because he is not a businessman." The nepmen may have been obnoxious "social swine," but they were performing a necessary function in restoring Russian industry, which Lenin admitted had degraded so terribly that Russia's dwindling industrial labor force had "ceased to exist as a proletariat." In one of his saltier moods, he said that his own government's employees "should all be hanged for creating all this unnecessary red tape." Try though they mightily did, it turned out that "we [Communists] cannot run an economy. This has been proved in the past year." Having swallowed his pride, Lenin now wanted Russia's Communists to swallow their own, exhorting them to "get down to business, all of you." He added, "You will have capitalists beside you, including foreign capitalists, concessionaires, and leaseholders. They will squeeze profits out of you amounting to hundreds per cent; they will enrich themselves, operating alongside of you. Let them. Meanwhile you will learn from them the business of running the economy, and only when you do that will you be able to build up a communist republic."[4]

A non-Marxist might object here that, if central planning of all economic activity—now retroactively disowned as "War Communism"—had caused Russia's economy to collapse in ruins in three years, perhaps there was something wrong with Communism. But this is not to reckon with the suppleness of dialectical materialism, which sees in every failure the seeds of some future triumph. As Lenin explained, "capitalism," in a backward country like Russia, could serve as "the connecting link between small-scale production and socialism, as the means, path, and method of increasing the productive forces." Still, Lenin was game enough to abandon the Communist label for now, calling his strange new hybrid of NEP "state capitalism."[5]

Necessary though it was to enable Russia's economy to recover from the depths of famine and industrial depression, NEP was never meant to be permanent. How long would it take, though? Back in March 1921, when the tax in kind was first introduced, Lenin warned that restoring large-scale industrial production would mean tolerating private trading for "many years, not less than a decade, and probably more given our economic havoc." That June, he described NEP as a policy that had been "adopted seriously and for a long time." Addressing the Ninth All-Russian Congress of Soviets in December, he said that Communists should be "reckoning the task in decades, not months." At the Eleventh Party Congress in March 1922, Lenin reassured Russian Communists that the "last and decisive battle" with "Russian capitalism" would take place "in the near future," but he cautioned that "it was impossible to determine the date precisely." By January 1923, after moneyed transactions had fully replaced rationing and Russia's market economy was back in force, Lenin conceded that restoring the state-planned economy originally envisioned under War Communism might require a "whole historical epoch, lasting one or two decades."[6]

However long it would last, NEP was a painful compromise for the Communist party, a constant reminder of failure. Communists despised the nepmen. As a shocked German Communist visitor observed while visiting one showcase "workers' restaurant" in April 1923, the old Marxist banner over the entrance ("Proletarians of the world, unite!") had been replaced with what he gamely admitted were "agreeably sensuous decorations" of the kind preferred by its new nepmen clientele. Authentic workers, the German complained, could no longer afford to eat there.[7]

Although the Communist government strictly censored the Soviet press, stories like this were hard to hide. The ostentatious behavior of the nepmen, Germany's ambassador reported to Berlin, has "aroused deep resentment among the workers and rank and file of the Party, who are asking whether they made the Revolution to enrich a host of private profiteers." A Menshevik exile publication in Berlin, *Sotsialisticheskii vestnik* (Socialist herald), reported that Russian party cadres had begun demanding "the closing of all 'NEP restaurants,' the taxation of nepmen for hundreds of millions, and so on." Owing both to the unpopularity of NEP with Communists and Lenin's incapacitation in his last months, party leaders began quietly backtracking over the winter of 1923–1924, first withholding state credits and contracts from private traders and then shutting many of them down entirely. A Russian American named William Reswick traveled to Russia in 1922 to take advantage of opportunities presented by NEP and returned to New York for two months in late 1923. When he went back to Russia, he was astonished by the change in the business climate that had taken place between October and December. The famous Sukharev Market, where Russians and foreigners alike had browsed for bargains on artwork and collectibles, was now "deserted." When Reswick asked a friend what had happened, he was told that "the victims of this wave of terror" were "nearly all Nepmen, who had invested their capital in reliance on existing laws and acted in good faith." Tens of thousands of private businesses were shuttered in the first half of 1924, some of them following acts of sabotage that were either encouraged, or at least not discouraged, by the authorities. The crackdown was hardly subtle: one Moscow restaurant popular with both nepmen and the foreign diplomatic and press corps, the Hermitage, was raided by the State Political Directorate (Gosudarstvennoe politicheskoe upravlenie)—or GPU—as the CHEKA had been renamed, during its New Year's Eve party of 1923–1924. While the foreigners were left alone, Russian nepmen were forced to prove that they had paid their taxes. Presumably not everyone had, as the restaurant was closed down.[8]

Some of the Communist policy confusion in 1924 reflected political uncertainty following Lenin's death. While never stipulating an expiry date, Lenin had implied that Communists would have to tolerate private trading for a longer period than they were probably comfortable with. Perhaps inevitably, the question of whether to continue NEP became entangled with the issue of Soviet leadership succession in the Political Bureau, or "Politburo," as the party's ruling cabinet was called. No one, not even Trotsky, who usually took the most aggressive revolutionary line, had come out openly against NEP, although he had begun quietly hinting that Lenin's concessions might have gone too far and that the "socialist offensive" should resume. Lev Kamenev and Grigory Zinoviev, party bosses of Moscow and Leningrad, respectively, were wary of either repudiating Lenin or openly siding with Trotsky, who had made a catastrophic political error in failing to attend Lenin's funeral in January 1924. Nor did Trotsky participate in the Politburo meetings where the embalming of Lenin's body was planned out. His absence allowed Stalin to reap the benefits of organizing the elaborate rite that turned Lenin into a deity of Communism. Because Stalin controlled appointments in the party bureaucracy—hiring and firing—through its Organization Bureau (Orgburo), a job that won him the nickname "Comrade Card Index" (*tovarisch kartotekov*), he had little trouble isolating Trotsky, his most flamboyant rival, whose goateed features had turned him into a symbol of world revolution. Foolishly, Kamenev and Zinoviev, after helping Stalin destroy Trotsky as part of a short-lived Politburo "Triumvirate," began moving closer to Trotsky's critical "hard left" position on NEP in 1924–1925. It was therefore the logical move for Stalin to team up with the more NEP-tolerant Communists on the "right," such as Nikolai Bukharin, to see off his fellow Triumvirs. By 1925, NEP was on its second wind, while Trotsky, Kamenev, and Zinoviev, its failed "Left Opposition" critics who had lined up against the wishes of the deceased Lenin, were on the path to political oblivion.[9]

Despite appearances, Stalin had not really embraced NEP on principle. His alliance with Bukharin was purely tactical, allowing him to see off three dangerous political rivals. Unlike Trotsky, who had run the Red Army, and Kamenev and Zinoviev, who had urban political machines behind them, Bukharin had never taken on practical governing responsibility. A true Marxist intellectual, he was great at arguing his positions, becoming almost emotionally invested in doctrine—even if the doctrines he embraced did not always seem to line up coherently. A radical "left" Communist in the debates over whether to sign the Brest-Litovsk Treaty or launch a revolutionary war against Germany in January 1918, Bukharin had then become the party's foremost theoretician of War Communism, arguing in favor of what he called "'Extra-Economic' Coercion in the Transition Period." After Lenin embraced NEP in 1921, Bukharin shifted over to the "right." For the time being, Bukharin's defense of NEP was useful to Stalin, who let the party's leading thinker have his moment in the spotlight. Under War Communism, Bukharin explained in 1925, "we believed it possible to destroy market relations immediately with a single stroke. As it turned out, we will reach socialism only through market relations." Translated into the cruder language of party agitprop, this meant that Russia would grow into Communism gradually, achieving "socialism in one country"—rather than, as the discredited Trotsky had advocated, resuming the "socialist offensive" immediately while fighting for "permanent revolution" everywhere.[10]

Was a "Bukharin alternative" version of Communism ever real? Certainly the Soviet regime might have continued tolerating private trading in grain and consumer goods for a few years longer, even for the "decade" or more Lenin had spoken of. This might have allowed more scope for peasant smallholders to raise yields and produced genuine Russian, as opposed to forced or imported, technological innovation. It might also have allowed for more tolerance for dissent and, if not freedom in the Western sense, then at least something less than what Bukharin himself later denounced (shortly before being purged) as the "cruel, uncultured provincialism" of Stalin's "revolution from above." Bukharin's first Western biographer, the late historian Stephen Cohen of Princeton, quoted a Russian Communist dissident from the Brezhnev years as saying, "Without Stalin we [Communists] undoubtedly could have attained much greater success."[11]

Even granting Bukharin the benefit of the doubt, as Cohen suggests we should, the viability of his supposed "alternative" depended on the huge assumption that central planners and state collectives could improve on the output of private producers once Communists learned the secrets of capitalist production from them. As Bukharin explained, the goal of NEP was "not to trample the [nepman private trader] and close his shop, but . . . to produce and sell cheaper and better than [he]." Speaking to party activists in April 1925, Bukharin exhorted them to "enrich yourselves!" Once Gosplan had shown that "the state economy is better able to satisfy the daily demands and needs of the peasantry than is the private capitalist, private trader, private merchant, or private middleman," then peasants would willingly join lushly stocked state cooperatives, rather than bringing their produce to private markets. Russian capitalists and Russian Communists, Bukharin proposed, would compete to see who could achieve better economic performance.[12]

Bukharin should have been careful what he wished for. Scarcely three years into the "second wind" of NEP, signs were multiplying that peasants had little interest in the puny and unappealing consumer offerings of Russian state collectives. Although manufacturing was still expanding from the extremely low levels of 1920–1921, growth rates had leveled off, and the consumer sector in particular remained perishingly weak. Private retail sales, after rising gradually between 1924 and 1926, began dropping in 1927 and then fell off a cliff in 1928. In the wooden language of Communism, the economic downturn of 1927–1928 was referred to as a "scissors crisis," the idea being that the two scissor blades of the economy—agriculture and manufacturing—were diverging, according to a dialectical formula clever Communists could master. In reality, peasants were simply withholding their produce, as they had often done during the world war and revolution and civil war period, because there was so little to buy with the cash they could get for it.

Although farmers were growing enough grain to feed themselves, they were increasingly disinclined to ship it to market. In the fall of 1927, grain deliveries to state collection centers plummeted so severely—from 6.8 million tons the previous year to 4.8 million—that famine again threatened urban Russia.[13]

Bukharin, as the public face and theoretician of NEP, could not escape responsibility for the food shortages in Russia's cities. It did not help his case that Bukharin, as part of the Politburo shake-up, had replaced Zinoviev as head of the Communist International. The Comintern had a particularly rough year in 1927, when both Britain and China broke off relations with Moscow in retaliation for its meddling in their internal affairs. Once Stalin had completed the formal expulsion of his "Left Opposition" rivals, Trotsky and Zinoviev, from the Communist Party in December 1927 (Kamenev, though still in the party, was expelled from the Central Committee), there was no political reason for him to defend Bukharin. Realizing this, Bukharin meekly offered his own resignation, writing to Stalin, in June 1928, "I'll be prepared to go wherever you like, without any scuffles, without any noise and without any struggle." Though pleased to hear this, Stalin subjected Bukharin to plenty of abuse as he prepared to purge his last rival among the Old Bolsheviks of 1917 for "right deviation and conciliationism." A year later, having endured enough abuse and scapegoating, Bukharin and his two remaining loyalists on the Central Committee signed a forced confession of "error," stipulating that his "right deviation" had "turned out to be mistaken." Stalin's authority in the party was now supreme, just in time for the fulsome state celebrations of his fiftieth birthday on December 21, 1929, which marked the onset of the Stalin cult.[14]

Beyond the failure of state producers to outcompete the more nimble nepmen, NEP was always a political dead end for Communists. Stalin, a more experienced politician than Bukharin, knew this instinctively, and it is not surprising that he jettisoned the "Bukharin alternative" as soon as NEP became a serious political liability. Just as he and his advisers had done after the first wind of NEP in 1923–1924, Stalin ordered repression of private traders to ramp up after the terrible harvest figures came in for 1927, with his secret police (the GPU) arresting an astounding 2,687,000 nepmen in 1928 and 1929. Contrary to a widespread belief that the Soviet forced-labor-camp network, or Gulag (derived from the acronym for the Russian name of the Chief Administration of Corrective Labor Camps), dated to the Terror of the 1930s, it was actually the mass arrests of nepmen in 1928–1929 that midwifed it into existence. The arrested private traders supplied the bodies for the camps, which were built for the purpose of enforcing uncompensated corrective work "in industry, on construction projects, or in forestry work" (decree of March 26, 1928) and for "the development of the natural resources of the northern and eastern regions of the country" (June 27, 1929).[15]

At the Fifteenth Communist Party Congress, held in December 1927, Stalin reminded Russia's Communists that Lenin had never intended NEP to be permanent. The essential question of the Marxist dialectic, Stalin argued, was *Kto-kogo*, or *Who-whom*: Who would vanquish whom, Communism or private capital? To resume the offensive, he proposed the forcible collectivization of agriculture at a Central Committee plenum in July 1928. Part of his rationale was to secure a state-controlled grain reserve to feed Russia's cities and supply the Red Army in case of war with the capitalist world, but he also insisted—ominously, in view of Russia's already thin grain surpluses, which he freely admitted were running at less than half of prewar levels—that the state must also *export* grain in order to "import equipment for industry."[16]

Lenin had given up temporarily on planned state agricultural and industrial production under NEP. Stalin would now try to achieve both simultaneously. It took remarkable chutzpah to do this at a time when the vast majority, in fact nearly all, of Russia's prime farmland remained in private hands—and in far more peasant hands than ever before, as so many of the noble landlords of great estates had fled after the revolution. In theory, the new state grain collectives would be mechanized, deploying modern tractors in place of traditional wooden plows drawn by horses (or drawn by peasants themselves if they did not own horses), thereby fulfilling Marx's demand in the *Communist Manifesto* for "industrial armies" for agriculture. And yet the entire Soviet Union, the largest country on earth, with a predominantly rural population of some 150 million, possessed, in 1928, all of about 28,000 tractors, and was producing only 1,200 new ones a year. True, Stalin planned to "import agriculture machines, tractors and spare parts for them," along with regular industrial inputs, with the grain surplus he expected mechanized agriculture to produce. But this was putting the tractor before the horse cart, assuming exportable grain surpluses into existence based on a massive mechanization-modernization drive that had not happened yet.[17]

Posing an even bigger obstacle was the likely hostility of Russia's peasant farmers, who had put up such fierce resistance to the first effort to seize their meager grain surpluses in Lenin's time. Before relenting with NEP in 1921, Lenin had used the term *kulak* to describe recalcitrant peasant farmers who refused to turn over their produce to Bolshevik food-army requisitioners—and he did not mean it as a compliment.* In a now notorious telegram to Soviet officials in Penza province from August 1918 published after the fall of the USSR, Lenin had ordered that "the kulak uprising in your five districts must be crushed without pity. . . . You must

---

* Literally translated as "fist," the word *kulak* had acquired a colloquial meaning as "tight-fisted," an epithet used by socialists to stigmatize wealthy peasants or landowners as stingy "capitalists."

make an example of these people. Hang (I mean hang publicly, so that people see it) at least 100 kulaks, rich bastards, and known bloodsuckers. . . . Publish their names. . . . Seize all their grain. . . . Do all this so that for miles around people see it all, understand it, tremble." In a "top secret" instruction to the Politburo in March 1922, issued after he learned that peasant parishioners were resisting the Bolsheviks' campaign to loot Russia's churches, Lenin illustrated what the Communists' attitude should be toward "kulaks": "The present moment . . . offers us a 99% chance of overwhelming success in shattering the enemy [e.g., Russia's peasant masses] and assuring our position for decades. It is now and only now, when in the famine regions there is cannibalism, and the roads are littered with hundreds if not thousands of corpses, that we can (and therefore must) carry through the confiscation of Church valuables with the most rabid and merciless energy."[18]

The peasant masses of Russia and Ukraine were no more pleased to be conscripted into Stalin's forced march to industrialized state agriculture than they had been in Lenin's time. Stalin's own offensive began fitfully, with peasants arrested or deported, nepmen-style, for "taking part in commerce," that is, selling grain privately; or for employing hired hands and thus qualifying as petty capitalist "kulaks"; or, in a few cases, for possessing more than one samovar, the traditional Russian tea-brewing stove. Stalin made the war semiofficial when he demanded, on December 27, 1929, "the eradication of all kulak tendencies and the elimination of the kulaks as a class," leading to brutal repression in the countryside that sparked fierce peasant resistance. The GPU recorded 7,978 peasant revolts and mass protests in just the first three months of 1930, which cost Soviet state organs 1,500 casualties. Peasant resistance inspired the passage of ever-more-explicit Communist decrees that winter, such as one on the "elimination of kulaks as a class" in a Politburo resolution of January 6, 1930. Even a seemingly moderate Central

Committee resolution of April 2, 1930, stipulating the need for a tactical "alliance with the middle peasants" (i.e., those not quite poor, but not rich either), reaffirmed the imperative of "a merciless struggle against the kulaks" and demanded the "liquidation of bourgeois elements in the cities."[19]

In a notorious *Pravda* editorial in early March 1930, Stalin did hint, in the style of the pretend-remorseful authoritarian, that repression had gone too far. He condemned "the numerous abuses of the principle of voluntary collectivization" by local party bosses who were "drunk [or "dizzy"] with success." The temporary mass exodus from state collectives inspired by Stalin's fake *mea culpa* resulted in yet another round of state repression. That same month saw the first "deportation quotas" with numeric targets—for example, "60,000 kulaks of the first category"; "15,000 of the most diehard and active kulaks"; or 30,000 to 35,000 "kulak families." Like the nepmen before them, these unlucky kulaks—if they first survived summary shootings—were sent off to distant forced-labor camps, often in the inhospitable and frigid wastes of the Soviet arctic region, where they would be put to work in forestry, in road construction, or in the deadly and soon infamous construction of a canal 240 kilometers (150 miles) long linking the Baltic to the White Sea, which ultimately employed some 125,000 slave laborers allowed only hand tools for the task.[20]

By singling out the most productive peasant smallholders for "elimination" and confiscating their land and produce, Stalin's collectivization drive had catastrophic effects on the food situation in Ukraine, Russia's adjoining Black Earth region, and other grain-producing areas. By the winter of 1932–1933, a terrible famine had descended on the areas of "comprehensive collectivization" affecting more than 70 million people, from Ukraine through the Black Earth belt to the North Caucasus to Central Asia. Cannibalism was commonly observed in the Soviet secret police reports, particularly in Ukraine, where at least 3 million or 4 million victims starved to death, often in gruesome conditions. The tragedy is still remembered today as the "Holodomor," or "Terror-Famine."* Owing to lack of access to archives, historians are only now reckoning with the catastrophic results of collectivization elsewhere in the Soviet Union, such as in Kazakhstan, where as many as 2 million starved to death in 1932 and 1933. Stalin's collectivization drive destroyed the nomadic way of life in Soviet Central Asia, as the policy was, of course, designed to do.[21]

As if starting a new civil war with Russia's peasant masses in 1930 were not enough, Stalin simultaneously launched a great industrialization drive, meant to be capitalized by exporting the grain reserves he was squeezing out of the peasantry at gunpoint (though, in practice, more capital was raised by Soviet art and antiquities auctions). The First Five-Year Plan, launched in April 1929—though backdated to October–November 1928—aimed to turn Soviet Russia into a first-class industrial power in order to catch up with and then surpass its Western capitalist rivals. The stated goals were breathtaking, from 20 percent annual growth in industrial output to more specific targets in selected categories, such as 50,000 tractors a year, 17 million tons of pig iron, 200,000 cars and trucks, 50,000 tanks, and 40,000 warplanes per year. Graduates of the new Industrial Academy in Moscow would be the "shock brigades" of the "Red offensive" against capital, foot soldiers in a forced march to socialism, with the targets of each year's march set, raised, and then raised again. The pace of production was never enough for Stalin, who proposed the slogan "Five Years in Four."

---

* Owing to the lack of dramatized content, the Holodomor remained little known to the Western public until fairly recently. A film called *Mr. Jones*, telling the story of the Welsh journalist Gareth Jones who first broke the story in March 1933, came out in the winter of 2019–2020. Alas, the timing was not ideal, in a year when a global pandemic killed off public moviegoing.

The saying became so ubiquitous that kindergarten children would "march around their schools waving little banners and chanting" it:

> Five in four,
> Five in four,
> Five in four,
> *And not in five!*[22]

It might seem overambitious that Stalin would try to collectivize agriculture at the same time that he was embarking on an industrialization drive, but the first project fed the second. Seizing control of the country's grain supply was necessary to feed industrial workers, even while deported Russian and Ukrainian "kulaks" and Central Asian nomads, like the nepmen before them, furnished an almost bottomless supply of forced labor for Stalin's industrialization drive. Many famous Soviet "public works" projects, from the Baltic–White Sea Canal to the Moscow Metro, still used and admired by millions of daily riders today, were built by conscripted, unpaid workers—that is, slave laborers. Children worked, too, particularly on the collective farms, where the twelve-hour day was common for farmhands under fourteen, as in the worst days of the Industrial Revolution in England.[23]

Brutal as working conditions were in Stalin's merciless state-planned Communist economic system, the results were promising, at least in material terms. Annual growth rates approached 10 percent, if not 20 percent. The Siberian goldfields alone yielded about 100 million rubles' worth per year of salable bullion, which came in handy for importing foreign equipment and hiring foreign managers who demanded to be paid in hard currency. Colossal new electric utilities and mining combines soon graced (or marred) the landscape of eastern Ukraine, while tractor and auto factories sprouted up in the growing industrial suburbs of Moscow and Leningrad. Magnitogorsk, a fully planned Soviet industrial city near Orenburg, soon housed the largest iron- and steelworks in the entire world, employing nearly 250,000 people. Yekaterinburg, where Nicholas II and the Romanovs were murdered in July 1918, was now known for housing "Uralmash," the world's largest factory complex for the construction of heavy machinery. At least on the surface, the Soviet Union was the fastest-growing economy on the globe, putting the "capitalist" world to shame with its "full employment" policy. It even began attracting migrant laborers from the burgeoning ranks of the unemployed in Europe and the United States. True, Soviet laborers might not have been well paid by Western standards—many of them were not being paid at all—but they were *working*.[24]

For all the boastful agitprop about "building Communism" and "Five years in four," and the multiplication of economic planning ministries under VSNKh and then Gosplan (which grew from three in 1932 to twenty by 1939), the painful truth was that nearly all of Stalin's great new industrial works were modeled on or designed by Western capitalist firms. The State Institute for the Design of Metallurgical Factories (Gipromez) in Leningrad had the state monopoly, but its construction work was carried out by the Freyn Engineering Company of Chicago, Illinois. Magnitogorsk was designed by the Arthur G. McKee Corporation of Cleveland, Ohio, based on a prototype from Gary, Indiana. The MacDonald Engineering Company of Chicago supervised the construction of the four main Soviet cement combines. The gigantic new Soviet hydroelectric plant on the Dnieper River in Ukraine—likely the inspiration for the dam in the 1965 film *Dr. Zhivago*—was designed and built by the Hugh L. Cooper engineering firm of New York City. Russia's bauxite-mining and aluminum-smelting industry, critical in the construction of Soviet tanks and warplanes, was designed from scratch by Frank E.

Dickie of the American Alcoa Corporation. A Soviet chronicle of the First Five-Year Plan published in 1933, *Za industrializatsiiu*, admitted that it was "a combination of American business and science with Bolshevik wisdom" that had "created these [industrial] giants in three or four years." So ubiquitous were American "specialists" in Stalin's Russia that they had their own newspaper, the *Moscow News*, aimed at "American engineers, specialists and miners working in the USSR." Even the ubiquitous emblem of Stalinist central planning, the state collective farm, or *kolkhoz*, was modeled on a "capitalist" farm owned by Thomas Campbell, the "Wheat King" of Montana, which at 95,000 acres was sprawling enough to satisfy Stalin's grandiose vision of Marx's "industrial armies" in the countryside.[25]

If the material results of Stalin's industrialization drive were real, so was the price paid by millions of Soviet traders, peasants, and workers to achieve them. Whenever onerous production targets went unmet, "wreckers" and "saboteurs" were blamed, as if they had been spies from the capitalist world—notwithstanding the fact that the Communist government itself had recruited hundreds of foreign engineers and managers to design Stalin's new industrial combines. Fifty-three "bourgeois specialists" from the Shakhty region in the Ukrainian Donbass were put on trial in April 1928, and 11 of them were condemned to death. Another innovation in the "Shakhty show trial" was the use of children as witnesses to denounce their parents. In May 1929, 112 more "wreckers" were arrested at a metallurgical plant in Dnepropetrovsk. By 1931, the practice of rounding up industrial "saboteurs" had become institutionalized, with 7,000 of the country's estimated 35,000 trained engineers under arrest. The lethal flavor of the scapegoating was captured in the trial of "The Industrial Party" in November–December 1930. The defendants were engineers charged with "wrecking . . . the Five-Year Plan in order to produce an economic crisis." After the engineers, the economists and academics were hauled in, too, accused of "scientific-theoretical wrecking."[26]

As terrifying as the treatment of white-collar "wreckers" was, far more Gulag victims were snared up in Stalin's peasant collectivization drive—1,803,392 in 1930 and 1931 alone, according to the regime's figures. In addition to "kulaks," the GPU also rounded up "kulak accomplices" (*podkulachniki*)—that is, anyone who resisted state grain and livestock requisitions or helped the victims. The model informer was Pavlik Morozov, a thirteen-year-old Communist hero-martyr, replete with statues and memorials across the USSR, who was celebrated for having denounced his own father to the authorities. Thrown together in crowded cattle cars and shipped off to distant labor camps in the arctic Far North or the frigid far reaches of Siberia, peasant and nomad deportees were fortunate to survive the journey; many tens of thousands did not. Still more perished in the hours and days after arrival from simple frostbite. In one report sent to Stalin by a Communist official in Novosibirsk in southwestern Siberia in May 1933, we learn that out of a convoy of 6,114 deportees arriving in *late May*—far from the coldest time of year, and in one of the warmer and more hospitable areas of Siberia—"on the first day, 295 people were buried," and after that, the "daily mortality rate" mercifully declined to only about "35–40 people." It was not simply exposure to the cold that killed them, but the effects of incipient starvation, which led many desperately hungry deportees to ingest raw flour; some, as a result, "choked to death." "It was not long," the report to Stalin from Novosibirsk dryly concluded, "before the first cases of cannibalism occurred." In the first three months, nearly two-thirds of the deportees died, leaving only 2,200 alive by August 20.[27]

Those who survived the harrowing journey into Stalin's burgeoning Gulag network were put to work at backbreaking tasks; ill-fed; exposed unprotected to cold, sun, and wind; and driven to exhaustion by camp guards eager to pounce on anyone who slacked off or complained. One Polish Gulag survivor recalled that he "never came across a prisoner who had worked in the forest for more than two years." Those who survived one year might be transferred to brigades performing slightly easier work, but "from these they soon 'retired'—to the mortuary." At one camp, a deportee who worked in the "death registration office" observed that two filing cabinets, both "the height of a normal man," were "filled with three vertical stacks of death certificates." The Siberian goldfields at Kolyma and Chukotka were notorious for their horrendous work conditions. Death rates in Kolyma topped 50 percent in the early 1930s, reaching 70 percent by decade's end. As a survivor recalled typical Kolyma scenes, "a man pushing a wheelbarrow up the high runway . . . would suddenly halt, sway for a moment, and fall down. . . . And that was the end. Or a man, loading a barrow, prodded by the shouts of a foreman or a guard . . . would sink to the ground [and] blood would gush from his mouth." Nurses at the Kolyma camp infirmary, camp inmates themselves, could scarcely keep up with the intake of sick and wounded camp laborers, or *zeki*. As the survivor recalled, the real job of the "nurses" was "counting the dead who had escaped the misery of the gold mines." Crude hearses left every night, "piled high with naked bodies."[28]

As if the horrors of the Holodomor and Gulag were not enough, Stalin found yet more categories of people to punish for his regime's failures after the suspicious murder of Sergei Kirov, Zinoviev's successor as Leningrad party boss, on December 1, 1934. Many of the practices associated with the resultant "Great Terror" (c. 1936–1938), such as public show trials, had first emerged in the anti-NEP crackdown and "wrecker" trials of 1928–1931. Still, the escalation in the wake of the "Kirov affair" was unmistakable, ultimately engulfing the upper ranks of the Communist Party leadership, including "Old Bolsheviks" such as Kamenev, Zinoviev,

Radek, and Bukharin—who were hauled in for spectacular show trials that riveted the attention of Moscow (and bewildered its foreign residents) between 1936 and 1938—the secret police, and, after the downfall of Marshal Mikhail Tukhachevsky in May 1937, the Red Army. Charges leveled against Old Bolshevik defendants were a mishmash of political vituperation—conspiracies involving the long-exiled Trotsky and a "united Trotskyite-Zinovievite Center," insinuations of complicity in the Kirov murder, or alleged spying for a foreign power. Whether out of party loyalty, a sense of guilt for their own role in terrorizing the country, or because they had been tortured in the notorious cells of the Lubyanka prison, defendants invariably confessed all, enabling Stalin's prosecutor general, Andrei Vishinsky, to produce a guilty verdict for Stalin, which always concluded, "I recommend VMN—death by shooting." In a particularly sinister touch, the Soviet government published a decree in April 1935 extending the death penalty for "offenses against the state" to minors as young as twelve years old. This allowed Stalin to threaten political opponents with the murder of their children, in case guilt and torture were not enough to induce show-trial confessions.[29]

Numerous theories have been advanced to explain the Moscow show trials and "Great Terror" they inaugurated, from Stalin's alleged jealousy of Kirov (likely exaggerated), which may have led him to order the murder of his rival (an unproven case now suspected by scholars not to be true); to the hardening of Stalin's heart after the suicide of his second wife, Nadya Alliyuyeva, in November 1932 (plausible enough, but hardly definitive); to the Soviet leader "learning" from Hitler's purge of the fanatically Nazi Sturmabteilung (SA) in the "Night of the Long Knives," on June 30, 1934, that the best way to ensure loyalty in the violent milieu of totalitarianism was to keep everyone guessing by targeting even the truest of true believers. This last theory may help to explain some of the odder features of Stalin's Terror, including the execution of enthusiastic secret police chiefs such as Genrikh Yagoda (March 1938) and Nikolai Yezhov (February 1940), who were both drenched in the blood of Terror victims, or the arrests of the wives of loyal henchmen such as Marshal Budyonny (June 1937) and President M. I. Kalinin (October 1938). Many have proposed an ethnic animus on Stalin's part, in that whole national groups, such as Poles, Germans, and Koreans, were subjected to mass deportations (usually as alleged spies)—as many as 144,000 Poles were arrested in one operation, and 110,000 of them were executed. Indeed, despite the attention given to the Moscow show trials of mostly Russian "Old Bolsheviks," according to the historian Tim Snyder more than 90 percent of those executed for "political crimes" in 1937 and 1938, fully 625,483 out of 681,692, were targeted on national grounds or as "kulaks" (in the latter case meaning mostly Ukrainians).[30]

Significantly, victims targeted on an ethnic basis included Soviet Jews, despite Stalin's public disavowal of antisemitism as "an extreme form of racial chauvinism," and his claim, in a public interview with the Jewish Telegraphic Agency, that "under USSR law active anti-semites are liable to the death penalty." One scholar, reckoning between 500,000 and 600,000 Jewish victims of the Great Terror, has claimed that "the ratio of Jewish victims was probably the highest among all the Soviet nationalities," whether because of or despite the fact that so many architects of the Terror were themselves Jews, such as Yagoda, Operations Chief K. V. Pauker of the NKVD, and the secret policeman in charge of foreign espionage and executions, A. A. Slutsky. All three of these Jewish mass executioners had been executed themselves by 1938, as had myriad other Jewish party bosses, army officers, intellectuals, and—in an eerie foreshadowing of Stalin's postwar paranoia—several Jewish Kremlin doctors accused of poisoning or mistreating Soviet leaders.[31]

However outlandish some of the allegations now seem, the metastasizing Terror under a centralizing strongman like Stalin followed a certain logic systemic to Communism. Whether it was the violent suppression of the Constituent Assembly in January 1918, the unleashing of Red Terror after the assassination attempt on Lenin that fall, the Red Army rounding up Whites in Siberia in 1919 and Crimea in 1920, Trotsky crushing the Kronstadt rebels in 1921, the anti-NEP crackdowns of 1923–1924 and 1928–1929, or the murderous collectivization drives in Ukraine and Kazakhstan in the early 1930s, the template was broadly similar. Until the planned economic utopia was achieved, those standing in the way might become casualties in the war between Soviet Communism and its enemies, be they "capitalist" agents, spies of "imperialist" powers, industrial "wreckers," saboteurs, or mere troublemakers. "Class enemies" might unmask themselves by complaining about the seizure of their grain or livestock, the treatment of their loved ones, their workload or food rations, their lack of freedom of movement, or basic living standards: average living quarters, by 1937, had fallen to three square meters per person. It was common for 15 Soviet families to share an urban "communal" apartment with, as one state housing official noted, "an overflow . . . sleeping on boxes in the corridor, on the kitchen floor, on the common oven." In a damning verdict on the first decade of Stalin's Communist "offensive" and a crude gauge of its lethality, the Soviet census of 1937 came in at 162 million people, 15 million lower than expected. With black humor, Stalin had the census board arrested for "treasonably exerting themselves to diminish the population of the USSR."[32]

Of course, not everyone in the Soviet Union was suffering. One of the curious aspects of the Great Terror was that, by bringing low so many of the high and mighty of the Communist regime, Stalin provided a psychological release for ordinary Russians, who may have enjoyed seeing their tormentors suffer—or at least did not especially mind, so long as they and their loved ones remained untouched. Aleksandr Solzhenitsyn later recalled of the purges that "Black Marias [police vans] were going through the streets at night . . . [but] how could we know anything about those arrests and why should we think about them? Two or three professors had been arrested, but after all they hadn't been our dancing partners, and it might even be easier to pass our exams as a result. Twenty-year-olds . . . we were the same age as the Revolution, the brightest of futures lay ahead."[33]

Just as Solzhenitsyn suggested, social climbers could now climb into the dead boots of those purged or "disappeared." Kliment Voroshilov, the party hack "general" who directed Stalin's army purges, boasted in November 1938 that he had done away with 40,000 Soviet officers—and promoted 100,000 new men to replace them. Reliably Communist graduates of new technical academies might rise like meteors through the Soviet bureaucracy, such as V. A. Malyshev, a 1932 graduate of Moscow's Bauman Mechanical Engineering Institute, who was people's commissar for heavy machine construction by 1939, or A. N. Kosygin, who graduated from the Leningrad Textile Institute in 1935 and had become commissar of the textile industry by 1939 and a member of the Central Committee of the Communist Party. The star engineers and managers of Stalin's industrialization drive were given fancy new suits from party stores as the taste for "bourgeois" standards returned. The benefits even seemed to accrue to family life, with the early Soviet tolerance for divorce giving way to the idea that marriage had "positive value for the Soviet socialist state." Greater ceremony began to be attached to weddings, epitomized in the relegalization of gold wedding rings. With abortion, the shift was more dramatic still, from state-subsidized abortion-on-demand to an outright ban in 1936, in order to reverse a falling birth rate (in 1934 abortions had outnumbered live births in Moscow clinics by nearly 3 to 1,

154,000 to 57,000). To encourage productivity and family formation, Stalin declared the "equalization of pay" to be a "petty bourgeois prejudice" and approved salary increases for engineers, who
received four to eight times more pay than unskilled workers; and
managers, who might earn twenty or thirty times as much. Skilled
workers who outperformed norms were given bonuses, better
apartments, and more generous pensions. Labor mobility was not
unknown, although seeking a better job was made more difficult
by the introduction of internal passports (*propiski*) in 1932, which
meant that workers needed government permission to move from
town to town. This policy strongly encouraged party membership,
as advancement depended on ideological compliance as much as—
or more than—skill or productivity.[34]*

Still, despite the social mobility and increasingly "bourgeois" living standards of skilled workers, engineers, managers, and party
hacks, we should not exaggerate the material achievements of Soviet
Communism. A revealing snapshot of Soviet living standards was
compiled by two Russian-speaking British officers sent to Finland in early 1940, who interviewed a representative cross-section
of 2,075 Soviet war prisoners captured in the Soviet-Finnish or
"Winter War." "Twenty years of underfeeding," the officers concluded, had resulted in "a very low standard of physique and lack
of stamina." Interviewees expressed no patriotism or pride in the
achievements of Communism, showing only the "obvious fatalism"
of men who "accept the persecution in civil life and the brutal discipline of military life, the permanent shortage of food and clothes,
and the ordering, herding and hectoring by the Soviet state as being
the dictate of an unkind fate."[35]

---

* In a sign that party loyalty trumped engineering talent, the technical academy students who rose the furthest in the Communist hierarchy, such as Nikita Khrushchev
and Leonid Brezhnev, were mediocre students at best: Khrushchev dropped out of the
Moscow Industrial Academy in 1931.

Back home, even those fortunate Soviet subjects who avoided the perils of military service or the terrors of deportation were living under the kind of all-out mobilization conditions most countries saw only in the darkest depths of war and invasion. In June 1940, Gosplan, the Soviet Planning Ministry in charge of economic life across the entire USSR, extended the official workweek from six to seven days—eliminating even the token day of rest Russians had previously enjoyed on Saturdays (except when conscripted into unpaid *subbotnik* projects). In October 1940, Gosplan established a "strategic labor reserve" of Soviet teenagers between the ages of fourteen and seventeen, with an annual target of "800,000 to 1 million." Each of these teenage labor-draftees, after completing their training in advanced military-production techniques, was conscripted for *four years* of service in the Soviet war industry—at a time when the USSR was nominally at peace.[36]

Communism might have been advancing in Russia under Stalin's leadership, but at an almost unfathomable human price, and with a disappointing level of buy-in from the people being Communized—judging, at least, from the regime's forced-labor approach to economic production and its mass repression of sundry opponents. If Communism was to spread beyond the borders of the USSR, it would do so not by persuasion or example, but by force of arms.

9
HIGH NOON

COMMUNISM FROM PEAK TO TROUGH, AND BACK AGAIN

For all the failures of Communism at home, the Soviet government was considerably more successful in promoting its image abroad. In view of what we know today about the suffering of Holodomor and Terror victims, it is astonishing to reflect that this period of high Stalinism, c. 1928–1938, also marked a peak in Communist prestige internationally judged on almost any criterion, from the inward migration of Western laborers and managers to design and man Stalin's blast furnaces and factories to the singing of the regime's praises by Western "fellow travelers" such as George Bernard Shaw.* Communist party membership figures grew, as did the ranks of Western agents who enlisted to spy for Stalin—often

---

* It was Trotsky who first used the term *poputschiki*, or "fellow travelers," to describe the Western intellectuals who, despite never joining the Communist party, performed such useful service to Communism by praising the Soviet Union and its works abroad. By the 1930s, the phenomenon had become institutionalized, with the Soviet government inviting fellow travelers on "Potemkin village" tours of showcase industrial facilities and plants, carefully shielding them from any unpleasantries involving forced-labor camps or starving kulaks.

free of charge. For the fellow travelers and economic migrants, it was Stalin's forced-industrialization drive that drew them in, coupled with the slide of Western economies into the Great Depression in the early 1930s. For Communist party recruits and spies, it was more a matter of foreign affairs, as Hitler's German rearmament began to pose a threat after 1933. Stalin's belated decision to allow a "Popular Front" of left-wing parties against fascism after 1935, following a period when the Comintern Executive in Moscow had forbidden Communists from collaborating with socialists in any way, convinced sympathizers that supporting Soviet foreign policy was not just a matter of conscience, but a geopolitical imperative.[1]

The rising of Communist prestige in the West in the 1930s was welcome and extremely useful to the Soviet government. It did not necessarily reflect, however, any great perspicacity on Stalin's part. The Comintern did not abandon the hard-left line established at its Sixth Congress in 1928, which required Communists to denounce socialists as "social fascists" more dangerous than real ones, such as the Nazis, until the Seventh Congress met in July 1935—more than two years after Hitler had come to power. Not even after the Nazi crackdown on the KPD following the Reichstag fire of February 28, 1933, did Stalin ease up on "social fascists." To widespread surprise, four out of the five Communist defendants accused of setting the Reichstag fire were exonerated at the Leipzig trial in December 1933, including the Bulgarian Georgi Dimitrov, who was flown to Moscow on a special plane arranged by Hitler in February 1934 and became secretary of the Communist International. The USSR was the first government to sign a "non-aggression pact" with Nazi Germany, in May 1933. Even so, Hitler's persecution of Communists and other Nazi crimes against human decency, from book burnings to attacks on Jews, offered Communists such a perfect ideological counterfoil that not even Stalin's cooperation with Hitler could ruin it.[2]

Making it easier for Communists to pose as principled anti-fascist martyrs was the fact that the Soviet government made no public acknowledgment of the concentration camps in which it had been interning "enemies of the people" since 1918, or the burgeoning Gulag forced-labor network dating to 1928–1929, or the horrors of the Holodomor or Great Terror (aside from the Moscow show trials, which were defended by foreign Communists and some fellow travelers). While a few Soviet exiles lucky enough to escape the USSR, and several Western journalists brave enough to question the claims of government minders, such as Malcolm Muggeridge and Gareth Jones, published critiques of the Soviet famine-genocide, these accounts were drowned out by the pleasing lies of Stalin-friendly journalists such as Walter Duranty at the *New York Times*.[3]*

Hitler's aggressive posture abroad also made Stalin's diplomatic offensive in the Popular Front era far easier than it should have been. As with flagrant domestic repression in the wake of the Reichstag fire, Hitler scarcely bothered to conceal his foreign designs, from overturning the Versailles Treaty and repudiating the reparations burden imposed on Germany, to pursuing rearmament far beyond the limits imposed by the Allied Control Commission, to stirring up German "irredentist" minorities in Poland and Czechoslovakia with the aim of revising Germany's truncated postwar eastern borders. Combined with Nazi brutality at home, Hitler's rearmament drive and assertive foreign policy allowed Stalin and his Jewish commissar for foreign affairs, Maxim Litvinov, to pose as principled opponents of Nazi German aggression. Making Litvinov's job

---

* Neither Duranty nor the *New York Times* ever returned the Pulitzer Prize he was given for his whitewashing of the famine ("Russians are hungry, but not starving," he wrote at the height of the famine on March 31, 1933). Duranty was finally given the treatment he deserved in a sinister performance by Peter Saarsgard in the 2020 film *Mr. Jones*, which salutes Gareth Jones for his courage in exposing the Holodomor (though exaggerating his scoop—in fact, Malcolm Muggeridge broke the story first, as Jones himself graciously acknowledged at the time).

still easier, Hitler voluntarily withdrew Germany from the League of Nations in October 1933, confessing his hostile intent toward the status quo—to be replaced, with elegant symmetry, by Stalin's USSR, which joined the League of Nations in September 1934. By the time the Popular Front was announced in Moscow in July 1935, Stalin had already won the public relations battle with Hitler, with his once pariah state devoted to world Communist revolution entering the ranks of international respectability even as Nazi Germany was thrust out into the cold.[4]

The Popular Front was a godsend for Soviet foreign relations. Even the countries most hostile to Communism saw an explosion of sympathy with the USSR. In the United States, which had recognized Stalin's government only in November 1933, the Soviet Union gained support especially after October 1935, when the once-tiny Communist Party USA, or CPUSA, received instructions from Moscow about the new "Popular Front" doctrine. The new policy meant, among other things, that Communists no longer had to denounce the wildly popular US president, Franklin Delano Roosevelt, as a "fascist." Coupled with this concession to political reality, the plausible (though dubious) idea that Stalin's USSR was the most principled opponent of Hitler's Germany seduced thousands of Americans into the Communist orbit. While many of these were "fellow-traveling" sympathizers who showed up at a few meetings, many others were card-carrying party members (the number of the latter had risen from 13,000 to 80,000 by 1938). Still others were paid Soviet informants working inside the US government: according to contemporary NKVD records, there were 221 of these, though, according to the "Venona" telegrams later decrypted by US intelligence, there may have been as many as 329. The most highly placed Soviet spies were Alger Hiss, who headed the Office of Special Political Affairs in the State Department from 1936 to 1947, where he had access to classified material relating to

US military strategy, and Harry Dexter White, assistant secretary and second-in-command at the Treasury Department under Henry Morgenthau, a close friend of President Roosevelt's.[5]

Although President Roosevelt's hands were tied, owing to congressional and public opposition, from forging an alliance with Moscow, he strove to improve relations. In November 1936, the president appointed a full-throated Soviet sympathizer, Joseph Davies, as his ambassador in Moscow, after his predecessor, William Bullitt Jr., had become openly critical of the Moscow show trials. Davies would make no such mistake, fawning over Stalin as "a greater leader than Catherine the Great, than Peter the Great, a greater leader even than Lenin." Inviting Stalin to intervene in US foreign policymaking, Davies warned him that President Roosevelt was "surrounded by reactionary elements." Taking Davies's hint, Roosevelt's undersecretary of state, Sumner Welles, purged "Stalin-phobes" in the State Department's East European Affairs Division in 1937. The division's library of Soviet newspapers and journals was dismantled.[6]

The Comintern made huge Popular Front strides in Britain, too, despite Downing Street then being in the hands of the Conservative governments of Stanley Baldwin (1935–1937) and Neville Chamberlain (1937–1940). It was the heyday of Soviet espionage in Britain, headlined by the "Cambridge Five": Anthony Blunt, Guy Burgess, John Cairncross, Kim Philby, and Donald Maclean. The real number of Soviet agents was not five but ten, including also James Klugmann, Michael Straight, Leo Long, Tom Wylie, and Alistair Watson. These "Cambridge spies" infiltrated the top ranks of the British establishment, including the Foreign Office (Maclean), MI6 (Philby and Burgess), the BBC (Burgess again), British army intelligence (Klugmann), and the War Office (Wylie, who supplied classified information to Burgess and Philby). By 1939, as official MI6 historian Christopher Andrew later reported, "the volume of high-grade intelligence [these men] supplied was to become so large that Moscow sometimes had difficulty coping with it."[7]

Meanwhile, in France and Spain, broad "anti-fascist" coalitions of the Left actually came to power in 1936. In the case of Spain, this brought Communists answering to ECCI in Moscow into a Western ruling cabinet for the first time. True, Communists had little real influence over policy, at least at first. In a sign of the continued wariness of European socialists abused for so long as "social fascists" by their Communist rivals, the French Popular Front government of Léon Blum refused to appoint a single Communist to head a government ministry. Nor did Blum offer financial or armed support for France's neighboring Popular Front government in Spain, which *did* have two Moscow-aligned Communist ministers in it, after General Francisco Franco's nationalist forces rebelled against Madrid in July 1936, owing to a growing wave of wild-cat strikes, property seizures, attacks on churches and monasteries, and general anarchy across the country. Blum's refusal to support his politically aligned Left Popular Front government in Madrid offered Stalin yet another opportunity to promote Communism— by embracing the "Republican" cause in Spain. As with the belated Comintern shift to anti-fascism, it was not prescience on Stalin's part that produced the Spanish opportunity. In fact, Moscow did not even have diplomatic relations with Madrid at the time of Franco's rebellion, which meant that the Spanish government's request for arms, after being denied by Blum, had been kicked over to the Soviet embassy in Paris.[8]

If Stalin was not always a Nostradamus of international politics, however, he knew how to capitalize on an opportunity when a door was opened up for him. Not only did Soviet backing of the Republican cause earn the USSR huge popularity and prestige on the left in Europe and America, but it proved to be a gold mine for Stalin's government in the literal sense. Unlike Hitler and Mussolini, who allowed Franco to purchase arms on credit, thus giving them a vested interest in him winning the war (so they could recoup payment), Stalin insisted on payment up front, and not in soggy paper, or even hard Western currencies, but in gold. By the end of 1936, he had secured 463 tons of bullion from Franco. In exchange, Moscow sent 320 Soviet warplanes, 350 tanks, 1,900 guns, 15,000 machine guns, 500,000 rifles, and 250 grenade launchers to Spain. This was a substantial number of arms, and sorely needed, but not the all-out commitment Madrid might have expected after handing the country's gold reserves over, and Soviet war supplies largely dried up after the first war winter of 1936–1937. Stalin did send 2,082 Soviet troops and military technicians—again a significant number, but only a fraction of the military manpower that Hitler's Germany (16,000) and Mussolini's Italy (70,000) had devoted to Spain—and of these 2,082, only 700 or 800 would remain permanently in Spain.[9]

More significant for the spread of Communist influence in Spain was the fact that Stalin blanketed the country with political advisers and spies, who infiltrated the Spanish government and military leadership and seized political control of Republican Spain. To some extent, the ruthlessness of the purges in Spain during its Civil War period owed to the unfortunate timing of the war, coinciding as it did with the acceleration of the Great Terror in the USSR. The Soviet army purges at home kicked off in May 1937 with the spectacular downfall of Mikhail Tukhachevsky, civil war hero and marshal of the Soviet Union, after the annual May Day parade—the same month that saw bloody street fighting in Barcelona. The events in Barcelona, in turn, kicked off a brutal Soviet-directed purge of "Trotskyists" and anarchists from Spanish Republican forces, which left something like 500 dead and 1,000 wounded. George Orwell, a socialist who had enlisted in the allegedly "Trotskyist" Spanish militias, wrote a searing memoir account of the Republican "tragedy," *Homage to Catalonia*, which helped inform popular accounts of the Spanish Civil War, such as those of Hugh Thomas. Orwell and Thomas popularized the idea of "two Spanish Counter-Revolutions," one Franco's, the other the Communists', who snuffed out the early idealism of the Republican cause of Spanish socialists, anarchists, and foreign volunteers in the "International Brigades." The Communists, we are told, clamped down on property seizures and popular militias, bringing "an end to the social revolution" that had spread across Spain in 1936, in the interest of military and political discipline.[10]

There is some truth in this story of the Soviet betrayal of the Spanish Revolution, but more that is obscured. Setting aside the always questionable idea, first propagated by Orwell and other wide-eyed Western volunteers, that the chaotic property seizures (i.e., thefts), manor and monastery burnings, and often violent assaults on churches, priests, and nuns that erupted in Spain in 1936 represented a lost socialist Eden before Stalin's men arrived and put a halt to "innocent" revolutionary idealism, the lasting importance of the Soviet intervention in Spain lay not in ephemeral decisions on the political line of the day, but in the institutional innovations for Communism. International Brigades for Spain, like the fellow travelers, were useful up to a point, but political fashions like this came and went; it would hardly do for Moscow to rely on volunteers. Nor did Stalin's people in Spain trust the International Brigades, which were all fully infiltrated by Soviet minders. These Soviet insiders kept personnel files on every volunteer (including those in the American "Abraham Lincoln Battalion") and purged the brigades of unreliables, from drunkards and deserters to "fascist spies and Trotskyites." There were two Spanish prisons used to house renegade International Brigade volunteers. Eventually, over 500 of the volunteers were put to death—a small but significant fraction of the 10,000 to 15,000 political prisoners executed by Moscow's puppet Republican government during the war.[11]

The point of these Spanish Republican purges, however genuinely terrifying to once-naïve volunteers like Orwell (who himself escaped arrest and fled Barcelona before it was too late), was not a paradoxical Communist "counter-revolution," but to ensure Madrid's compliance with the ECCI as Moscow established a "democratic parliamentary republic of a new sort," or "people's democracy," in Spain, the evolving prototype of what would later be called "people's republics" in Eastern Europe, Korea, and China. The novel element in Spain involved an established "Republican" government with non-Communist cabinet members. Neither of the two premiers who held power in Madrid from the fall of 1936 until Franco's victory in March 1939, Francisco Largo Caballero or his successor Juan Negrín (handpicked by Stalin's agents), were Communist Party members. Spain thus maintained a facade of "bourgeois" parliamentary democracy even as shadowy Communist advisers and agents—some Spanish, some foreign European, some Soviet Russian—ruled behind the scenes. Stalin really did introduce to the world a "democratic parliamentary republic of a new sort" in Spain—that is, a sham Communist one, answering to Moscow. True, the experiment failed in the end, just as the Soviet Republics in Bavaria and Hungary had, but this was due to Franco's thumping military victory in March 1939, not to flaws in the political model as such. In longevity, the Communist-dominated Spanish Republic had outlasted Béla Kun's Hundred Days by two years. If the Soviets could improve their clients' military performance, the next "people's democracy" might last longer still.[12]

The success of Communism as a political doctrine, as shown in the Red victory in the Russian Civil War, the rapid Soviet defeat in Bavaria, Kun's slightly less swift collapse in Hungary, and the slower-burn failure in Spain, depended ultimately on the force of arms. Stalin, a keen student of history and politics, understood this intuitively, which is why almost the entire Soviet economy had been on war footing since the inauguration of the First Five-Year Plan in 1928. The production targets of the Third Five-Year Plan, launched in 1938, were mind-bogglingly ambitious, envisioning the production of 50,000 warplanes annually by 1942–1943, along with 125,000 air engines and 700,000 tons of aerial bombs; 60,775 tanks; 119,060 artillery systems; 450,000 machine guns; 5.2 million rifles; 489 million artillery shells; 120,000 tons of naval armor; 1 million tons of explosives; and 298,000 tons of chemical weapons. Although not all of these targets were met, progress in some critical areas was striking, with annual production of warplanes ramping up from 4,270 in 1936 to 10,362 by 1939.[13]

Roping in new party members, fellow-traveling sympathizers, and International Brigade volunteers with Popular Front "anti-fascism" was well enough, but Stalin never lost sight of the ultimate purpose of the Comintern, outlined in number 14 of the "21 Conditions" for member parties: foreign Communists were to "give every possible support to the Soviet Republics in their struggle against counter-revolutionary forces." In an elegant, if cynical, demonstration of the logic of this Comintern rule, Stalin used the gold bullion he acquired from Madrid in 1936–1937 to modernize the Soviet Air Forces, developing a DB-3 bomber after a million-dollar deal with the Glenn L. Martin Company of Baltimore and purchasing a license to build a Soviet version of the DC-3 transport plane from Douglas Aircraft of Southern California for $207,500. Stalin also placed expensive new Soviet aviation orders with European firms such as Renault (for warplanes and aviation engines), Ratier Figeac (aviation propellers), and Hotchkiss (plane-mountable machine guns). It was at least in part due to these new foreign acquisitions that Soviet warplane production took such a dramatic leap forward in 1938–1939, just as Europe stood on the precipice of war.[14]

More cynically still, though wholly in line with Comintern logic, Stalin began negotiating arms deals with Nazi Germany in the winter of 1938–1939, even as Franco's German-supplied forces were rolling up his beleaguered clients in Spain. On January 28, 1939, Stalin's commissar of foreign trade, Anastas Mikoyan, and his defense commissar, Klim Voroshilov, presented the German government with a military-technological wish list *seventeen pages long*, including 112 items judged to be priorities for Soviet military modernization. On the list were "four complete fighter and bomber prototypes, seven engine designs, thirteen different machine gun and bomb designs, nine types of laboratory equipment, and ten kinds of optical and electrical equipment."[15]

Stalin's wish list for German military technology was not the only sign he was growing impatient with the strategic limitations of the Popular Front. True, by showing up the passive "liberal democracies" in Spain Stalin had won press accolades in the West. His Jewish foreign affairs commissar, Maxim Litvinov, had helped win praise for the Soviet Union in the press as well, by loudly championing "collective security" against Nazi Germany. This was especially the case after Britain and France succumbed to Hitler's intimidation at Munich in September 1938, enabling Germany to absorb the Czech Sudetenland without a fight. Following this act of craven appeasement, Stalin and Litvinov might have won still more prestige had they backed up, or surpassed, British prime minister Neville Chamberlain's soon-notorious guarantee of "Polish independence" in the House of Commons on March 31, 1939. But they did no such thing. Baldly, on April 1 Litvinov informed Britain's ambassador in Moscow that Britain "could pursue [its] own [Polish] policy: the Soviet Government would stand aside." Stalin wanted no part of Chamberlain's Polish guarantee.[16]

The reason was not hard to fathom for anyone familiar with Soviet history. The USSR had never recognized Poland's eastern borders as legitimate, accepting the verdict of the Soviet-Polish War of 1920, which had deprived the USSR of thousands of square miles of territory east of the Curzon Line and 3 million inhabitants, only as a second Brest-Litovsk, a tactical retreat allowing the Red Army to finish off General Pyotr Wrangel's forces then encamped in Crimea. Stalin himself, at the time the Red Army's political commissar on the southwestern front, had felt this Polish defeat keenly, and he was determined to avenge it. As early as February 1938, the head of the European desk in the Soviet Commissariat of Foreign Affairs, V. P. Potemkin, informed the Bulgarian minister in Moscow that Stalin might be interested in a partition of Poland. "Hitler aims to let Poland loose against the Soviet Union," Potemkin wrote in an April issue of the Soviet theoretical journal *Bol'shevik*. The Polish would inevitably be defeated, but this would "clear the pathway [eastward] for Germany": "So let the Polish army be shattered. Let [Poland] again, as in 1920, begin to tremble under the hooves of the Soviet columns," Potemkin said. "Hitler wants Poland ground to dust between the millstones. . . . He is preparing [Poland's] fourth partition. Let history be repeated." In November 1938, *Izvestiya* argued in favor of a Polish partition plan whereby the northeastern section would join Soviet Belorussia, eastern Galicia would be annexed to Soviet Ukraine, and the area west of the Vistula would be assigned to Germany. The partition of Poland was Stalin's idea, not Hitler's.[17]

Of course, for Stalin to court arms deals and Polish partitions with Adolf Hitler—sponsor of Franco and bête noire of socialists, liberals, and progressives across the Western world—threatened to undermine all the political gains Communists had achieved in the Popular Front era. For this reason, negotiations between Berlin and Moscow remained secret well into 1939. There was no formal announcement that the Popular Front was dead in the wake of Franco's routing of Republican forces in March, no Comintern

Congress heralding a new political line. Communist and Nazi propaganda messaging alike remained opaque, a matter of symbolic moves. When Stalin sacked his Jewish Foreign Affairs commissar, Litvinov, for example, on May 3, replacing him with his right-hand man, the gentile Vyacheslav M. Scriabin (who had taken the name "Molotov," meaning "Hammer," as a pseudonym), Hitler responded to the gesture two days later by ordering his own propaganda chief, Joseph Goebbels, to instruct Nazi journalists to suspend their "sharp attacks on the Soviet Union until they received new instructions." At least publicly, Stalin remained open to negotiations with the Western powers, which, in the wake of Hitler's absorption of rump Czechoslovakia (alongside Poland and Hungary, which also seized Czech territory) in March 1939, were increasingly desperate to recruit possible allies against Hitler. Significantly, however, Stalin signaled his own aloofness by instructing his representatives in Paris and London to "leave the initiative to the British and French."[18]

At least until Hitler's foreign minister, Joachim von Ribbentrop, flew into Moscow on August 23, 1939, and was given the red-carpet treatment by Stalin and Molotov, it was possible for Western Communist sympathizers to believe in the promise of a Popular Front against Nazi Germany. For all his authoritarian tendencies, Stalin had apparently turned the USSR into an industrial-military juggernaut with his Five-Year Plans. Meanwhile, the Western liberal democracies had exposed their impotence by allowing Hitler to rearm, march troops into the Rhineland (March 1936), absorb Austria in the "Anschluss" (March 1938), and seize the Sudetenland (October 1938), and then rump Czechoslovakia (March 1939). Britain, France, and the United States had left the Spanish Republic in the cold while Stalin had taken up the fight against Franco, suggesting that Soviet Communism had both principles and the arms to back them up. True, anyone with knowledge of the brutal xenophobia animating the Great Terror, or able to parse Soviet press reports for Stalin's hints about foreign policy revanchism, would have been skeptical about Stalin's alleged commitment to "collective security"—a word that nowhere appears in the *Short Course*, a kind of "bible" of Communism Stalin published in 1938, officially titled *History of the All-Union Communist Party (Bolsheviks)*. (He instead spoke of a "new period" in world affairs, declaring that the "Second Imperialist War has actually begun.") But for the casual observer of European news in England or North America, who had either a predisposed sympathy to Communism or little curiosity about how it really worked in practice, it was not unreasonable to view Stalin's USSR as a likeable protagonist and critical ally against Nazi Germany once Hitler began making his aggressive moves on the European chessboard.[19]

The news of the Moscow Pact of Non-Aggression Between Nazi Germany and Soviet Russia, more commonly known as the Molotov-Ribbentrop Pact—trumpeted in the world press after its signing in the Kremlin on August 23, 1939—was therefore a bombshell not just for the peace of Europe, but for the international image of Communism. True, the secret clauses dividing up Poland, the Baltic states, Finland, and Romania into spheres of influence were not announced to the world, but the "non-aggression" clauses were published proudly in *Pravda* as well as in Berlin, suggesting that Poland, at least, was in danger of imminent invasion. But Stalin's government was now hitched to Hitler, requiring Communists to defend Nazi Germany even as much of the world recoiled in horror at Germany's actions. In a speech on August 31, 1939, laying down the Comintern line, Molotov blamed the European war that was about to break out on British imperialists, who he said had been trying for years to "embroil Germany and Soviet Russia in war, in order to kill two birds with one stone." Instead, the Soviets had turned the table on the Western imperialist powers with their "peaceful" non-aggression pact. Anyone who criticized the Molotov-Ribbentrop Pact, Molotov instructed Communists to say, was a "warmonger, trying to bring about a global bloodbath."[20]

Not every Communist was loyal enough to Moscow to swallow this hogwash without retching. In France, where the ECCI line required members of the French Communist Party to defend Hitler and the Nazis *even after the Germans invaded France in May 1940*, up to and including passing out antiwar leaflets to soldiers and sabotaging French munitions factories, hundreds of Communists, including 21 of the party's 73 parliamentary deputies, tore up their party membership cards in disgust. (On the other hand, 2,500 French party members were deprived of their municipal posts, and another 3,000 were arrested for treasonous support of the German invader.) The political price Communists paid for endorsing German armed aggression was not quite as obvious in a neutral country, as the United States was at that time, but even so, the party's dramatic membership growth during the Popular Front era, which had peaked at nearly 80,000 in 1938, reversed sharply after Stalin's unsightly deal with Hitler was made public, plummeting below 50,000.[21]

Still, despite the political disadvantages for Communist recruitment abroad, the Moscow Pact made possible the most dramatic Soviet territorial and material gains since the Civil War. After invading an almost prostrate Poland on September 17, 1939, whose armed forces had been largely obliterated by the German Wehrmacht and Luftwaffe, the Red Army rolled up Stalin's promised eastern half of the country, not only reconquering territory lost to Poland in 1920 but going well beyond the Curzon Line. As Molotov boasted in a speech to the Supreme Soviet in October 1939, in Stalin's undeclared war against a largely undefended country, which cost the Red Army only about 737 dead and 1,862 wounded, the USSR had enlarged Soviet Belorussia by 108,000 square kilometers

(41,700 square miles), on which lived 4.8 million people, and "Western Ukraine" by 88,000 square kilometers (34,000 square miles), on which lived another 8.4 million.[22]

Stalin's 13 million new subjects in what had been eastern Poland could now enjoy the same advantages of Communism his other subjects had been enjoying. Just as in Russia in 1917, the first priority was the banks. In Polish Galicia (now "western Soviet Ukraine"), *Pravda* reported in March 1940, the Soviet occupiers took over 414 banking and 1,500 credit institutions, "opened the vaults[,] and helped themselves to the greater part of the contents deposited there." In the more rural area of formerly Polish "western Belorussia," Soviet occupation brought a reenactment of the Holodomor: private landholdings were divided up into 605 collective farms, and local farmers and peasants were herded onto them. Naturally, there was resistance to these policies, which gave the occupiers cause to set up special occupation tribunals and round up resisters and "class enemies" for deportation to Stalin's Gulag camps, where Polish prisoners were put to work building roads and military bases near the new frontier with Hitler's Reich—or, in more sensitive cases involving high-ranking politicians and military officers, farther east in the remote areas of northern Russia and Siberia, usually to work in forestry. Over the next eighteen months, nearly 1.5 million unfortunate Polish souls (including Polish Jews, many of whom fled the German occupation zone hoping for better treatment in the USSR) were shipped eastward into Stalin's Gulag network. An idea of the scale of the Polish deportations can be gleaned from a Politburo resolution from December 1939 stipulating that captured Polish officers and other prisoners assigned to work in forestry would be distributed in Siberia on the basis of "100 to 500 families per village."[23]

Because much of the world's attention was focused on the "official" German invasion of Poland, which had led Britain and France to declare war on Germany on September 3, 1939 (though doing almost nothing to help Poland), Stalin paid little price for his Polish invasion. Britain's War Cabinet refused to issue even a diplomatic protest or withdraw its ambassador from Moscow (the French ambassador did submit a mild protest note). Stalin might have lost Western sympathizers by signing a pact with Hitler, but he had avenged the Soviet defeat of 1920, expanded the USSR's borders westward, acquired millions of new subjects and slave laborers, and avoided incurring hostilities with Britain and France, both of them at war with Nazi Germany (and hoping to defeat or at least seriously weaken it), and had not even received a slap on the wrist for it.[24]

Stalin was not quite so lucky when he tried to move against Finland, which the Molotov-Ribbentrop Pact had assigned to the Soviet sphere of influence. The Finnish government, to Stalin's shock, refused his demands for territory, and the Soviets invaded Finland on November 30, 1939—only for this to bog down into a quagmire. By December, Soviet losses were running at 70 percent in many units, and wounded Russians had overwhelmed the hospitals of Leningrad: one overworked Soviet surgeon complained that he was treating 400 wounded Red Army soldiers a day. In the first two weeks of January 1940, Stalin received twenty-two NKVD reports on army discipline problems, which prompted the creation of his infamous disciplinary NKVD battalions (*kontrolno-zagraditel'nyie otryadyi*) inside each Red Army unit. Made public on January 24, 1940, to enhance their deterrent effect on desertion and a growing epidemic of Russian "self-wounding," the disciplinary battalions did ultimately shore up Soviet fighting morale in Finland. But the human price was horrific, and the advent of NKVD terror battalions, once word of them spread, damaged Communist prestige. As one Swedish volunteer told a British journalist, "The Russian soldiers [are] being driven forward like cattle with machine guns behind them, and they were stumbling forward hiding their faces with their arms and the Finns just mowed them down." "The whole world is watching us," Stalin admonished his generals on January 7. "If we get stuck in the face of such a weak opponent, that will arouse the anti-Soviet forces of imperialist circles." Declining Soviet prestige took concrete form in December 1939 when the USSR was expelled from the League of Nations—the first country so punished. As the general secretary dryly observed, "Germany, Italy and Japan had at least the decency to resign from the League before committing flagrant aggressions."[25]

Staring defeat in the face, Stalin cut his losses in Finland. First he reshuffled the Red Army command, appointing Semyon Timoshenko, who had helped direct the brutal mop-up operations in eastern Poland in September 1939, to command a new army group massing nearly 600,000 troops into the narrow Karelian Isthmus. Giving up on a war of maneuver, Timoshenko bludgeoned the Finns into submission, losing nearly 200,000 men by the end of February 1940—but "gnawing through." Stalin then surprised the world by suing for peace on March 12 on terms milder than expected, acquiring the Karelian Isthmus, where the worst fighting had taken place—though, as a Soviet general lamented, it was only "just about enough ground to bury [the] dead."[26]

Meanwhile, Stalin used the smokescreen of the Soviet-Finnish war—and the threat of Allied intervention, embodied in British surveillance flights over Soviet oil installations and refineries in Baku and Batumi—to order a purge of Polish officers and elites who had been deported to labor camps in the fall of 1939 to preempt a fifth column in case Britain and France declared war on the USSR. The "Katyn Forest massacre" (named after the forest where the bodies were dumped, although the executions took place elsewhere) was not carried out until April 1940, after the Finnish war was over, but NKVD Directive No. 794/B was signed by NKVD chief Lavrenty Beria on March 5. It sentenced 25,700 Polish elites to the "highest measure of punishment—execution." Beria's executioners complied, though not quite meeting the target ("only" 22,892 Poles were executed, 15,000 of them military officers). Still, Beria and Stalin, nothing if not thorough, had NKVD squads track down the wives and children of executed Poles, 60,667 in all, and deport them to special labor camps in Kazakhstan. For good measure, another 78,000 Polish nationals who had been granted refugee status in 1939, so loyal to Poland they had refused to accept Soviet citizenship, were rounded up and sent to Gulag camps. Some 84 percent of these victims, along with 8 percent of the Katyn Forest victims, were Polish Jews.[27]

The very brutality of the Finnish war, though hardly a boon to Soviet military prestige, greased the wheels for Stalin's next moves in his efforts to expand the boundaries of Communism in Europe. In June 1940 he turned his attention to the three Baltic states and Romania—but their leaders, after witnessing the terrible suffering of Poland and Finland, submitted to Stalin's bullying almost without resistance. It helped the Soviets that, just as in Poland in September 1939, world media attention was focused on the unfolding drama in France as the German armies approached Paris: it was on the day Paris fell (June 14, 1940) that Molotov submitted Stalin's ultimatum to Estonia, Latvia, and Lithuania, accusing these tiny states of making "war preparations" against the USSR. On the next day, 300,000 Soviet troops entered Lithuania, a country of 2 million, and the Soviet fleet sealed off all Baltic ports in case anyone tried to escape by sea. Between June 16 and 18, the Red Army crashed into Latvia and Estonia. On June 21, Stalin had Timoshenko draw up orders to commanders of the Red Army's new Baltic military district to "disarm the population" and to "shoot anyone who resist[ed]." Stalin then assigned three NKVD chiefs who had "blooded" themselves in the Terror to rule over these former countries: Andrei Vishinsky, the public prosecutor of the Moscow show trials, was assigned to Latvia; Stalin's loyal stooge Andrei Zhdanov was given Estonia; and Beria's trusted Georgian aide Vladimir Dekanozov would run Lithuania. The state gold reserves of Estonia, Latvia, and Lithuania were "nationalized."[28]

Then the purges began. A typical NKVD directive of July 7, 1940, targeted Lithuanians: "Preparatory to liquidation. Active abolition of the leading influence of parties hostile to the State." Those arrested were often brutally tortured. As Juozas Viktoravicius later recalled of his treatment in a Kaunas jail, "My hands were put into iron chains and wrenched. . . . [W]ith their thumbs they squeezed my abdomen, with a press they repeatedly struck my shoulders and tore at the injured places. . . . [T]hey noosed my sex organs with a piece of cord and pulled at them." "Questioned" like this for *forty-five hours*, Viktoravicius fainted repeatedly before having his hands and feet bound and being dropped "into cold water in the basement of the NKVD building," left for dead. As an Estonian woman recalled of the terrible summer of 1940, "People began disappearing at night and were never seen again." "Night after night," a Latvian witness recalled, "the dreaded black vans of the secret police raced through the streets. . . . [H]undreds upon hundreds of men, women and children were spirited away into the vastnesses of the Soviet Union." At least 34,250 Latvians were either killed or vanished without a trace, more than 2 percent of the country's population.[29]

Romania was next in line. On June 26, 1940, Molotov handed Romania's ambassador an ultimatum, giving Romania twenty-four hours to pull troops back from the Soviet border and cede Bessarabia to the USSR. On June 28, the Red Army rolled into Romania, allowing Stalin to seize 51,000 square kilometers (19,700 square miles) of territory and another 3.7 million "proletarian" subjects, as Molotov crowed in the Supreme Soviet. In just over ten days, counting the Baltic annexations, Stalin had acquired 10 million new subjects for Communism, on top of the more than 13 million he had acquired the previous fall in eastern Poland (minus those crushed underfoot in the invasions, executed, or tortured to death). The "Ukrainian and Moldavian inhabitants" of the new Soviet province known as "Moldavia SSR," Molotov added proudly, would now enjoy "the blessings of Communism"—from the nationalization of banks, factories, and farms to mass arrests: 200,000 Romanians were taken into custody in July, the first of 300,000 deported to Soviet Gulag camps by the end of 1940.[30]

It had been a heady year for Communist expansion. But there were warning signs on the horizon, beginning with the lopsided outcome of the European war, which had seen Hitler make still more dramatic gains. Stalin and Molotov had been supportive of Hitler during the German invasion of France and the Low Countries, but the ease of the German victory was alarming. According to Nikita Khrushchev, after learning of the extent of the Allied debacle, Stalin "cursed the French and he cursed the British, asking how they could have let Hitler smash them like that."[31]

Hitler and Ribbentrop, for their part, accepted Stalin's cheap victories in Eastern Europe, but with increasing annoyance. Stalin's final list of terms for joining "Tripartite Pact" with Germany, Italy, and Japan, delivered by Molotov to the German ambassador in Moscow on November 25, 1940, included the right to station Soviet troops in Bulgaria and on the Bosporus in Turkey, coupled with the insulting demand that "all German troops must be withdrawn from Finland without delay." After reading over Stalin's terms, Hitler raged at the Bulgarian minister in Berlin on December 3 "that he now well understood Russia's real intentions." Hitler now made the fateful decision to break with Stalin, issuing "Order No. 21" on December 18, which inaugurated planning for the German invasion of the USSR known as "Operation Barbarossa."[32]

Despite enduring claims that Stalin was caught off guard by this "betrayal," after the diplomatic break the Soviet dictator stepped up his own war preparations no less dramatically than Hitler did. Three decades of research in previously inaccessible Russian archives has greatly enhanced our understanding of both the scale of Stalin's military preparations in the first half of 1941 and the deployment of most of the new Soviet air bases (199 out of 251) and armor in districts abutting the German frontier. In the order of battle, Soviet matériel advantage was, or should have been, decisive, with a five-to-one edge in tanks (more than 15,000, out of a Red Army tank park of 25,000, to 3,300 German ones), and a seven-to-one edge in warplanes (15,000 out of a Soviet reserve of 23,245 against the mere 2,250 belonging to the Luftwaffe, which had sustained serious losses in the Battle of Britain in 1940). In artillery, 7,146 German artillery pieces faced 37,000 Soviet guns at the front—with another 110,000 Soviet cannon and mortars in reserve. This was not to mention qualitative advantages, such as the superior armor and maneuverability of the Soviet T-34 tank.[33]

Despite this contrast, the initial verdict on this dangerously forward Soviet military posture was damning. The German Luftwaffe all but destroyed the gargantuan Soviet air force on the ground in the hours after Barbarossa was launched on June 22, 1941, seizing control of Soviet airspace, which allowed German bombers to blow up Soviet tank parks, fuel stations, and weapons depots. Enjoying air supremacy, the infantry and armored divisions of the Germans and their allies-in-arms (Romania, Hungary, Slovakia, and Finland) swiftly advanced hundreds of miles into the Baltic region, Soviet Belorussia, and Ukraine, crossing six major rivers in stride, seizing Smolensk in mid-July, encircling Kiev and crossing the Dnieper River into Left Bank Ukraine in September, and reaching the outskirts of Leningrad and Moscow by October. In a worrying sign for Soviet morale, and a damning political verdict on the willingness of Stalin's subjects to fight for Communism, more than 3.5 million Red Army troops, including 15,179 officers, were taken prisoner in 1941, often captured (or surrendering) with their arms.[34]

Whatever they may have said later, at the time Stalin and his advisers were, if not as shocked by the German invasion as historians used to believe, genuinely terrified by these losses. Not even the most ruthless measures—such as executions of Red Army officers whose men had pulled back; the introduction of NKVD "Special Section" disciplinary battalions in July 1941, authorized to "arrest deserters," and if necessary, "to shoot them on the spot"; or the now infamous Order No. 270, signed by Stalin on August 16, which declared that any soldier who surrendered "should be regarded as a malicious deserter whose family is to be arrested as a family of a breaker of the oath and betrayer of the Motherland"—could stem the tide of Soviet retreat. As early as the first week of July, the Politburo ordered the evacuation of 500,000 skilled military-industrial employees and their families from Moscow and Leningrad, along with cash and gold reserves from the State Bank and Lenin's embalmed body from Red Square, which was shipped east under a heavily armed NKVD guard to Tyumen. On October 15, when the Germans were close enough to the capital that Muscovites could hear artillery fire, Stalin signed a decree evacuating foreign missions and embassies 1,050 kilometers (650 miles) east to Kuibyshev (formerly Samara) on the Volga, along with the offices of the Soviet government and the Political Administration of the Red Army. With tantalizing ambiguity, the decree noted that "comrade Stalin will evacuate either tomorrow or later, depending on circumstances" (*smotrya po obstanovke*). With Metro service halted, panic engulfed Moscow. At NKVD headquarters in the Lubyanka, smoke poured out from the windows. Communist slogans were defaced, and hammer-and-sickle flags torn down from factories and apartment buildings. Muscovites burned their party membership cards. After all the political gains of the Popular Front years and the territorial advances since 1939, Soviet Communism now seemed a spent force, with its Moscow epicenter about to fall to the Nazis.[35]

But Stalin did not leave. The Soviet dictator directed the city's defense alongside Georgy Zhukov, who had the army command, and Beria, running the NKVD, while huddling with them and other top advisers in the Moscow Metro, built deep underground to double as a bomb shelter. Defiantly, he appeared in public to address the crowd that had gathered for the parade in Red Square on November 7 commemorating the 1917 October Revolution. Reinforced by the timely arrival of fresh troops from Siberia (a critical maneuver enabled by Stalin's Tokyo spy Richard Sorge, who assured him that Japan intended to attack the United States that year, not the USSR), Soviet lines west of Moscow held. It helped, too, that Anglo-American Lend-Lease aid to the USSR, requiring no payment up front, and authorized by the Roosevelt administration in secret without the knowledge of Congress or the US public, was now arriving at the Soviet-German front, including warplanes, tanks, and trucks to be used in the Soviet counteroffensive launched outside Moscow on December 5, 1941, along with huge volumes of American "aluminum, tin, lead, nickel and rubber." These metals were desperately needed to restart Stalin's own war factories, which had evacuated east to the Ural Mountains, as Stalin himself informed his Politburo colleagues in November. Nonetheless, we should not discount the critical role that Stalin's courageous decision to stay in Moscow played in shoring up Soviet fighting morale.[36]

The Battle of Moscow was a critical turning point in the Second World War and in the history of Communism more generally. For the first time in the war, the Germans were thrown backward, puncturing the Wehrmacht's reputation for invincibility. On December 8,

1941, Hitler ordered his armies to assume a defensive position on the Eastern Front. Although the Germans would recover and mount a major offensive from Left Bank Ukraine in the summer of 1942, reaching Stalingrad on the Volga in early September, this proved to be the high-water mark of the *Drang nach Osten*. Zhukov engineered the turnaround, a flanking operation called "Uranus" that cut off Stalingrad, forcing the surrender of the entire German Sixth Army, in the greatest single victory of the war. The last German armored offensive on the Eastern Front, launched in July 1943 against the Soviet salient at Kursk, was decisively repulsed, following which the Red Army began its long march to Berlin. Stalin's armies, to be sure, continued to hemorrhage soldiers and equipment at horrific rates, losing more men and matériel than the Germans in nearly every engagement, even after morale improved from the depths of 1941. In the Kursk campaign, one of the most famous Red victories of the war, Soviet casualties are estimated at nearly 1,677,000, plus the loss of 5,244 guns, 4,108 warplanes, and 6,064 tanks, against German losses of 170,000 casualties, 760 panzers, and 524 warplanes. Nonetheless, by 1944–1945, the Soviet armies appeared unstoppable as they reconquered Ukraine and then crashed into Belorussia, Poland, Hungary, the Balkans, and then Germany, their mobility enhanced by Lend-Lease trucks, jeeps, and motorcycles from America, riding on American rubber.[37]

The story of the Soviet triumph against Nazi Germany is well worn into popular legend, nowhere more dramatically than in Russia itself, where the "Great Patriotic War" narrative has sustained rulers from Stalin to Putin. In view of the stupendous sacrifice of the Soviet peoples, who lost somewhere between 25 million and 30 million war dead between 1941 and 1945, it is not hard to see why the story retains its epochal significance for Russians and the other peoples of the former Soviet Union. Westerners, too, have tended to view the Soviet victory as a heroic blood sacrifice almost too sacred to question, no matter how oppressive the treatment by Stalin's regime of its own people might have been, even—indeed especially—when they were resisting, and ultimately defeating, the most barbaric invasion in human history. The Great Patriotic War was both the finest moment of Soviet history, the one unquestionable geopolitical achievement Communists everywhere could claim as their own, and the movement's most harrowing and near-fatal episode.

In view of the human losses, it may seem impolitic to throw shade on Stalin's victory, but there has always been something dubious about his regime's claim to have proved itself, to have demonstrated the supremacy of Communist central planning and social organization, by "winning" a war while losing nearly 30 million people, of whom 15 million or 16 million were civilians. As Max Hastings pointed out in his best-selling war history *Inferno*, the number of Red Army soldiers *shot by their own side* alone (about 300,000) is "more than the entire toll of British troops who perished at enemy hands in the course of the war." Then there is the awkward circumstance that saw the Soviet war economy become almost wholly reliant on "capitalist" Lend-Lease supplies from 1941 to 1945, from raw materials and foodstuffs to industrial inputs and finished products. Oblivious to both horrendous NKVD disciplinary measures and the Lend-Lease story, which was little reported at the time, many westerners generously credited Stalin and his government with the victory. It was, after all, the Red Army that conquered Berlin, albeit in part because General Dwight Eisenhower and the US command refused to contest the city, and Stalin's men shed considerable blood in Berlin alone, with 361,367 casualties, including nearly 100,000 dead. As in the war on the Eastern Front more generally, the horrors of the Battle of Berlin demonstrated Soviet grit, heroism, and determination—though not military efficiency.[38]

Coupled with the contributions of underground Communist resistance fighters inside Nazi-occupied countries such as France and Italy—at least after the Comintern reversed its line on Hitler following the German invasion of the USSR—the raising of the hammer-and-sickle flag over the ruins of the Berlin Reichstag in May 1945 restored all the prestige Communism had lost in the Molotov-Ribbentrop period, and then some. In France's elections of October 1945, the French Communist Party (PCF), no longer saddled with defending the German invaders as in 1940, received the largest share of the vote at 26 percent, enough for Communists to enter the cabinet for the first time. The Italian Communist Party (PCI) did not do quite as well in its first postwar election, held in June 1946, netting just 19 percent of the vote; even so, it had cabinet members after renewing a Popular Front with the Italian socialists, who won 20 percent. True, the PCF and PCI were expelled from the French and Italian cabinets in 1947, as Cold War tensions heated up and a harsh new line was laid down by Stalin, requiring them to oppose their governments with violence if necessary. PCF leaders vowed to develop "new forms of struggle" that were "not parliamentary," and the PCI envoy promised Stalin that Italian Communists would unleash "a wave of demonstrations, land-seizures, [and] economic and political strikes." Many historians now suspect that, absent a massive influx of American subsidies and "covert assistance" from US spy agencies, the PCI might have come to power in Rome through the ballot box in the Italian elections of April 1948. If it had occurred, it would have been an unheard-of political achievement for Communism—Communists having failed to do so in Russia in 1917 or anywhere else where genuine democratic elections were held.[39]

This remains counterfactual speculation, however. Despite Stalin relenting enough to allow the PCI to join socialists again in a Popular Front, the Italian Left coalition lost 8 percent of its previous vote share in April 1948, allowing the pro-American Christian Socialists of Alcide de Gasperi to claim a real popular mandate, winning nearly 50 percent outright. The fact remains that, even with Soviet prestige and popularity peaking in Western Europe in the years after 1945, Communists did *not* come to power there by winning free and fair elections. As shown in Russia between 1917 and 1920, in Hungary in 1919, in Spain from 1936 to 1939, and in eastern Poland, Finland, the Baltic states, and Romania from 1939 to 1941, Communist fortunes still depended on military force—on the successes and failures of the Red Army and its clients. Fortunately for international Communism, the Red Army had crashed into Eastern Europe from the Baltic to the Adriatic, carrying vast military stores in its baggage train, including regiftable American trucks, jeeps, and motorcycles along with well-funded Soviet spies, political advisers and agents, and Moscow-trained foreign Communist leaders ready to take power. After the near-debacle of October 1941, which had brought the movement to its lowest ebb since 1917, Communism was on the march again.[40]

10
"PEOPLE'S DEMOCRACY"
COMMUNISM BEHIND THE IRON CURTAIN

O n V-E Day, when the war in Europe officially ended (May 8, 1945), Germany and many of the countries it had occupied lay in ruins. The devastation was perhaps worst of all in Berlin, where the Red Army and fanatical rearguard Nazi Schutzstaffel (SS) units had fought a brutal street-by-street battle until the bitter end. East Prussia, Poland, and Hungary, which had seen fighting on a similar scale over the past year, were little better off. War losses were bad enough in Britain and France, which had lost hundreds of thousands of war dead, but this was nothing like the apocalypse that had ravaged Poland, which had lost some 5.5 million people, or 20 percent of its population (about 3 million Jews and 2.5 million gentiles), or Hungary (1 million dead, including 400,000 Jews, in all one-eighth of the population). Aside from war casualties and damage to roads, bridges, buildings, and movable property, there were the Nazi death camps of Auschwitz, Belzec, Majdanek, Sobibor, and Treblinka, their few emaciated Jewish Holocaust survivors liberated by the Red Army in its long march through occupied

Poland, along with untold numbers of Nazi political prisoners and forced laborers. Then there were the victims of the Red Army itself, including at least 2 million rape victims. None of this was to account for refugees expelled or uprooted from their homes, whether from recent war trauma, having been conscripted into German or Soviet forced-labor camps, or in the new wave of forced expulsion of between 12 million and 14 million ethnic Germans from Poland and Czechoslovakia that followed the war. Across Central and Eastern Europe, it was as though the four horsemen of the apocalypse had swept through, as the brutal armed clash of two would-be conquerors, Hitler and Stalin, had left behind little but famine, pestilence, and human misery.[1]

Horrific as these scenes were for anyone caught up in them, the collapse of civilization across the once-prosperous lands of Central Europe augured well for Communist fortunes. The arrival of the Red Army into devastated cities such as Warsaw and Budapest in 1945 brought not just political prestige in the abstract, as in France and Italy, but the promise of the restoration of law and order—of a sort—along with the promise of retribution for the war's victims. Many of those who had suffered the horrors of Nazi occupation viewed the Red Army as liberators, even many Poles, who might have resented the role Stalin's armies played in the destruction of their country in September 1939, but had suffered for far longer (so far, at least) under the German yoke. Polish cities and towns in the German zone had seen their names Germanized, and Poles had been banned from shops and restaurants labeled "for Germans only." Jewish Holocaust survivors had the most obvious reasons for gratitude to the Soviets, followed by those liberated from Nazi prisons and camps, but even "gentile" Poles living at large had reason to rejoice. As late as 2007, one elderly Polish survivor interviewed by an American journalist still viewed the Red Army occupiers of 1945 with gratitude, insisting, "We had no mixed feelings towards them. They liberated us." In Czechoslovakia, occupied by the Germans even sooner than Poland—and, unlike Poland, not invaded by the USSR in 1939—there were even fewer "mixed feelings" about Soviet liberation. Hungarians, whose country had been allied to Nazi Germany until March 1944 and participated in the Barbarossa invasion, had more reason for trepidation about the Red Army, which showed little mercy as it crashed into the country later that year, surrounding Budapest in December and laying siege to the city until February 13, 1945. Nonetheless, many Hungarians still viewed the Russians as liberators, at least at first. "I ran out in the courtyard and hugged the first Soviet soldier I saw," one Budapest resident recalled decades later. At least the war and the siege were over.[2]

The Soviet occupiers wore out their welcome quickly, however, undermining the reputation and popularity of Communism in Eastern Europe just when it should have been peaking after the great Soviet victory over Nazi Germany. That the Red Army carried out mass rapes and looting in Berlin, the belly of the Nazi beast, was not surprising in view of the horrendous suffering of the Soviet peoples at the hands of the Barbarossa invaders, but rapacious Russian behavior was not limited to Prussia. Not just Germans but thousands of Polish, Hungarian, Romanian, and Czech women were raped as the Red Army crashed into Central Europe in 1945. In Yugoslavia, despite this Soviet-friendly country being liberated by the Red Army and the Partisans of Stalin's client Tito, Tito's own officials reported 1,204 cases of looting with assault and 121 cases of rape by Red Army soldiers, of which 111 were rape-murders. As one of Tito's Partisans observed, they were "witnessing a return to the administrative methods of Attila and Genghis Khan."[3]

The Genghis Khan treatment by the Soviet occupiers extended to property theft as well, establishing a precedent that did not bode well for the popular reception of Communism. Officially, each Red

Army soldier was limited to five kilograms of loot after conquering Berlin, Budapest, and other large cities, although most Red Army officers hardly bothered to search their men. Watches were especially prized, so commonly stolen that by the summer of 1945 it was hard to find a Russian without one. The iconic Soviet photo of the raising of the hammer and sickle over the Reichstag had to be "airbrushed" to remove the looted wristwatches on the soldier's arm. In Poland, schoolchildren playacting the part of Soviet soldiers in the early postwar years would shout, *"Davai chasyi"*—Give me your watch! As in 1940, when the Red Army had marched into the Baltic countries and Romania, it was not just greed but cultural shock that motivated Soviet looting, as serving men and officers alike were bewildered by the material wealth of the capitalist countries, replete in so many things Communist Russia lacked, from toys and bicycles to varieties of liquor, from kitchen accoutrements to men's and women's clothing, perfume, and lingerie.[4]

Property "nationalization" had been shocking when the Soviets applied it to occupied Poland, Estonia, Latvia, Lithuania, and Romania in 1939–1940 after two decades of relative peace and prosperity. In 1945, after five or six terrible years of war, the violent seizure of property had become numbingly routine. The Nazis had "nationalized" banks and businesses no less assiduously than the Communists had, usually targeting those owned by Jews first, but not stopping there as the needs of the German war machine grew more voracious each year and the economies of occupied countries were "Germanized." Indeed, in some ways the economic side of Nazism began to resemble its Soviet Communist antipode during the war, from its increasingly statist control over production targets and nationalization of key industries to its massive use of slave labor. The economies of Poland, Czechoslovakia, and Hungary were thus ripe for Communist picking in 1945: Soviet nationalization commissars often simply replaced the German occupation bosses who had either been killed or fled. Many German-owned factories were broken down and physically carted back home to the USSR by Red Army "looting" detachments, amounting to 3,024 entire factories and nearly 10 million tons of industrial goods removed from Germany by the end of 1946.[5]

The Soviet looting campaign, like the mass rapes, was not confined to Prussia. Red Army looting battalions took industrial property from Poland, Czechoslovakia, Austria, and Hungary, too, along with huge quantities of oil, foodstuffs, and vehicles. All of this was justified as "reparations," although the volumes looted from each country bore little resemblance to Soviet reparations claims. Hungary, as a full Barbarossa participant between 1941 and 1944, was supposed to pay the most, $300 million of reparations—but supplied Stalin only 2,800 railway wagons of loot. Czechoslovakia, in contrast, though charged with ten times less in reparations ($30 million)—Slovakia had participated in Barbarossa, even if the rest of the country had been German- or Hungarian-occupied—supplied more than twice as much (6,500 railway wagons). The most absurd disconnect lay in Poland, victimized by both Nazi Germany and the USSR in 1939, but now forced to cough up "reparations" to its Soviet occupier amounting to 211,500 railway wagons' worth of industrial property—more than Hungary by a factor of 100.[6]

The use of both industrial property and slave labor as "reparations in kind" had actually been codified into the Yalta agreement of February 1945, approved by both Franklin Roosevelt and Winston Churchill, and Stalin was not shy about exploiting either resource. Romania was especially targeted, both in that it had participated in Barbarossa, and in that its meager industrial wealth was less enticing than that of Hungary, Czechoslovakia, Prussia, and Poland (though Stalin still levied a reparations charge of $125 million on Bucharest). In addition to the 190,000 Romanian troops taken prisoner by the Red Army since 1941, 130,000 Romanian soldiers were deported into the USSR at war's end, along with 100,000 Romanian nationals serving in the Hungarian army. In all, some 420,000 Romanians were sent to Gulag camps. Hungary was not spared either, supplying Stalin with 600,000 slave laborers in 1945. Predictably, Germans supplied the most slave laborers to Stalin, nearly 2 million. Poland, though contributing the most industrial property other than Germany, was "spared" from postwar human reparations, furnishing only 91,000 new Gulag victims in 1945 (although over 1 million Poles had been sent to labor camps in 1939–1940). Far from camouflaging his use of war prisoners as slave laborers, Stalin boasted about the practice to Harry Hopkins, envoy of US president Harry Truman, on May 28, 1945, even joking that Italian POWs (mostly volunteers captured on the Eastern Front) were more productive than his German and East European victims—because Soviet camp guards actually fed them halfway decently.[7]

Of course, Stalin's mass looting operations, however ostensibly justified when carried out in Nazi Germany, were not much of an argument for the beneficence of Communism when they crashed into Poland, Czechoslovakia, Hungary, Yugoslavia, and Romania. But the Soviets had other benefits to offer Communist protégés, including the "regifting" of surplus American Lend-Lease vehicles, and the sharing of looted apartments and country houses. In Poland, the "Lublin Committee" of Communist puppets Stalin established in the summer of 1944 to rule over postwar Poland (formally named the Polish Committee of National Liberation), led by Bolesław Bierut, was given 485 Dodge trucks, 300 Jeep "Willys," and 350 motorcycles from Soviet Lend-Lease stocks in November 1944, plus 850 more American trucks in January 1945, in order to help Bierut's police forces hunt down Polish Home Army fighters who had escaped the clutches of Hitler and Stalin after the tragic and abortive Warsaw Uprising of 1944. A special Polish War

Trophy Commission was established in March 1945 to adjudicate property disputes between the Red Army and the Lublin Committee, setting an important precedent for the "people's democracies" to come. In theory, Poland was entitled to a 15 percent share of the reparations Germany owed the USSR, according to an agreement finalized at the Potsdam Conference in July 1945, although in practice the Soviets coughed up only 8.5 percent, most of it sent not in cash but in looted German industrial goods. The needs of Stalin's puppet Communists remained secondary. To furnish Bierut's new Polish presidential palace, the Red Army commandant agreed to part with only cheap modern tables and chairs, reserving "valuable antiques" for himself.[8]

In some cases, Stalin was willing to share scarce resources with favored East European clients, such as Marshal Tito, whose Communist Partisans had helped defeat the German (and Bulgarian) occupiers of Yugoslavia—thanks in large part to British and American support airlifted to Tito's men in 1943 and 1944, before the Red Army arrived in force in October 1944. While the Red Army requisitioned the Yugoslav grain and vegetable harvest that fall for Soviet consumption, Stalin compensated Tito by sharing looted Hungarian coal with the Partisans, so they could take credit for helping desperate Yugoslavs heat their homes that winter. Stalin even encouraged Tito to levy his own reparation claims against Hungary and Germany.* Nonetheless, when Tito's representatives in Moscow asked Stalin, in January 1945, to share more reparations with Yugoslavia, Stalin balked. In an elegant statement of the principles of Communist armed conquest, Stalin explained that "trophies belong to the army that captures them."[9]

---

* Though, significantly, not against Bulgaria, which had actually supplied more occupation troops in wartime Yugoslavia than the Germans. Bulgaria was poorer than Hungary or Germany, making it less promising as a piggy bank; it was also occupied by fewer Soviet troops, which meant Stalin had less leverage in Sofia and had to tread more carefully in Bulgaria.

Stalin's brutal rebuke of Tito was a shot across the bow, and it showed how difficult it would be for even his proudest Communist clients to achieve real independence from the USSR. Tito was not just a successful guerrilla leader but a Communist with seniority in the movement. Born Josip Broz in Habsburg Croatia in 1892, Tito had joined the Yugoslav Social Democratic (i.e., Marxist) party as early as 1910, fought in World War I, and been taken prisoner by the Russians, whereupon, like Béla Kun, he had thrown in with the Bolsheviks in the revolutionary whirlwind of 1917. A member of the Yugoslav Communist Party since 1920, Tito had been promoted to party leadership during the Terror years, helping purge the party and thus proving himself a loyal Stalinist. Even during the wartime years when he was receiving vast military stores from "capitalist" Britain's Cairo command, Tito remained fiercely loyal to Stalin, although his British handlers, such as Churchill's personal envoy, Fitzroy Maclean, were oblivious to this. Comintern files now available in the Soviet archives in Moscow show that Tito discussed Maclean's every move with Georgi Dimitrov and Stalin, provided detailed reports on everything the British airlifted to him, and demanded instruction from Moscow on even the smallest matters of protocol.[10]

Tito, to be sure, was stubborn and proud. But his independent streak, such as it was, led him not to question Stalin's orders but often to exceed them. In parallel to the Soviet operations carried out by "SMERSH"—the military counterintelligence organization that Stalin had created by April 1943 to hunt down (among others) White Russian and Cossack émigrés who had enlisted in the notorious Osttruppen (Eastern troops) of the German Wehrmacht— Tito established his own Partisan hit squad in Yugoslavia. In the infamous "Kočevski Rog massacre" of June 2, 1945, Tito's men herded between 12,000 and 18,000 alleged Nazi collaborators— mostly members of the collaborationist "Slovenian Home Guard" but also Croats, Serbs, Montenegrins, and a few Bulgarians, Germans, and Italians—into a series of underground caverns, pits, and mines; hurled grenades and smoke bombs into them; "spray[ed] the general area with machine-gun fire"; and dynamited the entrances to prevent escape. Those few victims who managed to crawl out of the pits were beaten, stabbed to death, and thrown back in (except for one or two survivors who escaped to tell the tale). By the fall of 1945, between 30,000 and 50,000 alleged collaborators had been killed by Tito's Partisans without trial. Tito did, at least, show his main wartime rival in the Yugoslav armed resistance, Colonel Draža Mihailović, who had commanded the "Chetnik" forces on behalf of Yugoslavia's London government-in-exile only to be abandoned by the British, the courtesy of a treason trial for "collaboration" in 1946, after which Mihailović and most of his senior officers were executed. Here, too, Tito was a pioneer, carrying out his own "show trials" several years before Stalin's less independent Communist satellites held their own.[11]*

If any of the countries liberated and now occupied by the Red Army had a chance to avoid the worst aspects of Stalinism in 1945, it was Czechoslovakia. Despite Nazi reprisals carried out against Czechs after the assassination of SS officer Reinhard Heydrich in Prague in 1942, only rump Slovakia had participated in Barbarossa, and both Prague and the Czech industrial heartland of Bohemia had been spared the worst destruction during the war. Stalin imposed a fairly light reparations burden of $30 million on Czechoslovakia, and Red Army looting battalions carried off a relatively modest 6,500 tons of its industrial goods. The country's prewar president, Edvard Beneš, no Communist, was one of the first victims of Nazi aggression—refusing to recognize the German annexation of the Sudetenland, Beneš fled to London shortly after

---

* Mihailović's treason conviction was posthumously overturned by Serbia in 2015.

Munich—and thus had more seniority than any other exiled resistance leader in Europe. Stalin had no animus against Beneš as he did toward the London Poles, who, by demanding an investigation into the Katyn Forest massacre in 1943, had incurred Stalin's wrath. Beneš had bent over backward to appease Stalin, corresponding regularly from London with the main Czech Communist leaders in Moscow, Klement Gottwald and Rudolf Slánský. Unlike Poland's London government-in-exile, Stalin recognized Czechoslovakia's as fully legitimate, along with the country's pre-Munich borders. In a series of agreements hammered out in Moscow in March 1945 and in the eastern Slovak town of Košice that April, Beneš was allowed to form a genuine "National Front" coalition government, with his longtime non-Communist foreign minister, Jan Masaryk from the London exile government, retaining his position. Although eight cabinet members, including the ministers of defense, interior, information, education, and agriculture, were Communists, the prime minister, Zdeněk Fierlinger, was a Social Democrat (though he, like Gottwald and Slánský, had spent the war years in Moscow under Stalin's thumb). In a sign that Stalin was willing to tolerate some level of Czech independence, the Red Army withdrew from Prague in December 1945. Beneš was then resoundingly reelected as president in June 1946. In parliamentary elections held that May, the Communists won a plurality of 38 percent, allowing Gottwald to take over as prime minister. Still, so long as Beneš and Masaryk were in office, there was a hope that liberal democratic institutions might endure. As late as April 1947, Beneš and Masaryk informed the US ambassador in Prague, Laurence Steinhardt, that Stalin was not interfering with the Czech government.[12]

These reassurances were misleading. Just as in Spain during the Civil War, Stalin was willing to tolerate non-Communist front men at the head of a satellite government only as long as they carried out the policies he wanted them to. For all the hopes many British and American officials expressed for Czechoslovakia as a rare case of Communist pluralism, the reality was that Beneš and Masaryk had signed off on policies no less ruthlessly retributive than Stalin's own. In an interesting confluence of timing, Beneš delivered a radio address from Brno shortly after V-E Day, on May 12, 1945, the same day Churchill first road-tested his soon-to-be-famous phrase about an "Iron Curtain" descending in Central Europe between the Western democracies and Stalin's new satellites. Beneš declared that the Germans who had helped dismember his country "must pay for all this with a great and severe punishment," adding, "We must liquidate the German problem definitively." Within days some 20,000 German nationals had been evicted from Brno alone, the first of nearly 2.5 million ethnic Germans to be expelled from Czechoslovakia by October 1946. Roughly 1.6 million of these went to the American zone (the future West Germany), and 800,000 into the Soviet zone (the future East Germany). The largest number of German expellees came from the Sudetenland used by Hitler to pry apart the country in 1938, where 1.7 million Czech farmers were resettled onto lands owned by expelled Germans, a policy soon extended to other border regions denuded of Germans and to as many as 1 million Czech Hungarians, particularly numerous in Slovakia, and ultimately to all large Czech landed estates.[13]

Far from objecting to any of this, Beneš signed off on the ethnic expulsions in a series of 143 executive resolutions known to history as the "Beneš decrees." No. 12 ordered the "seizure of agricultural property belonging to traitors, enemies of the state, Germans or Hungarians." Beneš's decree no. 5 also nationalized "any company owned by an enemy of the state" or by anyone listed in the 1929 census as a German or Hungarian national. Other decrees nationalized Czech banks, insurance companies, and large industrial enterprises, placing 60 percent of industrial production, and a similar percentage of workers, under state control. Another decree (no. 115) nationalized the production and distribution of coal and firewood. Even the decrees dealing with matters of culture and education were reminiscent of Soviet practice, from the nationalization of primary schooling to the creation of state art academies and orchestras. Beneš himself might have euphemized all of this top-down reordering of Czechoslovak society as "socializing democracy," but to anyone familiar with Soviet history, it looked a lot like Communism.[14]

By pursuing such policies and reassuring Stalin about their goodwill, Beneš and Masaryk hoped to retain some freedom of action. As Masaryk had told Beneš back in London, "I'd rather go to bed with Stalin than kiss Hitler's behind." But the deck was stacked against them. Beneš signed the decrees expelling Czech Germans and Hungarians and "enemies of the state," but it was the Communist-controlled Ministry of Agriculture that oversaw the redistribution of land and took the credit. The Communists in charge of the Economics Ministry expanded the state agencies overseeing the economy—installing nearly 140,000 party members in this metastasizing Gosplan-style Czech bureaucracy by 1947, as Slánský proudly informed Stalin that September. Just as predictable, in view of Communists having been given the Defense and Interior Ministries, was the flooding of the Czechoslovak army and police with loyal party members.[15]

The Communists therefore held all the cards when Beneš and Masaryk first tried to buck Stalin's authority in July 1947 by accepting the US offer of financial assistance made in June by US secretary of state George Marshall, known to history as the Marshall Plan. As this was preeminently a matter of foreign policy, it was Masaryk's brief, his chance to shine. Summoned to Moscow, he was brutally dressed down by Stalin. Whether out of fear or loyalty, Masaryk was forced to assent to the statement, according to his delegation's own minutes of the meeting, that "all political parties are agreed that Czechoslovakia may not undertake anything which would be against the interests of the Soviet Union," such as accepting American economic aid. As Masaryk later recalled, "I left for Moscow as a Czechoslovak Minister, I returned as Stalin's lackey."[16]

The political fallout was predictable. Even though Beneš and Masaryk swallowed Stalin's insults and rejected the Marshall Plan, their initial openness to it was used to discredit all non-Communist parties in Czechoslovakia, who were now smeared as collaborators with American "imperialist aggression." Soon thereafter the same applied throughout the rest of Eastern Europe, especially after September 1947, when the newly created Communist Information Bureau, or Cominform, in Moscow drafted a resolution laying down a new line condemning Popular Front–style coalitions with "bourgeois" parties. In May 1943, Stalin had abolished the Comintern as a diplomatic sop to US president Roosevelt. (At a time when the Anglo-Americans were generously supplying his armies and factories, overthrowing the US and British governments was counterproductive.) Now that a different president had proclaimed (in February 1947) the anti-Communist "Truman doctrine" of support for "free peoples . . . resisting armed subjugation by armed minorities or outside pressures," and the United States was backing this up with the Marshall Plan of economic aid to Europe, Stalin decided it was time to bring back the Comintern in new clothing, beginning with no. 14 of the old "21 Conditions" establishing the subservience of foreign Communists to Soviet foreign policy needs.

The difference now was that, with Soviet troops occupying most of Stalin's new East European satellites, and loyal Communists controlling the police and armed forces in those few places from which the Red Army had withdrawn (such as Prague), parties taking orders from the Cominform could actually *rule*. In Czechoslovakia, this meant purges of non-Communists from the "National

Front" government, carried out under threat of a huge Communist mob mobilized in Prague in the "coup" of February 25, 1948, and then the removal of 30,000 remaining non-Communist employees of the state bureaucracy. Beneš, initially so shocked that he refused to accept cabinet resignations, limped on as president for a few months, but even he lost heart after his friend and colleague Masaryk jumped (or was thrown) from a window in the courtyard of the Czech Foreign Ministry in his pajamas in March.[17]*

With any possible opposition ousted—most members of the parliamentary opposition fled to London, where they hoped to be recognized again as a government-in-exile—Gottwald and the Communists then completed the work of Stalinizing Czechoslovakia. A Five-Year Plan that focused on heavy industry, an extension of the workweek to six out of seven days, and Gulag-style forced-labor camps were all decreed in October 1948. The collectivization of agriculture was on hold for now, with small-scale holdings under 125 acres protected, but otherwise the Sovietization of the Czechoslovak economy was nearly complete. Gosplan in Moscow set production and trade targets for Stalin's satellites, with each allotted shares in key sectors. Twenty-three percent of the Czech production in "tubes, tracks, metal-sheets, heavy industrial engines, power station equipment, dredgers and motors" was to be shipped to Russia, along with 72 percent of Czech production in consumer goods such as boots and rubber, cigarettes and parchment paper, textiles and woolen goods, and plate glass and china. In exchange, Czechoslovakia would import Soviet foodstuffs such as wheat, meat, fats, sunflower seeds, and peas to help feed the tens of thousands of forced laborers now working for the state along

---

* The Czech line on Masaryk's death has changed repeatedly, with the Communists concluding it was clearly a suicide, and the post-Communist government reversing course after the "Velvet Revolution" of 1989, declaring it a murder. Yet another investigation inaugurated in 2019 concluded that no one knows for sure.

with the 100,000-plus political prisoners held in Communist jails by the early 1950s.[18]

If this was the fate of the satellite whose leaders had tried the hardest to appease Stalin, it is not hard to imagine what was in store for countries that had joined Operation Barbarossa, such as Hungary and Romania. Both countries, as we have seen, supplied Stalin with "reparations" of looted industrial property and slave labor. The German minority in both countries was also subjected to brutal treatment under Soviet auspices (although in this case the other locals had less reason to object). Ethnic Germans furnished one-sixth of those expelled from Romania into the USSR, while 200,000 Germans were expelled from Hungary. Even those allowed to stay suffered the torments of a hostile Soviet military occupation, from requisitions and rapes to reprisals against partisans, particularly in Romania, where resistance was widespread. By 1948, when most of the last resistance had been snuffed out, more than 1 million Romanians—not counting those deported to the USSR—had been either imprisoned, sent to forced-labor camps, or executed. Romania also endured a reenactment of Stalin's White Sea Canal forced-labor project of the early 1930s, as tens of thousands of conscripted Romanians died building a new Danube–Black Sea Canal. Perhaps the worst crime committed by Romanian Communists was the "Piteşti Prison Experiment," conducted between December 1949 and September 1951, when more than 1,000 political prisoners (some, though not all, of whom had belonged to the fascist "Iron Guard" during the war) were forcibly "reeducated" by an "Organization of Prisoners with Communist Conviction" through physical and psychological torture, the horrors of which have only recently come to light.[19]

Soviet retaliation in occupied Hungary was not as swift as in Romania, although this was in part because, as in Poland, so many thousands of Hungarians who might have resisted a postwar Soviet

Expansion of Communism into Europe, 1944–1948

NORWAY
Oslo•

Stockholm•
SWEDEN

FINLAND
Helsinki•
•Leningrad

Tallinn•
Estonia

Latvia
Riga•

Russia
•Moscow

NETHERLANDS
UNITED
KINGDOM
Amsterdam•

DENMARK
Copenhagen•

Hamburg•

Gdańsk •

Lithuania
Kal. Vilnius•

•Minsk

UNION OF SOVIET
SOCIALIST REPUBLICS

British
Zone
Brussels •
BELG. Bonn
GERMANY
•Paris
LUX. Fr.
US
FRANCE Zone
SWITZ.

Berlin•
Russian Zone
(SBZ)

Prague •

Warsaw•
POLAND

Belarus

•Kiev

CZECHOSLOVAKIA

•Lyon
•Milan

Vienna•
AUSTRIA

•Bratislava
•Budapest
HUNGARY

Ukraine
Dnepropetrovsk •

Moldova
Kishinev•

Rostov-
Na-Donu

Marseille

Ljubljana•
Zagreb•

•Odessa

ROMANIA

ITALY
Rome•

Belgrade•
Sarajevo•
YUGOSLAVIA

•Bucharest

•Constanta

Naples•

Tirana•
ALBANIA

BULGARIA •Varna
Sofia

Thessaloniki•

•Istanbul

TURKEY
•Ankara

•Tunis

GREECE

•Athens

Expanded Soviet borders, 1945

Communist satellites, c. 1948

Electoral near misses for
Communist parties

0   300 miles

occupation had perished already as the Red Army fought its bloody way into the country, inflicting more than 100,000 Soviet casualties themselves. As one of Hitler's key Barbarossa coalition partners, Hungary was treated as an enemy country, pillaged at will by the Red Army's looting battalions. It was granted formal independence only in February 1946, and that under enduring Soviet occupation.

The Hungarian Communists, led by Mátyás Rákosi, a veteran of the Kun government, did not have a whiff of popular legitimacy, winning only 17 percent of the vote in the first postwar elections, held in November 1945. The poor Communist performance was due in part to the bad odor left by Soviet looting, as Rákosi complained to his Soviet handlers. One of them confirmed to Stalin that "arbitrariness, pillage and violence on the part of certain Soviet soldiers" had doomed Communist chances. Not that Rákosi, a loyal Comintern agent since 1919, was about to rebuff Stalin. Instead, Rákosi plowed on ahead with his "Hungarian salami tactics," as he colorfully euphemized his politics. By this he meant infiltrating the opposition parties with Communist agents and "slicing away" the opposition elements from the government one by one, imprisoning those who objected too vigorously. The salami tactics worked: In May 1949, Rákosi's Communists improved their electoral performance, now taking 95 percent of the vote instead of 17 percent. There was never a dramatic Hungarian Terror, more like death by a million salami cuts: the best estimates show that a million or more Hungarians had been imprisoned, deported, or sent to forced-labor camps at home by 1953.[20]

Bulgaria, which, despite joining Hitler's Tripartite Pact, had declined to participate in Barbarossa, might have been expected to receive more lenient treatment. The country enjoyed historic ties to Tsarist Russia, which had liberated it from the Ottoman Turkish yoke in the war of 1877–1878. It also had a certain prestige in the Soviet era. One reason was that the Bulgarian Communist Party had pulled off a spectacular act of interwar political terrorism when it bombed Sofia's Sveta Nedelya Cathedral in April 1925 during a state funeral, with almost the entire Bulgarian government in attendance.[*] Moreover, party leader Georgi Dimitrov had embarrassed

---

[*] The Sveta Nedelya bombing, carried out by the Bulgarian Communist Party's military organization, did miss the primary targets, as King Boris III was attending another

the Nazis at the Reichstag fire trial and had been Popular Front secretary of the Comintern. Dimitrov, resident in Moscow since the Nazis had flown him there in 1933, had become a close confidant of Stalin's during the war—his diaries are among our best sources on Stalin's thinking. Encouragingly, Stalin informed Dimitrov that postwar Bulgaria would be accorded some political leeway, and specifically, that the three non-Communist "anti-fascist" parties from the wartime underground Fatherland Front (including the Social Democrats, the Agrarian National Union, and the more bourgeois "Zveno Circle") would be tolerated in order to provide Dimitrov's regime-to-be with "a broader base and a convenient disguise." Communist Bulgaria was created in a matter of days—the four days, to be exact, between the Soviet declaration of war on Bulgaria, on September 4, 1944, and the pro-Soviet coup that toppled the pro-German government of King Boris III on September 8 and invited in the Red Army, which lost less than 1,000 casualties. Even more remarkable was the low cost of the Communist takeover, which set Stalin's treasury back only $50,000. The United States and Britain had not even contested it. (In the "naughty document"—or "percentages agreement"—that Churchill handed Stalin in October 1944, the Soviets were given 75 percent of Bulgaria.) Bulgaria had a relatively clean Holocaust record, having leveraged its friendly relations with Berlin to postpone deportation orders and protect nearly all of its Jewish subjects (although Bulgarian troops occupying Greece and Yugoslavia did send more than 11,000 Jews to Treblinka in 1943). For all these reasons, there seemed little cause for Bulgarians to expect unduly harsh treatment under Communism.[21]

---

funeral, and all the government ministers miraculously survived. Still, the bomb killed four Bulgarian generals, the mayor of Sofia, the chief of police, a regional governor, three parliamentary deputies, and 141 other civilians. Five hundred people were also wounded, some quite seriously.

It was all the more shocking for both Bulgarians and those few foreign observers left in the country, then, to see it suffer arguably the earliest wave of Communist Terror. New research in Bulgarian archives has confirmed that between 25,000 and 30,000 people were "killed or disappeared" in just the first half of September 1944. As the Central Committee reported proudly to Dimitrov (who was personally overseeing the purges on Stalin's behalf) on September 13, "In the first days of the Revolution we squared accounts with the most malicious enemies, fallen into our hands." But, he added, "the fight is not over," and "armed members of the Party" would "form striking commands for particularly important assignments." This was extrajudicial killing. As the Bulgarian Communist Party's Central Committee explained to Dimitrov on October 1, "Despite the discontent of our feeble allies [e.g., the three non-Communist groups in the wartime Fatherland Front] at our revolutionary liquidation of the fascist *agentura*, we decided that the purge will go on for one more week. After that the purge will continue by lawful means."[22]

The "lawful" purges were only marginally less bloody than the lawless ones had been. On October 6, the Bulgarian Communist Party established "people's tribunals" to try cases against fascists, "monarcho-fascists," and other collaborators, soon working at full blast. By April 1945, these tribunals had processed 135 "cases" involving more than 11,000 defendants, of whom 2,730 were executed, 1,516 acquitted, and the rest imprisoned or sent to labor camps. Here, too, Bulgaria's Communists were ahead of the curve, establishing "Work Education Centers" as early as December 20, 1944. The network soon included 88 Gulag-style forced-labor camps housing 184,000 "politically dangerous" Bulgarians, from employees of the royal government to army officers and Orthodox clerics. The purges worked, too. In the first postwar parliamentary elections, held in October 1946, the Communists won with

53.5 percent of the vote—though, in the atmosphere of terror it is remarkable that opposition parties did this well. Changing his tone, Stalin informed a triumphant Dimitrov, "The elections are over and your opposition can go to hell." The purges were extended to Bulgaria's Fatherland Front opposition parties, beginning with the arrest of Agrarian Party leader Nikola Petkov on June 5, 1947, and the onset of public show trials, which in Bulgaria marked not the beginning of Stalinist terror, as in Czechoslovakia, but its culmination.[23]

Bulgaria was ahead of the Communist curve in economic policy as well. Collectivization of agriculture began in 1945, much sooner than in more industrialized satellites, such as Czechoslovakia— although, in a small mercy to Bulgarians, the Communists declared only "Two-Year Plans" instead of the five-year ones in Prague. Rather than working to meet onerous industrial targets for the USSR like the Czechoslovaks, Bulgarians endured a small-scale Holodomor. Peasant resistance to collectivization was fierce enough that it inspired show trials, such as the Dimitar Gichev trial that opened in April 1948, in which Gichev, an Agrarian Party leader, and his party associates were accused of "conspiring . . . to instigate the peasants to hide and destroy their food and to sabotage the economic policy of the government" in order "to undermine the Two-Year Plan and to jeopardize the planned foundation of the country's economy." As Dimitrov himself vowed in a speech to the party faithful in October 1947, "the steam roller of historical development will mercilessly crush all enemies who would dare attempt to destroy [the] unity [of the people] while those who are still firmly sitting on the fence will be thrown away like useless lumber." By the time Dimitrov died in July 1949, he had turned Bulgaria into a model people's democracy, from collectivization and plants to labor camps and giant public-works projects. The country's showcase hydroelectric dam, today's Iskar

Reservoir, was even named after Stalin, as was its highest peak in the Rhodope Mountains, and its largest port, Varna on the Black Sea coast.[24]

If Bulgaria was Stalin's most loyal Communist satellite, then Poland was the most unruly. In view of Stalin's brutal treatment of Poles under Soviet occupation in the Molotov-Ribbentrop period, the Red Army and its Polish Communist clients could hardly expect a warm welcome. Then, too, there was the refusal of the Red Army, despite reaching the Vistula (Wisła) River in late July 1944, to aid the Polish Home Army (Armia Krajowa, or AK) during the Warsaw Uprising against the Nazis launched that August 1. It was not merely that Stalin's commanders on the ground had refused to help, leaving the Polish rebels at the mercy of the Nazis: the NKVD had issued orders to disarm and arrest AK fighters in areas of eastern Poland under Soviet control on the very day the uprising began. By October, the Soviet NKVD had arrested around 25,000 AK fighters and sent them to internment camps—more men than the Home Army lost fighting the Germans in Warsaw (about 16,000). Another 17,000 AK fighters were arrested that winter by a special standing NKVD division created on October 15. They were charged with taking part in Polish counterinsurgency operations and deported to Gulag camps inside the USSR. By the time the Red Army finally marched into the depopulated rubble of Warsaw on January 17, 1945, the city's population was down from a prewar figure of 1.3 million to under 150,000. The Red Army, alongside the NKVD and the security forces of Bierut's puppet Lublin government (commanded by Zygmunt Berling, and thus popularly known as "Berling's men" [berlingowcy]), continued hunting down Polish Home Army patriots long after the Nazis were expelled from Poland in January 1945. The "Augustów operation," carried out by the NKVD and the berlingowcy in the Augustów (now Podlaskie) region of northeastern Poland between

July 10 and 25, 1945, is today remembered by Poles as a "second Katyn." Nearly 600 arrested fighters, including 27 women, some of them pregnant, and 15 minors, were deported into the USSR and never seen again. They were presumed dead. In November, AK resistance in the area around Liski, in former East Prussia, grew so hot that the Red Army sent in nine regular divisions to crush Polish rebels. In December, six months after V-E Day, the Soviets started bombing AK strongholds from the air. Although the fighting was most intense in 1945 and 1946, the Polish Home Army continued resisting into 1947, losing 8,700 fighters while inflicting thousands of Soviet and Polish Communist casualties themselves.[25]

The imposition of Communism on Poland, under a hostile Soviet military occupation falling somewhere between civil war and colonial counterinsurgency,* was never likely to be accepted by a majority of Poles as legitimate. To the extent the Soviets had anything positive to offer Poles, it was property seized from the German occupiers, "shared" from German industrial reparations, or, in the case of the area of Prussia east of the Oder-Neisse line (transferred to Poland to "compensate" it for Stalin's annexation of eastern Poland), farmland and real estate emptied by the Germans being cleansed. To be sure, the new ex-German Poland was scarcely half the size of the area of eastern Poland absorbed by Stalin.[†] Still,

---

* Because so many of the forces engaged in anti-partisan operations were Soviet army, NKVD, or SMERSH, and so many of the deportations and executions were carried out by them, many Poles today find even the suggestion of a "civil war" in postwar Poland to be offensive. Nonetheless, some of the atrocities were clearly committed by the *berlingowcy* and the secret police of the Ministry of Public Security (MBP)—that is, by Polish Communists.

† Although the Western Allies later signed off on this cynical territorial swap, as on the German expulsions, the details were quietly negotiated between Stalin and Bierut in 1944, including the bartering of Königsberg (which became Soviet and is still Russian Kaliningrad) for the port of Stettin (now Polish Szczecin)—the Stettin later invoked by Churchill in his "Iron Curtain" speech ("from Stettin on the Baltic . . ."). Stalin, underrating Churchill's knowledge of geography, assured Bierut at the time that "Churchill will never notice the difference." He did.

the new western Poland should have had enough vacant property and land to house Polish settlers, as nearly 7 million Germans had either fled the advancing Red Army or been expelled by the new Polish Communist government. They had left behind a mere rump of 200,000 or 300,000 ethnic Germans, making "room" for 2.7 million Poles who had been expelled by the Russians from lands absorbed by the USSR, alongside 1.5 million Polish survivors returning from forced-labor camps in Hitler's Reich. When these Polish settlers arrived in formerly German Pomerania in 1945, some from the west and some from the east, they were greeted with Communist pamphlets heralding "the great Agricultural Reform in Pomerania. Under a state decree, all post-German and landed territories pass into your hands, into the possession of agricultural workers, landless, small and middle-class peasants."[26]

To their shock, however, Poles moving into Pomerania found that the Soviet occupiers tended to favor the rump German minority, as if to remind Poles of the horrors of the Molotov-Ribbentrop era, when Soviet-German collaboration was summed up in the hideous pidgin slang phrase "Germanski und bolsheviki zusammen stark!" (Germans and Bolsheviks strong together!). As Władysław Gomułka, Bierut's deputy prime minister, complained to Marshals Georgy Zhukov, Konstantin Rokossovsky, and the Soviet ambassador in Warsaw on January 10, 1946,

> The attitude of the Red Army units to the Polish population in the area of the regained territories is often reluctant, thus evoking in Polish society an atmosphere of bitterness and discouragement. The actions of some units of the Red Army, who engage in rapes, robberies, plunder and killings against the Polish population, make Polish actions in the regained territories difficult, and the pro-German policy of some war commanders intensifies the difficulties that we have to overcome in the development of these areas.[27]

Delicately, Gomułka requested a "ban on private accommodation" of Red Army units in ex-German western Poland, to "prevent fraternizing with the Germans and favoring them over the Polish population." In addition, he requested the replacement of "hitherto stationed Red Army troops, consisting mostly of front soldiers [who] treat areas recovered as captured territory, by troops from the depths of Russia," whose fresh perspective might be a "contributing factor to Polish-Soviet friendship."[28]

The Soviet occupiers deployed the same kind of cruelty with Polish political prisoners, who were sometimes forced to share cells with their former German tormentors. The most famous instance was the confinement of Kazimierz Moczarski, an AK resistance hero (code-named "Borsuk," or badger), in a cell in Mokotów Prison with SS general Jürgen Stroop, the man who had brutally crushed the Warsaw Ghetto Uprising in 1943. For 225 days, Stroop was given generous food rations and treated humanely while Moczarski was slowly starved; deprived of fresh air, water, and soap; and subjected (in his memoir recollection) to "forty-nine different types of tortures and beatings." Mokotów Prison, formerly used by the Nazis, was soon the showcase Communist political prison in Warsaw, where hideous new tortures were tried out and perfected. The most notorious involved light deprivation, from contorted physical confinement inside cabinets; sleep deprivation, in which the prisoner was "forced to stand upright in a dark cell and . . . kept awake with blows to the face"; and a Communist version of waterboarding, where prisoners were confined in pitch-black cellar chambers slowly filling with fetid water from the city sewage system, which belched forth hungry rats to gnaw on their legs and vitals. Mokotów Prison was also the site of the Katyn-style execution of seven "doomed soldiers" of the AK resistance carried out on March 1, 1951. The facility, now a museum, has become sacred ground for Poles, who come to lay flowers in the cells and cellars where their family members were so cruelly tortured by the Polish Communist government, acting in obeisance to Poland's Soviet occupiers.[29]

If there was any mercy shown to Poles in their new "people's democracy," it lay in the hesitation of Bierut, Berling, Gomułka, and others to pursue the Communist transformation of society too far, owing to Poles' orneriness. Less than 9 percent of the arable land in Poland was enrolled into "collective farms." Another 10 percent was state-owned but not collectivized, though even this low figure was distorted upward by state ownership of a third of the arable land in formerly German west Poland. Although private farmers were subjected to requisitions quotas, there was no "anti-kulak" terror like the one that had taken place in Soviet Ukraine in the early 1930s. The Polish Communists, as in all the other "people's democracies," controlled the press and flooded the country with pro-Soviet, anti-American propaganda, especially after the Marshall Plan brouhaha broke in 1947. But few Poles bought what the Communists were selling. A Polish émigré visiting Cracow reported to the British Foreign Office in April 1948 that, upon hearing the suggestion that "some people at least must believe in the wickedness of the Marshall Plan," a nearby village innkeeper "roared with laughter."[30]

Yugoslavia, too, was beginning to chafe under Soviet domination, although in Yugoslavia's case it had more to do with Tito's own ambitious brand of Communism than popular resistance as such. As we saw in the story of the Kočevski Rog massacre of June 2, 1945, Tito stood out from the pack in the "people's democracies" not because he was morally opposed to Stalinism, but because he was a pioneer in political terror himself. The same was true in the economic sphere, where Tito nationalized more businesses than any other satellite leader, boasting 100 percent state control by 1948. Tito showed the same initiative in foreign policy, signing a bilateral agreement with Dimitrov's Communist Bulgaria in August 1947, and then intervening in the ongoing Greek Civil War by sending aid to the Communists there. This was despite Stalin having promised the Anglo-Americans that he accepted Greece as part of their sphere of influence, and in defiance of a pointed rebuke that Molotov delivered to Tito on the issue in February 1948. To Stalin's annoyance, Tito's boldness was infectious. A report reached him that Sofia's central railway station was plastered with posters glorifying Tito. Neighboring Albania, which Tito granted independence in exchange for Albanian Communists contributing two divisions to his Partisans in November 1944, began to chafe under the Communist dictatorship of the loyal Stalinist Enver Hoxha, whose opponents lined up with Tito. Even Hungary's party supremo, Mátyás Rákosi, known for his "slavish loyalty" to Moscow since Lenin's day, had spoken admiringly of Tito in a private Kremlin audience with Stalin. With Tito refusing to back down, Stalin withdrew all Soviet troops and advisers from Yugoslavia on March 18 and organized a ritual condemnation by all Cominform member countries in Moscow in June 1948.[31]

By holding his ground against Stalin, Tito impressed many Western observers with his "independent" streak, giving hope that a crack might be opening in Winston Churchill's Iron Curtain. Intrigued, the Truman administration offered Tito a watered-down version of the Marshall Plan, in the form of food aid to help Yugoslavia overcome bad harvests between 1948 and 1950, and even backed the country's bid for a seat on the UN Security Council in 1949 (Stalin said no). Churchill had taken a fancy to Tito during the war, instructing Britain's Cairo command to ship his Partisans nearly 23,000 tons of war supplies in just the first nine months of 1944. This was one hundred times more than he had sent to Mihailović's Chetniks during the entire war, and it had contributed mightily to Tito's victory in the Yugoslav Civil War. Celebrating his own prescience in the manner of a self-fulfilling prophecy, after returning to office in Downing Street in 1951 Churchill invited Tito on an official visit to London in March 1953.[32]*

Viewed without Churchillian sentimentality, the "Tito-Stalin split" actually reinforced the Iron Curtain rather than rending it. In his political and economic policies Tito was arguably more Stalinist than Stalin. The Tito case also provided Stalin with a useful litmus test of loyalty: party leaders in each of the other satellites were now forced not only to denounce Tito but to purge experienced, battle-hardened Communists who might have become Titos, on the same logic as the targeting of Old Bolsheviks in the Great Terror of 1936–1938. Albania's Hoxha passed the test, purging the Tito faction in Tirana and having its ringleader, Koçi Xoxe, hanged on June 13, 1949. Next to fall was Gomułka in Poland, who, unlike Bierut and Berling, had not spent the war under Stalin's thumb in Moscow. Gomułka had shown teeth in complaining about Soviet behavior in Pomerania, and he had resisted collectivization even before falling afoul of Stalin by not denouncing Tito loudly enough. Although he was not arrested, Gomułka was sacked as secretary general of the party and ritually denounced in party circulars. In Bulgaria, the scapegoat was a lifelong party activist named Traicho Kostov, who, like Gomułka, had toiled away in the underground during the war rather than toadying up to Stalin in the Kremlin. Unlike Gomułka, Kostov was not left at large; instead, he was beaten into "confessing" to conspiring with Tito to surrender

---

* Revealingly, Tito did not visit London until eighteen months after Churchill returned to power in October 1951—arriving eleven days after Stalin's death on March 5, 1953. Tito's visit was certainly provocative: "Hundreds of letters" were sent to Downing Street by Britons offended that a Communist dictator who had violently overthrown the Yugoslav monarchy had been invited to dine at Buckingham Palace, and Churchill vowed that a Soviet invasion of Yugoslavia would occasion a military response. For all his vaunted independence from Stalin, Tito had not dared to provoke Moscow this directly while the Soviet dictator was alive.

the Balkans to the Anglo-Americans, and then hanged after a Sofia show trial in December 1949 (to his credit, Kostov refused to repeat his confession-under-torture on the witness stand). It was a similar story in Hungary, where Interior Minister László Rajk, a lifelong Communist who had spent the war in the underground rather than in Moscow, was made the scapegoat for an alleged Tito-Anglo plot to subject Hungary to "a bloodthirsty dictatorship on the fascist pattern, the betrayal of the independence of the country, and colonization on behalf of the imperialists." The "only defense against mad dogs," the prosecutor announced during Rajk's October 1949 show trial, was "to beat them to death."[33]

Just as in the Great Terror, the purges in Stalin's satellites did not stop with "mad dog" mavericks but enveloped secret policemen and senior Communists. In Hungary, Rajk's execution was followed by that of Lieutenant General György Pálffy, founder and head of the Hungarian military's Political Department (Katonapolitikai Osztály, or Katpol), and of Colonel Ernö Szücs, deputy chief of the Hungarian Secret Police (Államvédelem Hatóság, ÁVH), who had both helped direct the purges in 1949. By 1951, even the founder of the ÁVH, János Kádár, was in jail awaiting execution. In Czechoslovakia, the Prague show trials continued well into 1952, culminating in the purges of nearly all of the founding members of the Czech Communist secret police (Státni Bezpecnost, StB), who had directed the purges from 1948 to 1950, along with Rudolf Slánský, general secretary of the Czechoslovak Communist Party. The Slánský trial rolled together all the bugaboos of postwar Stalinism, from antisemitism to anti-Americanism. The trial summation was almost a parody of Stalinist vituperation, declaring that "Zionist organizations" in Slánský's "conspiratorial center" had "always been linked with world capitalism by a thousand ties," serving "the efforts of American imperialism to dominate the world and unleash a new war," and thus proving themselves "a

dangerous enemy of the liberation struggle of the working class."
Somehow Slánský, a Czechoslovak Communist Party member in
good standing since 1921, who had spent the war in Moscow working for Stalin, had become infected with "cosmopolitanism . . . and
Jewish bourgeois nationalism," which were "only two sides of the
same coin, minted in Wall Street."[34]

Czechoslovakia's descent from a semi-independent country enjoying postwar prestige as the first victim of German armed aggression
into Communist show-trial parody and Stalinist satrapy was sadly
revealing. From Beneš and Masaryk to Slánský, any Prague politician remotely independent of Moscow had been sidelined just
as ruthlessly as their counterparts in Poland and Hungary. Surely,
even Georgi Dimitrov, the Bulgarian hero of the Reichstag fire,
would have been purged too had he not conveniently died of natural causes in July 1949. Tito himself was the exception that proved
the rule, his own survival serving as a useful cudgel with which
Stalin and Molotov could browbeat the other satellites into submission. By the time the show trials were up and running in 1949,
the "people's democracies" were thoroughly Stalinized, with nearly
identical secret police forces, all thoroughly penetrated by and
loyal to their Soviet handlers, answering to the Comintern-esque
"Cominform" in Moscow, and with state-planned economies that
had production targets and mandatory trade quotas coordinated
by Gosplan in the USSR via the Council for Mutual Economic
Assistance (Comecon), created in January 1949. The creation of the
North Atlantic Treaty Organization (NATO) under US auspices
in April 1949 to defend Western Europe against Soviet aggression,
sparked by Stalin's closing of the rail and road links to West Berlin
in June 1948 and the ongoing Berlin airlift, only further hardened
the Iron Curtain.

By 1949, only the Soviet Occupation Zone in Germany (the
Sowjetische Besatzungszone, or SBZ), remained outside the

Cominform and Comecon—owing not to any independent streak in German Communism but to the provisional nature of the Soviet milch-cow occupation regime. Political purges were hardly necessary in a country occupied by twenty Red Army divisions, beyond the public exclusion of former Nazi party members from public life (although, in practice, out of necessity, many were secretly hired anyway, just as they were in West Germany). In addition to the 2 million German prisoners toiling away in Soviet labor camps, 240,000 Germans were housed in ten "special Soviet camps" (*Speziallager*) in the SBZ, of which between 78,500 and 95,643 died from starvation or disease before the camps were phased out in 1950. The East German rump of the old German SPD was simply merged together with the KPD in April 1946 into the thoroughly Stalinist Socialist Unity Party of Germany (Sozialistische Einheitspartei Deutschlands, SED). Led by Walter Ulbricht, who had helped purge the KPD in the Great Terror years, the SED was so rigidly controlled that show trials were not really necessary, although Ulbricht did proactively purge the party's lower ranks. Illustrating both the party's true nature and that of the state it ruled, the SED was simply told by Colonel Sergei Tyul'panov of the Red Army's propaganda department, in May 1948, "to view the division of Germany into two blocs as an accomplished fact," and to "orient itself along strictly Leninist-Stalinist lines with a policy of ensuring law and order in the Soviet occupied zone, rejecting 'people's democracy' in the aim of acquiring statehood." The German Democratic Republic (Deutsche Demokratische Republik, DDR) formed in October 1949 was a Communist satellite par excellence, created on an express pledge to reject any hint of the people's democracy implied in its name. Even the infamous East German "Stasi" secret police (short for Ministerium für Staatsicherheit, Ministry of State Security), founded in February 1950, was a thoroughly Soviet import, growing out of the 15,000-strong NKVD occupation squadron led by the fearsome Ivan Serov.[35]

Owing to Soviet military conquest, Eastern Europe had been Communized. Before long, China would experience a similar fate, as the carnage of the Second World War created the conditions allowing Mao's Communists to conquer the country by force.

11
MAO'S MOMENT

COMMUNISM ARRIVES IN ASIA

Since Chiang Kai-shek had crushed the Communist uprising in Canton (Guangzhou) in 1927, the Chinese Communist Party (CCP) had patiently bided its time, going underground in Juangxi province in southern China, where party leaders Mao Zedong and Zhu De formed a "Chinese Soviet Republic" (Zhonghua Suwei-ai Gongheguo). Although Chiang's governing Kuomintang (KMT) party broke off diplomatic relations with Moscow in the aftermath of Canton, Stalin did not authorize further CCP revolutionary adventures in China. Gradually Stalin's Comintern men and military advisers resumed ties with Chiang's Nationalists, even while subvening his archenemies in the CCP. Stalin funded other Chinese warlords, too, including Zhang Zuolin, whose forces operated in Manchuria and North China until he was assassinated in June 1928; Feng Yuziang, who controlled much of "Inner" (i.e., Chinese) Mongolia bordering the (Soviet-controlled) Outer Mongolian "People's Republic"; and Sheng Shicai, who controlled the Muslim-Tatar-majority Chinese-Soviet border province of Xinjiang, which by the 1930s was a Russian Soviet protectorate with a heavy NKVD presence on the ground securing coal, oil, and tin for the USSR. Because the weakened Chinese Communists, based in China's deep south after their expulsion from Canton, were so far from the Soviet frontier, they had become a low priority for Soviet foreign policy in Asia, which was increasingly focused on containing Imperial Japan.[1]

The invasion of Manchuria by Japan's Kwantung Army in September 1931 presented both danger and opportunity for Communist expansion in Asia. The Japanese army's Northern Advance scheme envisioned a rapid conquest of Siberia as far west as Lake Baikal to "eliminate the Communist threat to Asia." The presence of 250,000-odd Red Army troops in the Soviet Far East abutting Chinese Manchuria to the north and in the "Mongolian People's Republic" to its east helped to redirect Japanese attention south, toward less well-defended Manchuria (or "Manchukuo," as Japan called it), the richest and most industrialized area in China. Still, Japan's thrust into Manchukuo was hardly reassuring to the Soviet army command, which now faced a formidable, battle-hardened modern army 100,000-plus strong by 1932–1933 on two separate land frontiers. As Stalin told his adviser Sergo Ordzhonikidze in June 1932, "the Japanese are certainly (certainly!) preparing for war against the USSR, and we have to be ready for anything."[2]

Soviet security concerns aside, Japan's Manchurian incursion also breathed new life into Chinese Communism. Kuomintang forces had been on the cusp of crushing the CCP partisans in their "Third Encirclement Campaign" before the Japanese invasion to the north forced Chiang to call it off in January 1932. There was even something of a truce in the Chinese Civil War when the CCP joined the KMT in declaring war on Japan that April, trying to capitalize on growing popular anti-Japanese sentiment. Chiang, however, did not want to be drawn into a Manchurian war his forces would not likely win—a war that could only strengthen his Communist enemies. As he had told aides in January, despite commanding armies much larger than Japan's Kwantung Army, the reality was that China did not possess "real military power." If he reactivated the Manchukuo front by declaring war on Japan, "within three days Japan would vanquish the coastal areas and the Yangtze river basin." Stalin, too, was wary of engaging the Kwantung Army, lest a direct Soviet-Japanese clash free up Chiang's own troops defending northern China to crush the Soviet-subsidized CCP partisans in the south (who were only nominally at war with Japan, having no point of contact with Manchukuo). In 1933, Stalin even offered Japan a non-aggression pact, hoping to turn the attention of Kwantung Army commanders southward toward Chiang's Nationalists—which would also benefit the CCP.[3]

Chiang Kai-shek, however, was wise to Stalin's imperialist wiles disguised in Communist clothing. He signed his own truce with Kwantung Army commanders on May 31, 1933, which made possible the Kuomintang's Fifth Encirclement Campaign, pitting 1 million KMT troops against 200,000 Communists. In savage fighting, Chiang's men finally dislodged CCP partisans and chased them into their legendary "Long March" along a circuitous path nearly 9,700 kilometers (6,000 miles) long, from China's deep south, east through Guangxi and Guizhou provinces, northward via Sichuan and Gansu, and finally into the rural hinterland surrounding Yan'an in Shaanxi province of northeastern China, a frontier province abutting the Soviet Mongolian Republic. Mao's idea was to establish contact with the Soviet armies posted there to regroup and rearm—Moscow having covered his expenses along the way, paid in Mexican silver dollars. (Mao himself had been on the Soviet payroll since 1921, when a Comintern agent bought his ticket to the CCP founding congress in Shanghai.) The Long March, a term popularized by the Mao-admiring American journalist Edgar Snow in his 1937 bestseller *Red Star over China*, did far more for Mao's reputation than for his partisans themselves, who died in droves.* Out of Mao's original force of 200,000 Communist partisans in Jiangxi province (already halved in the military phase of the Great Encirclement Campaign of 1933), only 7,000 survived the grueling trek to Yan'an. In November 1935, Mao was named the undisputed leader of the CCP, a legend in the making, whether because of or despite the attrition rates of the forces he led and his abject dependence on Moscow funds.[4]

Stalin was not sold on Mao yet, however. As long as the Kwantung Army posed a serious threat to his strategic position in the Far East, Soviet foreign policy needs took priority. When Japan and Germany signed the Anti-Comintern Pact on November 26, 1936, Stalin faced the prospect of a two-front pincer war against the Soviet Union—a genuine strategic danger, as opposed to the largely phantom threat of capitalist encirclement that had animated much Comintern agitprop since 1919. Unable to trust Britain, the United States, or even Popular Front France (which had signed a toothless Mutual Assistance Pact with the USSR that February, only to do nothing to resist Hitler's invasion of the Rhineland in March) to distract German strategic attention westward, Stalin's only recourse was to try to further embroil Japan in China. The Popular Front doctrine offered the prospect of an Asian realignment if Stalin's agents could broker a truce between Chiang and Mao to unite China against Japanese aggression. It would not be easy, however. Mao, weaker and more isolated since the devastating Long March, was enthusiastic about a truce, because he expected Chiang's Nationalists to do the real fighting against Japan—allowing

---

* Edgar Snow sold Western readers an uncritical version of partisan legends fed to him by Mao and his aides, describing a Long March he did not witness in person. Snow arrived at Mao's headquarters only in July 1936, more than a year after the Communists arrived in Yan'an.

him to husband his own forces. Chiang was less keen, reasoning that a full-on war with Japan could only benefit Mao and the Communists. Accepting a Popular Front might open the floodgates for Soviet arms deliveries, but then Mao, whose partisans were now close to the Soviet border, would likely receive just as much, if not more, Soviet largesse. Chiang therefore wanted guarantees that Mao's men would fight loyally under his command before he agreed to a truce in order to fight Japan. He also wanted to make sure Stalin's own armies would tie down the Kwantung Army in Manchukuo if China went to war with Japan. As Chiang's ambassador in the USSR, Jiang Tingfu, reported from Moscow, "Soviet authorities on the one hand hope that we will resist Japan . . . but they have never discussed concrete steps. They want to avoid war with Japan."[5]

Chiang's hesitation before embroiling China in a terrible war with Japan speaks well of his strategic sense and his humanity. But the political pressure was growing. In the "Xi'an Incident" of December 12, 1936, some of Chiang's top generals either mutinied or acted on behalf of Mao, arresting him and turning the Kuomintang leader over to Mao's diplomatic envoy, Zhou Enlai. Informed of Chiang's capture, Mao sent a telegram to Moscow rejoicing in news of "the arrest of the mother of all criminals." On December 15, the CCP requested that the KMT mutineers "hand [Chiang] over to a people's tribunal." But Stalin insisted on Chiang's release from CCP custody, after Chiang agreed to release his own Communist prisoners and open a "United Front" against Japan. In a brilliant rejoinder to the Anti-Comintern Pact, Stalin's diplomatic coup ensured, as S. C. M. Paine argues in a 2012 study, that "Chinese not Russian soldiers would die fighting Japan."[6]

It worked. Japan responded to the United Front by invading the North Chinese mainland after an incident at the Marco Polo Bridge, on the outskirts of Peking (Beijing), on July 7, 1937, that

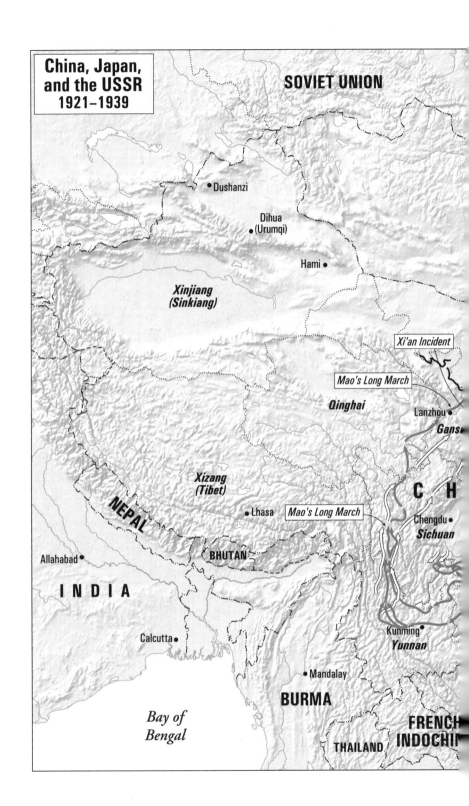

China, Japan,
and the USSR
1921–1939

SOVIET UNION

• Dushanzi

Dihua
• (Urumqi)

Hami •

Xinjiang
(Sinkiang)

Xi'an Incident

Mao's Long March

Qinghai

Lanzhou •

Gans

C H

Xizang
(Tibet)

• Lhasa

Mao's Long March

Chengdu •
Sichuan

NEPAL

Allahabad •

BHUTAN

I N D I A

Calcutta •

Kunming •
Yunnan

• Mandalay

BURMA

FRENCH
INDOCHII

Bay of
Bengal

THAILAND

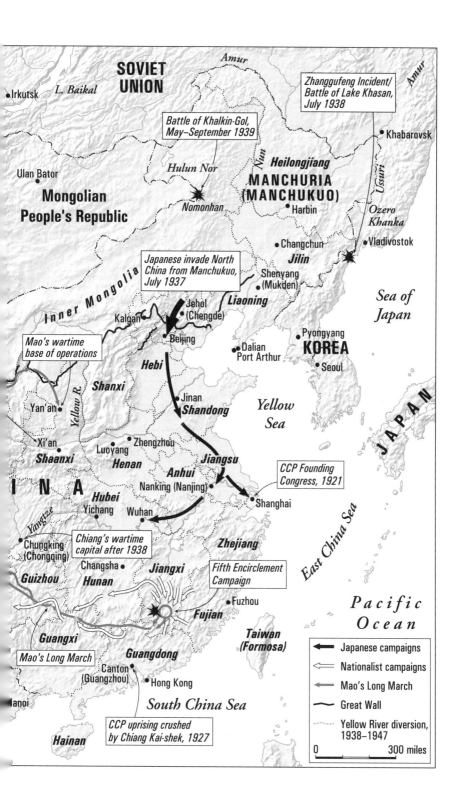

SOVIET
UNION

•Irkutsk   *L. Baikal*   Amur   Amur

Zhanggufeng Incident/
Battle of Lake Khasan,
July 1938

Battle of Khalkin-Gol,
May–September 1939

•Khabarovsk

Ulan Bator

Hulun Nor   Nun   *Heilongjiang*
MANCHURIA
(MANCHUKUO)

Mongolian
People's Republic

•Nomonhan   •Harbin   *Ozero
Khanka*   •Vladivostok

•Changchun   *Jilin*

Japanese invade North
China from Manchukuo,
July 1937

Shenyang
(Mukden)   Sea of
Japan

Kalgan•   *Jehol
(Chengde)*   *Liaoning*   •Pyongyang
KOREA

Mao's wartime
base of operations   •Beijing   •Dalian
Port Arthur   •Seoul

Hebi

Shanxi

•Yan'an   *Yellow R.*   •Jinan
Shandong   *Yellow
Sea*

JAPAN

•Xi'an   •Zhengzhou
Shaanxi   Luoyang•   *Henan*   *Jiangsu*   CCP Founding
Congress, 1921

I N A   *Anhui*
Nanking (Nanjing)•   •Shanghai

Hubei
•Yichang   •Wuhan   East China Sea

Yangtze

•Chungking
(Chongqing)   Chiang's wartime
capital after 1938   *Zhejiang*

Changsha•   *Jiangxi*

Guizhou   *Hunan*   Fifth Encirclement
Campaign   Pacific
Ocean

•Fuzhou

Guangxi   Mao's Long March   *Guangdong*   *Fujian*   *Taiwan
(Formosa)*

Canton
(Guangzhou)•   •Hong Kong

Japanese campaigns

Nationalist campaigns

•anoi   South China Sea   Mao's Long March

Great Wall

CCP uprising crushed
by Chiang Kai-shek, 1927   Yellow River diversion,
1938–1947

Hainan   0   300 miles

would soon become infamous. By November, the Kwantung Army had incurred 40,000 casualties, including 9,115 dead, which forced Japan to send in reinforcements, committing nearly 600,000 troops by year's end. With the bulk of Japan's land forces and armor now tied down in Mainland China, the Mongolian People's Republic and the Soviet Far East were safe from any serious Japanese offensives for the foreseeable future. Chinese losses were heavier still, amounting to 187,200 in the first four months, including 70 percent of Chiang's Nationalist officers. Just as Stalin had intended and Mao's own passivity now ensured, it was the Nationalists who did the fighting and dying against Japan, not the Communists. As Nelson T. Johnson, the US ambassador in China, observed of Stalin's strategy in February 1938, "Communist Russia expects to profit by the chaos that Japan is creating, and sees safety for itself in a Japan that is exhausting itself in China."[7]

Stalin did send Soviet fighters, heavy guns, machine guns, trucks, and about eighty-two light and medium tanks to support Chiang's beleaguered Nationalist forces. But a more substantial commitment, let alone outright Soviet military intervention to support China, did not follow. By the time Shanghai fell to Japan in November 1937, Chiang's ambassador in Moscow had grown desperate, demanding that the Red Army intervene before it was too late. But Stalin, who had a sleeper agent in Chiang's inner circle (Commander General Zhang Zhizhong), and thus knew where things stood on the ground, maintained his own freedom of action. On November 18, Stalin promised explicitly—and rather cynically—to authorize a Soviet incursion across the border into Manchukuo only if the collapse of the entire Chinese national government (now relocated inland at Chungking, out of the path of Japanese advance along the coast) was imminent.[8]

Stalin was good to his word. When the Japanese swept up the Yangtze and began bombing Chungking in June 1938, Stalin authorized an incursion south of Vladivostok, at the Soviet-Korean border town of Zhanggufeng. The "Zhanggufeng Incident" pitted 21,000 Red Army troops against 3,000 Japanese, who held out long enough to force a postponement of their Yangtze campaign. The following spring, the same pattern emerged when Japanese forces threatened to outflank Chungking. In May 1939, Stalin again authorized a small incursion against Japanese Manchukuo on the western side of Mongolia near the Khalkin-Gol River, where Soviet Mongolian cavalry advanced to the village of Nomonhan before being pushed back by the Japanese. The Red Army's 57th Special Corps then brought in tanks and warplanes to support them, giving the game away.[9]

In this way Stalin prolonged the Sino-Japanese War of 1937, ensuring that the Imperial Japanese Army would grind down Chiang's Nationalist forces and vice versa, while Mao's Communists observed from the sidelines. In October 1940, Stalin made this policy explicit, brokering a secret deal offering Mao's forces "sanctuary" from Japanese aggression. He offered Chinese Communists still more favorable terms in the Soviet-Japanese Neutrality Pact he signed on April 13, 1941, which pledged both Moscow and Tokyo to protect Mao's forces in Yan'an. That May, Japan even launched an offensive against Chiang's Nationalists in southern Shanxi province in coordination with Mao and Stalin, in order to free up Mao's eastern and southern flanks. Once the Nationalists were ejected from Shanxi, Japan withdrew.[10]

The Japanese attack on Pearl Harbor in December 1941 completed the circle for Stalin's Communist strategy in Asia, now coming up roses in all directions. With the United States and Britain at war with Tokyo and committed to supplying Chiang's armies, Stalin no longer needed to support the Kuomintang. In a sign of things to come, he responded to Chiang's plea for help after Pearl Harbor with the blunt warning that China "should not count on Soviet participation in the war against Japan anytime soon." So true was Stalin to the Neutrality Pact with Japan that he refused to meet with Chiang throughout the entire duration of the war. By the fall and winter of 1944–1945, with German forces on their heels in Europe, Stalin began contemplating a north Asian offensive to wrest Manchukuo, North China, Sakhalin, the Kurile Islands, and Korea away from a Japan whose naval and air forces were already fatally weakened by the long war of attrition it was fighting against the Anglo-Americans. Once the Allies' "island-hopping" campaign brought the US Air Force close enough to rain firebombs down on Tokyo and other Japanese cities, Japan began transferring land forces, too, home from the Asian mainland, stripping Manchukuo and North China of nearly a million troops, all but waving the red flag before the Soviet Communist bull.[11]

Stalin was hardly going to resist a golden opportunity like this. In October 1944, his military advisers had presented the US military liaison in Moscow, General John Deane, with a list of material requirements for equipping a Soviet "force of 1.5 million men" in the Far East with food, fuel, and "transport equipment" sufficient for a two-month offensive, along with 2 million pairs of boots. This "special" aid protocol was added to 2.7 million tons of war matériel sent by "regular" Lend-Lease protocols that winter, not including 7,995 American fighter planes and bombers flown into the Soviet Far East from Alaska. Stalin's Far Eastern Armies had received 150,000 American trucks, jeeps, and tanks just since the summer of 1944. As they prepared to storm into Manchuria, North China, Korea, Sakhalin, and the Kurile Islands, spreading Communism across northern Asia, Stalin's Far Eastern Armies, with more than 1.5 million men, rode on Lend-Lease vehicles, wore American boots and shoes, and were fed, fueled, and munitioned by the "capitalist" Americans.[12]

What should have been the triumphal moment for Chiang Kai-shek and China's national government curdled instead into a sour strategic defeat. It was not the Kuomintang, which had been

fighting against rapacious Japanese armies since the Japanese invasion of Manchuria in 1931, that would liberate Manchukuo from
the occupier, but rather the Communist armies of Stalin's USSR,
which had actually been *helping* Japan for more than four years—for
example, by interning hundreds of US pilots who had crash-landed
on Soviet soil in the Far East. Because the KMT, Britain, and the
United States had spent four years softening up Japan's forces on
land, air, and sea, the US-funded, US-munitioned, and US-fueled
Soviet offensive (August Storm), launched on August 9, 1945, came
with relatively light casualties (36,653, including 12,103 deaths).
Adding insult to this injury to the Chinese Nationalist cause, Mao's
Communist partisans, protected from Japanese attack in the "sanctuary" Stalin had negotiated for them with Tokyo, would soon
march into Manchuria unopposed at the invitation of the victorious
Red Army, to claim the fruits of a military victory to which they
had contributed nothing. Stalin had played his cards perfectly.[13]

Still, Stalin and Mao had to proceed cautiously, lest too obvious
cooperation between the Soviet armies and Mao's partisans (now
restyled the People's Liberation Army, or PLA) rouse the new US
president, Harry Truman, to resist. In the Sino-Soviet Agreement of
August 14, 1945, signed when his armies were still advancing into
Manchuria, Stalin recognized Chiang's government and agreed to
give it formal political control over Manchuria. In exchange, Chiang was forced to agree to a Soviet naval base at Port Arthur and
Soviet control of the modern port of Dalian—giving Stalin's forces
control over Manchurian communications with the outside world.
Stalin even coaxed a pledge out of Mao, signed under duress in Chiang's wartime capital of Chungking on September 18, that his PLA
forces would "stop the civil war" and "all parties must unite under
the leadership of Chairman Chiang to build a modern China."[14]

This pledge was misleading. With control of China in the balance, Stalin was never likely to settle for just Manchuria. Quietly,

Red Army commanders in Manchuria established contact with Mao's armies and began sharing arms with the Chinese Communists, some regifted from American Lend-Lease surplus, others from stocks confiscated after Japan's surrender. The Russians, of course, did not turn everything over, keeping much of the best American, Japanese, and Soviet equipment for themselves. Nonetheless, Mao's armies were given 700,000 rifles, as many as 18,000 machine guns, and 4,000 field artillery pieces, along with 11,052 grenade launchers, 3,078 trucks, 14,777 horses, 21,084 supply vehicles, 860 warplanes, and 287 command cars. Stalin also agreed to hand over Kalgan, a critical gateway in the Great Wall of China guarding the northern approaches to Beijing, to Mao's PLA. Soviet sources now prove that Mao's pledge of unity with Chiang on September 18 was insincere, because the day before this he had received orders from Stalin to "expand towards the north" into Soviet-occupied Manchuria to load up on arms and supplies—orders Mao passed on to his armies after returning to Yan'an on September 19. His September 18 pledge, Mao assured his generals, was "a mere scrap of paper." On October 4, Stalin ordered Mao to move his forces into Manchuria, promising that Red Army commanders would provide arms for the PLA, which promptly expanded to half a million men.[15]

By October, Manchuria, the richest and most industrialized region in China, was likely lost for good to the Chinese national government, owing to Soviet wiles and American naïveté. Even had Chiang convinced Truman to go all in to support a massive offensive to regain Manchuria, much of the economic point was already lost, as the Soviet occupiers had carted off much of the industrial wealth worth having, almost $900 million worth of goods and equipment by later US estimates, and sabotaged or destroyed the rest (total damages were estimated at $2 billion). In all, the Soviets helped themselves to between 70 and 90 percent of

Manchuria's industrial capacity, including 83 percent of the electrical power generation equipment, 86 percent of the mining equipment, 82 percent of cement production, 80 percent of metallurgy, and 65 percent of the processing equipment for petroleum fuel and lubricants. As an American adviser to Chiang, James McHugh, observed on entering Soviet-occupied Mukden (Shenyang), "Factories lay like riddled skeletons, picked clean of their machinery," even while Red Army grunts "stole everything in sight, broke up bathtubs and toilets with hammers, pulled electric wiring out of the plaster," and set fire to whatever they didn't rip out. Reconquering the now ruined Manchuria from Mao's lavishly supplied PLA would be a massive military undertaking, not least because the Soviets controlled its principal ports and Mao controlled Kalgan and the main roads from Beijing heading north into Manchuria overland. In a clear sign of hostile intent, Stalin informed Chiang, on October 17, that he would not share any captured Japanese war matériel with Nationalist China, and that he would not withdraw Soviet troops three months after the war as he had pledged to do in the Sino-Soviet Agreement.[16]

For all these reasons, Truman's new military liaison to the Chinese national government, General Albert Wedemeyer, urged Chiang Kai-shek to be cautious and not walk into Stalin's Manchurian trap. Wedemeyer, unlike his predecessor, the salty-tongued General "Vinegar Joe" Stilwell, who had called the generalissimo "peanut," actually liked Chiang and wanted him to succeed in salvaging what he could of China from Stalin and Mao. Unfortunately for Wedemeyer and Chiang, the Truman administration, despite cooling on Soviet expansionism in Europe, was taking the opposite tack in Asia. On November 10, a White House directive to Wedemeyer stipulated that "American military aid to China will cease immediately if evidence compels the U.S. government to believe that [Chinese troops] receiving such aid are using it . . . to conduct civil war." Undercutting Wedemeyer's authority still further, President Truman sent his army chief of staff, General George Marshall, to Chungking as a "special presidential envoy" in December with instructions to establish a coalition government between Chiang and Mao—two mortal political enemies whose civil war had just bloodily resumed. Marshall even sent American officers to Kalgan, the Great Wall gateway city Stalin had handed over to Mao, to train Mao's PLA soldiers. On Marshall's watch, US financial aid to Chungking was slow-walked and arms shipments kept to a trickle—and then cut off entirely in September 1946. US troop strength on the ground in China plummeted from 63,000 in September 1945 to 10,000 by January 1946, heading toward zero. By 1947, the proxy conflict in China was wholly one-sided: Stalin provided Mao with whatever he needed in Manchuria, from Soviet and (captive) Japanese engineers to fix and modernize the arms factories of Dalian to Soviet tanks and artillery, even while the United States *forbade* Chiang to use American arms to defend his government against the Communists. Making this betrayal more painful, it was the same year the United States announced the "Truman doctrine," taking up the banner of "free peoples" in their struggle against Communist subversion or armed aggression. But there was no Truman doctrine for China. Asked by a friend to explain why the Kuomintang had lost China, Wedemeyer dryly observed that Marshall and the US government had "announced we would not support Chiang Kai-Shek and his government."[17]

In a last gasp to salvage China from Communism, Truman sent Wedemeyer back on a fact-finding mission in July 1947 and temporarily lifted the US arms embargo on Chiang's government. What Wedemeyer reported back, however, was not encouraging. Owing to the lack of financial support from Washington, Chiang's government had resorted to the printing press, paying its soldiers, officers, and civil servants in Chinese paper yuan rapidly dwindling in purchasing power. Something like 70 percent of expenses were now devoted to the war against the Communists, despite support drying up from the US government, which sent only about 1 percent of the aid to Nationalist China between 1945 and 1949 (about $225 million) as was sent to Europe ($25 billion including Marshall Plan funds). "Under the impact of civil strife and inflation," Wedemeyer informed Truman, "the Chinese economy is disintegrating." The "ruthless tactics of land distribution and terrorism" practiced by Mao's Communists had "alienated" the better-off Chinese farm families whose land had been taken. Nonetheless, many landless peasants, particularly those in the impoverished rural hinterland of Shanxi province, which furnished Mao's political base, were warming to the Communist message of land reform. Popular support was anyhow largely irrelevant in an asymmetric civil war in which Mao's PLA deployed "hit and run tactics, adapted to their mission of destruction at points or in areas of their own selection," which gave them "a decided advantage over the Nationalists, who must defend many critical areas including connecting lines of communication." The "overall military position of the National Government," Wedemeyer concluded, "has deteriorated in the past several months and the current military situation favors Communist forces." Absent a resumption of US aid, including food deliveries to alleviate hunger in China's coastal cities, and arms deliveries on a massive scale, Chiang would lose Manchuria, and he would struggle to hold on to North China for much longer.[18]

No such American aid was forthcoming. Although the US Congress approved one final $125 million aid package for Chiang in April 1948, the money arrived too late to affect either plummeting urban living standards or the military balance. Stubbornly, Chiang continued sending reinforcements into the teeth of Communist strength in Manchuria, rather than retreating behind the Great Wall to hold down Beijing. First the Nationalist stronghold of Changchun was surrounded by the armies of Mao's top commander, Lin Biao, who had been trained by Soviet officers at the Whampoa Military Academy. After being informed that Chiang's commander, Zheng Dongguo, would not surrender, General Biao ordered his PLA forces, 200,000 strong, to "turn Changchun into a city of death." They complied, closing all roads in and out, cutting off the city's water, and turning back hungry town dwellers trying to flee. Meanwhile, an advance guard of Lin Biao's forces proceeded south to Shenyang and cut the rail connection south to Beijing. By September, the PLA had encircled Jinzhou, the last Nationalist stronghold in southern Manchuria outside the Great Wall. After Jinzhou capitulated on October 15, Chiang finally gave General Zheng permission to evacuate Changchun after a 150-day siege that had cost the lives of 160,000 civilians and retreat. It was too late: Zheng's emaciated troops, unable to break through Communist lines, either surrendered or deserted over to the victorious forces of Lin Biao. Now trapped in between PLA pincers north and south, brave Nationalist fighters in Shenyang held out for two weeks. But on November 1, Shenyang, too, fell. Asked by Chiang whether, in view of the Manchurian collapse, Chinese Nationalist forces might still be able to hold on to Beijing, Zheng replied acidly, "No place in China will be safe."[19]

Chiang's Nationalist government was now at Mao's mercy. Chiang had lost his best troops, and most of his best armor and equipment, in a forlorn campaign to win back Manchuria. Lin Biao now commanded a conquering Communist army, 750,000 strong and gaining strength every day, while Chiang had only 240,000 or so underpaid troops defending Beijing. Would China's storied capital, too, become a "city of death"? The terrible fate of Changchun helped convince Chiang's commander in Beijing, Fu Zuoyi, to surrender (after a mere forty-day siege) to preserve the city from destruction and its civilian population from starvation—including nearly all of his 240,000 Nationalist troops, who were simply absorbed into the PLA under Lin Biao. While fierce fighting continued in central China near the railway linking Beijing to Nanking (Nanjing) and Shanghai, the fall of Beijing on January 22, 1949, was an unmistakable triumph for Lin Biao and Mao, as Chiang acknowledged by resigning his office as president. It seemed that nothing could now stop the Communists in their march across China.[20]

So rapid was the advance of Mao's Communist armies that Stalin himself was taken aback. While Soviet advisers, arms, and funds had played a huge role in turning the PLA into a formidable fighting force, the farther this army advanced south into China, the farther Mao would recede from the Soviet frontier and from Soviet influence and control. Sensing that a triumphant Mao would be tempted to go Tito's way—the Tito-Stalin split had just lit up the European sky in 1948—Stalin tried clumsily to intervene, sending Mao a telegram in January 1949, after the fall of Beijing, urging that the PLA halt at the Yangtze River and negotiate a settlement with Chiang, which might have left Nanjing, Shanghai, Canton (Guangzhou), and southern China in Nationalist control. The Yangtze was a formidable strategic barrier, a river so wide and deep that it is navigable by massive ocean liners nearly 950 kilometers (600 miles) inland. A fleet of some thirty Kuomintang naval vessels plied the river. As Wedemeyer observed, despite their failures in Manchuria and North China, Chiang's Nationalist forces "could have defended the Yangtze river with broomsticks if they had the will to do so." But such will was lacking after the humiliating failures in the north—and after Chiang's failure to pay his flag officers for months: the promised aid from Washington had not yet arrived. To emphasize the hopelessness of the cause, PLA forces amassed on the northern banks of the river for miles on end, mustering a million men by early March 1949. After a mutiny aboard

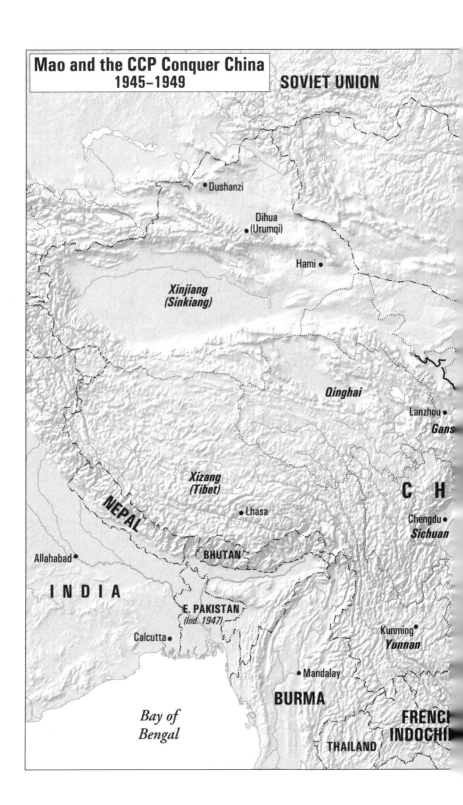

Mao and the CCP Conquer China
1945–1949

SOVIET UNION

• Dushanzi

Dihua
• (Urumqi)

Hami •

Xinjiang
(Sinkiang)

Qinghai

Lanzhou •
Gans

C H

Xizang
(Tibet)

• Lhasa

Chengdu •
Sichuan

NEPAL

Allahabad •

BHUTAN

I N D I A

E. PAKISTAN
(Ind. 1947)

Kunming •
Yunnan

Calcutta •

• Mandalay

BURMA

Bay of
Bengal

FRENC
INDOCHI

THAILAND

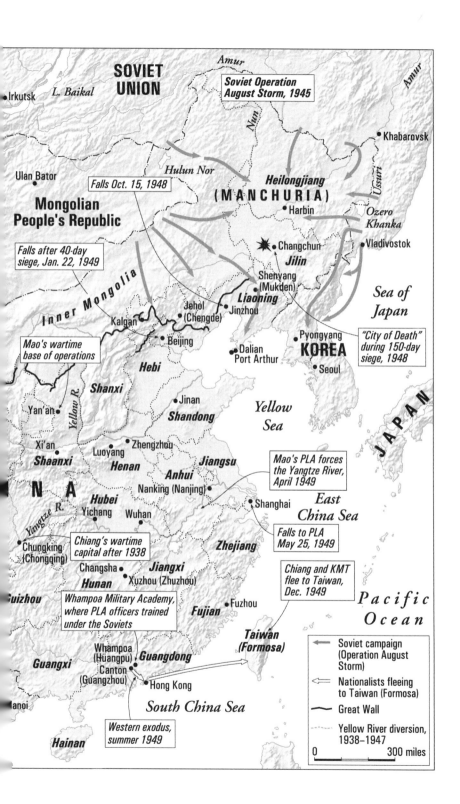

Soviet Operation
August Storm, 1945

SOVIET UNION

Irkutsk

L. Baikal

Amur

Amur

Khabarovsk

Ulan Bator

Hulun Nor

Falls Oct. 15, 1948

Mongolian
People's Republic

Heilongjiang
(MANCHURIA)

Harbin

Ozero
Khanka

Vladivostok

Falls after 40-day
siege, Jan. 22, 1949

Inner Mongolia

Changchun

Jilin

Shenyang
(Mukden)

Kalgan

Jehol
(Chengde)

Liaoning

Jinzhou

Beijing

Dalian
Port Arthur

Pyongyang
KOREA

Sea of
Japan

"City of Death"
during 150-day
siege, 1948

Mao's wartime
base of operations

Hebi

Seoul

Shanxi

Jinan

Shandong

Yellow
Sea

Yan'an

Yellow R.

Xi'an

Shaanxi

Luoyang

Zhengzhou

Henan

Jiangsu

Anhui

Nanking (Nanjing)

Mao's PLA forces
the Yangtze River,
April 1949

East
China Sea

J A P A N

N A

Hubei

Yichang

Wuhan

Shanghai

Falls to PLA
May 25, 1949

Chungking
(Chongqing)

Chiang's wartime
capital after 1938

Zhejiang

Chiang and KMT
flee to Taiwan,
Dec. 1949

Changsha

Jiangxi

Xuzhou (Zhuzhou)

Hunan

uizhou

Whampoa Military Academy,
where PLA officers trained
under the Soviets

Fujian

Fuzhou

Taiwan
(Formosa)

Pacific
Ocean

Guangxi

Whampoa
(Huangpu)

Canton
(Guangzhou)

Guangdong

Hong Kong

anoi

South China Sea

Soviet campaign
(Operation August
Storm)

Nationalists fleeing
to Taiwan (Formosa)

Great Wall

Hainan

Western exodus,
summer 1949

Yellow River diversion,
1938–1947

0   300 miles

303

Chiang's Yangtze flagship on February 25, the fight had gone out
of the Nationalist navy, which soon melted away just as Chiang's
armies had done in the north, turning their river vessels over to the
PLA and enabling Communist troops to cross the river unopposed
in April.[21]

Chiang's wartime capital of Chungking, Wuhan (both cities upriver on the Yangtze), and the other great trading cities of
South China were now under the gun. A great southward exodus of prosperous Chinese traders and European businessmen and
missionaries toward Shanghai, Canton, and finally Hong Kong
was underway. After only a few days of token resistance, Nanjing
fell on April 23, 1949, Shanghai on May 25, and finally Canton
(Guangzhou) on December 10, on which date Chiang Kai-shek
fled to Formosa (Taiwan), establishing a Nationalist government
in exile that still exists today. All of Mainland China, excepting
only the British crown colony of Hong Kong, whose sovereignty
Mao conceded, had now been "liberated" by Mao's armies, many
of them "teenagers in the first flush of youth," as one foreign diplomat observed.[22]

Wherever the loyalties of China's people had lain during the
Civil War, Mao's Communists enjoyed a honeymoon of sorts in
their first days in power. Like the arrival of the Red Army in Eastern Europe, the PLA takeover meant, in the first place, an end to
the war—to a series of wars that had plagued China for nearly four
decades, ever since the dissolution of the Qing dynasty in 1912.
The era of "warlordism" was now over, along with the Nationalist
ascendancy in the Kuomintang era, which, despite Chiang's promises to wean China of foreign influence, had led instead to levels of
dependence on foreign influence and investment greater than ever
before. China's coastal cities had become thronged with westerners, from American bankers and arms dealers to White Russian,
Jewish, and other civilian refugees from Europe: Shanghai now

had the second-highest foreign-born population of any city in the world, just behind New York. Indeed, foreign dependence ultimately proved Chiang's undoing once American aid dried up after 1946.[23]

It helped the Communist cause immensely that Beijing, the ancient capital, had been spared, including the Imperial Palace, or "Forbidden City" (Gu Gong), which had stood for millennia. Although dilapidated, dirty, and overgrown with weeds after years of war and neglect, Tiananmen Square in front of the Palace Gates was still a grand setting for an imperial procession, and Mao used it to spectacular effect when he proclaimed the formation of the People's Republic of China (PRC) there on October 1, 1949. Huge crowds, 300,000 strong, attended the founding ceremony, shouting out slogans such as "Long live the Chinese Communist Party" and "Long live Chairman Mao." Mao, now fifty-six years old, was in fine form addressing the masses, flanked by troupes of dancers, costumed stilt walkers, and more than 16,000 PLA soldiers, on foot and mounted, accompanied by tanks and warplanes screaming overhead. A young Chinese doctor named Li Zhisui, who had returned from Australia to attend the ceremony in Beijing after hearing the news of the end of the Civil War, later recalled, "I was so full of joy that my heart nearly burst out of my throat, and tears welled up in my eyes. I was so proud of China, so full of hope, so happy that the exploitation and suffering, the aggression from foreigners, would be gone forever." Thousands more felt the same way, judging by the enthusiastic reception of the crowd.[24]

Just as in Eastern Europe, the honeymoon with Mao's conquering Communist army was short-lived. Soldiers, supporters, and hangers-on of the defeated Kuomintang, of course, never welcomed the Communists at all. Those who could get out, did, with as many as 2 million refugees pouring out of China via Hong Kong, some settling there under British protection but most of them following

Chiang into exile. Chinese urbanites of means who stayed behind hoped for the best, but they found themselves harassed, their apartments and homes searched and looted of "forbidden items" such as radios, and were often arrested on suspicion of sympathy with the Kuomintang. As in Russia after the Revolution, strict food rationing was introduced, as households were registered with the government, censorship and state control of print media and radio were introduced, industry nationalized, and young students and workers were mobilized into *subbotnik*-style work battalions to clean up and rebuild the infrastructure of a war-damaged country. Mao introduced Communist innovations, too, dividing families up into sixty social "classes," with a clear proletarian hierarchy between "revolutionary" cadres, soldiers, martyrs, and industrial workers at the top, and bourgeois capitalists, "landlords," and "rich peasants" at the bottom. Mass arrests of class enemies began almost immediately on the pretext that, despite Chiang's departure to Taiwan, the war with the Nationalists was still ongoing. In Hebei province, home to the capital, Beijing, some 20,000 "counter-revolutionaries" were executed in the first twelve months after Mao proclaimed the PRC. Social "parasites," such as prostitutes, beggars, and vagrants, were rounded up in the thousands and sent off to prison or re-education camps. Brothels and gold and jewelry shops were closed down as Western "capitalist" excrescences. Women abandoned lipstick and makeup, and everyone either hid away or sold off their jewelry, watches, and rings. "The fashion was simplicity almost to the point of rags," one female Communist recalled of the liberation years. Regime agitprop was simpler still. As another young Communist observed, "There is very little subtlety involved. Good and bad, friend and foe, are defined in terms of black and white." Maoism left no room for doubt.[25]

Stringent as the new regime's imposition of control was during its first year in power, the fall of 1950 saw more draconian measures still after the PRC invaded Tibet (on October 7) and Korea (on October 18). While the Tibet campaign was small in scale, though bloody enough, China's entry into the Korean War to bail out Communist North Korea, after Kim Il-sung's invasion of South Korea on June 25 was countered by a broad US-led United Nations coalition, marked an obvious escalation of global tensions between the Communist and "capitalist" worlds. The fighting in the Korean War cost the PLA some 400,000 deaths out of 3 million troops deployed in Korea, against a tenth of that many killed on the US-allied side (a bit under 40,000, of whom 36,000 were Americans)—not to mention several million Korean civilians and soldiers. In military terms, all this bloodshed led to a stalemate at the 38th parallel, which endures today as the border and "demilitarized" zone between North and South Korea. But the PLA proved its ability to fight the Americans and their allies to a standstill, winning great prestige for Mao's government at home—while furnishing the backdrop for a new agitprop campaign ("Resist America, Aid Korea," and later, "Hate America") to justify arresting alleged American spies and sympathizers, 13,800 just by the end of 1950. Americans and other foreigners were harassed; their bank accounts frozen; their apartments, villas, businesses, and cars seized; and were then still often arrested, beaten, and denied exit visas until they would agree to give up whatever cash, jewelry, and other valuables they still had. Often they departed with just the clothes on their backs and whatever small items they could fit in a suitcase. As a Beijing newspaper warned foreigners, "When the tables are turned / We Chinese have no further need for you knaves. Imperialists beware / All is not well with you anymore."[26]

Traumatic as this treatment was for foreigners from the old Western missions and trading colonies who had lived their entire lives in China, native Chinese suffered far worse horrors as paranoia ramped up in the Korean War years. A critical escalation occurred in March 1951, when a ranking CCP general, Huang Zuyan, was shot by a protester in Jinan, in Shandong province. In retaliation, Mao demanded "several batches of big killings" in China's cities, writing to one of his provincial party secretaries that "the people say that killing counter-revolutionaries is even more joyful than a good downpour." In its inspiration by an assassination attempt, the CCP terror that followed was similar to Lenin's Red Terror, but in its scale, and the use of provincial death and deportation quotas, it soon resembled Stalin's Great Terror, with the sinister new twist that quotas were set per thousand residents (i.e., 1 killed per 1,000 and 9 deported to labor camps). To summon the necessary hatred, mass rallies were held in Chinese cities, with CCP spokesmen asking crowds what should be done with "spies and special agents hiding in Beijing," or to "feudal remnants" such as "fishmongers, real-estate brokers, water carriers and nightsoil scavengers." The answer that usually came back was "Execute them by firing squad." Like Stalin chiding his NKVD henchmen for "Dizzy with Success" excesses against kulaks, Mao chided his Beijing executioners in April 1951, ruling that, in this city of 2 million residents, of whom 10,000 had been arrested, 700 killed, and 700 more scheduled for dispatch, "killing roughly 1,400 should be enough." But the momentum of terror was hard to stop. At a CCP convention in 1954, Chinese bureaucrats reported having executed 710,000 people—a figure historians now think is too low—and sent millions more to forced-labor camps. Mao himself boasted, at one point, that 800,000 "counter-revolutionaries" had been "liquidated."[27]

As if this were not enough, October 1951 saw a "Three-Antis" campaign to purge the PRC government of corruption, waste, and bureaucracy, and January 1952 the "Five-Antis" campaign against "bribery, tax evasion, pilfering government property, cheating on contracts, and stealing state secrets." In an interesting update to

Soviet secret police informers, the PRC provided "denunciation boxes, bright red with a small slit at the top," allowing anyone in China to denounce anyone else of thought crimes. One PRC report in October 1952 listed 1.2 million such "corrupt individuals" who had been denounced by volunteer spies in the government alone. As for the private sector, PRC files show that some 450,000 businesses were targeted, while at least 2.5 million people were imprisoned or sent to reeducation or forced-labor camps, roughly 1.2 percent of the rural population but fully 4 percent of China's urban population. China's people paid a heavy price for Mao's triumphant fighting-to-a-draw with the Americans in Korea.[28]

The end of the Korean War with the ceasefire of July 1953 brought little relief to China's harassed and hectored people. Even as anti-American war hysteria subsided, a new agitprop campaign was launched against a mythical internal conspiracy labeled the "attack of the right opportunist cold wind." Later simplified into a movement for "thought reform" (*szuhsiang kaitsao*), the new targets were dissident party members or "hidden counterrevolutionaries" (*sufan*). Intellectuals and schoolteachers, too, were subject to arrest quotas, about one in ten among middle school instructors (85,000 in all), and still more primary school teachers (roughly 170,000). In the cultural sphere Mao channeled Hitler more than Stalin. The anti-intellectual thought-reform campaign saw public book burnings so colossal that they were measured by volume. In Shanghai, 237 metric tons of books were torched. In Shantou, a coastal port where European influence had been marked, 300,000 volumes were thrown onto a giant bonfire that raged for three days. Western-style books, music, and films were either destroyed or hidden away in CCP archives, replaced by new Communist tunes, hymns, and newsreels as the new Sino-Soviet Friendship Association, with 120,000 branches in China, launched the "Learn from the Soviet

Union" campaign, which flooded the country with Soviet Communist literature, films, and school textbooks.* While some enduring Chinese cultural traditions, such as Confucianism and Buddhism, were reluctantly tolerated for the time being, Taoism and Chinese Christianity, minority but mainstream faiths, were ruthlessly persecuted. The Catholic Church, with 3 million adherents, saw nearly 13,000 of its 16,000 churches shut down, torched, or razed to the ground, enough to reduce the number of parishioners by nearly half.[29]

The first hint of relief came in May 1957, when the "Hundred Flowers Campaign" promised greater freedom to party members and others to air grievances. Whether or not Mao genuinely wanted to hear constructive criticism of his government's policies—his motivation seems to have been staving off criticism of his own leadership inside the party—CCP bureaucrats interpreted the policy as cynically as possible, encouraging critics to speak out—whereupon their names were taken down and put onto lists of dissidents who had expressed "evil thoughts." At a village meeting in southern China near Macao, a schoolteacher named Hsiao Jo-ping lamented the persecution of his father in the Terror, declaring bravely that the "Communist regime was the most disastrous tyranny in Chinese history." His brother Hsiao Chung-yao then spoke up in the same vein, followed by several others. "The Communists," an eyewitness named Lee Ke-chiang recalled after escaping to Hong Kong, "kept a record of every word. Later all of them were sent to a labor camp." By July 1957, the Hundred Flowers Campaign had served its purpose, rooting out even mild "rightist" opposition among party cadres and

---

* Unlike other foreigners in Communist China, Soviet nationals were given protected legal status, akin in many ways to the "extraterritorial" rights of Europeans in the old days, and were even allowed to shop in special stores where imported consumer goods were available.

schoolteachers: between 400,000 and 700,000 of them had voluntarily confessed their thought crimes and been sent off to re-education camps.[30]

The Hundred Flowers hiccup out of his system, Mao returned full-bore to the Communist offensive. The Cold War was entering peak hysteria, with the Soviet launch of Sputnik in October 1957, the first Earth-orbiting satellite, prompting the United States to spend massively to catch up in the space race. Mao himself visited Moscow that November, and he was impressed with the Soviet achievement, along with Nikita Khrushchev's boast that the USSR would catch up with the United States in the production of meat, milk, and butter "in a few short years," and would outstrip the Americans in overall economic output "within the next fifteen years." Perhaps Communist China could not match this, but Mao vowed that it "may well catch up with or overtake Britain." Ominously, he hinted that the ultimate goal was for the Communist world to win a world war with the capitalist powers—a war that, he predicted with curious confidence, would kill "a third," or "if it is a little higher it could be half," of the world's population, which he reckoned at "2.7 billion people." A billion or more might die, but the happy result would be that "imperialism would be erased and the whole world will become socialist. After a few years there would be 2.7 billion people again." More elegantly, Mao retooled a traditional Chinese proverb as a Communist battle slogan: "East Wind Prevails over West Wind" (*Tung-Feng-Ya-Tao-Si-Feng*).[31]

Mao declared production targets of breathtaking audacity. He vowed to double, then triple, Chinese steel output, from 5.2 million metric tons annually to "10 or 15," in the first five years, then double that again in the five after that, to reach "30 to 40 million" within fifteen years. Grain output would double by 1958 from 195 million to 375 million tons. Collectivization would not serve as a prelude or complement to industrialization as in Stalin's USSR;

rather, everything would happen all at once, pell-mell, "industry and agriculture, heavy and light industries," through a mixture of "modern and indigenous methods of production." China would show the world that true Communists were capable of "walking on two legs" at once (*Liang-T'iao-T'ui-Ch'o-Lu*).[32]

China's people, already exhausted by a decade of invasive governance, were now sent into an abyss of forced-labor madness. First came the massive dam projects to harness China's rivers for electric power and irrigation. This initiative gave its name to Mao's broader push, the "Great Leap Forward" (*Ta-Yo-Tsin*). With a certain callous honesty, Mao's commissars did not even pretend, like Stalin's agricultural planners in 1928, that they would be able to deploy hundreds of thousands of tractors to till the soil. Rather, China would deploy its one comparative advantage—its hundreds of millions of people, perhaps numbering about 650 million, the vast majority of them illiterate, desperately poor farmers and villagers—to transform the landscape with muscle power and crude hand tools. The rural population would dig up soil and rocks during the slack winter months to build dams and reservoirs and irrigation channels. Mao himself beatified a showcase reservoir project outside Beijing, at the "Ming Tombs," by chipping in half an hour's work digging, which left him "dripping with sweat." As always, his real talent was in coining a slogan. To justify the backbreaking labor of his people, who were expected to work day and night, in all weather conditions, he came up with "Three Years of Hard Work Is Ten Thousand Years of Happiness." Not everyone agreed. So many emaciated laborers, unable to quit after half an hour like Mao, were collapsing from overwork that CCP officials in Jiangsu devised a formula to estimate labor wastage rates: one dead worker for each million cubic meters of soil moved. For example, one overseer "claims he can move 30 billion cubic meters," which meant "30,000 people will die." Another promised to move "20 billion," such that "20,000 will die." No one knows for sure how many people died digging up China's earth with "picks, shovels, baskets and poles" between 1957 and 1960, but new research suggests the number of victims was in the hundreds of thousands.[33]

Unfortunately for China's people, this was only the beginning of their agony. To raise agricultural yields, party planners demanded that the fields be plowed deeper and deeper, to an almost unheard-of depth of a meter below the surface, and rice and other crops planted more densely in the field through "close cropping" of seeds (just one Chinese inch apart, about 1.5 US inches). Mao's command was to "use human waves, turn every field over," and then flood the tilled fields with as much fertilizer as possible to drive up yields. Local party activists, encouraged to "launch a Sputnik" by breaking yield barriers, sent Chinese farm workers out to conjure up every kind of "fertilizer," from seaweed and garbage to mud, straw, or bucketloads of "animal and human excrement," even women's hair—sheared off and ground up to feed the inexhaustible maw of organic waste material thrown on the fields. As Li Jingquan, the Communist party boss in Sichuan province, explained, "Even shit has to be collectivized!" Chicken coops, cattle barns, and pigpens were torn down for the trace amounts of excrement or urine they contained. Before long even human dwellings were torched and churned into semi-organic fertilizer, on the logic that shelter for living animals and humans was less important than a theoretical increase in future agricultural yield on the new Chinese collective farms. As the Maoist slogan had it, "Destroy Straw Huts in an Evening, Erect Residential Areas in Three Days, Build Communism in a Hundred Days." Chinese farmers too poor to have smeltable iron gates on their houses were forced to throw their kitchenware, forks, spoons, and knives into backyard "furnaces" to smelt steel. As one Communist activist later recalled after leaving the country in disgust, without "pots, pans, and utensils" to cook and dine with, peasants now "had no choice but to eat in commune mess halls."[34]

While digging up and carting around soil and rock, collecting animal and human waste, tearing down chicken coops, and even melting down utensils and tools in backyard furnaces could be done with muscle power and simple tools, ramping up Chinese industrial production to Western levels would require imported machinery. As Mao confessed in October 1957, "If we want to build socialism, we need to import technology, equipment, steel, and other necessary materials." Like Stalin's First Five-Year Plan, Mao's ambitious industrial targets necessitated cruel triage, as the only things China produced in enough quantity to export were grain, rice, pork, nuts, seed oils, and clothing—the very things people needed to survive. And so China ramped up food exports in 1958 and 1959 to pay for industrial imports even as food shortages began to bite, shipping 4.2 million metric tons of grain abroad in 1959 alone. Unlike Stalin, who had manipulated gullible (or cynical) Western journalists like Walter Duranty to camouflage his murderous food-export triage, Mao and his advisers *boasted* about it. As Zhou Enlai wrote in November 1958, "I would rather that we don't eat or eat less and consume less, as long as we honor contracts signed with foreigners." Deng Xiaoping, general secretary of the Party Secretariat, insisted that "if everybody could just save a few eggs, a pound of meat, a pound of oil and six kilos of grain the entire export problem would simply vanish." Mao proposed at a party congress in Shanghai in April 1959 that the nation could "save on clothing and food to guarantee exports, otherwise if 650 million people start eating a little more our export surplus will all be eaten up." In fact, he added, "horses, cows, sheep, chicken, dogs, pigs: six of the farm animals don't eat meat, and aren't they all still alive? Some people don't eat meat either. . . . [C]an we pass a resolution that nobody should eat meat, that all of it should be exported?"[35]

The result of the radical overturning of traditional Chinese agriculture, and the forced export of dwindling yields of grain, seed oils, and pork to pay for industrial imports, was a famine of unprecedented scale, dwarfing even the horrors of the Soviet Holodomor. China, to be sure, had known terrible famines before, as recently as 1928–1930, which had cost the lives of 2 million or 3 million. But this was nothing like the humanitarian catastrophe that spread across the country from 1958 to 1962. While, owing to CCP control of the central archives, we may never know the full extent of China's suffering, intrepid researchers have been working for years to collate material from local archives, including at least one major CCP semiofficial investigation conducted in 1979, during a post-Mao thaw, along with death certificate records for the years before and after 1958, which allow demographers to estimate "excess deaths." The "normal" death rate across the country, already hugely elevated in 1957 owing to years of privation and repression, was something like 11 percent; this rose to an average of 15 percent during the Great Leap Forward years, peaking at 29 percent in 1960. In Anhui province, in North Central China, the death rate soared to an almost unfathomable 68 percent of the population in 1960. Not all regions in China suffered equally horrific starvation rates, but the overall story is clear: even the Chinese government admitted in 1988 that there had been at least 20 million famine deaths. The best independent estimates for excess Chinese deaths during the Great Leap years come out between a low end of 32 million, calculated by a Chinese demographer, Cao Shuji, who worked with local party records, and the "43 to 46 million" estimated by Chen Yizi, who headed the CCP research team in 1979–1980 (a figure Chen Yizi published only after fleeing China following the Tiananmen Square massacre of 1989). Frank Dikötter, in his groundbreaking 2010 study *Mao's Great Famine*, concluded after years of researching all available datasets that "the death toll stands at a minimum of 45 million excess deaths." Even Mao, the architect of the greatest man-made famine in history, was forced to admit it was happening, writing, in November 1960, as deaths were peaking, that "bad people have seized power, causing beatings, deaths, grain shortages and hunger." More pithily, as a Chinese refugee from Shanghai told the American journalist Stanley Karnow in 1965, "We tried a great leap but broke our bones."[36]

So over-the-top was Mao's Great Leap Forward that it came in for criticism from Nikita Khrushchev, of all people, the Soviet Communist strongman so obsessed with agricultural modernization— from the milk and meat race with America to the plowing of "virgin lands" to plant corn as feedstock—that Russians had begun referring to him as *Kukuruznik*, or "corn freak." Whether out of jealousy over Mao's still greater ambition and the publicity it was generating,[*] concern over Mao's saber-rattling on the Chinese-Indian border and with the United States over the Taiwan Strait, or genuine horror at the humanitarian disaster unfolding in China, Khrushchev rebuked Mao's Great Leap Forward in July 1959 and backed up his criticism by withdrawing Soviet nuclear cooperation with Beijing. Their differences on this matter were the first sign of the emerging "Sino-Soviet split" in the Communist camp that would shake up the Cold War in the years to come. As Khrushchev later wrote, the Soviets had produced their own famine horrors in Ukraine in the early 1930s, "but there was no excuse for the Chinese to be repeating our own stupid mistakes." Mao responded in kind when Khrushchev visited Beijing that September. "You have accused us of quite a lot," Mao told his Soviet counterpart. "You say . . . that the Great Leap was wrong, that we brag

---

[*] Khrushchev may also have been annoyed by the "summit swim" Mao had cleverly staged in Beijing. Mao, a champion swimmer who showed off his best stuff, embarrassed poor Khrushchev, who could only "flop around" in the pool's shallow end.

about ourselves as orthodox Marxists. Therefore I have an accusation for you, too: that you are guilty of 'time-serving.'"[37]

The USSR, once the Communist movement's sole standard-bearer, now had a younger rival on the global stage, breathing renewed, if slightly manic, energy into the cause. With European empires crumbling in Asia and Africa, new vistas for Communist expansion were opening for Moscow and Beijing, working sometimes in collaboration, more often in competition.

12
"THE WORLD WAS TURNING IN OUR DIRECTION"
COMMUNISM GOES GLOBAL

At least part of the reason Nikita Khrushchev began seeking new Soviet clients in Asia and Africa in the 1960s is that the prestige of Communism in Europe had crested and was now eroding. While it is difficult to pinpoint the exact moment of the peak, one could easily mark Stalin's death on March 5, 1953, as a catalyst in its decline. For a quarter of a century, Soviet and European Communism had revolved around the ferocious will of one man—sometimes capricious, but always bold and sure. Whatever their true feelings about Stalin, many Europeans genuinely mourned the loss of the conqueror who had defeated Hitler, pouring out into the streets in Berlin, Budapest, and Prague to pay their respects. Stalin's funeral on March 9 brought Communist statesmen from across the world together in Moscow, including the East European Stalinists Bolesław Bierut of Poland, Mátyás Rákosi of Hungary, Walter Ulbricht of East Germany, Klement Gottwald of Czechoslovakia, and Enver Hoxha of Albania; Mao Zedong and Zhou

Enlai from China; and the West European Communist leaders Palmiro Togliatti from Italy and Maurice Thorez from France. It also brought thousands of Russian mourners onto the streets of central Moscow, their bodies packed in ever tighter between buildings and rows of trucks lined up to secure the dignitaries at the funeral. The crowding resulted in a terrible stampede killing dozens in a tragedy somehow appropriate to the murderous dictator being mourned. So overwhelming was the occasion that Gottwald, the Stalinist who had helped purge Czechoslovakian Communism, suffered a heart attack and died five days later.[1]

In the initial confusion over the succession, it appeared that Lavrenty Beria, Stalin's longtime secret police chieftain, was in pole position as he now became minister of internal affairs and first deputy chairman of the Council of Ministers. To the surprise of his colleagues, who had long feared Beria's power of life and death over Stalin's rivals and opponents, Beria distanced himself radically from Stalin, declaring that the "Doctors' Plot" paranoia of 1951–1953—in which a group of mostly Jewish doctors were accused of conspiring to assassinate Stalin and other Soviet leaders, inspiring a spasm of antisemitic terror—was a fabrication. Beria then floated a general amnesty for Gulag prisoners, whose numbers he estimated at 2,526,401, including 438,788 women. Nearly 1.2 million of the prisoners were duly released. To drive the amnesty home, Beria ordered an end to "cruel beatings" and other abuses. Oversight of the remaining "corrective labor camps" was transferred from Beria's Ministry of Internal Affairs to the Soviet Justice Ministry. In an amazing repudiation of his longtime patron, Beria shared classified documents with the Central Committee proving that Stalin had demanded that confessions be tortured out of political prisoners. "Stalin was a scoundrel, a savage, a tyrant! He held us in fear, the bloodsucker. And the people too," Beria roared. "Fortunately we're now rid of him. Let the snake rot in hell!"[2]

Over the next few months, Beria extended liberalization to Stalin's satellites, all but repudiating Communism and the Cold War. Summoning Hungarian and East German Communist leaders to Moscow in June 1953, Beria dressed down Rákosi for terrorizing Hungarians on Stalin's orders. "How could it be acceptable," he berated Rákosi, "that in Hungary, a country with 9,500,000 inhabitants, 1,500,000 were persecuted?" Explaining, from personal experience, that "a person who's beaten will make the kind of confession that interrogating agents want," Beria demanded that Rákosi grant amnesty to political prisoners—and then sacked him anyway, elevating the agriculture minister, Imre Nagy. Addressing Ulbricht, Beria went further, demanding that the DDR repudiate Communism, or what he called "forced socialism," entirely. The DDR, Beria pointed out, was "not even a real state": "It's only kept in being by Soviet troops, even if we do call it the German Democratic Republic." When Vyacheslav Molotov objected that removing the "force" must lead to the end of socialism in the DDR, Beria doubled down on his "New Course." "All we need," Beria proposed, "is a peaceful Germany; whether or not it is socialist isn't important to us."[3]

The Beria thaw, alas, was short-lived. Even *talking* about withdrawing Soviet military protection from the DDR was to play with fire. Nearly half a million East Germans had fled into West Germany since 1950, and a token reduction in the Soviet military presence was enough to accelerate the outflow of East Germans voting with their feet. Fifty-eight thousand left in March 1953 alone, which would have annualized to 700,000, almost quadruple the already robust numbers from 1952. On June 17, 1953, matters came to a head when thousands of Germans in East Berlin, excited about Beria's New Course but disappointed that Ulbricht's policies did not seem to include lower work quotas or better wages, took to the streets to protest. The protests soon spread across the DDR, with 500,000 workers going on strike in 600 different factories. The uprising was serious enough that 13 Stasi stations and 12 prisons were overwhelmed by rioters. Ulbricht left Berlin to go into hiding in nearby Karlshorst, effectively abdicating to the Soviet ambassador, who declared martial law and deployed the Red Army to restore order. T-34s and other Soviet tanks rumbled into Berlin. At least 50 Germans were killed in the fighting, and nearly 10,000 arrested, of whom perhaps 200 "ringleaders" were then shot. Among the victims was Beria himself, who was arrested by Khrushchev and other Politburo members on June 26 in retaliation for his reckless attempt, as Khrushchev put it, to "hand over 18 million East Germans to American imperialist rule." After a secret trial held that December, Beria was stripped, hog-tied, gagged, and shot in the back of the head, as so many of his own victims had been. So died the Beria thaw.[4]

Unwinding the systematic mass terror that had come to define Communism in Stalin's era would not be easy. To loosen the machinery of repression, as Beria had done in East Germany, threatened to capsize the system if enough people rose up together for freedom. Had the Berlin uprising and its bloody aftermath not killed off Beria's New Course, the thaw might well have spread to Poland, Czechoslovakia, and Bulgaria. Indeed, the leaders of those nations had been invited to Moscow in July 1953 to discuss similar reforms only for the invitations to be called off after Beria's arrest. Still, no matter how dangerous it was to lift the veil on Stalin's crimes, even the most staunch Stalinists had been scarred by the Terror. Khrushchev, like Beria, had sent thousands of people "to the next world," as Molotov once dryly put it. In 1938 alone, when Khrushchev was purging Ukraine, 106,119 people were arrested, and at least 54,000 put to death. Far from bashful about his role in the purges, Khrushchev had informed comrades at the Fourteenth Ukrainian Party Congress in June 1938 that "the struggle is still being carried out too weakly. We must . . . mercilessly smash spies and traitors." Khrushchev later boasted of how many "vermin" he had exterminated. Perhaps to expiate his own guilt, in October 1955, after outmaneuvering rivals such as Georgy Malenkov, who had overseen the development of Soviet military aircraft production during the war and directed the Soviet nuclear weapons program alongside Beria before briefly succeeding Stalin as premier in 1953, for party leadership, Khrushchev established a commission to investigate Stalin's Great Terror. The commission, granted unprecedented access to NKVD files, concluded that 1,920,635 people had been arrested for "anti-Soviet activity" between 1935 and 1940, and 688,503 executed.[5]

Armed with the evidence, Khrushchev denounced Stalin in a closed session of the Twentieth Soviet Communist Party Congress on February 25, 1956, for the late dictator's "intolerance, his brutality and his abuse of power." Embracing a "cult of personality," Stalin had "ignored the norms of party life and trampled on the Leninist principle of collective party leadership." Instead of "mobilizing the masses," Khrushchev continued, Stalin "often chose the path of repression and physical annihilation, not only against actual enemies, but also against individuals who had not committed any crimes against the party and the Soviet Government." Of course, what most animated Khrushchev and his audience, judging by the commotion reported in the minutes, was not Stalin's crimes against the Soviet people as such, but his treatment of *Communists*, such as the 1,108 delegates to the Seventeenth Party Congress in 1934 (out of 1,966) arrested in 1937 and 1938, and the 98 Central Committee members (of 139) who had been shot. Nonetheless, Khrushchev's "secret speech," as it came to be called, was a bombshell, so shocking that Poland's leading Stalinist, Bierut, who listened in person, was hospitalized that night; he died of a heart attack two weeks later. Such explosive revelations could not remain secret for long. Khrushchev approved the printing and distribution of the text to party committees across the USSR, likely suspecting the news would ultimately spread beyond Soviet borders—as it did on June 4, when the *New York Times*, handed a copy via a Polish source (by way of the CIA), blasted it on the front page.[6]

Russians were and remain grateful for Khrushchev's exposure of (some) of the crimes of Stalinism, but his denunciation of Stalin could not help but dent Soviet prestige internationally. Beria might have liberated Gulag prisoners, rebuked Rákosi as a Stalin stooge, and encouraged Ulbricht to de-Communize East Germany, but his remarks about Stalin had been issued in private. Khrushchev's February 1956 speech aired Communist dirty laundry in public for the world to see, and many Communist leaders were livid about it. As Mao chided Chinese Communist Party colleagues that November in his inimitably earthy language, they must not fall into "uncritically thinking that everything in the Soviet Union is perfect, that all their farts are fragrant." Russian Communists might be done with the "cult of personality," but, as one loyal Chinese Communist responded to Mao's chiding, "we must have blind faith in the Chairman! We must obey the Chairman with total abandon!"[7]

Mao was not wrong that Communist self-criticism threatened the party's monopoly on power. Just as Beria's brief thaw had unleashed chaos in Berlin, Khrushchev's speech energized protesters across Eastern Europe, beginning in Poland, where Bierut's death had already shaken the Communist government. Already known inside the party, the text of Khrushchev's speech was widely distributed after it hit world newswires in early June, sparking furious debates at public meetings. On June 28, when workers at the Stalin Locomotive Works in Poznań went on strike, they were soon joined by workers from nearby factories and other passersby, until 100,000 people had joined in. The swelling crowds sang the old Polish national anthem, chanted anti-Communist slogans—"Down with the Russkis! Free Elections!"—and attacked the local secret police (Służba Bezpieczeństwa, or Security Service, SB) headquarters in scenes reminiscent of those in the DDR three years before. Just as in June 1953, the army crushed the uprising as tanks rumbled into the city. About seventy civilians were killed, and hundreds more wounded. While the units deployed to Poznań were nominally Polish, the orders to fire were given by Soviet officers. Seventy-six of these officers had ranking positions in the Polish army, including Marshal Konstantin Rokossovsky, who had more or less ruled the country since 1944. Although the bloodbath in Poznań quieted popular protests for a time, resentment of Soviet domination continued to smolder, even inside the party. In October 1956, Władysław Gomułka, the Communist leader purged in 1949, was rehabilitated and named first party secretary, a development alarming enough that Khrushchev flew to Warsaw on October 19 to lay down the law. With Soviet troops and armor moving toward the Polish capital, it appeared that another violent crackdown was imminent. Gomułka convinced Khrushchev to back down in exchange for a pledge that Poland would remain a loyal member of the Warsaw Pact.[8]

Meanwhile, an even more serious crisis was brewing in Budapest. For many Hungarians, Imre Nagy, the agricultural minister promoted to chairman during Beria's thaw in June 1953, had become a symbol of hope after he was sacked on Soviet orders in April 1955 and the unpopular Rákosi returned to power. As reverberations from the Khrushchev speech spread across Hungary in June 1956, crowds started shouting for Nagy, only to be disappointed when a Soviet envoy, sent by Khrushchev to appease the crowds, fired Rákosi but replaced him with Ernö Gerö, the nondescript interior minister who had helped direct the party purges. In early October, long-simmering popular resentment boiled over at a public funeral held for László Rajk, the "mad dog" scapegoat of the Hungarian show trials. When news of Gomułka's defiance of Khrushchev in Warsaw reached Budapest on October 22, thousands of Hungarians gathered to pay tribute before the statue of a brave Polish general, József Bem, who had fought with Hungarians against Russian troops during the revolution of 1848. Shouting "Russians go home!" the crowds sacked a Russian bookstore and tore down a statue of Stalin in Hero Square, the first of hundreds of symbols of Soviet power defaced and destroyed in the coming days. As in East Germany and Poznań, secret police headquarters were stormed, along with a villa belonging to Rákosi. Nagy, at first reluctantly, then loudly, embraced the revolution, announcing that Hungary was withdrawing from the Warsaw Pact. On October 24, Soviet tanks crashed into Budapest accompanied by thousands of Red Army regulars. Twenty-five Hungarians were killed the first day, and hundreds more over the next week, but still resistance continued. A tense standoff endured until November 5, when Khrushchev gave unequivocal orders to fire upon and disperse the crowds in Budapest. The resulting Soviet offensive cost the lives of nearly 20,000 Hungarians and 15,000 Soviet troops and advisers.[9]

The bloodbath in Budapest, following on the heels of similar Soviet crackdowns in Poznań and East Germany, dashed the hopes of reform-minded Communists across Eastern Europe while gravely damaging the Soviet image in the West. The Berlin rising is best remembered today by a famous Bertolt Brecht poem asking, in view of a Communist leaflet announcing that the "people had forfeited the government's confidence / and could only win it back / by redoubled labor," "wouldn't it be simpler in that case if the government dissolved the people and elected another?" If Brecht, a German playwright who had been a committed Communist for his entire adult life, had lost faith, then ill winds were blowing for the cause.[10]

Because of its strategic location and bifurcation into a Soviet-occupied Eastern zone and a Western zone occupied by the

United States, Britain, and France, Berlin had turned into a symbolic Cold War battleground. Like Korea, which had been split since the 1953 armistice into rival countries north and south of the 38th parallel, divided Germany was a living economic experiment, with people sharing a history and culture living on opposite sides of an artificial frontier under different political systems—and, in Berlin, cheek by jowl in the same city. So far, it was not going well for the Communists. West Berlin, flooded with US dollars, had been rebuilt and turned into a glitzy capitalist showcase, its riches beckoning cruelly across an uneasy frontier of military checkpoints to impoverished East Berliners. The East Berliners remained cramped among the unreconstructed ruins of war—but for a few grandiose Stalin wedding-cake buildings built to house Soviet occupiers and their East German puppets. East Germans were voting "with their feet" as they fled in the thousands, then millions, from the Communist DDR into the capitalist Federal Republic of Germany (FRG), with the largest outflow in Berlin itself. Although the outflow was briefly stanched by the crackdown that followed the June 1953 uprising, by 1955 it was again up to a steady 20,000 per month, a rate of 240,000 per year. By 1961, nearly 2.7 million people had fled the DDR. With the East German population now falling in absolute terms, from 18.4 million in 1950 to 17.2 million by 1960, even as West Germany's had grown from 51 million to 56 million, this was more than bad publicity for Communism. The country was literally emptying of people.[11]

Scrambling to explain the embarrassing defection of German "proletarians" to the capitalist enemy, Ulbricht's Communist propagandists blamed the FRG's sophisticated American-style television programs broadcast across the frontier, which displayed the gaudy (but presumably fake) wealth of West Germans (*Wessis*) to East Germans (*Ossis*). In April 1960, the Socialist Unity Party's (SED's) agit-prop department appropriated 18 million Ostmarks to revamp East

German television at Berlin's Johannisthal studios, including 8.5 million for importing studio equipment from the West, with the aim of doubling the volume of TV programming by October 1961. However worthy the goal, the effort to polish the DDR's image among its own people was baldly undermined on August 13, 1961, when Soviet sappers threw up barbed wired around East Berlin to stem the metastasizing outflow of Ossis into West Berlin: 30,415 had left in July, and 47,433 in just the first twelve days of August— at a rate that would have annualized to 1.4 million. Once it was clear that the United States had not responded to the provocation with force, but only with a symbolic deployment of Marines to hold down West Berlin, Khrushchev gave orders to make the new barrier permanent. An imposing series of concrete walls, barbed wire, and guard towers encircled West Berlin. Try though Ulbricht and his Soviet sponsors did to claim that the Berlin Wall had been built to keep capitalist West Berliners *out of*, rather than impoverished Ossis *in*, East Germany, the persistent efforts of Ossis to leave gave the game away. Some 700 of them died over the next twenty-eight years trying to get over the heavily fortified wall. Until August 1961, West Berlin had provided a pressure valve of sorts for Ossis, who could cross over to work or visit, whether or not they stayed on and defected. Now the DDR's prison walls had closed in. Even so, Ossis had to foot the bill for spruced-up TV programming, still as lousy as before, only with much higher fees. The issue occasioned nationwide protests in 1962 so serious that the television fee crisis was discussed at the SED Party Congress.[12]

The prospects for Communist expansion into Western Europe looked increasingly dim in the wake of Khrushchev's "secret speech," the bloodbath in Budapest, and the construction of the Berlin Wall. Elsewhere in the world, however, promising new vistas were opening for Communist expansion owing to the eclipse of the empires of those same Western European powers. Khrushchev's speech had come on the heels of the widely publicized April 1955 Asian-African Conference in Bandung, in formerly Dutch and now independent Indonesia, which helped launch the idea of a "Third World" being liberated from Western imperialism at long last. True, the leading statesmen at Bandung, such as the Indonesian host Sukarno; Jawaharlal Nehru, prime minister of formerly British India; and Colonel Gamal Abdel Nasser, of formerly British Egypt, had taken pains to declare that they were "non-aligned" in the Cold War between East and West. But it did not take a savant to detect that the real animus of the gathering was with the West, and with Britain in particular. In a little-noticed passage in the "secret speech," Khrushchev noted with approval, with a nod to Bandung, that "the peoples of the East" were "becoming a new mighty factor in international relations." The ex-colonies of Britain, France, and the Netherlands in Africa and Asia, he declared, "need not go begging for up-to-date equipment to their former oppressors. They can get it in socialist countries, without assuming any political or military commitments." Nasser had already taken the lead in June 1955 when, following a rebuff from several Western ambassadors, he had "told the Soviet Ambassador frankly that I wanted to arm quickly."[13]

The timing was fortuitous for Khrushchev's pivot away from Europe. Lenin had tried to launch a "Muslim-Communist holy war" against the British Empire with the Baku Congress of September 1920, only to see Soviet expansion stopped by Poland and the British Empire reach its greatest extent ever. Willi Münzenberg had kicked the tires again with his Anti-Imperialism Congress in Brussels in February 1927, but the initiative was forgotten after Chiang Kai-shek, Moscow's most promising anti-imperialist client, broke with Stalin. The post–World War II era, by contrast, had seen the cratering of one European empire after another, from the British withdrawals from Palestine and India in 1948 and Egypt in 1951 to Dutch recognition of Indonesian independence in 1949, the French withdrawal from Indochina in 1954, France's violent disengagement from Algeria and French North Africa between 1958 and 1962, and British recognition of an independent Ghana, led by the charismatic Kwame Nkrumah, in 1957. In February 1960, hoping to avoid the violence that had plagued Palestine, India, Indochina, and Algeria, Britain's prime minister, Harold Macmillan, delivered his "Winds of Change" speech in Pretoria, South Africa, promising to relinquish what remained of the British Empire in Africa.

Khrushchev knew an opportunity when he saw one. With Europe's "capitalist" empires all but declaring bankruptcy, the USSR could embrace the cause of the colonized peoples. On his visit to the United States in 1959, he addressed the UN General Assembly in New York, saluting "the heroism of those who led the struggle for the independence of India and Indonesia, the United Arab Republic [as the union of formerly French Syria and formerly British Egypt under Nasser was then called] and Iraq, Ghana, Guinea and other states." Still, although these colonized peoples had "won independence," Khrushchev continued, they were still "cruelly exploited by foreigners economically." "Their oil and natural wealth is plundered," he said. "It is taken out of the country for next to nothing, yielding huge profits to foreign exploiters." By working together with leaders of newly independent colonies, the Soviets could reverse their exploitation, helping them nationalize resources and providing the technology they needed—absent a "capitalist" profit motive (though still taking payment, presumably). Basking in applause after this anti-imperialist pitch, Khrushchev enjoyed himself so much that he returned to New York in the fall of 1960, bear-hugging all the new national leaders from Africa and delivering twelve speeches to the General Assembly.* In

---

* During one of these speeches, on October 12, 1961, Khrushchev, confronted with a question from the Philippines delegate about Soviet hypocrisy in "swallowing up"

January 1961, he made the "sacred" anti-imperialist struggle of the Third World a state priority of the Soviet Union, vowing to "bring imperialism to its knees."[14]

This was more than rhetoric. By 1964, the Soviet Union had undertaken more than 6,000 economic development projects in the former colonies of the Third World while signing lucrative arms deals, beginning with Nasser's Egypt. Nasser may not have been a Communist, but his nationalization of the Suez Canal in July 1956, which prompted a humiliatingly inept response from Britain, France, and Israel to reconquer the canal that November, in what was called "the Suez Crisis," turned Nasser into an "anti-imperialist" hero on the world stage and Moscow's most promising client. The arms and funds Khrushchev sent to Cairo represented nearly 46 percent of all Soviet foreign aid between 1954 and 1961. In addition, he sent KGB bodyguards and Soviet political advisers, who ultimately numbered more than 20,000. In 1958, Nasser was invited for a state visit to Moscow, where he was treated to a three-week VIP tour of the country and declared a Hero of the Soviet Union. In homage to his Communist sponsors in Moscow, Nasser nationalized Egyptian industry in 1961. Egypt (and Syria, which Nasser absorbed into his new "United Arab Republic" in 1958) may have been "non-aligned," but Nasser had clearly chosen sides in the Cold War, and not with the Americans, despite the fact that US president Dwight D. Eisenhower had opposed the British-French-Israeli moves in the Suez Crisis no less fervently than Khrushchev had. As Nasser told a cheering crowd in Cairo in May 1958 after returning from his triumphant visit to the USSR, the USSR was "a friendly country with no ulterior motive" that held the entire Arab nation "in great esteem."[15]

Eastern Europe while espousing anti-imperialism, banged his shoe on a table, unintentionally proving the delegate's point about Soviet bullying.

Khrushchev was no less fortunate in Cuba, where another promising client fell into his lap. Fidel Castro, the guerrilla leader whose
forces had toppled the increasingly unpopular government of Ful-
gencio Batista, may have been an "anti-imperialist" motivated by a
desire to unshackle Cuba from dependence on the nearby United
States, but his 26th of July Movement (named after the date commemorating a guerrilla attack on a Cuban army base in 1953) was
endorsed by neither the Cuban Communist Party nor by Moscow.
As late as October 1958, Khrushchev dismissed Castro's movement as "heroic but unequal." Only on December 27, 1958, did the
Soviet government authorize the first limited shipment of weapons
to Castro, and this was of German weapons captured in 1945, sent
not by Moscow but Prague, to preserve Soviet deniability. Because
these arms arrived only *after* Batista fled Havana on January 1,
1959, it is a curious fact that Fidel Castro conquered Cuba with
not Soviet but American support: the United States had cut off its
previous client, Batista, in 1958, and at the same time had begun
secretly providing funds (about $50,000) and arms to Castro
through the CIA.[16]

If Castro was not yet a Soviet client in January 1959, it did not
take long for him to be recruited. In view of Cuba's sensitive location, with its capital, Havana, just 160 kilometers (100 miles) from
Key West, Florida, and 320 kilometers (200 miles) from Miami,
Khrushchev at first proceeded with caution. On his US visit in September 1959, he declared that the USSR would not send military
aid to Cuba. He quietly reversed course after returning to Moscow,
however, approving the dispatch of weapons from Warsaw Pact
countries and authorizing back-channel contacts through Fidel's
brother Raúl, who, unlike Fidel, was a committed Communist.
Khrushchev sent the Soviet trade commissar, Anastas Mikoyan, to
Havana, but the deal Mikoyan struck covered only Cuban sugar
exports and a $100 million Soviet loan. Not until March 1960 did

Khrushchev send a personal message to Fidel Castro, and even this was delivered "verbally" by the KGB *resident* in Cairo, Aleksandr Alekseyev (operating undercover as a journalist). Nonetheless, Khrushchev made clear his own commitment, vowing to a gathering of Soviet schoolteachers that June that "if need be, Soviet artillerymen can support the Cuban people with their rocket fire, should the aggressive forces in the Pentagon dare to start intervention against Cuba." As if to goad the US government into intervening in Cuba, Khrushchev publicly embraced Castro during his visit to the United Nations in September.[17]

The Americans took the bait. On April 17, 1961, nearly 1,400 armed Cuban exiles waded ashore on the southern coast of Cuba in a CIA operation aimed at toppling Castro's government—although, in a forlorn effort to give Washington plausible deniability, without US air support, which left the men cruelly exposed to strafing from the Cuban air force. More than 100 exiles were killed in the ensuing rout, and the rest herded into captivity. The American "Bay of Pigs" fiasco was the best possible publicity for Castro and his Soviet backers, who now moved in for the kill, pumping arms, advisers, and weapons into Cuba. By the fall of 1962, when the first nuclear-armed Soviet missiles arrived, Cuba was a Cold War flashpoint even more dangerous than Berlin. Owing to their defiance of the imperialist "Yankees"—notwithstanding the Soviet sponsorship that made this defiance possible—Castro and his charismatic Argentinian adviser and chief executioner, the former doctor Ernesto "Ché" Guevara, became romantic heroes of anti-imperialism.

To be sure, Castro was taken down a notch when US president John F. Kennedy called Khrushchev's bluff in the Cuban Missile Crisis of October 1962. The confrontation only concluded when Moscow agreed to withdraw all its nuclear missiles from Cuba in exchange for the United States pulling back its own medium-range

Jupiter missiles from Turkey (although this part of the deal was not acknowledged publicly, to avoid giving the impression of a quid pro quo). Khrushchev himself became a casualty when he was forced out of power by the Politburo in October 1964, largely (though not exclusively) because of his failed Cuban gambit, which was condemned as one of his "hare-brained schemes." Castro himself, who, according to Khrushchev, had "openly advised us to use nuclear weapons," was aghast that the Soviets had withdrawn "his" missiles. The Soviet climbdown, Castro complained to Khrushchev, had brought tears to "countless eyes of Cuban and Soviet men who were willing to die with supreme dignity." Castro called Khrushchev a "son of a bitch" who had "no *cojones*." To placate Castro, Soviet archives have revealed, Soviet technicians tried to hide 100 nuclear warheads (without missiles to deliver them) in Cuba in November 1962, hoping the Americans would not notice (they did). In the end Castro was fobbed off with a forty-day consolation tour of the USSR in April and May 1963. Losing the missiles might have wounded his pride, but Castro must have enjoyed reviewing the Red Army in the May Day parade alongside Khrushchev, who made him a Hero of the Soviet Union. Castro expressed his "profound and eternal gratitude for the Soviet Union."[18]

Almost lost in the drama of nuclear brinkmanship in 1962 was that Khrushchev had negotiated a significant concession from Kennedy: a "no-invasion" pledge allowing Castro to remain in power in Cuba, as he did for more than half a century. He remained a sharp Communist thorn in the side of the United States. Castro's one-party dictatorship imprisoned and tortured thousands of dissidents, epitomized in the mass executions of nearly 700 political prisoners on Ché Guevara's orders in La Cabaña prison in 1959. Some 1.4 million Cubans had left Cuba by 1962, nearly a fifth of Cuba's population of 7.14 million, the vast majority of them heading for South Florida, where Cuban exiles would soon predominate in and run the great city of Miami. But however sordid the reality of Castro's rule, and however many Cubans voted with their feet by fleeing, Cuba's prime strategic location neighboring the arch-capitalist United States ensured Castro endless publicity. Ché saw his fame ratchet up to even higher levels after he died a martyr's death trying to export Communist revolution to Bolivia—and thereafter the rest of South America—in 1967, when he was captured and executed by US-trained Bolivian soldiers in October. Although Ché had the blessing of the USSR for his Bolivian scheme—he had received instructions, and a new passport, in Moscow the previous October—it is curious that his death was mourned by more people in Washington, DC (50,000), than in Moscow, where Khrushchev's successor, Leonid Brezhnev, rebuked Ché's "conspiracy of heroes." Ché was the single most admired celebrity among American college students in a 1968 poll, and he has never since lost his mojo. Guevara, as the commentator Alvaro Vargas Llosa observed in a sardonic tribute, became and remains the "quintessential capitalist brand" of global Communism: "His likeness adorns mugs, hoodies, lighters, key chains, wallets, baseball caps, toques, bandannas, tank tops, club shirts, couture bags, denim jeans, [and] herbal tea," Vargas Llosa wrote, along with "those omnipresent T-shirts" with the famous Alberto Korda photo of the bearded "socialist heartthrob in his beret."[19]

Ché may have failed to ignite a Communist revolution in Bolivia, but he and Castro had turned Havana into a Moscow of the Western Hemisphere, both inspiration and source of funds (usually funneled via the KGB) for aspiring revolutionaries. As early as January 1959, emissaries from a radical Nicaraguan organization opposed to the pro-American Somoza dynasty had arrived in Havana, where Ché, on behalf of Castro, promised them "all possible support." This was the Sandinista National Liberation Front (Frente Sandinista de Liberación Nacional, FSLN, also known as the Sandinistas, named after Augusto César Sandino, who had led Nicaraguan resistance to US occupation in 1927–1933). When their leader, Carlos Fonseca Amador, had visited Moscow in 1957 to attend a World Youth Festival, he had been put on the KGB payroll. "With the victory of the Cuban Revolution," he had declared, "the rebellious Nicaraguan spirit recovered its brightness." The Marxism of Lenin, Castro, and Ché Guevara, he added, had been "taken up by the Sandinista National Liberation Front." The KGB provided $10,000 to the FSLN for "weapons and ammunition"; further funds from Moscow were initially channeled through Havana or the KGB residency in Mexico City ($25,200 by 1964), and later via the Soviet-backed government of José Figueres Ferrer, who came to power in neighboring Costa Rica in 1970. Figueres also allowed the Sandinistas to set up a rear base of operations (at a cost of $300,000). Although it took twenty years, thanks to Soviet funding and Cuban logistical support the Sandinistas finally toppled Anastasio Somoza Debayle's government in July 1979, dealing a major blow to US prestige in Central America.[20]

Castro further justified his Moscow subsidies by supporting Communist revolutionaries in Africa. To be sure, many of the early Soviet moves in Africa, such as the embrace of Nasser after the Suez Crisis of 1956, predated the Cuban Revolution. With newly independent Ghana in 1957, Khrushchev barely had to try, as Kwame Nkrumah, though denying that he was a Communist, declared his allegiance to the Soviet Bloc anyway and invited in Russians and East German technicians and military advisers. There were drawbacks to such pro-Soviet "anti-imperialism," however, not least that it looked—well, imperialist. After Nkrumah was overthrown in a military coup in 1966, the new government in Ghana expelled 1,000 Soviet advisers and terminated all agreements with Moscow. Far better, the KGB leadership resolved in the Brezhnev era to camouflage Soviet influence operations in Africa via Cuban agents and auxiliaries—who spoke Spanish but were not "Euro-pean." Many Cubans even *looked* African, or at least more closely so than pale-faced Russians. In the late 1960s Castro began sending Cuban troops and advisers to Africa, ramping up his commitment in 1974 and 1975, when Portugal, the last remaining European empire, began to disengage from Angola and Mozambique. By the late 1970s, there were 750 Cuban soldiers and advisers to Mozam-bique, 19,000 Cuban troops and 8,500 "technicians" in Angola, and 16,000 Cuban troops in Ethiopia—a country never formally colonized but prioritized by Moscow owing to its strategic loca-tion. All three countries turned into solid Soviet allies, owing in part to the "camouflage" effect provided by Cuban auxiliaries. By contrast, the largely Cuban-free Soviet intervention to prop up the Mohamed Siad Barre government in neighboring Somalia back-fired when Somalia broke with the USSR in 1977. Barre had been the first African leader to sign a formal alliance treaty with the USSR, which had in turn flooded the country with arms, KGB men, and 3,600 Russian advisers. KGB director Yuri Andropov had conducted a personal tour of inspection.[21]

In order to increase his diplomatic leverage, Castro declared Cuba "non-aligned" in the Cold War, a kind of Kremlin inside joke that allowed him to grandstand on Moscow's behalf at non-aligned conferences, like the fellow travelers of the 1920s and 1930s. At the Fourth Conference of the Non-Aligned Movement in Algiers, the capital of formerly French Algeria, in 1973, Castro gave the keynote address, asking African and other Third World leaders, "How can the Soviet Union be labelled imperialist? . . . Where is its participation in multinational corporations? . . . What worker is exploited in any country of Asia, Africa or Latin America by Soviet capital?" Castro proposed an "alliance among all the progressive forces of the world" in order to "overcome the still-powerful forces of imperialism, colonialism, neocolonialism and racism." While not

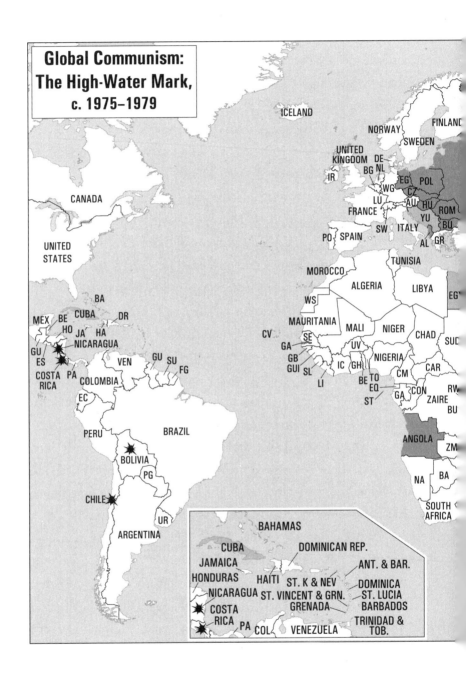

Global Communism:
The High-Water Mark,
c. 1975–1979

ICELAND

NORWAY
SWEDEN
FINLAND

UNITED
KINGDOM   DE
            BG NL
IR   WG   EG   POL
            LU   CZ
FRANCE   AU HU   ROM
                  YU   BU
PO   SPAIN   SW ITALY   GR
                      AL   GR

CANADA

UNITED
STATES

TUNISIA

MOROCCO
ALGERIA   LIBYA
WS   EG
MAURITANIA   MALI   NIGER   CHAD   SUD
CV
GA   SE   UV
GB   NIGERIA
GUI SL   IC   GH
     LI   CM   CAR
          BE TO
          EQ   RW
               GA   CON   ZAIRE
          ST   BU

BA
CUBA   DR
MEX   BE   HA
HO   JA
GU   NICARAGUA
ES
COSTA   PA
RICA   COLOMBIA
EC
VEN   GU SU
          FG

PERU   BRAZIL

BOLIVIA
PG
CHILE

ANGOLA   ZM

NA   BA

SOUTH
AFRICA

ARGENTINA
UR

BAHAMAS

CUBA   DOMINICAN REP.
JAMAICA   ANT. & BAR.
HONDURAS   HAITI   ST. K & NEV   DOMINICA
NICARAGUA ST. VINCENT & GRN.   ST. LUCIA
           GRENADA   BARBADOS
COSTA   TRINIDAD &
RICA   PA   COL   VENEZUELA   TOB.

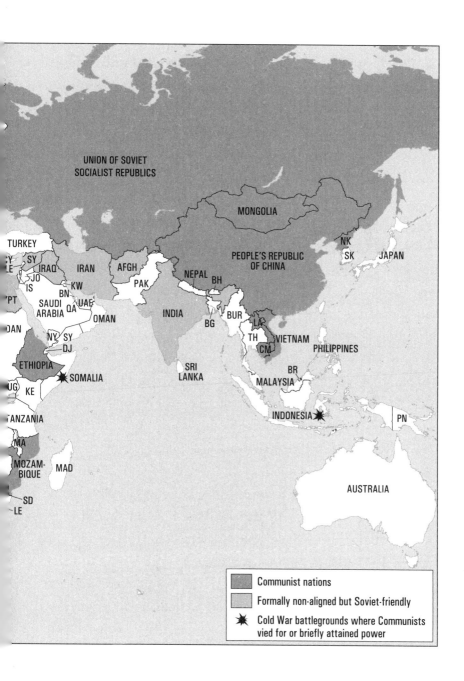

convincing everyone to become Soviet clients, the rousing speech ensured that the conference communiqué denounced the "aggressive imperialism" of the United States and its allies while refusing to criticize the Soviet Union. Like Nasser before him, Castro had chosen the Communist side in the Cold War while camouflaging this choice behind "non-aligned" anti-imperialism. Small wonder that the Soviet KGB, in its internal evaluations, described the Non-Aligned Movement as "our natural allies."[22]

Moscow pulled off the same trick in Southeast Asia, where the July 1969 Non-Aligned Conference, held in Belgrade, the capital of (ostensibly) non-aligned Yugoslavia, endorsed the struggle of "the heroic people of Vietnam" against American imperialism—even though the USSR and Communist China had intervened no less massively in North Vietnam than the United States had in the South. Because neighboring China had split the costs of arming him, and sent more military personnel than the Soviets, Ho Chi Minh of North Vietnam was one of the most valuable Soviet assets in the Cold War, a competent and less histrionic Castro or Nasser—especially since the latter's crushing defeat in the Six-Day War against Israel in 1967 had dealt a considerable blow to Soviet military prestige. Unlike Nasser or Castro, Ho Chi Minh (born Nguyen T'at-Than) was a committed Communist already when he came to power in the North after the French withdrawal in 1954. He had studied in Moscow after attending the Comintern Congress in 1922 (the "Communist University of the Toilers of the East"), and had served as the leader of the Comintern's Southeast Asia bureau in 1928–1930. He had even attended Lenin's funeral in January 1924, waiting so long in line to view the embalmed body that "his fingers and nose became frostbitten."* He and other Asian

---

* The plaque commemorating Ho Chi Minh's residency in Moscow still stands on the block between the Lenin Library and the Kremlin.

revolutionaries, Ho later wrote, saw Lenin as "the personification of universal brotherhood."[23]

Ho's first Comintern posting was in China, where he helped its Executive Committee liaise with Chiang Kai-shek (until 1927) and the CCP. In 1930, he founded the Indochinese Communist Party among exiles in Hong Kong. Ho also founded Communist parties, all Moscow-funded, in Siam, Malaya, and Singapore. Not until the Japanese moved into Indochina in 1941 did Ho return to his native land. He mostly bided his time during the war years, holing up in the interior much like Mao did in Yan'an, recruiting followers by denouncing the Japanese occupiers without actually fighting them. Also like Mao, Ho set up his base near a friendly frontier—an area of northern Vietnam abutting China. An adept politician, Ho played the French off against Chiang's Kuomintang forces (from whom he received funds in 1942, on a false promise that he would use them to fight Japan), inviting the French army to reoccupy North Vietnam in 1946 and stave off a possible Chinese incursion, despite having spent much of his career denouncing French imperialism. As Ho colorfully explained to aides, "It is better to sniff French shit for a little while than to eat Chinese shit all our lives." Nor did he sniff French shit for long, launching an uprising against France in the North Vietnamese capital of Hanoi in December 1946 that soon grew into a full-on insurgency.[24]

What Ho was decrying in his off-color remarks about China, of course, was the spread of *Nationalist* Chinese influence into Vietnam. After Mao conquered China for Communism in 1949, he sang a different tune. "Brotherly relations," Ho announced in a dramatic about-face, "have existed between the Vietnamese and Chinese nations during thousands of years of history. Henceforth these relations will be even closer." By 1950, both the USSR and Maoist China had recognized Ho's "Democratic Republic of Vietnam" and, following Ho's visits to Beijing and Moscow, began to flood his growing armies with funds and weapons, including 14,000 rifles, 1,700 machine guns and recoilless rifles, 60 artillery pieces, and 300 bazookas just in the first installment. "From now on, you can count on our assistance," Stalin promised Ho in Moscow. "Our surplus materials are plenty, and we will ship them to you through China. But because of limits and natural conditions, it will be mainly China that helps you. What China lacks, we will provide." Ho's signature victory in his war to expel the French occupiers, at Dienbienphu in 1954, was a case in point, won by a combination of Vietnamese Communist manpower, Chinese trucks, howitzers, and heavy artillery, and Soviet Katyusha rockets—operated by Chinese experts.[25]

Historic though Dienbienphu was, it was after the mighty United States was sucked into direct involvement in the Vietnamese war in the early 1960s that the Soviet-Chinese investment in Ho bore the most fruit. To be sure, much of the strategic payoff resulted from American blundering, above all in the foolish and self-defeating coup to oust the Americans' own client ruling non-Communist South Vietnam, Ngo Dinh Diem, in November 1963. In the political chaos that followed, the South Vietnamese military position deteriorated so severely that President Kennedy's successor in the White House, Lyndon Johnson, committed tens of thousands of US ground troops beginning in 1965, in an open-ended intervention that ultimately cost Washington more than $140 billion between 1961 and the US withdrawal in 1975—the current equivalent of well over $1 trillion—along with 58,000 American war dead, not to mention rampaging inflation. But we should not forget that American blundering was provoked by the impressive performance of both the regular North Vietnamese Army (NVA), or "People's Army," and Ho's Viet Cong guerrilla forces in the South, which kept up ferocious pressure on the South Vietnamese government in Saigon and its US sponsor. Even the greatest defeat of

Ho's forces, in the Tet Offensive launched in January 1968, turned into a strategic victory for North Vietnam and global Communism. Media coverage of dramatic early Viet Cong gains and American reverses helped turn the US public against the war, a political reaction severe enough that Johnson chose not to seek reelection later that year.[26]

Ho's victories did not come cheaply for Moscow. While Maoist China did split the expense, at times covering half or more, the Soviet government spent a billion rubles propping up and arming Ho's People's Republic of Vietnam between 1953 and 1967. According to the official exchange rate of 0.90 rubles to the dollar, that was $1.11 billion—the equivalent of $15 or $20 billion today.* In 1968 alone, the Soviets spent 357 million rubles on North Vietnam (then $396.7 million at nominal exchange), a considerable expense by any reckoning. So substantial was Moscow's commitment by 1967–1968, when the Vietnam War was entering its most critical stage, that at least some Soviet advisers began to complain that Ho's officers were not showing them enough deference—for example, by not allowing them to debrief captured American war prisoners or examine captured US war matériel. Although Ho denounced Moscow's bêtes noires like Tito, and publicly backed the USSR during its ugly interventions in Budapest in 1956 and in the Prague Spring, crushed by Soviet tanks in August 1968, in general he was less slavishly obedient than Castro. In one 1968 report from Hanoi, a Soviet correspondent for *Izvestiya* complained that, despite accounting for "75–80 percent" of foreign assistance for Ho's war against South Vietnam, the USSR enjoyed only "4–8 percent" of

---

* Dollar figures for Soviet expenditures must be approached with caution, as the black-market dollar-ruble exchange rate inside the USSR was often ten times the official one. Nonetheless, using official ruble-dollar parity, as the Soviet government did in its own accounting, is still helpful in assessing comparative expenditures compared to gross domestic product in the United States and the USSR—that is, how easily the costs could be borne by each government.

political influence in Hanoi. Still, in terms of strategic payoff, the 357 million rubles Moscow spent on Hanoi in 1968 may have been the best investment the Soviets ever made in the Cold War.[27]

It was in the years of the post-Tet slow-motion US disaster in Vietnam, from 1968 to 1975, that Soviet global influence and the popularity of the Communist cause likely peaked. Perhaps the greatest political triumph of all came with the election of Salvador Allende to the presidency of Chile on behalf of a Popular Front–style Unidad Popular (Popular Unity, UP) coalition of Communist, Socialist, and Radical parties in September 1970, with a plurality of 36.3 percent of the vote. Chilean electoral law ensured that Allende was formally voted president by the Chilean Congress in the capital, Santiago, that October. While Allende defeated his US-backed Independent opponent, Jorge Allesandri, by only 39,000 votes, and fell well short of a majority, this was still a unique pro-Communist (if not literally Communist) plurality won at the ballot box in a free election. Not even Ho Chi Minh, despite his widespread popularity as the man who had ejected the French from Indochina in 1954 and stood up to the Americans who replaced them, had ever won a genuine contested popular election.* Allende's many admirers could crow that the CIA had spent at least $425,000 trying to defeat him. Fewer know that the KGB spent more than this ($450,000) supporting Allende in 1970, and another $18,000 persuading a UP-aligned Chilean senator not to run in the election and split the left-wing vote.[28]

Allende's narrow plurality was not exactly a popular mandate for Communism, but he plowed ahead anyway with what he called

---

* It is likely true that Ho would have won the "Vietnamese unification elections" prescribed by the Geneva Accords of 1956, had they ever been held, as countless critics of the US intervention in Vietnam have pointed out. Nonetheless, this remains just as hypothetical as a Communist victory at the polls in postwar France or Italy absent CIA or US meddling. Ho *might* have won a fair and contested election that year, but there is no way of knowing for sure.

the "Chilean path to socialism" ("*La vía chilena al socialismo*"). That path included the nationalization of key Chilean industries (such as copper production and coal mining) and health care, state-mandated wage increases, and Soviet-style land reform, with large estates nationalized or broken up. Many of these measures proved popular, but they were expensive, and it did not help that the administration of US president Richard Nixon, angry at being outmaneuvered by the Soviets, cut off foreign aid to Chile. (Nixon further instructed his advisers to "make the [Chilean] economy scream.") With budgetary pressure mounting rapidly, Allende's government defaulted on Chile's external debts in November 1971. Meanwhile, inflation, already running at 23 percent when Allende had taken office that January, exploded to 163 percent by 1972 and nearly 200 percent by 1973. Labor strikes and demonstrations, at least some of them CIA-supported, rocked the country, and the Chilean Congress censured Allende over his nationalization and redistribution measures, which had "subject[ed] all citizens to the strictest economic and political control by the state and, in this manner, fulfill[ed] the goal of establishing a totalitarian system."[29]

Allende toyed with the idea of scheduling a referendum to decide between him and the Congress, threatening to mobilize his supporters against the parliament. "If the hour comes, the people will have arms," Allende vowed—perhaps overoptimistically. To the disappointment of his KGB backers, whose warnings about an impending military coup he failed to heed, Allende instead holed himself up in the presidential offices in La Moneda that September, defended by his Cuban-trained bodyguards. There, he quietly awaited his fate as the long-predicted coup, led by General Augusto Pinochet (whom Allende had himself appointed), spread out across Santiago, surrounded and stormed the palace, and ousted Allende's government. Allende committed suicide during the coup, falling on his sword so gallantly that he was "instantly canonized," as the chief foreign correspondent of the British *Sunday Times*, David Holden, wrote, "as the most potent cult figure since his old friend, Ché Guevara." The brutality of the Pinochet counter-revolution, which, according to an investigation by Chile's government in 1990, carried out 3,197 extrajudicial executions and "disappearances," and burned Marxist books in Nazi-style bonfires in Santiago, helped to crystallize the Allende legend. Millions of admirers took as a matter of faith that Allende himself was gunned down by Pinochet's men (not implausibly either, as the official story was that Allende shot himself with an AK-47). Soviet files have now revealed that at least some of the Western demonization of Pinochet was seeded by KGB "active measures," such as a forged letter implicating Pinochet in foreign assassinations in 1976 (in Operation TOUCAN).[30]

In truth, though, the Soviets did not have to try very hard to convince large swaths of the Western public that Pinochet was a villain and Allende a fallen hero, a misunderstood idealist. It was a similar story in Indonesia, where, as in Chile, the Sukarno government, ostensibly non-aligned but in fact pro-Communist, and backed by Hanoi, Beijing, and Moscow, was toppled in a US-backed military coup led by General Suharto in 1965, followed by Pinochet-style anti-Communist purges. It was emblematic of Cold War politics that millions of westerners came to idolize these fallen "martyrs" with only slightly less fervor than in the Ché Guevara cult, helped along by Hollywood movies such as *The Year of Living Dangerously* (1982), starring Mel Gibson, which dramatized alleged American perfidy in Indonesia in 1965, and *Missing* (also released in 1982), starring Jack Lemmon, which did the same for Pinochet's Chile of 1973. Even when their clients lost, the Soviets won in the arena of public opinion. Small wonder the former head of the International Department of the Central Committee of the Soviet Communist Party, Karen N. Brutents, later recalled of the heyday of Soviet global operations in the mid-1970s that "the world was turning in our direction." Certainly no satellites were *leaving* the Communist Bloc, as the Soviets had assured with the crushing of the Prague Spring, establishing the precedent referred to as the "Brezhnev doctrine."[31]

Still, despite the solidifying of the Eastern Bloc, robust Soviet expansion into Southeast Asia, Africa, and the Caribbean, and propaganda triumphs in Indonesia and Chile, trouble was brewing in the Communist heartland in Eurasia, where the Sino-Soviet split was deepening. Even in Vietnam, where Moscow and Beijing were ostensibly collaborating to support Ho Chi Minh against the Americans and their South Vietnamese clients, Chinese officials were poisoning the well, frequently accusing the Soviets of "selling out" North Vietnam every time the latter conducted talks with Washington. In one bitter argument with the Soviet ambassador to China in 1966, Mao's foreign minister, Zhou Enlai, had accused the Soviets of "treason" for contacting the US government "behind the back of China and Vietnam." In March 1969, the war of words between Moscow and Beijing heated up into an armed border skirmish near Zhenbao Island on the Ussuri River in Manchuria, in which at least thirty-one Soviet troops were killed. The border standoff lasted for months, growing serious enough that the Soviet government canvassed opinion among its Warsaw Pact allies about whether they would support "a conventional attack to destroy China's nuclear weapons center at Lop Nor"—a threat that led Mao to order general mobilization. Not until May 1970 had the war scare calmed down enough for Mao to receive a Soviet delegation in Beijing, announcing that the two Communist rivals should "only fight with words."[32]

Lending frisson to the Sino-Soviet split was Mao's ongoing Cultural Revolution in China, which had frightened Brezhnev and his advisers no less seriously than the Great Leap Forward had alarmed Khrushchev. Mao had always been a loose cannon, and his latest radical experiments threatened to spoil the image of Communism in the West just when it seemed to be recovering from the aftershocks of Stalin's death, Khrushchev's secret speech, and the bloody crackdowns in the East European satellites in 1953, 1956, and 1968. Soviet Communism may have lost the deadly zeal of the Stalin era, but Maoism continued to test the limits of collectivist political activism—and human depravity.

13

RED GUARDS AND THE KHMER ROUGE

COMMUNISM *AD ABSURDUM*

Since Stalin's death in 1953, Beijing had emerged as a genuine rival to Moscow for leadership of the Communist world, with Mao displaying the energy and ambition that were fading in the Soviet Union. Khrushchev had a certain crude peasant energy, but not even this could be said of Leonid Brezhnev, whose fondness for gifted baubles, imported cars, and elegant villas epitomized the creeping corruption and complacency. A popular joke had Brezhnev proudly showing his mother around his luxurious hunting lodges and dachas, only for her to whisper, "Well, it's good, Leonid. But what happens if the Communists come back?"[1]

Mao, by contrast, was a picture of manly vigor, never complacent, never satisfied, always keeping his aides and rivals on edge as he lurched from one madcap scheme to another. Just in the two years following Khrushchev's "secret speech" of 1956, the "Socialist High Tide" of collectivization in the PRC's agricultural sector gave way to the Hundred Flowers Campaign, Mao's liberalizing invitation for party members and citizens to air grievances, with the motto "Let a Hundred Flowers Bloom." That invitation belched forth enough anti-Communist sentiment to fill reeducation camps with hundreds of thousands of dissenters and justify the Great Leap Forward, launched in 1958. The ensuing nationwide famine provoked pushback from Mao's advisers as early as the CCP conference held in Lushan in the summer of 1959, which in turn prompted Mao to crack down on recalcitrant party members. He purged nearly 3 million commissars and replaced them with younger and more ruthless activists willing to push the Great Leap through without questioning it. The results were so appalling that Mao reversed course again in 1960, allowing peasants forced onto state communes to grow food on private plots, relegalizing local food markets, and authorizing grain imports to alleviate shortages. In April 1961 Mao even requested that some of his critical Politburo colleagues, such as head of state Liu Shaoqi, visit the countryside to investigate shortages and find someone to blame—not Communists, of course, but "feudal forces, full of hatred towards socialism," who must be "stirring up trouble."[2]

Liu did as he was told, but his findings were not to Mao's liking. In January 1962, Liu shocked delegates to the party's "Seven Thousand Cadres Conference" by describing the ongoing famine as a "man-made disaster" (*renhuo*), implying some responsibility on the part of the CCP, although Liu still defended Mao's Great Leap Forward on the grounds that *some* regions of China had seen gains in agricultural production. In private, Liu was far more critical, telling Mao in Beijing that July that "so many people have died of hunger. History will judge you and me, even cannibalism will go into the books!" Mao was offended enough that he now defended the Great Leap unequivocally, blaming Liu for backing down. Going on the offensive, Mao announced a new slogan in August 1962: "Never Forget Class Struggle." Private plots would be outlawed again, the land returned to the state communes. By 1963 the Great Leap was back on again, with a chastened Liu sending his own wife out to lead a Communist "work team" in recollectivizing a rural village and "taking power back from class enemies." Mao's new watchword was a war against "revisionism," to ensure that no "Khrushchev" emerged to de-Stalinize China.[3]

One might have expected that Khrushchev's fall in October 1964, and the rehabilitation of Stalin under Brezhnev, would have reassured Mao about the risks of Chinese Communists backsliding into "revision." Instead, Khrushchev's ouster fueled Mao's paranoia still further, as it provided a model of how he might himself be treated. It did not help matters that, at a Kremlin reception that November, a drunken Soviet official told Zhou Enlai, "We've already got rid of Khrushchev; you ought to follow our example and get rid of Mao Zedong. That way we'll get on better." In his inimitably earthy fashion, Mao expressed his fears that December by complaining, after a fractious party meeting, that "somebody is shitting on my head." In January 1965, Mao had the guidelines of the Socialist Education Campaign rewritten to focus on the failings of high party leadership instead of provincial cadres. The goal now was to "rectify those people in positions of authority within the party who take the capitalist road."[4]

Lending frisson to Mao's latest agitprop offensive was the ramping up of the Vietnam War. In July 1964, Mao had promised Ho that, if the Americans "start[ed] bombing or landing operations" against North Vietnam, the PRC would "fight them." His confidence and belligerence were buoyed by China's successful detonation of an atomic bomb on October 16 on a salt lake in the Muslim-majority frontier province of Xinjiang. Mao's foreign policy slogan, corollary to domestic attacks on "capitalist roaders," was "Resist America and Assist Vietnam." At a summit with Ho Chi Minh in Beijing in May 1965, he promised Ho that China would provide "whatever support was needed by the Vietnamese." In addition to Chinese shipments of guns, artillery pieces, shells, and ammunition, this support soon included the dispatch of entire Chinese antiaircraft artillery divisions and engineering troops to Hanoi, peaking at 170,000 Chinese forces on the ground in North Vietnam in 1967. Mao was good to his word. Unlike the Soviets, who kept a certain public distance from Hanoi and avoided engaging the Americans directly in Vietnam, Chinese antiaircraft gunners participated in more than 2,000 active firefights, during which they shot down 1,707 US warplanes over the next four years and damaged another 1,608.[5]

As his vow to fight the Americans in Vietnam shows, Mao's threats were rarely idle: he meant what he said. Unfortunately for thousands of CCP leaders and millions of ordinary Chinese people, he also meant what he said about rooting out "capitalist roaders" at home. Mao had dropped hints for several years about what was coming, from crackdowns on Confucianism and Christianity to an ominous declaration, in June 1963, that an "acute class struggle" was "taking place in the country relating to ideology, education, theory, science, arts, newspapers, periodicals, broadcasting, publishing," and "other fields." That November, Mao attacked the Chinese Ministry of Culture, which, he said, should be renamed the "Ministry of Dead People" in view of its reactionary tendencies. Among these benighted tendencies was the old "mandarin" examination system for enrolling Chinese government bureaucrats, which Mao weakened by dumbing down the exams, insisting that, to avoid any advantage for "bourgeois" children, students be given the questions in advance and be allowed to copy clever students' answers—that is, cheat on class grounds. Even dozing off in class Mao praised: there was no reason for good proletarian children to "have to listen to nonsense, you can rest your brain instead." In May 1964, a mimeographed compendium of Mao's quotations was distributed to the People's Liberation Army. Officially titled *Quotations from Chairman Mao Zedong*, but soon known colloquially as the "Little Red Book," it included this unsubtle inscription: "Read Mao's book, listen to Chairman Mao's words, act according to Chairman Mao's instructions and be a good fighter for Chairman Mao." As with his populist attacks on schooling, traditional religion, and high culture, the "Little Red Book" targeted the impressionable young, with the added menace that the young people were to be armed. Mao was training ideological foot soldiers for a new Communist crusade.[6]

The first shoe dropped when Mao attacked a historical play written by Wu Han, a Communist history professor who was also deputy mayor of Beijing, at a CCP conference in October 1965. *The Dismissal of Hai Rui*, an allegory about a sixteenth-century mandarin who had fought against the exploitation of peasants as a kind of Chinese "Robin Hood," had premiered in 1961 and was initially praised by party propagandists. Mao (and his wife, Jiang Qing, a former actress, to whom he had given the theater-purging brief) now decided that this "poisonous weed" of a play actually "cast aspersions on Communism's failures in agriculture," by using "historical events and characters to mock, attack and slander the realities of present day socialism." Wu Han's play was then used as an ideological litmus test, with an "anti-party clique of four" who had allegedly endorsed it sacked on May 23, 1966, in a purge Zhou Enlai saluted as a "victory for Mao Zedong thought." In a lead editorial promoting International Children's Day on June 1, the *People's Daily* exhorted young Communists to "Sweep Away All Monsters and Demons," by which was meant "bourgeois specialists" like Wu Han, and, more generally, "to destroy the four olds" (*P'o-Szu-Chiu*): Old Thought, Old Culture, Old Customs, and Old Habits. Students were put to work creating "big-character posters" (*Ta-Tzu-Pao*) with menacing slogans printed in large Chinese characters, such as "Smash the Black Gang!," "Down with the Anti-Socialist Cabal!," and "Carry the Revolution Through to the End." In a sign of things to come, Peking University, where another history professor had been denounced for defending the study of Chinese classics against comrades who insisted they were all a "pile of garbage," was singled out for big-character denunciation as a hotbed of "Khrushchev-type revisionist elements." The university was shut down by decree on June 2, and its closure was soon followed by the suspension of all classes in Beijing. The Great Proletarian Cultural Revolution of 1966 was underway.[7]

Many of the themes of Mao's new agitprop offensive, such as xenophobia and the purging of "elites" and intellectuals, were familiar from the early Stalin era in the USSR. This was not entirely an accident, as the man chosen to lead Mao's "Cultural Revolution Group," and author of the "Four Olds / Sweep All Monsters Away" *People's Daily* editorial, Chen Boda, had studied for four years in Moscow in the early 1930s before becoming Mao's stenographer and the CCP's first official historian. The "Little Red Book," which became the bible of young Maoist militants during the Cultural Revolution, recalled Stalin's *Short Course* of 1938, just as the plastering of Beijing and other Chinese cities with giant portraits of Mao, "flanked by red flags with hammer and sickle," recalled the aesthetics of high Stalinism. Likewise, the ruthless CCP leadership purges that accelerated to fever pitch in 1966, enveloping even high-ranking Communists—such as Peng Zhen, a longtime member of the CCP Central Committee and Politburo, and General Luo Ruiqing, chief of the Joint Staff of the People's Liberation Army and a former head of State Security, who were both scapegoated as cardinal members of the "anti-party clique of four"—were a small-scale simulacrum of the fate of former Soviet Politburo and Red Army heroes in Stalin's Great Terror.

Nonetheless, there was something new in Mao's Cultural Revolution, a ramping up of generational conflict against everything "old," which represented an escalation in Communist radicalism. To be sure, future party bosses like Khrushchev, Brezhnev, and Georgy Malenkov had stepped into the boots of dead older men in the Stalin era. But they weren't exactly children when they did so. Khrushchev was forty when he oversaw construction of the Moscow Metro by forced laborers in 1934–1935, and forty-three when he directed the Moscow purges in 1937. Malenkov was forty when he joined the Politburo in 1941. Even Brezhnev, youngest of the three, was thirty-three when Khrushchev appointed him as regional party secretary in Ukraine in 1939. The foot soldiers who manned Mao's big-character poster campaign launched in May–June 1966, by contrast, were mostly teenagers at secondary school, who were told by the government, in a June 3 decree launching the Cultural Revolution in schools, to stop attending class and start denouncing their teachers. Teachers and principals were heckled and forced to wear "dunce camps" or self-denouncing big-character posters ("I am a Black Gang Element!," or "I am an Anti-Party Intellectual") tied around their chests or necks with weights, and were then assigned menial and humiliating work tasks, or in some cases "forced to kneel on broken glass." Fellow students, too, were denounced if they refused to join the terror campaign against teachers. The Cultural Revolution Group set a quota mandating that 1 percent of students and teachers nationwide be labeled "rightists" or "counter-revolutionaries" and ritually abused, with a target goal of 300,000 victims. On June 13, China's university exam system was declared null and void, and it was announced that fall enrollment would be postponed by at least six months: school was out not just for summer, but for the rest of the year.[8]

Curiously, Mao himself was out of public sight as China's Great Proletarian Cultural Revolution was launched, as if to let his actress wife, Jiang Qing—a prominent member of the Cultural Revolution Group—assume the spotlight. But Mao was too vain to let her steal the show for long. On July 16, 1966, he staged one of his favorite spectacles, a public swim of the Yangtze, with photographers capturing his buoyant ruddy-cheeked face as he emerged, having allegedly swum fifteen kilometers (ten miles) in sixty-five minutes (in fact he had basically just floated downstream in an area of the river known for a strong current). A great swimming craze gripped Beijing as thousands of young Chinese, including soldiers in uniform, rushed to show that they had no less vigor than Mao: many drowned, happy to sacrifice themselves for the Cultural Revolution. On July 29, Mao addressed 10,000 secondary school and college students in the Great Hall of the People in Beijing, denouncing "old counter-revolutionaries," and "old revolutionaries," too, for that matter—including Liu Shaoqi, China's head of state, third only to Mao and Zhou Enlai in the CCP hierarchy, and Deng Xiaoping, party general secretary and Liu's closest ally in the Politburo. Calling in Lin Biao, the PLA commander-in-chief, for reinforcements, Mao sidelined Liu and Deng at a secret Party Plenum on August 6 and made the purge official in an August 8 "Decision on the Great Proletarian Cultural Revolution," which denounced "those in power within the party taking the capitalist road" and instructed party cadres to "trust the masses" and their "big-character posters" instead. Deng, Mao told Lin Biao with a hint of menace, "was to be treated as an enemy." Mao wrote his own big-character poster with the headline, "Bombard the Headquarters!"[9]

It was now open season on unpopular, hesitant, or simply elderly Communist party leaders in China, whom angry young students and soldiers, forming armed groups called "Red Wind" or "East Wind," devoted to Chairman Mao's Cultural Revolution (soon shortened to simply "Red Guards" [*Hung-Wei-Ping*]), were exhorted to smoke out. The first victim of the Red Guards was the female vice principal of a girls' school in Beijing, Bian Zhongyun, who on August 5 was splashed with ink, forced to kneel, beaten with nail-spiked clubs, and dumped in a garbage cart, where she died of her wounds. Among the schools that saw similar horrors that August was Beijing's 101st Middle School, where Mao himself had sent his own children. Ten unfortunate teachers of this junior high school were ritually tortured and then "forced to crawl on a path paved with coal cinders," after which their Red Guard tormentors wrote "Long Live the Red Terror" with their victims' blood on the wall of the room where they had tortured them.[10]

Taking his own advice to "trust the masses," Mao summoned more than a million children and teenage students to Beijing's Tiananmen Square (meaning "Heavenly Peace," it was now renamed *Dongfanghung*, or "The East Is Red" Square) on August 19, 1966, where he, Lin Biao, and Zhou Enlai exhorted these future Red Guards to "strike down all power-holders walking the capitalist road, all bourgeois reactionary authorities, all bourgeois royalists, all bourgeois rightists, all freaks and monsters," and "to destroy all old ideas, old culture, old customs and old habits of the exploiting classes." It was an invitation to ritualized violence, not just against an alleged social class of oppressors, as in Lenin's Red Terror, or recalcitrant party leaders or generals, as in Stalin's Great Terror, but against anyone older or old-fashioned, or who annoyed the Red Guards by their very manner of being. Teachers, school principals, prominent writers, filmmakers, musicians, adults who wore eyeglasses, women who wore high heels, and men with "long, western haircuts" were surrounded, ritually denounced, beaten, and tortured. Hundreds were killed each day in Beijing, peaking at 200 a day toward the end of August, adding up to 1,700 killed by late September. In Daxing, a rural village near Beijing, 300 "landlords" were killed along with their families, their corpses hurled into "disused wells and mass graves." Scenes of horror abounded, epitomized in the eyes of one British diplomat by the "sight of two old ladies being stoned by small children."[11]

While elderly or "bourgeois" Chinese furnished most of the victims, not even the foreign community was immune. On August 25, 1966, Red Guards broke into the fortified Beijing compound hosting the Sacred Heart Academy, a Catholic school operated by French nuns, and plastered the walls with posters reading, "Get out, foreign devil!" and "Chase out running dogs of imperialism." The Red Guards then took hostages and presented an ambitious list of demands:

Abolish the taxis and send the cars to villages.
Prohibit the sale of gold, fish, birds, antiques and foreign goods . . .
Bicycles should be free.
House owners should transfer their property to the state . . .
Bourgeois element should be made to do manual work.
Cinemas, theaters and bookshops should be decorated with portraits of Mr Mao.
Luxury restaurants abolished, business must serve workers, peasants, soldiers.
Loudspeakers set up on every street to broadcast directives.
Perfumes, jewellery and non-proletarian clothes and shoes surrendered.
No more first-class rail wagons and seats.
All paintings of bamboo and non-political themes abolished.
All books not representing Mao's thought should be burned.
Bourgeois actors should only be allowed to play unsympathetic characters.
All pedicabs should be peddled by bourgeois themselves.[12]

Even *Communist* foreigners were attacked. The East German military attaché was surrounded by Red Guards and physically assaulted in front of the Soviet embassy. The DDR issued a sharp protest, but received no apology from Mao. Embassies of other Communist powers, such as Hungary and North Vietnam, issued strong protests. Even the radical and generally pro-Maoist Communist dictator of Albania, Enver Hoxha, chided Mao for the "dangerous" actions of the Red Guards, which were "undertaken outside the Leninist norms of the party and the laws of the dictatorship of the proletariat." In the most shocking act of Communist lèse-majesté, Red Guards unfurled a giant big-character poster in front of the Soviet embassy in Beijing, addressed "to the Soviet people." "All old and new hatreds," the Red Guards informed their onetime Soviet benefactors, "have been cut into our hearts. We shall not forget them—not in 100, 1,000, or 10,000 years! One day, when the time comes, we shall cut the skin off you. We shall tear your sinews out, we shall burn your corpses and disperse your ashes in the wind!" To ensure that this blood-curdling message was received in Moscow, *Komsomolskaya Pravda* reported from Beijing on September 20, 1966, the Red Guards shouted it aloud from loudspeakers.[13]

The Sino-Soviet split was already well underway by 1966, but the Cultural Revolution deepened the fracture still further. Soviet students studying in Chinese universities, sent home early that year as their schools were shuttered before fall classes, were not amused by the Red Guards, or by Mao's soon infamous explanation for the school closures, announced in early September, namely that "the more you study, the stupider you become." One frustrated Russian student informed a Soviet journalist that he had witnessed Red Guards beating a pregnant woman and a "famous 70-year-old professor." One of his teachers, the Russian continued, "welcomed the cultural revolution until her own children denounced her in a Red

Guard leaflet." All through 1966 and 1967, the Soviet press ran horror stories about Mao's Cultural Revolution no less disapproving than those in the Western media. The Soviet news agency TASS took note of an alarming incident that took place in Changzhou, northwest of Shanghai, in September 1966, when Red Guards had broken into an electrical engineering school shouting, "It is necessary to fight with weapons, not words." Among the Red Guard victims were three elderly women and an old factory worker who, the Soviet journalist noted, was overheard wailing, "Before liberation, I was beaten by capitalists. Now you have beaten me." At the height of Cultural Revolution hysteria that fall, recalled then chief of the Soviet KGB Vladimir Semichastny, there was genuine fear in the Kremlin that the Chinese Red Guard hysteria would spill over the border into Soviet Siberia. "What if," he recalled warning his colleagues, "a storming crowd of Chinese moved on foot and without any armament to the north, to our border? What could be done against the storming of a fanatical crowd?" Mao responded to Russian criticism by labeling the USSR a "socialist-imperialist country."[14]

Soviet and Western journalists alike were horrified when reports emerged of Red Guard assaults on libraries as repositories of "old" culture, often accompanied by book burnings. A library in Xiamen, a coastal city near the Taiwan Strait, was lit up in a fire that leapt "three storeys high," as Red Guards fed the conflagration with more than sixty liters of kerosene. In Shanghai, a library opened by Jesuits in 1847, which housed more than 200,000 volumes, saw its priceless collections burned as a symbol of foreign "capitalism." Christian churches and cathedrals were torched, along with ancient Chinese pagodas, Buddhist temples, and other cultural monuments. Even the sacred Confucius cemetery in Qufu, final residence and resting place of the great teacher, was not immune: a band of some 200 Red Guards broke in and desecrated the tombs.

Foreign cemeteries, especially those in Shanghai, were specially targeted, with thousands of headstones defaced or smashed to pieces. Flower shops, too, were targeted for destruction, on the idea that ornamental plants and flowers were wasteful "bourgeois" indulgences. Cats, seen as decadent "bourgeois" pets, were massacred in Shanghai and other cities. Apartments were searched for "capitalist" extravagances, from paintings and pianos to musical instruments, antiques, porcelain, and silverware. Like Bolshevik looters in revolutionary Russia, Red Guards kept much of the loot for themselves, including more than 4 metric tons of gold jewelry and coin. In addition to being deprived of their property and often their shoes, as many as 400,000 of their "bourgeois" urbanite victims were expelled from their homes and frog-marched, barefoot, into the countryside to work on state and collective farms. Unsurprisingly, urban dwellers who survived these terrors tended to hunker down and avoid drawing attention to themselves. Women ceased wearing makeup or heels or braiding their hair, and men adopted bland "proletarian haircuts." Household items, from sinks to silks to pillows to children's toys, were redesigned to look as bland and functional as possible. Even socks were jettisoned as remnants of benighted "old" feudalism.[15]

While no one could really be said to have controlled the armed children who terrorized China into drab proletarian conformity in their war against the "four olds," Chairman Mao was unquestionably their inspiration. He personally reviewed over 12 million Red Guards on the march in Beijing in the months following the official rollout in August 1966, and he ensured that they could travel easily across China by decreeing that all Red Guards could ride for free on public buses and trains, and stay for free in hotels—at least until the last week of November, when a series of decrees began to rescind the privileges Red Guards had become accustomed to. On November 23, Red Guards were ordered to leave Beijing. On

November 28, free national transport for them was withdrawn, and the next day Zhou Enlai announced that schools across China would soon be reopening, as if to inform Red Guards (of whom an estimated 95 percent were students) that, their service to the cause appreciated, it was time to turn in their weapons and go back to class. On December 21, free board in state hotels and hostels was withdrawn, too. Not all of these juvenile class warriors, however, obliged. Many thousands kept moving, intimidating their way onto buses and trains with their weapons, slowly transitioning from angry class warriors to accidental "red tourists." Others heeded instructions issued by Mao's Cultural Revolution Group in October to wander around China on foot, proving their strength and endurance by reenacting a version of Mao's legendary "Long March." In Changzhou, the same city where Red Guards had invaded the electrical engineering school to the horror of Soviet observers in September, defiant Red Guards threatened, in a big-character poster plastered around the city in December, that they were ready to "unfurl the victorious flag over the White House" (Zhongnanhai), referring to the Beijing compound adjacent to the Forbidden City housing CCP headquarters and government offices, "and if necessary stain the whole Pacific with blood."[16]

Before it came to that, Mao was able to bring the Red Guards to heel—but not before using them to unleash a brutal round of purges. In the winter of 1966–1967, as juvenile Red Guards slowly began to self-dissolve and go home, the Cultural Revolution spread to China's factories in a wave of protests and strikes. In Shanghai, rebellious workers, assisted by Red Guards, seized control of several party newspaper offices and then city hall, in a kind of armed uprising against the CCP establishment. Curiously, despite being the chairman of the ruling party against which radical "proletarians" were now doing battle, Mao praised the Shanghai rebellion as a "January storm" and exhorted workers and students across

China to emulate it. The new watchword was "Seize power!" In effect, what Mao was encouraging was civil war, as radical elements aligned with himself toppled whichever CCP bureaucrats happened to be in charge at the time.[17]

At first, it seemed that the PLA, led by loyal Maoist Lin Biao, was on the side of the rebels—but tensions inevitably arose between the regular army and the ragtag bands of rebels rampaging across the country, looting and destroying as they went. In Qinghai, the interior province east of Xinjiang, the PLA violently crushed a radical uprising and sent nearly 10,000 rebels off to labor camps. In February 1967, Mao signaled a possible shift when he chided Chen Boda and other members of the Cultural Revolution Group for excesses, even criticizing his own wife, Jiang Qing, for arrogance ("You look down on everyone else"). Deftly, Mao was able to rally support from Zhou Enlai and Lin Biao for continuing course with the Cultural Revolution, though with the PLA authorized to keep order whenever things got out of hand. A kind of martial law descended on China in March as nearly 3 million troops left their barracks to guard key strongpoints, CCP offices, and other urban power bases. But the situation remained tense, and civil violence flared up all spring and summer. Embassies of "foreign imperialist" governments in Beijing, including the Soviet one, remained under siege. Rebels actually set fire to the British embassy on August 22 in an act of terrorism so brazen that Mao finally reined in the Cultural Revolution Group, denouncing a faction led by Wang Li as "bad people." It was a signal to cool down the fervor, tear down the big-character posters, and obey the PLA. The last remaining Red Guard units were disbanded by force in July 1968. In a turnabout their "bourgeois" victims might have enjoyed, had they still been alive to witness it, on December 22, 1968, Mao issued a decree sending urban *students*, many of them former Red Guards, into the countryside for "reeducation." They were now forced to work the fields with their hands instead of "lazing about in the city."[18]

And so Mao's Cultural Revolution churned on. Red Guards had come and gone, but in a way Mao's turn against the students was consistent with arming them in the first place: the idea was to do away with book learning and "bourgeois" civilization more generally, to force everyone (excepting Mao and his trusted Communist party cadres, of course) to get dirty and work with their hands. Not just children but entire families were deported from the cities in a reverse urbanization that ultimately saw 17 million city and town dwellers expelled from their homes before the campaign finally petered out in the mid-1970s. Mao's Cultural Revolution, in the end, cost far fewer lives than earlier convulsions like the Great Leap Forward—the best current estimates of the death toll come out at around 1.5 to 2 million—but the impact on China's material civilization and culture was devastating. In many ways, the country is still recovering from the trauma.[19]

Even as it was calcifying at home, Mao's Cultural Revolution spread beyond China's borders into neighboring Cambodia, by way of a virulent, Red Guards–inspired Communist movement known as the Khmer Rouge or "Red Khmer" (Khmer is the language spoken by Cambodians). Although China's government has sought to distance itself from the Khmer Rouge since its genocidal crimes were exposed, it is a matter of public record that its French-educated Communist founder and leader, Pol Pot (born Saloth Sâr), visited Beijing for three months in the winter of 1965–1966, at the height of Mao's Cultural Revolution, and was trained, educated, and later funded by the Chinese Communist Party. Recent archival research by Andrew Mertha has demonstrated how critical CCP support for Pol Pot's regime was. China provided 90 percent of the foreign funding of "Democratic Kampuchea" between 1975 and 1979, trained its soldiers, and sent, Mertha discovered, everything from foodstuffs and construction equipment to T-54 and T-63 tanks, warplanes, helicopters, VPBE patrol boats, AK-47s, field artillery, and antiaircraft guns.[20]

To be sure, the Khmer Rouge could never have emerged as a serious fighting force in the first place without the spillover of the Vietnam War into Cambodia in 1970. The North Vietnamese Communist regime had long used Cambodian territory to evade US airpower, both to route supplies to South Vietnam and increasingly as an actual rear base, stationing elements of five army divisions, nearly 50,000 troops, on Cambodian soil by 1969. As part of a new strategy (known as "Vietnamization") to use US airpower more aggressively to cover a phased-out withdrawal of American ground troops from South Vietnam, the administration of President Richard Nixon authorized bombing raids on North Vietnamese bases and supply routes in Cambodia—which alarmed Cambodia's head of state, Prince Norodom Sihanouk, who wished to remain neutral. Annoyed with Sihanouk's wavering, the Cambodian defense minister and prime minister, Lon Nol, engineered a parliamentary vote of no confidence in March 1970 in a rolling coup that brought him to power as a "president," basically a pro-American dictator. While Sihanouk was not a Communist himself, he publicly accused the American CIA of arranging his ouster. Taking refuge with Mao in Beijing, he threw his support and considerable prestige behind the "Khmer Republic"—a Cambodian opposition to Lon Nol led by Communist forces aligned with North Vietnam and China, of which the most prominent faction was Pol Pot's Khmer Rouge. As Sihanouk told the Agence France-Presse in Beijing on September 26, 1970, "The majority of the Royal Government of [Cambodian] National Union is now Red Khmer, and the power already belongs to the Cambodian Communist Party. I am giving everything to the Red Khmers." Three years later, a chastened but still unrepentant Sihanouk told the Italian journalist Oriana Fallaci that his name was being used by the Khmer Rouge to recruit peasants and expand their ranks to 35,000 armed actives, but "when they no longer need me, they will spit me out like a cherry pit."[21]

Not everyone was as sanguine about the Khmer Rouge as Prince Sihanouk. By 1973, Pol Pot's Communist guerrillas had already begun emptying towns, such as Kompong Cham, that they had captured—deporting *everyone*, that is, not just "class enemies." In March 1974, the Khmer Rouge sacked and looted the ancient Cambodian royal capital of Oudong, home to a "revered seventeenth-century complex of Buddhist temples and tombs" where priceless Buddhist relics were kept, along with the tombs of many Khmer kings, and then deported 20,000 people into the countryside, of whom few survived. The nearby towns of Prek Kdam and Kompong Luong were emptied, too, as were "a number of villages in between." As one terrified survivor told a *New York Times* reporter, Sydney Schanberg, after the area was retaken by Lon Nol's troops in July, "Forests have been mowed down. Schools, pagodas, mosques and hospitals have been flattened. The remains are skeletal—a staircase going nowhere, a wall holding up nothing."[22]

Schanberg was bewildered by the devastation he observed, but an American expert named Kenneth Quinn at the State Department, who had been studying the actions and publications of the Khmer Rouge for years, had issued a prescient warning in early 1974. Pol Pot and his adjutants, all Communists educated in Paris but aligned with Mao's Cultural Revolution, were, in Quinn's view, committed to a "total social revolution." The Khmer Rouge idea of Cultural Revolution entailed "stripping away, through terror and other means, the traditional bases, structures and forces which have guided an individual's life," from parental authority, religion, and royal tradition to even things such as "traditional songs and dances," until "he is left an atomized, isolated individual unit; and then rebuilding him according to party doctrine and substituting a series of new values." To achieve this, the Khmer Rouge would destroy *everything* that made up Cambodian tradition and civilization, which was all "anathema that must be destroyed."[23]

When the decade-old US military intervention in Vietnam and Cambodia went belly-up in April 1975, encapsulated in unforgettable scenes as the last American soldiers and diplomats were airlifted by Marine helicopters out of both Phnom Penh (on April 13) and Saigon (April 29–30), Pol Pot and the Khmer Rouge were given the chance to put their plans for "total social revolution" into practice. The Cambodian capital was already swollen with refugees from the ongoing Cambodian Civil War, with nearly 3 million people now huddled in Phnom Penh to escape the fighting—and the mercies of the Khmer Rouge, whose forces began entering the now defenseless capital on April 17. "Their faces [were] cold," and there was "a deadness in their eyes," wrote Schanberg of the Khmer Rouge before he was arrested. The city's communications were cut off, and there were no Western eyewitnesses for much of what followed. Schanberg, who was later transported to Thailand and released, was one of the last Western reporters to leave. Along with John Barron, Anthony Paul, and a few other journalists, he was later able to help debrief survivors. Among those who were left behind was Dith Pran, Schanberg's Cambodian photographer, who, because he was not a US citizen, could not evacuate with him. Dith's story, told by Schanberg, inspired the 1984 film *The Killing Fields*.[24]

Barron and Paul, who interviewed over 300 Cambodian refugees, mostly at a border camp in Thailand in October 1975, were the first to piece together the harrowing story. The first Khmer Rouge squads, composed of ten to twelve soldiers each, marched into Phnom Penh around 7:00 a.m. on April 17. Most were "small men and women from peasant stock," who were "dressed in black pajamalike uniforms, peaked Mao caps and Ho Chi Minh sandals carved from rubber tires." Many of them were as young as thirteen or fourteen years old, and thus "scarcely taller than the Chinese AK-47 or American M-16 rifles they carried." But they were hardened combat veterans, fearless and intimidating, 10,000 strong. Bewildered city residents at first welcomed the strange conquering army, hoping, like the Chinese who saluted Mao in 1949, that the long civil war, which had cost the lives of more than half a million Cambodians, was over. As one middle-class twenty-three-year-old university student, Ung Sok Choeu, recalled, "That morning we were shouting, 'Victory! Victory!' And I joined in with great glee. People were happy. . . . [T]hings could only become better now."[25]

Ung Sok Choeu's euphoria did not survive the day. Despite proclaiming the death penalty for "looters," Khmer Rouge soldiers were soon looting everything in sight, from cars and bicycles—confiscated at gunpoint—to watches, transistor radios, jewelry, and liquor. Around 8:30 a.m., the killing began. The first victims were recognizable officials of the Lon Nol regime, mostly older men. Nearly twenty civil servants, exiting a government building, were machine-gunned down. Other elderly officials, or wounded or decommissioned Cambodian soldiers unlucky enough to be wearing their uniforms, were beaten, tortured, and shot. Some of these atrocities might have been random, or at least spontaneous, rather than specifically ordered from above, but at around 9:00 a.m. the Khmer Rouge got serious, putting into action what was clearly a systematic evacuation plan. Door by door, house by house, the young armed guerrillas went, forcing everyone out onto the streets and "shooting in the air, shouting that everybody should leave the city." Khmer Rouge soldiers then "evacuated" Phnom Penh's hospitals, including the wounded. Bursting into Preah Ket Melea Hospital, armed teenage Communist warriors shouted, "Out! Everybody out! Get Out!":

Hundreds of men, women and children in pajamas limped, hobbled, struggled out of the hospital into the street where the midday sun had raised the temperature to over 100 degrees Fahrenheit [37.8 degrees Celsius]. Relatives or friends pushed the beds of patients too wounded, crippled or enfeebled to walk, some holding aloft perfusion bottles dripping plasma or serum into the bodies of loved ones. One man carried his son, whose legs had just been amputated. The bandages on both stumps were red with blood, and the son . . . was screaming, "You can't leave me like this! Kill me! Please kill me!"[26]

Ostensibly, insofar as any explanation was offered by its largely mute teenage foot soldiers, the Khmer Rouge was evacuating Phnom Penh (including its wounded hospital patients) to "protect" everyone from American bombing raids—a curious pretext, in that the United States had already evacuated the city and was in the process of withdrawing from Indochina entirely. But this can hardly explain the looting, ransacking, and wanton destruction the Khmer Rouge carried out, or the time that was taken to burn down bookstores and libraries (including a medical library in a Soviet-built hospital), or to throw thousands of books into the Mekong River. Whereas the Bolsheviks, and Mao's Communists, had taken care to secure gold and cash reserves in the banks they nationalized, the mostly teenage thugs of the Khmer Rouge, after bursting into the Banque Khmer de Commerce, set fire to huge piles of Cambodian riels and threw the rest out the windows. When it came to household property, the story was similar: Khmer Rouge girls and boys smashed up the crockery and bedding and threw whatever they could lift out into the streets to rot away. By nightfall, about 10,000 people had been killed or left for dead in the city, while several hundred thousand Cambodians had already been forced onto the roads leaving the city. By the end of April, an American F-4 Phantom—not a bomber, a reconnaissance aircraft—circled the skies over Phnom Penh for the better part of a day, but "its cameras could detect almost no signs of life of any kind." The Cambodian capital, recently home to 3 million people, including 20,000 wounded or ill hospital patients, had been transformed, as these surveillance photos demonstrated, "into a vast, still wasteland occupied primarily by corpses, stray dogs, pigs, ducks, chickens and [Khmer Rouge] patrols standing guard to ensure that human life did not return."[27]

The fate of Phnom Penh was only the beginning. Nearly every city in Cambodia was forcibly emptied by the Khmer Rouge, with something like 3.5 million people, or half the national population, herded by heavily armed teenage soldiers—most between twelve and fifteen years old—into jungles and rice paddies, nearly all of the victims "trembling," as one former philosophy professor who had initially welcomed the Khmer Rouge later recalled, "like half-drowned baby mice." Emaciated and half-starving adults who complained were beaten with "big sticks and hoes,"* as Dith remembered, so as to "save bullets," or had their heads covered with a plastic bag and pushed down to drown in the wet rice paddies. Sometimes the capital offense was something as simple as a man and woman "holding hands." To discourage this kind of "unauthorized break from work," families were separated, wives from husbands and both from children, so no one would waste time kissing or caressing or hugging, or simply talking, instead of tilling the fields. "Anyone they didn't like," Dith recalled, "they would accuse of being a teacher or a student or a former Lon Nol soldier, and that was the end." Others just starved to death, hundreds of thousands in 1975 alone. No one knows for sure how many Cambodians died

---

* In a rare Chinese admission of complicity, China's ambassador to Cambodia, Zhang Jinfeng, admitted in an interview in 2010 that Beijing had sent aid to the Khmer Rouge, but that it consisted only of "scythes and hoes." These were often the very weapons of choice used by Khmer Rouge thugs in rural beatings and executions.

at the hands of the Khmer Rouge during their four-year reign of terror, but that the scale was genocidal is not in dispute. The tales of horror told by witnesses and refugees were so overwhelming that the Communist government of North Vietnam, which had helped arm the Khmer Rouge, invaded Cambodia largely out of mercy in December 1978 to put an end to Pol Pot's murderous regime. (While at least 200,000 South Vietnamese elites had been sent to "reeducation camps" after the Communist takeover of Saigon in April 1975, and hundreds of thousands more "boat people" had fled, there were no mass atrocities like the ones seen in Cambodia under the Khmer Rouge.) The *Communist* government that now took over Cambodia on behalf of Hanoi, then known as the People's Revolutionary Party of Kampuchea (PRPK), estimated that the Khmer Rouge had killed 3.1 million people, although most Western scholars think the figure is too high, reckoning the real number somewhere between 1 million and 2 million—which is still between one-seventh and one-third of the entire population.[28]

As staggering as these figures are, it is not really the raw number of victims that stands out in the Khmer Rouge's reign of terror in Cambodia. Far more people died from the convulsions of Mao's Great Leap Forward, the famines of the Stalin era in Ukraine and Kazakhstan, or in the Holocaust; on the Eastern Front in the Second World War; or on the Western Front in the First. The twentieth century did not lack for crimes against humanity.

What was singular in Cambodia was the all-encompassing "year zero" ambition of the Khmer Rouge. Here Communism was reduced to its essentials, as a negation of everything existing, a war of the young on the old, a social leveling of society down to equality in abject poverty and misery. Pin Yathay, a Cambodian engineer whose family was wiped out by the Khmer Rouge before he escaped and staggered on foot across the mountains to Thailand, later recalled of life in "Democratic Kampuchea," "There were no schools, no money, no communications, no books, no courts. . . . [S]urveillance was constant and mutual. . . . [W]e were warned to be vigilant and invited to denounce friends." Because so many children "denounced their parents, simply in order to 'purify' them," "adults became wary of talking freely in the presence of children." At compulsory political meetings, adults were told that "the perfect revolutionary . . . should not experience any feeling, was forbidden to think about spouse and children, could not love." In the "often-heard Khmer Rouge parable, the individual was compared to an ox": "You see the ox, comrades. Admire him! He eats when we command him to eat. If we let him graze on the field, he eats. If we take him to another field where there is not enough grass, he grazes all the same. He cannot move about, he is supervised. When we tell him to pull the plough, he pulls it. He never thinks of his wife or his children."[29]

Unlike Lenin, Stalin, or Mao, Pol Pot and the Khmer Rouge scarcely tried to justify their methods with happy talk about industrial progress, aside from vague chatter about (in Yathay's words) the "perfect communist country" they were building. The coercion itself was the point, the reduction of free-willed humans to animals, enslaved by robotic, heavily armed children who had themselves been deprived of any kind of genuine education, human warmth, or feeling. Small wonder the North Vietnamese Communists intervened to put this embarrassing fellow Communist regime out of business, or that after 1979 the Khmer Rouge was quietly disowned by its CCP sponsors in Beijing, who have been on alert ever since for news stories exposing China's role in training and propping up this hideous genocidal regime. Fortunately for the image of Communism, outside of Hanoi and Beijing, a few refugee camps in Thailand, and Cambodia itself, there were very few people who had genuine knowledge of what was happening in Cambodia between 1975 and 1979. Sydney Schanberg, the reporter best known for exposing what is now generally referred to as the "Cambodian genocide," did not actually break the story until 1980.[30]

Even when the truth about what happened in Cambodia under the Khmer Rouge emerged in the 1980s, many westerners subsumed it inside the more general tragedy of Indochina, putting as much blame on the Americans, Soviets, and Chinese as on the ideological beliefs that had animated Cambodian Communism. As Schanberg himself wrote, after the military coup of 1970 Cambodia was turned into "a surrogate Cold War battlefield," with "the Chinese backing the Khmer Rouge, the Soviets backing Hanoi, and the Americans backing the Lon Nol regime." Many popular histories of the Vietnam War are more reductionist still. In *Vietnam: An Epic Tragedy, 1945–1975* (2018), Max Hastings declares blandly that "the US and North Vietnam shared responsibility for the tragedy that engulfed Cambodia," ignoring the Chinese role entirely, and not even mentioning the Communist beliefs animating the Khmer Rouge. In this way the Cambodian genocide has come to be dismissed as a tragic and accidental spillover from the proxy war in Vietnam, rather than genuine Communism in practice. Even the Western press tended to devote more scrutiny to American war crimes in Vietnam and the abuses of US client regimes, such as Pinochet's Chile, than to the suffering in Communist countries such as Cambodia that were all but closed off to Western journalists, few of whom, in the wake of the US withdrawal from Vietnam, were all that interested in Cambodia anyway. The Cold War was still on, after all, and in press-friendlier spheres of international competition such as the Olympics, the arms race, and the convening of "peace congresses" and "nuclear freeze" demonstrations against American (but not Soviet) missiles, the Communists were winning.[31]

14

FROM SELLING JEWS AND GERMANS TO SPORTS SUMMITS, SOCIALIST FEMINISM, AND THE STASI

COLD WAR COMMUNISM IN ACTION

By the 1970s, Soviet and East European Communism may have lacked the kind of radical élan that Mao's Cultural Revolution and its Khmer Rouge offshoot in Cambodia projected, but this was not necessarily a bad thing for the cause. The very aging of the Soviet leadership in the Brezhnev era—which saw the average age of Politburo members approach geriatric levels before the admission of forty-eight-year-old Mikhail Gorbachev in 1979 dropped it to a mere seventy—had the effect of moderating the ambitions of Soviet Communist leaders to radically transform their society and the world. Whereas Khrushchev had helped launch the space race and brought the world to the brink of nuclear Armageddon in the Cuban Missile Crisis, Brezhnev was content to let the Americans crow about putting a man on the moon with the Apollo 11 mission in July 1969, so long as the Soviets continued making strides in the

Third World and quiet economic progress at home. Thousands of Soviet Jews emigrated to the West, enabled by the Nixon-Kissinger policy of détente, which was institutionalized in the Jackson-Vanik amendment to the US Trade Act of 1974 tying US trade concessions to Communist policies on Jewish emigration and human rights. But even this did not unduly discomfit Brezhnev or his advisers. The Soviets were happy to exploit more generous US loan packages to ramp up spending on nuclear missiles, reaching parity with the United States. This achievement was recognized in the 1972 Strategic Arms Limitation Talks (SALT) Treaty, wherein Nixon and Brezhnev agreed that neither side would seek "unilateral advantage." The only real price Brezhnev paid for détente was Western scrutiny of certain Soviet human rights abuses, such as the diagnosis of dissidents such as Vladimir Bukovsky, and ordinary Russians who simply tried to leave the USSR, with phony mental illnesses such as "sluggish schizophrenia." They were invariably sent to one of eleven KGB-run "special psychiatric hospitals," where they were injected repeatedly with dangerous mind-altering drugs—a Soviet practice that the World Psychiatric Association condemned in 1977.[1]

The softer era in East-West rivalry was best encapsulated in the Ostpolitik, or "Eastern Policy," of West German Social Democratic Party chancellor Willy Brandt, whose years in office neatly paralleled the détente years of the Nixon administration (1969–1974). Like Senators Henry Jackson and Charles Vanik with their US Trade Act amendment, Brandt hoped to ameliorate social conditions and human rights inside the DDR through proactive economic diplomacy, or, as Brandt's elegant German phrase had it, *Wandel durch Handel* (Change through trade). Brandt, a socialist since his teen years, was less instinctively pro-American and correspondingly less anti-Soviet than Konrad Adenauer, the first leader of the Christian Democratic Union of Germany (Christlich Demokratische Union Deutschlands, CDU), who had served as chancellor from 1949 to

1963, and Adenauer's CDU successors between 1963 and 1969. While Brandt was not actually, as was alleged in a sensational report in the German newsmagazine *Focus* in 1998, a Soviet spy, he had been well known to Soviet intelligence since the 1930s, given the code-name POLYARNIK (Polar). The NKVD had drawn on intelligence tips Brandt had shared with the Soviet residency in Stockholm during the war, although Brandt had also shared tips with US and British intelligence. After Brandt became mayor of West Berlin in 1957, the KGB tried to blackmail him by threatening to reveal his wartime communications with the Soviets (including a receipt showing that Moscow had paid him 500 kroner), only for Brandt to refuse to play ball. As foreign minister of the CDU-led "Grand Coalition" government of Kurt Kiesinger from 1966 to 1969, Brandt had proactively regularized West German (FRG) relations with Communist Romania and Yugoslavia and opened trade relations with Czechoslovakia. When Kiesinger developed cold feet about going further, the KGB took a hand, leaking German files captured by the Red Army in 1945 exposing Kiesinger's Nazi ties. The revelation critically damaged Kiesinger's reputation before the September 1969 elections, allowing Brandt's SPD to win a plurality of 44 percent and to form a coalition government excluding the CDU.[2]

Brandt introduced Ostpolitik in his Inaugural Address as chancellor in October 1969. The concept entailed recognition of the legitimacy of the DDR and other Soviet satellite regimes and renunciation of West German nuclear ambitions. This meant signing the Nonproliferation Treaty, which had been adopted by the United Nations in June 1968. Brandt sent his adviser Egon Bahr to Moscow in January 1970 to open talks. More sensitively and significantly, Brandt signed a treaty with Communist Poland in Warsaw that December recognizing the new Polish frontier, including the areas of formerly German Prussia and Silesia that had been absorbed into Poland in 1945, as legitimate. In a symbolic act of contrition for Germany's wartime crimes committed on Polish territory, Brandt fell to his knees before the memorial to the murdered Jews of the Warsaw Ghetto, a gesture that was both moving and diplomatically adroit.[3]

So far as we know, despite the surreptitious role of the KGB in smoothing his path to power, the motivations behind Brandt's Ostpolitik were honorable. West Berliners like Brandt had a genuine desire to help out their fellow Berliners and the other Ossis who had been cut off from them by the Berlin Wall. For this reason, Brandt focused his primary energies on opening up the DDR, beginning with the replacement of the crusty old Stalinist Walter Ulbricht as head of the Socialist Unity Party with a younger and more pliable Erich Honecker in 1971, which Brezhnev arranged for him. Although his efforts to legitimize the Communist dictatorship of the DDR remained controversial in West Germany, leading to a no-confidence vote in the Bundestag in April 1972 that fell only two votes short, Brandt plowed ahead, buoyed by an impressive SPD showing in the September 1974 FRG elections that he had called as a referendum on his Ostpolitik policies. A mutual recognition treaty was signed between the FRG and the DDR on December 21, 1972, paving the way for the entry of both states into the United Nations in 1974; much easier travel regulations, enabling nearly 4 million Germans to cross over the Berlin Wall in 1973 alone; and a quadrupling of bilateral trade. Billions of marks in low-interest loans also allowed the DDR to import goods from Western Europe and the United States, with huge benefits for the East German standard of living. A secret deal brokered by Bahr in Moscow in February 1970 led to increases in Soviet natural gas exports through pipelines that had been under construction since the late 1950s. These exports supplied the West German industrial heartland with cheap energy from western Siberia and gave the Soviets desperately needed hard currency income. For his efforts to dial down tensions between the hostile military blocs in Europe, Brandt was named *Time* magazine's "Man of the Year" for 1970 and awarded the Nobel Peace Prize for 1971.[4]

There was a darker side to détente and Ostpolitik, however. Although the DDR was happy to welcome cash-spending West German tourists on short-term (usually one-day) tourist visas, there was no loosening of the Berlin Wall in the other direction. In 1975, 3.5 million curious Wessis visited the DDR, while only 40,000 Ossis were allowed to cross in the other direction, and only if they could document "urgent family matters," such as the death of a relative. Meanwhile, the supposedly softer Honecker government of the DDR used Brandt's Ostpolitik to ramp up its spying operations in West Germany, doubling the contingent of Stasi agents abroad between 1972 and 1982 and suborning Bundestag deputies. Much of the luster of Brandt's Nobel Prize was dimmed in April 1974, when his top aide, Günter Guillaume (code-named HANSEN), was arrested and exposed as a Stasi spy. Guillaume had been reporting regularly to his Stasi handlers since the 1950s, as he openly and proudly confessed—and Brandt had apparently known about it for at least a year. It later emerged that the Stasi had bribed two CDU deputies to break with their party in not voting "no confidence" against Brandt in April 1972—an incriminating deposit slip for 50,000 deutsche marks (DM) was published in the Munich weekly *Quick* in June 1972—which seemed to compromise Ostpolitik altogether. Scarcely had Brandt established diplomatic relations between Bonn and East Berlin than these were thrust into the cooler over a massive Stasi spying and bribery scandal.[5]

No less sordid was the story behind the thawing of relations between Bonn and Bucharest, where the US government had followed Willy Brandt's lead. The Romanian Communist government of Nicolae Ceaușescu (1965–1989) was one of the most grotesque tyrannies in Eastern Europe. Ceaușescu, who drew inspiration from a state visit to Beijing during Mao's Cultural Revolution in 1971, embraced a Mao-style personality cult and carried out full-spectrum surveillance of the entire Romanian Politburo and government officials, whose offices and homes were bugged with the latest Soviet listening devices (the KGB had developed a pin-size, almost undetectable bug, used everywhere in the USSR from offices and train stations to trains and trams, with a range of 500 meters). As Ceaușescu explained to his trusted adviser Ion Mihai Pacepa, deputy chief of foreign intelligence of the fearsome Romanian secret police, or Securitate, in 1972, "We should not trust anyone, family members included, before checking on their thoughts."[6]

As suggested by his toadying up to Mao instead of Brezhnev during the years of the Sino-Soviet split, Ceaușescu's diplomatic strategy was to distance himself from the increasingly sclerotic Soviet government—he even denounced the Warsaw Pact invasion of Prague in 1968—to demonstrate his "independence" in the Eastern Bloc. Even the most famous physical legacy of the Ceaușescu era in Romania, the gargantuan "People's Palace" (Casa Poporului), built at colossal state expense at a time when Romanians were the poorest people in all of Europe, was inspired not by the Kremlin but by the American Pentagon, which it uncannily resembles. (Although the Pentagon houses more office space, Ceaușescu's version is heavier, weighing in at a Guinness World Record of 9.04 billion pounds, or 4.1 million metric tons.) And yet somehow, Ceaușescu's corrupt and utterly undemocratic Balkan dictatorship was given the honor of a summit with US president Richard Nixon in 1969. When Nixon traveled to Romania that year, it was the first time the leader of a Communist country had been visited by a US president since the Yalta Conference in 1945—it preceded Nixon's more famous summits in Beijing and Moscow in 1972. On the strength of this shuttle diplomacy and Ceaușescu's pledge to "contribute to the solution of humanitarian problems" in accordance with the Jackson-Vanik amendment, Romania was granted a coveted "most favored nation" (MFN) status by the United States in 1975.[7]

Ceaușescu was not lying about allowing Romanians to emigrate—for a price. The "exit visa bribe," a long-standing practice of Communist regimes, dated back to Lenin's time, when the Soviet Finance Ministry had charged as much as 1 million rubles to wealthy émigrés trying to flee. As early as 1949, the Romanian Communist Party had authorized the emigration of Romanian Jews to the new state of Israel, though charging Israel's government a hefty fee of $100 for each emigrant. By the early 1950s, Romania had come to depend on, as an internal accounting report admitted, "a yearly income in hard currency of about two million [dollars]" from Israel. In a sign of how cash-poor Communist Romania was by the late 1950s and early 1960s, Bucharest began to accept agricultural products instead of cash in exchange for Jewish exit visas to Israel, including Dutch cattle and, in one deal with the London-based Hungarian Jewish businessman Henry Jacober in 1964, prefabricated French food-processing plants, a "fleet of refrigerated Mercedes trucks" to import packaged meat, and a Kellogg's Corn Flakes factory, all of it "paid for by Henry Jacober in exchange for exit visas for Romanian Jews." "If you cannot find the [Jews] you need in the jails," Ceaușescu's predecessor, Gheorghe Gheorghiu-Dej, instructed his interior minister, "just arrest the ones you need and then use them." It was under Ceaușescu, who formalized diplomatic relations with Israel in 1969 as part of the diplomatic initiative that helped Romania attain MFN status, that the sale of Romania's Jews started bringing in serious money, with the price of individual exit visas surpassing $2,000, and reaching as high as $50,000, or even $250,000, in the case of Romanian Jews of especially high status or educational attainment.[8]

No less lucrative for Ceaușescu was the ransoming of Romanian Germans made possible by Romania's regularization of relations with the FRG as part of Brandt's Ostpolitik in 1967. Because Romania had joined the ultimately victorious Entente Powers in the First World War in 1916, despite performing ineptly on the battlefield it had been given huge swaths of Transylvania and other formerly Hungarian territory in the Treaty of Trianon of 1920. Along with Hungarians, huge numbers of mostly Saxon Germans, who had been settling the region since the twelfth century, lived in these regions. Nearly a million ethnic Germans lived in Communist Romania—a number easily dwarfing the 350,000 or so Romanian Jews who survived the Holocaust (out of a prewar population of 757,000). In March 1969, Ceaușescu's government negotiated a deal in Stockholm to send 3,000 Romanian Germans to the FRG over the next year, with exit visa prices ranging from 1,700 DM for elderly uneducated subjects to 5,000 for university students and 10,000 (then worth $2,500) for those with degrees or jobs. A new agreement followed this one's expiration in March 1970, with exit visa prices raised to 1,800, 5,500 and 11,000 DM, respectively, to be paid in lump-sum installments of 600,000 DM, with a guaranteed West German investment of 4 million DM once 40,000 ethnic Germans were exported. As added inducement, Brandt also offered Bucharest a low-interest loan of 100 million DM, along with special-order BMWs and Mercedes, hunting rifles, and other gifts for Ceaușescu valued at 2.1 million DM. Exit visa sales of Romanian Germans ramped up further after the United States extended MFN status to Romania in 1975, reaching more than 12,000 per year in 1978. Small wonder Ceaușescu told Pacepa in 1975 that "oil, Jews and Germans are our most important export commodities."[9]

In addition to exploiting Western naïveté for trade concessions, the Honecker and Ceaușescu regimes were also pioneers in one of the highest-profile realms of Cold War competition, international sports. While the Brezhnev regime in Moscow had backed down in the increasingly expensive space race, allowing the Americans to seize media headlines with a series of six human-crewed moon landings between 1969 and 1972, it judged the quadrennial Olympic Games, televised to the world, to be a more cost-effective opportunity for Soviet and Eastern Bloc athletes to shine. In view of the location of the USSR itself, stretching nearly 9,200 kilometers (5,700 miles) across far northern latitudes, and the size of the Soviet population (which by the early 1970s surpassed 250 million people), it was perhaps unsurprising that Soviet athletes tended to dominate the Winter Olympics in the 1960s and 1970s. But even in the higher-profile Summer Olympics, the success of smaller Communist regimes, especially Romania's in gymnastics, was striking. One recent calculation shows that Eastern Bloc countries won 169 of the 174 gymnastics medals awarded in Cold War Olympics from 1952 to 1988 (excepting 1984, when all the Eastern Bloc countries boycotted the Los Angeles games)—or 97.13 percent of them—and 55 of the 56 gold medals (98.21 percent). East German Olympic domination was not as statistically extreme as Romania's in gymnastics, but it was broader and deeper. Despite hailing from a country with a declining population of less than 17 million, DDR athletes somehow took home 66 medals (including 20 gold medals) at the 1972 Summer Olympics in Munich, 90 medals (of which 40 were gold) at the Montreal Olympics in 1976—including a borderline suspicious 11 of 13 gold medals in women's swimming events—and a truly astonishing 126 medals, including 47 gold medals, at the Moscow Olympics of 1980. So impressive was the performance of Eastern Bloc athletes in the television era of Olympic competition that it furnished one of the main themes of Joseph Nye's celebrated 2004 study *Soft Power: The Means to Success in World Politics*.[10]

At least some of these Eastern Bloc Olympic triumphs owed to the transcendent skill of athletes such as Romania's star gymnast Nadia Comăneci (now Conner), who scored the first-ever perfect 10 at the Montreal Olympics in 1976. There was a great deal more to Communist Olympic success, however, than talent and hard work. The International Olympic Committee (IOC) introduced "doping" rules—performance-enhancing drug controls—at the Mexico games in 1968, and began full-scale testing of Olympic athletes in 1972. But the effects of anabolic steroids were still little understood: they were only banned in 1975, and serious testing for them began only in the 1980s. Not until Ben Johnson, a Canadian sprinter, was stripped of his gold medal in the 100-meter dash at the Seoul Olympics in 1988 did the international press cotton to the importance of doping in international competition, and even then many athletes were able to skirt by the controls.[11]*

In the years between the introduction of anabolic steroids in the 1960s and the blockbuster Seoul scandal of 1988, Soviet Bloc countries took advantage of lax enforcement and Communist state planning controls to punch way above their weight in the Olympics. The DDR, drawing on Germany's robust, if not always ethical, scientific tradition, was the pioneer, running a special program known as "State Planning Theme 14.25" to inject "more than ten thousand unsuspecting young athletes" with "massive doses of performance-enhancing anabolic steroids," as a series of spectacular trials revealed after German unification. While not as murderous as the experiments carried out on human prisoners in Nazi Germany, the systematic doping of DDR teenagers, of minors as young as twelve who were isolated from their parents in elite state

* It was thanks to the eye-popping levels of banned anabolic steroids that the visibly altered Johnson had ingested, along with testosterone and human growth hormone (HGH), that the Canadian sprinter was caught. It is now believed that the next three finishers behind him, including substitute gold medalist Carl Lewis, may also have used banned substances.

sports academies, was still shockingly unethical. As Christiane Knacke-Sommer, a former East German Olympic swimmer who won a bronze medal at the Moscow Olympics in 1980, recalled at a Berlin criminal trial in 1998, she was told that the "little blue pills" she was forced to take at an elite sports academy near Dresden consisted of "vitamin tablets, just like they served all the girls with meals." These tablets actually contained Oral Turinabol, a powerful anabolic steroid, a substance that helped her ascend the Olympic podium—but also took a heavy toll: "They destroyed my body and my mind," she testified at the trial, referring to her coach and doctor. Another DDR athlete, Heidi Krieger, who trained at the same academy and won the gold medal in the shot put at the European Championships in 1986, testified that she had injected almost 2,600 milligrams of steroids that year alone—nearly twice as much as Ben Johnson took in 1988. The "little blue pills" Heidi took also contained 5 milligrams of testosterone, enough to elevate her testosterone levels to thirty-seven times that of an average woman. Heidi later experienced severe muscle pains and gender dysphoria before transitioning to a man in 1997 (Heidi is now Andreas Krieger). But not even Krieger was doped as intensively as a male East German weight lifter, Gerd Bonk, who ingested 12,775 milligrams of various anabolic steroids in a twelve-month stretch from 1978 to 1979. While Bonk did win an Olympic silver medal, the price he paid was severe: he ended up diabetic and in a wheelchair, dying in severe and chronic pain in 2014 at the age of sixty-three. One of the East German swimming stars who helped the DDR dominate the medal count at the Montreal Olympics with two golds, Andrea Pollack, later suffered a miscarriage, then died of cancer at age fifty-seven. Other East German women who took the "little blue pills" gave birth to children with "club feet or other defects." Nearly all of them suffered side effects ranging from acne and deepened voices to "excess growth of leg and pubic hair," hepatitis, heart disease, and liver tumors.[12]

While the sophistication of the DDR sports science program and lax Olympic controls allowed most of these athletes to escape sanction while they competed, the Eastern Bloc doping machine was not exactly unknown at the time. Ivan Drago, the Soviet boxer who kills an American boxer in the ring before sparring with the eponymous Rocky in 1985's *Rocky IV*, is shown injecting massive amounts of anabolic steroids into his muscles. YouTube viewers can still enjoy an American beer commercial from 1986 featuring a muscle-bound East German called Helga (played by Joe Piscopo) flanked by other male actors playing her fellow female Olympic swimmers. Helga informs us that Miller Lite "tastes great but [is] also less filling, which is important to comrades and I so to keep the girlish figure." A *Saturday Night Live* comedy skit from 1988 featured a roided-up Soviet weight lifter whose arms fall off when he tries to deadlift 1,500 pounds. While the Ben Johnson bust received the most headlines in 1988, no less than four Eastern Bloc athletes, including two Hungarian and two Bulgarian weight lifters, also tested positive for banned steroids at the Seoul Olympics. Perhaps the most revealing homage to the DDR doping machine at those now infamous Olympic Games were the world records set in the 100-meter (10.49 seconds) and 200-meter (21.34 seconds) dashes by the American female sprinter Florence Griffith Joyner ("Flo Jo") at Seoul, which still stand today—the longest-held records in the history of track and field. Whether or not Flo Jo cheated is unknown, but one can hardly blame her for being annoyed that she kept finishing second to suspiciously large East German *Fräuleins* between 1984 and 1987. Those years were part of a bizarre stretch from 1970 to 1989 that saw DDR women set 49 new world records in sprints and relays, and 71 out of 84 Olympic records overall, at distances from 100 to 1,500 meters.[13]

Because of the outsized effect of steroids and testosterone on female athletes, compared to the higher (and more easily detectable) levels required to improve male performance, it required little more than ruthlessness and deception for DDR doping doctors to conquer women's swimming and sprinting. This is not to say, however, that Soviet and East German sports commissars did not try to game other events and men's sports, too. In 1967, the Russians opened the Central Physical Culture Institute, which enrolled 1,000 Soviet and Eastern Bloc athletic trainers and doctors annually for an intensive degree program. It required 100 hours of study in "medical-biological disciplines (physiology, biochemistry, sports medicine, anatomical-morphological problems, medical control, [athlete] suitability and selection)," and 130–140 hours of instruction in "current problems of Marxist-Leninism." Communist sports commissars were expected to renew their training credentials every five years to stay on top of their training game—and international doping controls. As Grigory Rodchenkov, director of what he himself now calls the "ironically named Moscow Anti-Doping Center" in the 1980s, later recalled, among themselves Soviet trainers referred not to their athletes' fitness levels, but to their "pharmacology."[14]

Overseeing the sprawling Soviet sports complex as chairman of the Committee for Physical Culture and Sport was a Communist party careerist named Sergei Pavlov, who had previously headed the Komsomol, a Soviet organization aimed at enrolling teens fourteen and older into the party. (The All-Union Lenin Pioneer Organization, or Pioneers, did the perhaps more important work of indoctrinating children ages nine to fourteen.) Unlike his more notorious East German co-conspirator Manfred Ewald, who was convicted by a German court in 2000 as an accessory to the "intentional bodily harm of athletes, including minors," Pavlov, who headed the Soviet delegations to every Olympics between 1968 and 1980, suffered little more than forced retirement in 1989.[15]

Together, Pavlov and Ewald presided over a vast Communist sports empire, which planned everything from recruitment and doping to political messaging and cultivating warm relations with (that is, bribing) members of the IOC. The stunning medal counts of the USSR, East Germany, Romania, and other Eastern Bloc countries in certain events was no accident. Each Communist regime was given specific events to focus on and train for. The Soviets were assigned Nordic skiing, track events such as the 1,500- and 3,000-meter runs, the discus and hammer throw, and the 3,000-meter steeplechase. The Czechoslovak SSR was given the long and high jumps in the summer games, and Nordic ski jumping in the winter games. Hungarian trainers were told to recruit and train fencers. Ceaușescu's Romania, predictably, was assigned women's gymnastics—and less predictably, luge and bobsledding in the winter games. Todor Zhivkov's Bulgaria was to handle wrestling and weight lifting. Castro's Cuba was told to train boxers and cyclists.[16]

Central sports planning extended even to manufacturing. Each Communist Bloc country was assigned production tasks—for example, wrestling and volleyball uniforms in Bulgaria; fencing "electric hit indicators" in Hungary; children's ski equipment and roller skates in East Germany; wooden tennis rackets in Poland; snowmaking machines, hockey sticks, and track and soccer shoes in Czechoslovakia; and everything from figure and ice hockey skates to dumbbells and gymnastics equipment and uniforms in the USSR. (Ceaușescu's Romania, despite dominating gymnastics, was such a manufacturing basket case that it was not trusted to produce the requisite materials for its national sport.) For the most part, this planning worked well—well enough to ensure a steady mix of Olympic medalists. There were plenty of mishaps, however, and not just those suffered by the athletes themselves. In 1980, a Soviet doctor named Lev Korobochkin, whom Pavlov had tasked with developing "new pharmacological schemes" in the lead-up to that summer's Moscow games, a kind of drug-mixing that Grigory Rodchenkov compared to "making borscht," died suddenly at the age of forty-nine—having apparently gotten his "borscht" mixture wrong.[17]

By the time of the showcase Moscow Olympics of 1980, sports mania had become an integral part of Communist societies from Berlin to Beijing. Even Kim Il-sung's hermit Communist Kingdom of North Korea regularly sent delegations to annual "Socialist Sports Summits" held in Prague, Berlin, Moscow, and Havana. At these conferences, sports commissars, doctors, and trainers would assign country targets for specific Olympic disciplines, compare notes, and share important tips on evading the IOC's anti-doping protocols. In the mid-1980s, the Eastern Bloc sports machine invested heavily in beta-blockers to keep blood pressure down in high-pressure events such as biathlon, archery, and skeet shooting, as beta-blockers had been left out of the IOC's list of proscribed substances. Still, Communist party congresses being what they were, the attendees usually spent the bulk of their time listening to turgid speeches denouncing capitalist treachery. At the Moscow summit in March 1986, the host, Marat Gramov, president of the Soviet Olympic Committee, reminded delegates that the anti-doping initiative of the IOC was a "phenomenon, which capitalism has brought forth," that "quickly spread to the socialist countries and took them by surprise." By way of reply, the East German doping impresario Manfred Ewald insisted that anti-doping controls "must be carried out according to the principles of political-geographical and technical balance, and deception of the socialist countries [by capitalist powers] must be prevented." Communist sports commissars still wanted to cheat, but not to be caught doing so.[18]

Ewald and the Russians did not always see eye to eye on doping politics. Generally speaking, Pavlov, Gramov, and other
Soviet commissars wanted to maintain the appearance of pro-
priety at high-profile sporting spectacles such as the Olympic
Games, lest they give ideological ammunition to the American
enemy if Communist athletes violated drug protocols. In the latter half of the 1980s, when the new general secretary, Mikhail
Gorbachev, began courting Western governments for desperately
needed loans, the Soviet position softened still further. Before the
1988 Summer Olympics, according to Rodchenkov, Soviet athletes, hitherto accustomed to being given "an intravenous shot of
Stromba [the anabolic steroid stanozolol] or a quick hit of testosterone before a big competition," were all "told to stop taking pills
30 days before travelling to Seoul," and warned that anyone who
tested positive for "banned substances before the Games would
be left in Vladivostok." After the Ben Johnson scandal forced
the IOC to get serious about doping controls in the fall of 1988,
Gramov actually joined the IOC. He confessed publicly on the
record that Communist countries had practiced "state doping"
(as compared to the "individual doping" characteristic in capitalist lands) and vowed that the USSR would now "disarm in the
international 'medal war' and work towards worldwide unity in
the fight against the doping epidemic," a statement seen across
the Eastern Bloc as a betrayal. Romania and East Germany both
protested Gramov's admission, and the East German news agency
ADN retorted that "the athletes of the DDR are responsible for
their own sports, and Mr. Gramov only for the USSR." Defiantly,
Ewald's press agents declared that "as for the entry of doping
inspectors into the DDR, this not a matter for sport, but solely
for the [East German] Ministry of Foreign Affairs." As the writer
from ADN observed with a note of Schadenfreude, if the Soviet
Union indeed "disarmed" in the sports-doping race, as Gramov

had vowed to do, "the number one sporting power in the Olympics will probably lose its position to the DDR."[19]

Industrial-scale state cheating aside, international sport was clearly an arena where Communist countries competed well in the Cold War era. The Eastern Bloc had a similar kind of soft-power success in the realm of international "peace congresses," notwithstanding the massive ramping up of the Soviet nuclear and naval arsenal in the 1970s, the Soviet invasions of Hungary in 1956 and Czechoslovakia in 1968, and the military involvement of the USSR and China in Vietnam, Cambodia, and other proxy wars. With the cynicism Communist propagandists excelled in, the vaunted "Soviet Peace Committee" was created in August 1949 in response to the creation of the North Atlantic Treaty Organization that April—as if the Soviets planned to counter the US-backed military alliance with pacifist slogans and youth peace congresses, rather than with the more than 2.5 million troops and vast amounts of armor the Red Army was then deploying in Eastern Europe and the USSR's own heavily armed military alliance: the Warsaw Pact, though long in gestation, was formalized in 1955. (The US government responded to this cynical maneuver by creating the "Congress of Cultural Freedom" in 1950, a CIA front organization that funded left-leaning but anti-Communist intellectuals.) At regular intervals during the Cold War, the Soviets convened a Cominform-controlled body called the World Peace Council to oppose NATO military actions such as France's anticolonial campaigns in Vietnam and Algeria, Britain and France at Suez in 1956 (which occurred at the same time as the brutal Soviet invasion of Budapest, which the council ignored), the United States in Vietnam and Cambodia, and so on. Although entirely Soviet-funded, the World Peace Council often convened congresses in neutral cities such as Helsinki, Vienna, and Stockholm, giving it a patina of fake independence that appealed to Western sympathizers. But it was usually committed party members who gave teeth to Soviet antiwar propaganda, such as the Indian Communist leader Romesh Chandra, who thundered at the World Peace Congress in Budapest in 1971 that "the forces of imperialism and exploitation, particularly NATO . . . bear the responsibility for the hunger and poverty of hundreds of millions all over the world."[20]

The crowning jewel of Soviet peace propaganda was the "nuclear freeze movement" that swept across Western Europe and the United States in the early 1980s. Much of the energy behind the protests, to be sure, was organic, growing out of the genuine fears and anxieties Europeans and Americans felt about the terrifying prospect of nuclear war. But when the Soviet archives were opened in 1991 it was revealed that the campaign was also highly organized and funded by the Kremlin. According to US government analysts spooked by its success, the Soviet Union spent nearly $600 million on the peace movement in the years before it peaked in 1983, the equivalent of more than $1.8 billion today. Even the airplane travel of political activists to peace and disarmament conferences was subsidized, in the form of thousands of free tickets on Aeroflot, the official Soviet airline.[21]

The purpose of the Soviet peace campaign was to lull Western Europeans to sleep as Moscow deployed a new arsenal of mobile, medium-range SS-20 missiles targeting their capital cities, ideally causing a NATO split between the United States and its European allies, whose leaders might not trust that American presidents would really risk courting the obliteration of Washington, New York, Chicago, and other US cities with a retaliatory nuclear missile strike to defend Bonn, Paris, or London. The two initiatives, we now know, were planned out together. In May 1976, just as the first SS-20s were beginning to roll out, a resolution of the Soviet Communist Party's Central Committee launched a "global campaign for cessation of the arms race and for disarmament," with the goal of "isolating the bellicose forces of imperialism"—that is, the NATO alliance. The public launch of the campaign came with a World Conference "For a Peaceful and Secure Future for Our Children" convened under United Nations Educational, Scientific and Cultural Organization (UNESCO) auspices in Moscow in August 1979. After the Soviet deployment of SS-20s provoked Washington into stationing the first of its own medium-range "Pershing" missiles in Western European capitals, the Kremlin resolved, on April 15, 1980, that "Soviet public organizations should make full use of planned contacts and exchanges with West European countries, and also the additional proposals of Soviet embassies in these countries for the purpose of ensuring that the campaign against the NATO military continues to grow and reach maximum intensity by the time of the spring session of the main [NATO] agencies (May–June of this year)." Soviet-sponsored events in this vein included a "public movement on questions of security, cooperation, and disarmament" in Brussels in November 1980, a World Forum of Youth and Students for Peace, Détente, and Disarmament in Helsinki in January 1981, and a Congress of the International Democratic Federation of Women in Prague in October 1981.[22]

The nuclear freeze movement built toward a dramatic finale in October 1983, when more than a million people poured into the streets of Bonn, Berlin, and Hamburg in a cascading protest against the plan to station US Pershing missiles in the FRG that December. Similar marches were held simultaneously in NATO capitals—London, Paris, Rome, Brussels, and The Hague in the Netherlands—as well as in neutral capitals such as Stockholm and Vienna. Significantly, none other than Ostpolitik designer Willy Brandt, who was corresponding regularly with Soviet officials about the nuclear freeze movement, headlined the anti-Pershing protests in Berlin. Remarkably, owing to the genius of Soviet propaganda, the millions of Europeans gathering in and near NATO capitals (excepting those in neutral cities) were protesting not the regime whose deadly arsenal of mobile, medium-range SS-20 nuclear missiles were now aimed squarely at them (i.e., the Soviet Communist one in Moscow) but rather the US government trying to defend them.[23]

The Soviet peace campaign of the early 1980s might have been still more successful had it not been overshadowed by still larger demonstrations in Poland, which, unlike the heavily Soviet-subsidized anti-Pershing protests, were almost entirely organic. The precipitating event occurred in August 1980, when a female crane operator, Anna Walentynowicz, was fired in the Lenin shipyard of the Baltic port of Gdańsk just weeks before retirement, along with a shipyard electrician named Lech Wałęsa, bringing on a dockyard strike that led to the formation of the Solidarność (Solidarity) movement. Spurred on by sympathy strikes in Warsaw and Łódź; Wałęsa's charisma and organizing skill; widespread Polish disaffection with declining living standards (in particular, a sharp rise in meat prices); and, not least, by the inspiration of the new Polish pope, John Paul II (r. 1978–2005), who addressed an adoring crowd of 400,000 in Warsaw, Solidarity helped galvanize millions of Polish Catholics against Communism (including Wałęsa, a Catholic father of eight who was grandly received at the Vatican in January 1981). Solidarity ultimately enrolled some 9 million members, becoming a cross between a national political party and a shadow Polish opposition government.[24]

Like Kronstadt for the Bolsheviks in the 1920s, Solidarity was a black eye to Communism. Here was a general strike of the laboring masses against "proletarian dictatorship," giving the lie to the claim of Communists to rule in the name of the workers. The Soviet government tried as hard as it could to put a lid on the story, especially at home, where the Politburo strictly censored press reports from Warsaw and slashed tourist exchanges with Poland in half. But it was tough going. Instructions were issued to the Italian Communist Party to run interference during Wałęsa's January 1981 visit to the Vatican, but the PCI could hardly suppress favorable news coverage in Italian or Western media. In September 1981, Wałęsa got under the Russians' skin by issuing a dramatic public plea titled "Appeal to the Workers of Eastern Europe." In the Politburo, Brezhnev denounced the appeal as a "brazen challenge" that aimed "to provoke unrest in socialist countries and stir up grounds of all kinds of renegades."[25]

The growth of Solidarity was also a potential security threat to the Kremlin: if the Communist government in Warsaw was toppled, the Soviet Union faced the prospect of a huge and proud, patriotic and traditionally anti-Russian country, 35 million strong, on its border. By early 1981, the KGB and its Polish offshoot, the SB, were in panic mode, warning Brezhnev that 150 Western journalists in Poland were connected to the CIA, which had allegedly "acquired firm agent position in Solidarity." To appease Russian concerns, General Wojciech Jaruzelski, already serving as Polish defense minister, was appointed prime minister in February (while retaining the Defense Ministry), and there was loud talk in Warsaw of the imposition of martial law after Solidarity called a general strike on March 27. In early April, Jaruzelski was summoned to a Soviet railway car at Brest-Litovsk and personally dressed down by KGB chairman Yuri Andropov for his lack of resolution. By summer, Jaruzelski was complaining that the Russians were "hammering me into the ground."[26]

There were good reasons for Jaruzelski's hesitations—which also explained why Brezhnev and Andropov were reluctant to send in Soviet armor. Communism simply had no political purchase in Poland, and any effort to crush the burgeoning popular protests would likely fail. The Polish SB was just as well armed as the German Stasi, but it had nowhere near the numerical strength; nor did it have the same level of commitment from its officers. It has been estimated that the Stasi employed "seven times as many informers per head of population" as in Nazi Germany, and that it amassed detailed files on about 5.6 million people through its spying operations. Even the official rolls show that the number of "unofficial collaborators" (*inoffizielle Mitarbeiter*) of the Stasi hit 180,000 by 1975—in a country with a population of around 17 million—and never again dipped below 174,000 until 1990 when the DDR and the Stasi itself officially ceased to exist.* By contrast, the number of SB collaborators in Poland, a country with a population twice that of the DDR, peaked at a modest 25,000 in 1985 after five intense years of recruitment. Instead of Stasi-style spying, the SB mostly just opened Poles' mail in times of crisis. It opened 82 million letters, for example, at the height of Solidarity mania in 1982—and even that was only 15 percent of the true volume, as Poles are a literate people who loved writing letters.[27]

Solidarity, as even the most purblind Polish and Russian Communists realized, had the support of the vast majority of the Polish people. Jaruzelski was no Stalin, not even a Khrushchev or a Brezhnev, for that matter. A loyal Communist who reported regularly to the Soviet ambassador and to Brezhnev personally, he would have preferred that the Red Army do his dirty work for him—in fact, he *requested* a Soviet invasion of Poland to restore order only to be turned down, as neither Brezhnev nor Andropov wanted to court the risk of a bloodbath, which would ruin the gains the Soviets were making with the nuclear freeze movement. Rebuffed in the Kremlin, Jaruzelski tried the opposite tack, offering to bring Solidarity into his government, only for Wałęsa to refuse no less categorically than Brezhnev had. Running out of options and with Soviet pressure to act mounting, Jaruzelski decreed martial law on

---

* As late as 2009, after two decades of efforts by the government and private employers to purge spies, 17,000 more German civil servants were exposed as former Stasi employees.

December 13, 1981, blanketing Poland's cities with 1,750 tanks and 1,400 armored vehicles and unleashing the SB onto Solidarity's offices across the country, confiscating its files and funds. The SB arrested 10,000 activists and conducted 150,000 "prophylactic discussions," meaning interrogations. Still, there were discordant notes. Wałęsa was not so much interned as put under house arrest in a villa in rural Poland near the Ukrainian border, and several Polish army generals visited to pay homage to him and apologize for the hassle. By the time Wałęsa was released in November 1982, and certainly by the time he was awarded the Nobel Peace Prize in 1983, he had become Poland's de facto political leader, even if the Jaruzelski-led Communist martial-law regime held formal sovereignty.[28]

In view of the historic hostility between Warsaw and Moscow, which had been further exacerbated by Stalin's manifold crimes, Soviet-style Communism never had much chance of gaining a popular foothold in Poland. The Tito-Stalin split had likewise hamstrung the Soviet position in Yugoslavia from the earliest days of the Cold War, and Romania was now courting Beijing and Washington more fervently than Moscow. Nor was the DDR a political success story. East German sporting dominance notwithstanding, it was difficult for Communist propagandists to sell the idea that the DDR, a prison-garrison state of 17 million people occupied by hundreds of thousands of Soviet troops spread out over hundreds of sprawling military bases, was a real country. In reality, the DDR had been ruled since 1957 not by Honecker and the Socialist Unity Party, but by a body called the Mixed Soviet-German Commission (Gemischte Deutsch-sowjetische Kommission), which allocated state resources and real estate between DDR bureaucrats, the Stasi, the Red Army, and the KGB. The Russian occupiers did not even follow DDR law, enjoying privileges such as free train travel and exemption from traffic fines.[29]

If there was any Eastern Bloc country Moscow could point to as a success story, it was Bulgaria. Since Georgi Dimitrov's day, Bulgaria had been the most loyal Soviet satellite state. Among the most politically stable as well, it had been ruled with an iron hand by Todor Zhivkov from 1954 to 1989 in the era of "eternal Bulgarian-Soviet friendship." In August 1968, when Romania's Ceaușescu was denouncing the Soviet invasion of Czechoslovakia, Zhivkov had not only backed Brezhnev but offered to use the Bulgarian State Security secret police (Darzhavnaya sigurnost, DS) to overthrow the pro-American Greek military junta that had taken over in Athens in 1967 (his offer was politely declined). More notoriously, a Bulgarian diplomat and colonel were reported to have been involved in the assassination attempt on Pope John Paul II in St. Peter's Square in front of the Vatican on May 13, 1981, by a Turkish national, Mehmet Ali Ağca, after the pope had become such a thorn in the Kremlin's side, as Ağca himself testified in an Italian courtroom (the Bulgarians have always insisted on their innocence). So close was the collaboration between the DS and its Soviet sister agency that the KGB provided DS agents with a poison-tipped umbrella to murder a rare Bulgarian dissident named Georgi Markov, on Waterloo Bridge in London in September 1978, for "slandering Comrade Zhivkov."[30]

Bulgaria was a key Soviet asset in the soft-power realm as well. Sofia, a lower-cost alternative to Moscow, frequently hosted congresses such as the UNESCO International Children's Assemblies in 1979 and 1981. Thousands of Third World students came to Bulgaria to study Marxism-Leninism and a Slavic language, Bulgarian, which was very close to Russian. Although Zhivkov had little charisma himself, his daughter Luidmila Zhivkova, who took over the Bulgarian Culture Ministry in 1975 at the age of thirty-three, had beauty, intelligence (she did a D. Phil at Oxford), and charm, and she used these to promote Communism and Bulgaria on the world stage. Zhivkova's vision of "aesthetic education" was fresh in the sclerotic Brezhnev era of Soviet Communism, and far less dogmatic and frightening than what was coming out of Maoist China. Zhivkova decreed that Communist schools should "teach people how to feel, think, act and live according to the laws of beauty," so that citizens would acquire "harmonically developed personalities." Promoting the arts was central to Zhivkova's vision, even if many of the artists came from non-Communist countries. Highlights included an exhibition of the artwork of Leonardo da Vinci in Sofia and performances by the American singers Tina Turner and Ray Charles. While Communist milestones such as Lenin's birthday were still marked, Bulgarian students were also taught to revere Saint Cyril, father of the Cyrillic alphabet, and other Slavic heroes. The 1,300th anniversary of the foundation of Bulgaria in 1981 furnished an excuse for a vast cultural mobilization in Sofia, generating mostly positive headlines in Europe. Whereas East Germany, by the early 1980s, was known for the Stasi, Romania for the Securitate, and Poland for Solidarity, Bulgaria did not even seem to have dissidents (other than the late Markov). Zhivkova's public image was that of a charming and beautiful English-speaking cultural ambassador.[31]

Although she was hardly a proletarian herself, Zhivkova's brand of Communism had considerable appeal beyond the Iron Curtain. It blended together two themes dear to Western progressives: secularized state education and feminism. Bulgaria pioneered the most generous maternity leaves, family planning clinics, and childcare programs in the Eastern Bloc after a Politburo resolution on "Enhancing the Role of Women in the Building of a Developed Socialist Society" was passed in March 1973. (Romania was more notorious for its state orphanages—more than 500,000 children are estimated to have cycled through them by 1989, when the first published images of emaciated children in these "slaughterhouses of souls" shocked the world—but these were not seen as "progressive," as it was not feminism but the restrictions Ceauşescu placed on abortion to keep the Romanian birth rate high that had fueled their growth.) The Committee of the Bulgarian Women's Movement (CBWM), which published a feminist journal called *Zhenata Dnes* (Woman today), with a circulation of 400,000 (120,000 copies were printed in Russian translation, too), spearheaded Communist outreach, countering American feminist organizations during the UN Decade for Women (1975–1985). Bulgarian mothers might have known that, despite the Zhivkov-Zhivkova regime's boast that it was making their lives better, the Communist planned economy had so far been unable to produce a disposable diaper, meaning that they still had to wash soiled diapers every day by hand. But feminists from the non-Communist world, who, unlike their Bulgarian sisters, were allowed to import American disposable diaper brands, did not know this.[32]*

Bulgarian feminism also had geopolitical importance, owing both to the country's significant Muslim minority and to its location neighboring Turkey. In the "northern tier," as American Cold War strategists referred to the countries stretching from Turkey and Iran to Afghanistan and Pakistan that bordered the USSR, Communism had considerable appeal as a modernizing force, with its emphasis on state secular education, mass literacy, and women's rights serving as a bulwark against traditionalist Islam. Observing sepia-toned photographs from the 1960s and 1970s of unveiled women happily attending college in now-Islamicized cities such as Kabul, Islamabad, and Teheran, one can understand the appeal of a movement that promised universal state-subsidized education and culture to all, including girls. In Iran and Turkey, socialist feminism gave frisson to factional struggles between conservative

---

* Rather like Russians betraying an inferiority complex vis-à-vis Americans by calling a photocopy a *kseroks* (Xerox), older Bulgarians still refer to disposable diapers as *Pampers*.

nationalist and Islamic groups, which tended to align with the United States, and secular-progressives, who looked to the Eastern Bloc for inspiration. By the late 1970s, this political war had spilled out onto the streets.

The results were mixed. Secular-minded Iranian university students and women's rights activists, along with Communists from the banned Tudeh Party of Iran, were prominent in the burgeoning crowds protesting the regime of Shah Mohammad Reza Pahlavi in the fall and winter of 1978–1979, but they were not the ones who inherited power after the shah—installed in power in a CIA-backed coup in 1953—was toppled in February. The Shia preacher who did, Ayatollah Ruhollah Khomeini, was no friend of the Americans. It was the ayatollah's supporters who in November 1979 stormed the US embassy in Teheran and held fifty-two Americans hostage for over a year. Viewing the Iranian Revolution as a body blow to the United States, and appreciative that the ayatollah lifted the ban on Iran's pro-Moscow Tudeh Party, the USSR was the first country to recognize Khomeini's Islamic Republic. Brezhnev congratulated Khomeini and expressed the wish that "good neighborliness will fruitfully develop." Still, relations were guarded, as Khomeini's regime was Islamic rather than socialist, and he was wary of Soviet atheism.[33]

In Turkey, by contrast, where conditions in the streets and even many schools and universities were beginning to resemble a low-boil civil war, Communists lost across the board. In 1977 alone, some 230 people were killed in street riots. In 1978, casualty numbers spiked into four digits and fistfights broke out in the Turkish parliament. By September 1980, deaths were being counted by the day, with 20 killed on the 2nd, 29 on the 3rd, and 18 more on the 4th. Leftists attacked police buildings and prisons; right-wing nationalists targeted Communists; and Islamists held up green flags and posters of Ayatollah Khomeini. On September 12, as the Turkish military finally intervened, General Kenan Evren announced on television that more Turks had been killed in civil violence over the past two years than in the three-week Battle of the Sakarya in 1921, when the Greek invasion of Anatolia had been repelled. Casualty figures on the Left to date were far higher than on the Right, but it was the Left that bore the wrath of the Turkish army, which arrested hundreds of thousands of people and ruled the country for nearly three years.* Whatever else it was, the "Generals' Coup" of September 1980 was a US victory in an important proxy Cold War struggle, which kept Turkey firmly in NATO and the US camp.[34]

"Socialist feminism" and state-funded cultural initiatives gave Communism real soft-power appeal in the West, and to many who aspired to educational attainment in the Middle East as well. In the Islamic world, however, promoting atheism and feminism was playing with fire, as shown in Iran and Turkey in different ways—and as the Soviets were about to discover in Afghanistan.

---

* Several hundred ringleaders of a far-right nationalist militia called the "Grey Wolves" were arrested, too, but, in general, Turkish nationalists and Islamists involved in street violence got off with much lighter sentences than Marxists and other left-leaning activists and guerrillas did.

15
RECKONING

COMMUNISM UNDER CHALLENGE, FROM AFGHANISTAN AND
THE REAGAN RATCHET TO TIANANMEN SQUARE

H ard as it may be to believe today, after nearly five decades of
war and failed Great Power intervention have crystallized the
cliché about conservative-tribal Afghanistan as the "graveyard of
empires," there was a time when its capital, Kabul, was the shin-
ing hope of Communist modernizers. Ghazi Amanullah Khan's
Afghanistan was one of the first foreign countries to recognize and
sign a Treaty of Friendship with the USSR in 1921, which paved
the way for decades of Soviet investment in the country. By 1928,
the USSR had opened consulates in Herat and Mazar-i-Sharif and
there was regular flight service from Moscow to Kabul, carrying
Soviet engineers and military advisers in one direction and young
Afghan officers-on-the-make, and later students, in the other.
While the United States made some inroads in Kabul in the 1950s
with the aim of enlisting Afghanistan alongside Iran and Turkey
in the "northern tier" to contain Soviet expansion into the Middle
East, the deepening US involvement in Vietnam precluded a larger

commitment. That allowed the Soviets to retain prime position in Kabul, not only in trade and military aid but in education. A Polytechnic Institute was founded in the city, with a mostly Russian faculty, in 1967, and growing Soviet influence at Kabul University helped seed the new Afghan Communist Party (formally called the People's Democratic Party), founded in 1965 by Nur Mohammad Taraki and Hafizullah Amin. The number of Afghans enrolled in secular state secondary schools exploded in the 1960s and 1970s, with thousands of Afghan students enrolling at Soviet-tinged universities at home or studying in the USSR itself. Communism began to seem like the wave of the future in Afghanistan, especially after an April 1978 coup in Kabul that toppled the monarchy and brought Taraki and Amin to power. It was an attractive future, too, judging by the numbers of Western backpackers who visited the relatively safe and still largely intact Afghan capital on the "hippie trail" in the 1970s, an era many later viewed as a lost golden age.[1]

Like the British before them and the Americans after, the Soviets swiftly discovered that political coups or regime changes in Kabul did not necessarily register in the Afghan countryside. Afghanistan is and always has been a fiercely tribal country, defined by the blood feuds between ethnic clans such as Pashtun, Tajiks, and Uzbeks even more than by the Sunni Muslim faith practiced by the vast majority of its inhabitants. Both tribal and religious identity tap deeper veins in popular sentiment than modern ideologies, whether nineteenth-century British liberalism, twentieth-century Soviet Communism, or twenty-first-century American neoliberal progressivism. As early as 1923, Amanullah (emir from February 1919 to June 1926 and then king until January 1929) had attempted to modernize, emulating Mustafa Kemal's secular reforms in Turkey. But enrolling Afghan girls in school and establishing a minimum age for them to marry enraged Afghan tribal chiefs, who declared a *jihad*, or holy war, burned down the royal palace in Jalalabad,

marched on Kabul, and forced Amanullah to flee the country. Stalin ordered Soviet troops into Afghanistan in April 1929 in a futile
effort to restore him to his throne. In an eerie replay of the same
political dynamic fifty years later, the efforts of Communist officials
in Herat to enroll Afghan girls in school in March 1979 sparked
an uprising of *mujahideen*, or Islamic-tribal warriors, who, in the
words of one of them, Sher Ahmad Maladani, "rose up, killed the
Communists, killed the girls for good measure, and marched on
the city." As the mujahideen entered Herat, their ranks were swelled
by local residents, including 5,000 soldiers from the Afghan army
garrison, who defected to the rebels. The burgeoning mob then
"tore down the red flags and the portraits of the Communist leaders" and hunted down and killed state officials. Although reports of
"the mutilated bodies of . . . Soviet advisers, their wives and children" being "paraded through the streets" were exaggerated, the
Soviet government took the Herat debacle seriously enough that the
Politburo called a crisis meeting. Soviet leaders discussed Afghanistan for three whole days before resolving to reinforce Taraki's
beleaguered government in Kabul with arms and 500 Soviet military specialists and KGB officers.[2]

In view of the consequences for Communism and geopolitics
more generally, it is worth revisiting the historic Politburo discussions of March 17–19, 1979. KGB chairman Yuri Andropov, the
best-informed member of the Politburo about the true state of the
Soviet planned economy and the world outside the USSR, warned
his colleagues that they had better think long and hard about "why
and for what purpose we are sending troops into Afghanistan." It
was clear, Andropov continued delicately, that "Afghanistan was
not yet ready to solve all questions in a socialist way," owing to the
"huge dominance of [the Islamic] religion and the almost complete
illiteracy of the rural population." The only way to achieve a real
Communist revolution in Afghanistan, he insisted, "was with the

bayonet"—that is, by military force—and, "for internal [Soviet] reasons" (although he did not elaborate on these), "this is inaccessible to us. We cannot take that risk." Speaking for the Foreign Affairs Commissariat, which he had headed since 1957, Andrei Gromyko declared his "complete agreement" with Andropov, observing frankly that "any army, which we send to Afghanistan, will be viewed as aggressors." To defend the Communist regime in Kabul would require Soviet soldiers "to fight against the Afghan people, first of all, and it will be necessary to shoot at them." "All non-aligned countries," Gromyko predicted, "will be against us," putting at risk all of the USSR's recent gains in the international arena. After other members of the Politburo chimed in, making similar points, Brezhnev declared the resolution of the Soviet government, on March 18, 1979, "that we should not be drawn into the war [in Afghanistan]."[3]

And then the USSR was drawn in anyway. The story of the tragic and ultimately failed Soviet intervention in Afghanistan was broadly similar to that of the United States getting pulled into Vietnam in the early 1960s (or into Afghanistan in the years after 9/11, for that matter), involving a toxic blend of wishful thinking, panic, and doubling down on failure. What makes the Soviet miscalculation surprising is that it so closely followed the American Vietnam debacle, and that members of the Politburo seemed, at first, so clear-headed about the risks. In their discussion about the likely consequences of Soviet invasion, Andropov, Gromyko, and Brezhnev appeared to be under no illusions that the tribal peoples of Afghanistan had much interest in, let alone support for, Communism. At their advanced age—Andropov was sixty-five in 1979, Gromyko turned seventy, and Brezhnev was a positively ancient seventy-two—Soviet leaders were wizened cynics who understood the limits of Soviet power and propaganda. They still cited Lenin out of habit, but the zeal was gone. Since the Cuban Missile Crisis provoked by the discredited (and since 1971, deceased) Khrushchev, there had been no real existential crisis with the capitalist world, only a series of Asian, African, and Latin American proxy wars leavened by détente, Ostpolitik, periodic summits, and a few arms control agreements. The real center of gravity in the Cold War, at least until the SS-20 and Pershing deployments ratcheted up tensions again in the early 1980s, had shifted onto the symbolic terrain of Olympic competition, where the Soviets were pretty thoroughly winning.

Nonetheless, there were limits to Soviet patience, and by the fall of 1979 both the Afghan mujahideen and the Soviet client regime in Kabul had reached them (the latter owing to its ineptness and brutality—"Lenin taught us to be merciless towards the enemies of the revolution," Taraki had told the Russian ambassador). In a pattern familiar to students of the Vietnam War, each detachment of Soviet military advisers, trainers, and supplies flown into Bagram Air Base north of Kabul had led to demands for more, from helicopters and warplanes to paratroopers and special operations forces, and finally regular ground troops. Soviet reinforcements, in turn, exposed the weakness and dependence of the Amin-Taraki government, fueling both the mujahideen rebellion in the countryside and factional struggle in Kabul. In September, political tensions boiled over in Kabul, leading to a bizarre coup that saw Taraki allegedly trying to have Amin assassinated, and Amin retaliating by arresting Taraki—who was then, to the horror of his Soviet advisers, bound and smothered to death under a pillow.[4]

Brezhnev, who had repeatedly met with Taraki and promised to back him to the hilt, took the news as a personal affront. "What a bastard, Amin," Brezhnev told Andropov when he heard the news, "to murder the man with whom he made the revolution." "Who will now believe my promises," Brezhnev asked, "if my promises of protection are shown to be no more than empty words?" To restore

Soviet credibility—and to fend off any American attempt to muscle into Afghanistan to avenge the ongoing US debacle in Iran (the US embassy hostage crisis in Teheran had just gotten underway)— Brezhnev and Andropov resolved, at a series of Politburo meetings between December 8 and 12, 1979,* to send enough Red Army troops and KGB men to secure Kabul, topple Amin, and install a loyal Afghan Communist named Babrak Karmal in power. On the night of December 24–25, armor from the Soviet Fortieth Army poured across the border into Afghanistan, even as "Soviet aircraft landed practically non-stop at Kabul and Bagram airports," carrying nearly 8,000 paratroopers and assault forces, who swiftly secured the capital, stormed the palace where Amin was holding out, and shot him. The Russian invasion of Afghanistan had begun.[5]

In a flash, all the political gains the Soviets had made globally since the Prague Spring of 1968 evaporated. It was no longer the United States being vilified in the world press over Vietnam, but the USSR for its invasion of Afghanistan. As Anatoly Chernyaev, deputy director of the Russian Communist Party's International Department responsible for the international Communist movement, wrote in exasperation in his diary on December 30, "Everyone is furiously condemning the occupation, intervention, interference in the internal affairs of a small and weak country. . . . [B]y the power of the mighty mass media, the rest of the world has turned against us." All of the "détente capital we accumulated" in recent years, Chernyaev observed acidly, "is shot to hell." Because "our unwavering friends" in the press now must "rebut comments about 'Soviet aggression,' nobody will listen to campaigns against American missiles." By January 1980, the USSR

* Or at least Andropov did. The Politburo resolution authorizing the Soviet invasion of Afghanistan did not even mention the country, referring to it simply as "A," and did not mention troops. Although Brezhnev was almost certainly aware of the invasion plan, including the targeting of Amin, Andropov underplayed its scale to ensure the general secretary's compliance.

had lost the General Assembly at the United Nations, previously a reliably anti-American body, where a vote of 104–7 condemned Soviet aggression. Even the Italian, Spanish, and British Communist parties had denounced the Soviet government "for aggression, for violating all international norms, for occupation, for undermining détente, for provoking an arms race, for encroaching on the Muslim world." Whatever goodwill the Soviets had with Ayatollah Khomeini and the new Islamic Republic of Iran was now gone, despite Iran's visceral hostility to the United States. Iran's foreign minister, Sadegh Ghotbzadeh, denounced the Soviet invasion of Afghanistan as "a hostile measure not only against the people of the country but against all Moslems of the world."[6]

Just as in 1956 and 1968, Soviet hard power had undermined Soviet soft power—but this time the hard power, too, began to falter. Securing bases in and around Kabul and other large Afghan towns to defend the puppet government was not especially difficult; rooting out mujahideen rebels in the villages and mountains was much harder. The rebels found a commander of genius in Ahmad Shah Massoud, the "Lion of Panjshir," whose defense of the Panjshir Valley in northeastern Afghanistan after Soviet operations began there in April 1980, marked by terrifying ambushes, became legendary. The Red Army endured its most serious losses since the Second World War, losing an average of nearly 150 dead every month, more than 1,700 a year.[7]

Afghanistan became, in short, an open strategic wound for the USSR, and a golden opportunity for the United States to avenge its humiliation in Vietnam. What made the Afghan operation especially hazardous for Moscow was that the Soviet economy was already tottering before the Red Army waded in. The global run-up in petroleum prices in the wake of the oil embargo of 1973 from the Organization of the Petroleum Exporting Countries (OPEC) did buy some time for Soviet planners, who, owing to

TO OVERTHROW THE WORLD

the construction of a network of pipelines to Europe by German firms, could count on export earnings of $15 billion for oil alone by 1980, and another $4 billion in natural gas revenue, to pay for imports. Soviet arms exports, from the legendary "Kalashnikov" AK-47 gas-operated assault rifle to MiG fighter planes, brought in another $5.6 billion that year. Other than energy and weapons, however, Soviet factories mostly produced junk—and not enough of it, either. While there had been gains during the early Brezhnev years in the production of foodstuffs, consumer durables, and appliances, Soviet refrigerators, sewing machines, and televisions lagged far behind Western "capitalist" standards in both quality and quantity. By the late 1970s, growth across the board, even in the food sector, had flatlined. Russians might still enjoy the proverbial "3 ruble vodka," cheap rents, and state-subsidized utilities, but basic foodstuffs were now scarce. A "weekly shopping" basket in Moscow cost the wage equivalent of forty-two hours' labor in 1979, nearly four times what it cost in Washington, DC. Far from surpassing the Americans in milk production, as Khrushchev had vowed to do in 1957, Soviet collective and state farms could barely produce enough to feed a growing population; dairy production actually declined between 1975 and 1980. Were it not for private plots, which Communist planners reluctantly tolerated, the country would have starved: despite taking up only 3 percent of the arable land, these supplied 25.3 percent of Soviet milk, 29 percent of meat, 30 percent of eggs, and 42 percent of fruits and berries. Meanwhile, in the increasingly critical sector of data processing and computing, which should have been a huge priority in a planned economy, the Soviets were so far behind the Americans by 1980 that comparison is basically impossible. Not until 1986 did the Soviets produce the first home computer (the "Agat"), which was ten times more expensive than contemporaneous IBM or Apple desktops, and for which no floppy disks were available. As Soviet programmers liked to joke, they had fewer computers than the Americans, but theirs were heavier![8]

Well-traveled Soviet leaders like Chernyaev knew perfectly well how poorly the Soviet economy was performing even before the metastasizing Afghan intervention began draining state coffers. "We have fallen terribly behind capitalism," Chernyaev observed after visiting Berlin and Frankfurt in November 1979, noting how far ahead of the Soviet Bloc countries the West Germans were in every possible measurement, despite Germany having been "wiped off the face of the earth" in the war. Wages and living standards in the FRG were vastly superior to those in the USSR, and yet somehow, Chernyaev marveled, "their workers have six weeks of vacation." He described how "their 'iron battalions of the proletariat' . . . [got] in their personal cars to drive to work in the morning and home in the evening. . . . Their roads are so well maintained that you can drive at 160km/h with a full cup in the car and not spill a drop." The Communist countries, despite all the boasting about building socialism, had "no social or economic advantage to show."[9]

If Soviet economic performance was this poor *before* the invasion of Afghanistan in December 1979 killed off détente, it was not hard to imagine the economic strain the Kremlin would be under once the Cold War ratcheted up again. And ratchet up it would, owing to US support for the mujahideen, the Solidarity crisis in Poland (1980–1982), and the Reagan administration's huge conventional arms buildup. Reagan's Strategic Defense Initiative (SDI), announced in 1983, threatened to nullify the Soviet nuclear deterrent entirely with missile defense. It did not help matters for Moscow that oil prices, after shooting up from 1973 to 1975 and spiking all the way to $40 per barrel (the current equivalent of $148) in June 1980, fell precipitously to just above $10 in 1985–1986 (the current equivalent of $29), costing the USSR tens of billions annually in hard currency revenue even as expenditures on the Afghan war and the arms race were skyrocketing. Gold prices, too, were cratering, after a mega-spike to more than $800 per ounce in January 1980 (the current equivalent of $2,554), falling below $300 per ounce in 1985 (current value $853)—with similar consequences, as the USSR was the world's second leading producer of the shiny metal behind South Africa. Indeed, substantial increases in Soviet gold sales to raise funds were largely responsible for the severe drops in the gold price between 1980 and 1985. Because oil, like gold, mostly trades in dollars, and is therefore something of a reverse indicator of the strength of the US currency, the dramatic price rises in both commodities from 1973 to 1980 provide a neat illustration of the declining American position in the world in those years while also helping to explain why the Soviets were able to expand the Communist map with new commitments in Latin America, Asia, and Africa. The sharp reversal in these trends from 1980 to 1985 likewise illustrates both American recovery in the Reagan years and the rapidly worsening financial and strategic position for Moscow.[10]

No one felt this more keenly than Mikhail Gorbachev, who took over as general secretary of the Soviet Communist Party at the relatively young age of fifty-four after the deaths of the elderly Brezhnev in 1982, his successor Andropov in 1983, and the scarcely sentient Konstantin Chernenko in March 1985. At the Reykjavik summit with President Reagan in October 1986, Gorbachev all but accused the president of economic sabotage against the USSR, raging that "we know who started beating down the oil price, and who benefits from it!" The general secretary was not wrong, either: by encouraging Saudi Arabia to ramp up its spare production capacity, the Reagan administration was putting the squeeze on Soviet oil export earnings, even as increases in US military spending, the SDI program, and support for the anti-Soviet Afghan resistance drove Soviet state expenditures through the roof. (In

1986 the first portable Stinger rocket launchers arrived, allowing mujahideen fighters to shoot down Soviet helicopter gunships with relative ease.)[11]

A protégé of the longtime KGB chairman Andropov, Gorbachev had been appointed to the Politburo in 1980 as minister of agriculture. He was well informed about the woeful state of the Soviet economy, famously declaring, "Our rockets can find Halley's Comet and reach Venus. But our fridges don't work." This is not to say, however, that Gorbachev understood *why* the planned economy was failing consumers. In his first year in power, he lashed out at scapegoats, from Reagan manipulating oil prices to excessive Soviet drinking, which prompted him to launch a full-scale temperance campaign in 1985. Vineyards were plowed under, state liquor shops shuttered, and 627,000 illegal home distillers prosecuted. Alcohol consumption duly dropped by an impressive 34 percent across the USSR as a whole, and an amazing 68 percent in Russia proper— but the impact on economic productivity was minimal. Moreover, closing liquor stores, perhaps predictably, cost the state billions in revenue, fueling inflation. Gorbachev's other bright idea was to improve product quality by establishing a central State Quality Control Committee (Gospriemka) in May 1986 to reject inferior consumer goods—which turned out to be most of them, with rejection rates as high as three-quarters in some regions. By the end of 1987, 6 billion rubles' worth of consumer goods had been discarded as "scrap," costing the state still more income. Shortages of milk, meat, and durables were so common that many urbanites carried a "by chance" bag around, in case something—anything—was available to buy. Meanwhile, Soviet fridges still did not work well— because, with guaranteed sales in a captive domestic market and no competition, state monopoly producers had no incentive to improve them. (Soviet assault rifles and warplanes sold on the international arms market, by contrast, had to work, or foreign customers would not buy them.) Because there was no real price discovery for domestically produced consumer goods and durables, quality failed to improve even after a frustrated Gorbachev decentralized decision-making to regional party bosses. Rather than investing in new plants, Communist managers preferred to use state funds to raise wages to appease angry workers, or simply stole them. A committed Communist with no grasp of market incentives, Gorbachev could only tilt at windmills like Don Quixote.[12]

It is important to understand that, despite presiding over the ultimate demise of the USSR and Soviet Communism, Gorbachev did not set out to do these things. He had taken the reins of power at a tense moment in the Cold War, with Soviet casualties in Afghanistan mounting and Reagan's SDI threatening to upend the delicate strategic doctrine of Mutually Assured Destruction (known by the apposite acronym MAD, the idea was that neither side would risk a first nuclear strike, as retaliation would ensure the other side's obliteration). His main objective was thus to revitalize the Soviet economy in order to ramp up military spending. As he told Reagan at the Geneva summit in November 1985, referring to the missile shield that had become SDI's main feature, "We will build up in order to smash your shield."[13]

The watchword of the Soviet Twelfth Five-Year Plan, launched in 1986, was *acceleration* (*uskoreniye*). The goal of *perestroika*, as Gorbachev grandly renamed his economic reforms in 1987 (literally "reconstruction," although at times he meant by it something like "new thinking"), was not economic liberalization for its own sake, but to facilitate rearmament. It was not an end to planning, but a drive to plan more efficiently—for example, by importing Western technology, especially computers, to bring Soviet factories up to date. Likewise, *glasnost*, or "openness," a complementary policy Gorbachev announced after the devastating (and humiliating) Soviet nuclear accident at Chernobyl in April 1986, was not meant to abandon censorship and Communist control of the press, but to shine light on sectors of the economy performing badly. While Gorbachev's stated goal of reaching "world standards" in Soviet consumer goods failed badly, this was not true in the military sector, which was his real priority. By 1988 and 1989, the Soviets were producing 3,500 tanks a year—450 percent more than the United States—along with 5,700 armored personnel carriers (8.7 times more than the United States) and 1,850 field artillery guns (11.5 times more than the United States). The Soviets were building three times as many nuclear submarines as the Americans, too, utterly erasing the former US naval advantage, just as ramped-up production of intercontinental ballistic missiles (ICBMs) and SS-20s had erased the former missile gap. *Perestroika* was working: in terms of raw military hardware, the Soviets were winning the Cold War. Of course, this all cost Moscow a fortune—in 1989, 220 billion rubles, 50 percent of Soviet state expenditure, was spent on the military, which sucked in 80 percent or more of industrial capacity. By 1991, the exorbitant military spending and runaway inflation threatened to capsize the entire Communist system. As Gorbachev ruefully admitted, the USSR had "the most militarized economy in the world and the largest defense expenditures."[14]

In fairness to Gorbachev and his predecessors, after the ructions of the Maoist era the economy of the USSR's main Communist competitor, the People's Republic of China (PRC), was in even worse shape than the Soviet one. Whereas the USSR could boast of an improvement in material living standards under Brezhnev, by the time of Mao's death in September 1976 China was poorer than before the Communist takeover in 1949. Per capita calorie consumption was lower than in 1933, although higher than in 1960, one of the worst famine years. Entire provinces had reverted to primitive autarky after the violent disruptions to internal trade during the Great Leap Forward and the Cultural Revolution. In once wealthy trading cities along the Pearl River delta near Hong Kong there were perennial shortages of basic staples, from soap and toothpaste to matches and cloth. Although production and consumption recovered a bit after 1970 as the Cultural Revolution petered out, and the opening of relations with the United States stimulated foreign trade, as late as 1985 there were only 20,000 passenger cars *total* in a country with a population of more than 1 billion. Meanwhile, the USSR was producing 1.3 million cars a year. The PRC was a poor country.[15]

China had one huge advantage over the USSR, however. Aside from the Korean War, which had ended in 1953, the occupation of tiny Tibet, a short border conflict with the Soviets in 1969, and relatively inexpensive subventions of Communist North Vietnam and "Democratic Kampuchea," Beijing had avoided the costly global security commitments Moscow had assumed. Indeed, since Nixon had "opened" China, a process consummated in the formal establishment of diplomatic relations in 1978, the United States had been transformed from an enemy into a friendly strategic partner of sorts against the Soviets. These developments obviated the need for China to compete in the hugely expensive nuclear arms race, the space race—or the Olympics, for that matter (where the PRC was not allowed to represent China until 1980). Cambodia, to be sure, was a Chinese headache, but it was a cheap client—it was largely to save scarce resources that Mao had switched from subvening Hanoi to the Khmer Rouge in the early 1970s. Even after Communist Vietnam invaded Kampuchea in December 1978 to topple Beijing's Khmer Rouge clients, China's reaction was measured, limited to a symbolic punitive invasion launched in February 1979 that was called off after twenty-nine days. It was a sign of China's modest ambitions that Mao's successor, Deng Xiaoping, had asked US president Jimmy Carter for permission to invade Vietnam while visiting Washington in late January (Deng interpreted Carter's silence as assent). He had also reassured Brezhnev that Chinese troops would not stay long, and had then ordered his troops to withdraw before the Soviets intervened. So long as Deng and his colleagues avoided antagonizing Washington or Moscow,* they could tinker as they pleased with the Chinese planned economy, and even invade small neighboring countries, without having to worry about the expenses and pretenses of superpower competition.[16]

Securing US backing for his planned invasion of Vietnam was not the only reason Deng came to Washington. He had once been a dogmatic Maoist, and whether or not he was now truly a Communist "revisionist" at heart, his denunciation by Mao and Lin Biao as a "capitalist roader" in 1966 did have the perhaps unintended effect of turning him into a skeptic of sorts. Although Deng had survived the Cultural Revolution, he had genuinely suffered at Mao's hands, having been placed in a kind of house arrest and separated from his personal secretary, his bodyguard, his children, and his grandmother, who were forbidden to visit him for nearly two years. Weirdly, Deng was still paid his senior class party salary of 404 yuan a month at that time—ten times what ordinary Chinese workers earned—but as he was unable to leave the house, there was not much he could do with the money. Even after Mao rehabilitated him in 1974, Deng was kept on a tight leash and frequently criticized in the Politburo, which contributed to the impression in China and abroad that he was a closet reformer.[17]

Once Deng had climbed his way to the top of the CCP hierarchy in 1978, he was able to use this impression to China's advantage. On a state visit to Japan that October, Deng was amazed by

---

* Annoyed that China had invaded a Soviet client state, Brezhnev phoned President Carter on the "hotline" installed after the Cuban Missile Crisis to ask whether the United States had authorized its incursion into Vietnam. Carter denied it with enough conviction that Brezhnev, although not fully convinced, declined to intervene. It was a sign of China's diminished stature in 1979 that neither the Soviet nor the American leader took the invasion seriously.

Japanese bullet trains and electronics factories such as Panasonic, which churned out fax machines, microwave ovens, and especially color televisions at a time when even well-off Chinese citizens did not have basic black-and-white models. On his American tour in late January and early February 1979, Deng was overwhelmed by the grandeur of Washington, DC, the colossal Ford and Boeing plants, the Houston Space Center, and a Texas rodeo, where he charmed the crowd by donning a ten-gallon cowboy hat. There was method to his charm offensive. Japan granted Most Favored Nation status to the PRC and flooded China with trillions of yen in loans, aid, and infrastructure investment. In the United States, Deng went out of his way to win over the famously anti-Communist senator Henry "Scoop" Jackson of Washington State, who had been critical of détente and sponsored the Jackson-Vanik amendment tying US trade concessions to human rights policy. To win over Jackson, Deng traveled to Seattle and gave him a bear hug. With Jackson neutralized, in February 1980 the United States, too, gave the PRC MFN status, leavened by agreements on student and scientific-technological exchange. The Communist and former Maoist Deng was the toast of Washington, and *Time* magazine's "Man of the Year."[18]

Like Khrushchev marveling at the productivity of the American corn belt, Deng was genuinely impressed with what he saw. "We thought capitalist countries were backward and decadent," as a CCP colleague who traveled with him to Japan later recalled, but "when we left our country and took a look, we realized things were completely different." Swallowing his pride, Deng admitted at a public meeting in Japan, "We [Chinese] are very poor. We are very backward. We have to recognize that. We have a lot to do, a long way to go and a lot to learn."[19]

To catch up with the Japanese and Americans, Deng realized that Communist China would have to borrow—or buy, or copy—technology and ideas from them. With Communist naïveté, Deng initially thought he could just butter up the director of the lead-ing Japanese electronics company, Matsushita Konosuke (whom he saluted as the "god of technology"), to come to China and teach trusted CCP managers and engineers how Panasonic built its world-class products, only to be informed by Matsushita that, in the capitalist world, profitable industrial processes and technolo-gies were patented intellectual property, trade secrets that were pre-ciously guarded.[20]

Clearly it would not be easy, but Deng did have significant advantages enjoyed by neither Khrushchev, with his plans to flood the world with corn, meat, and milk, nor Gorbachev, with his *perestroika*. It was not only that Beijing did not face the terrible "guns-versus-butter" dilemma of the Soviet superpower, but that China was still, despite all the Maoist sound and fury of the 1950s and 1960s, only three decades removed from an unplanned, tradi-tional, pre-Communist economy. There were still millions of peo-ple in China, or Chinese émigrés in nearby capitalist hubs such as Hong Kong, who had lived experience of farming, small-scale manufacturing, private enterprise, and retail, whose skills and instincts the CCP might be able to tap—with the party, of course, still retaining ownership of their production. Deng's goal was not, despite the gushing of his growing ranks of Western admirers, to unleash private enterprise, but to establish "special economic zones" (SEZs) to experiment with new techniques and encourage Japa-nese and Western capital investment. In fact, contrary to legend, he never actually uttered the famous exhortation to CCP members that "to get rich is glorious," but he did reassure them that "to get rich through diligence is appropriate." The first SEZs were in the coastal areas of Guangdong province near Hong Kong—a natural transit point for these exchanges, as so many wealthy Chinese émi-grés lived there, many of them keen to resume contacts with family and friends on the mainland.[21]

More broadly, Deng sought to decentralize management of state enterprises from Beijing to local party committees, and in agriculture from the huge state collectives to individual households, in a series of regional trials of semi-privatized agriculture. "The practice of fixing farm output quotas on a household basis," Deng announced on May 31, 1980, "has been adopted in some localities [e.g., in Feixi county, Anhui province]. It has proved quite effective and changed things rapidly for the better." In the industrial sector, the results were more mixed. CCP factory managers tended to spend resources buying finished products from Japan, such as TVs and pocket calculators, rather than investing in domestic plants. Inevitably, they kept demanding more funds from Beijing. To cover a growing deficit, the CCP started floating government loans in 1981 for the first time in decades, raising 12 billion yuan, which Deng hoped would be spent on domestic industrial production rather than on imports. Much of the state budget, however, still had to be spent importing basic foodstuffs. While the new "household" plots Deng had introduced in trial regions were helping stimulate production, they were also fueling a massive black market in grain that accounted for nearly 70 percent of domestic consumption. And it was still not enough. In 1979 alone, Beijing imported 12 million metric tons of grain from Australia and Canada. Communist China was not growing anywhere near enough food to feed its population.[22]

Still, there was no doubt that Deng had introduced a new course in economic policy, a kind of Chinese version of Russia's New Economic Policy (NEP) from the 1920s. The resemblance was not accidental. Although some Chinese technocrats became enamored with an American futurist named Alvin Toffler, whose *Third Wave* (a follow-up to his 1970 bestseller *Future Shock*)—filled with jargon about discarding "old ways of thinking, old formulas, dogmas and ideologies"—was published in 1980, the party's in-house academics were more enamored with Nikolai Bukharin, the prophet of the Soviet NEP policy, martyred by Stalin in the 1930s. New CCP editions of Bukharin's works were published in China in 1980 and 1981, along with dozens of articles discussing his ideas, and even a translation of the admiring 1973 Bukharin biography by the American Sovietologist Stephen Cohen of Princeton. CCP historian Zheng Yifan, who had studied at Leningrad University in the 1950s, took special note of Bukharin's exhortation to Russian peasants: "Enrich yourself, accumulate, develop your farms." In 1985, Deng himself said that, although Mao was still the standard-bearer for Chinese Communism, Bukharin's New Economic Policy was "perhaps" the "most correct model of socialism."[23]

In some ways Deng's economic reforms also paralleled Gorbachev's nearly concurrent *perestroika* in the USSR—for example, both recommended the decentralization of industrial decision-making and the use of imported technology. Deng's reforms, however, were clearly more successful than Gorbachev's. In part this was owing to the intensive level of Western, particularly Japanese, investment in Chinese industry, which took off in the years after 1982, and in part it reflected the brazen attitude of Chinese Communist managers toward Western copyright law. If Japanese and American firms would not share trade secrets, as Deng initially hoped, then, he concluded, there was no reason not to steal them. Chinese planning documents from the period, later uncovered by historians, reveal a systematic approach to industrial espionage, with the Panasonic facilities Deng had visited in Japan the first and highest-priority target (the Chinese replica was euphemistically named the "Yingkou Washing Machine Plant"). "We need a unified approach towards copying," one SEZ manager in Shanghai wrote, so that "the quality of the copied equipment can be guaranteed." Another party boss in Tianjin wrote that the fourteen special economic zones offered "ideal conditions for copying consumer goods and advanced technology." Boldly, the Shanghai

Committee on Computing opened an industrial espionage warehouse in San Francisco, in the heart of California's Silicon Valley during the computer chip boom, an operation greased along by then mayor of San Francisco (and later senator from California) Dianne Feinstein. Feinstein embraced her "mayoral" counterpart from Shanghai, Jiang Zemin, a future CCP general secretary and future president of China, and declared Shanghai the "sister city" of San Francisco. Wining and dining CCP officials and engineers, in exchange she saw her husband Richard Blum given sweetheart concessions in China, including an 18 percent stake in the Shenzhen Development Bank—the first stake given to a Western "capitalist" by the CCP.[24]

Starting from such an abysmally low base, it was not hard to achieve head-turning growth rates on paper with these policies, such as a 15 percent increase in China's gross domestic product (GDP) in 1984, or a reported increase in industrial output of 23.4 percent in the second quarter of 1985. In addition to the SEZs, in 1984 the CCP began allowing hybrid partnerships called "township and village enterprises," or TVEs. By 1985 they employed 4.75 million people out of a nationwide total of 22 million "private employees." It was in 1984 that Deng first used the phrase "socialism with Chinese characteristics," a hint that the CCP was no longer beholden to Marxist dogmas about state ownership of *all* the means of production or to Soviet-style planning of the entire economy (rather than just most of it). Whatever it was called, it seemed to be working. Shenzhen, a showcase SEZ city in southeastern China near Hong Kong (where Senator Feinstein's husband had a stake in the development bank), saw an increase by a factor of *seventy* in foreign direct investment inflows between 1979 and 1985, annualized economic growth of 58 percent, and gains in per capita average annual incomes by a factor of ten, from $122 to $1,279 (despite the population growing by 500 percent).[25]

Unlike Gorbachev, however, who allowed *glasnost* to deepen to the point where Soviets were reading Solzhenitsyn's *Gulag Archipelago* and other dissident literature on the Moscow Metro—and by 1989 voting in semi-democratic elections for a new Congress of People's Deputies—Deng never made so much as a nod toward political liberalization. Along with economic reforms and foreign investment, the Deng era also brought with it ghastly innovations in statist repression—such as the "one-child policy," inaugurated in January 1980, which decreed that couples could have no more than one child (or perhaps a second in some cases, if the first was a daughter—and if the parents applied to the state for permission). Babies born without CCP authorization might be allowed to live, but without rights of citizenship: barred from attending state schools and from getting jobs in state enterprises, essentially they had to be hidden from the authorities. The one-child policy led to thousands of gruesome coerced late-term abortions, many conducted as late as the eighth month of pregnancy. In one commune in east Guangdong, 316 out of 325 pregnancies in 1981 were thus "terminated." In 1983 alone, Communist China reported, proudly, that state clinics had carried out 14.4 million abortions and 20.7 million sterilizations.[26]

For all the excitement in the Western business press about Deng's economic "transformation" of China, the draconian one-child policy should have sounded a note of caution. The CCP had not surrendered an inch of its political authority. When China's GDP growth began to slow after 1987, the CCP faced a political reckoning. Just as in the USSR at the same time, the combination of looser economic controls and a sharp rise in imported Western goods was fueling drastic inflation. China's GDP still grew by a nominal 11.3 percent in 1988, but this was easily outpaced by an 18.8 percent rise in the consumer price index. In theory, the state still controlled food and consumer prices—which meant that ordinary Chinese people knew whom to blame when their bills went up. It did not help that the *People's Daily* had gingerly announced, on August 19, 1988, that prices on food and many consumer goods would be gradually freed over the next five years, leading to a run on bank deposits and a wave of panic buying and hoarding of staples such as rice and soap—and, for those who could afford them, imported electronic devices and appliances. Store shelves were swept clean. Under mounting political pressure, Deng, now eighty-three years old and sensing that he was out of touch with the public mood, backtracked in December, restoring price controls in full on everything from foodstuffs to industrial inputs. To stanch public anger, he ordered factories to shift toward consumer production, redirecting steel and timber quotas from construction firms, for example, to factories making refrigerators and matches. All that this officious return to Communist central planning accomplished was confusion, along with retrenchment in heavy industry and declines in foreign investment. In 1989, even nominal growth leveled off to 4 percent, while inflation maintained its terrifying 18 percent clip. By March, at least 50 million laid-off factory workers were roaming the Chinese countryside looking for work.[27]

Numbers like this were a recipe for political turmoil, especially after news stories about liberalization in the USSR and its satellites began appearing in Beijing in the first half of 1989, fueling hopes among educated elites that China might follow a similar path. In February, Solidarity was legalized in Poland, with parliamentary elections announced for June. As with the elections to the Soviet Congress of People's Deputies, held on March 26, Communists were guaranteed a majority of seats—65 percent in Poland, and basically all of them in the USSR, although Communist "reformers," such as Boris Yeltsin, were allowed to run on an opposition platform. The idea was not to move toward genuine democratic pluralism, but to harness "party democracy" to lend legitimacy—in the case of Poland, to the martial law dictatorship of Wojciech Jaruzelski, and in the case of the Soviet Union, to Gorbachev's newly created office of Soviet "president." Indeed, Jaruzelski and Gorbachev were not on the ballots themselves; instead, they were asking to be "voted" into the offices they already held once the legislative bodies assembled. Yeltsin returned a thumping anti-Gorbachev mandate, however, receiving 89.4 percent of the vote in Moscow, and Solidarity candidates won 160 out of the 161 seats they were allowed to contest in the Sejm. Despite Communists retaining control, contested elections were held that allowed genuine public policy debates to take place in Poland and the USSR for the first time in decades.[28]

Still more dramatic headlines were rocking the Communist world in the realm of diplomacy and geopolitics. Under fierce pressure from the Reagan administration—which insisted on not just a complete Soviet withdrawal from Afghanistan in exchange for the extension of new loans to Moscow, but even that the withdrawal be "frontloaded"—Gorbachev had given up the ghost in Afghanistan, withdrawing the first half of Soviet occupation troops between May 15 and August 15, 1988, and the remainder, including every last single Red Army officer and grunt, by February 15, 1989. The blow to Soviet military prestige was profound, unleashing powerful centrifugal forces undermining Moscow's imperial authority, beginning with the three Baltic countries, which restored the primacy of their languages over Russian and then the primacy of each republic's laws over Soviet ones. These decisions amounted to a kind of declaration of autonomy if not yet sovereignty (in Estonia in November 1988, Lithuania in May 1989, and Latvia in July 1989). The catalyst in the East European satellites came when Hungarian border authorities turned off the electricity in the barbed-wire fence guarding the country's border with Austria in April, and then began dismantling the fence itself in May. Within days, thousands of Hungarians began pouring through this gap in the "Iron Curtain." Encouraged by the collapse of Soviet military power in Afghanistan, the satellites were spinning free from Moscow's orbit even as democratic reforms were about to crash into Moscow itself. The Congress of People's Deputies was scheduled to convene on May 25, 1989—200 years to the month after the French Estates-General had assembled, in a historical parallel few news editors could resist drawing. Was Communism about to stand in the dock for judgment?[29]

With eerie timing, the man presiding over what appeared to be the democratization of Soviet Communism arrived in Beijing for a summit with Deng on May 15, 1989. A wave of democratic protest, mostly on university campuses, had already been building in China since April 15, when the news broke of the death of Hu Yaobang, a former general secretary who had been forced to resign his position in 1987 because of the soft line he had taken during student protests the previous year. He had suffered a heart attack. On April 18, demonstrators grew bold enough to picket CCP headquarters at Zhongnanhai, next to Beijing's Forbidden City, shouting, "Long Live Democracy!" and "Down with the Communist Party!" On April 19, protesters tried to storm the gate, encouraged by others holding up streamers threatening to "Burn Zhongnanhai!" Whether or not Hu was really the democratic champion student protesters and liberal Chinese intellectuals made him out to be— after admitting his "errors" in January 1987, he had been allowed to stay on the Politburo, and he retained his seat until his death in April 1989—his death brought an outpouring of genuine grief. Hundreds of students laid wreaths in Tiananmen Square to honor him on April 21, many overheard shouting "We Want Democracy, We Want Freedom," and "Down with the Communist Party." The funeral, held in the Great Hall of the People on April 22, was more subdued, but the crowds were even larger, with as many as 200,000 straining to get in. "The honest man is dead," a Chinese poet wrote in Hu's honor. "The hypocrites live on."[30]

By the time Gorbachev arrived on May 15, the crowds in Tiananmen Square had grown to 300,000, including, according to an alarmed CCP official, "workers, peasants, government functionaries, working staff of democratic parties, children from kindergartens and elementary schools, and officers and men of justice departments and even of the military academies." On May 13, student leaders announced a hunger strike to capitalize on media attention they were receiving because of the summit. Even while the two "reformist" dictators were meeting to bury the hatchet in the Sino-Soviet split, hundreds of emaciated hunger strikers were being carried to hospitals. Western press photographers who had arrived to cover the summit captured the scene, and by May 18, the crowds in Tiananmen Square had mushroomed to 1.2 million, by Chinese secret police estimates. The throng was so immense that Gorbachev's motorcade could not make it through the square to the Great Hall of the People where he was scheduled to meet the press for the official end of the summit. The Soviet leader was supposed to visit Shanghai next to close out his China trip, but more than 100,000 protesters had flooded the downtown there, causing similar issues. Hundreds of thousands more protesters had gathered in Hangzhou, Jinhua, Ningbo, Wenzhou, and other provincial capitals.[31]

While Deng had thus far tolerated the metastasizing crowds in Tiananmen Square, so as not to sully the Gorbachev summit with ugly scenes of violent repression while the world press was watching, he had long wanted to throttle the protest. On May 13, the day the hunger strike began, Deng called in CCP general secretary Zhao Ziyang, who had begun to waver, just as Hu had in 1986. "The student slogans," Zhao bravely informed the chairman, "all support the [Chinese Communist] Constitution; they favor democracy and oppose corruption. These demands are basically in line with what the Party and government advocate, so we cannot reject them out of hand." Moreover, Zhao pointed out, "the number of demonstrators and supporters is enormous, and they include people from all parts of society." Deng was having none of this. "We can't be led around by the nose," he admonished Zhao. The movement had "dragged on too long," and "the senior comrades" were "getting worried." They would "have to be decisive": "I've said over and over that we need stability if we're going to develop." "These people," Deng concluded, "want to overthrow our Party and state."[32]

Once Gorbachev left, on the morning of May 19, 1989, Deng and his Politburo colleagues decided they could wait no longer. At 10:00 p.m. that evening, the CCP premier, Li Peng, announced that martial law would be imposed at 10:00 a.m. on May 20, and ordered 50,000 troops to surround Tiananmen Square. But the move came too late. Catching wind of the crackdown, a number of lorry drivers friendly to the protesters blocked the six main entrances to Beijing, allowing crowds to surge forth and surround army convoys, remonstrating with commanders to pause (and in some cases letting air out of truck tires if drivers refused to halt). Owing in part to the hesitation of at least one senior PLA officer, the commander of the Thirty-Eighth Army, Major General Xu Qinxian, who said he would not comply with a verbal order and demanded to see a written one instead from the People's Liberation Army high command before he would fire on demonstrators, these tactics worked. Disgusted with this insubordination,* Deng told Li that he feared "the soldiers' hearts may not be steady," and Li confessed he "had not expected that the troops would encounter such huge resistance." Backing down, Li and Deng instructed the PLA to withdraw from the city center on May 22 (though the units remained poised outside Beijing).[33]

It did not help Deng's cause that the Western media was still camped out in Beijing, cottoning on to what seemed to be an

---

* Major General Xu Qinxian was court-martialed, expelled from the Chinese Communist Party, and sentenced to five years in military prison.

even bigger story than the Gorbachev summit. Western photographers and TV crews were on high alert, hoping to be able to capture the moment when the regime wavered in the face of such huge protests. Surely, most Western journalists thought, the CCP would not fire into the crowds with the whole world watching.

For two weeks, the Chinese Politburo and the Tiananmen Square protesters eyed each other warily. On May 30, students unveiled a giant statue of the *Goddess of Democracy*, ten meters (thirty-three feet) high, made of Styrofoam, metal, plaster, and papier-mâché. They arranged her so that she was directly facing down the giant portrait of Mao looming menacingly over the square. The statue helped put steel in the protesters after many had been losing heart: after climbing steadily the first three weeks of May, the number of protesters had started to decline after the army withdrew on May 22, dwindling to less than 10,000 by month's end. Behind the scenes, Deng was readying for a confrontation, tripling the size of the PLA force outside Beijing to more than 150,000 and assembling hundreds of tanks and armored vehicles. On June 3, the first armed skirmishes were reported in central Beijing. Throngs of protesters surrounded military buses, smashed in windows, and started erecting barricades in the square. A confrontation took place outside CCP headquarters in Zhongnanhai, which led to multiple injuries on both sides. Whoever was responsible for breaking the uneasy truce, Deng and Li used this "counter-revolutionary riot" to justify a move they were planning anyway. Deng ordered PLA commanders to do "whatever was necessary" to restore order, dispersing the Tiananmen Square protest peacefully if possible—but authorized the use of force if they encountered serious resistance. Deng did warn the students about what was coming, broadcasting clear instructions over loudspeakers at 6:30 p.m. that the crowds must disperse and civilians should stay off the streets for their own safety.[34]

Over the night of Saturday, June 3–4, 1989, a long procession of tanks, armored vehicles, and PLA soldiers carrying assault rifles (including Soviet AK-47s) crashed into central Beijing. The Thirty-Eighth Army, its hesitating commander Xu Qinxian now replaced by officers willing to do Deng's bidding, was the first to engage protesters, opening fire on civilians with AK-47s and tank-propelled gas canisters at a huge roundabout called Gong-zhufen, or "Tomb of the Princess," at around 11:15 p.m. At each successive intersection, the Thirty-Eighth Army felled civilians and bystanders, including some killed in their own kitchens or bedrooms by stray bullets. The first tanks burst into Tiananmen Square around midnight, unleashing hell on the protesters, although some of the tanks were set on fire, too. All night loudspeakers blared out warnings that protesters must go home, but the warnings did not convince the diehards, mostly students, and 3,000 of them stayed in the square to the bitter end. Toward dawn, tense negotiations ensued between student leaders and PLA officers, who gave a grace period for students to leave if they wanted to. Some did, but most courageously stayed on to face the worst, huddling together and singing the old French socialist anthem "The Internationale" as the soldiers secured the square, demolished the tent city students had erected for shelter, and smashed the *Goddess of Democracy*. Sporadic violence continued throughout the day on Sunday, June 4, and Monday, June 5, some of which was caught on camera—including an indelible image of a man, holding two shopping bags, who stood bravely in a pedestrian crossing and forced a tank convoy to halt—before an uneasy peace fell upon Beijing. The butcher's bill was substantial. At least 310 students and other protesters (as Li informed the US government), and possibly as many as 2,600 (according to an ABC reporter who compiled this estimate from Beijing hospitals and the Chinese Red Cross), or even 3,400 (according to the

British ambassador, briefed by local sources), lay dead, and several thousand more had been wounded.[35]

Whatever the true casualty figures were in the Tiananmen Square massacre, the political verdict in China was clear and unambiguous. While economic reforms might or might not continue, democratic reform was off the table. Deng, no Gorbachev, had made certain of that. Communist rule in China would endure.

EPILOGUE

THE AUGUST COUP AND THE STRANGE
NON-DEATH OF COMMUNISM

For Americans and their Cold War allies, the Tiananmen Square massacre was a rare discordant note in an otherwise triumphant year. Gorbachev and the Soviets were giving in across the board. The USSR withdrew from Afghanistan on May 15, 1989. Hungary was allowed to punch a hole in the Iron Curtain in April, and that hole widened in September when Budapest announced that East Germans could cross the Hungarian border into Austria. Moreover, the Soviets refrained from interfering as Solidarity rode to electoral triumph in Poland in June, and in August a chastened Wojciech Jaruzelski allowed it to form the first non-Communist government in Poland since World War II. Gorbachev had signaled that the "Brezhnev doctrine" was obsolete, and on October 25, a Soviet Foreign Ministry spokesman, Gennady Gerasimov, made this official in a television interview on *Good Morning America*, announcing the "Frank Sinatra doctrine," by which he meant that Eastern Bloc countries were now free to go "My Way," that is, their own way. Gorbachev himself, on the same day, said, in a press conference in Helsinki, "I think the Brezhnev doctrine is dead." Absent

Soviet backing, even the Stasi was weakening its grip, epitomized in the resignation of DDR strongman Erich Honecker on October 18 in the face of burgeoning protests, and in the promise of his successor, Egon Krenz, to open "dialogue with the citizens." One could hardly blame Ossis for misinterpreting a DDR spokesman's imprecise remarks on November 9, when he was discussing a loosening of travel restrictions, to mean that the Berlin Wall was open. They began flooding across into West Berlin that evening.[1]

With no sign of Soviet military intervention after the Berlin Wall was breached and dismantled by Ossis alongside West German gawkers and tourists, it did not take long for the other satellites to fall, too. In Prague, a charismatic, chain-smoking dissident playwright named Václav Havel, who had first come to fame for opposing the Soviet invasion in 1968, formed a Solidarity-style opposition group called the Civic Forum to protest a government crackdown on student protesters on November 17. His group called a general strike on November 27 and began meeting underground in beer halls, then set up headquarters in a theater called the "Magic Lantern." The unloved Communist government of Gustáv Husák announced it would relinquish power on November 28, Husák duly resigned on December 10, and Havel was elected president on December 29. Prague's "Velvet" or "Gentle" Revolution, as Czechs and Slovaks called it, was perhaps the least violent, and certainly the most charming, political revolution of the twentieth century, given its own best-selling chronicle (*The Magic Lantern*) by a Western writer, Timothy Garton Ash, who befriended Havel and even fed him a pithy line that Havel repeated before the cameras ("In Poland it took ten years [i.e., since Solidarity emerged], in Hungary ten months, in East Germany ten weeks, perhaps in Czechoslovakia it will take ten days!").[2]*

---

* Although Ash has confirmed the accuracy of the quote Havel adopted, he has also been honest about its inaccuracy, not least vis-à-vis the Velvet Revolution itself, as he

As edifying as the story is, the parable of the Magic Lantern has misled many westerners about what was happening in Eastern Europe in 1989. Czechs and Slovaks certainly succeeded in throwing off the shackles of Communism, but they were able to do so only because the Afghan mujahideen, armed by the United States and Pakistan, had undermined Soviet military credibility, even while the strategic pressure applied by the Reagan administration had throttled the Soviet economy. These developments had left Gorbachev so desperate for Western approval of loans and aid that he had decided not to fight for the satellites after first Poland, then Hungary, and finally East Germany resisted Soviet domination. Nor did the Communists in the remaining satellites surrender power as easily as Husák did in Prague. In Bulgaria, Todor Zhivkov had cracked down violently on the country's Turkish minority in May, leading to the forced exodus of nearly 360,000 Muslims into neighboring Turkey—an operation so ugly that Gorbachev called for his ouster. On November 10, the day after the Berlin Wall fell, Zhivkov was forced to resign by the Bulgarian Politburo, which resolved to change the name of the Bulgarian Communist Party to "Socialist" and allow opposition groups to contest parliamentary elections the following June. In Romania, Ceaușescu ordered the Securitate, and then the regular army, to fire into a crowd of demonstrators in Timișoara on December 17–18. Although casualty figures are widely disputed, deaths were certainly in the high double digits and possibly well into the hundreds. Ceaușescu was able to restore control for a few days, only to be confronted with a massive crowd of hostile protesters in Bucharest. After fleeing the capital, Ceaușescu and his wife, Elena, were caught in Târgoviște. They were publicly executed on Christmas Day, in a gruesome finale to the revolutions of 1989. As in Bulgaria,

made the remark on "day 7" (November 23), and the quip was repeated on television to justify the general strike on day 11, not 10 (November 27), leading to the government's collapse on day 12 (November 28) and Husák's resignation on day 24 (December 10).

Romania's was not so much a popular revolution as a palace coup, with Communist insiders changing the name of the party to retain control. Most violent of all was the dissolution of Communism in Yugoslavia, where the leader of the League of Communists of Serbia (SKS), Slobodan Milošević, renounced Communism for revanchist nationalism. While serious ethnic violence did not break out until later, Milošević got the ball rolling with a Serbian economic boycott of Slovenia in December 1989, which broke apart the Yugoslav Communist Party and led Slovenia, Croatia, and then Bosnia-Herzegovina to secede from the union and find their own ex-Communist nationalists to counter Milošević's Serbian chauvinism. The result was predictable, as the persecution of minorities in each new independent Yugoslav republic led to retaliation and ethnic cleansing, and finally a genocidal war in Bosnia.[3]

The Velvet Revolution, we can now see, was the exception proving the rule. Communist leaders did not, and do not, generally surrender power peacefully owing to popular protests. The removal of the Soviet security guarantee left Eastern Bloc rulers vulnerable, but even so, most of them resigned only when forced to do so by colleagues maneuvering for power themselves, such as Honecker and Zhivkov, or chose to shed blood as Deng had done in Tiananmen Square, such as Ceaușescu, who bought himself another week in power, and Milošević, who lasted another decade. The important geopolitical question, in the wake of the dramatic events of 1989, was which path Moscow would follow. Would Gorbachev fight to defend Communist rule in the Soviet Union, if not in all the satellites? If so, where in the constituent Soviet Republics would he draw the line, and how much blood was he willing to shed to maintain the party in power?

Judging from the way he responded to the dissolution of the Soviet empire in Europe, Gorbachev seemed closer to Husák than to Deng or Ceaușescu. In negotiations over the future status of

Germany and NATO, Gorbachev barely put up a fight, although, in his defense, the new Bush administration in Washington, DC, manipulated him masterfully. Meeting with Gorbachev in Moscow on February 9, 1990, US secretary of state James Baker made the later infamous "offer" that, in exchange for the Soviets withdrawing troops from the DDR and allowing a "unified Germany to be tied to NATO," the United States would agree that "NATO would not shift one inch eastward from its present position." Gorbachev, not fully understanding this loaded question, replied that *any* expansion of the "zone of NATO" was unacceptable to the USSR, and in his own recollection, Baker replied that "we [Americans] agree with that." Acres of print have since been devoted to ascertaining what, exactly, Baker meant, and what Gorbachev thought he meant: Would a new, unified Germany renounce NATO membership? Or would this new Germany be allowed to join NATO, which would *then* not expand farther east than the old DDR-Polish—now unified German—frontier? Much of the fault lies with Baker, whose phrase "not one inch eastward from its present position" implied that only the half of Germany west of the Elbe River would remain in NATO (that was the "present position")—contradicting his proposal that "a unified Germany be tied to NATO." But Gorbachev, if his goal was to keep a unified Germany from joining NATO and thus setting a precedent for further NATO expansion eastward, should have teased out the contradiction—and gotten any US assurance on this front in writing, which he did not.[4]

Gorbachev had many cards to play in 1990, beginning with the more than 380,000 Red Army troops still occupying the DDR, for whose withdrawal, and ownership of the huge real estate holdings thereof, he could have bartered dearly. Instead, he received little more than economic aid from the FRG (including 1.2 billion DM in "stationing costs" to cover Soviet occupation expenses until the troops left, and a promise that the FRG would build 45,000 new apartments in Moscow and other Soviet cities to house Red Army officers returning home), in exchange for giving up the most important Soviet-controlled piece of the postwar European chessboard, when he agreed to let the DDR join a unified Germany on July 15, 1990. As Gorbachev told German chancellor Helmut Kohl in a painfully honest self-assessment, there were already "howls" from the Soviet military brass that he was "selling the Soviet victory in World War II for deutsche marks." President George H. W. Bush and subsequent US administrations, walking through the door Gorbachev left wide open by withdrawing the Red Army, plowed ahead with NATO expansion into the old DDR, the other Warsaw Pact satellites, and ultimately the former USSR republics of Lithuania, Latvia, and Estonia, with fateful consequences for US-Russian relations, and Ukraine in particular.[5]

Nor did Gorbachev seem to have much fight in him as the Soviet economy collapsed in upon itself, all but bankrupting the Kremlin as centrifugal forces in the constituent republics put a heavy strain on the overstretched Soviet military and security forces. First Lithuania, in March 1990, and then Latvia and Estonia (March 1991) and Georgia (April 1991), declared sovereign independence, with similar resolutions on the table in Central Asia, the Caucasus, and even Belarus and Ukraine. In just the first half of 1991, the Soviet GDP declined by 10 percent outright, even as inflation hit 2–3 percent per *week* and the government reached its expected annual deficit of 26.6 billion rubles by the end of January. Since 1989 the State Bank of the USSR had been forced to dump gold to prop up the ruble and cover the foreign trade deficit (state dollar reserves had likewise plummeted from $15 billion to $1 billion), shipping more than 1,000 metric tons of bullion abroad; Soviet gold reserves were all gone by November 1991. Whatever wealth the Soviet state still possessed was being spirited away into private hands, with more than $150 billion transferred to Western banks by Soviet individuals between the fall of the Berlin Wall and the final collapse of the USSR. Soviet Communist Party insiders and KGB agents were cashing in, fleeing the sinking Soviet ship— and all Gorbachev could come up with to stanch the bleeding of imperial authority was a popular plebiscite on a "Union Treaty" on March 17, 1991, which would keep the USSR together as a "union of sovereign equal states" with strong central power over the military and foreign policy.[6]

As for the money he needed to pay the army to shore up his crumbling empire, Gorbachev's plan was to beg the Americans to give it to him. Over breakfast in the US embassy in London that July, the president of the once-mighty Communist USSR asked the president of the country that the entire Soviet nuclear arsenal was directed against why, after he had "found 100 billion dollars to deal with one regional conflict," meaning the Persian Gulf War fought earlier that year, the US president could not devote a similar sum to "change the Soviet Union, to allow it to reach a new state, to become an organic part of the world economy and world community not as an opposing force or threat." After selling the Soviet position in Europe for deutsche marks, Gorbachev now wanted American dollars to surrender the Cold War. It was such a stunning and embarrassing request that President Bush, according to Chernyaev, who had already heard Gorbachev beg Bush in a similar manner *three previous times* that year, "turned crimson before my eyes." Suppressing his shock and agitation, Bush quietly changed the subject. It was a no.[7]

Cleverly, Gorbachev's main political rival, Boris Yeltsin, had attached a rider to the March referendum allowing for the direct election of a Russian president, who might soon rival Gorbachev's authority as Soviet president. The dual referendum passed, and Yeltsin was elected with an impressive majority of 57 percent on the first ballot on June 12, 1991. On July 10, Yeltsin was sworn in

440

Communism in Retreat
1989–1991

Leningrad

Moscow, August 1991, the failed coup

Moscow

UNION OF SOVIET SOCIALIST REPUBLICS

Minsk

Belarus, independent September 1991

Belarus

Alma-Ata (Almaty), Kazakhstan, December 1986

Kazakhstan

Kiev

Ukraine, independent August 1991

Stalingrad

Ukraine

Dnepropetrovsk

Moldova, independent August 1991

Rostov-Na-Donu

Moldova

Kishinev

Odessa

Azerbaijan, independent December 1991

Constanta

Georgia, independent December 1991

Tbilisi

Georgia

Varna

Azerbaijan

Armenia

Yerevan

Istanbul

Armenia, independent September 1991

Ankara

TURKEY

IRAN

SYRIA

IRAQ

441

as president in a traditional Kremlin ceremony presided over by the Orthodox patriarch. His inauguration speech, Gorbachev's aide Chernyaev observed, "had something of Holy Vladimir the Baptizer," with scarcely a nod to Soviet Communist themes, not even the "Great Patriotic War" with Nazi Germany. "After the October Revolution," Chernyaev huffed, in Yeltsin's version of history "everything is black," and Communism "deserves to be trampled and cursed." Showing that this was not mere rhetoric, Yeltsin's first act in power was to prohibit the Communist Party from the Russian government and instruct the legislature to ban the party from the Russian army, security organs, and judiciary. The stage was set for a political showdown.[8]

Over the course of July, and with gathering momentum after Gorbachev left Moscow on a two-week vacation in a fancy new seaside state villa at Foros, near Yalta, in Crimea on August 5, a plot was hatched to declare martial law, arrest Yeltsin, and halt the disintegration of the USSR before the Union Treaty was signed on August 20. Although they met furtively in KGB safe houses, the plotters encompassed basically the entire Soviet Communist government, including Gorbachev's vice president, Gennady Yanaev; Prime Minister Valentin Pavlov; the defense minister, Marshal D. T. Yazov; Oleg Baklanov, the first deputy chairman of defense; Boris Pugo, head of the Soviet Interior Ministry and its troops; and Vladimir Kryuchkov, head of the KGB. To this day the precise role of Gorbachev, the man who had appointed all of these plotters, remains in dispute. Although Gorbachev was put under house arrest in Foros on August 18 and his phones were cut off, we know that he met with Baklanov and other plotters in Foros on August 18 and again on August 21. In between these two meetings, for which no good sources are available, the plotters, some of them drinking heavily, botched their attempted coup. After martial law was declared at 4:00 a.m. on August 19, a special KGB commando unit

("Alpha") sent to Yeltsin's dacha outside Moscow somehow failed to arrest him. The Russian president was able to race to the "White House" hosting Russia's parliament, now surrounded by armored units, where he famously climbed up onto a tank around noon and read out an "Appeal to Russia" denouncing the "right-wing, reactionary, anti-constitutional coup d'état." Deputies and Russian volunteers threw up barricades and gathered arms to defend the White House, holding on throughout the day on August 20. The tanks and army units called into Moscow by the plotters began leaving early the next morning, having inflicted only a handful of casualties (including three deaths). By the afternoon of August 21, it was all over. Yeltsin confirmed his political victory by sending a team to Foros to "rescue" Gorbachev from his own appointee-plotters—men who, after meeting with Gorbachev one last time, were taken into custody. Gorbachev was flown back to Moscow in Yeltsin's Russian presidential plane (a Tupolev) instead of his own, larger Ilyushin 62, the Soviet equivalent of US Air Force One—a plane he would never get to ride in again. Two days later, Yeltsin forced a diminished Gorbachev to read out, on television, the meeting transcript of his own cabinet ministers on August 19 as they committed what looked like treason. "On a lighter note," Yeltsin asked Gorbachev, "shall we now sign a decree suspending the Russian Communist Party?"[9]

So dramatic were the scenes in Moscow in the thwarted August 1991 coup that they came to define, for most Americans and Europeans, the triumph of "freedom" over Communist dictatorship: a heroic mass protest, channeled by a popular elected president, had taken down the USSR. Like the fall of the Berlin Wall, the image of Yeltsin bellowing on the tank provides a neat bookend to the Cold War and the history of Communism, a kind of retort to the Tiananmen Square massacre that kept the CCP in power in China. In the early triumphalism of the Yeltsin era, the Russian Communist

Party was even forced to defend itself in the courtroom in a trial conducted between August and October 1992, much of it televised. In an act of sublime symbolism, the Yeltsin government called in as expert witness on the legality (or criminality) of the Soviet Communist Party a famously anti-Communist American historian, Richard Pipes. Pipes had worked as an adviser to the Reagan administration during the years of Poland's Solidarity crisis in the early 1980s, and his best-selling history of the Russian Revolution, published in 1990, had made him a household name. In part owing to this heady experience, Pipes later opened a short popular history by declaring that he was writing not only "an introduction to Communism" but, "at the same time, its obituary." As the American political scientist Francis Fukuyama put it still more grandly in a 1992 bestseller, the Western victory in the Cold War marked "the end of history," with the demise of Communism marking "the endpoint of mankind's ideological evolution," as Western liberal democracy was revealed to be "the final form of human government."[10]

As understandable as this kind of chest-thumping triumphalism was after his big moment on the tank, Yeltsin had grossly overplayed his hand. Contrary to the perception in the Western media, which covered the 1992 trial with breathless anticipation as a Nuremberg for Communism, it was the *Communists* who had initiated legal proceedings against Yeltsin in the Russian Constitutional Court for his decision to outlaw the party in 1991. Though it is true that many of the party's crimes, including mass executions of dissidents, were discussed in the courtroom, on the legal point at issue—Yeltsin's claim that the Communist Party of the Soviet Union (CPSU) was "never a party," but a "special mechanism for shaping and exercising political power by fusing with state structures"—Yeltsin's government lost its case. In view of the composition of the court, on which twelve out of thirteen judges were current or former Communist Party members, this should not have been surprising. The outlawed CPSU became the fully legal Communist Party of the Russian Federation—a party soon outpolling Yeltsin, largely because of galloping inflation and economic chaos, but also owing to the political backlash sparked by the fact that he had outlawed the party and invited a notorious American Cold Warrior to testify in court.[11]

Even the story of the August coup is not as straightforward as many in the West first thought. Contrary to the popular impression many have of Gorbachev as a quasi-pacifist who surrendered the Cold War nonviolently—an impression reinforced by the Nobel Committee's curious decision to award him the Peace Prize in 1990—the Soviet president shed a considerable amount of blood trying to keep the Soviet empire together. Although Gorbachev read out harrowing letters in the Politburo from soldiers' mothers about the horrors their sons were experiencing in Afghanistan, tabling a possible withdrawal as early as October 1985, the fact remains that he continued prosecuting the brutal war there for nearly four more years. Gorbachev ordered brutal crackdowns against protesters in Alma-Ata (today's Almaty) in Kazakhstan in December 1986 (at least 2 were killed and likely far more), in Tbilisi in April 1989 (18 confirmed dead, including 12 young women, and 190 wounded), and in Baku in January 1990 (at least 100 and possibly far more dead, nearly 1,000 wounded). The significance of the latter two interventions was not that they failed—they did not—but that Gorbachev, increasingly concerned about his image in the West as he courted loans and approval, recoiled from the violence his own orders had produced, rebuking the responsible army commanders. His behavior after the Baku massacre was particularly damaging. He sent a team of 39 investigators to Baku with orders to inventory "crimes committed by the servicemen of the airborne forces," instructing them to "investigate immediately and to punish severely." When the investigators threatened to take custody of those responsible, the commander of the airborne troops, Lieutenant General Alexander Lebed, turned the tables on them and arrested the men on the investigators' security detail. Lebed believed that the incident was being used to victimize him, and he refused to let himself become Gorbachev's latest scapegoat (although he did in fact let the investigators have their security team back to protect them from "local marauders"). Armed interventions in January 1991 in Vilnius, Lithuania (16 dead and hundreds wounded), and Riga, Latvia (4 dead, 10 wounded), attracted more Western media attention, owing to their proximity to Europe—which led Gorbachev to denounce the commander of the Vilnius Red Army garrison, Major General Vladimir Uskhopchik, by name in public, as if he himself had nothing to do with the Vilnius crackdown. By the summer of 1991, Gorbachev had put himself in the position of Alexander Kerensky in 1917, alienating the very officers who had sworn to defend him and his government. Significantly, the Vilnius episode prompted Yeltsin, ironically playing the role of Lenin, to call on Russian soldiers not to obey unjust orders to fire on civilians—that is, to mutiny, as many of them soon did when, during the August coup, they refused to fire on the crowds and arrest Yeltsin.[12]

Viewed dispassionately, the failure of the August coup did not really mean, as many in the West believed, that the Russian people, enraged after decades of repression and fed up with the perennial shortages of foodstuffs and consumer goods in a Communist economy, had risen up en masse to topple an oppressive regime. Rather, it showed that Gorbachev in 1991, like Kerensky in 1917, had forfeited the loyalty of the men manning the empire's defenses, and so was unable to rely on main force when it counted. Communism had conquered Russia and its borderlands, after all, not by popular acclamation—the Bolsheviks lost the only genuine democratic poll contested in November 1917—but by the sword, and their regime vanished once the sword shattered.

In China, the sword was still there, and so the CCP stayed in power after the supposed "end of history" in 1989, as it does to this day. So did Communist parties ruling by the sword in Cuba, North Korea, Vietnam, and Laos (though mercifully not in Cambodia, where the monarchy was reinstated in 1993). Although an outside observer, whether sympathetic or hostile, might object that private firms, both domestic and foreign, are active on the ground in China and Vietnam (less so in Cuba, Laos, and North Korea), thus violating the core Marxist premise of state control of "the means of production," there was never a time in the history of Soviet Communism when this was not true—not even the high Stalinist years of the 1930s, when American investors and engineers dominated Soviet metallurgy and heavy industry. China and Cambodia, in the feverish years of Mao's Cultural Revolution and the Khmer Rouge, came closer to abolishing private economic activity and "bourgeois" family life altogether, but the civilizational collapse that resulted discredited these extreme literal-minded interpretations of Marxism. What made the USSR "Communist" is the same thing that defines the current governments of China, North Korea, Vietnam, Laos, and Cuba: rule by a single-party dictatorship that allows no legal opposition parties, that claims to direct and control the entire economy, that blankets society with all-encompassing rules and regulations, and that hectors, monitors, and surveils the people in whose name it claims to rule in minute detail. Who are we to argue that we know better than they do?

To be sure, there is considerable variation between Communist regimes today. North Korea remains the most Stalinist (or Maoist) dictatorship: public executions are common, and people can still be arrested for possessing forbidden "capitalist" items, such as American DVDs or video players, or for offenses such as butchering cows (owned by the state) without permission. Cuba, despite suffering a similar collapse in living standards as North Korea after

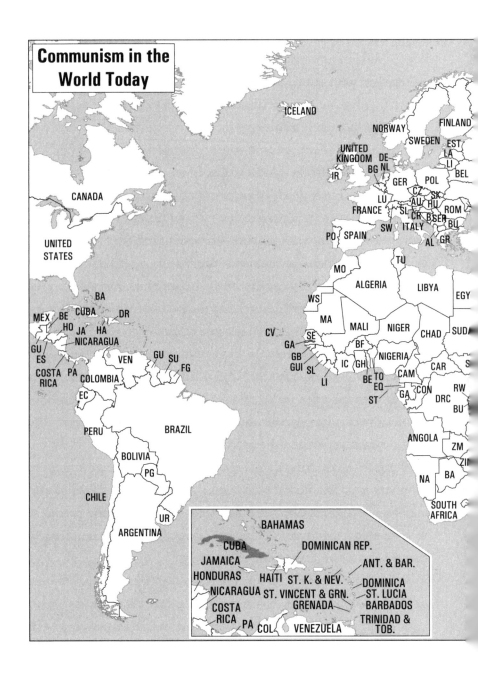

Communism in the World Today

ICELAND

NORWAY FINLAND

SWEDEN EST

UNITED LA
KINGDOM DE LI

IR BG NL BEL

GER POL

CANADA CZ SK

LU AU HU

FRANCE SL CR ROM

B SER

SW ITALY BU

UNITED PO SPAIN AL GR

STATES TU

MO

BA ALGERIA LIBYA EGY

WS

MEX BE CUBA DR MA

HO JA HA MALI NIGER CHAD SUD

NICARAGUA CV SE

GU GA BF

ES VEN GU SU GB NIGERIA CAR S

COSTA PA FG GUI SL IC GH

RICA COLOMBIA LI BE TO CAM

EC EQ CON RW

ST GA DRC

BU

PERU BRAZIL ANGOLA ZM

ZI

BOLIVIA

PG NA BA

CHILE SOUTH
AFRICA

UR BAHAMAS

ARGENTINA CUBA DOMINICAN REP.

JAMAICA ANT. & BAR.

HONDURAS HAITI ST. K. & NEV. DOMINICA

NICARAGUA ST. VINCENT & GRN. ST. LUCIA

COSTA GRENADA BARBADOS

RICA PA COL VENEZUELA TRINIDAD &
TOB.

448

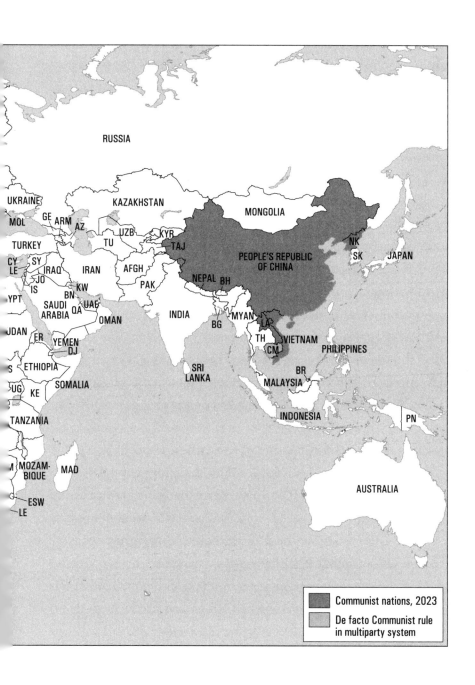

Soviet subsidies amounting to some $4.5 billion a year dried up in the Gorbachev era, achieved modest improvements in living standards once tourism resumed, reaching $10,000 in per capita income today—but the country is still desperately poor. One of the saddest features of the post-Soviet Cuban Communist economy is the ubiquity of *jiniterismo*, or what is sometimes called "sex tourism," although this does not always involve prostitution. As the Frommer's travel website explained in 2023, "Travelers of both genders and any sexual persuasion will encounter constant offers for companionship, and usually more. In some cases, the terms are quite clear and a cash value is set. In others, the *jinetera* or *jinetero* is just looking for some restaurant meals, drinks, store-bought clothing, food, [and] daily necessities." Communist Laos and Vietnam do not share Cuba's reputation for bottom-feeding sex tourism, but on paper they are even poorer than Cuba, boasting per capita annual incomes of only $2,000 despite native reputations for industriousness—better than the Asian Communist hermit kingdom of North Korea ($1,300), but a fraction of that of neighboring "capitalist" Thailand ($5,640).[13]

China is the most interesting case of all. In terms of raw GDP, after three decades of near double-digit or higher annual growth rates it now boasts the second-largest (or by some estimates the largest) economy in the world, with output of $18 trillion reported for 2022. This growth has been fueled both by Western investment and by the "outsourcing" of much of the American manufacturing base to China—from plastic toys and trinkets to household appliances, consumer electronics, and other high-end products. Even so, Chinese per capita incomes, even by official figures, are still five times lower than in the United States (c. $12,000 vs. $70,000, as of 2021 World Bank estimates, although the ratio is improving). So much of the data is opaque that there is really no way of knowing for sure how Chinese output and efficiency compares to American or Western counterparts, but the trend line of Chinese economic growth is impossible to ignore.[14]

More ominously for westerners, Chinese Communism has proved to be nearly as influential in the West as the Soviet version was at its various peaks, albeit with a critical difference: the Chinese model has been less successful than the Soviet one in the purely political sense of public relations. Not only has the tacit (if not official) abandonment of the "classless society" ideal since Deng's market reforms been illustrated by the conspicuous consumption of Chinese elites, but Chinese human rights abuses have been accorded greater publicity. Those who have been targeted include religious groups, such as Falun Gong; the Uighur population; and, more recently, dissidents in Hong Kong, who have been CCP subjects since 1997. Few hard-core Western Communists, and fewer still progressive reformers and women's rights activists, look to Beijing today for inspiration in the way so many did to Moscow in the 1930s and 1940s, or again in the 1970s and 1980s—or even afterward, in the case of widespread nostalgia in former Eastern Bloc countries for life under Communism (when, although there were fewer and thus less strain-inducing choices of consumer goods and careers, people did not have to work as hard as they did in the West to pay for state-subsidized shelter and utilities and health care).[15]

Still, in terms of raw economic power and the institutional and often personal leverage that comes with it, the CCP has been more successful than the Soviets ever were. Whether in buying up Western politicians, firms, and real estate; inviting Western aerospace companies, such as Boeing, to outsource sensitive manufacturing processes to China; sending students to top science programs in the United States and Europe and investing in research laboratories and "Confucian Institutes" in American universities; or simply poaching Western talent with generous salary offers, CCP leaders have relentlessly leveraged their economic power. From Hollywood studies to higher ed, from the American retail behemoth Walmart to the 5G telecommunications giant Huawei, from the search engine Google to the National Basketball Association (NBA), entities controlled by or kowtowing to the CCP, owing to the strategic stakes it holds in Western firms, or simply its control over access to the giant Chinese market, now dominate much of Western economic and social life.[16]

However striking its apparent success, the China model is not entirely new. We should not forget that the original Soviet Five-Year Plans, aimed at facilitating Stalin's hypertrophic arms buildup to prepare for war with the capitalist world, depended heavily on importing Western technology and hiring "capitalist" engineers, managers, and even agronomists (such as the "Wheat King" of Montana, who helped design the first *kolkhoz*). Even the most famous "Soviet" weapon of the Second World War, the T-34 tank, rode on a suspension designed by the US engineer J. Walter Christie (Stalin purchased the patent for it in 1930). Stalin's master aviation spy Stanislav Shumovsky placed agents in all the leading US aviation firms in the 1930s, from Douglas to Bell Aircraft to Wright Aeronautical, and these agents copied, stole, or reverse-engineered the designs on which most of the Soviet air force was based. In view of the horrendous human rights abuses in this era of high Stalinism, from the mass arrests of nepmen to the Holodomor, the Great Terror, and the Gulag, the US government might have blocked some or all of this industrial espionage and technology transfer, but owing to a mixture of naïveté and Soviet influence operations in the State Department, Treasury, and White House, it did not. After the Nazi invasion of the USSR, the Roosevelt administration let the Soviets "requisition" whatever they needed from US war industries free of charge—including enriched uranium, deuterium oxide ("heavy water"), and the other materials used to jump-start Stalin's atomic bomb program. The Soviet Communist superpower that contested the Cold War and brought the United States to the brink of nuclear war in 1962 could not have emerged without the contributions, both voluntary and involuntary, of American capitalists.[17]

The story of Communist China since 1989 has followed an eerily similar path. Rather than holding Deng's feet to the fire after the Tiananmen Square massacre, President Bush went on camera and vowed that he and his advisers would not "judge the Whole People's Liberation Army by that terrible incident." Bush's national security adviser, Brent Scowcroft, flew to Beijing in early July 1989, in secret, to reassure Deng privately that "President Bush is a true friend, a true friend of you and of China," adding that he and the president were both "close associates of Henry Kissinger"—the secretary of state who had helped Nixon "open" China, and much of whose subsequent career has been devoted to lobbying for Chinese interests in Washington. While these men were all Republicans, CCP-appeasing in Washington has been wholly bipartisan, with Democratic senator Feinstein of California repeatedly defending the Tiananmen Square massacre in public when arguing against rescinding MFN status for China. Bush's Democratic successor, Bill Clinton, ushered through the US-China Relation Act of 2000 granting Communist China permanent normal trade relations status, which made China's entry into the World Trade Organization (WTO) possible under President George W. Bush in 2001. In the détente years, the Jackson-Vanik amendment had required at least some policy concessions, and brought scrutiny of Soviet psychiatric and human rights abuses in exchange for loans. By contrast, in exchange for the United States granting China unprecedented access to its market and easing the legal path for US multinational corporations to outsource manufacturing to China, the CCP conceded—nothing.[18]

To promote Beijing's entry into the WTO at the turn of the millennium, Washington politicians promised Americans that opening

China for trade would moderate Communism. As Clinton's secretary of state, Madeleine Albright, put it, "By entering the WTO, China committed to free itself from the 'House that Mao Built,' including state-run enterprises [and] central planning institutes," leading to "more institutions and associations free from Communist party control." Nothing of the kind has happened. Instead of Communist China converging on Western liberal norms, Western technology has allowed the Chinese government to ratchet up surveillance of its citizens. It uses data mining made possible by US internet search engines, tracking features on smartphones, and the like to keep tabs on people's movements and activities in the most invasive "social credit system" in the world. Dissidents are denied access to jobs, travel, and credit cards. With "Zero COVID" contact tracing and forcible house quarantining, the CCP under China's increasingly authoritarian president, Xi Jinping, carried out population controls the KGB could only have dreamed of.[19]

Rather than recoiling in horror from the souped-up Communist surveillance state that US trade policy has helped facilitate, the United States and its allies have instead been "Sino-formed" themselves. To be sure, the US security state abuses exposed by Julian Assange, founder of WikiLeaks, whistleblower Edward Snowden, and others between 2010 and 2013—including electronic eavesdropping on ordinary Americans—were largely a result of Cold War–era paranoia, compounded by the US reaction (or overreaction) to the security failures that led to the 9/11 terrorist attacks of 2001 on the World Trade Center and the Pentagon. But in the years since this direct government spying was exposed, a subtler but deeper collaboration between social media companies and government spy agencies has emerged. The "Twitter files" released after Elon Musk's takeover of that company in 2022 revealed that Twitter was not only collaborating with the White House and other government agencies to censor or ban certain accounts and information, but was actually paid $3.4 million by the FBI to share confidential user information. Owing to the Twitter files exposé and a series of landmark court cases, we now know that social media companies, often on orders from the US government, have been monitoring and censoring dissident viewpoints on everything from largely imaginary Russian (or actual Ukrainian) influence operations in Washington (for example, the now infamous "Biden laptop" story), to COVID mask and vaccine mandates, to claims of electoral fraud during the 2020 presidential election.[20]

With the COVID-19 lockdowns of 2020–2022, the China model of Communist statist surveillance crashed into Europe, the United States, Canada, Australia, and New Zealand as once inviolable Western freedoms—of movement, travel, and association, of speech and robust debate over controversial public policies—were abandoned one by one. Even "social distancing," the now much-mocked craze of 2020—which, by making it illegal for humans to sit or congregate closer than six feet (in the United States) or one meter (most of Europe), shut down public schools and all but destroyed social industries, from cinemas, concert halls, and theaters to churches, gyms, restaurants, and nightclubs—was a CCP import. Contrary to the reassuring, though bizarre, story fed to us by a *New York Times* cover story in April 2020 and popularized by the Michael Lewis 2021 bestseller *Premonition* that "social distancing" was invented by a fourteen-year-old girl in a 2005 science fair project, "social distancing lockdown" (封锁 or Fēngsuô, originally a military term meaning "blockade" or "sealing off") was a Chinese Communist policy imposed in 2002–2003 in response to outbreaks of avian flu and severe acute respiratory syndrome (SARS). It was quietly, owing to CCP influence, incorporated into pandemic guidelines by the World Health Organization (WHO) and the American Centers for Disease Control and Prevention (CDC) in 2004, reversing decades of progressively more humane—and scientifically sound—policies on mitigating disease outbreaks. "Lockdown" had absolutely no basis in the Western tradition, not even in the more credulous times of the Black Death, when *sick* people might have been quarantined against their will, but never the entire healthy population.[21]

Social distancing lockdown, however, was a logical outgrowth of the statist population controls embraced by twentieth-century Communist regimes, such as the one in China where it first emerged. The Western adoption of CCP repression was perhaps best described by the British epidemiologist Neil Ferguson, whose frightening, wildly exaggerated COVID "death projections" helped scare westerners into surrendering their freedoms in March 2020. Ferguson told the *London Times* that, after learning about China's draconian lockdown in Wuhan, he and his colleagues in London and Washington first told themselves, "It's a Communist one-party state. . . . [W]e couldn't get away with it in Europe [or the United States], we thought . . . and then Italy did it. And we realized we could." They could, and they did. The world has never been the same since.[22]

After heady moments in 1989 and 1991 when it appeared that the fall of Communism would usher in an era of greater civil liberties and freedoms worldwide, most of the Western world is now converging instead on a hybrid Chinese Communist model of statist governance and social life. Private (or semi-private) social media and other tech companies are harnessed by the state to track, monitor, censor, and control private communications, speech, and political activity, mostly behind the scenes, although with periodic high-profile crackdowns to scare would-be dissidents into compliance. The CCP's social credit system, which sees those who fall afoul of the government or social media consensus denied access to schooling, travel, banking, or credit, has already been applied en masse to the "COVID unvaccinated" across the Western world, along with other dissidents. Such restrictions have now begun to extend into the banking system in the West. Funds raised to feed Canadian truckers participating in an outdoor winter protest against COVID vaccine mandates in early 2022, for example, were frozen by Canadian authorities in early 2022. When former Brexit Party chairman and European Parliament member Nigel Farage faced closure of his bank accounts, or "debanking," in the summer of 2023, he believed it was because of his political views. Similar crackdowns affected British and American journalists critical of the West's Ukraine policy in 2023.[23]

It is not hard to imagine "debanking" or other types of persecution being applied in the near future to people whose views dissent from the approved consensus of Western social and governing elites on a wider range of topics, such as "climate change," immigration, race, sexual orientation, or gender identification. It might once have sufficed for intellectual orthodoxy-enforcers that dissenters had trouble finding employment in government, in academe, or at white shoe corporate and law firms, but social access can now be restricted to many other areas of public life: not only the closure of bank accounts or refusal of service, but also social media bans, the seizure of funds collected via online platforms such as GoFundMe, the denial of passport or travel rights, or even, in some cases, interrogation and arrest. Americans have thus far been spared the cruder Communist injustice of "expropriation" of their assets, and the horrors of Stalin- or Mao-style Gulag camps and state-induced famines. In the social and intellectual sphere, however, the echoes of Cultural Revolution–style Communist totalitarianism have become too powerful—and painful—to ignore. Because modern-day thought commissars often work in the private sector (or for companies aligned with state intelligence), these new Western forms of social control may be more insidious than the cruder methods of physical intimidation and violence deployed by the NKVD, the Stasi, and Mao's Red Guards: many victims deprived of their jobs, funds, reputations, or basic civil rights may not even know who their accusers are. Far from dead, Communism as a governing template seems only to be getting started.

ACKNOWLEDGMENTS

The idea of writing a history of Communism grew out of a conversation I had with my fellow historian Nick Lloyd several years ago at the height of the COVID-19 lockdown, when the two of us were discussing how difficult it then was to conduct research, travel, or do much of anything, really. I am as astonished today as I was then that our two countries—Nick is English—had so easily and thoroughly surrendered our vaunted "Anglo-Saxon" freedoms dating back to the Magna Carta of 1215. While I still have no satisfying answer to the question of how that came to pass, writing this book has been an extremely helpful tonic keeping despair at bay, and I am grateful to Nick for providing the spark.

The subject also brought me back to my early passion for the history of international Communism, a subject I had not taught in twenty years. It was a great pleasure putting together an updated curriculum for a Bard College class on the revolutionary socialist internationals from 1864 to 1943 that I taught in the fall of 2022. My students rose brilliantly to the occasion, and I learned a great deal from them, especially from the brave debaters who vigorously defended Lenin and other Communist revolutionaries. It is difficult these days to get students to discuss controversial ideas at all, let alone with such verve and passion, and this was one of the most exciting classes I have taught for many years. I am grateful to each and every one of my students.

I would also like to extend thanks to Bard's undergraduate dean, Deirdre d'Albertis, who kindly approved my research agenda for this book, and to Rachel Price and Sherry Gildersleeve, who processed the requests. Richard Aldous is not just a brilliant historian but a prince of a colleague, who helps make Bard such a pleasant place to write. Cecile Kuznitz is a historian of great integrity and rare courage, with whom it is an honor to work. Seth Halvorson may have been a temporary neighbor in Aspinwall while another colleague was on leave, but his irrepressible spirit was invigorating over this past year as I hit crunch time drafting the book. I always learn a great deal from another Aspinwall neighbor, my colleague from medieval literature Karen Sullivan, whose sharp mind helps me refine my thinking. My ideas about the increasingly Soviet atmosphere of the contemporary West owe much to my conversations with Archie Magno, who is himself something of a dissident from Putin's increasingly chauvinistic Russia—though still Russian enough that he finds the contrary pieties of modern American culture bewildering.

It was not easy getting research done in the post-COVID era, and so I am especially indebted to archivists such as Roberto Welzel, who introduced me to the Stasi collections in Berlin, and Martin Kröger at the Political Archive of the Federal Foreign Office in Berlin. Bogdan Musial and Nick Siekierski both went out of their way to set me up in the Warsaw archives in the summer of 2022. Bogdan shared so much of his own work on Soviet, Polish, and East German Communism—from Communist land policy in Poland to the hidden underbelly of West German Ostpolitik and the real story behind Germany's multi-decade investments in Soviet oil and gas pipelines—that I often felt there was little left for me to discover on my own, although I did my best. Nick was a splendid host, a tireless interpreter, and also a historical tour guide, pointing out key memorials all over town from the doomed 1944 Warsaw

Uprising and from Polish Communist history more generally. Nick also introduced me to a brilliant young Polish historian named Witold Bagieński, who regaled me with fascinating tales about Polish secret police methods during the Communist era and kindly shared his library of new work in multiple languages on Polish Communism. Alex Richie also took time out of her busy schedule in Warsaw to arrange a private tour of the Mokotów Prison, where so many Polish dissidents were cruelly tortured and executed. Truly this was sacred ground, and I was honored and touched to be able to tread on it and pay my respects.

Sadly, owing to the deep freeze in US-Russia relations over the Ukraine war, which shows no sign of abating, I was unable to return to Moscow for this book, although I continue to mine material I have amassed over the many years I worked there, particularly at the old Russian State Archive of Socio-Political History, which also holds the Comintern records. I really do miss the place, even (perhaps especially) Misha, the tormented muse of the document registers, who bellows so violently when patrons do not heed his advice. Owing to the shutdown of access to Russia I am more indebted than usual to the archivists at the Hoover Institution Archives who microfilmed so much Soviet material back in the 1990s. At that time, Russia was more open to researchers than it is today, including allowing access to "Fond 89," the material declassified by President Boris Yeltsin to present his case when the Russian Communist Party sued his government for outlawing the party in 1992. Although they are now retired, Elena Danielson and Linda Bernard have provided invaluable assistance over the years in helping me prepare for my always rewarding visits to the Hoover Institution—including, in Elena's case, providing me, on my most recent visit, with the member introduction that is now necessary to get a room at the Faculty Club. Bert Patenaude also shared his deep familiarity with the Hoover Institution's Russian Communist collections, in particular the marvels of Fond 89, allowing me to exploit it in full.

My agent, Andrew Lownie, has supported this project wholeheartedly, even if my last book was so long that selling foreign rights was far more of a chore than it should have been. Lara Heimert of Basic Books is always a pleasure to work with, and she has played an especially active role in shaping this book. Of course, I could not write at all without the support, encouragement, and love of my beautiful wife, Nesrin, along with our two splendid children, Ayla and Errol. They, like Nesrin and her parents, who were refugees from Communist Bulgaria, often wonder why I spend so much time reading about Marx, Lenin, Stalin, and their works. I can only say that seeing them at the end of each day of writing or research helps keep me going. Thank you for everything.

ABBREVIATIONS OF ARCHIVES REFERENCED IN THE NOTES

AAN Archiwum Akt Nowych (Central Archives of Modern Records), Warsaw.

BB Bundesarchiv (Federal Archives), Bern.

DBB Deutsches Bundesarchiv (German Federal Archives), Lichterfelde, Berlin.

GARF Gosudarstvenny Arkhiv Rossiiskoi Federatsii (Government Archive of the Russian Federation), Moscow.

NAA National Archives Annex, College Park, Maryland.

PAAA Politisches Archiv des Auswärtigen Amtes (Political Archive of the Federal Foreign Office), Berlin.

PRO National Archives of the United Kingdom, Kew Gardens, London.*

QO Archives of the Quai d'Orsay, Paris.

RGAE Rossiiskii Gosudarstvennyi Arkhiv Ekonomiki (Russian Government Archive of Economics), Moscow.

RGASPI Rossiiskii Gosudarstvennyi Arkhiv Sotsial-Politicheskii Istorii (Russian State Archive of Socio-Political History), Moscow.

---

* Although it has been years now since the Public Record Office was renamed the National Archives, for the sake of tradition, and to preserve common currency, I continue to reference it in this book as the PRO.

RGVIA Rossiiskii Gosudarstvennyi Voenno-Istoricheskii Arkhiv (Russian Government Military-Historical Archive), Moscow.

RSU Riksarkivet Stockholm Utrikesdepartement (National Archives, Stockholm, Ministry of Foreign Affairs), Stockholm.

VSHD Vincennes, Service Historique de la Défense (Defense Historical Service, French military archives), Vincennes, Paris.

NOTES

Preface

1. Richard Pipes, *Communism: A History* (New York: Random House / Modern Library, 2001), ix.

2. Karl Marx, *The Eighteenth Brumaire of Louis Bonaparte* (New York: International Publishers, 1987 [1869]), 15.

Introduction: Social Equality

1. Aristophanes, *Ecclesiazusae* (*Assemblywomen*), trans. and ed. Eugene O'Neill Jr. (New York: Random House, 1938), lines 590–592, 617, 625, online at Perseus Digital Library, Tufts University, www.perseus.tufts.edu/hopper/text?doc=Perseus%3A text%3A1999.01.0030%3Acard%3D583; Plato, *Republic*, trans. G. M. A. Grube (Indianapolis: Hackett, 1992), Book V, 462b-c.

2. Cited in Tom Holland, *Dominion: How the Christian Revolution Remade the World* (New York: Basic Books, 2019), 148; Matthew 19:21 (ESV).

3. Koran 39:42; Gerhard Böwering, "The Concept of Time in Islam," *Proceedings of the American Philosophical Society* 141, no. 1 (March 1997): 55–66.

4. Letter from Columbus to King Ferdinand, c. 1493, online at Docplayer, https://docplayer.net/227211503-Christopher-columbus-letter-to-king-ferdinand-of -spain-1493.html.

5. Thomas More, *The Best State of a Commonwealth and the Island of Utopia* (1516), in *The Utopia Reader*, 2nd ed., ed. Gregory Claeys and Lyman Tower Sargent (New York: NYU Press, 2017), 97–98.

6. See Paul Ham's interesting study of the *New Jerusalem: The Short Life and Terrible Death of Christendom's Most Defiant Sect* (North Sydney, Australia: William Heinemann, 2018).

7. Denis Diderot, article entry "Encyclopédie," in *Encyclopédie*, vol. 5 (November 1755), 565.

8. Jean-Jacques Rousseau, *Discourse on the Origin and Foundations of Inequality Among Men* (1755), in *Rousseau: The Basic Political Writings*, 2nd ed., trans. and ed. Donald A. Cress, with an introduction and annotation by David Wootten (Indianapolis: Hackett, 2011), 69 (for "savages," see pp. 75, 98).

9. Rousseau, *Discourse on the Origin and Foundations of Inequality Among Men*; Jean-Jacques Rousseau, *On the Social Contract* (1762), in Cress and Wootten, *Rousseau:*

The Basic Political Writings, Book I, chapter 7 ("On the Sovereign"); Book I, chapter 9 ("On Real Property"); and Book II, chapter 5 ("On the Right of Life or Death") (pp. 167, 169, 177).

10. "Declaration of the Rights of Man and Citizen" (August 26, 1789), and Robespierre, *Report on the Principles of Political Morality* (February 5, 1794), in *The Old Regime and the French Revolution*, ed. Keith Michael Baker (Chicago: University of Chicago Press, 1987), 238, 374. Unless otherwise noted, emphasis is reproduced from the original.

11. On the Maximum and its fitful implementation, particularly its interaction with the mobilization of soldiers, war matériel, and labor for the war industry, see R. R. Palmer, *Twelve Who Ruled: The Year of the Terror of the French Revolution* (Princeton, NJ: Princeton University Press, 1970), 69–70, 239–41, and *passim*.

12. Étienne-Gabriel Morelly, *Code de la Nature, ou Le veritable esprit de ses loix*, ed. Gilbert Chinard (Paris: R. Clavreuil, 1950 [1755]), 171–72 (for authorship), and 184 and *passim* (for "savages").

13. Morelly, *Code de la Nature*, 214–17.

14. Morelly, *Code de la Nature*, 285–86, 291–92.

15. As noted by Alain Besançon in *The Rise of the Gulag: Intellectual Origins of Leninism* (New York: Continuum, 1981), 32.

Prologue: Conspiracy of the Equals

1. "Manifesto of the Directors" (November 5, 1795), in *The Old Regime and the French Revolution*, ed. Keith Michael Baker (Chicago: University of Chicago Press, 1987), 392.

2. Cited by John Anthony Scott, "Francois-Noel Babeuf and the Conspiration des Egaux," in *The Defense of Gracchus Babeuf Before the High Court of Vendôme*, trans. and ed. John Anthony Scott (Amherst: University of Massachusetts Press, 1967), 1.

3. Ernest Belfort Bax, *The Last Episode of the French Revolution* (London: Grant Richards, 1911), 64–69.

4. Cited in William Doyle, *The Oxford History of the French Revolution* (New York: Oxford University Press, 1990), 324.

5. Doyle, *Oxford History of the French Revolution*, 324–25; Bax, *Last Episode of the French Revolution*, 96–99.

6. Philippe Buonarroti, *Babeuf's Conspiracy for Equality*, trans. Bronterre O'Brien (New York: Augustus M. Kelly, 1965 [1836]), 89–90 and *passim*.

7. Sylvain Maréchal, *Le jugement dernier des rois* (1793), reproduced in full in the French original at Project Gutenberg, www.gutenberg.org/files/26124/26124-h/26124-h.htm.

8. Manifesto of the Equals, Piece No. VII, reproduced in the appendix of Buonarroti, *Babeuf's Conspiracy for Equality*, 314–17.

9. As translated and reproduced by Bax in *Last Episode of the French Revolution*, 114–16.

10. "Act of Insurrection," printed by "The Insurrectionary Committee of Public Safety to the People," c. April–May 1796, reproduced in Buonarroti, *Babeuf's Conspiracy for Equality*, 384–89. For the accompanying declaration seized by authorities, see Bax, *Last Episode of the French Revolution*, 127–29.

11. "Act of Insurrection."

12. Doyle, *Oxford History of the French Revolution*, 326.

13. Scott, *Defense of Gracchus*, 19–20, 47, 57.

14. Scott, *Defense of Gracchus*; Buonarroti, *Conspiracy for Equality*.

Chapter 1: Karl Marx and the Utopians

1. Cited in Walter Alison Phillips, *The Confederation of Europe: A Study of the European Alliance, 1813–1823, as an Experiment in the International Organization of Peace* (New York: Longmans, Green, 1920), 208–9.

2. Henri Comte de Saint-Simon, *Selected Writings*, trans. and ed. F. M. H. Markham (Oxford: Basil Blackwell, 1952), 116.

3. Citations in Joshua Muravchik, *Heaven on Earth: The Rise and Fall of Socialism* (San Francisco: Encounter Books, 2002), 41, 46, 50.

4. Cited in Charles Fourier, *The Utopian Vision of Charles Fourier*, trans. and ed. Jonathan Beecher and Richard Bienvenu (Columbia: University of Missouri Press, 1983), 20–21.

5. Martin Malia, *The Soviet Tragedy: A History of Socialism in Russia* (New York: Free Press, 1994), 37 and *passim*; Alexis de Tocqueville, *Democracy in America*, trans. Stephen D. Grant (Indianapolis: Hackett, 2000), 5–6. On electoral law, see François Furet, *Revolutionary France, 1770–1880* (Oxford: Blackwell, 2007), 333.

6. Pierre-Joseph Proudhon, *What Is Property? An Inquiry into the Principle of Right and of Government*, trans. Benjamin R. Tucker (New York: W. Reeves, 1902 [1840]), 37, 69, 241, 248–51. "Anarchist": Proudhon, *First Memoir* (1840), in Pierre-Joseph Proudhon, *Selected Writings of Pierre-Joseph Proudhon*, ed. Stewart Edwards, trans. Elizabeth Fraser (New York: Doubleday, 1969), 88.

7. G. W. F. Hegel, *Elements of the Philosophy of Right*, ed. Allen W. Wood, trans. H. B. Nisbet (Cambridge: Cambridge University Press, 1991), sec. 258, p. 267. "Moral dignity" and "equality before the law": G. W. F. Hegel, *The Philosophy of History*, trans. J. Sibree (Kitchener, Ontario: Batouche Books, 2001), 165. "The history of the world is not a scene of happiness": cited in Leszek Kolakowski, *Main Currents of Marxism*, trans. P. S. Falla (New York: Norton, 2005 [1978]), 60–61. "World history": G. W. F. Hegel, *Reason in History: A General Introduction to the Philosophy of History*, trans. Robert Hartman (New York: Macmillan, 1987), 24.

8. Karl Marx, *Theses on Feuerbach* (c. 1845), and for earlier citations in this paragraph, "Contributions to the Critique of Hegel's *Philosophy of Right*: Introduction," in Karl Marx and Friedrich Engels, *The Marx-Engels Reader*, 2nd ed., ed. Robert C. Tucker (New York: Norton, 1978) (henceforth *Marx-Engels Reader*), 53–54, 145.

9. Cited Jonathan Sperber, *Karl Marx: A Nineteenth-Century Life* (New York: Liveright, 2014), 54 (for details on Marx's doctoral work, see pp. 66–70).

10. Cited in Paul Johnson, *Intellectuals* (New York: Harper and Row, 1988), 54–55. "Met in beer cellars": Isaiah Berlin, *Karl Marx: His Life and Environment* (New York: Norton, 2013), 69.

11. Marx to Arnold Ruge, c. September 1843, in the *Marx-Engels Reader*, 13. Marx's disappointing inheritance and "My family" and "wretched conditions": cited in Sperber, *Karl Marx*, 72.

12. See Sperber, *Karl Marx*, 100–104.

13. Sperber, *Karl Marx*, 110–11.

14. Proudhon, *Second Memoir* (1841), in Proudhon, *Selected Writings*, 288; Sismondi: as paraphrased by H. W. Spiegel, cited in Ross E. Stewart in "Sismondi's Ethical Critique of Early Capitalism," *Journal of Business Ethics* 3, no. 3 (August 1994): 228.

15. Marx, "Contributions to the Critique of Hegel's *Philosophy of Right*," 64–65.

16. Marx, "Preface," "Estranged Labor," "Private Property and Communism," "Economic and Philosophic Manuscripts of 1844," and "The Meaning of Human Requirements," in the *Marx-Engels Reader*, 67–74, 79, 84, 93, 99.

17. Citations in Sperber, *Karl Marx*, 179–80. For more on this trip, see also H. F. Peters, *Red Jenny: A Life with Karl Marx* (New York: St. Martin's Press, 1987), 64.

18. Marx to Proudhon, from Brussels, May 5, 1846, and Proudhon to Marx, from Lyon, May 17, 1846, in Proudhon, *Selected Writings*, 147–48, 150–51.

19. Marx, *The Poverty of Philosophy* (1847), in the *Marx-Engels Reader*, 218–19.

20. Marx, "Manifesto of the Communist Party," based on but heavily revised from Engels's original draft, in the *Marx-Engels Reader*, 473.

21. Marx, "Manifesto of the Communist Party," 473–74.

22. Marx, "Manifesto of the Communist Party," 475–77, 482, 484.

23. Marx, "Manifesto of the Communist Party," 490.

24. Marx, "Manifesto of the Communist Party," 486–89.

25. Marx, "Manifesto of the Communist Party," 492–99.

26. Marx, "Manifesto of the Communist Party," 500.

27. Cited in Sperber, *Karl Marx*, 236.

Chapter 2: The First International and the Bakunin Prophecy

1. Jonathan Sperber, *Karl Marx: A Nineteenth-Century Life* (New York: Liveright, 2014), 258–59.

2. Sperber, *Karl Marx*, 260, 282–85, and *passim*.

3. Karl Marx, *Eighteenth Brumaire of Louis Bonaparte* (New York: International Publishers, 1987 [1869]), 15–16.

4. Marx, *Eighteenth Brumaire*, 75–76.

5. Marx, *Eighteenth Brumaire*, 123–24.

6. Karl Marx, *Capital: A Critique of Political Economy*, ed. Friedrich Engels, trans. from the 3rd German ed. by Samuel Moore and Edward Aveling, vol. 1 (New York: Modern Library / Random House, 1906 [1867]), Part IV, chapter 15 ("Machinery and Modern Industry"), section A ("Appropriation of Supplementary Labour-Power by Capital. The Employment of Women and Children"), 431 and *passim*, and Part V, chapter 16 ("Absolute and Relative Surplus-Value"), 558 and *passim*.

7. Marx, *Capital*, vol. 1, Part VII, chapter 25 ("The General Law of Capitalist Accumulation"), 678–80.

8. Marx, *Capital*, vol. 1, Part VII, chapter 25, 682, 686–87.

9. Marx, *Capital*, vol. 1, Part VII, chapter 25, 688, 703, 709.

10. Marx, *Capital*, vol. 1, Part VIII, chapter 32 ("Historical Tendency of Capital Accumulation"), 836–37.

11. On Marx and the *New York Tribune*, see Isaiah Berlin, *Karl Marx: His Life and Environment* (New York: Oxford University Press, 1963), 198–99, and Sperber, *Karl Marx*, 294–95 and *passim*.

12. Sperber, *Karl Marx*, 354–57; Berlin, *Karl Marx: His Life and Environment*, 223 and *passim.* "Not one single line": cited in Julius Braunthal, *History of the International*, vol. 1, *1864–1914*, trans. Henry Collins and Kenneth Mitchell (London: Thomas Nelson, 1966), 101.

13. Karl Marx, "Inaugural Address of the Working Men's International Association," c. October 1864, in the *Marx-Engels Reader*, 512–19.

14. Marx, "Inaugural Address," 518–19.

15. Details in H. F. Peters, *Red Jenny: A Life with Karl Marx* (New York: St. Martin's Press, 1987), 138–40.

16. Braunthal, *History of the International*, 1:106–7.

17. Cited in Sperber, *Karl Marx*, 360. For more details, see also Berlin, *Karl Marx: His Life and Environment*, 230–31.

18. The best single-volume history of the conflict is Geoffrey Wawro, *The Franco-Prussian War: The German Conquest of France in 1870–1871* (New York: Cambridge University Press, 2003).

19. Cited in Braunthal, *History of the International*, 1:145. "For my own part": Marx to Paul and Laura Lafargue, July 28, 1870 (in English), no. 200 in Karl Marx, *The Letters of Karl Marx*, trans. and ed. Saul K. Padover (Englewood Cliffs, NJ: Prentice-Hall, 1979), 275–77. "Hideous farce" and "French need a thrashing": cited in Sperber, *Karl Marx*, 374–75.

20. Citations in Berlin, *Karl Marx: His Life and Environment*, 252–54.

21. Braunthal, *History of the International*, 1:152–53. For general background on the Commune, see Furet, *Revolutionary France, 1770–1880* (Oxford: Blackwell, 2007), 500–506. Commune appeals for support: cited by Sperber, *Karl Marx*, 378.

22. Sperber, *Karl Marx*, 379.

23. Marx to Ludwig Kugelmann in Hanover, April 12 and 17, 1871, nos. 204 and 205 in Marx, *Letters of Karl Marx*, 279–81.

24. For details, and the Zola citation, see Furet, *Revolutionary France*, 504–5.

25. Marx to Kugelmann, July 27, 1871, no. 206 in Marx, *Letters of Karl Marx*, 281–82. "Vast conspiracy": cited in Sperber, *Karl Marx*, 380.

26. Marx, *The Civil War in France*, from the address originally read out "to the General Council of the International Working Men's Association on May 30, 1871," *Marx-Engels Reader*, 646–48, 650. "Monstrous gnome" and "lived in concubinage": cited in Sperber, *Karl Marx*, 380.

27. Marx, *Civil War in France*, 635, 638, 651–52.

28. Cited in Sperber, *Karl Marx*, 503. "Red Terror Doctor": cited in Berlin, *Karl Marx: His Life and Environment*, 259. "Monster": Marx to Kugelmann, no. 206, in Marx, *Letters of Karl Marx*, 281–82.

29. Marshall Schatz, introduction to Michael [Mikhail Aleksandrovich] Bakunin, *Statism and Anarchy*, trans. and ed. Marshall Schatz (Cambridge: Cambridge University Press, 1990 [1873]), xvii–xxi and *passim.*

30. Cited in Braunthal, *History of the International*, 1:163. Bakunin: Schatz, introduction to Bakunin, *Statism and Anarchy*, xxvi.

31. Citations in Sperber, *Karl Marx*, 512–13. "Dilettantist experiments and sects": cited in Berlin, *Karl Marx: His Life and Environment*, 262.

32. Cited in Braunthal, *History of the International*, 1:184.

33. Bakunin, *Statism and Anarchy*, 131–37, 177–81. On Marx's use of the term "dictatorship of the proletariat," see Monty Johnston, "The Paris Commune and Marx's Conception of the Dictatorship of the Proletariat," *Massachusetts Review* 12, no. 3 (Summer 1971): 447–62.

34. Cited by Sperber, *Karl Marx*, 516–17.

Chapter 3: The Second International and the Path Not Taken

1. "Gotha programme" (c. 1876), in *The Age of Bismarck: Documents and Interpretations*, ed. Theodore S. Hamerow (New York: Harper and Row, 1973), 230–32.

2. Cited in Jonathan Sperber, *Karl Marx: A Nineteenth-Century Life* (New York: Liveright, 2014), 526. Marx's marginal notes: Karl Marx, "Critique of the Gotha Program," in the *Marx-Engels Reader*, 533–34, 537–38.

3. Dieter Nohlen and Philip Stöver, *Elections in Europe: A Data Handbook* (Baden Baden: Nomos, 2010), 76. On the Bismarck ban and the social insurance laws meant to soften its blow, see Sidney B. Fay, "Bismarck's Welfare State," *Current History* 18, no. 101 (January 1950): 1–7.

4. Cited in the *Marx-Engels Reader*, 665. Marx learns Russian: Isaiah Berlin, *Karl Marx: His Life and Environment*, 273–74. Marx on Churchill, Disraeli, and the Russo-Turkish war: Sperber, *Karl Marx*, 521–24.

5. Karl Marx, *Secret Diplomatic History of the Eighteenth Century*, first published posthumously in 1897. On the tangled history of this manuscript in the Soviet period, and its embrace by Ukrainian scholars, see Thomas M. Prymak, *Ukraine, the Middle East, and the West* (Montreal: McGill-Queen's University Press, 2021), 18–20, 223–24 (footnotes 37 and 38).

6. The Erfurt program of 1891, translated by Thomas Dunlap, is reproduced at the Marxists Internet Archive, www.marxists.org/history/international/social-democracy/1891/erfurt-program.htm.

7. Citations in James Joll, *The Second International, 1889–1914* (Boston: Routledge and Kegan Paul, 1955), 15–16.

8. Joll, *Second International*, 32–35. For the numbers attending: Julius Braunthal, *History of the International*, vol. 1, *1864–1914*, trans. Henry Collins and Kenneth Mitchell (London: Thomas Nelson, 1966), 198.

9. Cited in *History of the International*, 1:196–97.

10. The "Proceedings of the International Working-Men's Congress in Paris (1889)," including the one cited ("Abolition of Standing Armies"), edited by Wilhelm Liebknecht and translated by Graham Seaman, are reproduced online at the Marxists Internet Archive, www.marxists.org/history/international/social-democracy/1889/marxists-congress/index.htm. See also Joll, *Second International*, 40.

11. Details in Joll, *Second International*, 51–53.

12. Cited in Braunthal, *History of the International*, 1:251.

13. Citations in Braunthal, *History of the International*, 1:254–55.

14. Citations in Barbara Tuchman, *The Proud Tower: A Portrait of the World Before the War, 1890–1914* (New York: Ballantine Books, 1996), 430–31.

15. Eduard Bernstein, *Evolutionary Socialism: A Criticism and Affirmation*, trans. Edith C. Harvey (New York: Schocken Books, 1961) (first published in 1899 as *Die*

Voraussetzungen des Sozialismus und die Aufgaben der Sozialdemokratie), xxix, 80–81, 107, 139, 147–48, 151–55.

16. Citations in Braunthal, *History of the International*, 1:261, 271.

17. Rosa Luxemberg, "Social Reform or Revolution," in *Selected Political Writings of Rosa Luxemburg*, ed. Dick Howard (New York: Monthly Review Press, 1971) (first published 1899 in Leipzig), 53.

18. Cited in Tuchman, *Proud Tower*, 431. "The conquest of State power": cited in Braunthal, *History of the International*, 1:272.

19. *Cinquième Congrès socialiste international tenu à Paris du 23 au 27 septembre 1900: Compte rendu analytique officiel* (Paris: Société nouvelle de librairie et d'édition, 1900), 4e Question ("Paix internationale. Militarisme. Suppression des armées permanentes") and 5e Question ("La politique coloniale").

20. Citations in Joll, *Second International*, 102–3.

21. Cited in Tuchman, *Proud Tower*, 436–37. "Participating in governmental power within capitalist society": from the SPD Dresden resolution of 1903, adopted at Amsterdam in 1904, cited in Joll, *Second International*, 101.

22. Cited in Joll, *Second International*, 112. "80 percent": cited in Tuchman, *Proud Tower*, 417–18.

23. For details, see Sean McMeekin, *The Russian Revolution: A New History* (New York: Basic Books, 2017), 34–42 and *passim*.

24. Cited in Joll, *Second International*, 135. Luxemburg: from "Mass Strike, Party, and Trade Unions" (September 1906), in Luxemburg, *Selected Political Writings*, 227.

25. Cited in Joll, *Second International*, 136. "Do not fool yourselves" / "It is not true": cited in Tuchman, *Proud Tower*, 448–49.

26. Cited in Joll, *Second International*, 141; Lenin, *What Is to Be Done?*, trans. Joe Finberg and George Hanna (London: Penguin, 1962) (originally published as *Chto delat?*, 1902); Luxemburg, "Organizational Questions of Social Democracy," in Luxemburg, *Selected Political Writings*, 283–306 (originally published in 1904 in *Neue Zeit*).

27. On these and other counterfactuals relating to the outbreak of war in 1914, see the epilogue in Sean McMeekin, *July 1914: Countdown to War* (New York: Basic Books, 2013).

28. On the might-have-beens of French politics in 1914, see McMeekin, *July 1914*, 62–68, 385.

Chapter 4: Turning the Armies Red

1. Cited in R. Craig Nation, *War on War: Lenin, the Zimmerwald Left, and the Origins of Communist Internationalism* (Durham, NC: Duke University Press, 1989), 22. For other details, see James Joll, *The Second International, 1889–1914* (Boston: Routledge and Kegan Paul, 1955), 177–81.

2. Cited in J. P. Nettl, *Rosa Luxemburg* (New York: Schocken Books, 1969 [1966]), 371n3. On the "Fourth of August betrayal," see Julius Braunthal, *The History of the International*, vol. 2, *1914–1943*, trans. John Clark (New York: Praeger, 1967), 1–8.

3. Willi Münzenberg, *Die dritte Front* (Berlin: NDV, 1930), 153. Britain: Joll, *Second International*, 183.

4. Nettl, *Rosa Luxemburg*, 371–74. For details on Liebknecht, see Braunthal, *History of the International*, 2:14, and Joll, *Second International*, 190.

5. Nation, *War on War*, 67–71. For the text of the youth congress's antiwar resolution, see Münzenberg, *Dritte Front*, 40–41.

6. Cited in Nation, *War on War*, 69.

7. Report of "K.k. Ministerium des Innern: Staatspolizeiliches Bureau," August 16, 1914, in RGASPI, fond 4, opis' 3, del' 48, list' 1, 2, 8, 9. "Even if the authorities released the spy": cited in Michael Pearson, *Lenin's Mistress: The Life of Inessa Armand* (New York: Random House, 2001), 131.

8. Cited in Nation, *War on War*, 37.

9. On Lenin's stage-managing, see Pearson, *Lenin's Mistress*, 134.

10. Citations in Nation, *War on War*, 87–90. On Liebknecht's antiwar activities and imprisonment, see also Nettl, *Rosa Luxemburg*, 377, 399–400.

11. Citations in Braunthal, *History of the International*, 2:47–48.

12. V. I. Lenin, *Socialism and War: The Attitude of the R.S.D.L.P. Towards the War*, written circa July–August 1915, first published in fall 1915 by the *Sotsial-Demokrat* Editorial Board in Geneva, reproduced in V. I. Lenin, *Collected Works*, vol. 21, *August 1914–December 1915*, trans. and ed. Julius Katzer (Moscow: Progress Publishers, 1980), 299.

13. Lenin, *Socialism and War*, 305.

14. Lenin, *Socialism and War*, 315.

15. Lenin, *Socialism and War*, 314, 316. "Transformation of the imperialist war into a civil war": cited in Nation, *War on War*, 81.

16. As translated by Nation in *War on War*, 1.

17. Sean McMeekin, *The Red Millionaire: A Political Biography of Willi Münzenberg, Moscow's Propaganda Tsar in the West* (New Haven, CT: Yale University Press, 2003), 26–27, 38. Lenin on Tripadvisor: www.tripadvisor.com/Attraction_Review-g188113 -d10354630-Reviews-Lenin_Apartment_Zurich-Zurich.html.

18. Cited in McMeekin, *Red Millionaire*, 38–39, 42.

19. Citations in Nation, *War on War*, 141–43. "Lay down your weapons": cited in Richard Pipes, *The Russian Revolution* (New York: Knopf, 1990), 383.

20. V. I. Lenin, *Imperialism, the Highest Stage of Capitalism* (New York: International Publishers, 1939 [1916]), 15, 99, 107. "Vain, hypocritical," and "epoch of wars": cited in Nation, *War on War*, 147. J. A. Hobson, *Imperialism: A Study* (New York: James Pott and Company, 1902), available at Online Library of Liberty, Liberty Fund Network, https://oll.libertyfund.org/title/hobson-imperialism-a-study.

21. V. I. Lenin, "Military Programme of Proletarian Revolution" (c. October 1916), in V. I. Lenin, *Collected Works*, vol. 23, *August 1916–March 1917*, trans. M. S. Levin, Joe Fineberg et al., ed. M. S. Levin (Moscow: Progress Publishers, 1964), 77–78.

22. Lenin, "Military Programme," 78–79.

23. "Military Programme," 79–81, 83.

24. "Military Programme," 82.

25. Pipes, *Russian Revolution*, 157–59. On the German Foreign Office subsidies for the January 1916 (but not January 1917) Bloody Sunday marches, see Minister in Copenhagen to the Chancellor, January 23, 1916, reproduced in Z. A. B. Zeman, ed.,

Germany and the Revolution in Russia, 1915–1918: Documents from the Archives of the German Foreign Ministry (London: Oxford University Press, 1958), 14–16, and Z. A. B. Zeman and W. B. Scharlau, *The Merchant of Revolution: The Life of Alexander Israel Helphand (Parvus), 1867–1924* (London: Oxford University Press, 1965), 187. "We of the older generation": V. I. Lenin, "Lecture on the 1905 Revolution," January 9 (22), 1917, in Lenin, *Collected Works*, 23:259.

26. See George Katkov, *Russia 1917: The February Revolution* (New York: Harper and Row, 1967), 143–44.

27. "Svodka Svedenii o sostoyanii i nastroenii nashei deistvuyushchei armii . . . prosmotrennoi za vremya s' 15 dekabrya 1916 g. po 1 yanvarya 1917 goda," in RGVIA, fond 2031, opis' 1, del' 1181, list' 20–22 (and backs), 23. "Full of fight": cited in Norman Stone, *The Eastern Front, 1914–1917* (London: Penguin, 1998 [1975]), 282. German soldiers begging for food and "Now our roles have reversed": "Doklad' o nastroenii voisk' 5-i armii po pis'mam za fevral' mesyats' 1917 g.," Brusilov Offensive, area conquered, and "Electrifying effect on Russian morale": citations in McMeekin, *Russian Revolution*, 75. On plans for the amphibious descent on Constantinople, see Sean McMeekin, *Ottoman Endgame: War, Revolution, and the Making of the Modern Middle East, 1908–1923* (New York: Penguin Press, 2015), chapter 14 ("Russia's Moment").

Chapter 5: The Bolsheviks Take Power

1. V. Zenzinov, "Fevral'skie Dni," entries for February 24 and 25 (March 9 and 10), 1917, and Okhrana report dated February 26 (March 11), 1917, in *The Russian Provisional Government 1917*, vol. 1, ed. Robert Paul Browder and Alexander Kerensky (Stanford, CA: Stanford University Press, 1961 [1927]), 27, 32–33, 37.

2. Diary entries of Frank Golder, an American historian in Petrograd during the Bolshevik revolution, for March 12 (February 27) and March 13 (February 28), 1917, in the Frank Golder collection, Hoover Institution Archives, box 2, folder 2.

3. Sean McMeekin, *The Russian Revolution: A New History* (New York: Basic Books, 2017), 118 and *passim*.

4. Cited in Richard Pipes, *The Russian Revolution* (New York: Knopf, 1990), 305. For the draft and final version of Order No. 1, see George Katkov, *Russia 1917: The February Revolution* (New York: Harper and Row, 1967), 370–73, and Allan K. Wildman, *The End of the Russian Imperial Army*, vol. 1, *The Old Army and the Soldiers' Revolt* (Princeton, NJ: Princeton University Press, 1980), 187–88. On Guchkov outmuscling Rodzianko over the army loyalty oaths, see McMeekin, *Russian Revolution*, chapter 7 ("Army in the Balance: March").

5. On Bonch-Bruevich and his role in publicizing Order No. 1, and in the launching of *Izvestiya* more broadly, see Katkov, *Russia 1917*, 369–73, and Vladimir Bonch-Bruevich, *Na boevyikh postakh fevral'skoi i oktyabr'skoi revoliutsii* (Moscow: Federatsiya, 1931), 12–13. On the Brusilov Offensive and its impact on Austria-Hungary, see Graydon Tunstall, "Austria-Hungary and the Brusilov Offensive of 1916," in *Historian* 70, no. 1 (Spring 2008): 30–53.

6. The final passage terms, confirmed by the German consul in Bern on April 5, 1917, are reproduced in Z. A. B. Zeman, ed., *Germany and the Revolution in Russia, 1915–1918. Documents from the Archives of the German Foreign Ministry* (London:

Oxford University Press, 1958), 38–39. For more on the negotiations and the appropriation of funds, see Z. A. B. Zeman and W. B. Scharlau, *The Merchant of Revolution: The Life of Alexander Israel Helphand (Parvus), 1867–1924* (London: Oxford University Press, 1965), 208 and *passim*. The original publication of German sources, on which these and other accounts are based, is Werner Hahlweg, *Lenins Rückkehr nach Russland: Die deutsche Akten* (London: Brill, 1957).

7. Memorandum by Ow-Wachendorf, Berlin, April 11, 1917, in Zeman, *Germany and the Revolution in Russia*, 44–45. Ow-Wachendorf insisted that the German hotel rooms in Sassnitz in which Lenin and the Russians had stayed were "locked" from the outside, but this is just as implausible as the "sealed train" legend. On Parvus's man joining the Russians, see Bussche to Bern, April 5 and 7, 1917, reproduced in Zeman, *Germany and the Revolution in Russia*, 37–38, 40. On the two German officers reporting to Ludendorff, see citations in Michael Pearson, *The Sealed Train: Journey to Revolution. Lenin, 1917* (New York: Putnam, 1975), 81–82.

8. Kamenev: cited in James Bunyan and H. H. Fisher, eds., *The Bolshevik Revolution, 1917–1918: Documents and Materials* (Stanford, CA: Stanford University Press, 1934), 7. Stalin: cited in Leonard Shapiro, *The Russian Revolutions of 1917: The Origins of Modern Communism* (New York: Basic Books, 1984), 59.

9. Grünau passing on Steinwachs from Stockholm, April 17, 1917, received at Spa, Belgium (German military headquarters), on April 21, 1917, reproduced in Zeman, *Germany and the Revolution in Russia*, 272–73. Golder: diary entry for April 18, 1917, in the Frank Golder collection, Hoover Institution Archives, box 2, folder 2.

10. On the Bolshevik purchase of the printing press and the print runs, see "Materialyi predvaritel'nogo sledstviya o vooruzhenom vyistuplenii v Petrograde 3 (16-I-1) (18) iyula 1917 g. tom 7. 24 July (5 Aug)–12/25 Aug 1917," in RGASPI, fond 4, opis' 3, del' 43. For the print runs of the other versions of *Pravda*, see Pipes, *Russian Revolution*, 410.

11. Evgeniya Ivanovna Shelyakhovskaya deposition, in "Materialyi predvaritel'nogo sledstviya o vooruzhennom vyistuplenii v Petrograde 3(16)–5(18) iyulya 1917 goda," in RGASPI, fond 4, opis' 3, del' 41, list' 112–13 (and back of 112).

12. Citations in Allan K. Wildman, *The End of the Russian Imperial Army*, vol. 2, *The Road to Soviet Power and Peace* (Princeton, NJ: Princeton University Press, 1987), 89–92. For more on the offensive, see also Robert S. Feldman, "Russian General Staff and the June 1917 Offensive," in *Soviet Studies* 19, no. 4 (April 1968): 539.

13. Baluev to Brusilov from Vorobin, June 23 (July 6), 1917, in RGVIA, fond 2067, opis' 1, del' 396, list' 13 and back. "Down with the War": cited in Wildman, *End of the Russian Imperial Army*, 2:98–99.

14. Afanasii Efimovich Zamyikin and I. P. Slesarenok depositions, July 15 (28), 1917, in RGASPI, fond 4, opis' 3, del' 41, list' 34, 42.

15. Zamyikin and Slesarenok depositions. For more details on the abortive July 4 (17) putsch attempt, see also N. N. Sukhanov, *Russian Revolution 1917: A Personal Record*, trans. Joel Carmichael (New York: Oxford University Press, 1955), 444–49 and *passim*.

16. Details in B. V. Nikitin, *The Fatal Years: Fresh Revelations on a Chapter of Underground History* (Westport, CT: Hyperion Press, 1977), 160–72 and *passim*. For the charges against the Bolsheviks, see excerpt from *Zhivoe Slovo* ("The Charges Against the Bolsheviks") in Kerensky and Browder, eds., *Russian Provisional Government*, vol. 3,

ed. Robert Paul Browder and Alexander Kerensky (Stanford, CA: Stanford University Press, 1961 [1927]), 1364–65.

17. Cited in Wildman, *End of the Russian Imperial Army*, 2:293. On the Kornilov affair, see McMeekin, *Russian Revolution*, 185–91.

18. Citations in Wildman, *End of the Russian Imperial Army*, 2:291–92.

19. Cited in Pipes, *Russian Revolution*, 480.

20. See Orlando Figes, "The Harmless Drunk," in *Historically Inevitable? Turning Points of the Russian Revolution*, ed. Tony Brenton (London: Profile Books, 2016), 123.

21. See "Order of the Commander of the Petrograd Military District" and "Petrograd Proclaimed in a State of Insurrection," October 24 (November 6), 1917, both reproduced in Bunyan and Fisher, *Bolshevik Revolution*, 85–91.

22. "Progress of the Insurrection," Levitsky to General Dukhonin by direct wire, on the morning of October 25 (November 7), 1917, and "The Taking of the Winter Palace," reproduced in Bunyan and Fisher, *Bolshevik Revolution*, 98–99, 107, 116–17. See also Mel'gunov, *Kak bol'sheviki zakhvatili vlast': Oktiabr'skii perevorot 1917 goda* (Paris: La Renaissance, 1953), 106–7.

23. "Transfer of Authority to the Soviets," "Lenin's Speech on the War Question," "Lenin's Speech on the Land Decree," "The Land Decree," and "The Soviet of People's Commissars (Sovnarkom)," in Bunyan and Fisher, *Bolshevik Revolution*, 124–33. "Dustbin of history": cited in Figes, "Harmless Drunk," 138.

24. Cited in Wildman, *End of the Russian Imperial Army*, 2:401. Wildman is paraphrasing here the eyewitness accounts of Krylenko's *supporters*, as there were no surviving witnesses from Dukhonin's side to tell the tale. For the back-and-forth, see "Order to Dukhonin to Open Armistice Negotiations," radiogram from Lenin, Trotsky; Krylenko to Stavka, November 8 (21), 1917; "Dukhonin Declines," conversation by direct wire, 2:00 a.m. on November 9 (22), 1917; "Lenin Urges the Soldiers to Negotiate with the Enemy," published in *Izvestiya*, November 9 (22), 1917, all in Bunyan and Fisher, *Bolshevik Revolution*, 233–36.

25. Krylenko directive no. 19018, December 8 (21), 1917; Novitskii telegram no. 6544, November 27 (December 10), 1917, and Lukirskii telegram no. 6033, November 28 (December 11), 1917, and accompanying documentation, in GARF, fond P375, opis' 1, del' 8, list' 1, 3, 8 (and back), 9 (and back). On the flight of Kornilov et al. to Rostov-on-Don, see German intelligence reports, November 27 (December 10), 1917, and December 4 (17), 1917; in BA / MA, RM 5 / 2596.

26. "Prikaz' vsem' voiskam' Voenno-Revolyutsionnago Komiteta," November 2, 1917, November 3 and 5, 1917, in GARF, fond P1, opis' 1, del' 3, list' 117, 135, 161.

Chapter 6: Communism in Power

1. "The October Revolution in Saratov," reproduced from the memoirs of Mikhail Vasiliev-Iuzhin, in *Russia in War and Revolution, 1914–1922: A Documentary History*, ed. Jonathan Daly and Leonid Trofimov (Indianapolis: Hackett, 2009), 117–20.

2. Commissar F. G. Luparev, "On Establishing Bolshevik Rule in Viatka Province, December 1917," in Daly and Trofimov, *Russia in War and Revolution*, 120–24.

3. "Reasons for the Strike," *Delo Naroda*, November 8 (21), 1917; "Strike of the State Employees of Petrograd," *Volia Naroda*, October 28 (November 10, 1917); "The Spread

of the Strike of State Employees," *Delo Naroda*, October 28 (November 10), 1917; "Vikzhel's Ultimatum to End the Civil War," October 29 (November 11), 1917, all in *The Bolshevik Revolution, 1917–1918: Documents and Materials*, ed. James Bunyan and H. H. Fisher (Stanford, CA: Stanford University Press, 1934), 155, 225–27.

4. V. I. Lenin, "Will the Bolsheviks Retain State Power?" (1917), in Bunyan and Fisher, *Bolshevik Revolution*, 318–19. Marx: from the *Manifesto of the Communist Party*, in the *Marx-Engels Reader*, 490.

5. Richard Pipes, *The Russian Revolution* (New York: Knopf, 1990), 528.

6. F. O. Lindley, "Report on Recent Events in Russia," November 12 (25), 1917, in PRO, FO 3000 / 3743. See also V. Obolensky-Osinsky, "How We Got Control of the State Bank," in Bunyan and Fisher, *Bolshevik Revolution*, 319. The 5 million ruble deal is mentioned in a German intelligence report, dated November 30, 1917, in BA / MA, RM 5 / 2596.

7. Cited by Nicolas Werth, "The Iron Fist of the Dictatorship of the Proletariat," in *The Black Book of Communism: Crimes, Terror, Repression*, by Stéphane Courtois, Nicolas Werth, Jean-Louis Panné, Andrzej Paczkowski, Karel Bartosek, and Jean-Louis Margolin, trans. Jonathan Murphy and Mark Kramer, consulting ed. Mark Kramer (Cambridge, MA: Harvard University Press, 1999), 103. For more on the bank strike, see also "The bank position," enclosure in Sir George Buchanan's dispatch of January 6, 1918, in PRO, FO 371 / 3294.

8. "Proekt dekreta o provedenii v zhizn' nationalizatsii bankov i o neobkhodimykh v sviazi s etim' merakh'," December 14 (27), 1917, and Undated Doklad, circa late December 1917, "Upravliaiushchemu Komissariatom byvsh: Chastnykh bankov tov. Sokolnikovu," all in RGASPI, fond 670, opis' 1, del' 35, list' 5–8 (and backs), 19–21, 54.

9. "Tablitsa tsennykh bumag' prinadlezhavshikh byvshimi chastnimi Bankami v Moskve na 15/31 dekabria 1917 goda / po nominal'noi stoimosti," in RGASPI, fond 670, opis' 1, del' 35, list' 35. Addresses and phone numbers: "Naimenovanie Bankov: Adres'. NoNo Telefonov . . . ," circa late December 1917, in RGASPI, fond 670, opis' 1, del' 35, list' 5–8 (and backs).

10. Sokolnikov, telegram sent from Petrograd to "Moskva, Ekaterinburg', Arkhangel'sk . . ." (etc.), December 8 (21), 1917, in RGASPI, 670-1-15, 29. "All holders": "Search of Safe Deposit Boxes: Decree of the Central Executive Committee, December 27, 1917," in Bunyan and Fisher, *Bolshevik Revolution*, 324.

11. "The bank position" and "Opening of safes at banks," enclosures in Sir George Buchanan's dispatches of January 5–6, 1918, in PRO, FO 371 / 3294; Report from the British Consulate General, Moscow, January 28, 1918, in PRO, FO 368 / 1965.

12. M. J. Larsons, *Im Sowjet-Labyrinth: Episoden und Silhouetten* (Berlin: Transmare Verlag, 1931), 64–65.

13. "Svedeniia o kolichestve osvobozhdennykh, vzlomanykh i podlezhashchikh vzlomu seifov vo vsekh stal'nykh kladovykh . . . g. Moskvy," in RGAE, 7733-1-248, 6 (and back), 7. Take for first six months of 1918: reported in the July 27, 1918, *Izvestiya*, in Bunyan and Fisher, *Bolshevik Revolution*, 324.

14. Figures in Tony Brenton, "The Short Life and Early Death of Russian Democracy," in *Historically Inevitable? Turning Points of the Russian Revolution*, ed. Tony Brenton (London: Profile Books, 2016), 155–56.

15. "Bolshevik Policies as to the Assembly," transcript of the "Meeting of the Bolshevik Central Committee, December 12 (25), 1917," reproduced from pro-Bolshevik press accounts in *Delo Naroda* and *Izvestiya*, in Bunyan and Fisher, *Bolshevik Revolution*, 361–62.

16. Details in Sean McMeekin, *History's Greatest Heist: The Looting of Russia by the Bolsheviks* (New Haven, CT: Yale University Press, 2008), 31–32; Pipes, *Russian Revolution*, 520, 552–55. On the dissolution of the Constituent Assembly, see German military intelligence reports dated January 5 (18) and 6 (19), 1918, in BA / MA, RM 5 / 4065. On the bank strike and how it ended, see Max Laserson (M. J. Larsons), *Expert in the Service of the Soviet*, trans. Angelo S. Rappoport (London: Ernst Benn, 1929), 19.

17. Winfried Baumgart, *Deutsche Ostpolitik 1918: Von Brest-Litowsk bis zum Ende des Ersten Weltkrieges* (Vienna: Oldenbourg, 1966), 224 and n50; Pipes, *Russian Revolution*, 641–42. "Down with the Traitor" and Brest-Litovsk: John Wheeler-Bennett, *Brest-Litovsk: The Forgotten Peace, March 1918* (New York: St. Martin's Press, 1956), 260, 279, 403–8.

18. Trotsky, "Death for Deserters," August 14, 1918, reproduced in *Intervention, Communism, and Civil War in Russia, April–December 1918: Documents and Materials*, ed. James Bunyan (Baltimore: Johns Hopkins University Press, 1936), 301. On Lenin's approach to the Red Army, see also Jacob W. Kipp, "Lenin and Clausewitz: The Militarization of Marxism, 1914–21," *Military Affairs* 49, no. 4 (October 1985): 188.

19. Sean McMeekin, *The Russian Revolution: A New History* (New York: Basic Books, 2017), 256–58.

20. "Yakov Yurovsky's Note on the execution of the imperial family," in *The Fall of the Romanovs: Political Dreams and Personal Struggles in a Time of Revolution*, by Mark D. Steinberg and Vladimir M. Khrustalëv (New Haven, CT: Yale University Press, 1995), 353–54.

21. "Seizure of the Gold Reserve at Kazan," report of Lebedev to the Samara government, and Trotsky, "Death for Deserters," August 14, 1918, both in Bunyan, *Intervention, Communism, and Civil War in Russia*, 292, 301.

22. "Red Terror Legalized," Sovnarkom resolution of September 5, 1918; "Red Terror in the Provinces," compilation of press reports in *Izvestiya*, September 10–29, 1918; and "Trotsky's Announcement," all in Bunyan, *Intervention, Communism, and Civil War in Russia*, 237–39, 242–43, 301.

23. See Richard Pipes, *Russia Under the Bolshevik Regime* (New York: Vintage, 1994), 51–53. On German plans to occupy Petrograd: Baumgart, *Deutsche Ostpolitik*, 116–17; "Treaty of Brest-Litovsk," Article 5, reproduced in Wheeler-Bennett, *Brest-Litovsk*, 406. On Bolshevik looting of German embassy bags in Moscow and Petrograd, see Franz Rauch's April 12, 1919, report to the German Foreign Office in Berlin, in DBB, R 901 / 82082, 22–25.

24. Pipes, *Russia Under the Bolshevik Regime*, 59–60; Stephen Kotkin, *Stalin*, vol. 1, *Paradoxes of Power, 1878–1928* (New York: Penguin, 2014), 297.

25. Details and citations in McMeekin, *Russian Revolution*, chapter 19 ("Red on White").

26. On factory nationalizations, closings, and layoffs in early 1918, see Pipes, *Russian Revolution*, 558; Silvana Malle, *The Economic Organization of War Communism,*

1918–1921 (Cambridge: Cambridge University Press, 1985), 50, 161. The decree on "Annulment of Russian State Loans," February 10, 1918, is reproduced in Bunyan and Fisher, *Bolshevik Revolution*, 602.

27. "The Functions of the Supreme Council of the National Economy," Sovnarkom decree of August 8, 1918, in Bunyan, *Intervention, Communism, and Civil War in Russia*, 405–6.

28. On VSNKh employment figures: Pipes, *Russian Revolution*, 691.

29. Gold used only for building toilets: cited in Pipes, *Russia Under the Bolshevik Regime*, 393–94. "Abolition of money payments": "Preparing for the Abolition of Money, January 1921," in Daly and Trofimov, *Russia in War and Revolution*, 324–25. For industrial production indices, see Pipes, *Russian Revolution*, 696.

30. Letter from Robert E. Olds, American Red Cross commissioner to Europe, to Dr. Livingston Farrand, April 15, 1920, in RSU, HP 494.

31. Letter from Olds to Farrand, April 15, 1920.

32. H. H. Fisher, *The Famine in Soviet Russia, 1919–1923: The Operations of the American Relief Administration* (New York: Macmillan, 1927), 51. "Crowds of thousands of starving peasants": cited in Nicolas Werth, "From Tambov to the Great Famine," in Courtois et al., eds., *Black Book of Communism*, 111. Antonov-Ovseenko: cited in Orlando Figes, *A People's Tragedy: The Russian Revolution, 1891–1924* (New York: Penguin, 1998), 754. Casualty figure from peasant wars: cited in Pipes, *Russia Under the Bolshevik Regime*, 373.

33. Cited in Fisher, *Famine in Soviet Russia*, 545.

34. Citations in Stephen Velychenko, *Life and Death in Revolutionary Ukraine: Living Conditions, Violence, and Demographic Catastrophe, 1917–1923* (Montreal: McGill-Queen's University Press, 2021), 7, 61, 91.

35. The decrees on universal labor duty ("The Unemployed Forbidden to Refuse Work," September 3, 1918; "Abolition of Workers' Control," October 18, 1918; "Relations Between Trade Unions and the Union of State Employees," October 18, 1918; and "Universal Labor Duty," Decree of Sovnarkom, October 31, 1918) are reproduced in Bunyan, *Intervention, Communism, and Civil War in Russia*, 407–8, 413, 417–19. Soviet labor code and days off: "Soviet Russia's Code of Labor Laws, 1919" and "Proletarian Holidays," March 1920, in Daly and Trofimov, *Russia in War and Revolution*, 317–19. Trotsky: cited in Pipes, *Russian Revolution*, 703.

36. "Communist Saturdays," c. March 1920, in Daly and Trofimov, *Russia in War and Revolution*, 316.

37. "Soviet Domestic Relations Law" and "The Legalization of Abortion," November 1920, in Daly and Trofimov, *Russia in War and Revolution*, 320–22.

38. "Eradication of Illiteracy in Cheropovets," c. December 1919 (with annotated statistics on the results), reproduced in Daly and Trofimov, *Russia in War and Revolution*, 322–24.

39. Citations in Pipes, *Russia Under the Bolshevik Regime*, 289–90, 293–94.

Chapter 7: The Communist International

1. "Manifesto of the Communist International to the Proletariat of the Entire World," in *The Communist International, 1919–1943: Documents*, vol. 1, *1919–1922*,

ed. Jane Degras (London: Oxford University Press, 1956), 38–47. For more details on the founding congress, see Julius Braunthal, *The History of the International*, vol. 2, *1914–1943*, trans. John Clark (New York: Praeger, 1967), 162 and *passim*, and Angelica Balabanoff, *Impressions of Lenin,* trans. Isotta Cesari (Ann Arbor: University of Michigan Press, 1964), 69 and *passim*.

2. Rosa Luxemburg, "Was Will der Spartakusbund?," first published in *Rote Fahne*, December 14, 1918, reproduced as "The German Spartacists: Their Aims and Objects," in *International Communism in the Era of Lenin*, ed. Helmut Gruber (Greenwich, CT: Fawcett, 1967), 123–31. On the principal events of the Spartacist uprising in Berlin and elsewhere in Germany, see Eric Waldman, *The Spartacist Uprising of 1919 and the Crisis of the German Socialist Movement* (Milwaukee: Marquette University Press, 1958), 161–97.

3. For a critical overview of casualty estimates in Munich, see the recent study by Eliza Ablovatski, *Revolution and Political Violence in Central Europe: The Deluge of 1919* (New York: Cambridge University Press, 2021), 66–71.

4. See Ablovatski, *Revolution and Political Violence in Central Europe*, 70.

5. Entry for "Béla Kun" in "Biographical Notes," in Gruber, *International Communism in the Era of Lenin*, 300–301.

6. Ablovatski, *Revolution and Political Violence in Central Europe*, 54–55. Only thirty minutes: see Franz Borkenau, *World Communism: A History of the Communist International* (Ann Arbor: University of Michigan Press, 1962), 118.

7. Borkenau, *World Communism*, 118–24, and, for Kun's arguments in the Council of People's Commissars, Braunthal, *History of the International*, 2:138.

8. Citations in Braunthal, *History of the International*.

9. Citations in Stéphane Courtois and Jean-Louis Panné, "The Comintern in Action," in *The Black Book of Communism*, by Stéphane Courtois, Nicolas Werth, Jean-Louis Panné, Andrzej Paczkowski, Karel Bartosek, and Jean-Louis Margolin, trans. Jonathan Murphy and Mark Kramer, consulting ed. Mark Kramer (Cambridge, MA: Harvard University Press, 1999), 273. For more details, see also Gruber, *International Communism in the Era of Lenin*, 124–25.

10. For a comparison of the Red Terror and the White Terror in Hungary, see Ablovatski, *Revolution and Political Violence in Central Europe*, 104–19. For thirty out of forty-eight commissars being Jewish, see 194n77, and for eighteen out of twenty-six commissars being Jewish, Richard Pipes, *Russia Under the Bolshevik Regime* (New York: Vintage, 1994), 171.

11. Cited in Borkenau, *World Communism*, 131–32.

12. Lukács, "Critical Observations on Rosa Luxemburg's 'Critique of the Russian Revolution,'" January 1922, in *History and Class Consciousness: Studies in Marxist Dialectics*, trans. Rodney Livingston (London: Merlin Press, 1968). "Revolutionary destruction": cited in Michael Löwy, *Georg Lukács from Romanticism to Bolshevism*, trans. Patrick Caniller (London: NLB, 1979), 93.

13. Cited in Branko Lazitch and Milorad M. Drachkovitch, "The Communist International," in *The Revolutionary Internationals, 1864–1943*, ed. Milorad M. Drachkovitch (Stanford, CA: Stanford University Press, 1966), 165.

14. Citation and details in Richard Ullman, *Anglo-Soviet Relations, 1917–1921*, vol. 3, *The Anglo-Soviet Accord* (Princeton, NJ: Princeton University Press, 1972), 51, 54.

15. V. I. Lenin, *"Left-Wing" Communism: An Infantile Disorder*, in V. I. Lenin, *Collected Works*, vol. 31, *April–December 1920*, trans. and ed. Julius Katzer (Moscow: Progress Publishers, 1966), 82, 85.

16. Evan Mawdsley, *The Russian Civil War* (Winchester, MA: Allen and Unwin, 1987), 250–53. "Corpse of White Poland": cited in Pipes, *Russia Under the Bolshevik Regime*, 180.

17. "Conditions of Admission into the Communist International," c. July 1920, in Gruber, *International Communism in the Era of Lenin*, 288, 290. Lenin "momentarily halted": citation in Braunthal, *History of the International*, 2:185–86 and, for context, n3.

18. "Conditions of Admission to the Communist International," 287–92.

19. Cited in Sean McMeekin, *The Red Millionaire: A Political Biography of Willi Münzenberg, Moscow's Propaganda Tsar in the West* (New Haven, CT: Yale University Press, 2003), 93–94.

20. Cited in Willi Münzenberg, *Die dritte Front* (Berlin, NDV, 1930), 321. Lenin and Zinoviev: cited in Braunthal, *History of the International*, 2:170.

21. Max Barthel, *Kein Bedarf an Weltgeschichte* (Wiesbaden: Limes Verlag, 1950), 103–12. On Makhno, see also Vladimir Brovkin, *Behind the Front Lines of the Russian Civil War: Political Parties and Social Movements in Russia, 1918–1922* (Princeton, NJ: Princeton University Press, 1994), 106–12, and Orlando Figes, *A People's Tragedy: The Russian Revolution, 1891–1924* (New York: Penguin, 1998), 662.

22. On the burning in effigy, see Ullman, *Anglo-Soviet Relations*, 3:318. "Holy war": cited in Stephen Kotkin, *Stalin*, vol. 1, *Paradoxes of Power, 1878–1928* (New York: Penguin, 2014), 369.

23. Mawdsley, *Russian Civil War*, 253–57.

24. On the Polish settlement and the evacuation of the Crimea, see, in particular, Ullman, *Anglo-Soviet Relations*, 3:310–12 and 311n.

25. Citations in Braunthal, *History of the International*, 2:201–6.

26. Braunthal, *History of the International*, 2:223–24, and Kevin McDermott and Jeremy Agnew, *The Comintern: A History of International Communism from Lenin to Stalin* (New York: St. Martin's Press, 1997), 19.

27. Cited in Braunthal, *History of the International*, 2:195.

28. Citations in Braunthal, *History of the International*, 207–8.

29. Figures in McDermott and Agnew, *Comintern*, 21–22. Delegates leaving the Second Congress with diamonds: Babette Gross, *Willi Münzenberg: A Political Biography* (East Lansing: Michigan State University Press, 1974), 99.

30. Levi, *Our Course Against Putschism* (1921), in Gruber, *International Communism in the Era of Lenin*, 334. Exploding toilet: Borkenau, *World Communism*, 217–18.

31. Braunthal, *History of the International*, 2:208–10.

32. Citations in Lazitch and Drachkovitch, "The Communist International," 168–69, 172. On "to the masses," see also McDermott and Agnew, *Comintern*, 27–29.

33. Cited in Werner T. Angress, *Stillborn Revolution: The Communist Bid for Power in Germany, 1921–1923* (Princeton, NJ: Princeton University Press, 1963), 428 and *passim*.

34. Citations in Lazitch and Drachkovitch, "The Communist International," 179–80.

35. McDermott and Agnew, *Comintern*, 173–79.

36. On the Brussels Congress and the "League Against Imperialism," see McMeekin, *Red Millionaire*, chapter 11 ("Pre-Empting the Peace"). Münzenberg appropriated 8,260 Reichsmarks to cover costs for Chiang Kai-shek, who never showed up. See IAH budget report for January 1, 1926, to September 30, 1927, in RGASPI, fond 538, opis' 2, del' 41, list' 9.

37. Cited in Drachkovitch and Lazitch, "The Communist International," 105.

Chapter 8: Stalin Resumes the Communist Offensive

1. Citations in Nicolas Werth, "From Tambov to the Great Famine," in *The Black Book of Communism: Crimes, Terror, Repression*, by Stéphane Courtois, Nicolas Werth, Jean-Louis Panné, Andrzej Paczkowski, Karel Bartosek, and Jean-Louis Margolin, trans. Jonathan Murphy and Mark Kramer, consulting ed. Mark Kramer (Cambridge, MA: Harvard University Press, 1999), 112.

2. Cited in Richard Pipes, *Russia Under the Bolshevik Regime* (New York: Vintage, 1994), 383–86.

3. V. I. Lenin, "The New Economic Policy and the Tasks of the Political Education Departments," in V. I. Lenin, *Collected Works*, vol. 33, *August 1921–March 1923*, trans. and ed. David Skvirsky and George Hanna (Moscow: Progress Publishers, 1973), 64. On the implementation of NEP, see Alan Ball, *Russia's Last Capitalists: The Nepmen* (Berkeley: University of California Press, 1987), 18–21, and Pipes, *Russia Under the Bolshevik Regime*, 394. On the reintroduction of hard currency and Bolshevik finances, see Sean McMeekin, *History's Greatest Heist: The Looting of Russia by the Bolsheviks* (New Haven, CT: Yale University Press, 2008), 211–12.

4. V. I. Lenin, "The New Economic Policy and the Tasks of the Political Education Departments," in Lenin, *Collected Works*, 33:71–72. "One of the most underdeveloped countries," "how to carry on trade," "social swine," and "ceased to exist as a proletariat": citations in Ball, *Russia's Last Capitalists*, 15, 18–19. "Childish, completely childish," and "cannot run an economy": V. I. Lenin, "Political Report of the Central Committee of the RCP (B) to the Eleventh Congress of the RCP (B)," in Lenin, *Collected Works*, 33:273, 290. "Should all be hanged": cited in Victor Sebestyen, *Lenin: The Man, the Dictator, and the Master of Terror* (New York: Pantheon, 2017), 485.

5. Citations in Ball, *Russia's Last Capitalists*, 15, 17.

6. Citations in Ball, *Russia's Last Capitalists*, 26–27, 176–77, n26–27.

7. Cited in Sean McMeekin, *The Red Millionaire: A Political Biography of Willi Münzenberg, Moscow's Propaganda Tsar in the West* (New Haven, CT: Yale University Press, 2003), 140.

8. Citations and details in Ball, *Russia's Last Capitalists*, 39–42.

9. On NEP and its relation to the succession struggle after Lenin's death, see, especially, Martin Malia, *The Soviet Tragedy: A History of Socialism in Russia* (New York: Free Press, 1994), chapter 5 ("The Road Not Taken: NEP, 1921–1928"). For details on the funeral and embalming of Lenin, and Trotsky's absence during all the critical meetings, see Politburo resolutions dated January 22 and 29, 1924, in RGASPI, fond 17, opis' 1, del' 110 and 111, respectively. Available in reproduction in the Hoover Institution Archives.

10. Cited in Ball, *Russia's Last Capitalists*, 45. "'Extra-Economic' Coercion" and "grow into Communism": cited in Stephen Cohen, *Bukharin and the Bolshevik Revolution: A Political Biography* (New York: Knopf, 1974), 92, 384.

11. Citations in Cohen, *Bukharin and the Bolshevik Revolution*, 363, 386.

12. Cited in Ball, *Russia's Last Capitalists*, 45–46. "Enrich yourselves": cited in Lars Lih, "Bukharin's 'Illusion': War Communism and NEP," *Russian History* 27, no. 4 (Winter 2000): 427n24.

13. Figures in Nicolas Werth, "From the Truce to the Great Turning Point," in Courtois et al., *Black Book of Communism*, 142. On the broader production indices, see Ball, *Russia's Last Capitalists*, 101–3.

14. Citations in Cohen, *Bukharin and the Bolshevik Revolution*, 299–300, 335. "Prepared to go wherever you like": cited in Kevin McDermott and Jeremy Andrew, *The Comintern: A History of International Communism from Lenin to Stalin* (New York: St. Martin's Press, 1997), 76–77.

15. Citations in Werth, "From the Truce to the Great Turning Point," 144; Lih, "Bukharin's 'Illusion,'" 427n24. "Gulag" stands for "Glavnoye Upravleniye Ispravitelno-Trudovykh Lagerei."

16. Cited in Robert C. Tucker, *Stalin in Power: The Revolution from Above* (New York: Norton, 1992), 71, and, for Stalin's invocation of the *Kto-kogo* paradigm, 86–87.

17. Figures in Tucker, *Stalin in Power*, 73–74.

18. The original can be found in RGASPI, 2-1-22947, 1–4. "Kulak uprising": cited in Werth, "Red Terror," in Courtois et al., *Black Book of Communism*, 72.

19. "Zakryitoe pis'mo TsK VKP 'O zadachakh kolkhoznogo dvizheniya v svyazi s bor'boi s iskrivleniyami partinoi linii," April 2, 1930 (referencing also the Politburo resolution of January 6, 1930), in RGASPI, fond 17, opis' 86, del' 7.

20. Figures and citations in Werth, "Forced Collectivization and Dekulakization," in Courtois et al., *Black Book of Communism*, 150–51.

21. The most prominent example of the new "ethnic animus" argument is Anne Applebaum's revealingly titled *Red Famine: Stalin's War on Ukraine* (New York: Doubleday, 2017). Robert Conquest's pioneering work *The Harvest of Sorrow* (New York: Oxford University Press, 1986) is still worth reading, along with his responses to critics after the Soviet archival revelations following the fall of the USSR. The archival documents tended to support most (if not quite all) of his contentions. See, for example, Robert Conquest, "Excess Deaths and Camp Numbers: Some Comments," in *Soviet Studies* 43, no. 5 (1991): 949–52. In more recent work drawing on archival documents, Timothy Snyder's *Bloodlands: Europe Between Hitler and Stalin* (New York: Basic Books, 2010), marked a notable advance, although his death figures, slightly lower than Conquest's, occasioned protests from some Ukrainian scholars.

22. Tucker, *Stalin in Power*, 96. Targets for tanks and warplanes: Stephen Kotkin, *Stalin*, vol. 2, *Waiting for Hitler, 1929–1941* (New York: Penguin, 2017), 51.

23. Memorandum to the TsK VKP (b) and J. Stalin from A. Vyshinskii, USSR prosecutor general, on "regulations for child labor in collective farms," March 23, 1939, in RGASPI, fond 89, opis' 55, del' 19 (this is the "fond 89" originally prepared for the trial of the Communist Party of the Soviet Union in 1992, now preserved in the Hoover Institution Archives).

24. For a poignant tribute to those hopeful westerners drawn in by the promise of employment in the workers' paradise, in particular African Americans, see Tim Tzouliadis, *The Forsaken: An American Tragedy in Stalin's Russia* (New York: Penguin, 2008).

25. Stephen Kotkin, *Stalin*, vol. 1, *Paradoxes of Power, 1878–1928* (New York: Penguin, 2014), 700. For other joint ventures, in particular those involving mining and metals, see Antony Sutton, *Western Technology and Soviet Economic Development, 1930 to 1945* (Stanford, CA: Hoover Institution, 1968–1973), 1, 44–60. Freyn and Gipromez: Stephen Kotkin, *Magnetic Mountain: Stalinism as a Civilization* (Berkeley: University of California Press, 1997), 37. See also "Soviet Contract Let to Americans: $110,000,000 Order for Industrial and Grain Plants Goes to Chicago Company," *New York Times*, November 12, 1929. On the *Moscow News*, see David Caute, *The Fellow Travelers: A Postscript to the Enlightenment* (New York: Macmillan, 1973), 79.

26. Cited in Tucker, *Stalin in Power*, 100–101. Children denouncing their parents at the Shakhty trial: Conquest, *Harvest of Sorrow*, 295. Figures on Shakhty and Dnepropetrovsk: cited in Werth, "From the Truce to the Great Turning Point," 143.

27. Cited in Werth, "Forced Collectivization and Dekulakization," in Courtois et al., *Black Book of Communism*, 153–54.

28. Cited in Nikolai Tolstoy, *Stalin's Secret War* (London: J. Cape, 1981), 28–29. On the Siberian goldfields, see also Kotkin, *Stalin*, 2:133 and *passim*.

29. Citations in Simon Sebag Montefiore, *Stalin: The Court of the Red Tsar* (New York: Knopf, 2004), 189–90. April 1935 decree extending the death penalty to minors: cited in Robert Conquest, *The Great Terror: Stalin's Purge of the Thirties* (New York: Macmillan, 1968), 86–87.

30. Cited in Snyder, *Bloodlands*, 107. On the Polish arrests and executions, see Bogdan Musial, "The 'Polish Operation' of the NKVD: The Climax of the Terror Against the Polish Minority in the Soviet Union," *Journal of Contemporary History* 48, no. 1 (2012): 98–124. For Nadya's suicide and the arrests of the wives: Montefiore, *Stalin*, prologue and 229, 229fn, 240–41, 317. For a more straightforward explanation of the Terror, noting that Stalin really did come to believe "that enemies were all around," see Oleg Khlevniuk, *Stalin: New Biography of a Dictator* (New Haven, CT: Yale University Press, 2015), 157–62. For the most authoritative study of the Kirov murder, see Matthew Lenoe, *The Kirov Murder and Soviet History* (New Haven, CT: Yale University Press, 2010).

31. Citations and details in Louis Rapoport, *Stalin's War Against the Jews: The Doctors' Plot and the Soviet Solution* (New York: Free Press, 1990), 49–51, 54.

32. Cited in Brian Moynahan, *The Russian Century* (New York: Random House, 1994), 106. "An overflow": cited in Tolstoy, *Stalin's Secret War*, 22.

33. Aleksandr Solzhenitsyn, *Gulag Archipelago, 1918–1956*, vol. 1, *An Experiment in Literary Investigation*, trans. Thomas P. Whitney (New York: Harper and Row, 1973), 160–61. For an interesting account of how ordinary Russians coped with life under the Terror, see Sheila Fitzpatrick, *Everyday Stalinism: Ordinary Life in Extraordinary Times* (New York: Oxford University Press, 1999), 209–17. On the Red Army purges, see Montefiore, *Stalin*, 223–26; Mikhail Mel'tiukhov, *Upushchennyi shans Stalina: Sovetskii soiuz i bor'ba za Evropu, 1939–1941* (Moscow: Veche, 2000), 368; and David M. Glantz and Jonathan M. House, *When Titans Clashed: How the Red Army Stopped Hitler*, rev.

ed. (Lawrence: University Press of Kansas, 2015), 9. Not all the purged officers were executed, and 11,500 were later reinstated.

34. Details and citations in Geoffrey Hosking, *The First Socialist Society: A History of the Soviet Union from Within* (Cambridge, MA: Harvard University Press, 1985), 156–57, 206–7, 214–15.

35. "Report on the Political Conditions in the USSR," by Major R. O. A. Gatehouse and Captain C. H. Tamplin, February 22, 1940, in PRO, FO 371 / 24850.

36. Gosplan resolution "O Gosudarstvennyikh Trudovyikh Rezervakh SSSR," ratified by President Kalinin on October 2, 1940, and Kalinin labor *ukaz* on the seven-day week dated June 26, 1940, both in GARF, fond 4372 (Gosplan), opis' 38, del' 1, list' 72 (and back), 133–35.

Chapter 9: High Noon

1. The classic study of the *poputschiki*, or "fellow travelers," is David Caute's *The Fellow-Travelers: A Postscript to the Enlightenment* (New York: Macmillan, 1973).

2. On the Reichstag fire trial and what Hitler and Stalin may have agreed to, see Marin Pundeff, "Dimitrov at Leipzig: Was There a Deal?," *Slavic Review* 45, no. 3 (Autumn 1986): 545–49. On the Soviet-German agreement of May 1933, see Edward E. Ericson III, *Feeding the German Eagle: Soviet Economic Aid to Nazi Germany, 1933–1941* (Westport, CT: Praeger, 1999), 15–16. On the Comintern's "social fascism" doctrine and its significance in Germany, see Julius Braunthal, *The History of the International*, vol. 2, *1914–1943*, trans. John Clark (New York: Praeger, 1967), 364–80.

3. Walter Duranty, "Russians Hungry but Not Starving," *New York Times*, March 31, 1933, www.nytimes.com/1933/03/31/archives/russians-hungry-but-not-starving-deaths -from-diseases-due-to.html. For the Pulitzer committee's decision not to revoke Duranty's prize despite hundreds of scholars thoroughly debunking his reporting, see "Statement on Walter Duranty's 1932 Prize," November 20, 2003, The Pulitzer Prizes, www .pulitzer.org/news/statement-walter-duranty.

4. On the League of Nations exchange and its significance, see, especially, Jonathan Haslam, *The Soviet Union and the Threat from the East, 1933–41: Moscow, Tokyo, and the Prelude to the Pacific War* (Pittsburgh: University of Pittsburgh Press, 1992), 43–44.

5. See Christopher M. Andrew and Vasili Mitrokhin, *The Sword and the Shield: The Mitrokhin Archive and the Secret History of the KGB* (New York: Basic Books, 1999), 106, and more broadly, chapter 7 ("The Grand Alliance"). For a useful table of party members and their dates of service in government, see Herbert Hoover, *Freedom Betrayed: Herbert Hoover's Secret History of the Second World War and Its Aftermath*, ed. George H. Nash (Stanford, CA: Hoover Institution Press, 2011), 36–46.

6. Details in Martin Weil, *A Pretty Good Club: The Founding Fathers of the U.S. Foreign Service* (New York: Norton, 1978), 92–93. For Davies to Stalin: transcript of Kremlin meeting of June 5, 1938, in RGASPI, fond 558, opis' 11, del' 375, list' 1–7.

7. Andrew and Mitrokhin, *Sword and Shield*, 58. For more on the Cambridge recruits, see Andrew Lownie, *Stalin's Englishman: Guy Burgess, The Cold War, and the Cambridge Spy Ring* (New York: St. Martin's Press, 2015), 51–57 and *passim*.

8. Cited in Stanley G. Payne, *The Spanish Civil War, the Soviet Union, and Communism* (New Haven, CT: Yale University Press, 2004), 126.

9. Payne, *Spanish Civil War, the Soviet Union, and Communism*, 153–56, 161. Gold shipped to Moscow: Robert C. Tucker, *Stalin in Power: The Revolution from Above* (New York: Norton, 1992), 351. Hitler and Mussolini financing Franco: Pierpaolo Barbieri, *Hitler's Shadow Empire: Nazi Economics and the Spanish Civil War* (Cambridge, MA: Harvard University Press, 2015).

10. In this vein, see George Orwell, *Homage to Catalonia* (London: Secker and Warburg, 1938), and Hugh Thomas, *The Spanish Civil War* (London: Eyre and Spottiswoode, 1961). "End to the social revolution": cited in Braunthal, *History of the International*, 2:461. The Spanish militias were under the umbrella of the Workers' Party of Marxist Unification (Partido Obrero de Unificación Marxista, POUM).

11. Citation and figures in Stéphane Courtois and Jean-Louis Panné, "The Shadow of the NKVD in Spain," in *The Black Book of Communism: Crimes, Terror, Repression*, by Stéphane Courtois, Nicolas Werth, Jean-Louis Panné, Andrzej Paczkowski, Karel Bartosek, and Jean-Louis Margolin, trans. Jonathan Murphy and Mark Kramer, consulting ed. Mark Kramer (Cambridge, MA: Harvard University Press, 1999), 343, 351. For Soviet surveillance and disciplining of the brigades, including the Abraham Lincoln Battalion, see "List of Suspicious Individuals from the XVth Brigade," document 48 in *The Secret World of American Communism*, ed. Harvey Klehr, John Earl Haynes, and Fridrikh Igorevich Firsov (New Haven, CT: Yale University Press, 1995), 164–83.

12. On Negrín being handpicked by Stalin's agents, see Walter Krivitsky, *In Stalin's Secret Service: An Exposé of Russia's Secret Policies by the Former Chief of the Soviet Intelligence in Western Europe* (1939; repr., New York: Harper and Brothers, 1985), 99–101.

13. Third Soviet Five-Year Plan targets: cited in Lennart Samuelson, *Plans for Stalin's War Machine: Tukhachevskii and Military-Economic Planning, 1926–1941* (London: Palgrave Macmillan, 2000), 191. Figures on Soviet warplane and tank production: Table 11 in Bogdan Musial, *Kampfplatz Deutschland: Stalins Kriegspläne gegen den Westen* (Berlin: Propyläen, 2008), 303. Annual Soviet tank production actually declined between 1936 (3,981) and 1939 (3,107).

14. Glenn Martin deal: Antony Sutton, *Western Technology and Soviet Economic Development, 1930 to 1945* (Stanford, CA: Hoover Institution, 1968–1973), 220–21. Douglas DC-3 deal: Svetlana Lokhova, *The Spy Who Changed History: The Untold Story of How the Soviet Union Stole America's Top Secrets* (New York: Pegasus, 2019), 270. French deals: "Commandes de materiel de guerre faites en France par l'URSS," summary by the French chargé d'affaires in Moscow, January 6, 1939, in VSHD, 7 N 3124.

15. Ian Johnson, *Faustian Bargain: The Soviet-German Partnership and the Origins of the Second World War* (New York: Oxford University Press, 2021), 202.

16. Cited in Adam Ulam, *Expansion and Coexistence: Soviet Foreign Policy, 1917–1973*, 2nd ed. (New York: Praeger, 1974), 268.

17. Citations in Richard Raack, "His Question Asked and Answered: Stalin on 'Whither Poland,'" *Polish Review* 55, no. 2 (2010): 198–200, 207–8 (brackets in original).

18. Cited in Jonathan Haslam, "Soviet-German Relations and the Origins of the Second World War: The Jury Is Still Out," *Journal of Modern History* 69, no. 4 (December 1997): 793. Hitler's instructions to Goebbels and Nazi journalists: Schulenberg to

Weizsäcker from Moscow, May 22, 1939, document no. 8 in *Die Beziehungen zwischen Deutschland und der Sowjetunion, 1939–1941: Dokumente des Auswärtigen Amtes*, ed. Alfred Seidl (Tübingen: H. Laupp, 1949), 9.

19. As noted by Raack in "Question Asked and Answered." "Second Imperialist War": Commission of the Central Committee of the C.P.S.U., *History of the Communist Party of the Soviet Union (Bolsheviks): Short Course*, commissioned by Joseph Stalin, edited by the Central Committee of the C.P.S.U. (New York: International Publishers, 1939 [1938]), 333.

20. "Molotow-Rede vor dem Obersten Sowjet," August 31, 1939, clipped and translated into German by the German Foreign Office, in PAAA, R 261183.

21. Eric Breindel and Herbert Romerstein, *The Venona Secrets: Exposing Soviet Espionage and America's Traitors* (Washington, DC: Regnery, 2000), 32–33. French party figures: Nikolai Tolstoy, *Stalin's Secret War* (London: J. Cape, 1981), 193–94. On dissension in the French Communist ranks, see Roger Moorhouse, *The Devils' Alliance: Hitler's Pact with Stalin, 1939–1941* (New York: Basic Books, 2014), 111–12. CPUSA membership figures: John Haynes, "CPUSA Membership After Nazi-Soviet Pact," published at H-net, https://networks.h-net.org/node/6077/discussions/4021026 /cpusa-loss-membership-after-nazi-soviet-pact.

22. Molotov speech to Supreme Soviet, October 31, 1939, translated (into German) by the Wilhelmstrasse, in PAAA, R 261183.

23. "Proekt polozheniya NKVD SSSR 'o spetsposelakh i trudovom ustroistve osadnikov, vyiselyaemyikh iz zapadnyikh oblastei USSR i BSSR," December 29, 1939, reproduced as no. 2.4 in N. L. Pobol' and P. N. Polyan, eds., *Stalinskie deportatsii, 1928–1953* (Moscow: Mezhdunarodnyi fond demokratiia, 2005), 112–14. For Poles sent to work in road construction: Beria order no. 315, September 25, 1939, and Politburo protocol for October 1, 1939, point 260, in RGASPI, fond 17, opis' 162, del' 26. Estimates of Poles and Jews deported east: Keith Sword, "The Welfare of Polish-Jewish Refugees in the USSR, 1941–43," in *Jews in Eastern Poland and the USSR, 1939–46*, ed. Norman Davies and Antony Polonsky (London: Palgrave Macmillan, 1991), 145.

24. British and French reactions on the day of the Soviet invasion of Poland: British War Cabinet minutes, September 17, 1939, in PRO, CAB 65/1. French reservations (and the mild protest): Charles Corbin to Georges Bonnet, September 20, 1939, in QO, 92 CPCOM/286 ("Grand-Bretagne 1930–1940. Dossier general").

25. Cited in Patrick R. Osborn, *Operation Pike: Britain Versus the Soviet Union, 1939–1941* (Westport, CT: Greenwood Press, 2000), 39. "The whole world is watching us": cited in Stephen Kotkin, *Stalin*, vol. 2, *Waiting for Hitler, 1929–1941* (New York: Penguin, 2017), 736. "Driven forward like cattle": from a report collected by British army intelligence on February 15, 1940, in PRO, FO 371 / 24792. The Stalin decree of January 24, 1940, on creating the disciplinary battalions is cited in Vadim J. Birstein, *SMERSH: Sekretnoe oruzhie Stalina* (Moscow: Airo-XX, 2018), 149. On Soviet casualties at the front, see William R. Trotter, *Frozen Hell: The Russo-Finnish Winter War of 1939–1940* (Chapel Hill, NC: Algonquin Books, 1999), 72–73; Bair Irincheev, *War of the White Death: Finland Against the Soviet Union, 1939–40* (Barnsley, UK: Pen and Sword Military, 2011), 26–27. Soviet doctor treating 400 wounded soldiers a day in Leningrad: Seeds to Halifax, December 7, 1939, in PRO, FO 371 / 24791.

26. Trotter, *Frozen Hell*, 206–9. The Soviet-Finnish peace treaty is available online at Battles of the Winter War, www.winterwar.com/War%27sEnd/moscow_peace _treaty.htm.

27. Beria to Stalin, top-secret directive no. 794/B of March 5, 1940, reproduced in its entirety as document no. 216 in Rudolf Pikhoya et al., eds., *Katyn': Plenniki neob'yav-lennoi voinyi* (Moscow: Mezhdunarodnyi fond demokratiia, 1999), 384–90. The editors have produced a photostat of the original. For more on the Katyn murders and parallel deportations, see Timothy Snyder, *Bloodlands: Europe Between Hitler and Stalin* (New York: Basic Books, 2010), 135–41, and Moorhouse, *Devils' Alliance*, 45.

28. Molotov telegram to "Polpredam SSSR v Litve, Latvii, Estonii and Finlandii," June 14, 1940, document no. 10, in L. E. Reshin et al., eds., *1941 God. Dokumenty*, vol. 1 (Moscow: Mezhdunarodnyi fond 'demokratiia,' 1998), 29–32. On the gold reserves, see Walter Thurston from US Embassy Moscow, August 1, 1940, in NAA, T 1248, "Relating to the Political Relations Between the Soviet Union and Other States, 1940–44."

29. Citations in Tolstoy, *Stalin's Secret War*, 200–201, and Moorhouse, *Devils' Alliance*, 85.

30. Molotov speech before the Supreme Soviet, August 1, 1940, translated by the German Foreign Office and preserved in PAAA, R 261183. On property nationaliza-tions, see German military intelligence report, November 20, 1940, "Umsiedlungsver-handlungen für die baltischen Staaten," in PAAA, R 101388. Romanians deported: Tolstoy, *Stalin's Secret War*, 205–6.

31. Cited in Kotkin, *Stalin*, 2:768.

32. "Führerweisung vom 18: Dezember 1940," document no. 13 in Walter Post, *Unternehmen Barbarossa: Deutsche und sowjetische Angriffspläne, 1940/41* (Berlin: E. S. Mitler, 2001), 390–92. Hitler to Bulgarian minister: Parvan Draganov from Berlin, December 3, 1940, in BGA, fond 316K, opis' 1, del' 273, list' 25. Stalin's terms on Tri-partite Pact relayed by Molotov on November 25, 1940: Schulenberg handwritten report of Molotov's reply to Ribbentrop in PAAA, Botschaft Moskau 544.

33. The most detailed estimates of Soviet war matériel on the eve of the German invasion, based on Soviet and German archival sources, are Bogdan Musial, *Stalins Beu-tezug: Die Plünderung Deutschlands und der Aufstieg der Sowjetunion zur Weltmacht* (Ber-lin: Propyläen, 2010), 69–70. On 199 out of 251 air bases in frontier districts: "Spisok zashifrovannyikh aerodromov, naznachennyikh stroitel'stvom po Glavnomu Upravl-eniyu Stroitel'stva Aerodromov NKVD SSSR na 1941 god," April 1, 1941, in GARF, fond 8437, opis' 1, del' 1, list' 43–47 (and backs).

34. Soviet soldiers taken prisoner in 1941: Bogdan Musial, *Stalins Beutezug*, 69 (cit-ing the *Kriegstagebuch des Oberkommandos der Wehrmacht, 1940–1941*, vol. 1, 1106). Soviet official estimates were naturally lower, although, even so, they were embarrass-ingly high, ranging from 2.3 million to 3.3 million. See V. V. Litvinenko, *Tsena Voinyi: Lyudskie poteri na sovetsko-germanskom fronte* (Moscow: Veche, 2013), 50.

35. Special Section authorized to "shoot them on the spot": cited in Birstein, *SMERSH*, 190. Order no. 270: cited in Simon Sebag Montefiore, *Stalin: The Court of the Red Tsar* (New York: Knopf, 2004), 379n. Lenin's body to Tyumen: Resolution 176 on July 2, 1941, in RGASPI, fond 17, opis' 162, del' 36 (folder 1). Evacuation of skilled

workers and families: Resolutions 196 and 197 on July 7, 1941, in RGASPI, fond 17, opis' 162, del' 36 (folder 1). State cash and gold reserves evacuated June 28: Musial, *Stalins Beutezug*, 82. Moscow evacuation: Montefiore, *Stalin*, 392, 396–97; Rodric Braithwaite, *Moscow 1941: A City and Its People at War* (New York: Knopf, 2006), 227.

36. Cited in Alexander Werth, *Russia at War, 1941–1945: A History* (New York: Skyhorse, 2017 [1964]), 247. For the role of Anglo-American Lend-Lease aid in the Battle of Moscow, see Sean McMeekin, *Stalin's War: A New History of World War II* (New York: Basic Books, 2021), chapter 22.

37. For official Soviet estimates of Kursk losses, see David M. Glantz and Jonathan M. House, *When Titans Clashed: How the Red Army Stopped Hitler*, rev. ed. (Lawrence: University Press of Kansas, 2015), Table Q (in appendix). For German figures and different estimates for Soviet figures, see Musial, *Stalins Beutezug*, 97. On the role of Lend-Lease tanks, trucks, jeeps, and motorcycles in Stalin's armies on the Eastern Front, see McMeekin, *Stalin's War*, chapters 24 (for Stalingrad), 26 (for Kursk), and 29 (for Bagration, the Belorussian offensive of July–August 1944).

38. These are the estimates in Glantz and House, *When Titans Clashed*, 340. For 300,000 shot by their own side and "entire toll of British troops," see Max Hastings, *Inferno: The World at War, 1939–1945* (New York: Vintage, 2011), 148. Losses of Soviet armor: Evan Mawdsley, *Thunder in the East: The Nazi-Soviet War, 1941–1945* (London: Hodder Education Publishers, 2006), 392.

39. Citation and details in William Hitchcock, *The Struggle for Europe: The Turbulent History of a Divided Continent* (New York: Doubleday, 2002), 73–74, 83–84, 90. On "covert assistance" and the importance of US financial aid and political support for de Gasperi, see James E. Miller, "Taking Off the Gloves: The United States and the Italian Elections of April 1948," *Diplomatic History* 7, no. 1 (Winter 1983): 35–55.

40. Hitchcock, *Struggle for Europe*, 92.

Chapter 10: "People's Democracy"

1. On the apocalyptic atmosphere of Europe at the end of the war, see Ian Buruma, *Year Zero: A History of 1945* (New York: Penguin, 2013). Casualty figures: cited in Anne Applebaum, *Iron Curtain: The Crushing of Eastern Europe, 1944–1956* (New York: Doubleday, 2012), 9. Poland's war losses have recently become a political football, as Warsaw has tried to use new estimates as the basis for per capita reparations claims from Germany. The issue is complex, as some relatives of the 3 million or so Polish Jewish victims have received some compensation, via either German Holocaust reparations or forced-labor camp settlements (i.e., as "Jews" rather than as "Poles"), and the current Polish government wants to include Jewish victims in the final tally of "Polish" deaths to increase the per capita sum owed from Berlin. On deportations of ethnic Germans, see R. M. Douglas, *Orderly and Humane: The Expulsion of the Germans After the Second World War* (New Haven, CT: Yale University Press, 2012).

2. Citations in Applebaum, *Iron Curtain*, 27.

3. Cited in Nikolai Tolstoy, *Stalin's Secret War* (London: J. Cape, 1981), 268.

4. "*Davai chasyi*": cited in Applebaum, *Iron Curtain*, 27.

5. Bogdan Musial, *Stalins Beutezug: Die Plünderung Deutschlands und der Aufstieg der Sowjetunion zur Weltmacht* (Berlin: Propyläen, 2010), 338–39, 390–97 (Tables 11–22).

6. Musial, *Stalins Beutezug*, 274–77. The corporate files of Siemens, BMW, Allianz, and other German firms that Stalin's men looted are housed in Moscow at the Special Archive for Foreign Trophy Records (formerly TsGOA, then TsKhIDK, now subsumed into RGVIA).

7. "Zapis' Besedyi tov. I. V. Stalina s G. Gopkinsom, Lichnyim Predstavitelem Trumena, i Garrimanom, Poslom (USA) v USSR," May 26, 1945, in RGASPI, fond 558, opis' 11, del' 376, list' 18. Romanian and Hungarian deportation figures: Tolstoy, *Stalin's Secret War*, 267–68.

8. Bierut to Zhukov, March 8, 1945, and Zhukov to Bierut, March 15, 1945, in AAN, 2/579/0/2/933, list' 16–17, and Vasilevski to Shatilov, May 29, 1945, in AAN, 2/579/0/2/934, list' 20. Regifted Lend-Lease vehicles: Bulganin to Bierut, November 17, 1944, in AAN, 2/579/0/2/933, list' 30. German reparations shared by USSR with Poland, in the form of industrial goods: see Zhukov to Ulbricht, c. early January 1950, and Ulbricht's reply dated January 6, 1950, in BB, DE 1 / 11520. The list of materials Ulbricht agreed to ship to Poland, typed out over forty-eight pages, was, admittedly, impressive in length and variety. But in dollar terms, it amounted to just 8.5 percent of the value of German goods shipped to the USSR.

9. "Zapis' besedyi tov. Stalina" with Tito's representative, A. Khebrang, on January 9, 1945, in RGASPI, fond 558, opis' 11, del' 397, list' 1–16.

10. See, for example, Tito to Dimitrov (for Stalin), October 2, 4, 7, 12, 13, and 30 and December 28, 1943, all in RGASPI, fond 82, opis' 2, del' 1369.

11. Mihailović was put on trial for treason on June 10, 1946, and sentenced on July 17, 1946. On the Kočevski Rog massacre and other Partisan executions in 1945, see Nikolai Tolstoy, *The Minister and the Massacres* (London: Century Hutchinson, 1986), 176–207.

12. William Hitchcock, *The Struggle for Europe: The Turbulent History of a Divided Continent* (New York: Doubleday, 2002), 110–13.

13. For estimates of ethnic Germans expelled from Czechoslovakia, see "Memories of World War II in the Czech Lands: The Expulsion of Sudeten Germans," Radio Prague International, April 14, 2005, https://english.radio.cz/memories-world-war-ii -czech-lands-expulsion-sudeten-germans-8097851. Churchill uses the "Iron Curtain" phrase in cable to Truman on May 12, 1945: cited in David Reynolds and Vladimir Pechatnov, *The Kremlin Letters: Stalin's Wartime Correspondence with Churchill and Roosevelt* (New Haven, CT: Yale University Press, 2018), 588. "Must pay" and "liquidate the German problem": cited in Applebaum, *Iron Curtain*, 120.

14. Details in Bradley Adams, "Hope Died Last: The Czechoslovak Road to Stalinism," in *Stalinism Revisited: The Establishment of Communist Regimes in East-Central Europe*, ed. Vladimir Tismaneanu (Budapest: Central European University Press, 2009), 347–48. Beneš decrees nos. 5, 12, and 115 are excerpted in a recent article, "The Beneš Decrees," Living Prague, accessed November 17, 2023, https://livingprague.com /politics-and-history/the-benes-decrees.

15. Citation and details in Hitchcock, *Struggle for Europe*, 110–12.

16. Citations in Adams, "Hope Died Last," 350–51.

17. See "Smrt Jana Masaryka kriminalisté v dalším vyšetřování neobjasnili," March 8, 2021, Novinky, www.novinky.cz/clanek/domaci-smrt-jana-masaryka-kriminaliste -v-dalsim-vysetrovani-neobjasnili-40353297.

18. Report on the Czech parliamentary package passed on October 27, 1948, prepared by the Czechoslovak Social Democratic Party in Exile, in PRO, FO 371 / 71331A (Czechoslovakia). The decree on forced-labor camps is cited in Adams, "Hope Died Last," 360. On 100,000 political prisoners: Tony Judt, *Postwar: A History of Europe Since 1945* (New York: Penguin, 2006), 192.

19. Judt, *Postwar*, 92. For more on the deportations, see Applebaum, *Iron Curtain*, 117–23. On the Pitești Prison Experiment, see Roland Clark, "Romania's History Wars: On the Sufferings of Fascist Saints," Open Democracy, December 4, 2019, www.opendemocracy.net/en/countering-radical-right/romanias-history-wars-on-the-sufferings-of-fascist-saints.

20. Judt, *Postwar*, 192. On Rákosi's "salami tactics," see Hitchcock, *Struggle for Europe*, 108–9 and *passim*.

21. The "naughty document" is cited in Reynolds and Pechatnov, *Kremlin Letters*, 482–83. For more on the Allied agreement with Stalin over Bulgaria, see Ekaterina Nikova, "Bulgarian Stalinism Revisited," in Tismaneanu, *Stalinism Revisited*, 288. On the coup in Sofia and the money allotted to it, see Dimitrov to Molotov, September 6, 1944, in RGASPI, fond 82, opis' 2, del' 1130, list' 18–19. "Broader base and a convenient disguise": cited in Georgi Dimitrov, *The Diary of Georgi Dimitrov*, ed. Ivo Banac (New Haven, CT: Yale University Press, 2003). On the Sveta Nedelya bombing, see Franz Borkenau, *World Communism: A History of the Communist International* (Ann Arbor: University of Michigan Press, 1962), 242. On Bulgaria's mixed Holocaust record, see "A Short History of Bulgaria and the Holocaust," World Jewish Congress, accessed November 17, 2023, www.worldjewishcongress.org/download/niHdRsTz0Ml6P5dvhNAURQ.

22. Citations in Nikova, "Bulgarian Stalinism Revisited," 290.

23. Nikova, "Bulgarian Stalinism Revisited," 289–94.

24. Nikova, "Bulgarian Stalinism Revisited," 300. "Instigate the peasants" and "undermine the Two-Year Plan": "Speech for the Prosecution in the Dimiter Gichev case," *Rabotnichesko Delo*, April 16, 1948, clipped and translated in PRO, FO 371 / 72132. "Steam roller of historical development": "Dimitrov's New Year Message to Bulgaria" for 1948, clipped and translated in PRO, FO 371 / 72131.

25. See Red Army field report from occupied Poland, December 17, 1945, in AAN, 2/579/0/2/933, list' 57–58. Nine regular divisions: "Dlya Pamyati," November 23, 1945, in AAN, 2/579/0/2/934, list' 31–32. On 25,000 AK fighters being disarmed and interned by the NKVD, and 8,700 resistance fighters killed by 1948, see Andrzej Paczkowski, "Poland, the 'Enemy Nation,'" in *The Black Book of Communism: Crimes, Terror, Repression*, by Stéphane Courtois, Nicolas Werth, Jean-Louis Panné, Andrzej Paczkowski, Karel Bartosek, and Jean-Louis Margolin, trans. Jonathan Murphy and Mark Kramer, consulting ed. Mark Kramer (Cambridge, MA: Harvard University Press, 1999), 373, 376–77. On special NKVD division arresting AK fighters and deporting them to Soviet labor camps, see Andrzej Paczkowski, *The Spring Will Be Ours: Poland and the Poles from Occupation to Freedom*, trans. Jane Cave (University Park: Pennsylvania State University Press, 2003), 130. For estimates on casualties and deaths in the Warsaw Uprising of 1944, see Musial, *Stalins Beutezug*, 221.

26. "Biuletyn Informacyjny Reformy Rolnej: Województwa Pomorskiego," March 20, 1945, in AAN, 2/579/0/1.2/230. For land area and population transfers,

see Paczkowski, *The Spring Will Be Ours*, 146–51, and on Stalin bartering Königs-berg for Stettin and assuming Churchill would not notice, see Douglas, *Orderly and Humane*, 82.

27. Gomułka to Ambassador Lebiediwa, Zhukov, and Rokossovsky, January 10, 1946, in AAN, 2/196/0/2/61. "Germanski und Bolsheviki zusammen stark": cited in Roger Moorhouse, *The Devils' Alliance: Hitler's Pact with Stalin, 1939–1941* (New York: Basic Books, 2014), 39.

28. Gomułka to Ambassador Lebiediwa, Zhukov, and Rokossovsky, January 10, 1946.

29. Moczarski's memoir account is cited at length in Paczkowski, "Poland, the 'Enemy Nation,'" 377–78. On the Mokotów executions and other torture methods deployed, see "The Craft of Breaking a Man: Torture Methods Used by UB (Urzad Bezpieczenstwa, Bezpieka) Against Polish Underground Soldiers, and Democratic Opposition in Poland Between 1944 and 1963," The Doomed Soldiers: Polish Under-ground Soldiers, 1944–1963—the Untold Story, accessed November 17, 2023, www.doomedsoldiers.com/torture-methods-of-ub.html. Other details were shared with me on a guided tour of Warsaw's Mokotów Prison in July 2022, kindly arranged by Alex Richie.

30. Report of Michael Winek to Robin Hankey of the Foreign Office via Britain's Warsaw embassy, April 23, 1948, in PRO, FO 371 / 71529. Percentage of land collectiv-ized and state-owned in Poland and in formerly German West Poland, lack of anti-kulak campaign, and requisitions: Paczkowski, *Spring Will Be Ours*, 214 and *passim*.

31. Hitchcock, *Struggle for Europe*, 117–18. "Slavish loyalty" and posters in the Sofia railway station: Judt, *Postwar*, 142. Businesses nationalized by Tito by 1948: see the chart reproduced in John Connelly, "The Paradox of East German Communism: From Non-Stalinism to Neo-Stalinism?," in Tismaneanu, *Stalinism Revisited*, 179.

32. For estimates on how much war matériel Churchill supplied Tito with, see "Report on Mission to General Mihailović . . . By Colonel S. W. Bailey, O.B.E.," circa April 1944, in PRO, HS 7/202. For "Hundreds of letters" and details of the Tito visit to London in March 1953, see Andrew Harrison, "A Cold War Visitor in London: Mar-shal Tito of Yugoslavia," UK National Archives, March 15, 2018, https://blog.national archives.gov.uk/cold-war-visitor-london-marshal-tito-yugoslavia.

33. Cited in Hitchcock, *Struggle for Europe*, 122.

34. Cited in Hitchcock, *Struggle for Europe*, 124. For StB members purged, see Petr Blazek and Pavel Zácek, "Tschechoslowakei," in *Handbuch der kommunistischen Geheimdienste in Osteuropa, 1944–1991*, ed. Lukasz Kamínski, Krzysztof Persak, and Jens Gieseke (Göttingen: Vandenhoeck and Ruprecht, 2009) (henceforth *Geheimdienst Handbuch*), 397 and *passim*. On the KatPol and ÁVH purges in Hungary, see Krisztian Ungváry and Gabor Tabajdi, "Ungarn," in *Geheimdienst Handbuch*, 488.

35. Jens Gieseke, "Deutsche Demokratische Republik," in *Geheimdienst Handbuch*, 203. "To view the division" and "in the aim of acquiring statehood": cited in Ulrich Mählert, *Kleine Geschichte der DDR, 1949–1989* (Munich: C. H. Beck, 2010), 37. On "special Soviet camp" internees and deaths, see Norman Naimark, *The Russians in Ger-many: A History of the Soviet Zone of Occupation, 1945–1949* (Cambridge, MA: Belknap Press of Harvard University Press, 1995), 378, Table 2. On the SED and the formation

of the DDR, see Connelly, "The Paradox of East German Communism," 178–79, and Mark Kramer, "The Soviet Union and the Founding of the German Democratic Republic," *Europe-Asia Studies* 51, no. 6 (1999): 1093–1124. On 1.7 million Germans in Soviet labor camps, see "Zapis' Besedyi tov. I. V. Stalina s G. Gopkinsom . . . ," May 26, 1945, in RGASPI, fond 558, opis' 11, del' 376, list' 18.

Chapter 11: Mao's Moment

1. S. C. M. Paine, *The Wars for Asia* (New York: Cambridge University Press, 2012), 88–89.

2. Cited in Oleg Khlevniuk, *Stalin: New Biography of a Dictator*, trans. Nora Seligman Favorov (New Haven, CT: Yale University Press, 2015), 123.

3. Paine, *Wars for Asia*, 89. "Real military power": cited in Hans van de Ven, *War and Nationalism in China, 1925–1945* (London: Taylor and Francis / RoutledgeCurzon, 2003), 151.

4. On the Long March and Snow legend, see Paine, *Wars for Asia*, 74–75, 92–93, 115–16. On Mao being on the Soviet payroll, and Soviets paying for the Long March, see Frank Dikötter, *The Tragedy of Liberation: A History of the Chinese Revolution, 1945–1957* (London: Bloomsbury, 2013), 121.

5. Cited in van de Ven, *War and Nationalism in China*, 174.

6. Paine, *Wars for Asia*, 103. For more details on the negotiations and the Xi'an Incident, see also van de Ven, *War and Nationalism in China*, 183–88.

7. Cited in Greg Kennedy, *Anglo-American Strategic Relations and the Far East, 1933–1939* (London: Routledge, 2011), 108.

8. Details in Paine, *Wars for Asia*, 103, 132–33. On Soviet arms shipments, see Jonathan Haslam, *The Soviet Union and the Threat from the East, 1933–41: Moscow, Tokyo, and the Prelude to the Pacific War* (Pittsburgh: University of Pittsburgh Press, 1992), 93–94. On the Stalinist sleeper agent in Chiang's inner circle, see Antony Beevor, *The Second World War* (Boston: Little, Brown, 2012), 58.

9. Paine, *Wars for Asia*, 141–49.

10. Paine, *Wars for Asia*, 228–29. The terms of the Soviet-Japanese Neutrality Pact of April 13, 1941, are reproduced as Document No. 384 in L. E. Reshin et al., eds., *1941 God. Dokumenty*, vol. 1 (Moscow: Mezhdunarodnyi fond 'demokratiia,' 1998), 74–75. On the implications of the key clauses, see also Hubertus Lupke, *Japans Russlandpolitik von 1939 bis 1941* (Frankfurt: Alfred Metzner, 1962), 100–101.

11. Paine, *Wars for Asia*, 215. "Should not count on Soviet participation": Stalin to Chiang, December 11, 1941, in RGASPI, fond 558, opis' 11, del' 326, list' 34–35.

12. Lend-Lease protocol figures in Robert Huhn Jones, *The Roads to Russia: United States Lend-Lease to the Soviet Union* (Norman: University of Oklahoma Press, 1969), 167 and Appendix A, Tables I, II, and VIII. US warplanes flown to the Soviet Far East: "Minutes of the Twenty-Third Meeting of the Protocol Subcommittee on Supplies Held May 16, 1945," in FDR Library, Hopkins Papers, Box 309, Book 5 ("Aid to Russia"), Folder 2, part 1.

13. For Soviet casualty estimates during August Storm, see David M. Glantz and Jonathan M. House, *When Titans Clashed: How the Red Army Stopped Hitler*, rev. ed. (Lawrence: University Press of Kansas, 2015), Table Q (in appendix). US pilots arrested

and interned: John R. Deane, *The Strange Alliance: The Story of American Efforts at War-time Co-operation with Russia* (London: John Murray, 1946), 59–62.

14. Citations in Dikötter, *Tragedy of Liberation*, 13.

15. Paine, *Wars for Asia*, 238–39. "Mere scrap of paper": cited in Dikötter, *Tragedy of Liberation*, 13.

16. Cited in Dikötter, *Tragedy of Liberation*, 15. For estimates on Soviet looting reparations and other details, see Paine, *Wars for Asia*, 240–41 and *passim*.

17. Albert Wedemeyer, "Answers for Miss Gretta Palmer," and, on plummeting US troop levels in China, Wedemeyer, "The China Theater Today," c. January 1946, in the Hoover Institution Archives, Wedemeyer Collection, Box 5, Folders 5.11 and 6.31, respectively.

18. "The Wedemeyer Report—China and Korea," September 1947, in the Hoover Institution Archives, Wedemeyer Collection, Box 5, Folder 7.33. For more details on financial aid, see Dikötter, *Tragedy of Liberation*, 19.

19. Cited (with accompanying details) in Dikötter, *Tragedy of Liberation*, 7–8, 20–21. For more on the collapse of the Chinese economy in the early postwar years, particularly agricultural yields, and the paltry amount of food aid that arrived, see van de Ven, *War and Nationalism in China*, 297–98.

20. On the central Chinese campaign, see Paine, *Wars for Asia*, 258 and *passim*.

21. Citation and details in Paine, *Wars for Asia*, 259–60, and Dikötter, *Tragedy of Liberation*, 27.

22. Cited in Dikötter, *Tragedy of Liberation*, 30.

23. Dikötter, *Tragedy of Liberation*, 107.

24. Cited in Dikötter, *Tragedy of Liberation*, 41.

25. Citations and details in Dikötter, *Tragedy of Liberation*, 49–62.

26. Cited in Dikötter, *Tragedy of Liberation*, 110.

27. Cited in Jean-Louis Margolin, "China: A Long March into Night," in *The Black Book of Communism: Crimes, Terror, Repression*, by Stéphane Courtois, Nicolas Werth, Jean-Louis Panné, Andrzej Paczkowski, Karel Bartosek, and Jean-Louis Margolin, trans. Jonathan Murphy and Mark Kramer, consulting ed. Mark Kramer (Cambridge, MA: Harvard University Press, 1999), 483. For 700,000, regional death quotas/estimates, and "killing roughly 1,400 should be enough," see Dikötter, *Tragedy of Liberation*, 97, 100.

28. Figures in Margolin, "China: A Long March into Night," 482–83. Denunciation boxes, "bribery, tax evasion, pilfering government property," and 1.2 million "corrupt individuals": citations in Dikötter, *Tragedy of Liberation*, 163–64, 168.

29. Dikötter, *Tragedy of Liberation*, 127–28, 189–91, 201–4. On "thought reform," see also Franz Schurmann, *Ideology and Organization in Communist China* (Berkeley: University of California Press, 1968), 47 and *passim*. "Right opportunist cold wind": "Communist China's Agricultural Revolution," in the Karnow Collection, Hoover Institution Archives, Box 1, Folder 1.

30. Figure in Margolin, "China: A Long March into Night," 485. "Kept a record of every word": "Interview with Lee Ke-Chiang," Karnow Collection, Hoover Institution Archives, Box 4, Folder labeled "China: Cultural Revolution, 1965."

31. Citations in Frank Dikötter, *Mao's Great Famine: The History of China's Most Devastating Catastrophe, 1958–1962* (London: Bloomsbury, 2010), 12–13. "In a few short

years": cited in William Taubman, *Khrushchev: The Man and His Era* (New York: Norton, 2004). "East Wind Prevails over West Wind": cited from Mao's speech to Chinese students in Moscow, November 17, 1957, in "Glossary of Chinese Communist Terms," in the Karnow Collection, Hoover Institution Archives, Box 4, Folder labeled "China: Cultural Revolution, 1965."

32. "Glossary of Chinese Communist Terms," Karnow Collection, Hoover Institution Archives, Box 4, Folder labeled "China: Cultural Revolution, 1965." Production targets, Dikötter, *Mao's Great Famine*, 14 and (for agriculture), Margolin, "China: A Long March into Night," 488.

33. Citations in Dikötter, *Mao's Great Famine*, 30–33.

34. "Former Communist cadre" interviewed by Stanley Karnow, c. 1965, in the Karnow Collection, Hoover Institution Archives, Box 4, Folder labeled "China: Cultural Revolution, 1965." Other citations and details in Dikötter, *Mao's Great Famine*, 37–39, 53, 62.

35. Citations in Dikötter, *Mao's Great Famine*, 82–83.

36. Interview with "Mr Chen from Shanghai" conducted by Stanley Karnow, c. 1965, in the Karnow Collection, Hoover Institution Archives, Box 4, Folder labeled "China: Cultural Revolution, 1965." "Bad people have seized power": cited in Frank Dikötter, *The Cultural Revolution: A People's History, 1962–1976* (New York: Bloomsbury, 2016), 15. Figures from 1928–1930 famine, and baseline and elevated "death" rates from 1957 to 1960: Margolin, "China: A Long March into Night," 469, 495. Cao Shuji and Chen Yizi estimates, and "stands at a minimum of 45 million": Dikötter, *Mao's Great Famine*, 324–25, 333.

37. Citation and details in William Taubman, *Khrushchev: The Man and His Era* (New York: Norton, 2004), 391–95. "Repeating our own stupid mistakes": cited in Lorenz M. Lüthi, *The Sino-Soviet Split: Cold War in the Communist World* (Princeton, NJ: Princeton University Press, 2008), 109.

Chapter 12: "The World Was Turning in Our Direction"

1. Anne Applebaum, *Iron Curtain: The Crushing of Eastern Europe, 1944–1956* (New York: Doubleday, 2012), 435–36. On the stampede at Stalin's funeral and casualty estimates (Khrushchev gave a figure of 109), see Oleg Khlevniuk, *Stalin: New Biography of a Dictator* (New Haven, CT: Yale University Press, 2015), 317. For a firsthand memoir account, see Evgenii Evtushenko, "Mourners Crushed at Stalin's Funeral," in *Precocious Autobiography* (New York: Dutton, 1963), 88–102, available online at Seventeen Moments in Soviet History, https://soviethistory.msu.edu/1954-2/succession-to-stalin /succession-to-stalin-texts/mourners-crushed-at-stalins-funeral.

2. Citations in William Taubman, *Khrushchev: The Man and His Era* (New York: Norton, 2004), 246. On the Doctors' Plot, see Louis Rapoport, *Stalin's War Against the Jews: The Doctors' Plot and the Soviet Solution* (New York: Free Press, 1990), and Jonathan Brent and Vladimir Naumov, *Stalin's Last Crime: The Plot Against the Jewish Doctors, 1948–1953* (New York: Harper Perennial, 2004).

3. Cited in Taubman, *Khrushchev*, 247–48. For Ulbricht and the East German perspective, see Ulrich Mählert, *Kleine Geschichte der DDR, 1949–1989* (Munich: C. H. Beck, 2010), 71–72.

4. Taubman, *Khrushchev*, 257–58 and (for "hand over 18 million East Germans"), 249. For more details on the abortive East German uprising, see Mählert, *Kleine Geschichte der DDR*, 73–76, and Applebaum, *Iron Curtain*, 438–44. On 58,000 East Germans leaving in March 1953 alone, and 13 Stasi stations and 12 prisons overwhelmed, see Jens Gieseke, *Die Stasi, 1945–1990* (Munich: Pantheon, 2011), 61–62.

5. Taubman, *Khrushchev*, 116, 120, 278–79. For more on Khrushchev's role in the Terror, see Simon Sebag Montefiore, *Stalin: The Court of the Red Tsar* (New York: Knopf, 2004), 271.

6. "Khrushchev's Secret Speech, 'On the Cult of Personality and Its Consequences,' Delivered at the Twentieth Party Congress of the Communist Party of the Soviet Union," February 25, 1956, online at Wilson Center Digital Archive, https://digital archive.wilsoncenter.org/document/khrushchevs-secret-speech-cult-personality-and -its-consequences-delivered-twentieth-party. For more on the speech's reception, see Taubman, *Khrushchev*, 283–84. On Bierut's death, see Applebaum, *Iron Curtain*, 454.

7. Cited in Frank Dikötter, *Mao's Great Famine: The History of China's Most Devastating Catastrophe, 1958–1962* (London: Bloomsbury, 2010), 19.

8. Andrzej Paczkowski, *The Spring Will Be Ours: Poland and the Poles from Occupation to Freedom*, trans. Jane Cave (University Park: Pennsylvania State University Press, 2003), 272–77.

9. Taubman, *Khrushchev*, 295–99. See also Applebaum, *Iron Curtain*, 455–58.

10. Cited in Tony Judt, *Postwar: A History of Europe Since 1945* (New York: Penguin, 2006), 277. Anne Applebaum also uses the Brecht poem as the epigraph to her concluding chapter of *Iron Curtain* (p. 435).

11. Mählert, *Kleine Geschichte der DDR*, 79 and *passim*. For the demographic comparison, see Aaron O'Neill, "Population in the Former Territories of the Federal Republic of Germany and the German Democratic Republic from 1950 to 2016," Statistica, June 21, 2022, www.statista.com/statistics/1054199/population-of-east-and-west-germany.

12. "Auszüge aus den Berichten der Bezirksleitung Karl-Marx-Stadt vom 28.6.1962 und der Hauptverwaltung der Deutschen Volkspolizei vom 27. Und 29.6.1962 über Stimmung und Argumente für Bevölkerung," from the SED's Agitprop Department (Bereich Agitation), in DBB, DY 30 / 82800. For the new television spending, see "top secret" report from the SED Agitation Department on "Das II. Fernsehprogramm und sein Stand in Westdeutschland und der DDR," April 19, 1960, in DBB, DY 30 / 82730. On the construction of the wall and estimates of DDR refugees who died crossing it, see Mählert, *Kleine Geschichte der DDR*, 98–100. On Khrushchev's role, see Taubman, *Khrushchev*, 505–6.

13. Cited in Uri Ra'anan, *The USSR Arms the Third World: Case Studies in Soviet Foreign Policy* (Cambridge, MA: MIT Press, 1969), 59. "Peoples of the East" and "need not go begging": cited in Christopher Andrew and Vasili Mitrokhin, *The World Was Going Our Way: The KGB and the Battle for the Third World* (New York: Basic Books, 2005), 5.

14. Andrew and Mitrokhin, *World Was Going Our Way*, 7–8.

15. Andrew and Mitrokhin, *World Was Going Our Way*, 149–51.

16. Andrew and Mitrokhin, *World Was Going Our Way*, 33 and *passim*. On Khrushchev's suspicions of Castro, see also Taubman, *Khrushchev*, 532–33. On the CIA funding Castro, see "CIA Helped Fund Castro in 50's, Author Contends,"

Washington Post, October 19, 1986, Internet Archive Wayback Machine, https://web.archive.org/web/20170123223511/https://www.cia.gov/library/readingroom/docs/CIA-RDP90-00965R000706570004-6.pdf.

17. Cited in Taubman, *Khrushchev*, 533. On the KGB and the back channel through Raúl, see Andrew and Mitrokhin, *World Was Going Our Way*, 34–36.

18. Cited in Andrew and Mitrokhin, *World Was Going Our Way*, 45–46. "Openly advised us": cited in Taubman, *Khrushchev*, 579. "Hare-brained schemes": cited in John Keep, *Last of the Empires: A History of the Soviet Union, 1945–1991* (Oxford: Oxford University Press, 1995). On the 100 nuclear warheads initially left behind in Cuba, as later revealed from Soviet archives, see Sergo Mikoyan and Svetlana Savranskaya, *The Soviet Cuban Missile Crisis: Castro, Mikoyan, Kennedy, Khrushchev, and the Missiles of November* (Stanford, CA: Stanford University Press, 2014).

19. Alvaro Vargas Llosa, "The Killing Machine: Che Guevara, from Communist Firebrand to Capitalist Brand," first published in the *New Republic*, July 11, 2015, reproduced at Independent Institute, www.independent.org/news/article.asp?id=1535. For a moving account of what life for dissidents was like under Castro and Ché, see Armando Valladares, *Against All Hope: The Stunning Exposé of Life in Castro's Prisons*, trans. Andrew Hurley (New York: Knopf, 1986). On Brezhnev rebuking Ché, who was mourned by 50,000 in Washington, DC, see Andrew and Mitrokhin, *World Was Going Our Way*, 51–52.

20. Citations and details in Andrew and Mitrokhin, *World Was Going Our Way*, 42–43, 67, 116–18.

21. Andrew and Mitrokhin, *World Was Going Our Way*, 447–49. For Cuban deployment figures in Africa, see David Ottaway and Marina Ottaway, *Afrocommunism* (New York: Africana Publishers, 1986), 168, 171, 175.

22. Citations in Andrew and Mitrokhin, *World Was Going Our Way*, 12, 90.

23. For details on Ho's time in Moscow, see the memoir essay by Ruth Fischer, "Ho Chi Minh: Disciplined Communist," *Foreign Affairs* 33, no. 1 (October 1954): 86–97.

24. Citations in Mark Moyar, *Triumph Forsaken: The Vietnam War, 1954–1965* (New York: Cambridge University Press, 2006), 9–11.

25. Citation and details in Moyar, *Triumph Forsaken*, 22, 24. On the battle of Dienbienphu, see Fredrik Logevall, *Embers of War: The Fall of an Empire and the Making of America's Vietnam* (New York: Random House, 2012), 524–34.

26. See "U.S. Spent $141 Billion in Vietnam in 14 Years," *New York Times*, May 1, 1975, www.nytimes.com/1975/05/01/archives/us-spent-141billion-in-vietnam-in-14-years.html.

27. Figures in Ilya Gaiduk, *The Soviet Union and the Vietnam War* (Chicago: Ivan R. Dee, 1996), 58–59, 177. For "75–80 percent" of foreign assistance as against "4–8 percent" influence in Hanoi, see Andrew and Mitrokhin, *World Was Going Our Way*, 265. On Ho denouncing Tito and supporting Soviet invasions of Budapest, etc., see Moyar, *Triumph Forsaken*, 9.

28. Andrew and Mitrokhin, *World Was Going Our Way*, 71–72.

29. "Agreement of the Chamber of Deputies of Chile," August 22, 1973, translated by José Piñera, available online at Wikisource, https://en.wikisource.org/wiki/Agreement_of_the_Chamber_of_Deputies_of_Chile.

30. Citations in Andrew and Mitrokhin, *World Was Going Our Way*, 84–85.

31. Cited in Odd Arne Westad, "Moscow and the Angolan Crisis, 1974–1976," *Cold War International History Project Bulletin* 8–9 (Winter 1996–1997): 21.

32. Citations in Lorenz M. Lüthi, *The Sino-Soviet Split: Cold War in the Communist World* (Princeton, NJ: Princeton University Press, 2008), 326, 342, 344.

Chapter 13: Red Guards and the Khmer Rouge

1. Cited in Brian Moynahan, *The Russian Century* (New York: Random House, 1994), 215.

2. Cited in Frank Dikötter, *The Cultural Revolution: A People's History, 1962–1976* (New York: Bloomsbury, 2016), 15.

3. Citations in Dikötter, *Cultural Revolution*, 15, 18–19, 22.

4. Cited in Dikötter, *Cultural Revolution*, 26.

5. Citations and details in Chen Jian, *Mao's China and the Cold War* (Chapel Hill: University of North Carolina Press, 2001), 209, 217, 219, 226–29.

6. Citations in Dikötter, *Cultural Revolution*, 30, 36–38.

7. Stanley Karnow dispatch from Hong Kong for the *Washington Post*, May 6, 1966, in the Karnow Collection, folder labeled "China: Cultural Revolution, 1965," and on the "four olds": "Glossary of Chinese Communist Terms," folder 1 of 2 marked "December 1966," both in the Karnow Collection, Hoover Institution Archives, Box 4. "Victory for Mao Zedong thought" and "Sweep Away All Monsters": cited in Dikötter, *Cultural Revolution*, 50, 54, 57.

8. Stanley Karnow, "Major Current Events as Revealed in the Press and Radio of the Chinese People's Government: Chronology of Major Recent Events Relating to Cultural Revolution," c. March 1967, in Hoover Institution Archives, Box 4, Folder "China: Cultural Revolution, 1965." "Forced to kneel on broken glass": cited in Dikötter, *Cultural Revolution*, 62–63.

9. Dikötter, *Cultural Revolution*, 68–69. Deng "treated as an enemy": cited in Alexander V. Pantsov and Steven I. Levine, *Deng Xiaoping: A Revolutionary Life* (New York: Oxford University Press, 2015), 249–50. On Mao's swim, see also Karnow, "Major Current Events."

10. Dikötter, *Cultural Revolution*, 69–73.

11. Cited in Dikötter, *Cultural Revolution*, 77.

12. Karnow dispatch from Hong Kong, passing on wire report from Beijing, August 25, 1966, in the Karnow Collection, Hoover Institution Archives, Box 4, Folder "China: Cultural Revolution, 1965."

13. *Komsomolskaya Pravda* dispatch from Beijing, September 20, 1966, clipped and translated by Stanley Karnow, in the Karnow Collection, Hoover Institution Archives, Box 4, Folder "China: Cultural Revolution, 1965." DDR military attaché: Serbian news service dispatch from Beijing to Belgrade, August 29, 1966, filed in the Karnow Collection, Hoover Institution Archives, Box 4, Folder "China: Cultural Revolution, 1965." Hoxha: cited in Lorenz M. Lüthi, *The Sino-Soviet Split: Cold War in the Communist World* (Princeton, NJ: Princeton University Press, 2008), 299.

14. Cited in Chen, *Mao's China and the Cold War*, 243. Semichastny: cited in Lüthi, *Sino-Soviet Split*, 299. "Fight with weapons, not words": TASS dispatch, September 22,

1966, and "70-year-old professor": "Red Guard 'Cruelties' Bared: Russian Student Gives Eyewitness Account," in "China Mail" report datelined Moscow, December 16, 1966, both in the Karnow Collection, Hoover Institution Archives, Box 4, Folder "China: Cultural Revolution, 1965."

15. Details and citations in Dikötter, *Cultural Revolution*, 83–95.

16. "China Topics," reports filed by Stanley Karnow on November 11, 23, 28, 29, and December 23, 1966, in the Karnow Collection, Hoover Institution Archives, Box 4, Folder "China: Cultural Revolution, 1965." Reenacting the Long March: Dikötter, *Cultural Revolution*, 112.

17. Dikötter, *Cultural Revolution*, 132–35.

18. Dikötter, *Cultural Revolution*, 157–63, 177, 192, 201.

19. Dikötter, *Cultural Revolution*, xviii and *passim*.

20. Andrew Mertha, *Brothers in Arms: Chinese Aid to the Khmer Rouge, 1975–1979* (Ithaca, NY: Cornell University Press, 2014), 81–82 and *passim*.

21. Citations in John Barron and Anthony Paul, *Peace with Horror: The Untold Story of the Cambodian Genocide* (London: Hodder and Stoughton, 1977), 55–56.

22. Sydney Schanberg, "Town Is Devastated in Cambodian 'Victory,'" *New York Times*, July 28, 1974.

23. Cited in Barron and Paul, *Peace with Horror*, 59–60.

24. Sydney Schanberg, *Beyond the Killing Fields: War Writings* (Washington, DC: Potomac Books, 2010), 3 and *passim*; Robert D. McFadden, "Sydney H. Schanberg Dies at 82; Times Reporter Chronicled Khmer Rouge Terror," July 9, 2016, www .nytimes.com/2016/07/10/business/media/sydney-h-schanberg-is-dead-at-82-former -times-correspondent-chronicled-terror-of-1970s-cambodia.html.

25. Citations in Barron and Paul, *Peace with Horror*, 3, 9.

26. Barron and Paul, *Peace with Horror*, 14–17.

27. Barron and Paul, *Peace with Horror*, 20–21, 25, 38.

28. For an overview of all the studies on Khmer Rouge victims in Cambodia between 1975 and 1979, see Jean-Louis Margolin, "Cambodia: The Country of Disconcerting Crimes," in *The Black Book of Communism: Crimes, Terror, Repression*, by Stéphane Courtois, Nicolas Werth, Jean-Louis Panné, Andrzej Paczkowski, Karel Bartosek, and Jean-Louis Margolin, trans. Jonathan Murphy and Mark Kramer, consulting ed. Mark Kramer (Cambridge, MA: Harvard University Press, 1999), 589–91. "Big sticks and hoes" and "Anyone they didn't like": cited in Schanberg, *Beyond the Killing Fields*, 92–93.

29. Pin Yathay, with John Man, *Stay Alive, My Son*, 1st Touchstone ed. (New York: Simon and Schuster, 1987), 169–71.

30. Schanberg's "Life and Death of Dith Pran," which ultimately inspired the 1984 film *The Killing Fields*, was published in the *New York Times Magazine* on January 20, 1980.

31. Schanberg, *Beyond the Killing Fields*, 4 and *passim*; Max Hastings: *Vietnam: An Epic Tragedy, 1945–1975* (London: Williams Collins, 2019), 481.

Chapter 14: From Selling Jews and Germans to Sports Summits, Socialist Feminism, and the Stasi

1. John Keep, *Last of the Empires: A History of the Soviet Union* (Oxford: Oxford University Press, 1995), 191–92. For a harrowing memoir account of Soviet psychiatric

abuse, see Vladimir Bukovsky, *To Build a Castle: My Life as a Dissenter* (New York: Viking, 1979). David Satter interviewed Bukovsky and other psychiatric abuse victims and reported his findings in *Age of Delirium: The Decline and Fall of the Soviet Union* (New York: Knopf, 1996), 265–74. On the politics of Jackson-Vanik and the Soviet Jewish persecution that lay behind it, see Gal Beckerman, *When They Come for Us, We'll Be Gone: The Epic Struggle to Save Soviet Jewry* (New York: Houghton Mifflin, 2010), esp. chapter 8 ("Linkage, 1972–1975"), 273–310.

2. See Vladimir Bukovsky, *Judgment in Moscow: Soviet Crimes and Western Complicity*, trans. Alyona Kojevnikov (Westlake Village, CA: Ninth of November Press, 2019 [1996]), 297. Bukovsky has reproduced a facsimile of the key documents online. See WordPress, accessed November 23, 2023, https://bukovskyoldarchive.files.wordpress .com/2015/07/27-may-69-231-z.pdf. On the *Focus* story, and what KGB files actually reveal about Brandt's complicated relationship with the Soviets, see Christopher Andrew and Vasili Mitrokhin, *The Sword and the Shield: The Mitrokhin Archive and the Secret History of the KGB* (New York: Basic Books, 1999), 17–18, 441–43.

3. William Hitchcock, *The Struggle for Europe: The Turbulent History of a Divided Continent* (New York: Doubleday, 2002), 293–97. On Bahr and Brandt's courting of Moscow, see Norman Stone, *The Atlantic and Its Enemies: A History of the Cold War* (New York: Basic Books, 2010), 344–46.

4. Stone, *The Atlantic and Its Enemies*, 297–300, and Ulrich Mählert, *Kleine Geschichte der DDR, 1949–1989* (Munich: C. H. Beck, 2010), 123–26. On the natural gas deal, see Bogdan Musial, "Die westdeutsche Ostpolik und der Zerfall der Sowjetunion," Bundeszentrale für politische Bildung, Deutschland Archiv, August 2, 2011, www.bpb.de/themen /deutschlandarchiv/54107/die-westdeutsche-ostpolik-und-der-zerfall-der-sowjetunion.

5. Citations in Andrew and Mitrokhin, *Sword and Shield*, 443–45. For more on the Guillaume/Brandt spy scandal, see Jens Gieseke, "Deutsche Demokratik Republik," *Geheimdienst Handbuch*, 230–31. On the doubling of Stasi agents abroad between 1972 and 1982, see Gieseke, *Die Stasi, 1945–1990* (Munich: Pantheon, 2011 [2001]), 216. On tourist and visa traffic in 1975, see Mählert, *Kleine Geschichte der DDR*, 131.

6. Cited in Ion Mihai Pacepa, *Red Horizons: The True Story of Nicolae and Elena Ceausescus' Crimes, Lifestyle, and Corruption* (Washington, DC: Regnery, 1987), 131. On the capacities and deployment of Soviet listening devices, see Keep, *Last of the Empires*, 185–86.

7. Cited in Dennis Deletant, "New Evidence on Romania and the Warsaw Pact, 1955–1989," Cold War International History Project, Wilson Center, accessed November 23, 2023, www.wilsoncenter.org/publication/new-evidence-romania-and -the-warsaw-pact-1955-1989.

8. Pacepa, *Red Horizons*, 74–75. "Yearly income in hard currency": cited in Radu Ioanid, *The Ransom of the Jews: The Story of the Extraordinary Secret Bargain Between Romania and Israel* (Chicago: Ivan R. Dee, 2005), 63 and *passim*. On early Soviet exit visa bribes, see Sean McMeekin, *History's Greatest Heist: The Looting of Russia by the Bolsheviks* (New Haven, CT: Yale University Press, 2008), 49–50.

9. Cited in Pacepa, *Red Horizons*, 73, 76. Photostats of Romania's German export deals are reproduced in Heinz Günther Hüsch, Pieter-Dietmar Leber, and Hannelore Baier, *Wege in die Freiheit: Deutsch-rumänische Dokumente zur Familienzusammenführung*

und Aussiedlung, 1968–1989 (Aachen: Hüsch and Hüsch, 2016), 78–79, 86–89. On Romania's Holocaust deaths, see "Murder of the Jews of Romania," World Holocaust Remembrance Center, accessed November 23, 2023, www.yadvashem.org/holocaust /about/final-solution-beginning/romania.html.

10. Joseph S. Nye Jr., *Soft Power: The Means to Success in World Politics* (New York: PublicAffairs, 2004), 73–75 and *passim*. For gymnastics medal counts, see Mike Davis, "How Dominant Was the Eastern Bloc in Gymnastics?," Medal Count, December 2, 2020, https://themedalcount.com/2020/12/02/how-dominant-was-the-eastern-bloc -in-gymnastics. For DDR medal counts, see Isaac Eger, "The Recent Russian Doping Scandal Is a Throwback to Soviet Bloc Olympic Medal Politics: When East German Super Swimmers Dominated the Pool," Medium, July 20, 2016, https://timeline.com /russian-doping-scandal-germany-bbbe6645baa7.

11. On Johnson, see, for example, Skip Myslenski, "Johnson Admits Steroid Use," *Chicago Tribune*, June 13, 1989, www.chicagotribune.com/news/ct-xpm-1989-06 -13-8902090266-story.html. On the likely steroid use of his fellow finalists in 1988, see "Smith True Winner of 'Dirtiest Race' in History," Reuters, September 23, 2013.

12. Lucas Ackroyd, "Health Consequences of PEDs Continue to Plague Ex–East German Athletes," Global Sport Matters, November 7, 2019, https://globalsportmatters .com/health/2019/11/07/ex-east-german-athletes-struggle-with-health-problems -due-to-the-consequences-of-ped-taking. On Krieger, see Catrien Spijkerman, "How East and West Germany Abused and Drained Their Athletes," trans. Annemarie van Limpt, Iron Curtain Project, accessed November 23, 2023, www.ironcurtainproject .eu/en/stories/ive-given-my-blood-for-union/how-east-and-west-germany-abused -and-drained-their-athletes. On Christiane Sommer, see Steven Ungerleider, *Faust's Gold: Inside the East German Doping Machine* (New York: St. Martin's Press, 2001), 5–6.

13. See Steve Sailer and Stephen Seiler, "Track and Battlefield," *National Review*, December 31, 1997. On Bulgarian and Hungarian weight lifters testing positive at Seoul, see Grigory Rodchenkov, *The Rodchenkov Affair: How I Brought Down Putin's Secret Doping Empire* (London: Penguin / Random House, 2020), 50. For popular culture references to East German doping, see Ackroyd, "Health Consequences of PEDs." "Helga Piscopo": "Miller Lite Parody: 'Helga' Piscopo (1986)," YouTube, posted by Marketing the Rainbow, November 4, 2021, www.youtube.com/watch?v=ofyMrLnYrXc.

14. Rodchenkov, *Rodchenkov Affair*, ix, 31. "Medical-biological disciplines" and "current problems of Marxism-Leninism": "Treffen der Dopingexperten beider Länder zur Erarbeitung eines Vorschlags für die Internationalisierung," in file on "Beratungen zwischen DTSB und dem sowjetischer Komitee für Körperkultur und Sport," c. April 23–25, 1981, in DBB, DY 30 / 5071.

15. Eger, "The Recent Russian Doping Scandal."

16. "Treffen der Dopingexperten."

17. Rodchenkov, *Rodchenkov Affair*, 13. For an example of sports and equipment production targets, see "Arbeitsplan der Kommission für Spezialisierung und Kooperation für 1981–1982," Anlage no. 8 to the file on "Beratungen zwischen DTSB und dem sowjetischer Komitee für Körperkultur und Sport," in DBB, DY 30 / 5071.

18. From the Protocol of the Sports Summit held in Moscow March 13–14, 1986, Section 14 ("Zu Problemen der Dopingkontrolle"), in DBB, DY 30 / 5072. On beta-

blockers, see "Niederschrift über ein Gespräch . . . am 25.4.1984 in Havanna/Kuba zur Vorbereitung auf die Olympischen Spiele 1984 in Los Angeles," in DBB, EY 30 / 5066.

19. Günter Deister, "Gewandelter Gramow als Hoffnungsträger in Wien," and accompanying Dienstmeldung (ADN-Information), December 5, 1988, reproduced in DBB, DY 30 / 5072. "Shot of Stromba," "stop taking pills," and "left in Vladivostok": cited in Rodchenkov, *Rodchenkov Affair*, 45.

20. Cited in Christopher Andrew and Vasili Mitrokhin, *The World Was Going Our Way: The KGB and the Battle for the Third World* (New York: Basic Books, 2005), 324.

21. Bukovsky, *Judgment in Moscow*, 425. On $600 million spent on the peace movement, see John Kohan, "Eyes of the Kremlin," *Time*, February 14, 1982.

22. Soviet Communist Party Central Committee resolutions "On Additional Measures for Activating Public Manifestations Against the NATO Decision to Manufacture and Deploy New American Missiles in Western Europe," April 15, 1980, and "On Measures for the Further Activation of Manifestations by Peace-Loving Peoples," November 18, 1980, reproduced in Bukovsky, *Judgment in Moscow*, 413, 415. On the Soviet deployment of the SS-20s, see Raymond L. Garthoff, "The NATO Decision on Theater Nuclear Forces," *Political Science Quarterly* 98, no. 2 (Summer 1983): 197–214.

23. On Brandt, see instructions sent to him by the Politburo, February 1, 1980, cited in Bukovsky, *Judgment in Moscow*, 393–94. On the 1983 protests more generally, see April Carter, *Peace Movements: International Protests and World Politics Since 1945* (New York: Longman, 1992), 120–21. On Brandt headlining the Berlin protest, see William Drozdiak: "More Than a Million Protest Missiles in Western Europe," *Washington Post*, October 23, 1983.

24. On the emergence of Solidarity, see Andrzej Paczkowski, *The Spring Will Be Ours: Poland and the Poles from Occupation to Freedom*, trans. Jane Cave (University Park: Pennsylvania State University Press, 2003), 405–10 and *passim*. On Pope John Paul II addressing 400,000 and 9 million members of Solidarity, see Stone, *The Atlantic and Its Enemies*, 533–34. On Wałęsa being received by Pope John Paul II, see Andrew and Mitrokhin, *Sword and Shield*, 520.

25. Politburo minutes on January 13 and September 10, 1981, cited in Bukovsky, *Judgment at Moscow*, 446–48.

26. Cited in Andrew and Mitrokhin, *Sword and Shield*, 524. On the Soviet censorship of Polish news and the crackdown on tourist traffic, see Bukovsky, *Judgment at Moscow*, 446. On the general strike on March 27 and Soviet pressure on Jaruzelski to act, see Paczkowski, *Spring Will Be Ours*, 423 and *passim*.

27. Antoni Dudek and Andrzej Paczkowski, "Polen," in *Geheimdienst Handbuch*, 291–96. Stasi figures: Gieseke, "Deutsche demokratische Republik," in *Geheimdienst Handbuch*, 241. For 5.6 million files and 17,000 former Stasi German civil servants still employed in 2009, see Cathrin Schaer, "Stasi Files Reveal East Germany's Dirty Reality," *Spiegel International*, July 17, 2009.

28. For details on the imposition of martial law, see Paczkowski, *Spring Will Be Ours*, 447–48 and *passim*. On Jaruzelski trying to bring Solidarity into his government, Wałęsa refusing, and Polish officers visiting Wałęsa, see Stone, *The Atlantic and Its Enemies*, 534. On Jaruzelski reporting to the Soviet ambassador and Brezhnev, see

transcript of Jaruzelski-Brezhnev phone calls, October 19 and 29, 1981, reproduced in Bukovsky, *Judgment in Moscow*, 456–59.

29. See complaint filed by the East German Defense Ministry to the Foreign Ministry, November 3, 1988, and accompanying protocols of the "Gemischte Deutsch-sowjetische Kommission" for 1986–1988, in PAAA, M 38 264–98.

30. Citations in Andrew and Mitrokhin, *Sword and Shield*, 375, 388–89. On the assassination attempt on the pope, see "Agca Asserts Bulgarian Told Him When and Where to Attack Pope," *New York Times*, July 3, 1985.

31. Citations in Theodora Dragostinova, *The Cold War from the Margins: A Small State on the Global Cultural Scene* (Ithaca, NY: Cornell University Press, 2021), 10–11, 34–40.

32. Dragostinova, *Cold War from the Margins*, 14. For the 1973 Bulgarian Politburo resolution and its impact, see Kristen Ghodsee, *Second World, Second Sex: Socialist Women's Activism and Global Solidarity During the Cold War* (Durham, NC: Duke University Press, 2018), 66–75. On Romanian orphanages, see Vlad Odobescu, "Half a Million Kids Survived Romania's 'Slaughterhouse of Souls.' Now They Want Justice," December 28, 2015, The World, December 28, 2015, https://theworld.org/stories/2015-12-28/half-million-kids-survived-romanias-slaughterhouses-souls-now-they-want-justice.

33. Cited in Alvin Z. Rubinstein, "The Soviet Union and Iran Under Khomeini," *International Affairs (Royal Institute of International Affairs)* 57, no. 4 (Autumn 1981): 599–602.

34. On the Generals' Coup, see Stone, *The Atlantic and Its Enemies*, 463–66 and *passim*.

Chapter 15: Reckoning

1. Rodric Braithwaite, *Afgantsy: The Russians in Afghanistan, 1979–1989* (New York: Oxford University Press, 2011), 15–17, 28–31.

2. Citations and details in Braithwaite, *Afgantsy*, 5–7, 15–16, 49–50.

3. Politburo minutes for March 17 and 18, 1979, in RGASPI, fond 89, opis' 25, del' 1, reproduced and stored at the Hoover Institution Archives, reel 1.988 (this is the collection assembled for the would-be trial of the Soviet Communist Party in 1992).

4. Braithwaite, *Afgantsy*, 72–73. "Lenin taught us to be merciless": cited in Christopher Andrew and Vasili Mitrokhin, *The World Was Going Our Way: The KGB and the Battle for the Third World* (New York: Basic Books, 2005), 389.

5. Citations and details in Braithwaite, *Afgantsy*, 84–89.

6. Cited in Alvin Z. Rubinstein, "The Soviet Union and Iran Under Khomeini," *International Affairs (Royal Institute of International Affairs)* 57, no. 4 (Autumn 1981): 606–7. Chernyaev: diary entries for December 30, 1979, and January 28, 1980, trans. Anna Melyakova, donated to the National Security Archive, online at National Security Archive, https://nsarchive.gwu.edu/document/19326-diary-anatoly-s-chernyaev-1979 and https://nsarchive.gwu.edu/document/20313-diary-anatoly-chernyaev-1980.

7. Braithwaite, *Afgantsy*, 141–43.

8. Citation and data tables on Soviet consumer goods sector (including "weekly shopping" basket comparison) in John Keep, *Last of the Empires: A History of the Soviet Union* (Oxford: Oxford University Press, 1995), 224–31, 248–49. On German-built

pipelines and Soviet oil revenue, see Bogdan Musial, "Die westdeutsche Ostpolitik und der Zerfall der Sowjetunion," Bundeszentrale für politische Bildung, Deutschland Archiv, August 2, 2011, www.bpb.de/themen/deutschlandarchiv/54107 /die-westdeutsche-ostpolitik-und-der-zerfall-der-sowjetunion. On natural gas exports c. 1980, see Nadia Kampaner, "Evropeiskaia energobezopasnost' i uroki istorii," *Rossiya na global'noi politike*, no 6 (November 2007), https://globalaffairs.ru/articles /evropejskaya-energobezopasnost-i-uroki-istorii. On Russian weapons export revenue during the 1970s, see Ian Anthony, "Economic Dimensions of Soviet and Russian Arms Exports," Stockholm International Peace Research Institute, accessed November 25, 2023, www.sipri.org/sites/default/files/files/books/SIPRI98An/SIPRI98 An04.pdf.

9. Chernyaev diary entry for November 20, 1979, trans. Anna Melyakova, donated to the National Security Archive, https://nsarchive.gwu.edu/document/19326-diary -anatoly-s-chernyaev-1979. In an aside, he pointed out that "iron battalions of the proletariat" was "[Ilya] Pomnomarev's favorite phrase, a quote from Lenin."

10. For oil prices, see "Gold Prices: 100 Year Historical Chart," Macrotrends, accessed June 2023, www.macrotrends.net/1333/historical-gold-prices-100-year-chart. (The data can be displayed with and without inflation adjustments.) The data for gold is charted on the same page. On Soviet gold sales affecting the world price, see Steven Rattner, "Impact of Soviet Gold Sales," *New York Times*, January 5, 1982.

11. Cited in Jack Matlock, *Reagan and Gorbachev: How the Cold War Ended* (New York: Random House, 2004), 227. On the Stingers and their impact on the battlefield in Afghanistan, see Braithwaite, *Afgantsy*, 203–4.

12. On Gorbachev's temperance campaign and Gospriemka, see Keep, *Last of the Empires*, 337–42.

13. Cited in Matlock, *Reagan and Gorbachev*, 157.

14. Figures in Yevgenia Albats, *The State Within a State: The KGB and Its Hold on Russia—Past, Present, and Future*, trans. Catherine Fitzpatrick (New York: Farrar, Straus, and Giroux, 1994), 188–89.

15. Figures in Lein-Lein Chen and John Devereux, "The Iron Rice Bowl: Chinese Living Standards, 1952–1978," *Comparative Economic Studies* 59, no. 3 (September 2017): 261–310. On 20,000 cars and shortages in the Pearl River delta, see Frank Dikötter, *China After Mao: The Rise of a Superpower* (New York: Bloomsbury, 2022), vii, 5.

16. On the strange diplomacy of the Sino-Vietnamese War of 1979, in particular Deng's courting of Carter and the Americans, see Alexander V. Pantsov and Steven I. Levine, *Deng Xiaoping: A Revolutionary Life* (New York: Oxford University Press, 2015), 349–50 and *passim*.

17. Dikötter, *China After Mao*, 4–12. On Deng's house arrest, see Pantsov and Levine, *Deng Xiaoping*, 258–59.

18. Pantsov and Levine, *Deng Xiaoping*, 347, and, for more on the Japan and US trips, Ezra Vogel, *Deng Xiaoping and the Transformation of China* (Cambridge, MA: Belknap Press of Harvard University Press, 2011), 305–10, 335, 340–45.

19. Cited in Vogel, *Deng Xiaoping*, 304. "We thought capitalist countries were backward": cited in Pantsov and Levine, *Deng Xiaoping*, 336.

20. Cited in Vogel, *Deng Xiaoping*, 306.

21. On the SEZs and the Hong Kong connection, see Vogel, *Deng Xiaoping*, 399–403 and *passim*. On the history of the likely phony "get rich is glorious" quote, see Evelyn Iritani, "Great Idea but Don't Quote Him," *Los Angeles Times*, September 9, 2004.

22. Citations in Vogel, *Deng Xiaoping*, 440–41. New loan of 12 billion yuan and 12 million metric tons of wheat: Dikötter, *China After Mao*, 40, 44.

23. Citations in Pantsov and Levine, *Deng Xiaoping*, 371–73.

24. Citations in Dikötter, *China After Mao*, 77. For more on Feinstein and the "sister city" deals with Jiang Zemin and the Shanghai CCP, see Peter Schweizer, *Red Handed: How American Elites Get Rich Helping China Win* (New York: Harper Collins, 2022), 47–51 and *passim*.

25. Julian Gewirtz, *Never Turn Back: China and the Forbidden History of the 1980s* (Cambridge, MA: Belknap Press of Harvard University Press, 2022), 97–98, 101. On the 15 percent rise in GDP in 1984, see Vogel, *Deng Xiaoping*, 467.

26. Dikötter, *China After Mao*, 51–53.

27. Dikötter, *China After Mao*, 103. For the decisions on price controls and GDP numbers, see Vogel, *Deng Xiaoping*, 470–73.

28. William Hitchcock, *The Struggle for Europe: The Turbulent History of a Divided Continent* (New York: Doubleday, 2002), 361–62, and Andrzej Paczkowski, *The Spring Will Be Ours: Poland and the Poles from Occupation to Freedom*, trans. Jane Cave (University Park: Pennsylvania State University Press, 2003), 499–504. For Soviet figures, see Keep, *Last of the Empires*, 357–58.

29. For details on the Soviet withdrawal, see Braithwaite, *Afgantsy*, 281–93. On US pressure and the "frontloading" of the Soviet pullout, see Matlock, *Reagan and Gorbachev*, 286–88.

30. Citations in Dikötter, *China After Mao*, 112–13.

31. "Workers, peasants" and protests in Shanghai and other cities: cited in Dikötter, *China After Mao*, 123, 126. Other citations and details in Vogel, *Deng Xiaoping*, 579–81, 597–98, 609–15.

32. Cited in Pantsov and Levine, *Deng Xiaoping*, 411–12.

33. Cited in Vogel, *Deng Xiaoping*, 621. "Had not expected": cited in Dikötter, *China After Mao*, 128.

34. Dikötter, *China After Mao*, 133–34. "Whatever was necessary": cited in Vogel, *Deng Xiaoping*, 625.

35. Li to US government and other details in Vogel, *Deng Xiaoping*, 630–31. On the ABC reporter and the British ambassador's estimates, see Dikötter, *China After Mao*, 138. On the tent city and the demolition of the *Goddess of Democracy*, see Pantsov and Levine, *Deng Xiaoping*, 416.

Epilogue: The August Coup and the Strange Non-Death of Communism

1. Gorbachev, Krenz, and DDR spokesman: cited in William Hitchcock, *The Struggle for Europe: The Turbulent History of a Divided Continent* (New York: Doubleday, 2002), 366. Gerasimov: "'Sinatra Doctrine' at Work in Warsaw Pact, Soviet Says," *Los Angeles Times*, October 25, 1989.

2. Timothy Garton Ash, *The Magic Lantern: The Revolution of 1989 Witnessed in Warsaw, Budapest, Berlin and Prague* (New York: Random House, 1990). For more on Ash's

own role in the events he helped mythologize, see Ash, "The Revolution of the Magic Lantern," *New York Review of Books*, January 18, 1990.

3. For details, see Hitchcock, *Struggle for Europe*, 367–77, 385–95, and *passim*. On Zhivkov's persecution of Turkish Muslims in Bulgaria, see Tomasz Kamusella, *Ethnic Cleansing During the Cold War: The Forgotten 1989 Expulsion of Turks from Communist Bulgaria* (London: Routledge, 2019).

4. For the relevant Baker citations and thorough annotation of how Baker's and Gorbachev's recollections diverged in the sources, see M. E. Sarotte, *Not One Inch: America, Russia, and the Making of Post–Cold War Stalemate* (New Haven, CT: Yale University Press, 2021), 1, 54–55, 365n1, 387–88n66–69.

5. Sarotte, *Not One Inch*, 92, 95. On 45,000 Soviet apartments paid for by the FRG, see William E. Odom, *The Collapse of the Soviet Military* (New Haven, CT: Yale University Press, 1998), 279.

6. For GDP, inflation, budget data, and referendum citation and results, see John Keep, *Last of the Empires: A History of the Soviet Union* (Oxford: Oxford University Press, 1995), 398–99. For figures on disappearing Soviet gold and dollar reserves and capital flight, see Martin McCauley, *Bandits, Gangsters and the Mafia: Russia, the Baltic States and the CIS Since 1992* (London: Pearson, 2001), 74–75.

7. Chernyaev diary entry for July 20, 1991, trans. Anna Melyakova, donated to the National Security Archive, reproduced online at https://nsarchive2.gwu.edu/NSAEBB /NSAEBB345/The%20Diary%20of%20Anatoly%20Chernyaev,%201991.pdf.

8. Keep, *Last of the Empires*, 401. Chernyaev: diary entry for July 11, 1991, trans. Anna Melyakova, donated to the National Security Archive, reproduced online at https://nsarchive2.gwu.edu/NSAEBB/NSAEBB345/The%20Diary%20of%20 Anatoly%20Chernyaev,%201991.pdf.

9. Citations in Brian Moynahan, *The Russian Century* (New York: Random House, 1994), 251–52. For more details on the August coup, see McCauley, *Bandits, Gangsters and the Mafia*, 57–58; Keep, *Last of the Empires*, 402–4; and Odom, *Collapse of the Soviet Military*, 305–8.

10. Francis Fukuyama, *The End of History and the Last Man* (New York: Free Press, 2006 [1992]), xi. This book was an expansion of his essay "End of History?," in *National Interest* 16 (Summer 1989): 3–18. "At the same time, its obituary": Richard Pipes, *Communism: A History* (New York: Random House / Modern Library, 2001), ix. For his trial testimony and real-time commentary, see Pipes, "The Past on Trial: Russia, One Year Later," *Washington Post*, August 16, 1992.

11. For a shrewd analysis of the legal issues and the political implications of the trial, see Sergey Toymentsev, "Legal but Criminal: The Failure of the 'Russian Nuremberg' and the Paradoxes of Post-Soviet Memory," *Comparative Literature Studies* 48, no. 3 (2011): 296–311.

12. Odom, *Collapse of the Soviet Military*, 250–51 (on Gorbachev reading soldiers' mothers' letters in the Politburo in October 1984); 251–52 (on the Alma-Ata affair); 252–60 (Tbilisi); 260–68 (Baku including Lebed's insubordination); and 268–71 (crackdowns in Lithuania, Latvia, and Yeltsin's intervention).

13. The World Bank's national per capita income figures for 2021 are available online at Datacommons.org (simply enter each country). On public executions and state crimes

in North Korea, see Yeonmi Park with Maryanne Vollers, *In Order to Live: A North Korean Girl's Journey to Freedom* (New York: Penguin, 2015), 50–51 and *passim*. "Both genders": "Tips for Single Travelers in Cuba," Frommers, 2023, www.frommer's.com /destinations/cuba/planning-a-trip/tips-for-single-travelers.

14. For China's GDP for 2022, see "Gross Domestic Product (GDP) at Current Prices in China from 1985 to 2022 with Forecasts Until 2028," Statistica, 2023, www .statista.com/statistics/263770/gross-domestic-product-gdp-of-china.

15. On the various kinds of Eastern Bloc nostalgia still prevalent to this day, see Kristen Ghodsee and Mitchell A. Orenstein, *Taking Stock of Shock: Social Consequences of the 1989 Revolutions* (New York: Oxford, 2021). For an amusing, if slightly trivializing and borderline offensive, cinematic take on *Ostalgie*, see *Good Bye Lenin!* (2003), a German film directed by Wolfgang Becker and produced by Stefan Arndt, X-Filme Creative Pool.

16. There are many studies in this emerging genre of "Sino-forming." See, for example, David Goldman, *You Will Be Assimilated: China's Plan to Sino-Form the World* (New York: Bombardier Books, 2020), and Peter Schweizer, *Red Handed: How American Elites Get Rich Helping China Win* (New York: Harper Collins, 2022).

17. See Sean McMeekin, *Stalin's War: A New History of World War II* (New York: Basic Books, 2021). On Shumovsky in particular, see Svetlana Lokhova, *The Spy Who Changed History: The Untold Story of How the Soviet Union Stole America's Top Secrets* (New York: Pegasus, 2019).

18. On Bush and Scowcroft, see Frank Dikötter, *China After Mao: The Rise of a Superpower* (New York: Bloomsbury, 2022), 144–45. On Feinstein, see Schweizer, *Red Handed*, 50, 55, and *passim*.

19. On China's "Zero COVID" policy at its most extreme, see Jeff Brown, "'Zero COVID' Lockdowns Spark Fury in China," Brownstone Research, November 28, 2022, www.brownstoneresearch.com/bleeding-edge/zero-covid-lockdowns-spark -fury-in-china. On Albright, see Schweizer, *Red Handed*, 159–60.

20. See Steven Lee Myers, "Appeals Court Rules White House Overstepped 1st Amendment on Social Media," *New York Times*, September 8, 2023, and Jacob Gershman, "Biden Administration's Policing of Online Content Likely Violated Free-Speech Rights, Court Rules," *Wall Street Journal*, September 8, 2023. On the FBI and Twitter, see Elizabeth Nolan Brown, "The FBI Paid Twitter $3.4 Million," *Reason*, December 19, 2022.

21. Eric Lipton and Jennifer Steinhauer, "The Untold Story of the Birth of Social Distancing," *New York Times*, April 22, 2020; Michael Lewis, *The Premonition* (New York: Norton, 2021). On the real Chinese precedent, as opposed to the more innocent (albeit self-incriminatingly stupid) fourteen-year-old science project story, see Michael Senger, "The Deeper History of 'Social Distancing'—the Western Term for Lockdown," Brownstone Institute, September 13, 2022, https://brownstone.org/articles /real-story-of-social-distancing.

22. Tom Whipple, "Professor Neil Ferguson: People Don't Agree with Lockdowns and Try to Undermine the Scientists," *London Times*, December 25, 2020.

23. On the Canadian truckers being cut off, see Brian Platt and Jen Skerritt, "Banks Freeze Millions in Convoy Funds Under Trudeau Edict," BNN Bloomberg,

February 22, 2022, www.bnnbloomberg.ca/banks-freeze-millions-in-convoy-funds -under-trudeau-edict-1.1727032. On the "debanking" of Nigel Farage, see Iain Withers, "UK Watchdog Steps into Row over 'Debanking' of Nigel Farage," Reuters, July 19, 2023, www.reuters.com/world/uk/farage-makes-fresh-allegations-against-uks -coutts-over-account-closures-2023-07-19. On journalists critical of the West's Ukraine policy seeing their funds seized, see Max Blumenthal, "Gofundme Freezes Grayzone Fundraiser 'Due to Some External Concerns,'" Grayzone, August 28, 2023, https:// thegrayzone.com/2023/08/28/gofundme-freezes-grayzone-fundraiser.

INDEX

abortion: one-child policy and, 423; Romanian policy on, 400; Soviet policies on, 166, 222–223

Adenauer, Konrad, 376–377

Afghanistan, 403–409, 408n, 412; Soviet withdrawal from, 425, 433, 445; US support of mujahideen, 411, 412–413, 435

Africa, 336–337; Cuban troops in, 337. *See also* individual nations

Ağca, Mehmet Ali, 398

agricultural collectivization, 209–214, 216–217, 221; in Bulgaria, 272; in China, 311–316, 349–350; famine and, 212–213, 314–316, 350; Gulag victims of, 217–218; in Poland, 277

Albania, 278–279

Albright, Madeleine, 454

Alekseev, Mikhail, 155

Alekseyev, Aleksandr, 333

d'Alembert, Jean, 13

Alexander II, 82, 87

Algeria, 330, 337

Allende, Salvador, 344–346

Allesandri, Jorge, 344

Alliyuyeva, Nadya, 219

All-Russian Extraordinary Commission to Combat Counterrevolution, Speculation, and Sabotage (CHEKA):

challenges to Bolshevism and, 199–200; founding of, 146–147; Red Terror and, 156

Amanullah (King of Afghanistan), 404–405

American Relief Administration (ARA), 163

Amin, Hafizullah, 404, 407–408

Anabaptists, 12–13

anarchism, 87–88, 103

Andrew, Christopher, 229

Andropov, Yuri, 337, 395, 412; Afghanistan and, 405–408, 408n

Angola, 337

anticolonialism, 329–331. *See also* anti-imperialism

Anti-Comintern Pact, 288

anti-imperialism, 329–331; in Africa, 331, 336–337; anti-imperialist congress, 195–196, 329; in China, 195; in Cuba, 332–333; non-aligned movement and, 340; Soviet Union and, 330–331, 330n, 336, 340; WWI as anti-imperialist war, 157, 187

Anti-Imperialism Congress (1927), 329

antisemitism: Dreyfus affair and, 89; Holocaust and, 253–254, 270, 371; in Hungary, 179, 181n;

death of, 412; détente and, 376;
Iranian Revolution and, 401;
Polish Solidarity movement and,
395–396; Sino-Soviet relations
and, 347; Soviet economy and, 410
Brezhnev doctrine, 347, 433
Britain: anticolonial movement
and, 329–330; Chinese Cultural
Revolution and, 363; Eastern
Europe and, 259–261, 270,
278, 279n; Hong Kong and,
304–305; as imperial power, 112,
116–117, 187, 238, 329–330; labor
movement in, 63, 65, 68, 72–73,
77, 79, 182–184; Marxist analysis
of, 61–62; relations with USSR,
208, 229–230, 241; WWI and, 98,
101, 106; WWII and, 235–236,
240–241, 245–246, 250, 253,
293, 295
Brousse, Paul, 84–85
Broz, Josip. See Tito
Brusilov, Aleksei, 131
Brusilov Offensive, 120–121
Brussels "anti-imperialist" Congress
(1927), 195–196
Brutents, Karen N., 346
Budyonny, Marshal, 220
Bukharin, Nikolai, 150, 205–206;
China and, 196; Chinese economy
and, 420–421; Comintern and,
208; New Economic Policy (NEP)
and, 205–208, 421; purging of, 219
Bukovsky, Vladimir, 376
Bulgaria, 398–400; break with Soviet
Union, 435; Communist Terror in,
271; international sport and, 386,
388; postwar purges in, 279–280;
post-WWII Soviet occupation of,
259, 259n, 269–273, 269n
Bullitt, William, Jr., 229
Buonarroti, Philippe, 24, 27, 29

Burgess, Guy, 229
Burns, Mary, 44
Bush, George H. W., 438–439, 453
Bush, George W., 453

Caillaux, Henriette, 102
Caillaux, Joseph, 101–102
Cairncross, John, 229
Calmette, Gaston, 102
Calvin, Jean, 12
Cambodia, 364–373, 416, 447
Cambridge Five, 229
Campbell, Thomas, 216
Canada, 455–457
Canovas del Castillo, Antonio, 88
Cao Shuji, 315
Carter, Jimmy, 416–417, 417n
Castro, Fidel, 332–337; Cuban
Missile Crisis and, 333–334;
Non-aligned movement and,
337, 340
Castro, Raúl, 332
Catherine the Great, 13–14
Ceauşescu, Elena, 435
Ceauşescu, Nicolae, 379–382, 388,
398, 400, 435–436; Romanian
orphanages and, 399–400
Central Physical Culture
Institute, 387
Chamberlain, Neville, 229, 235
Chandra, Romesh, 392
Charles, Ray, 399
CHEKA. See All-Russian
Extraordinary Commission to
Combat Counterrevolution,
Speculation, and Sabotage
Chen Boda, 354, 363
Chen Yizi, 315
Chernenko, Konstantin, 412
Chernobyl nuclear accident, 414
Chernyaev, Anatoly, 408, 411,
439, 442

gymnastics, 383–384, 388
György Pálffy, 280

Haase, Hugo, 106–107
Hague Congress of 1872, 74, 77
Hastings, Max, 250, 373
Havel, Václav, 434, 434n
Hegel, Georg Wilhelm Friedrich, 37–38
Herzen, Alexander, 74
Hess, Moses, 40
Heydrich, Reinhard, 261
Hiss, Alger, 228–229
History of the All-Union Communist Party (Bolsheviks) (Stalin, 1938), 238
Hitler, Adolph, 193–194, 226–228; cooperation with USSR, 236–238; Operation Barbarossa and, 245–246; Spanish Civil War and, 230–231; Stalin and, 226–227, 245–246; Western appeasement of, 235
Hobson, John, 116–117
Ho Chi Minh, 340–344; elections and, 344, 344n; Lenin and, 340–341, 340n
Holden, David, 346
Holocaust, 253–254, 270, 371
Holodomor, 212–213, 213n, 227, 240; compared with Chinese famine, 315
Homage to Catalonia (Orwell), 231–232
Honecker, Erich, 378–379, 382–383, 434, 436
Hong Kong, 451
Hopkins, Harry, 258
Horthy, Miklós, 179–180
Hoxha, Enver, 278–279, 319; Cultural Revolution and, 359
Hsiao Jo-ping, 310
Huang Zuyan, 308

Humbert, King of Italy, 88
Hundred Days (Hungary), 180–181, 191, 233
Hundred Flowers Campaign, 310–311, 349–350
Hungary: 1956 uprising in, 325–326; Beria and, 321; break with Soviet Union, 433, 435; dismantling of Iron Curtain, 425–426, 433; Hungarian Revolution (1918), 174–181; Hungarian Soviet Republic, 175, 178, 180, 233; imposition of Communism in, 5; international sport and, 386, 388; Jewish population of, 179, 179n; maps, 176; postwar deportation of Hungarians, 258; postwar purges in, 280; postwar reparations and, 257, 259, 267; post-WWII Soviet occupation of, 255–259, 263, 267–269; Red Terror in, 179
Husák, Gustáv, 434–435
Hu Yaobang, 426–427

immiseration thesis, 62
Imperialism, the Highest Stage of Capitalism (Lenin, 1916), 116–117
Inaugural Address of the Working Men's International Association (Marx), 63–64
Independent Social Democratic Party of Germany (Unabhängige Sozialdemokratische Partei Deutschlands, USPD), 189–190, 192, 378; post-WWII, 282
India, 329–330
Indonesia, 330, 346
industrial espionage, 234–235, 421–422, 452
international sports, 382–391; performance-enhancing drugs and, 384–387, 384n, 389–390

Slutsky, A. A., 220
Smith, Adam, 60–61
Snow, Edgar, 287–288, 288n
Snowden, Edward, 454
Snyder, Tim, 220
Social Democratic Party
(Sozialdemokratische Partei
Deutschlands, SPD), 80–87,
94–95, 102, 189–190; Erfurt
program and, 83–84, 95; founding
of, 80; Gotha program and, 81–83;
WWI and, 105–106, 111, 131
social distancing, 455–456
Socialism and War (Lenin, 1915),
111–113
Socialist Revolutionary Party (Parti
Socialiste Revolutionnaire,
PSR), 84
Socialist Revolutionary Party
(Russian, SR), 150
Socialist Unity Party of Germany
(Sozialistische Einheitspartei
Deutschlands, SED), 282, 327–328
social media bans, 457
Society of the Pantheon, 23
Sokolnikov, Gregory, 147–149
Solidarity movement (Poland),
394–397, 424–425, 433
Solzhenitsyn, Aleksandr, 222
Somalia, 337
Sorge, Friedrich Adolph, 77
Sorge, Richard, 248
Soviet-Japanese Neutrality Pact,
293–294
Soviet of People's Commissars. *See*
Sovnarkom
Soviet Peace Committee, 391
Soviet Union. *See* Union of Soviet
Socialist Republics (USSR)
Sovnarkom (Soviet of People's
Commissars), 138, 151–152, 161,
164; bank wars and, 145, 159;

election of 1917 and, 150; Red
Army and, 153
Spain: anti-fascist coalitions in, 230;
Spanish Civil War, 230–233, 252
Spartacus program, 171–172. *See also*
German Communist Party
special economic zones (SEZs), 419,
421–422
Sputnik, 311
Stalin, Joseph, 197, 319; Afghanistan
and, 405; agricultural
collectivization and, 210–213;
Brezhnev and, 351; Chiang
and, 287–288, 289, 297; China
and, 195–196, 287–298, 301;
Comintern and, 234, 265;
consolidation of power by, 208;
contemporary views of, 1–2;
Cultural Revolution and, 354;
Czechoslovakia and, 261–262;
death of, 319–320; German putsch
(1923) and, 194; Great Terror and,
218–221, 323; Gulag system and,
217–218; industrialization drive
and, 213–215, 226; international
Soviet prestige and, 226–228,
233; Japanese war aims and,
287–288, 292–294; Khrushchev's
denunciation of, 323–324; Mao
and, 293, 295–296, 301; Nazi
Germany and, 226–228, 236–242,
245; New Economic Policy
(NEP) and, 205–206, 208–209;
Operation Barbarossa and,
247–250; postwar reparations and,
259; relations with US, 229, 452;
Russian Revolution of 1905 and,
97; Soviet military and, 234–235,
452; Spanish Civil War and,
230–233; succession of Lenin and,
205; Tito and, 259–261, 278–279,
281, 301, 397

Sean McMeekin is a professor of history at Bard College. The award-winning author of several books, including *Stalin's War*, *The Russian Revolution*, *July 1914*, and *The Ottoman Endgame*, he lives in Clermont, New York.